INEQUALITY, GROWTH, AND POVERTY IN AN ERA OF LIBERALIZATION AND GLOBALIZATION

UNU WORLD INSTITUTE FOR DEVELOPMENT ECONOMICS RESEARCH (UNU/WIDER)

was established by the United Nations University as its first research and training centre and started work in Helsinki, Finland in 1985. The purpose of the institute is to undertake applied research and policy analysis on structural changes affecting developing and transitional economies, to provide a forum for the advocacy of policies leading to robust, equitable, and environmentally sustainable growth, and to promote capacity strengthening and training in the field of economic and social policy-making. Its work is carried out by staff researchers and visiting scholars in Helsinki and through networks of collaborating scholars and institutions around the world.

World Institute for Development Economics Research of the United Nations University (UNU/WIDER)
Katajanokanlaituri 6 B, FIN-00160 Helsinki, Finland. www.wider.unu.edu

Inequality, Growth, and Poverty in an Era of Liberalization and Globalization

Edited by

GIOVANNI ANDREA CORNIA

A study prepared by the World Institute for Development Economics Research of the United Nations University (UNU/WIDER)

OXFORD

UNIVERSITY PRESS

OXFORD
UNIVERSITY PRESS

Great Clarendon Street, Oxford OX2 6DP

Oxford University Press is a department of the University of Oxford.
It furthers the University's objective of excellence in research, scholarship,
and education by publishing worldwide in

Oxford New York

Auckland Bangkok Buenos Aires Cape Town Chennai
Dar es Salaam Delhi Hong Kong Istanbul Karachi Kolkata
Kuala Lumpur Madrid Melbourne Mexico City Mumbai Nairobi
São Paulo Shanghai Taipei Tokyo Toronto

Oxford is a registered trade mark of Oxford University Press
in the UK and in certain other countries

Published in the United States
by Oxford University Press Inc., New York

© United Nations University/World Institute for Development Economics Research
(UNU/WIDER) 2004

British Library Cataloguing in Publication Data

Data available

Library of Congress Cataloging in Publication Data

Data available

ISBN 0–19–927141–0

3 5 7 9 10 8 6 4

Typeset by Newgen Imaging Systems (P) Ltd., Chennai, India
Printed in Great Britain
on acid-free paper by
Biddles Ltd., King's Lynn, Norfolk

Contents

List of Figures

List of Figures ix

List of Tables

List of Abbreviations and Acronyms

AD	Acción Democrática (Venezuela)
ANC	African National Congress
CES	Constant Elasticity of Substitution
CGE	Computable General Equilibrium
COPEI	Partido Social-Cristiano (Venezuela)
CPIAL	Consumer Price Index for Agricultural Labourers
CPIIW	Consumer Price Index for Industrial Workers
CTV	Confederación de Trabajadores de Venezuela (Confederation of Venezuelan Workers)
CWS	Current Weekly Status
DAC	Development Assistance Committee
ECLAC	Economic Commission for Latin America and the Caribbean
ESIF	Emergency Social Investment Fund
FAES	Economic and Social Assistance Fund
FAO	Food and Agricultural Organization
FDI	Foreign Direct Investment
FIRE	Finance, Insurance, and Real Estate
FIS	Fondo de Inversión Social
FISE	Emergency Social Investment Fund
FONCODES	Fondo Nacional de Compensación y Desarrollo Social (Peru Social Fund)
FOSIS	Fondo de Solidaridad e Inversión Social
FSU	Former Soviet Union
GATT	General Agreement on Tariff and Trade
GDP	Gross Domestic Product
GEAR	Growth Employment and Redistribution
GEE	Generalized Estimating Equation
GNP	Gross National Product
GRP	Gross Regional Product
HSL	Household Subsistence Level
IDB	Inter-American Development Bank
i.i.d	identically independently distributed
ILO	International Labour Organization
IMF	International Monetary Fund
LIS	Luxembourg Income Study
MENA	Middle East and North Africa
MLL	Minimum Living Level
MTEF	Medium-Term Expenditure Framework
NDP	Net Domestic Product

NGO	Non-Governmental Organization
NNP	Net National Product
NSS	National Sample Survey
OCEA	Oficina Central de Estadística e Informática
OECD	Organization for Economic Cooperation and Development
OLS	Ordinary Least Squares
OTI	Offsetting Trends in Inequality
PA	Poverty Assessment
PADS	Social Development Action Project
PAMSCAD	Programme of Action to Migrate the Social Consequences of Adjustment
PDS	Public Distribution System
PGI	Poverty–Gap Index
PIT	Personal Income Tax
PPP	Purchasing Power Parity
RBI	Reserve Bank of India
RER	Real Exchange Rate
SALDRU	Southern African Labour & Development Research Unit
SAR	Special Administrative Region of the People's Republic of China
SARS	South African Revenue Service
SE	Social Expenditure
SEF	Social Emergency Fund
SIF	Social Investment Fund
SF	Social Fund
SMEs	Small and Medium-Sized Enterprises
Sida	Swedish International Development Cooperation Agency
SIS	State Institute of Statistics (Turkey)
TCM	Transatlantic Consensus Model
UNCTAD	United Nations Conference on Trade and Development
UNDP	United Nations Development Programme
UNESCO	United Nations Educational, Scientific, and Cultural Organization
UNICEF	United Nations Children's Fund
UNIDO	United Nations Industrial Development Organization
VAT	Value-Added Tax
WIDER	World Institute for Development Economics Research
WIID	World Income Inequality Database
WTO	World Trade Organization

List of Contributors

Tony Addison is Deputy Director of the World Institute for Development Economics Research (WIDER) in Helsinki. He was previously on the economics faculty of the University of Warwick, UK, where he directed the programme in quantitative development economics. His main research interests are conflict and post-conflict reconstruction as well as macroeconomic policy for developing countries.

Anthony B. Atkinson is Warden of Nuffield College, Oxford. He has previously been a professor of economics at the University of Cambridge and the London School of Economics. He has been President of the Royal Economic Society, of the Econometric Society, of the European Economic Association, and of the International Economic Association.

Michael Carter is a professor of agricultural and applied economics at the University of Wisconsin-Madison, USA. He is also director of the BASIS Collaborative Research Support Program that studies rural poverty alleviation strategies in Africa, Asia, and Latin America. His research focuses on the nature of growth and transformation in low-income economies, giving particular attention to how inequality in the distribution of land and other assets shape, and are shaped by, economic growth.

Daniele Checchi is a professor of economics at the University of Milan, Italy. He works on intergenerational mobility and inequality transmission. He has also published on trade union presence in Europe.

Ke-Young Chu, who was a senior advisor at the Fiscal Affairs Department, IMF, Washington DC, when he coauthored chapter 10, is now a visiting professor of economics, Wesleyan University, Connecticut. His research interests are in social protection, income distribution, economic and social implications of globalization, and the effects of cultural values on the evolution of institutions in economic development.

Giovanni Andrea Cornia is a professor of economics at the University of Florence, Italy. He was the Director of WIDER in Helsinki during 1996-9, and has held research positions for UNICEF, UNCTAD, and UNECE. He is widely published in development economics, particularly within his main research areas of macroeconomics, poverty, and inequality.

Hamid Davoodi is an economist at the International Monetary Fund (IMF). Prior to joining the IMF, he was on the staff of the Federal Reserve Bank of San Francisco, the World Bank, and Georgetown University. He has worked on the economies of Zambia, Tanzania, West Bank and Gaza Strip, Kazakhstan, Malawi, and Albania. He has published articles on economic growth, governance, corruption, fiscal decentralization, demographic dynamics, expenditure policy, and military spending.

Rahul Dhumale graduated with honours from Duke University and then earned his MSc in Economics from Oxford University and his PhD from Cambridge University. He was a fellow at the Judge Institute at Cambridge University before taking up his current position as a senior economist at the Federal Reserve in New York.

Robert Eastwood is a senior lecturer in economics at the University of Sussex. His recent publications are in quantitative development economics, concerning in particular the links from fertility to poverty and from financial market constraints to investment.

Sanjeev Gupta is an assistant director and Chief of the Expenditure Policy Division of the Fiscal Affairs Department at the IMF. Prior to joining the Fund, he was a fellow of the Kiel Institute of World Economics, Germany; Senior Faculty in the Administrative Staff College of India, Hyderabad; and Secretary of the Federation of Indian Chambers of Commerce and Industry, New Delhi. He has written extensively on fiscal issues, particularly in developing countries and transition economies.

Carolyn Jenkins is at the Centre for the Study of African Economies, University of Oxford, and at the Centre for Research into Economics and Finance in Southern Africa, LSE. She has been a consultant to business, governments, and international institutions on macroeconomic issues, trade policy, and regional integration in southern Africa.

Raghbendra Jha is a professor and Executive Director at the Australia South Asia Research Centre, Australian National University. He has previously taught at Columbia University and Williams College in the United States, Queen's University in Canada, University of Warwick in the United Kingdom, and Delhi School of Economics and Indira Gandhi Institute of Development Research in India. He works on public economics and macroeconomics issues related to economic development.

Sampsa Kiiski is a senior application specialist at Nokia Corporation, Switzerland. He was a junior researcher at WIDER (1998–2000), focusing on quantitative analysis and the World Income Inequality Database (WIID). His research interests include development economics, the new economy, and financial economics.

Michael Lipton is a research professor of economics, Poverty Research Unit, Sussex University. His books and papers deal mainly with the effect on poverty of alternative paths, outcomes, and policies affecting agricultural technology, farmland distribution, demography, nutrition, and rural–urban relations and resource allocations. Recently he led the EU study of the impact of rural asset size and distribution on fertility and migration in rural drylands.

Sanjay Reddy is an assistant professor of economics at Barnard College, Columbia University. His areas of work include development economics, international economics, economics and philosophy, and economics and social theory. His recent research focuses on the political economy, measurement and dynamics of poverty, and inequality. He has a PhD in economics from Harvard University, an MPhil in social anthropology from the University of Cambridge, and an AB in applied mathematics with physics from Harvard University.

Francisco Rodríguez is Chief Economist of the Venezuelan National Assembly. He has previously taught at University of Maryland, College Park. His areas of research are economic growth and income inequality, with special focus on political economy issues.

Catherine Saget has been a labour economist at the International Labour Office since 1998. She holds a PhD from the European University Institute in Florence on labour markets in transition economies. Her recent fields of interest are in wage policy issues, particularly the impact of the minimum wage on the level of poverty, formal employment, productivity, and social dialogue in developing countries.

Isra Sarntisart is an associate professor of economics and the Chairman of the Master of Economics Program at the Faculty of Economics, Chulalongkorn University, Thailand. His main research interests are in economic welfare analysis, sin tax, general equilibrium modelling, as well as poverty and income distribution for Thailand.

Ajit Singh is a professor of economics, University of Cambridge and Senior Fellow at Queens' College, Cambridge. He has been a senior economic advisor to the governments of Mexico and Tanzania and a consultant to various development organizations, including the World Bank, the ILO, UNCTAD, and UNIDO. He has published widely on finance, industry, and economic growth in advanced as well as developing countries.

Lance Taylor is the Arnhold Professor of International Economics, Cooperation and Development at the Graduate Faculty of New School University in New York. He is Director of the Center for Economic Policy Analysis, New School University.

Lynne Thomas is a research officer at the Centre for Research into Economics and Finance in Southern Africa at the London School of Economics. Her main research interests include the impact of capital flows in the South African economy; the characteristics of cross-border investment in southern Africa; and the prospects for regional integration and macroeconomic convergence in southern Africa.

Rolph van der Hoeven is Manager of the Technical Secretariat of the World Commission on Globalization, established by the International Labour Organization in Geneva. Previous positions include Chief of the Macroeconomic and Development Policy Group, Employment Strategy Department at ILO, Senior Economic Adviser to UNICEF in New York, and economist at ILO's Employment Team in Ethiopia and Zambia. He is widely published on employment, poverty, inequality, and economic reform issues.

A. Erinc Yeldan is professor and chair, Department of Economics, Bilkent University. He received his PhD from University of Minnesota, USA, and joined the Department of Economics at Bilkent in 1988. His recent work focuses on empirical, dynamic general equilibrium models of the Turkish economy, and macroeconomics of financial crises.

Foreword

After three decades of relative neglect, the issues of income inequality, its changes over time and its impact on poverty alleviation, and growth are again at the centre of the attention of scholars, policy-makers, and the public at large. The lively debate in refereed journals and books, as well as the growing discussions in the public policy arena and among new political movements focusing specifically on these issues, confirms the renewed interest in distributional questions.

One of the factors responsible for this revival of interest is the marked and undisputed rise in income inequality observed in the vast majority of the most populous and richest countries including the United States, China, Brazil, Russia, and more recently and less pronouncedly, India. Similar increases in inequality have also been evident in many other small and medium-sized developing, developed, and, especially, transitional economies. At the same time, countries with explicit distributional objectives, such as France and Malaysia, have been able to avoid adverse changes in income concentration, signalling that public policy can avoid or limit a shift towards higher inequality.

A second factor is the growing debate on the distribution across countries of the benefits of globalization and of the policies that drive it. While the issue of global inequality is not dealt with in this volume, the growing interest surrounding the subject has drawn attention also to the issue of rising inequality within countries, the central topic of this study. Further stimulus has been provided by the ongoing debate concerning the distributive impact of the Washington Consensus policy reforms that have dominated the scene during the last 20 years. Packages aimed at liberalizing foreign trade and capital movements have been introduced throughout Latin America, Eastern Europe, Asia, and Africa, and were in most cases preceded by the privatization of state enterprises and domestic deregulation. While these changes mark a dramatic switch in development policy away from traditional policy regimes, their impact on inequality, poverty, and human well-being are still being assessed.

The recent empirical analyses of inequality, particularly those dealing with the industrialized countries, tend to focus on changes in the wage premium by skill, which are usually explained in terms of growing flows of imports and immigrants from labour-abundant countries, or of the skill bias introduced by technical progress in the field of telecommunications and information. Other potentially relevant factors, such as high-land concentration, educational inequality, spatial inequality, or policy changes inspired by the Washington Consensus, are much less emphasized or ignored altogether. Likewise, analyses of changes in factoral distribution are conspicuously absent from the debate, in spite of the fall of the wage share and the rise of capital incomes frequently observed in recent years.

This collection of studies, assembled by my predecessor as Director of UNU/ WIDER, attempts to bridge this gap by providing a systematic analysis of the main potential causes of the recent rise in income inequality. In contrast to most of the recent literature in this area, the volume pays particular attention to the relationship between inequality changes and public policy changes in the field of domestic and external liberalization, taxation and income transfers, labour market institutions, and safety nets. In a sense, the unifying theme connecting the chapters in the volume is the question of what are the links between economic growth, inequality, poverty, and public policy.

The volume finds that over the last two decades income inequality has risen in two-thirds of the over seventy countries analysed; that the deterioration in the distribution of income was in several cases driven by a rise in the capital share; and that the overall rise in inequality is associated in many (if not all) cases with the unanticipated side effects of policy reforms introduced in recent years. Such hypotheses have never previously been explored in such general terms across a wide cross-section of countries. This volume also argues that in countries where the rise in inequality was small, or started from a relatively low level, its impact on poverty reduction and growth has probably been insignificant or even benign (as in some economies in transition). But where the increase was sizeable or began from already high levels of inequality, the impact on poverty reduction and growth has been—or will be after some lag—significant. In this respect, the volume argues that it might be impossible to achieve the poverty targets now firmly adopted by many national policy-makers and the international community unless the issue of high and rising inequality is dealt with explicitly.

The research agenda documented in this volume has entailed not only the preparation of the sixteen published studies but also the development of a database of income inequality statistics—the World Income Inequality Database (WIID)—a facility that is being regularly updated by UNU/WIDER to facilitate further research in this important topic. Other recent UNU/WIDER projects on Growth and Poverty and on Spatial Dispersion of Human Development continue this interest on distributional issues from a global perspective.

The findings of this original study will be very useful to policy-makers who seek to achieve their often-elusive growth and poverty reduction objectives as well as to practitioners and researchers in international agencies, and scholars interested in the income distribution and poverty alleviation debate. I strongly recommend this study not only to all these groups of people, but also to the general reader interested in the core questions of development and social justice.

Tony Shorrocks
Director, UNU/WIDER

Acknowledgements

This volume would not have seen the light of the day without the contribution of many people. To start with, my sincere professional appreciation goes to the entire project team—particularly to the chapter authors for their precious time and scholarly application, their original analyses and patience in revising twice the early versions of their chapters. My gratitude goes also to the participants of the two workshops held in Helsinki in July and December 1999. These gatherings offered the opportunity to provide helpful comments and frank critique on early chapter drafts, and on the articulation of the project as a whole. As this volume was being written while the debate on inequality was gathering momentum, a number of updatings and revisions were called for to which the chapter authors responded quickly and favourably.

Throughout the life of the project I was provided with constructive comments, useful literature and detailed data also by people other than the chapter authors. Among them are Andrea Brandolini, Stephen Brown, Klaus Deininger, Almas Heshmati, Juha Honkkila, Nilufer Kagatay, Mumtaz Keklik, Terry McKinley, Branko Milanovic, and Gianni Vaggi, to name a few. These colleagues provided insightful comments and advice on the scope and structure of the volume as well as on several specific points. Sincere thanks go also to two anonymous referees for their detailed and constructive comments on the first version of this volume. Its structure and content has substantially benefited from this peer review process.

Heartfelt thanks go to Juha Honkkila, Renato Paniccià, and Sampsa Kiiski for their key contribution to the development of the World Income Inequality Database (WIID), which has constituted the empirical basis for the analyses carried out in several of the chapters of this study as well as for their work on the initial imputation of inequality data in the database. My deepest gratitude goes to Sampsa Kiiski and later on to Maiju Perala for their continuous updating and improvement of WIID. Many sincere thanks go also to UNDP/SEPED that cosponsored the development of WIID and to its staff who contributed numerous important suggestions on how to improve its design and make it more user friendly. Finally, in the concluding research and editorial stages of this study following my transfer from World Institute for Development Economics Research (WIDER) to the University of Florence, Matti Pohjola first, and then Tony Shorrocks, ensured that my work could proceed smoothly and provided steady encouragement and intellectual stimulation for the conclusion of the volume. I am deeply indebted to them for their intellectual guidance and organizational support.

In WIDER, constant, enthusiastic, and efficient support was also provided by Suzsanna Oinas and Taina Iduozee who helped greatly with bibliographical research in this area. I would also like to express my deepest and most heartfelt gratitude to Lorraine Telfer-Taivainen for her expertise, patience, and cheerfulness in editing and formatting various versions of this volume, and for her efficient management of the project and working relations with its many contributors. I am deeply indebted to her for the truly excellent and tireless support she always provided.

The UNDP Division for Social Development and Poverty Elimination took special interest in this research, and acted both as participant and co-sponsor of the overall project. Finally, I would also like to express my most sincere gratitude to the Swedish International Development Cooperation Agency (Sida), which provided financial support to this study.

Giovanni Andrea Cornia
University of Florence
September 2003

PART I

INCOME DISTRIBUTION TRENDS, THEORIES, AND POLICIES

1

Inequality, Growth, and Poverty: An Overview of Changes over the Last Two Decades

GIOVANNI ANDREA CORNIA

1.1. INTRODUCTION: HISTORICAL CONTEXT, RATIONALE, AND PURPOSE OF THE STUDY

The last decade has witnessed a blossoming of research on poverty-related topics as well as a surge in attention towards the issue of poverty reduction by governments, the international financial institutions, the United Nations, and social scientists. These bodies rightly see the persistence of mass poverty not only as a major ethical and political problem but also as a serious threat to macroeconomic stability and a brake on long-term growth. This new awareness has triggered a few potentially important changes, including the UN General Assembly's adoption of Millennium Development Goals on poverty reduction, the creation of new World Bank and International Monetary Fund (IMF) facilities dealing with poverty alleviation, the preparation of poverty reduction framework papers, and so on. While it is too early to assess the real impact of these developments, they have the potential to seriously dent the long-lasting problems of poverty and underdevelopment.

A similar shift in focus and policy stance has yet to take place in the case of income inequality. While research in this field has made considerable strides, the policy reforms inspired by the Washington Consensus have broadly ignored the issues of high and rising inequality, of its impact on poverty and growth, and of the measures required to contain it. Some proponents of the Washington Consensus view high inequality either as a non-issue or an important issue about which nothing much can be done. Others see it as a source of incentives and capital accumulation leading to faster income growth for all, including the poor, or as a stimulus to upward mobility for low-income groups. Meanwhile, in the countries in transition, rising inequality is seen as a normal side-effect of the unwinding of socialism's artificial compression of earnings.

The neglect of rising high inequality has meant that over the last decade poverty reduction has been mainly pursued through economic growth and safety nets targeted at the poor. While growth is essential for poverty reduction, a strategy that relies solely on it is flawed in several respects. To start with, when the initial asset inequality is high and economic improvements are concentrated within few groups, the poverty reduction elasticity of growth is low. Such growth bypasses smallholders and microentrepreneurs and creates little employment for the unskilled workers. Second, high inequality may lower the growth rate of gross domestic product (GDP) itself. It is not surprising, for example, that in high-inequality Latin America growth has remained sluggish for decades, and the number of the poor in the region has declined only slowly. Third, the view that inequality is either neutral or even good for growth is now challenged by most of the recent theoretical and applied research (Benabou 1996; Aghion *et al.* 1999) that sees high 'vertical inequality' as unambiguously bad for growth and poverty reduction. New approaches also highlight the negative effects of high 'horizontal inequality' (such as among social groups) on the risk of civil conflict (Nafziger *et al.* 2000). In sum, ignoring high or rising inequality may entail large economic, social, and political costs.

The recent rise in within-country inequality has coincided with the emergence of a new policy paradigm—generally referred to as the Washington Consensus—that advocates the removal of barriers to international trade, the liberalization of capital flows, and the creation of a strong patent regime regulating technology transfers and intellectual property. Such reforms were adopted by a large number of countries in the 1990s and were often preceded in the 1980s by the liberalization of domestic markets and privatization of state assets. Not all countries, however, followed closely the prescriptions of the Washington Consensus. For instance, Raghbendra Jha argues in Chapter 12 that the policy approach followed in India (the 'Delhi Consensus') avoided liberalizing the capital account, downplayed the speed of reforms, and relied little on external resources.

Lance Taylor notes in Chapter 7 that the old policy paradigm inspired by import-substituting industrialization had been criticized for failing to achieve sufficiently rapid growth and to reduce high levels of inequality and poverty. Has the new Washington Consensus-inspired policy paradigm helped meet the goals of reducing inequality and poverty to which the international community is now firmly committed? The main official justification for the recent reforms was stated in terms of an acceleration in economic growth, less so in terms of an improvement in income inequality. While it was recognized that inequality might have worsened in advanced nations importing labour-intensive goods from developing countries, it was also emphasized that inequality was expected to fall in poor nations and on the global scale. As shown in this book, however, the distributive impact of domestic and external liberalization has turned out to be less favourable.

This volume attempts to bring together the three debates alluded to above, namely the recent rise in domestic income inequality, the likely impact of these changes on poverty alleviation, and the distributive impact of the Washington Consensus. If it is demonstrated that the last raises perceptibly income inequality, and that high inequality affects poverty alleviation directly and through a lowering of the growth rate, a profound conflict would become evident between the stated poverty alleviation objectives of the international community and the economic policies of the Washington

Consensus. Although analysis of the recent inequality changes raises many contentious theoretical, technical, and policy problems—including about the impact of the Washington Consensus—this issue has to be clarified directly and urgently, as little progress can be achieved on the poverty reduction front if the high inequality problem continues to be ignored.

1.2. RESEARCH METHODOLOGY

This volume has two main objectives. First, it aims at documenting and analysing the recent changes in within-country income inequality against the background of changes occurring in this area during the two prior decades. Chapter 2 provides an extensive review of the literature on income inequality since the end of the Second World War on the basis of country studies and regional reviews carried out by universities and institutions such as ECLAC and the Inter-American Development Bank (IADB) in Latin America, Organization for Economic Cooperation and Development (OECD), and LIS in the industrialized countries, the World Bank for sub-Saharan Africa and Eastern Europe, and so on. While these studies rely on income concepts, sample sizes, methods for the computation of inequality indexes, etc. that vary from one country to another, standardized and time-consistent approaches are used within each country in most cases. Changes in income inequality were explored also through an econometric analysis of the trends in Gini coefficients of seventy-three countries included in the World Income Inequality Database (WIID) codeveloped by the World Institute for Development Economics Research (WIDER) and United Nations Development Programme (UNDP) with the purpose of creating a time-consistent and regularly updated dataset available online.

The second objective of the study is to identify the causes of the changes in income inequality recorded during the period under observation. To do so, the volume relies on three sets of studies. A first group (Chapters 3–5) evaluates whether the recent rises in inequality can be explained by an intensification of the disequalizing effect of structural causes of high inequality—for example, high land concentration, unequal access to education, and the urban bias of public policy. While these factors explain the level of inequality in the early 1970s, it is not clear whether they also explain its surge over the last 20 years. In turn, a second group of chapters (Chapters 6–11) evaluates the extent to which the recent income polarization could be explained by new factors such as skilled-biased technical progress or the Washington Consensus policies. The relation between policy reform and income inequality has received comparatively little attention in the literature and for this reason it is especially emphasized in this volume. A third set of chapters (Chapters 12–16) comprises five country studies analysing inequality changes over the last 20 years. These studies follow a similar research methodology adopting a common periodization (before and after the early 1980s) and evaluating the impact of a common set of potential causes of inequality.

The five country studies mentioned above were selected because they illustrate particular aspects of recent distributive changes. India exemplifies the case of a country where inequality rose moderately in the 1990s following the partial liberalization of the economy. South Africa, in turn, highlights the distributive impact of political liberalization and of the subsequent economic reforms. And the studies on Thailand, Turkey, and Venezuela respectively depict the effects of a regionally imbalanced development strategy, financial liberalization, and the capital share surge in an oil-dominated economy.

While most of the recent literature focuses on changes in earnings differentials by skill, this volume tries to capture also the impact of changes in factor shares, taxes, and transfers. As noted in Chapter 9 by Anthony Atkinson, income distribution is often treated as synonymous with the wage distribution but a number of other factors need to be brought into any explanation of the changes in income distribution, including movements in factor shares and real interest rates, and the impact of government budgets.

1.3. MAIN FINDINGS

Notwithstanding the difficulties involved in summarizing the evidence provided in the subsequent fifteen chapters, six main conclusions, and a number of sub-points, emerge.

1.3.1. *A Fall in Inequality during the Golden Age is Followed by a Rise over the Last Two Decades*

In Chapter 2, Giovanni Andrea Cornia, Tony Addison, and Sampsa Kiiski examine changes in domestic income inequality based on the relevant literature and econometric analysis of inequality trends for seventy-three countries. They argue that, with the exception of Latin America and part of sub-Saharan Africa, a move towards lower inequality was recorded in the most developed, centrally planned, and developing countries during the 1950s, 1960s, and most of the 1970s, but the early 1980s saw this trend being halted or reversed in many countries. In the OECD region, the distribution of both net and gross incomes started to become more skewed in the early 1980s (to stabilize in the 1990s) in the Anglo-Saxon countries that were among the first to embrace neoliberal policies. The Scandinavian countries and the Netherlands followed suit, though in this case the reversal in inequality took place from lower levels and was less marked. Also Japan experienced in the 1980s and 1990s a turnaround in its inequality trend owing to the abandonment of the old egalitarian, lifetime employment system, and a prolonged stagnation. Only Germany and France—that is, countries with centralized wage-settings, a high union density and sizeable minimum wages—avoided a reversal of inequality trends.

The most striking inequality reversal was observed on the introduction of market reforms in the former socialists countries. Since 1989, the distribution of both net and gross income has widened moderately in Central Europe and massively (i.e. by 10–20 Gini points) in the former USSR and southeastern Europe. In the first year of reform, for instance, Russia experienced a worsening of its income distribution equivalent to that recorded by the United Kingdom over the entire 1980s. Also in this group, the growth of earnings inequality played an important role in the surge of income inequality (see Chapter 2). While this was expected because of the change in wage-setting norms and privatization, other policy factors contributed to the polarization of incomes, including a fall in the minimum wage relative to the average, the informalization of the economy, and a surge in interindustrial wage dispersion unrelated to changes in productivity differentials. In many instances, inequality also rose due to a capital share surge following inequitable privatization.

Inequality has also risen during the last 20 years, if moderately, in the Southeast and East Asian economies. The reversal of stable–declining inequality trends started in the late 1980s and was exacerbated by the 1997 Asian crisis. In this region, inequality rose in line with the development of the urban-based, capital- and skill-intensive sector, a slowdown in agriculture, and the retrenchment of rural development programmes. While export expansion and fast growth helped in reducing the incidence of poverty, equity could not be achieved due to the absence of effective mechanisms for the redistribution of the fruits of growth. The Asian crisis impacted inequality via a surge in full capacity unemployment, the spread of part-time and temporary jobs, the widening of the wage gap by employment type, and the differential impact of price changes on the poor.

In India (Chapter 12) the acceleration of growth of the 1990s was accompanied by a moderate rise in recorded consumption inequality and, possibly, by a larger one in unrecorded inequality, as the National Sample Survey seems increasingly unable to account for some types of incomes in the expanding urban sector. All this has led to a recorded modest rise in rural inequality, a more significant one in urban inequality, and a widening of the urban–rural income gap. Because of the shift of growth to the urban sector, the retrenchment of rural development programmes, the stagnation of agricultural wages, and the rise of food prices rural poverty declined little throughout the 1990s.

In the 1980s, all but three Latin American countries experienced a rise in their already high inequality levels owing to strong external shocks, the recessionary adjustment introduced to respond to them, and the debt crisis. During the 1990s inequality rose in half of them, mainly because of a rise in the capital share and the polarization of the wage gap by education (Szekely and Hilgert 1999). In Chapter 13, Francisco Rodriguez analyses the inequality surge recorded in Venezuela owing to the rising capital share in the oil sector and the financial crisis of 1994. Contrary to the widespread opinion that inequality rose in Africa during the last two decades, this volume is unable to identify a clear regional trend based on the limited evidence available. For instance, Carolyn Jenkins and Lynne Thomas show in Chapter 15 that overall inequality first fell with the abolition of apartheid but then rose because of the stringent policy reforms adopted by the postapartheid government. For the rest of the region the picture is a composite one. Overall inequality seems to have fallen in half of the cases and risen in the other half. Rural inequality rose in liberalizing countries characterized by high land concentration or collapsing marketing arrangements but fell where peasant agriculture was favourably impacted by domestic trade liberalization and agricultural procurement policies. This nuanced picture is confirmed by a recent

World Bank study of the impact of liberalization in seven sub-Saharan countries (Christiaensen *et al.* 2002).

Chapter 2 also formally tests the hypothesis that income inequality has risen during the last twenty years. To this extent, 770 reliable Gini coefficients for seventy-three countries spanning the period 1950–95 were extracted from the November 1998 version of the WIID (www.wider.unu.edu) and interpolated by means of linear and quadratic functions so as to capture possible reversals in inequality trends. Such analysis confirms the conclusions arrived at on the basis of the review of the literature (see Table 2.8 of Chapter 2), as inequality was found to have risen in forty-eight of the seventy-three countries analysed, remained constant in sixteen, and declined in nine. These conclusions are increasingly confirmed by most recent studies in this area (see for instance Sala-i-Martin 2002). As the November 1998 version of WIID includes data only up to 1995, these econometric results do not capture the distributive changes of the last five years and the impact of the recent financial crises in particular. Thus, if the countries that experienced inequality surges after 1995 are moved to the rising inequality category, the number of nations in this group rises to fifty-three. The surge was universal in the transition economies, almost universal in Latin America and the OECD, and increasingly frequent, if less pronounced, in South, Southeast, and East Asia.

1.3.2. *Sources of Inequality Changes*

Most of the literature on recent income inequality changes focuses on shifts in wage inequality by skill level and, in particular, on the so-called 'skill premium' that is alternatively attributed to trade liberalization or skilled-biased technical change and only seldom to other factors. Such literature broadly ignores changes in the factoral distribution of income and the redistributive effects of taxes and transfers. Such an approach can, however, steer to misleading conclusions. In Chapter 6, Ajit Singh and Rahul Dhumale warn that both the trade liberalization and skill-biased technical progress hypotheses hardly explain the inequality rises of the 1980s as in both industrialized and developing countries these were strongly influenced by a rise of the share of capital income in the total. For instance, as argued by Rodríguez in Chapter 13, while the Gini coefficient of the distribution of wages oscillated for many years in the range 0.35–0.40, the factor shares moved sharply against labour, causing in this way a rise in overall inequality.

In Turkey, the capital share increase was driven by financial liberalization as, in the presence of large budget deficits, this measure raised substantially the interest rate on the public debt and the share of budgetary resources absorbed by its servicing. In Chapter 14 Erinc Yeldan argues that while income distribution improved in Turkey in the 1970s, the liberalization and globalization of the late 1980s and 1990s fostered a rise in the share of non-wage incomes, the widening of the wage gap between skilled/organized and unskilled/marginal segments of the urban labour force, and a surge in the income share of the top population quintile. Chapter 12, in turn, suggests that the recent rise of inequality in India resulted from a shift in earnings from labour to capital income driven by the rapid service sector growth—particularly its finance, insurance, and real estate (FIRE) component—and by an increase in regional inequality. Finally, as Caroline Jenkins and Lynne Thomas show in Chapter 15, South Africa also experienced a significant redistribution of labour income towards profits, rents, and other property incomes, as indicated by the steadily rising share of property income from 18 per cent in 1981–2 to nearly 30 per cent in 2000 and by the corresponding 11 points fall in the wage share over the same period.

1.3.3. *Impact of the Observed Inequality Changes on Poverty and Growth*

One of the recurring themes throughout this volume concerns the impact of recent inequality rises on poverty alleviation and growth. The modest rises (i.e. of less than 3–4 Gini points) observed in a quarter of the fifty-three countries that experienced rising inequality (see Chapter 2) are unlikely to have affected growth and poverty rates in a significant way. In contrast, the hikes of 5–20 points or those recorded in countries with high initial inequality that were recorded in over half of the fifty-three countries mentioned above reduced the pace of poverty decline and may have affected the growth of the economy.

In this regard, Chapter 2 shows that, as expected, a rise in inequality lowers the poverty alleviation elasticity of growth. For instance, Table 2.10 in Chapter 2 shows during the 1980s and 1990s poverty dropped by 9.6 per cent in those developing countries where inequality fell, but by only 1.3 per cent in those where it rose. Similar conclusions are arrived at by Raghbendra Jha in Chapter 12, who argues that even the moderate rises in inequality recorded in India since the mid-1990s visibly eroded the poverty alleviation impact of growth in rural areas.

Chapter 2 argues further that rising inequality likely depressed growth in several countries. This is a controversial conclusion as there is no theoretical agreement on the shape of the relation between inequality and growth. The Keynesian and post-Keynesian literature posits a positive relation, while the political economy models and the analyses focusing on capital markets imperfections, political instability, and policy distortions suggest the opposite. Yet, none of these hypotheses has been satisfactorily tested. Also, the linearity and monotonicity of the inequality–growth relation assumed by these theories are counterintuitive. In this regard, Chapter 2 suggests that the inequality–growth relation is concave, and that 'too low' or 'too high' inequality are detrimental to growth that remains broadly invariant in an intermediate range. An artificially compressed distribution of income differs from the optimal distribution based on differences in talent, merit, and effort, and for this reason inhibits growth by affecting incentives, labour shirking, and free-riding behaviour. Conversely, when inequality rises beyond a given threshold (which varies with the characteristics of each country) growth turns negative. Also in this case, the observed distribution deviates markedly from the optimal one, thus causing an erosion of incentives, which may lead to output contraction among the self-employed and greater shirking among the dependent workers. A high level of inequality may also weaken social cohesion as, when the gap between rich and poor widens, predatory and criminal activities rise together with the transaction costs for business security and contracts enforcement. An empirical estimation of the concave relation between inequality and growth on a cross section of seventy-three countries suggests that the growth rate of GDP rises up to 4 points when the Gini coefficient increases between 0.15 and 0.30, is broadly invariant in the range 0.35–0.45, declines by 1 point when the Gini coefficient moves from 0.45 and 0.50, and declines another 4 when it reaches 0.60 (Addison and Cornia 2001). These results resemble those of Barro (2000), who found a significant negative relation between inequality and growth in low-income countries (that generally exhibit high inequality) and a positive one in countries with a high GDP per capita (that are characterized by low inequality). While these findings need further probing on broader datasets, they are nevertheless important as a conclusive testing of the inequality–growth relation along these lines would provide a strong rationale for adjusting public policy in the area of income distribution.

1.3.4. *The Contribution of Structural Factors to the Recent Surge in Inequality*

This volume explores in detail the degree to which recent increases in inequality were due to an aggravation of the structural factors responsible for the high inequality prevailing during the 1960s and 1970s. This hypothesis is discussed hereafter by considering the recent changes in each of these factors.

Unequal agrarian structures

In Chapter 3, Michael Carter explores the role of unequal land ownership in explaining not only historically high levels of income inequality but also the contemporary trend towards their rise. He identifies four channels of transmission between unequal agrarian structures and current inequality trends. First, in societies suffering from high land concentration, a decline of the agricultural share in GDP tends to reduce inequality, as the share of unequally distributed incomes declines. A second linkage is the 'legacy effect' by which the agrarian oligarchy is able to reserve for itself most opportunities for new industrial developments. A third pathway is represented by the 'exclusionary agrarian growth' in which capital market failures cause the displacement of smallholders by big farmers. This phenomenon has been observed in Latin America but not in India where rural growth was more equalizing than urban growth. Fourthly, in the presence of capital market imperfections, high land concentration can affect current inequality via past 'human capital accumulation failures' among low-income families.

Carter finds evidence of the negative effect of a drop in the agricultural share on current inequality. Over the last 40 years, the agriculture share in total output and employment declined substantially everywhere. In addition, land reforms over the 1950s and 1960s redistributed latifundia and state land in some thirty developing countries. As a result, land rents as a share of GDP declined in most countries. In

Latin America, for instance, they fell from 20 to 2–3 per cent of total income. Carter also finds evidence of the 'legacy effects' of unequal agrarian structure on current income inequality but considers this a spurious correlation. In contrast, he found no empirical verification for the other two effects. He concludes by noting that agrarian asset redistribution and corrections of financial market imperfections are two measures that would sever the linkage between high past land concentration and current high income inequality. Overall, however, he finds no evidence that recent inequality trends are explained by a worsening of land concentration.

Changes in educational inequality

The contribution of changing educational achievements to the recent rise of income inequality is explored by Daniele Checchi in Chapter 4. He constructs an index of average years of education and a Gini index of the distribution of educational attainments. He finds that the average years of education rose in all regions between 1960 and 1995 while educational inequality diminished until 1990 but rose rapidly between 1990 and 1995 in sub-Saharan Africa and East Asia, and moderately in Latin America and the OECD countries. His multivariate regression confirms prior findings about the inverted U-shape of the relationship between the average years of schooling of the workforce and income inequality. He also found that, after controlling for income per capita and average educational achievements, the relation between educational inequality and income inequality appears to be U-shaped, thus suggesting that a moderate increase in educational inequality from low initial levels reduces income inequality while larger increases (as those observed over 1990–5 in sub-Saharan Africa and, to a lesser extent, Latin America) raise it. Similarly, the decline in educational inequality he found in South Asia and the MENA region should have, ceteris paribus, reduced income inequality in these regions.

Thus, it would appear that changes in average years of education and educational inequality cannot explain the increase in income inequality observed during the last 20 years, with the possible exception of sub-Saharan Africa and, to a lesser extent, Latin America. Similar conclusions are arrived at by Cornia and Kiiski (2001), who underscore that in Latin America a rise in the average number of years of education was accompanied by growing educational inequality, as public policy emphasized the attainment of universal primary education (a measure that reduces educational inequality) and an expansion of university education while assigning low priority to secondary education (i.e. measures that raise educational inequality). In contrast, East and Southeast Asian and Middle Eastern countries focused on an expansion of universal secondary education and so helped reduce educational inequality and, ceteris paribus, income inequality.

An aggravation of the 'urban bias'?

In the 1960s and 1970s, income inequality in developing countries was strongly influenced by the 'urban bias' of public policy. Can a worsening of such bias explain the widespread rise in inequality observed over the last 20 years? This issue is explored by Robert Eastwood and Michael Lipton in Chapter 5 that analyses changes over time in intra-rural, intra-urban, and rural–urban income inequality for developing and transitional countries. The chapter evaluates the extent to which adjustment policies reduced, as expected, the urban–rural average income gap. Indeed, from 1980 many developing countries introduced structural adjustment programmes that were, inter alia, expected to reduced rural–urban inequality and overall income inequality. The findings of Chapter 5 suggest that the urban–rural gap declined in Brazil, Chile, Honduras, parts of Africa, Pakistan, Sri Lanka, and China (over 1978–84), but increased in Bangladesh, China (over 1985–2000), and Thailand. Eastwood and Lipton justify the failure of adjustment policies to narrow the rural–urban income gap by noting that the higher educational levels of the urban residents allowed them to better exploit opportunities brought about by price liberalization, that remote rural minorities (as in China) were not reached by the spread effects of urban growth, that the urban bias of public spending was unaffected by adjustment, and that farm prices continued their downward trend. All in all, there was no uniform shift in the urban–rural gap and it is therefore impossible to attribute to this factor the general rise in inequality of the last twenty years.

A worsening of the 'curse of natural resources'?

Countries endowed with abundant natural resources relative to other production factors tend to grow more slowly and have higher income and asset inequality than other economy types (Sachs and Warner 1995). In this sector, production requires a lot of capital but little labour. This compresses the demand for unskilled and semi-skilled labour, lowers the wage rate, and discourages investments in education. Second, the volatility of commodity prices reduces incentives to invest in education and may force poor families to pull children out of school in years of low prices. In this way, transitory shocks can cause permanent damage to the educational opportunities of the poor and raise the long-term dispersion of educational attainments. Third, ownership of assets and mining proceeds are highly concentrated due to the ease with which the related rents can be captured by élites.

To what extent did the distributive biases typical of countries endowed with natural resources intensify during the last two decades and so contribute to the recent rise in income inequality? This possibility is rejected as the 'mineral rent/GDP' ratio of most resource-rich countries fell steadily during 1980–5 due to a slowdown in new discoveries and because international commodity prices remained low in relation to their peak of the early 1980s. A simple bivariate regression of the mineral rent/GDP ratio on the Gini coefficient of the distribution of income per capita on a cross section of thirty-two countries for the periods 1970–4 and 1990–9 would show that in the latter period the mineral rent/GDP ratio explains a smaller proportion of overall income inequality than in the former.

1.3.5. *Recent Factors Influencing the Distribution of Income: Skilled-Biased Technical Change*

The new technologies, it is argued, generate a demand for skills and a distribution of earnings more skewed than those emanating from the old technologies. As a consequence, the demand for and wage of unskilled workers drop while that for skilled workers rise faster than their supply. As a result, wage dispersion rises in the sectors using the new technologies. Second, information technology reduces the cost of monitoring unskilled workers and minimizes labour shirking so reducing the wage premium needed to ensure their efficient performance. Finally, especially in the service sector and in a few industrial branches, new technologies replace unskilled labour with physical capital and in so doing push up the capital share and overall income concentration.

Chapter 6 by Ajit Singh and Rahul Dhumale reviews the plausibility of these hypotheses with particular attention to the middle- and high-income nations. The evidence they examine supports weakly the skilled-biased technical change hypothesis and suggests that other factors—such as changes in remuneration norms, labour institutions, and financial markets—may be more relevant in explaining the recent rise in wage inequality. They note that in the United States there was no trend increase in the relative demand for college-educated workers during the years of technical modernization. They note also that the earnings gap by education level rose in all industries, not only in those intensively using new technology. In addition, in the 1990s, the average wage of the bottom decile (unskilled workers) improved relative to the median while the latter declined in relation to that of the top decile, suggesting in this way that the cause of rising inequality cannot be due to a fall in unskilled wages.

Another weak element in the skill-biased technology hypothesis concerns the scarcity rents supposedly generated by a faster rise in the demand for skilled workers in relation to their supply. Comparisons between Canada and the United States in the 1980s to the 1990s and South Korea and Brazil in the 1960s to the 1970s illustrate this point. Murphy *et al.* (1998), for instance, compare the United States (where the skill premium rose by 20 per cent over 1980–95) and Canada (where it remained constant thanks to a steady supply of state-subsidized high school graduates). They conclude that, while the new technology raises the demand for educated workers, an increase in the skill premium mainly depends on the lack of public support to post-secondary education.

The World Bank (2000) suggests that the shift towards skill-intensive employment observed in the OECD nations in the 1970s and 1980s was matched in the 1990s in several developing countries and that this affected their distribution of income. This shift, however, cannot be a major factor in the developing countries where inequality rose already in the 1980s, or in regions such as Africa and the transition economies of Europe where the economic stagnation of the 1990s retarded technological modernization. Thus, with the partial exception of some sectors in the advanced countries, the evidence in favour of the hypothesis that technological change is the key factor behind the inequality rises of the last twenty years does not seem, on balance, sufficiently strong.

1.3.6. *Recent Factors Influencing the Distribution of Income: Policies towards Stabilization, Liberalization, and Globalization*

Policy reform began in the early 1980s with the implementation of stabilization pro-grammes aimed at tackling the large rises in the twin deficits caused by the second oil shock, the 1982–4 recession in the OECD countries and the debt crisis. These measures were followed by the liberalization of the products and factors markets and, in the 1990s, by that of external transactions. The starting year, pace, extent, and approach of these reforms varied from country to country, and in a few cases differed substantially from the mainstream approach. In India, for instance, policy reform began only in 1991 with fiscal consolidation, the abolition of export and fertilizer subsidies, and the phasing out of budgetary support to loss-making public enterprises. These measures were followed by a partial liberalization of industrial licensing, foreign investments, and imports, while changes in the capital account liberaliza-tion and patent legislation were minimal. In contrast, Chapter 15 shows that the postapartheid government in South Africa adopted policies closely inspired by the Washington Consensus. It committed itself to fiscal discipline, adopted low tariffs, and abolished exchange controls on non-residents in 1995 and on residents later on. In 1996 it pledged to reduce the fiscal deficit to 3 per cent of GDP, further opened its economy, and liberalized the labour market.

The distributive effects of the policies inspired by the Washington Consensus reviewed in this volume are summarized hereafter by main policy instrument.

Macroeconomic stabilization

When brought about through conventional instruments, stabilization quickly restores macroeconomic balance but causes large recessions and a deterioration in income distribution. The distributive impact of stabilization-induced recession is particularly pronounced in low-income countries. In industrialized nations, recessions have a greater impact on profits than wages due to the stickiness of the latter, to well-developed safety nets that cushion most of the loss in wage income, and to the fact that firms hoard labour during recessions that they perceive to be temporary to reduce the screening and training costs they face over the medium term. In contrast, in developing countries inequality tends to rise during recessions (as wages are downward flexible, social safety nets are little developed, and labour hoarding is rare) and fall during recoveries. This is well known to the IMF that pointed out some time back that the 'real wage rate may have to fall and real profit rates increase so as to encourage increased foreign capital inflow'—whether such tradeoff is unavoidable is however a matter of controversy (Johnson and Salop 1980: 23).

Inflation control was another key objective of the stabilization programmes introduced in the 1980s and 1990s. No doubt, high inflation (as in Bolivia in the mid-1980s or Russia in the early 1990s) sharply worsens income inequality as the poor are least able to index their incomes and maintain the real value of their assets, and unskilled labour is especially vulnerable to layoffs in recessions caused by ill-designed stabilization efforts. Finally, and most fundamentally, inflation rates of more than 40 per cent are costly as they reduce growth (Bruno and Easterly 1996). Yet, the orthodox approach itself to inflation control has not been immune from problems. First, the inflation target adopted was often single digit even though the literature shows that below the threshold of 40–50 per cent a year inflation does not cause losses of output (Stiglitz 1998). Second, such ambitious targets were achieved by means of large rises in interest rates and budget cuts—that is, measures that have negative distributive effects. Third, as evidenced by the allegedly successful Chilean and Mexican stabilization experiences of the 1980s, the monetary approach to control inflation generated unexpected monetary and fiscal side-effects (such as large falls in tax revenue) which required that austerity measures be kept in place for many years (up to seven in at least one instance) in order to push inflation below the established threshold (Solimano 1992).

An example of the limited success of the mainstream approach is illustrated in Chapter 15 on South Africa where, following the implementation of orthodox stabilization, output grew at a sluggish 2–3 per cent a year, income per capita stagnated, and income inequality rose. One reason for this substandard performance was contagion from emerging market financial crises. But the main factor was the policy followed. For example, a rapid deficit reduction penalized rather than stimulated private investment owing to the sharp contraction of the aggregate demand it brought about. Likewise, policy changes in the field of trade liberalization, relaxation of exchange controls, and deregulation increased uncertainty for investors. And the tight monetary stance adopted for years helped reduce inflation but severely retarded growth, employment creation, and savings.

Trade liberalization

The main rationale of trade liberalization are the Heckscher–Ohlin theorem and its Stolper–Samuelson corollary that show that, under restrictive assumptions, free trade raises the income of all trading partners and reduces the wage spread in the country exporting labour-intensive goods. A reformulation of this approach due to Wood (1994) suggests that in developing countries with an abundance of semi-skilled workers, trade liberalization leads to an expansion of labour-intensive exports, to an increase in the demand for unskilled but literate labour relative to that of skilled and illiterate labour, and to a fall in the wage differential between semi-skilled and skilled workers. Meanwhile, in the developed countries, a rise in labour-intensive imports reduces the demand for semi-skilled workers, depresses their wage rate, and raises wage inequality. Part of the empirical literature supports these predictions. For instance, Barro (1991) and Sachs and Warner (1995) found that trade distortions were associated with slow growth. Lately, Dollar and Kraay (2000) found that growth and poverty reduction were highest in the countries that significantly cut tariff rates or expanded trade volumes and that trade liberalization did not affect income distribution in these countries. These results, however, are biased by methodological problems. When the analysis was repeated with an unbiased procedure, there was no evidence that the globalizers grew faster than the other countries (Rodrik 2000). While trade and growth clearly correlate with each other, they both likely depend on the quality of a country's institutions.

Except for the studies just mentioned, the empirical record of the last twenty years does not generally corroborate the predictions of the neoclassical trade theory. For instance, wage inequality has been found to have increased in six out of seven liberalizing Latin American countries, the Philippines, and Eastern Europe (Lindert and Williamson 2001). Several explanations of the discrepancy between mainstream trade theory and observed outcomes have been put forward. First of all, as noted by Taylor in Chapter 7, trade liberalization was often accompanied by the opening of the capital account, a measure that tends to raise the real exchange rate. Under such circumstances, trade liberalization shifted the composition of demand towards imports and so encouraged the producers of traded goods to adopt cost-cutting measures (e.g. downsizing and subcontracting to informal-sector firms), restructure production, and rely on foreign outsourcing—that is, measures that reduced the absorption of unskilled labour, increased the size of the informal sector, and raised wage inequality. Trade and capital account liberalization also increased the pressure to weaken legislation on minimum wages and collective bargaining, altering in this way the factor distribution.

A second explanation is offered by the skill-enhancing trade hypothesis. One of the assumptions of the Hekscher–Ohlin theorem is that all trading countries share the same production technology, and that technology is not affected by trade. This assumption is clearly unrealistic. By relaxing foreign exchange rationing, trade liberalization can, for instance, enlarge the access of developing countries firms to formerly restricted technologies. Because of capital-skill complementarities, the latter are likely to raise the demand for skilled-labour. All this leads to a fall in the wage share, a rise in the demand for and wages of skilled workers, and a drop in the demand for and wages of unskilled workers.

A third explanation focuses on the problems faced by low-income countries specializing in the export of primary commodities. During the last two decades, these countries were hit by large price shocks and steadily declining terms of trade. Birdsall and Hamoudi (2002) provide evidence that this depressed their earnings and trade/GDP ratio despite the liberalization of their trade regime and the depreciation of the real exchange rate. In addition, these countries were often characterized by structural rigidities and governance problems that hampered the reallocation of resources towards the export sector. The impact of these rigidities on inequality is undetermined but that on poverty is clearly unfavourable. A third problem faced by countries exporting agricultural goods competing with Northern goods was persistent protectionism by OECD countries (Slaughter 2000). For all these reasons, in these countries, trade liberalization led to a fall in employment and earnings in the import-substituting sector without generating a corresponding rise in jobs in the export-oriented sector.

Fourth, the distributive impact of trade liberalization has been influenced by the historical context under which it took place. A big difference between Latin America in the 1990s and East Asia in the 1960s is the competitive pressures the former had to face owing to Asia's low-wage manufacturing exporters opening up to world trade. The point here is that the comparative advantage of a developing country may change because of the decision of other nations to enter the world market. Under these circumstances, the formal sector of middle-income countries lost its comparative advantage in labour-intensive exports. It either informalized its production or shifted it towards the skill-intensive sector where it had to face the stiff competition of the advanced economies. Finally, the neoclassical trade theory scarcely explains the inequality and employment changes intervened over the last 20 years in the OECD countries. As noted by Singh and Dhumale in Chapter 6, while the skill premium increased during this period in line with an expansion in manufacturing imports from the South, the starting volume of the latter in 1970 was so low that by the early 1990s the imports from developing countries constituted only 2 per cent of the GDP of the OECD group. Other factors, such as the changes in labour markets, remuneration norms, and social transfers, they argue, had a greater impact on inequality in these countries.

All in all, the predictions of standard trade theory were seldom confirmed in the 1990s. While trade liberalization likely improved the income distribution in the exporters of labour-intensive manufacturers with strong domestic institutions, it had the opposite effect in low-income, commodity-dependent countries. At the global level, it is thus difficult to identify a systemic effect of trade liberalization on inequality due to the heterogeneity of the situations analysed. Similar conclusions are arrived at for Latin America by Behrman *et al.* (2000), who found no statistically significant relation between trade liberalization and wage inequality. In contrast, a recent paper by Milanovic (2002) suggests that trade openness has had a negative impact on inequality in low- and middle-income countries but a favourable one in high-income ones.

Domestic financial reforms and capital account liberalization

In Chapter 7, Lance Taylor argues that during the past 15 years economic policy in developing countries was dominated by capital account liberalization. The freeing of capital movements was said to lead to a better international and intertemporal allocation of resources, greater overall efficiency, and the convergence of incomes per capita across countries. By increasing the absorption of unskilled labour, foreign direct investments and short-term portfolio flows were also supposed to improve the distribution of income in countries endowed with large labour stocks.

In reality, the impact of capital account liberalization has been different. To start with, the surge of capital inflows in developing countries often provoked credit booms associated with high interest rates and strong exchange rates, that is, changes that negatively affect exports, the current account balance, and income distribution. As a result, the traded sector suffered losses of employment and/or wages while the labour made redundant was absorbed in the non-traded sector where wages and employment conditions are less favourable. With rare exceptions, the wage differentials between skilled and unskilled workers thus rose in line with the liberalization of the capital account.

A second problem has been the instability of portfolio flows, as signalled by the rise in the frequency and severity of financial crises in recent years. As noted by Singh and Dhumale in Chapter 6, the movements of capital are intrinsically subject to problems of agency, incomplete information, markets and contracts, adverse selection, moral hazard, asset price speculation, and herd behaviour, that is, all factors leading to systemic instability. Evidence of the impact of instability on income inequality is limited but fairly consistent. The financial crises of the 1990s and 2000s entailed devastating losses of output and worsened income distribution via employment, wages, and price effects. Galbraith and Lu (1999) point to the close relation between capital account liberalization, the occurrence of financial crises, and the worsening of earnings inequality, particularly in countries with weak labour institutions and social safety nets. Diwan (1999) shows on international panel data that the labour share in GDP fell during financial crises, while in a subsequent paper finds that capital account restrictions help maintain it once a financial crisis occurs (Diwan 2000). In analysing the 1997–8 financial crisis in Indonesia, Levinshon *et al.* (1999) found that price increases had been significantly faster for poor and rural households. In analysing the impact of the liberalization package on wage differentials in eighteen Latin American countries over 1980–98, Behrman *et al.* (2000) found that the strongest disequalizing component of the reform package was precisely the capital account liberalization. Similar conclusions are arrived at in Chapter 7 by Taylor who notes that economies that combined growth with stable or declining income inequality adopted a policy mix that avoided the combination of high real exchange rate and domestic interest rate, maintained well-directed export incentives, and could count on a system of capital controls and financial regulation able to contain the consequences of capital surges.

The impact of capital account liberalization is best understood if seen against the background of domestic financial market liberalization introduced in Latin America in the mid-late 1970s, in Africa and Asia in the second half of the 1980s, and in Eastern Europe in the 1990s. Such changes entailed the lifting of interest rate ceilings, the market determination of interest rates, the lowering of reserve requirements, and easier norms for the establishment of new financial institutions. These policies, as well as the 1982 rise in US interest rates and the IMF policy of demanding large increases in interest rates in crisis countries, fuelled a worldwide rise in real interest rates that lasted over a decade. As noted in Chapter 14 by Erinc Yeldan, domestic financial liberalization in Turkey raised real interest rates to unprecedented levels and, as a result, the share of interests in total income rose between 1980 and 1998 from close to zero to 15.2 per cent of GDP, a figure equivalent to the value added of agriculture (a sector that employed 45 per cent of the labour force). Thus, financial deregulation led to a sharp increase in the rate of return on financial capital, a rise in the share of GDP accruing to non-wage incomes, and the redistribution via the budget of labour income to holders of state bonds. The net effect of all this was disequalizing, as in developing countries tax incidence is broadly proportional while ownership of financial assets is highly concentrated.

Changes in labour institutions and earnings inequality

The wage share, earnings concentration, and income distribution have also been influenced by reforms during the last 20 years, promoting wage and employment flexibility and an erosion of minimum wages and collective bargaining. As noted in Chapter 14, for instance, in early 1980s the Turkish government shut down the major labour unions, limited the right to strike, and created a supreme board of arbitration entrusted with the control of labour relations and the regulation of wage demands.

According to mainstream theory, the liberalization of the labour market is expected to simultaneously generate greater employment and higher wage dispersion. The overall impact depends on whether the wage-inequality effect or the employment-creation effect prevails. While such overall impact is in principle undetermined, Rolph van der Hoeven and Catherine Saget show in Chapter 8 that during the 1980s and early part of the 1990s the wage share declined in line with labour market liberalization in all countries under analysis with the exception of the East Asian ones. They find also that, on average, the Gini coefficients of the distribution of wages were below 0.30 in the countries with centralized wage-setting systems and over 0.45 in those with decentralized ones. However, in countries with dualistic labour markets, limited coverage of social security, and high wage inequality, the deregulation of the labour market was found to be equalizing. Mounting wage inequality was also found to be associated with a surge in the highest wages, a fact possibly related to the expansion of the FIRE sector and to changes in social norms on the remuneration of different skills. This point is discussed in Chapter 6 by Singh and Dhumale who note that the inequality rises observed in the United States and United Kingdom during the last two decades were led by a rise in high-income salaries, the spread of 'the winner takes all' type of remuneration, and greater use of stock options for executive compensation.

Van der Hoeven and Saget analyse also the relation between changes in minimum wages and earnings inequality. They suggest that the fall in minimum wages recorded in three African, nineteen Latin American, and three-quarters of the transition economies was a contributor to the recent rise in wage concentration. They test this relation formally on Mexican panel data for 1984–98 and show that the ratio of minimum to average wage is significantly and negatively correlated with an index of wage inequality. They present also regression results suggesting that the introduction of minimum wages does not reduce employment and cite ILO evidence suggesting that, contrary to the received wisdom, minimum wages of up to two-thirds of the unskilled wage do not lead to an informalization of employment.

Another institution considerably changed during the last two decades is unionization. The impact of this institution remains controversial. Some see unions as a source of distortion as they favour import protection. However, unions can also be an instrument for sustaining social cohesion and help containing real wages in periods of crises. Nevertheless, Chapter 8 provides evidence of a general non-uniform decline in union membership, which occurs irrespective of the type of industrial relation system. Finally, van der Hoeven and Saget find inconclusive evidence about the impact of changes in legislation on labour protection, job dismissals, and employment flexibility in OECD countries and Latin America. Studies cited in their chapter show that employment protection reduces short-term unemployment but may increase long-run unemployment among certain groups.

Changes in the redistributive role of taxes and transfers and the impact of the new safety nets

The last fifteen years has witnessed the introduction of tax and expenditure reforms in many countries. Direct and trade taxes were replaced with indirect taxes and tax systems were simplified. While the vertical progressivity of direct taxes was reduced, greater accent was generally placed on horizontal equity.

Past studies of industrialized countries show that while taxation had a limited redistributive impact, as the reduction in inequality associated with direct taxation was offset by indirect taxes, transfers were progressive and so was the overall impact of budgetary operations. In Chapter 9, Anthony Atkinson examines whether changes in this area contributed to the rise of income inequality recorded in the OECD countries during the past fifteen years. He notes that between 1980 and the mid-1990s the distribution of market incomes deteriorated in all countries analysed, such as the United Kingdom, the United States, Sweden, Canada, Germany, and Finland. He also finds also that while the latter three countries experienced no appreciable shifts in the concentration of disposable income owing to an increase in redistribution, the first three recorded a decline in redistribution and a rise in the inequality of disposable income greater than that of market incomes. Atkinson then analyses the specific contribution of the unemployment benefit and personal income taxation to the overall changes in redistribution mentioned above; he finds that for all six countries the generosity, coverage, and redistributivness of the unemployment benefit declined while the tax rate schedule became less progressive, though in Germany, Finland, and Canada this was accompanied by a broadening of the tax base which offset the negative effect of lower tax progressivity.

Studies for the 1960s and early 1970s on the net fiscal incidence of government taxes and transfers in developing countries indicated that here too the budget played a positive, if limited, redistributive role due to the broad proportionality of taxation and the moderate progressivity of public expenditure. In Chapter 10, Ke-Young Chu, Hamid Davoodi, and Sanjeev Gupta provide a systematic survey of tax incidence studies conducted in the developing and transitional economies from the mid-1970s to the mid-1990s. They show that of the thirty-six countries analysed, taxation was progressive in thirteen, proportional in seven, regressive in seven, and trendless in nine. In particular, direct taxes were found to be progressive in 12 of the 14 studies in this field.

The net impact of recent reforms in this area varied from country to country, but Tables 3 and 4 of Chapter 10 point to an average drop of one percentage point of the tax/GDP ratio over the 1980s–90s period (as opposed to a rise by 1.6 points between the 1970s and 1980s), a decline in the importance of direct taxes in the total and a fall in overall tax progressivity. For Latin America, for instance, Morley (2000) found that tax changes shifted on average the burden of taxation away from the high income groups and towards the middle classes and the poor. This trend is cause for concern as Chapter 10 shows that an increase in the ratio of direct to indirect tax revenue reduces, if moderately, income inequality. Altogether, Chapter 10 finds that tax and transfer policies in developing and transition economies were not sufficiently effective in offsetting the increase in inequality of market incomes.

The analysis of changes in redistribution presented in Chapter 10 is complemented in the volume by an analysis of the poverty and distributive impact of the extra-budgetary Social Funds increasingly introduced in the 1990s to offset the social costs of policy reform. As noted by Giovanni Andrea Cornia and Sanjay Reddy in Chapter 11, since 1987 over seventy Social Funds have been introduced to complement—through the launch of semi-autonomous, multisectoral, demand-driven, temporary, and fast-disbursing programmes administered by non-governmental actors—the formal social transfers that were generally seen as ineffective and poorly targeted. The evidence provided in Chapter 11, however, shows that notwithstanding the high visibility they enjoyed, Social Funds played a limited role in reducing adjustment-poor and chronic-poor, and in reversing the income inequality rises that often accompanied economic liberalization. The expenditures Social Funds mobilized never exceeded one per cent of GDP per year while the number of jobs created was generally less than one per cent of total employment and could hardly compensate for the cuts in jobs and essential expenditures recorded in many countries as a result, inter alia, of policy reform. In addition, Social Funds allocated their resources not to the poorest groups or activities with high social returns but to programmes that required limited preparation and were perceived as having large demonstration effects. The authors conclude that in order to generate a greater impact, the Social Funds should have counted on more resources, permanent relief structures, improved targeting, lower administrative costs, and limited reliance on demand-driven mechanisms in the distribution of the subsidies.

Impact of the overall liberalization package

The above overview has discussed the distributive impact of each of the main elements of the Washington Consensus.[1] It suggests that of the policy tools discussed in this volume, capital account liberalization appears to have had, on average, the strongest disequalizing effect, followed by domestic financial liberalization, labour market deregulation, and tax reform. At the aggregate level, trade liberalization has had unclear effects, likely owing to the heterogeneity of the experiences considered. The

---

[1] The distributive impact of privatization has been only tangentially discussed in this volume and is therefore ignored hereafter.

overview emphasized also that the impact on inequality varied substantially depending on the economic structure, institutions, and initial inequality of the countries considered.

These conclusions were reached on the basis of partial equilibrium analyses of the impact of specific measures in which second round effects were ignored. General equilibrium analyses or econometric analyses in which all measures part of the Washington Consensus are regressed simultaneously on the distribution of income are few and concern mainly Latin America and the economies in transition. One such study is that by Behrman *et al.* (2000) who assessed the impact on wage differentials of a synthetic reform index and specific indexes for each reform measure in eighteen Latin American countries over 1980–98. The study found that the overall reform package had a significant disequalizing effect but that this declined gradually over time. Broadly similar evidence is provided by Chapter 7, which analyses the effects of domestic and external liberalization during twenty-one reform episodes in eighteen countries. The chapter finds that inequality rose in thirteen cases, remained constant in six, and improved in two. In contrast, different results are arrived at by Morley (2000) in a review of the distributive impact of policy reform in Latin America. All studies underscore that each policy instrument has a distinct distributive effect and that the overall impact reflects a series of mutually offsetting impacts.

Cornia and Kiiski (2001) tried to explain the changes in income inequality over 1980–95 in thirty-two developing and transitional economies on the basis of the intensity of their liberalization measures proxied by a synthetic reform index (REFINDEX) developed by the World Bank; the initial value of income inequality ($GINI^0$), as even profound reforms are likely to generate a less marked increase in Gini coefficients in countries with high initial inequality; a dummy variable (DUMMYFSU) for the former Soviet Union transition economies where transformations induced by the transition, institutional weakness, and the low quality of the policy introduced heightened the impact of liberalization; and a dummy variable for Latin America (DUMMYLAC) as in this region the pervasiveness of the liberalization of the financial sector and capital account is not captured by the overall reform index. The regression results[2] confirm a significant impact of policy reform on income inequality, a significant effect of the dummy for the former Soviet Union, and

---

[2] $+ 0.32$ DUMMYFSU(3.95) $+ 0.07$ DUMMYLAC (1.43). The regression was run on a cross section of the 1980–95 changes in the Gini coefficients and made use of robust standard errors estimators and generated the following results: $\Delta \log GINI_{80-95} = -0.53$ $(0.86) - 0.23$ $\log GINI^0(2.51) + 0.13$ REFINDEX(3.07). All parameters have the expected sign and the t statistics of the first three variables (in parentheses) indicate that the parameters are statistically significant. The parameter of the Latin American dummy is significant at the 16% level. The F-test is highly significant—suggesting that the overall specification cannot be rejected—while the R square is a satisfactory 0.54. The inequality rises appear to often take the shape of a lagged, one-off, surge (spread over several years) following a change in policy regime, rather than a continuous increase over the two decades considered. They seem to reflect, in other words, a shift between two steady states characterized by different policy regimes. This point, however, has not been explored systematically.

a weak one of the Latin American dummy. The initial inequality level has also the right sign and is statistically significant. A ceteris paribus simulation shows that in a country with a Gini coefficient of 0.35, a shift of the liberalization index from 'no reform' to 'medium intensity reforms' raises the Gini coefficient by 3 points while a shift to 'strong liberalization' causes an increase of 5.5 Gini points. Stronger effects are evident in the former Soviet Union economies and, to a lesser extent, of Latin America.

These studies do not allow arrival at firm conclusions on the inequality impact of the policy reforms inspired by the Washington Consensus. More work is needed to refine the indexes of the extent and quality of specific reforms, to capture the interaction between single policy measures part of an overall package, to identify their mutually offsetting effects, and to analyse the time profile of the inequality rise. Yet, these initial results encourage a further probing of the hypothesis on the disequalizing effect of mainstream reforms, especially in countries with weak institutions, undergoing profound systemic transformations, or suffering from an unfavourable insertion in the international market.

1.4. UNANSWERED OR ONLY PARTIALLY ANSWERED QUESTIONS

The analyses in this volume have documented the rise in income inequality recorded over the last twenty years and assessed a series of potentially responsible factors. They have not, however, dealt with a number of crucial analytical points. First of all, the issue of the impact of rising inequality on growth and poverty reduction requires a more disaggregated treatment than that followed in this volume. The impact of inequality on growth (and, through it, on poverty alleviation) likely depends not only on the extent of its aggregate increase but also on the 'sources' of the inequality rise, that is, on the extent to which such increase reflects differences in efforts, talent, human capital, and natural resources, or whether it is the result of ascription, corruption, and rent-seeking activities made possible by the inaccurate design of policy reforms, as shown by the case of insider privatization. Presumably, an inequality increase of the first type has a less negative effect (or no effect) on growth than an increase due to spread of rent-seeking activities. This hypothesis has not been discussed or tested in this volume and this limits therefore the generality of the volume's conclusions about the need to contain inequality rises for efficiency reasons.

A second research issue that requires a more systematic investigation concerns the timing, sequencing, and interaction between, and the sequencing of, the different components of the Washington Consensus. Some of these reforms—for example, trade liberalization—may not be inherently inefficient or lead necessarily to adverse distributive effects but their success depends on other objective conditions or on prior introduction of complementary measures in related areas. The sizeable inequality rises observed in recent times may thus signal a premature, poorly sequenced, and unselective implementation of liberalization policies under weak institutional and incomplete market conditions rather than their inherent inefficiency. Thirdly, while the volume has hinted at the fact that the Washington Consensus needs to evolve in a more distributionally friendly direction, it has not attempted to specify alternative reform packages. While the broad direction of the alternative is to some extent implicit in the criticism of the orthodox approach, the formulation of consistent alternatives in the six areas has only been touched upon in this volume.

REFERENCES

Addison, A., and G. A. Cornia (2001). Income distribution policies for faster poverty reduction. WIDER Discussion Paper 2001/93, UNU/WIDER: Helsinki.

Aghion, P., E. Caroli, and C. Garcia-Penalosa (1999). Inequality and economic growth: The perspective of the new growth theories. *Journal of Economic Literature* 37, 1615–60.

Barro, R. (1991). Economic growth in a cross-section of countries. *Quarterly Journal of Economics* 106, 407–43

—— (2000). Inequality and growth in a panel of countries. *Journal of Economic Growth* 5: 5–32.

Benabou, R. (1996). Inequality and growth. In B. Bernanke and J. Rotemberg (eds.), *NBER Macroeconomics Annual 1996*. MIT Press: Cambridge MA, and London.

Behrman, J., N. Birdsall, and M. Székely (2000). Economic reform, and wage differentials in Latin America. Research Department Working Paper 435, Inter-American Development Bank: Washington, DC.

Birdsall, N., and A. Hamoudi (2002). Commodity dependence, trade and growth: When 'openness' is not enough. Centre for Global Development Working Papers 7, Centre for Global Development: Washington, DC.

Bruno, M., and W. Easterly (1996). Inflation crises and long-run growth. World Bank Working Papers 1517, World Bank: Washington, DC.

Christiaensen, L., L. Demery, and S. Paternostro (2002). Growth, distribution and poverty in Africa: Messages from the 1990s. Mimeo, World Bank: Washington DC.

Cornia, G. A., and S. Kiiski (2001). Trends in income distribution in the post-World War II period: Evidence and interpretation. WIDER Discussion Paper 2001/89, UNU/WIDER: Helsinki.

Diwan, I. (1999). Labour shares and financial crises (draft). World Bank: Washington, DC.

—— (2000). Labour shares and globalization. Paper presented at the Conference on Poverty and Inequality in Developing Countries: A Policy Dialogue on the Effects of Globalization, 30.11–1.12.2000, OECD Development Centre: Paris.

Dollar, D., and A. Kraay (2000). Trade, growth and poverty. Mimeo, World Bank: Washington, DC.

Galbraith, J., and J. Lu (1999). Inequality and financial crises: Some early findings. UTIP Working Paper 9, LBJ School of Public Affairs, University of Texas: Austin.

Johnson, O., and J. Salop (1980). Distributional aspects of stabilization programs in developing countries. IMF Staff Papers, IMF: Washington, DC.

Levinshon, J., S. Berry, and J. Friedman (1999). Impacts of the Indonesian economic crisis: Price changes and the poor. Mimeo, University of Michigan: Ann Arbor, MI.

Lindert, P., and J. Williamson (2001). Does globalisation make the world more unequal? Paper presented at the NBER Globalisation in Historical Perspective Conference in Santa Barbara, California, 3–6 May.

Milanovic, B. (2002). Can we discern the effect of globalization on income distribution?: Evidence from household budget surveys. World Bank Research Working Paper 2876, World Bank: Washington, DC.

Morley, S. (2000). Distribution and growth in Latin America in an era of structural reform. Paper presented at the Conference on Poverty and Inequality in Developing Countries: A Policy Dialogue on the Effects of Globalization, 30.11–1.12.2000, OECD Development Centre: Paris.

Murphy, K., C. Riddell, and P. Romer (1998). Wage, skills and technology in the United States and Canada. NBER Working Papers 6638, National Bureau of Economic Research: Cambridge, MA.

Nafziger, E. W., F. Stewart, and R. Väyrynen (eds.) (2000). *War, Hunger and Displacement: The Origins of Humanitarian Emergencies*, Vol. 1. Oxford University Press: Oxford.

Rodrik, D. (2000). Comments on trade, growth and poverty by D. Dollar and A. Kraay. Mimeo, Harvard University: Boston.

Sachs, J., and A. Warner (1995). Natural resource abundance and economic growth. NBER Working Papers 5398. National Bureau of Economic Research: Cambridge, MA.

Sala-i-Martin, X. (2002). The disturbing 'rise' of global income inequality. NBER Working Paper Series, Working Paper 8904, National Bureau of Economic Research: Cambridge, MA.

Slaughter, M. (2000). Protectionist tendencies in the North and vulnerable economies in the South. WIDER Working Paper Series 196, UNU/WIDER: Helsinki.

Solimano, A. (1992). After socialism and dirigisme, which way? Policy Research Working Papers 981, Country Economics Department, World Bank: Washington, DC.

Stiglitz, J. E. (1998). More instruments and broader goals: Moving toward the post Washington consensus, WIDER Annual Lectures 2, UNU/WIDER: Helsinki.

Szekely, M., and M. Hilgert (1999). The 1990s in Latin America: Another decade of persistent inequality. Working Paper of the Research Department 410, Inter-American Development Bank: Washington, DC.

Wood, A. (1994). *North–South Trade, Employment and Inequality*. Clarendon Press: Oxford.

World Bank (2000). *World Development Report 2000/1*. World Bank: Washington, DC.

2

Income Distribution Changes and Their Impact in the Post-Second World War Period

GIOVANNI ANDREA CORNIA, TONY ADDISON,
AND SAMPSA KIISKI

2.1. INTRODUCTION

This chapter analyses the trends in within-country inequality during the post-Second World War period, with particular attention to the last 20 years, on the basis of a review of the relevant literature and of an econometric analysis of inequality trends in seventy-three countries accounting for 80 per cent of the world's population and 91 per cent of world gross domestic product–purchasing power parities (GDP–PPP). The chapter suggests that the last two decades have been characterized by a surge in within-country inequality in about two-thirds of the developing, developed, and transitional nations analysed. It also suggests that in those countries where the upsurge in inequality was sizeable or where inequality rose from already high levels, growth and poverty alleviation slowed down perceptibly. While this trend towards higher inequality differs substantially across countries in its extent, timing, and specific causes, it marks a clear departure from that observed during the first 30 years of the post-Second Word War period during which, with the exception of Latin America and parts of sub-Saharan Africa, a widespread move towards greater egalitarianism was noted in the majority of the socialist, developing, and industrialized economies.

2.2. TRENDS IN WITHIN-COUNTRY INCOME INEQUALITY IN THE POST-SECOND WORLD WAR PERIOD

2.2.1. *The OECD Countries: Mostly U-Shaped Inequality Patterns*

The developed market economies emerged from the Second World War with a relatively high income inequality. Income concentration, however, declined steadily over the 1950s, 1960s, and most of the 1970s (Table 2.1). This view is confirmed by a review

Table 2.1. *Interdecile ratio[a] of pre-tax or post-tax income distribution in selected OECD countries*

Country	Canada (pre)	France (pre)	Germany (post)	Italy (post)	Japan (pre)	Holland (post)	UK (pre)	USA (pre)
Around 1950	19.6	—	13.9	—	—	17.6	—	23.8
Around 1960	16.6[b]	40.1	11.2	19.1[c]	8.5	12.5	11.5	25.0
Around 1970	26.5	26.6	11.7	15.8	6.6	10.6	11.8	23.4

[a] Ratio of the income shares of the top and bottom deciles.
[b] 1965.
[c] 1967.

Source: Authors' elaboration on data in Sawyer (1976).

of income distribution trends sponsored by the Organization for Economic Cooperation and Development (OECD) (Sawyer 1976: 26), which concludes that:

broadly, it would appear that through the 1950s there has been some movement towards greater equality almost everywhere. In the 1960s and early 1970s, the same remained true for France, Italy, Japan and the Netherlands. The picture is unclear in Germany ... and in the United Kingdom.... In North America, there seems to have been a marginal move away from inequality.

A steady decline in unemployment (which fell to an unweighted OECD average of 2.7 per cent by 1973), stable earnings inequality, and a rapid expansion of social security led to a steady rise in the labour share and to a drop in the concentration of the pre-tax or pre-transfer income distribution (Boltho 1997). In addition, the social security schemes introduced or expanded during the second Golden Age reduced even more rapidly the inequality of the distribution of post-tax or post-transfer income. Between 1951 and 1975, public expenditure on social security rose steadily from 3 to almost 12 per cent of GDP in the United States, from 7 to 14 per cent in Australia, Canada, New Zealand, and the United Kingdom, and from 8 to 20 per cent in eleven Western European countries (Cornia and Danziger 1997: figure 2.3). Thus 'despite a surprisingly stable pre-tax earnings structure, the distribution of post-tax income has nonetheless changed towards greater equality in those European countries for which reasonably reliable data are available. Fairly pronounced changes along these lines have taken place in Italy, the UK, and the Netherlands; more modest ones in France and Germany' (Sawyer 1976: 216–17).

Since the late 1970s this trend has been halted or reversed in most of the region: first, inequality started rising in the mid- to late-1970s in the United States, United Kingdom, Australia, and New Zealand, which were the first among the OECD countries to adopt a neoliberal policy approach (Brandolini 1998). The increase was particularly pronounced in the United Kingdom where the Gini coefficient of the distribution of net disposable income rose more than 30 per cent between 1978 and 1991; that is, twice as fast as that recorded in the United States during the same period, and double the fall registered in the United Kingdom between 1949 and 1976 (Fig. 2.1).

The Scandinavian countries and the Netherlands are part of a second wave of countries where, as in the Anglo-Saxon nations, inequality follows a U-shaped pattern,

Figure 2.1. *Trends in the Gini coefficients of the distribution of gross income in the USA (upper curve) and of net income in the UK (lower curve), 1944–97*

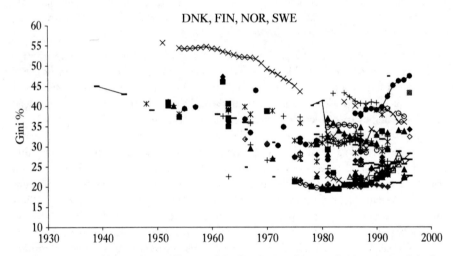

Figure 2.2. *Trends in the Gini coefficients of the distribution of income (various concepts) in the Nordic countries (Denmark, Finland, Norway, and Sweden), 1939–98*

though in these countries the trend reversal took place some 5–10 years later than in the first group, and the rise in inequality started from lower levels and was less pronounced (Fig. 2.2). A third wave of countries including Finland and, to a lesser extent, France experienced a gradual flattening of inequality indexes starting around 1975–80 (Brandolini 1998). In Italy, inequality rose by 4 points between 1992 and 1995, most likely as a result of the introduction in 1993 of measures to control the fiscal deficit as well as privatization and liberalization (ibid.). These overall changes are well described in Atkinson *et al.* (1995: 63), who notes that in the first half of the 1980s there was a marked rise in income inequality in Sweden and the UK. This rise is more striking in that it came after a period in which inequality fell: there was a reversal of the previous trend.... the pattern in the Netherlands, Norway and Denmark has some similarity... In Finland and France, it appears to be the case of a trend towards reduced inequality having come to a stop;... in Ireland and Italy the downward trend continued, in the latter one with a cyclical component.

Despite its reputation for having achieved fast growth with equity, Japan also experienced a rise in income inequality during the last two decades. Before the Second World War, Japan was characterized by a large income gap between the rich and the poor. These large differences were substantially reduced during the first three decades of the post-Second World War period. By the mid- to late-1970s, the Gini coefficient of net disposable income had fallen to around 0.30 (Ozawa and Kono 1997). However, since the early 1980s, this trend has been reversed, and in 1993, the Gini coefficient stood at 0.44, almost the same as the United States and far higher than that of countries such as Sweden and Denmark (Table 2.2). One of the recent factors contributing to this rise in inequality has been the policy to end Japan's decade-long economic slump by lifting restrictions on competition. This forced companies to scrap the old egalitarian lifetime employment system, with its age-based wage scales, in favour of rewarding productive workers with higher salaries. The ranks of those earning little or no income have also swelled as the economy's slide into recession has increased bankruptcies and the attendant job-cutting. The rise in inequality has also been influenced by the growing number of low-paid women entering the workforce and soaring land prices in the 1980s.

Most of this increase in *income* inequality in industrialized countries is explained by a rise in *earnings* inequality (Gottschalk and Smeeding 1997). Countries with centralized wage-setting institutions (Germany, Italy), a high union density, and comparatively high minimum wages (France) contained the pressures towards higher earnings inequality and experienced either smaller increases in earnings inequality or no increases at all. At the other end of the spectrum, the United States and other countries with decentralized wage negotiations and flexible labour markets experienced the largest rises. In the United States, respectively 30 and 20 per cent of the rise in earnings concentration is

Table 2.2. *Trend in the Gini coefficient of various income concepts in Japan*

Year	Before taxes, before transfers	After taxes, before transfers	After taxes, after transfers
1970s	0.300	—	—
1981	0.349	0.330	0.314
1984	0.398	0.382	0.343
1987	0.405	0.388	0.338
1990	0.433	0.421	0.364
1993	0.440	—	—

Source: Ozawa and Kono (1997).

explained by a 44 per cent fall in the minimum wage and the decline in unionization (ibid.).

Other factors contributed to the rising inequality. An upsurge in the share of financial rents, urban land rents, and profits depressed the wage share and contributed to the growing dispersion of market incomes. The profit share in industry, transport, and communication rose in the middle 1970s and early 1980s in all industrialized countries (UNCTAD 1997). In addition, returns to financial capital increased in line with the adoption of the policy of high interest rates which dominated the period 1982–93 and which induced an increase in the share of GDP assigned to financial rents, particularly in countries with a large domestic debt. Finally, the redistributiveness of the tax and transfer system declined, as the value of transfers fell relative to GDP and personal income tax became less progressive (see Chapter 9) and contributed, if modestly, to the increase in inequality of disposable incomes.

2.2.2. *The Widespread Rise of Inequality in the Former Soviet Bloc*

In these countries, the inequality of the distribution of net disposable income narrowed up to the mid- to late-1970s and increased moderately during the mid- to late-1980s owing to the spread of the 'second economy' in Hungary and Poland and the introduction of wage incentives during the Gorbachov era in the USSR (Atkinson and Micklewright 1992). Conclusions about the level and trend of inequality in the region would change somewhat, if not fundamentally, if the disequalizing impact of dual distribution systems and the growing regional differences in the supply of consumer goods were taken into account (Braithwaite and Heleniak 1989).

Since 1989, income concentration has risen moderately in the transition countries of Central Europe (Table 2.3) where earnings inequality rose less than anticipated and a comprehensive welfare state was preserved (Milanovic 1998). In contrast, in the

Table 2.3. *Gini coefficients of the distribution of net per capita disposable income over 1989–95*

Moderate increases	1989 Gini	1989–95 increase	Large increases	1989 Gini	1989–95 increase
Slovenia	23.7	1.3	Lithuania	27.5	8.5
Hungary	21.4	1.6	Latvia	22.5[a]	8.5
Slovakia	19.5	3.0	Estonia	27.7	11.9
Romania	23.5	4.9	Bulgaria	25.0[b]	12.0
Czech Republic	18.5	4.9	Moldova	26.7	13.3
Poland	24.9	5.1	Russia	25.7	15.2
			Ukraine	23.3[a]	24.1

[a] 1988: the data are not always comparable over time due to changes in sampling procedures. For a few countries and years the data refer to gross household income per capita.
[b] 1990.

Source: UNICEF (1995); Milanovic (1998) for Latvia and Ukraine.

former USSR and Southeastern Europe, the Gini coefficients rose on average by 10–20 points, 3–4 times faster than in Central Europe. In these countries, the transitional recession and fall in the wage share were very pronounced, social transfers declined, their composition and targeting deteriorated (Milanovic 1995; Cornia 1996), and privatization was far less egalitarian than in Central Europe.

Also in this region, rising earnings inequality seems to have played a central role in the surge of income inequality (Table 2.4). This rise has been attributed to the emergence of scarcity rents for professionals such as bankers and other specialists who were undersupplied during the socialist period and to a general rise in returns to education following liberalization (Rutkowski 1999). Such explanations, based on standard human capital theory, account, however, for less than half of the rise in earnings inequality. To start with, many highly educated state employees continued to receive very low wages. Earnings inequality appears to have risen also because of a fall in the minimum wage relative to the average (Standing and Vaughan-Whitehead 1995), the expansion of a highly inequitable informal sector, mounting wage arrears, and a surge in interindustrial wage dispersion unexplained by productivity differentials which favoured workers in politically influential sectors and penalized workers in sectors like health, education, and agriculture (Cornia 1996).

The limited contribution of the rise in capital incomes to the overall rise in income inequality suggested by the first column of Table 2.4 is perplexing and likely depends on the massive under-sampling and under-reporting of high incomes in household budget surveys, as suggested by the growing discrepancy between average income per capita derived from the national accounts and the household budget survey. The limited information available on the distribution of financial assets and bank deposits tend to support this view.

Table 2.4. *Decomposition of the increase in the Gini coefficient of the distribution of household incomes between the pre-transition period and the years 1993–6*

Country	Due to change in income structure	Due to change in concentration of:					Interaction term	Overall Gini change
		Wages	Social transfers	Pensions	Non-pension transfers	Non-wage private sector		
Hungary (1989–93)	−1.3	+5.9	−0.6	+1.4	−0.2	−0.6	−1.3	+2.2
Slovenia (1987–95)	−0.2	+3.6	−0.6	−0.1	−0.4	+0.4	−3.8	+2.6
Poland (1987–9)	−1.7	+3.4	+3.5	+3.2	−0.1	+0.8	+0.9	+7.0
Bulgaria (1989–95)	+1.4	+7.8	+0.9	+0.4	+0.4	−0.4	+0.3	+10.0
Latvia (1989–96)	−1.6	+15.0	−1.5	−2.0	+0.5	+1.4	−3.3	+10.0
Russia (1989–94)	−3.4	+17.8	+5.1	+3.9	+0.4	+3.0	+1.2	+23.6

Source: Milanovic (1998: table 4.2).

2.2.3. Latin America: A Rise in Inequality in the 1980s Followed by a Further Rise or Stagnation in the 1990s

With the exception of highly urbanized and educated Uruguay and Argentina, in the early- to mid-1950s Gini coefficients in Latin America traditionally ranged between 0.45 and 0.60—that is, among the highest in the world (Altimir 1996). This acute income polarization was rooted in a highly unequal distribution of land and educational opportunities, which benefited a tiny agrarian, mining, and commercial oligarchy. The rapid growth which followed the adoption of import substituting industrialization in the 1950s had, on the whole, a disequalizing impact. Of the twenty-one growth spells recorded over 1950–79, inequality fell in four cases, stagnated in five, and rose in eleven (Altimir 1994). In the 1970s, however, inequality declined moderately in most of the region except for the Southern Cone countries (Altimir 1996) following the introduction of extreme versions of neoliberal reform by military regimes. The combination of a rise over the 1950 to the 1960s and of a fall over the 1970s meant that by 1980, all medium- and large-sized Latin American countries had a greater concentration of income than in the early- to mid-1950s. From 1980 to the early 1990s, inequality in the region was affected by large external shocks and the recessionary adjustment introduced to respond to them, while a slow growth pattern dominated the rest of the 1990s. In the 1980s inequality declined in only three countries (Colombia, Uruguay, and Costa Rica) (Altimir 1996), a fact that made Iglesias (1998: 6) note '... at the end of the decade [of the 1980s], there was a substantial rise in inequality in most cases. That means that the recession of the 1980s hit the poor harder than the rich'.

Most importantly for this volume, income polarization did not decline and in some cases it worsened even with the resumption of growth, as shown by a recent review of inequality changes in the 1990s based on forty-nine nationwide representative household surveys covering 90 per cent of the population of the region (Székely and Hilgert 1999). The review shows that none of the countries examined recorded a distributive improvement during this period. In eight cases, significant increases in inequality were noted between the first and last observations of the 1990s, while in seven cases there was no change.

The income polarization of the 1980s (and likely of the 1990s) was the result of surges in inequality during recessionary spells and slow declines during periods of recovery. Cornia (1994) estimated, for instance, that in the 1980s the regional poverty elasticity of growth was 1.8 during recessions but only 0.6 during recoveries. In particular, the functional distribution of income worsened during recessions, as suggested by the decline by 5–6 percentage points in the labour share between 1980 and the late 1980s in Argentina, Chile, and Venezuela, and the 10-point decline of Mexico (Sainz and Calcagno 1992). Five structural labour market changes underlie this trend. These include a slowdown in job creation, a growing informalization of the labour market (due to a shift to the non-traded sector where lower productivity and wages are the rule), a slower rise in average formal sector wages in relation to GDP per capita, and a fall in the minimum wage in relation to the average wage (Tokman 1986; Sainz and Calcagno 1992; see also Chapter 8). The fifth structural change concerns a widening in wage differentials by skill and educational level (Székely and Hilgert 1999). This review may be concluded by noting with Altimir (1996: 59) that

Under these new economic modalities (characterized by trade openness, fiscal austerity, a prudent management of monetary policy, less public regulation of markets and more reliance on private initiative), the pattern of income distribution tends, as suggested above, to be unequal at the very least, and more unequal—in most cases, at least in urban areas—than those that prevailed during the last stages of the previous growth phase in the 1970s.

2.2.4. *China: A U-Shaped Trend Driven by Rising Regional and Urban–Rural Inequality*

In China too, income inequality followed a U-shaped pattern over the last 50 years, with the turnaround point located around the mid-1980s. While, at the beginning of the Maoist experiment in 1953, the nationwide Gini coefficient of the distribution of household incomes was equal to 0.56, the subsequent creation of agricultural communes, socialization of industrial assets, and development of an embryonic social security system reduced the index to 0.31 in 1964, and to 0.26 by 1975, despite the persistence of large regional differences in natural endowments (Table 2.5).

The agricultural reforms adopted since 1978 replaced the rural communes with an egalitarian family-based agriculture and introduced considerable price incentives for farmers. The result was a sharp acceleration of growth that was sustained at the 8–10 per cent level between 1978 and 2000. During the rapid agriculture-led growth

Table 2.5. *Evolution of the Gini coefficients and the income gap in China, 1953–98*

Year	Gini coefficient			Income gap, U/R[a]	Interprovincial income gap		
	Overall	Urban	Rural		Rural[b]	Urban[b]	Total[b]
1953	0.56[c]	—	—	—	—	—	—
1964	0.31[c]	—	—	—	—	—	—
1978	0.32	0.16	0.21	2.37	—	—	—
1981	—	0.15	0.24	2.05	2.80	1.81	12.62
1984	0.28[d]	0.16	0.26	1.71	3.16[e]	1.59[e]	9.22[e]
1988	0.38	0.23	0.30	2.05	—	—	—
1990	—	0.23	0.31	2.02	4.17	2.03	7.50
1995	0.43	0.28	0.34	2.47	4.82	2.34	9.79
1998	0.41[c]	—	—	—	—	—	—

[a] Ratio between the average urban and average rural income.
[b] Ratio between the average income of the highest to the lowest province, by rural, urban, and total area.
[c] Data for these years *are not comparable* with those of the other years and are provided only for illustrative purposes.
[d] Refers to 1983.
[e] Refers to 1985.

Source: Various data from China's state bureau of statistics and World Bank (2000).

years of 1978–84, there was only a modest upsurge in inequality in both rural and urban areas. As a result, the rural poverty rate fell precedentlessly from 30.7 per cent in 1978 to 15.1 per cent in 1984—literally halving the percentage of rural poor in just 6 years (Gustafsson and Zhong 2000). In turn, the urban Gini coefficient stagnated at a very low level,[1] as the introduction of various performance-related bonuses in urban-based state enterprises[2] did not apparently lead to any visible rise in the urban income disparity while transfer payments sheltered the registered urban population from the price and stabilization reforms of the 1980s (Ahmad and Hussain 1991).

In contrast, income concentration rose rapidly during 1985–90 and accelerated from 1990s onwards so that the national Gini coefficient reached 0.43 by 1995 and remained broadly at the same level until 1998 (Table 2.5). The rise in income disparity since the mid-1980s can be traced to a rise in the urban–rural gap driven by a faster expansion of urban activities (Ping 1997), a 30 per cent decline in agricultural prices over 1993–8, and a tripling of agricultural taxes levied by the central and local authorities (see Chapter 5). In view of the unequal spread of non-agricultural activities across provinces, inter-provincial inequality also became an important contributor to overall inequality, as indicated by the widening of the interprovincial income gap (last column of Table 2.5; see also Chapter 5: Section 5.3.2). Although incomes grew in less well-endowed provinces as well, the 1990s witnessed a rapid growth divergence between the rich coastal provinces and the poor interior ones. Finally, the 1988 and 1995 surveys of rural incomes suggest that widening rural inequality within some province was also due to a rise in earnings inequality in township and village enterprises (McKinley and Brenner 1998).

This rise in inequality had an obvious impact on poverty alleviation. The pace of rural poverty alleviation declined over 1984–95 as compared to 1978–84 despite a fall in the young age dependency ratio (Gustafsson and Zhong 2000). Furthermore between 1988 and 1995 the poverty rate rose in western China and several mountain locations (Gustafsson and Zhong 2000). Public policy was an important contributor to this income polarization. The fiscal decentralization of 1978 substantially reduced the ability of the central government to control regional inequality by means of transfers to poorer provinces. In addition, industrial policy played an even greater disequalizing role as it explicitly favoured the coastal provinces through the granting of special administrative and economic powers, tax privileges, and other benefits which facilitated the development of export industries and the inflow of foreign direct investment.

2.2.5. *East and Southeast Asia: A Common if Milder Reversal of Inequality Trends*

It is widely believed that the countries in this region were able to combine fast growth with equity. This view is, however, not entirely accurate. First of all, the initial level of income inequality varied considerably between the less egalitarian nations of Southeast Asia and the more equitable ones of Northeast Asia (see Fig. 2.3) that, in the

---

[1] The urban poverty rate does not take into account, however, the floating population which is much more likely to fall into poverty (Gustafsson and Zhong 2000).

[2] Industrial reforms were introduced starting from 1984.

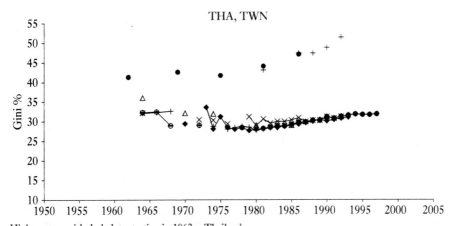

Higher curve with dark dots starting in 1962 = Thailand
The descending arm continuing in the lower curves = Taiwan

Figure 2.3. *Trends in the Gini coefficients of the distribution of gross income in Thailand and net income in Taiwan, 1953–97*

immediate post-war period, confiscated and redistributed land and other assets (like the 'zaibastu' in Japan), imposed steep wealth taxes, and ensured a widespread and equitable access to education. The Southeast Asian countries, in contrast, never undertook any reform to equalize rural incomes and relied for their development on resource rents which, *ceteris paribus*, increased inequality (Jomo 2000). Thus, in the 1950s and 1960s, Hong Kong, Thailand, Singapore, and Malaysia had Gini coefficients in the range 0.40–0.50 (Oshima, 1998; You 1998).

Second, and most importantly for the focus of this study, between the late 1950s and the mid-1990s, the Gini coefficient rose from 0.41 to 0.52 in Thailand (see Chapter 16) and from 0.34 to 0.39 in South Korea, and followed an inverted U-pattern in Malaysia (Oshima 1998). In South Korea, however, the trend towards greater *income* inequality was accompanied by a remarkable decline in *earnings* inequality, the Gini coefficient of which fell from 0.40 to 0.29 over 1976–93 owing to a narrowing of wage differentials between educational groups, occupations, and genders (Fields and Oyo 2000). In turn, Hong Kong, Taiwan, and Singapore show a mild U-pattern, with fairly rapid declines in inequality until the late 1970s and early 1980s, followed by moderate rises offsetting half of the earlier fall (Oshima 1998). In Taiwan, for instance, the Gini coefficients of the distribution of net income fell from 0.32 to 0.28 between 1964 and 1980 thanks to a rapid expansion of employment for both low-skilled and well-educated workers. While the demand for all types of labour expanded quickly, the demand and wages of low-skilled workers rose more than the average (Kanbur 2000). Over 1980–93, however, the development of skill-intensive sectors pushed up wage inequality again, while the share of capital and property incomes in the total surged in line with the development of large corporations and escalation of land prices. By 1993, Taiwan had again reached the level of inequality prevailing in 1964 though it was still below that of the 1950s.

Indonesia also follows a mild U-pattern with a Gini of total income of 0.35 in 1964–5 declining to 0.32 by 1987–90 to rise again to 0.38 by 1997 (Feridhanusetyawan 2000). During the first period, inequality fell thanks to the investment of oil surpluses in financing the green revolution. This substantially raised employment and production opportunities in the rural sector and, given a low land concentration, reduced the rural income inequality substantially. In contrast, the years from 1987 to 1996—during which the economy underwent a radical devaluation, tariff reform, and financial deregulation—were characterized by the development of the urban-based manufacturing and capital-intensive finance, insurance, and real estate (FIRE) sector, a slow down in agriculture, and a widening of the urban–rural gap (see Chapter 5). This trend was exacerbated by the lack of an effective income-transfer system and the retrenchment of strongly equalizing rural-development programmes. As a result, overall inequality rose from a low of 0.32 in 1987 to 0.38 in 1997 (Feridhanusetyawan 2000), although the fast growth of this period still achieved a cut in the overall poverty rate from 17 to 11 per cent over 1987–96.

The effect of the Asian crisis on poverty was immediate—due to a sharp output contraction—while that on inequality manifested itself in two stages. During the first, poverty remained constant or even declined marginally as the crisis hit hardest middle–high-income workers in the FIRE sector. In a second phase, however, inequality rose—especially in urban areas—due to the recession induced by the crisis, the stringent stabilization measures introduced to combat it, and the greater impact of price rises on the poor (Levinshon *et al.* 1999). In a summary analysis of the impact of the Asian crisis, Pangestu (2000) and Knowles *et al.* (1999) found that over 1997–8 inequality dropped marginally in Indonesia and rose in Thailand, the Philippines, and South Korea.

2.2.6. *The Late Liberalizers of South Asia*

The Washington Consensus has been slow to come to the region, and until the early 1990s all South Asian countries followed rather inward-looking policies. India, for instance, launched its first International Monetary Fund (IMF) stabilization programme in July 1991, while partial deregulation, trade liberalization, and privatization were introduced only in subsequent years. By and large, during the post-Second World War period, income distribution in the region changed less than elsewhere, but it too followed a mild U-pattern. In India, the Gini coefficient of household consumption expenditure fell from 0.36 to 0.31 over 1951–61 as a result of the limited land reform of those years as well as affirmative action in favour of low caste groups. It then broadly fluctuated in the range 0.29–0.32 until the onset of the stabilization and gradual liberalization in 1991. In the 1980s, stable inequality, substantial expenditure on rural development, and rapid agricultural growth (which rose to 4 per cent up from 1.8 per cent in the prior decade) reduced rural poverty from 50–55 to 35 per cent (see Chapter 12).

In the 1990s, the years of the gradual external and internal liberalization, GDP growth reached a respectable 5.6 per cent a year. Such growth was, however, far more concentrated in the urban sector, by region and income group. Urban inequality rose moderately from 0.34 to 0.36,[3] thus reducing urban poverty only from 33 to 28 per cent between 1991 and 1997. Rural poverty, in contrast, stagnated owing to slow agricultural growth, retrenchment of rural development programmes, and a rise in inequality (Mundle and Tulasidhar 1998; see also Chapter 12), and it is likely to have risen among agricultural labourers. To start with, the demand for labour and rural wages fell because of the slow agricultural growth. Poverty was also affected by cuts in public expenditure on rural infrastructure and food subsidies, and the government decision to raise food prices by 35 per cent in the outlets of the public distribution system (to which rural poverty is very sensitive). In sum, the experience of the 1990s points to a moderate rise in both urban and rural inequality, a larger rise in overall inequality due to a widening of the average urban–rural gap, and a decline in the poverty alleviation elasticity of overall growth (Ravallion and Datt 1999).

In Sri Lanka, Bangladesh, and Pakistan the inequality trend followed a typical, though little pronounced, U-shaped pattern. In Pakistan, the Gini coefficient declined moderately from 0.39 to 0.33 during the growth years of 1963–73 but gradually climbed back to reach 0.41 in 1993 (Banuri *et al.* 1997; Oshima 1998). The U-shaped pattern is more evident in the rural sector where an initial drop of 7 Gini points was followed by a rise of 12 points. Banuri *et al.* (1997) suggest that inequality rose during spells of slow growth and declined during periods of expansion and that social policies had only a limited impact on inequality. An unfavourable shift in the ratio of the rural wage to food prices and a rise in the share of GDP absorbed by interest payments on the public debt were other relevant factors.

2.2.7. *Sub-Saharan Africa: Falling Urban–Rural Gap, but Rising Intraurban and, at Times, Intrarural-inequality*

The limited statistical information on income inequality available for this region indicates that in the past overall inequality was the product of the large urban–rural income gap inherited from the colonial era and reinforced by the 'urban bias' of policies introduced by the new governments (see Chapter 5). In southern and eastern Africa, inequality was also due to high land concentration.[4] The 1980s, in contrast, were characterized by widespread adjustment programmes which aimed at reducing the urban–rural gap and stimulating growth and export orientation. These measures succeeded in liberalizing the economy, devaluing the real exchange rate (which fell on average by 30 per cent between 1980 and 1998), and opening African economies as the average import–export ratio to GDP rose from 51 to 62 per cent over the same years (Kayizzi-Mugerwa 2000). In spite of all this, growth remained modest at best and GDP per capita in the region stagnated with the exception of the years 1994–6. Even in the regional success stories of Mauritius, Uganda, Ghana, and, lately, Ethiopia, the

---

[3] Many argue that such modest increases in inequality contrast with other economic trends (e.g. rising capitalization of the stock market) and is the result of the exclusion of new high-income groups from national sample surveys.

[4] In countries such as Kenya, South Africa, Zimbabwe, and Malawi, the Gini coefficients of land concentration is in the range 0.6–0.8.

Table 2.6. *Gini coefficients of the distribution of income in the rural, urban, and overall economy*

Country	Year	Rural	Urban	Overall
Cote d'Ivoire	1970	—	—	0.53
	1985			0.39
	1995			0.37
Kenya	1982	0.40	—	0.52 ('76)
	1992	0.49		0.58 ('84)
Mauritius	1986	—	—	0.40
	1991			0.37
Ethiopia	1989	0.41	—	—
	1994	0.46		
Tanzania	1983	0.53	—	—
	1991	0.76		
Nigeria	1986	—	—	0.37
	1993			0.42
Uganda	1989	—	—	0.33
	1992	0.33	0.43	0.38
	1998	0.32	0.37	0.36
Zambia	1991	0.56	0.45	0.56
	1996	0.49	0.47	0.52
	1998	0.52	0.48	0.51

Source: World Income Inequality Database, UNU/WIDER, Helsinki, available at www.wider.unu.edu; Kayizzi-Mugerwa (2000); Bigsten (2000); McCulloch *et al.* (2000).

recovery remained fragile and donor-dependent while exports did not shift—with the exception of Mauritius—towards labour-intensive manufacturing.

The urban sector felt the hardest impact of adjustment policies. In several cases, the urban economy experienced both a drop in its domestic terms of trade and large income falls among most urban groups. While the urban economy generally deteriorated, the impact on the rural sector varied (Table 2.6). Intrarural inequality rose in countries characterized by high land concentration (as in Kenya) or a collapse of the food and inputs marketing arrangements (as in Zambia; see McCulloch *et al.* 2000) but it fell or remained constant in countries such as Mozambique and Uganda characterized by a peasant agriculture rebounding from years of civil strife (Addison 2003).

2.3. ECONOMETRIC ANALYSIS OF TRENDS IN WITHIN-COUNTRY INEQUALITY

The above review suggests that during the last two decades inequality increased—if from different levels and to different extents—in a good number of countries. These findings, however, run counter to some of the evidence found in the literature. Deininger and Squire (1996: 583), for instance, note that 'Decadal averages of inequality indexes across regions . . . are relatively stable through time, but they differ substantially across regions, a result that emerges for individual countries as well'. Another study comes to similar conclusions. After fitting linear trends to forty-nine country data the authors conclude that 'there is no evidence of a time trend in 32 countries, or 65 percent of our sample' (Li *et al.* 1998: 35). An examination of the estimation procedure followed by Li *et al.* suggests, however, that their conclusions are biased by the methodology adopted. To start with, some country trends are estimated on too few and poorly spaced data-points and are bound to yield statistically non-significant trends.[5] Second, the datapoints were fitted only with linear trends, a functional form, which does not permit the capture of trend reversals. Third, their sample did not include most economies in transition, the majority of which witnessed sharp rises in inequality in the 1990s. Fourth, their time series stopped in 1991–3 and therefore cannot capture the impact of external liberalization in many countries. Fifth, in assessing the global direction of the changes in inequality, the country results were not weighted by the share of the sample countries in world population and GDP–PPP.

Inequality trends were therefore re-estimated by means of an unbiased methodology on the basis of the World Income Inequality Database (WIID).[6] This allows us to increase the number of countries analysed to seventy-three and update the time series to 1995. The datapoints retained were interpolated country by country with linear and quadratic functions, so as to capture possible trend reversals. For each country, the 'best fit' functional form was chosen on the basis of the most significant *t* and *F* statistics and, as a subordinate criterion, the highest R^2. The results of this regression analysis are summarized in Table 2.7. They confirm the conclusions arrived at on the basis of the review of country studies and sharply differ from those of Li *et al.* (1998). In fact, inequality was found to have *risen* in forty-eight of the seventy-three countries analysed, and to have *remained constant* in sixteen (including Germany and Brazil as well as countries such India, Indonesia, and Tanzania—for which the recent trends discussed in Section 2.2 shows a rise in inequality). Only in nine small- and medium-sized countries such as Honduras, Norway, Malaysia, and the Philippines did income concentration decline over the long term. If these results are weighed by population size and GDP–PPP, these conclusions are strengthened (columns 2 and 4 of Table 2.7).

A comparison of the results in Table 2.7 with those of Li *et al.* (1998) indicates that the choice of the functional form used to interpolate the time trends explains over 40 per cent of the difference in the proportion of countries with rising inequality. Another 25 per cent is due to the increase in country coverage (from forty-nine to seventy-three) while the extension in the time series explain another 30 per cent of the overall difference (Cornia with Kiiski 2001).

---

[5] The time trend in Li *et al.* (1998) is statistically significant in 11% of the countries with 4–5 observations, and in respectively 37% and 42% of the countries with between 6 and 10 or more than 10 observations.

[6] The WIID database has been developed by WIDER and is accessible at www.wider.unu.edu.

Table 2.7. *Trends in the Gini coefficients of the distribution of income from the 1950s to the 1990s for seventy-three developed, developing, and transitional economies*

	Sample countries in each group	Share of			
		Population of sample countries	World population	GDP–PPP of sample countries	World GDP–PPP
Rising inequality, of which	48	59	47	78	71
Continuously rising or rising–stable	19	4	3	5	5
U-shaped	29	55	44	73	66
Falling inequality, of which	9	5	4	9	8
Continuously falling	6	3	3	7	7
Inverted U-shape	3	2	1	2	1
No trend	16	36	29	13	12
Not included in sample	—	—	20	—	9
Total	73	100	100	100	100

Notes: The results presented in the table are based on the interpolation of 770 'reliable observations' (out of a total of 3573 included in the WIID database) concerning the entire national economy of seventy-three countries for which at least seven well-spaced observations for the period 1960–95 or, at least, 1980–95 were available. These observations originate from documented and representative surveys of household incomes or expenditures, or of gross earnings, and broadly adopt the same definition of income or earnings and the same data collection methodology throughout the entire period analysed. The remaining observations included in the WIID database could not be used either because they were redundant, or because they did not concern the entire economy, or because some countries exhibited less than seven consistent observations over the period analysed, or because the data sources were poorly documented.

Out of seventy-three countries included in the analysis, thirty-three are developing, eighteen are from the OECD, and twenty-two are transitional economies. Except for Africa, these countries account for between 84% and 98% of the population of all regions, and between 82% and 98% of their GDP–PPP. For Africa, the five countries included in the analysis (see Table 2.8) account for 18% and 32% of its population and GDP–PPP.

The data interpolated refer to 'per capita household disposable income' in fifty-two cases (gross in twenty-eight cases, net in seventeen, unknown in seven), to 'per capita household consumption expenditure' in nine cases; and to 'gross earnings' in fourteen cases (mostly economies in transition).

The trend in the Gini coefficients were interpolated on a country by country basis by means of linear, hyperbolic, and quadratic functions so as to capture different trend shapes and possible trend reversals. The best results from these three types of interpolations were chosen on the basis of the combination of the best 't' and 'corrected R^2' statistics. Where the t statistics of the estimated parameters of these functions were not significant at the 5% level (and, for some ten countries, at the 10% level), the country analysed was assigned to the group 'no trend'.

Source: Authors' calculations on the November 1998 version of WIID (the world income inequality database) (available at www.wider.unu.edu). WIID includes the 2622 observations of the Deininger-Squire Database (1996 version) and 1131 observations collected by WIDER.

2.4. SUMMARY OF FINDINGS ABOUT INEQUALITY TRENDS

The analysis in Sections 2.2 and 2.3 leads us to the following conclusions:

1. Income inequality declined between the 1950s and 1970s although there were several exceptions to this rule in sub-Saharan Africa and Latin America.

Table 2.8. *Summary of changes in income inequality in seventy-three countries, 1960s to the 1990s*

| | Countries | | | |
	Developed	Developing	Transitional	Total
Rising inequality	12: Australia, Denmark, Finland, Italy, Japan, Netherlands, New Zealand, Portugal, Spain, Sweden, UK, USA	16: Argentina, Chile, China, Colombia, Costa Rica, Guatemala, Hong Kong, Mexico, Pakistan, Panama, Puerto Rico, South Africa, Sri Lanka, Taiwan, Thailand, Venezuela	20: Armenia, Azerbadjian, Bulgaria, Croatia, Czech Rep., Estonia, Georgia, Hungary, Kazakstan, Kirgistan, Latvia, Lithuania, Makedonia, Moldova, Poland, Romania, Russia, Slovakia, Ukraine, Yugoslavia	48
Constant inequality	4: Austria, Belgium, Canada, France	10: Bangladesh, Brazil, Cote d'Ivoire, Dominican Rep., El Salvador, *India*, *Indonesia*, Senegal, Singapore, *Tanzania*	2: Belarus, Slovenia	16
Declining inequality	2: Germany, Norway	7: Bahamas, Honduras, Jamaica, *South Korea*, Malaysia, *Philippines*, Tunisia	Nil	9
All	18	33	22	73

Notes: The length of the time series and the number of observations vary from country to country. For the countries in italic, there is very recent information (not yet included in the WIID database) that inequality has been rising over 1996–2000 (see Cornia and Kiiski 2001).

Source: Authors' compilation on background material prepared for Cornia and Kiiski (2001). All data come from the WIID of WIDER, accessible at www.wider.unu.edu.

2. Such a trend towards greater inequality was reversed over the last two decades in forty-eight of seventy-three countries included in Tables 2.7 and 2.8. As noted, the November 1998 version of the WIID only extends to 1995 and, because of this, the database does not reflect inequality changes occurring over 1996–2001—years which saw financial turmoil. If the countries that experienced inequality reversals after 1995 (India, Indonesia, South Korea, Tanzania, and the Philippines) are then added to the 'rising inequality' category, then the number of nations experiencing a surge in income concentration over the last 20 years rises to fifty-three out of a sample of seventy-three countries.

3. Out of the twenty-nine countries showing a U-shaped trend in income inequality, the trend reversal took place in the mid-1970s in Sri Lanka and Thailand, the 1970s in the early OECD liberalizers, the early- to mid-1980s in several Latin American countries, 1984 in China, 1985–90 in several European countries, 1989–92 in the European economies in transition, and 1992–3 in Italy and Finland. These findings contradict the view that within-country inequality remained broadly stable over the post-Second World War period.

G. A. Cornia et al.

Table 2.9. *Transition matrix of Gini coefficients for seventy-three countries between 1980 and the latest available year (mid- to late-1990s)*

Latest Gini / Gini 1980 or closest year	< 25	25.0–29.9	30.0–34.9	35.0–39.9	40.0–44.9	45.0–49.9	50.0–59.9	> 60.0	Total
<25	TTT O	TT O	TTTT O	TTTT	T	T			18
25.0–29.9		T OOOOO	TT R		TT O	T			13
30.0–34.9		R	OOO RR	OO R T	OO R				13
35.0–39.9				RRRR OO	RR L	L	R		11
40.0–44.9				RR	RR	LL	R LLL		10
45.0–49.9				R	R		R L		4
50.0–59.9						R	LL	L	4
Total	4	10	13	17	13	6	9	1	73

Notes: T = transition economies, O = OECD, L = Latin America, R = Others. Gini coefficients have been harmonized in terms of net income terms by adding 1 extra point to expenditure data and subtracting 5.5 points to gross income data.

Source: Authors' elaboration on WIID.

2.4.1. *The Intensity of the Rise*

The increase in the Gini coefficients during the period examined varied substantially. Of the forty-eight countries with rising inequality in Table 2.7, the change was of less than 5 Gini points in six countries, between 5 and 10 points in thirty countries, between 10 and 20 points in ten countries, and by more than 20 points in a few former Soviet Union transitional economies (Table 2.9). By the mid- to late-1990s, forty-six of the seventy-three countries analysed had Gini coefficients greater than 0.35–0.40— a threshold beyond which growth and poverty alleviation may start to be affected.

2.4.2. *Sources of the Rise in Overall Income Inequality*

The recent debate on inequality focuses overwhelmingly on market-determined changes in wage differentials by skills and ignores the changes arising from changes in factor shares and in redistribution through tax and transfer systems. In countries with a developed wage economy, the recent upswing in income inequality seems to have been driven by a fall in the labour share and a corresponding rise in the capital share as well as by a surge in earnings dispersion unexplained by increases in returns to education but attributable to market distortions, the decline in minimum informal sector and public sector wages, growing wage arrears and the abandonment of traditional remuneration norms. In a few countries, income concentration appears to have been also due to rising regional disparity (as in China and Thailand). The weakening of redistribution following the reform of the tax and transfer system and the boost in land and financial rents also contributed, if less crucially, to the recent rise in inequality.

2.5. RISING INEQUALITY AND POVERTY REDUCTION

The widespread rise in inequality discussed above has affected the achievement of the poverty reduction objectives adopted by the international community in the early 1990s. The *World Development Report 1990* (World Bank 1990: table 2) projected that the total number of people surviving on less than PPP $1 per day would have fallen from 1,125 to 825 million between 1985 and 2000. Yet, the Bank's 2000 assessment of poverty trends in the 1990s (World Bank 2000) indicates that such a target was missed by a considerable margin, as the number of worldwide poor was estimated at 1,214 million in 1998. If China is removed from the sample, the results appear even less satisfactory in terms of both poverty incidence—as the world poverty rate declined between 1987 and 1998 by only 2.3 percentage points (i.e. by an average of only 0.2 percentage points a year)—and of the absolute number of the poor, which increased by 100 million. At such a pace, the Development Assistance Committee (DAC) poverty target of reducing the incidence of poverty to 15 per cent by 2015 will be very difficult to reach. While countries such as China and a few others will reach this objective well before 2015, on current trends this target will remain out of reach for many others. Hanmer and Naschold (2001) estimate that if the 4 per cent growth in GDP per capita estimated for the years 2000–15 for the developing countries as a whole (World Bank 2000) is accompanied by medium inequality (i.e. Gini coefficients of less than 43), then the DAC target can be met. In contrast, if the projected 4 per cent growth is associated with higher Gini coefficients, then by 2015 the overall poverty rate for the developing and transitional economies taken together will still be in the vicinity of 20 per cent. In the high inequality scenario, the DAC poverty target will only be met if the growth rate of income per capita reaches a historically unprecedented 9 per cent a year.

That higher inequality does not help in reducing poverty in countries affected by rising inequality is also evident from the data in Table 2.10. The table refers to a large

Table 2.10. *Changes in poverty headcount ratios in 117 growth spells for forty-seven developing countries over the 1980s and 1990s*

Income inequality	Average household income/per capita	
	Falling	Rising
Rising	(17% of cases) poverty *rising* at 14.3% per year	(30% of cases) poverty *falling* at 1.3% a year
Falling	(26% of cases) poverty *rising* at 1.7 % a year	(27% of cases) poverty *falling* at 9.6% a year

Source: Ravallion (2001).

number of growth spells and shows that poverty rates rose in 43 per cent of cases (due to falling average income per capita and worsening inequality) and declined sharply (at 9.6 per cent a year on average) in 27 per cent of cases when a rise in income per capita was combined with a drop in inequality. It also shows that increases in income per capita per se did little to reduce poverty if accompanied by a surge in inequality (upper right quadrant of Table 2.10).

2.6. RISING INEQUALITY AND THE PACE OF GROWTH

The last decade has seen a blossoming of analyses of the inequality–growth relationship. Space limitations do not permit a review of them here—see instead Benabou (1996) and Addison and Cornia (2001) for a review of this literature. Yet, it is important to stress that all major new models on the inequality–growth relation—such as the new political economy models (Alesina and Rodrik 1994), the models focusing on capital market imperfections (Aghion *et al.* 1999), the social conflicts and political instability models (Venieris and Gupta 1986), and those concentrating on policy distortions and government failure (Alesina and Drazen 1993; Birdsall 2000)—posit a *negative linear relation* with growth over the entire income inequality range. The linearity of such a relationship is, however, counterintuitive. It is difficult to believe that a shift in the Gini coefficient from, say, 0.20 to 0.25 has the same impact on economic performance as one from 0.50 to 0.55. In addition, the sign of the relation between inequality and growth may change at different levels of inequality. Because of this, the approach proposed hereafter posits that the relationship between growth and inequality is concave, taking the form described in Fig. 2.4. Benabou (1996) and Banerjee and Duflo (2001) arrive at similar conclusions, if for different reasons, about the concavity of the inequality–growth relation.

In our approach, 'too low' or 'too high' inequality can, *ceteris paribus*, be detrimental to growth, which remains broadly invariant within a given growth-maximizing range. Such a range varies across countries depending on structural factors such as asset distribution, the share of agriculture in total output, natural resource endowment, the history of past policy decisions, and, thus, the accumulation and sectoral distribution of physical and human capital. Two main arguments underlie the concavity of the inequality–growth relation. First, let us assume a latent 'natural distribution of income rewards'. Under conditions of equal opportunities, such a latent distribution reflects the distribution of talent, effort, and merit, possibly corrected by social norms about the under-remuneration of the very talented and the over-remuneration of the least talented workers. Such a latent distribution is unobserved by the policy-maker but the economic agents perceive whether their position in the real distribution broadly corresponds to their relative effort, talent, and merit.

The real distribution of income often differs significantly from the latent one due to market imperfections and differences in the distribution of endowments. When the real income distribution is too compressed and only poorly reflects differences in talent, merit, and effort, growth may be inhibited by a weakening of individual work incentives, by attempts at labour shirking and free-riding, and by the search for a 'quiet

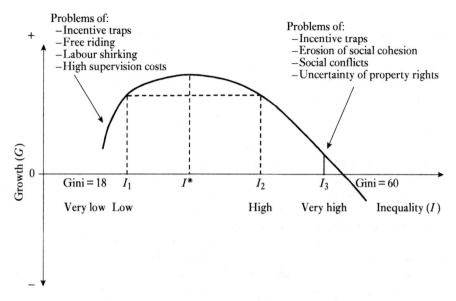

Figure 2.4. *Non-linear relation between inequality and growth*

working life'. Soviet-type pay arrangements, for instance, appear to have caused serious work disincentives, erosion of work discipline, and poor performance among workers and managers. Incentive loss can also occur if workers are subject to very high marginal tax rates (either by the state or by within-community mechanisms), the depressing effect of macroeconomic instability, or some combination of these mechanisms. Thus, growth suffers if inequality is artificially compressed and falls below I_1 in Fig. 2.4.

Conversely, as inequality rises there comes a point, I^*, at which the growth–inequality relationship starts to turn negative and, from inequality level I_2 onwards, growth turns sharply negative, as the observed distribution of income deviates markedly from the latent distribution of rewards based on talent, merit, and effort. This mainly happens because of the malfunctioning of labour, capital, and product markets, or because of unbalanced access to education, land, credit, and insurance or by sheer discrimination and segregation. This case is also characterized by an erosion of incentives which may lead to output contraction among the self-employed and to shirking and free-riding among dependent workers. In all cases where the output of the latter is not easily monitorable, the erosion of incentives deriving from large differences between the 'latent' and the 'real' distribution of rewards entails the introduction of costly labour-monitoring arrangements, which depress economic efficiency.

The empirical literature offers a number of microeconomic examples of such negative incentive effects. In labour surplus agriculture, for instance, high land concentration is generally associated with an inefficient use of labour, shirking by agricultural workers, high monitoring and supervision costs, and as a result of all this, low yields per hectare and total factor productivity (Cornia 1985). A high degree of asset concentration and landlessness may also force the poor to behave in ways that harm growth over the long term as observed in the case of over-exploitation of forests, pasture, and fisheries.

Low industrial wages, or large wage differentials unexplained by productivity differentials, could erode work incentives, increase shirking and supervision costs, and reduce efficiency in manufacturing as well. Large industrial firms relying on salaried workers generally face higher shirking and supervision costs than small firms where the distribution of rewards may be better aligned with that based on effort and talent and where, in any case, supervision costs are lower. In turn, in workers' cooperatives which rely on peer-group supervision, incentive structures are generally better and labour shirking is lower. But even these enterprises are not immune from incentive problems. For instance, Banerjee *et al.* (1998, cited in Banerjee and Duflo 2001), show, using panel data from sugar cooperatives in India, that the most unequal cooperatives are the least productive, with differences in output per capita of more than 50 per cent between the most and least egalitarian ones.

The erosion of work incentives described above can be accompanied by a weakening of 'the social contract' alluded to earlier when discussing social conflicts models. When the gap between rich and poor widens substantially, rent-seeking, predatory, and criminal activities rise. This increases transaction costs for business security and contract enforcement, while eroding the security of property rights. For instance, Fajnzylber *et al.* (1999) find evidence that high-income inequality is consistently associated with high violence levels across countries. In turn, Bourguignon (1998) and others measured the growing economic cost imposed on society by such violence in terms of lives lost, medical costs, and resources diverted from productive uses to prevent and repress criminal activities.

Figure 2.4 suggests that a moderate surge in inequality from a level lower than I_1 can improve incentives, accelerate growth, and contribute to poverty reduction.[7] Second, any country that intends to maximize poverty reduction within the growth-invariant inequality range should choose a lower level of inequality—I_1 over I_2 for example—as the former is associated with a higher poverty alleviation elasticity of growth than the latter. Finally, in the interval I_1-I^* the inequality level that optimizes poverty reduction varies in line with the slope of the curve. Further increases in inequality past I_1 are efficient as long as the growth-enhancing effect of higher inequality is greater than the decline in the poverty alleviation elasticity of growth due to a rise in inequality. Policy-wise, it is therefore necessary to identify for each group of countries an 'efficient inequality range' within which both growth and poverty reduction are maximized. In contrast, beyond I_2 there is both growth collapse and increasing poverty.

2.6.1. *An Econometric Test of the Non-linear Relation Between Inequality and Growth*

We regressed by means of ordinary least squares (OLS) with heteroschedastic correction the point-to-point changes over 1980 and 1998 (or most recent year) in the

---

[7] But an inequality level lower than I_1 might be chosen if society values lower inequality per se.

Gini coefficients ($\Delta\text{Gini}_{80-98}$) of the seventy-three countries analysed in Sections 2.2 and 2.3 on the average GDP growth rate realized over this period (G_{80-98}). The data were interpolated using both a linear function (numerical results not shown) and a quadratic function. The latter appears to fit the data substantially better than the former and identifies a statistically significant concave relation in ($\Delta\text{Gini}_{80-98}$)^2 that explains a satisfactory 57 per cent of the total variance in growth performance. The linear term $\Delta\text{Gini}_{80-98}$, in contrast, is almost equal to zero and has the wrong sign:

$$G_{80-98} = 4.52\ (11.67) - 0.0004\ (0.00)\ \Delta\text{Gini}_{80-98} - 0.410\ (8.69)\ (\Delta\text{Gini}_{80-98})^2$$
$$\text{for,}\quad R^2 = 0.57,\quad\text{no. of obs.} = 73.$$

This estimate suggests that, on average, the countries that experienced large increases in income inequality are likely to have suffered a slowdown in growth. There were, of course, important exceptions to this rule, as illustrated by the case of outliers such as China, which experienced fast growth despite a surge in inequality. As noted in Section 2.2, however, this was mainly due to a rise in inequality across regions, which is less likely to erode incentives and social cohesion and not to a surge in vertical inequality within all regions.

Inspection of Fig. 2.5 indicates, however, that the concave shape of the relation is due to the behaviour of the former socialist countries of Europe which—because of the one-off systemic changes entailed by the transition—recorded much larger falls in GDP per capita than other countries experiencing similar rises in Gini coefficients. To control this and similar systemic shocks—such as the 1980s debt crisis in Latin America—we expressed the average country change in GDP per capita over 1980–98 as an index number (with 1980 GDP/c = 100) and divided the value of the national index numbers so obtained for the regional average for the same indicator. We obtained in this way a standardized growth measure (SG_{80-98}) which takes into account the varying country exposures to regional shocks. Repeating the regression using the

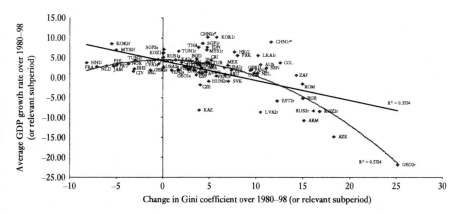

Figure 2.5. *Linear and non-linear relation between changes in Gini coefficients over 1980 and 1998 (or relevant subperiod) and changes in growth performance over the same period (or relevant subperiod)*

'standardized growth' variable improves the estimate of the inequality–growth relation. To start with, the sign of the variable $\Delta Gini_{80-98}$ now has the correct sign and its parameter is significant at the 83 per cent level. In addition, the parameter of the quadratic term declined substantially in relation to the prior formulation, a fact that reduces the steepness of the right arm of the function. In contrast, the fit of the data worsened:

$$SG_{80-98} = 1.040 \ (42.37) + 0.008 \ (1.38)\Delta Gini_{80-98} - 0.0012 \ (3.69) \ (\Delta Gini_{80-98})^2$$
$$\text{for,} \quad R^2 = 0.18, \qquad \text{no. of obs.} = 73.$$

Even after these corrections, this model still suffers from some specification problems. First of all, equal increases in inequality from different initial levels are likely, *ex ante*, to generate different impacts, a fact that is not captured by the above specification. The second problem concerns the direction of causation, a typical problem when dealing with synchronous cross-sectional data. A solution to this problem requires lagging the dependent variable, a change that could not be introduced given the cross-sectional nature of the data available.

To solve these problems we tested the relation between inequality and growth on a panel of 325 observations for twelve developed nations, six transitional economies, and seven large developing countries (Brazil, Chile, China, India, Pakistan, South Africa, and South Korea) for which at least seven well-spaced observations covering the years 1960–98 were available in the WIID database. Several estimation techniques were utilized to fit the relation $G_t = a + b\,Gini_t - c\,Gini_t^2$. All of them yielded similar and significant coefficients (not shown). Figure 2.6 presents the scatterplot of the above relation fitted with the estimate of such a quadratic function computed through a generalized estimating equation (GEE) panel data estimator with country-specific effects accounting for different average growth levels and Gini concepts. This estimation procedure is relatively robust to misspecification of the covariance matrix, an important issue when dealing with inequality datasets. The concave relation depicted in Fig. 2.6 shows that the growth rate of GDP rises on average by up to 5 points when the Gini coefficient rises from 15 to 30. Within the range 35–45 of the Gini coefficient, the average rate of growth is broadly invariant at around 5 per cent a year. Between 45 and 50 Gini points the GDP growth rate declines by 1 per cent, while another 4 percentage points of GDP growth vanish by the time the Gini coefficient reaches 60.

Similar results were arrived at by Barro (2000), who—after imposing all the necessary controls—found a significant *negative* relation between inequality and growth in countries with a GDP per capita of less than 2070 (in 1985 US$) and a significant *positive* relation in countries with a GDP per capita higher than the threshold. The countries covered by the first relation broadly corresponds to the high inequality countries in Fig. 2.6 (for which the relation is clearly negative) while the second corresponds to the low inequality countries in Fig. 2.6 (for which an increase in inequality is clearly pro-growth).

The results in Fig. 2.6 provide some initial support to the hypothesis that the relation between inequality and growth is concave, but several essential improvements are still necessary to confirm that this finding, at this stage, is of a highly tentative nature. Indeed, the above specifications still suffer from problems of multidirectional causality,

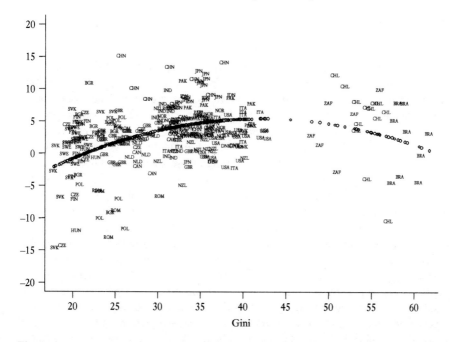

Figure 2.6. *Annual percentage growth of GDP, constant 1995 USD ((vertical axis) versus the level of the Gini coefficient of distribution of income (horizontal axis))*

simultaneity, and bias due to omitted variables.[8] Additional tests will have to focus in particular on tackling the simultaneity problem; including controls for convergence in GDP per capita and other unobserved effects correlated with it; including controls for the countries of the former Soviet Union; lagging of the dependent variable; averaging of the variables over quinquennial periods to reduce noise; and including in the analysis sample more developing countries. Most importantly, the model needs to be tested on microdata so as to isolate the specific incentives and social effects which lie behind the concave relation *I–G* discussed above. Mindful of all this, it must be noted that the simpler approach adopted was mainly due to problems of data availability and difficulties in the interpretation of the results of more complex specifications.

All in all, the above empirical tests do not provide conclusive evidence but encourage us to dig further in this direction. If successful, a more comprehensive testing of this relation might, in fact, substantially modify the policy approach in this crucial area.

2.7. CONCLUSIONS: IN SEARCH OF POLICIES FOR EGALITARIAN GROWTH AND POVERTY REDUCTION

While excessive egalitarianism stifles incentives and thus poverty reduction through growth, high inequality has a similar and more pronounced effect. For this, a genuine

---

[8] We are grateful to an anonymous referee for drawing our attention to this point.

attempt at alleviating poverty requires addressing both the traditional causes of high inequality as well as the sources of inequality that might be related to globalization and liberalization.

Much remains to be done to remove the sources of inequality analysed in Chapters 3–5 and 12–16 of this volume. A first step to achieve this objective would be implementing an agrarian reform in an incentive and power-compatible manner. The redistribution of large farms, plantations, and state-run farms to the landless and poor smallholders can improve both equity and efficiency in rural areas and raise urban unskilled wages which are often held down by the excess supply of landless labourers. Second, it is essential to rebuild human capital by refocusing public spending and mobilizing more revenue through progressive taxation. The present distribution of public spending and taxation in many countries is neither conducive to growth or poverty reduction. The fiscal system often distorts economic incentives, and contributes to an excessively high level of income inequality, damaging both growth and poverty reduction. Similarly, tax systems need institutional investment to provide the revenues to subsidize human capital formation among the poor. A third important policy measure is the correction of market failures in credit and insurance markets. Microcredit programmes are doing much to raise the incomes of the poor, especially among rural women. Less attention has been given to the development of insurance markets for smallholders and microentrepreneurs that would enable them to insure against both household-specific and covariant shocks. Finally, there is an urgent need to control regional and ethnic inequalities that cause poverty and social conflict. Urban and ethnic bias has been prevalent in public spending and public employment in countries such as Guatemala and apartheid South Africa. This has exacerbated horizontal inequality, leading to adverse growth effects through social conflict and localized violence.

Some of the recently observed rises in inequality are due to the way Washington Consensus policies have been conducted. Policy aiming at targeting poverty and the efficient inequality range will therefore need to introduce changes in this area as well. One first step is to design stabilization to avoid sharp compression in aggregate demand and pro-poor public spending. Stabilization can be undertaken in different ways, some of which are more protective of the poor than others—for example, reducing the fiscal deficit by mobilizing more public revenue to maintain pro-poor public spending or avoiding large rapid reductions in inflation rates below levels that have no discernible benefit for growth (Bruno and Easterly 1998)—while it does adversely affect income inequality and poverty through the recessions that it triggers. A second essential measure consists of investing in basic and technical education to raise the supply of skilled labour and thus spread the benefits of trade liberalization and technology investment more widely. East Asia's success in human capital investment illustrates one of the preconditions that needs to be met if countries wish to achieve global competitiveness and pro-poor growth. Third, the occurrence of financial crises and thereby sharp recession-induced rises in inequality need to be avoided. Premature financial liberalization, in the context of weak prudential regulation, has caused major crises in emerging economies but is also evident in low-income countries. Financial crises have large social costs. The social benefits of reducing output volatility are therefore considerable. Inter-American Development Bank (IDB) estimates that in Latin America, a 3 percentage point reduction in the volatility of real GDP growth would reduce the Gini coefficient by about 2 per centage points (IDB 1998: 100). In the absence of international action, national action must be taken. This includes strengthening prudential regulation, as well as the introduction of controls on destabilizing short-term capital flows. Finally, privatized enterprises need to be regulated. Realizing the social gains of privatization depends upon careful design of privatization itself, effective post-privatization regulation, and investment in an appropriate legal framework. While privatization is now a 'done deal' in many countries, regulation is the key entry point for getting equity objectives into policy. Privatized utilities illustrate the issues. With the privatization of state-owned utilities, the service access of the poor may improve after privatization, if substantial capital is invested. But, in practice, the service provided by privatized utilities to the poor has been mixed, leaving the poor, particularly in rural areas, with the worst access and services.

REFERENCES

Addison, T. (2003). *From Conflict to Recovery in Africa*. Oxford University Press: Oxford.

—— and G. A. Cornia (2001). Income distribution policies for faster poverty reduction. WIDER Discussion Paper 2001/93, UNU/WIDER: Helsinki.

Aghion, P., E. Caroli, and C. Garcia-Penalosa (1999). Inequality and economic growth: The perspective of the new growth theories. *Journal of Economic Literature* 37, 1615–60.

Ahmad, E., and A. Hussain (1991). Social security in China: An historical perspective. In E. Ahmad, J. Drèze, J. Hills, and A. Sen (eds.), *Social Security in Developing Countries*. Clarendon Press: Oxford.

Alesina, A., and A. Drazen (1993). Why are stabilizations delayed? *American Economic Review* 81(5), 1170–88.

—— and D. Rodrik (1994). Distributive politics and economic growth. *Quarterly Journal of Economics* 109, 465–90.

Altimir, O. (1994). Income distribution and poverty through crisis and adjustment. *Cepal Review* 52, 7–31.

—— (1996). Economic development and social equity. *Journal of Interamerican Studies and World Affairs*, Summer/Fall.

Atkinson, A. and J. Micklewright (1992). *Economic Transformation in Eastern Europe and the Distribution of Income*. Cambridge University Press: Cambridge.

Atkinson, A. B., L. Rainwater, and T. Smeeding (1995). Income distribution in European countries. In A. B. Atkinson (ed.), *Incomes and the Welfare State*. Cambridge University Press: Cambridge.

Banerjee, A., and E. Duflo (2001). Inequality and growth: What can the data say? Paper Presented at the WIDER Conference on Growth and Poverty, 25–26 May, UNU/WIDER: Helsinki.

—— D. Mookherjee, K. Munshi, and D. Ray (1998). Inequality control rights and rent-seeking: A theoretical and empirical analysis of sugar co-operatives in maharastra. Mimeo.

Banuri, T., S. R. Khan, and M. Mahmood (1997). *Just Development: Beyond Adjustment with a Human Face*. Oxford University Press: Karachi.

Barro, R. (2000). Inequality and growth in a panel of countries. *Journal of Economic Growth* 5, 5–32.

Benabou, R. (1996). Inequality and growth. In B. Bernanke and J. Rotemberg (eds.), *NBER Macroeconomics Annual 1996*. MIT Press: Cambridge, MA, and London.

Bigsten, A. (2000). Globalization and income inequality in Uganda. Paper Presented at the Conference on Poverty and Inequality in Developing Countries: A Policy Dialogue on the Effects of Globalization, 30 November–1 December, OECD, Paris.

Birdsall, N. (2000). Why inequality matters: The developing and transitional economies. Mimeo, February, Carnegie Endowment for International Peace, Washington DC.

Boltho, A. (1997). Growth, public expenditure, and household welfare in industrialized countries. In G. A. Cornia and S. Danziger (eds.), *Child Poverty and Deprivation in the Industrialized Countries: 1945–1995*. Oxford University Press: Oxford.

Bourguignon, F. (1998). Crime as a social cost of poverty and inequality: A review focusing on developing countries. Mimeo, DELTA, Paris.

Braithwaite, J., and T. Heleniak (1989). *Social Welfare in the USSR: The Income Recipient Distribution*. Centre for International Research, US Bureau of the Census, Washington, DC.

Brandolini, A. (1998). A bird's eye view of long-run changes in income inequality. Mimeo, Banca d'Italia: Rome.

Bruno, M., and W. Easterly (1998). Inflation crises and long-run growth. *Journal of Monetary Economics* 41(1), 3–26.

Cornia, G. A. (1985). Farm size, land yields and the agricultural production function: An analysis for 15 developing countries. *World Development* 13(4), 513–34.

—— (1994). Poverty in Latin America in the eighties: Extent, causes and possible remedies. *Giornale degli Economisti e Annali di Economia*, July–September.

—— (1996). Transition and income distribution: Theory, evidence and initial interpretation. WIDER Research in Progress 1, UNU/WIDER: Helsinki.

—— and S. Danziger (eds.) (1997). *Child Poverty and Deprivation in Industrialized Countries: 1945–1995*. Oxford University Press: Oxford.

—— and S. Kiiski (2001). Trends in income distribution in the post-World War II period: Evidence and interpretation. WIDER Discussion Paper 2001/89, UNU/WIDER: Helsinki.

Deininger, K., and L. Squire (1996). A new dataset measuring income inequality. *World Bank Economic Review* 10(3), 565–91.

Fajnzylber, P., D. Lederman, and N. Loayza (1999). Inequality and violent crime. Mimeo, World Bank, Washington, DC.

Feridhanusetyawan, T. (2000). Globalization, poverty and equity in Indonesia. Paper Presented at the Conference on Poverty and Inequality in Developing Countries: A Policy Dialogue on the Effects of Globalization, 30 November–1 December, OECD, Paris.

Fields, G., and G. Yoo (2000). Falling labour income inequality in Korea's economic growth: Patterns and underlying causes. *Review of Income and Wealth* 46(2), June, 139–59.

Gottschalck, P., and T. Smeeding (1997). Cross-national comparison of earnings and income inequality. *Journal of Economic Literature* June, 35(2), 633–87.

Gustafsson B., and W. Zhong (2000). How and why has poverty in China changed? *China Quarterly* 164(December), 983–1006.

Hanmer, L., and F. Naschold (2001). Attaining the international development targets: Will growth be enough? Paper Presented at the WIDER Conference on Growth and Poverty, 25–26 May, UNU/WIDER, Helsinki.

Iglesia, E. (1998). Income distribution and sustainable growth: A Latin American perspective. In V. Tanzi and K.-Y. Chu (eds.), *Income Distribution and High-Quality Growth*. MIT Press: Cambridge, MA.

IDB (1998). *Facing up to Inequality in Latin America: Economic and Social Progress in Latin America: 1998–1999 Report*, IDB: Washington, DC.

Jomo, K. S. (2000). Globalization, liberalization, poverty and income inequality in Southeast Asia. Paper Presented at the Conference on Poverty and Inequality in Developing Countries: A Policy Dialogue on the Effects of Globalization, 30 November–1 December, OECD, Paris.

Kanbur, R. (2000). Income distribution and development. In A. Atkinson and F. Bourguignon (eds.), *The Handbook of Income Distribution*. North Holland: Amsterdam.

Kayizzi-Mugerwa, S. (2000). Globalization, growth and income inequality: A review of the African experience. Paper Presented at the Conference on Poverty and Inequality in Developing Countries: A Policy Dialogue on the Effects of Globalization, 30 November–1 December 2000, OECD, Paris.

Knowles, J., E. Pernia, and M. Racelis (1999). Social consequences of the financial crisis in Asia. ADB Economic Staff Paper 60, Asian Development Bank, Manila.

Levinshon, J., S. Berry, and J. Friedman (1999). Impacts of the Indonesian economic crisis: Price changes and the poor. Mimeo, University of Michigan: Ann Arbor, MI.

Li, H., L. Squire, and H. Zou (1998). Explaining international and intertemporal variations in income inequality. *Economic Journal* 108(446), 26–43.

McCulloch, N., B. Baulch, and M. Cherel-Robson (2000). Globalization, poverty and inequality in Zambia. Paper Presented at the Conference on Poverty and Inequality in Developing Countries: A Policy Dialogue on the Effects of Globalization, 30 November–1 December 2002, OECD, Paris.

McKinley, T., and M. Brenner (1998). Rising inequality and changing social structure in China: 1988–95. Mimeo, UNU/WIDER: Helsinki.

Milanovic, B. (1995). Poverty, inequality and social policy in transition economies. Policy Research Paper Series 9, World Bank, Washington, DC.

——(1998). *Income, Inequality, and Poverty during the Transition from Planned to Market Economy*. World Bank, Washington, DC.

Mundle, S., and V. B. Tulasidhar (1998). Adjustment and distribution: The Indian experience. ADB Occasional Paper 17, Asian Development Bank, Manila.

Oshima, H. (1998). Income distribution policies in east Asia. *The Developing Economies*, XXXVI-4 (December).

Ozawa, M., and S. Kono (1997). Child well-being in Japan: The high cost of economic success. In G. A. Cornia and S. Danziger (eds.), *Child Poverty and Deprivation in the Industrialized Countries, 1945–1995*. Oxford University Press: Oxford.

Pangestu, M. (2000). Social impact of globalization in Southeast Asia. Paper Presented at the Conference on Poverty and Inequality in Developing Countries: A Policy Dialogue on the Effects of Globalization, 30 November–1 December 2002, OECD, Paris.

Ping, Z. (1997). Income distribution during the transition in China. WIDER Working Paper 138, UNU/WIDER: Helsinki.

Ravallion, M. (2001). Growth, inequality and poverty: Looking beyond averages. Paper Presented at the WIDER Conference on Growth and Poverty, 25–26 May, UNU/WIDER: Helsinki.

——and G. Datt (1999). When is growth pro-poor? Evidence from the diverse experience of Indian states. Mimeo, World Bank, Washington, DC.

Rutkowski, J. (1999). Wage inequality in transition economies of Central Europe: Trends and pattern in the late 1990s. Mimeo, August.

Sainz, P., and A. Calcagno (1992). Em Busca de Otra Modalidad de Desarrollo. *CEPAL Review* 48 (December).

Sawyer, M. (1976). Income distribution in OECD countries. *OECD Economic Outlook*, July.

Standing, G., and D. Vaughan-Whitehead (1995). *Minimum Wages in Central and Eastern Europe: From Protection to Destitution*. Central European University Press: Budapest.

Székely, M., and M. Hilgert (1999). Inequality in Latin America during the 1990s. Mimeo, Inter-American Development Bank: Washington, DC.

Tokman, V. (1986). Ajuste y Empleo: Los Desafios del Presente. Mimeo, PREALC, Regional Employment Programme for Latin America and the Caribbean: Santiago.

UNCTAD (1997). *Trade and Development Report*. UNCTAD, Geneva.

UNICEF (1995). Poverty, children and policy: Responses for brighter future. Regional Monitoring Report 3, UNICEF-ICDC, Florence.

Venieris, Y., and D. Gupta (1986). Income distribution and sociopolitical instability as determinants of savings: A cross-sectional model. *Journal of Political Economy* 94(4), 873–83.

World Bank (1990). *World Development Report: Poverty*. World Bank, Washington, DC.

——(2000). World development report 2000/1. Draft, 17 January, World Bank, Washington, DC.

You, I. (1998). Income distribution and growth in east Asia. *Journal of Development Studies* 34(6), 37–65.

PART II

TRADITIONAL CAUSES OF INEQUALITY: STILL RELEVANT FOR EXPLAINING ITS RISE IN THE 1980S AND THE 1990S?

3

Landownership Inequality and the Income Distribution Consequences of Economic Growth

MICHAEL CARTER

3.1. CAN AGRARIAN STRUCTURE EXPLAIN INCREASING INCOME INEQUALITY?

New data and the trends revealed by them have helped bring the economic analysis of income distribution in from the cold, to pinch Atkinson's (1997) phrase. Within development economics, the Kuznets (1955) inverted-U hypothesis, which had cooled and crystallized into a stylized fact of textbook orthodoxy, has been challenged anew. Among these newer studies, some show that there simply is no consistent relationship between inequality and growth, inverted-U shaped or otherwise (Li *et al.* 1998; Lundberg and Squire 1998). Others argue that the Kuznets relationship has been buried by a global trend of increasing, persistent, or excess inequality (Lodoño and Székely 1997; Cornia this volume; see also Chapters 2 and 9). Understanding these new patterns is both an academic challenge, and a matter of policy import. As Lodoño and Székely (1997) stress, understanding the 'surprises' of contemporary income distribution dynamics is vital in economies where high inequality calls into question the economic desirability and political legitimacy of the liberal policy regimes of the last two decades.

If new policies are justified,[1] designing them requires a sharper understanding of the factors that underlie the contemporary trends in income inequality. Land

The author thanks Pedro Olinto and Klaus Deininger for making available the data file used in their recent analysis of growth and inequality. Thanks are also due to Giovanni Andrea Cornia and to other participants in the World Institute for Development Economics Research (WIDER) Conference on Rising Income Inequality for their many useful and thought-provoking comments.

[1] The literature on income inequality has unfortunately paid little attention to distinguishing destructive from productive inequality. As described by Sheehan and Iglesias (1998), productive inequality results from the desirable operation of a socially legitimate incentive system that, say, encourages people to forgo income now in order to invest in education. Destructive inequality, on the other hand, reflects the operation of an economy in which some people are excluded from the opportunity to invest and otherwise to participate in the benefits of growth. Whether contemporary income inequality increases are economically costly and warrant policy remediation would seem to depend critically on the extent to which trends in aggregate inequality reflect increases in destructive or productive inequality components.

ownership inequality (agrarian structure) is one factor that has been traditionally taken to explain high *levels* of income inequality (especially in the lower income economies of the 1950s and 1960s where the agricultural sector predominated). But does agrarian structure have any role in explaining contemporary *trends* in income inequality? An affirmative finding might seem to indicate the appropriateness of policies to redistribute land, as Deininger (2001) advocates.

But it may also be that any contemporary impact of agrarian structure on income inequality takes place indirectly by conditioning the distributive consequences of economic growth, both agricultural and non-agricultural. This chapter conceptualizes and empirically explores two such indirect mechanisms: exclusionary agrarian transitions and household human capital accumulation failures. If it is through these indirect mechanisms that agrarian structure has its effect, then the array of new, ameliorative policy responses broadens beyond land redistribution to include measures that operate on these mechanisms.

Section 3.2 begins the chapter with a conventional income inequality accounting or Gini decomposition framework. Among other things, this decomposition provides a convenient vehicle to review the economic theory of the inverted-U, the assumptions under which it could be expected to hold, and, by implication, the likely reasons for its failure to hold in the contemporary world. This framework also makes clear that the *direct* explanatory power of land ownership inequality should diminish with the reduction in the share of national income generated in the agricultural sector.[2] These direct effects of agrarian structure on income inequality should thus be diminishing rapidly over time in those countries of Asia and Latin America where the weight of the agricultural sector in the overall economy has fallen off dramatically.

Figure 3.1, however, suggests a more complicated scenario. Each of the four panels pools together by decade the observations from an augmented Deininger and Squire (1996) dataset for which initial (~1965) agrarian structure data are available. The lines that are drawn in each panel show the estimated ordinary least squares (OLS) relationship between the Gini index for income inequality and the Gini index for landownership concentration. The curves are non-parametric kernel estimates using cross-validation to select the optimum bandwidth. Surprisingly, the data for the last decade (1985–95) show almost exactly the same statistically significant relationship as that for the earlier time periods. While there could of course be a myriad of factors that underlie the observed association, the failure of agrarian structure to wither away as an explanatory variable is provocative.

The notion that agrarian structure has deeper effects on economic performance is supported by recent empirical work that finds that landownership inequality retards the rate of economic growth. Deininger and Squire (1998) and Deininger and Olinto (1999) find that the same initial landownership inequality measure used in Fig. 3.1 statistically explains subsequent rates of economic growth, even when panel data methods are used to control for country heterogeneity. These authors argue that

---

[2] Agrarian structure could continue to exhibit a spurious statistical association with income inequality if it is correlated with inequality in the holding of industrial assets, as subsection 3.2.2 discusses.

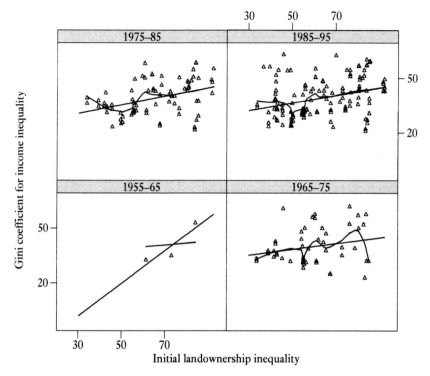

Figure 3.1. *Agrarian structure and income inequality*

landownership inequality creates low and insecure incomes for the rural poor, thereby retarding human capital accumulation and growth. These same mechanisms could also buttress high and potentially increasing levels of income inequality over time, creating what Birdsall *et al.* (1995) call a vicious circle of growth and inequality.

Building on the Gini decomposition framework, Section 3.2 draws on empirical and theoretical work about the nature of agrarian growth and transformation in the contemporary world. This chapter hypothesizes that landownership inequality can have continuing and perhaps increasing effects on income inequality because it can create exclusionary patterns of growth that deepen inequality over time. At the same time, these income distribution consequences of exclusionary growth are potentially magnified via their impacts on the accumulation of human and physical capital by the least well-off members of society. The role of these secondary effects in the explanation of contemporary income distribution dynamics is of course an empirical question.

Section 3.3 develops an econometric approach for answering this empirical question. Flexible estimation methods based on random coefficients or mixed effects models are employed to test for the effect of agrarian structure on income inequality. Section 3.4 summarizes the chapter by considering the implications for policy both inside and outside the agricultural sector.

3.2. DECOMPOSING THE EFFECTS OF AGRARIAN STRUCTURE ON INCOME INEQUALITY

As a basis for discussion of household income distribution, consider the following disaggregation of total income for a household, k, in country, i, in period, t:

$$Y_{kit} = Y_{kit}^A + w_{it}L_{it} + s_{it}H_{kit} + r_{it}K_{kit}, \tag{3.1}$$

where Y_{kit}^A is agricultural income and L_{kit}, H_{kit}, and K_{kit} are stocks of non-agricultural factors of production (unskilled labour, skilled labour or human capital, and physical capital) that are rewarded with factor payments, w_{it}, s_{it}, and r_{it}, respectively. While in practice it may be difficult to separate the returns from land and labour in agriculture, agricultural income can in principle be further disaggregated into returns from land and returns from labour:

$$Y_{kit} = [\tilde{p}_{kit}T_{kit} + \tilde{w}_{kit}F_{kit}] + w_{it}L_{it} + s_{it}H_{kit} + r_{it}K_{kit}. \tag{3.1'}$$

T_{kit} is the stock of land, $\tilde{p}_{kit}$ its rental price or shadow rate of return. F_{kit} is the stock of farmworkers, and $\tilde{w}_{kit}$ is the (shadow) value of agricultural labour, including labour which is self-employed on owner-operated production units. The Gini coefficient[3] for income inequality in country, i, in period, t, can be decomposed as follows:

$$G_{it} = \phi_{it}^A \tilde{G}_{it}^A + [\phi_{it}^H \tilde{G}_{it}^H + \phi_{it}^K \tilde{G}_{it}^K + \phi_{it}^L \tilde{G}_{it}^L], \tag{3.2}$$

using Eq. (3.1) for household income, or as

$$G_{it} = [\phi_{it}^T \tilde{G}_{it}^T + \phi_{it}^F \tilde{G}_{it}^F] + [\phi_{it}^H \tilde{G}_{it}^H + \phi_{it}^K \tilde{G}_{it}^K + \phi_{it}^L \tilde{G}_{it}^L] \tag{3.2'}$$

using Eq. (3.1'). Terms of the form ϕ_{it}^j are the shares of income type j in total gross domestic product (GDP), and the $\tilde{G}_{it}^j$ are the pseudo-Gini coefficients for income type j.[4] Note further that the pseudo-Ginis can be rewritten as

$$\tilde{G}_{it}^j = \rho_{it}^j G_{it}^j, \tag{3.3}$$

where G_{it}^j is the true Gini for income of type j and ρ_{it}^j is the rank order correlation between households' rank in the overall income distribution with their rank in the distribution of type j income. Note that the ϕ_{it}^j factor shares define the functional income distribution, while the pseudo-Ginis measure the endowment or asset inequality that is necessary to map functional income distribution into household income distribution. As subsection 3.2.1 now explores, the Kuznets hypothesis of an inverted-U-shaped relationship between income inequality and national income was largely rationalized in terms of a theory of the ϕ_{it}^j, the functional income distribution, while making rather strong assumptions on asset inequality, the G_{it}^j.

---

[3] The Gini coefficient has a number of well-known weaknesses as a measure of income inequality. It is used here because of the analytical convenience of its decomposability, as well as the empirical availability of Gini measures. Subsequent analysis should more carefully think through the appropriateness of the Gini measure for the questions being addressed here.

[4] The pseudo-Gini for income of type j is the Gini index that results when the Lorenz curve for income type j is constructed by placing people in rank order according to their position in the overall income distribution, not their position in the distribution type j income (e.g. see the discussion in Fields 1980).

3.2.1. *Asset Inequality and the Dual Economy Theory of Income Distribution Dynamics*

While earlier decades saw much debate concerning the merits of classical dual economy models (rooted in Lewis 1953) versus neoclassical dual economy models (rooted in the work of Jorgenson 1961), Taylor (1979) neatly demonstrates that basic models of both types have very similar income distribution implications. Both models predict that, in an initially poor rural economy, sustained capital accumulation and growth will bring a long period of constant or near-constant real wages for (unskilled) labour. In the classical models that assumed an institutionally fixed real wage, the reason for the trajectories of factor shares is obvious. In the neoclassical variants, which assumed an economically endogenous market-clearing wage, diminishing returns to capital would seem to imply that rapid capital accumulation would immediately shift income distribution in favour of labour. However, in the dual economy context, the shift from an agricultural to an industrial economy postpones the setting-in of diminishing returns to capital and generates increasing inequality in the factor distribution of income.

As a result of the constancy of the real wage in the face of economic growth, the income share of capital (ϕ_{it}^K in Eq. (3.2) above) and inequality in the functional income distribution rise. Both models do eventually reach a turning point, after which the real wage rises and (assuming inelastic capital–labour substitution in industry) the capital share, ϕ_{it}^K, and functional income inequality fall, creating an inverted-U-shaped dynamic in the *functional* income distribution. However, moving from this dual economy theory of functional income distribution to a theory of household income distribution requires information about asset distributions (the $\tilde{G}_{it}^j$ in Eq. (3.2) above).[5] Given the complexity of asset distributions and the intertemporal choices that underlie them, it is not surprising that the dual economy literature relied on highly simplified assumptions. With the exception of a few highly disaggregated computable general equilibrium (CGE) models, the dual economy literature assumed a simple polarized class structure persistent over the course of growth, whereby the few capitalist households own and mechanically accumulate all capital, while the numerically preponderant proletarian households[6] own only their labour such that:

$$\tilde{G}_{it}^K \approx 1 \ \forall \ t, \text{and,} \tag{3.4}$$

$$\tilde{G}_{it}^L \approx 0 \ \forall \ t. \tag{3.5}$$

---

[5] Also underlying the dual economy literature is a number of stark assumptions about technology and trade. In this literature, production technologies are typically modelled as constant returns to scale, with inelastic factor substitution in the industrial sector. Consistent with growth theory of the era, technology was exogenous and unbiased. Kelly *et al.* (1973), for example, show that exogenous technological change biased against labour will, if too high, defeat the Kuznets curve. In addition, the dual economy literature was largely a closed economy literature, and the returns to capital and labour were among those prices presumed to be set in the domestic economy. Factor shares were driven by domestic stocks of capital and labour, and the technological assumption of inelastic substitution between capital and labour in production (in at least one sector of the economy) meant that the returns to rapidly accumulated capital would eventually fall fast enough to shift functional income distribution.

[6] Note that these households are proletarian in the true meaning of the term as they serve the system only by bearing child-workers.

In his textbook analysis of income distribution in dual economy models, Taylor (1979) effectively assumes that agricultural income (labour and land rental) is distributed in an egalitarian fashion:

$$\tilde{G}_{it}^{A} \approx 0 \,\forall\, t. \tag{3.6}$$

More generally, at least implicit assumption in the literature seems to be the assumption that the landownership distribution is static, such that

$$\tilde{G}_{it}^{T} \approx \overline{G}^{T} \,\forall\, t. \tag{3.6'}$$

As discussed below, this assumption hides connections between landownership distribution and factor use and shadow factor prices ($\tilde{w}_{kit}$ and $\tilde{p}_{kit}$) in agriculture.

While Eq. (3.4) is at least a defensible simplification for physical capital, it makes little sense as an assumption about human capital (no slavery). While the classic dual economy literature ignored human capital (or, equivalently, subsumed it with physical capital), human capital does of course matter, and, importantly, its distributional dynamics cannot be adequately captured by a simple analogue assumption, either (3.4) or (3.5). Indeed, as the discussion in subsection 3.2.3 details, the dynamics of $\tilde{G}_{it}^{h}$ are likely to be influenced by agrarian structure.

In addition, Eq. (3.6) or (3.6') rules out a number of dynamic processes that are potentially relevant to the trajectory of income distribution. In classical and neoclassical models, the rural economy faithfully reproduces a stable reservation wage or living standard for the rest of the economy (i.e. $w = \tilde{w}$), generating what might be termed an 'inclusionary' agrarian transition. In the classical model, this result flows from the assumption of a socially embedded, precapitalist rural economy that guarantees all workers not demanded by the industrial economy a place and a subsistence standard of living. In the neoclassical model, the assumption of a simple Walrasian labour market (to use the language of Bowles 1985) assures that all workers are absorbed by the rural sector pending expansion of urban-industrial labour demand. Assumed away in these models is any process of institutional instability (such as that described by Collier *et al.* 1976 or Scott and Kerklievett 1975), or intrinsically imperfect rural factor markets that make labour demand and the reservation living standard a function of agrarian structure and make agrarian structure itself subject to independent, economically relevant dynamics. Violation of either assumption creates the prospect for exclusionary transitions and additional avenues by which the landownership distribution may shape income inequality.

However, before a discussion of ways in which agrarian structure may continue to shape the ongoing nature of agrarian growth (subsection 3.2.3) and human capital accumulation (subsection 3.2.4), the next section considers some direct impacts of agrarian structure on income inequality.

3.2.2. *Level and Legacy Effects of Agrarian Structure on Inequality in the Industrializing Economy*

While the previous subsection discusses the income distribution implications of the dual economy literature, that literature's original *raison d'être* was to explore the transformation of a 'traditional' agricultural economy into a 'modern' industrial economy. On the empirical side, the work of Hollis Chenery (e.g. Chenery and Syrquin 1973) documented this transformation, including the statistically regular withering away of agriculture as the predominant economic sector.

As is apparent from Eq. (3.2) above, the collapse of ϕ_{it}^A towards zero will make the level of agricultural inequality irrelevant from the perspective of overall income inequality in the industrializing economy. While a highly unequal agrarian structure (high G_{it}^T and $\tilde{G}_{it}^A$) will have a large effect in a predominately agrarian economy,[7] the direct inequality effect of a given level of agrarian inequality will eventually wither away with ϕ_{it}^A. In the following analysis, this direct impact of agrarian structure on the aggregate level of inequality will be called the 'self-dampening level effect'.

While this direct level effect will wither away, a bivariate statistical association between agrarian structure and income inequality could remain as a legacy of agrarian inequality (as in Fig. 3.1) if a highly unequal agrarian structure translates into a highly unequal initial distribution of industrial assets, $\tilde{G}_{it}^K$. If new industrial assets were acquired in proportion to agricultural assets, then such an outcome would be likely. Indeed, the correlation between $\tilde{G}_{it}^K$ and G_{it}^T would be further strengthened if an existing agrarian oligarchy is able to maintain its political power and reserve for itself new opportunities in the growing industrial economy. The popular portrayal of the economies of Central American (e.g. El Salvador and Nicaragua) as dominated by just a few oligarchic families (who control both agricultural and industrial wealth) illustrates this correlation. In this case, any relationship between agrarian structure and income inequality that survived the withering away of the agricultural share of GDP would be a spurious reflection of the initial relationship between agrarian and industrial asset ownership. Agrarian structure may have mattered for initial industrial asset inequality, but further intervention in agrarian asset ownership would not undo the concentration of industrial asset ownership or otherwise ameliorate income inequality.

However, it is not logically apparent that there should be a strong correlation between agrarian and industrial asset inequality, or that any persistent relationship between agrarian structure and income inequality is spurious. A strong correlation between agrarian and industrial asset inequality would seem to require highly imperfect financial markets such that only those families with strong initial wealth conditions are able to successfully accumulate. Subsection 3.2.3 below in fact considers the operation of this mechanism in the context of human capital accumulation, arguing that initial agrarian inequality will map into low and unequally distributed human capital accumulation. However, for physical capital, the requisite financial market imperfections seem much less likely to be important. Indeed, history abounds with counterexamples to the notion that a unified oligarchic interest creates a pathway between agrarian and industrial asset inequality. The most notable of these counterexamples is the nineteenth-century UK debate over the corn laws that pitted the old agrarian elite against the new industrial interests.

---

[7] Note that, when ϕ_{it}^A approaches 1 and agricultural income comprises nearly all of national income, then by definition ρ_{it}^A will also approach 1.

Closer in time, the political theory of land reform in Latin America in the 1960s was pinned on the notion that agrarian industrial asset correlation was low, such that the new industrial elite could be enlisted as allies against the rural elite in the battle for land reform. Land reform advocate Peter Dorner's 1965 open letter to the Chilean agrarian elite captures this notion with its portrayal of a politically insurmountable peasant–capitalist alliance that can, out of self-interest, overcome agrarian elite opposition to land reform (Castillo and Lehman 1983, quote Dorner's letter at length).

In the end, with the exception of a few, modestly industrialized economies, it seems hard to believe that landownership inequality will persistently influence income inequality through the correlation between agrarian structure and inequality in the distribution of industrial assets. However, given the absence of detailed country-specific historical inquiry and the paucity of data on asset ownership the statistical analysis later in this chapter will remain subject to the caveat that its results are possibly a spurious reflection of the correlation between agrarian structure and industrial asset inequality.

3.2.3. *Exclusionary Agrarian Growth and Landownership Inequality*

The historical experience of growth in Latin America's highly unequal agrarian economies contrasts with the dual economy portrayal of a stable rural sector that absorbs available labour at a constant real wage rate. In these economies, growth has often taken an exclusionary form, meaning that it has displaced peasants and tenants, prematurely mechanized the agrarian economy, and reproduced or even deepened rural inequality (e.g. see Williams 1985).

The term 'exclusionary growth' emerged in the empirical literature as a way to describe a growth process in which small-scale agricultural producers are displaced and the successor farm units respond to a different set of shadow factor prices such that the sector itself becomes labour-displacing. In terms of inequality decomposition in Eq. (3.2), exclusionary growth implies increasing inequality in the distribution of agricultural income, $\tilde{G}_{it}^A$. This trend would offset at least in part the tendency for the agricultural income distribution to matter less for aggregate inequality as the agricultural share of GDP falls. The goal of this section is briefly to review some of the theoretical and empirical literature that suggests that exclusionary growth is (a) possible, and (b) more likely in economies characterized by unequal landownership.

A number of authors have attributed the history of exclusionary agrarian growth patterns to a pernicious political economy that subsidized capital for the rich and depressed prices for labour-intensive exportables (see especially de Janvry and Sadoulet 1993; Binswanger *et al.* 1996). However, since the early 1980s, agricultural development policy has followed the general trend toward development liberalism, forcefully swinging toward laissez-faire throughout the developing world, changing relative prices, and opening up new markets and opportunities. Liberal policies have not always brought the increase in growth expected from them,[8] but, when they have spawned growth, the question has often been raised of whether the newly induced growth is exclusionary, deepening existing inequality in undesirable and socially problematic ways.

The authors de Janvry and Sadoulet (1993) argue that, while post-liberalization growth is at least potentially more inclusive of the poor so that growth will be relinked with poverty reduction (and diminished inequality), they also recognize that various constraints may prevent this happy outcome. In Latin America, countries that have vigorously and successfully pursued liberal, export-oriented agrarian growth strategies present a heterogeneous profile (Carter *et al.* 1996).[9] In some cases, growth has been broadly based and inclusive of small farmers and the rural resource poor. In others, the trajectory of growth has been narrow (based on a subset of wealthier producers), decidedly exclusionary, and socially problematic in the sense that it spills over through land and labour markets and negatively influences other individuals.

While sector-specific inequality data are scarce, the compilation of Eastwood and Lipton in Chapter 5 of the available measures reveals that rural inequality generally increased in the 1980s and 1990s in Asia, Latin America, and perhaps Africa.[10] Additional evidence concerning the exclusionary nature of agrarian growth comes from a time-series econometric study by de Janvry and Sadoulet (1996). They find that agrarian growth in Latin America is historically associated with sharply increasing rural inequality and that the association between agrarian growth and increasing rural inequality has been even stronger during recent post-liberalization growth spells than during earlier periods of growth. The increase in inequality has not been so sharp as to increase in rural poverty in the wake of agrarian growth, but it has clearly blunted the potentially positive impact of growth on rural poverty, as de Janvry and Sadoulet analyse in some detail.

Because the evidence of de Janvry and Sadoulet is on Latin America, it is hard to know whether the patterns they identify reflect on agrarian growth in general or on agrarian growth in environments of high land inequality. Evidence supporting the latter interpretation is found in a study by Ravallion and Datt (1995). In their analysis of income distribution and growth across Indian states, Ravallion and Datt find that agrarian growth in most states is more strongly associated with reduced poverty and inequality than is growth in other economic sectors. In other words, in most states agricultural growth appears to be inclusive of the poor. However, the exception to this pattern is the state of Bihar, the Indian state with the sharpest, near Latin American,

---

[8] The failure of agrarian liberalization to generate expected agricultural growth in some cases can be attributed to the failure of policies to generate stimulative market-level price signals to producers (see Barrett and Carter 1999) or to farm-level constraints *uniformly* blocking a positive supply response (Lipton 1993).

[9] Carter *et al.* (1996) summarize the results of coordinated microstudies of agrarian growth booms in Chile, Guatemala, and Paraguay. In two of the three cases (Chile and Paraguay), rapid growth brought increasing inequality in assets and probably in incomes. In Guatemala, the distributional outcome appears to have been much more favourable for low-wealth people.

[10] Increasing rural inequality is one of the trends that Eastwood and Lipton (this volume) hypothesize will offset the effect of diminished intersectoral inequality that liberalization can be expected to bring.

level of land inequality where agrarian growth appears to be exclusionary relative to urban growth and is not associated with diminished inequality and poverty.

From a theoretical perspective there are reasons for thinking that the loose empirical association between exclusionary growth and land inequality is not accidental. Assuming that technology is constant in returns to scale, all producers great and small would pursue identical resource allocation and production strategies in a world of full and complete markets. Growth booms occasioned by new prices, technologies, or markets would not be based on or biased against any particular wealth class of producers.

However, because of the spatially dispersed, biologically based, and stochastic nature of agricultural production processes, information asymmetries are likely to be especially problematic in rural areas. Hired labour, for example, is likely to be costly to supervise, implying that the labour market may reach an unemployment equilibrium with a wage above the Walrasian market clearing level (the higher wage and the threat of unemployment create work incentives). Among other things, this sort of labour market equilibrium will imply that family labour will be economically cheaper than hired labour. In addition, the sorts of information costs, which make rationing in credit markets likely (see earlier), apply with particular force to loans to small-scale farmers, especially in high risk environments (see Carter 1988).

Finally, the difficulty of distinguishing the effects of bad luck (e.g. localized weather disaster or bird damage) from the effects of sloppy effort and management would make insurance contracts costly to enforce.[11] In the actually existing world of asymmetric information and intrinsically imperfect and missing markets, a producer's specific endowment of family labour, savings, and risk-bearing capacity is likely to shape and distort economic behaviour. The more unequally distributed these endowments are, the more likely it becomes that growth will be exclusionary, with different groupings or classes of producers responding differently to apparently identical market or technological opportunities.

Systematic analysis of agrarian economic performance in the context of actually existing market imperfections highlights numerous issues about the growth and income distribution impacts of agricultural liberalization. In basically egalitarian economies (e.g. much of sub-Saharan Africa), economic liberalization may have modest growth effects if price liberalization magnifies price variability even as it improves average farmgate prices. As analysed by Barrett (1996) and Barrett and Carter (1999), the mixed (across countries and sectors) and often disappointing record of agricultural liberalization in Africa may reflect the microeconomic naivete of a policy regime designed around the presumptions that markets are full and complete. Improved agricultural growth will likely require a mix of ancillary, activist policies to complement the putatively stimulative signals induced by market liberalization and exchange rate

---

[11] Of course events such as generalized flooding or drought would be easy to observe for an insurance provider. However, the fact that there are generalized (or covariate) risks means that farmers form a bad and costly group for insurance purposes, rather like a group of individuals seeking cancer insurance when it is known that all group members will contract the disease at the same time. Binswanger and Rosenzweig (1986), for example, catalogue the impact of these information problems on the systematic imperfections and absence of numerous key markets in rural economies.

realignment. It may be that evidence on increased rural inequality in Africa reflects a reality in which only a small subset of producers have actually been able to respond at all to agricultural liberalization.

In inegalitarian economies (for instance, those of Latin America and parts of southern Africa), liberalization may be more likely to spawn rapid growth, but there are two fundamental breakdowns that may distort the income distribution consequences. First, production behaviour is likely to vary systematically across wealth-based classes of producers, with low-wealth producers behaving like prototypical peasants (pursuing labour-intensive, conservative, and non-commercial production strategies) and high-wealth producers behaving like entrepreneurial capitalists (see Eswaran and Kotwal 1986; Carter and Zimmerman 2000). In this circumstance, new economic opportunities may become differentially stimulative across classes, making possible the sorts of class-based growth booms referenced earlier.

Second, in addition to this sort of static differentiation in production behaviour, dynamic land, and asset accumulation strategies can also systematically differ across classes in actually existing market economies. When producer classes pursue distinct production strategies they are likely to value land and other assets differentially and exhibit differential competitiveness in asset markets. To the extent that land markets are well integrated, those producers positioned competitively to accumulate land will generate upward pressure on asset prices, which spills over and affects the land access of less competitive producers.[12] Microeconometric analyses of recent export booms in Guatemala and Paraguay indicate that differential production strategies have spilled over into distinctive class-based patterns of land accumulation. In addition, the decisions about how much to save and how to allocate savings across risky (land) and less risky (grain stores) assets become class-differentiated to the extent that the market economy has less than the full suite of Arrow–Debreu contingency markets. Thus, for example, low-wealth agents may find it entirely rational to devote their modest savings to low-return assets (e.g. grain stores which yield a negative rate of return) even as their current production is sharply capital-constrained and their land base meagre (for example, see the theoretical analysis in Zimmerman and Carter 2003).

Together, the various possibilities of differentiated production and accumulation strategies suggest that the process of agrarian growth and transformation in actually existing market economies can be an unsteady one and one in which initial levels of inequality are reproduced and deepened by a growth process. Such possibilities introduce the question of the degree to which the trajectory of agrarian growth itself becomes a function of the initial asset distribution in the agrarian economy. Can the relatively egalitarian growth paths of East Asian economies be understood as partially the result of their relatively equal initial distribution of land, as opposed to the continuing reproduction of inequality, which has characterized agrarian growth throughout much of Latin America?

---

[12] Lachmann's (1987) analysis of the English enclosure identifies increasing land rents as a key factor, which displaced and proletarianized the small farm class which was ill positioned to participate in the more remunerative activities which were driving the land price increase.

Another question concerns the breadth of asset inequality that is required to generate differentiated behaviour. Hence, while the range of agrarian asset inequality in much of West Africa appears narrow, econometric work suggests that, in these non-irrigated environments, the degree of risk faced by producers across that seemingly narrow range is broad enough that it could motivate sharply different production and accumulation strategies in a world of imperfect markets (Carter 1997).

In summary, while the level effect of unequal agrarian structure on income inequality is indeed self-dampening, it cannot be concluded that agrarian inequality is directly irrelevant to contemporary trends of increasing income inequality. Exclusionary agricultural growth—a prospect overlooked in the classic dual economy literature—will work to offset the dampening effect of a diminished agricultural share of GDP in the industrializing economies of Asia and Latin America. In the more highly agricultural economies of sub-Saharan Africa, Central America, and parts of Asia, exclusionary growth implies that the agricultural sector will become an increasingly important part of overall income inequality.

3.2.4. *Agrarian Structure and Unequal Human Capital Accumulation*

A number of microtheoretic studies have begun to explore the proposition that intertemporal borrowing constraints and other capital market imperfections can create a link between the initial distribution of wealth and the level and distribution of the human capital that is subsequently accumulated (see, for example, Chapter 4, as well as Lunqvist 1994; Chiu 1998). This section summarizes the two-period model developed by Carter *et al.* (2000) to highlight the investment and portfolio problems that confront rural households. The model explicitly establishes linkages between agrarian structure and the dynamics of growth, human capital accumulation, and income distribution.

Rural households in the Carter *et al.* model are endowed with different amounts of land, financial wealth, and family labour. In the first period of this model, households use their resources to generate income in the agrarian economy and must then decide how to allocate that income among consumption, precautionary savings, investment in education, and investment in agricultural capital. Returns to education occur in the second period and are uncertain. Educational investment has a fixed cost component, and both agricultural and educational investments are irreversible and cannot be sold or cashed in during the second period. As they make these first-period choices, households know that they face the risk of a second period 'marginal utility shock' in the form of increased consumption needs (or decreased work capacity). Financial markets are assumed to be imperfect. Households face intertemporal borrowing constraints (i.e. they cannot use second period earnings to finance first period investments). They also do not have access to insurance and must be prepared to deal autarchically with adverse shocks. In summary, as households contemplate investment in agriculture versus investment in education, they must not only be able to finance investment costs up front, they must also maintain a savings-investment portfolio that will permit them to manage shocks and survive if the educational investment does not pay off.

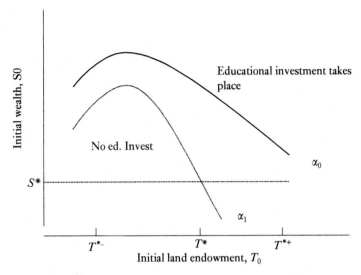

Figure 3.2. *Endowment space and human capital investment under risk and intertemporal borrowing constraints*

Because a household's initial endowments of land and financial wealth impinge on both its self-finance and its self-insurance capacities, a household's decision whether to invest in education will vary systematically over the space of these initial endowments. Assuming decreasing absolute risk aversion, the initial land-money endowment space (T_0, S_0) can be partitioned as shown in Fig. 3.2 into endowment combinations where households optimally choose to invest in education and those where they do not.

The solid line in Fig. 3.2 shows, for an initial level of agricultural productivity (α_0), the locus of initial endowments for which the household would be exactly indifferent whether to invest in education or not to invest in education.[13] Households with endowment positions above that locus will invest in education; those below it will not. As drawn, the indifference locus will initially slope upward because, as household land endowment increases from zero, it creates a competing demand for funds to invest in agriculture, and a greater amount of liquidity is needed before educational investment will occur.[14] At the same time, as land endowment increases, first-period income will increase, creating a larger pool of liquidity to allocate between consumption and the various savings and investment opportunities. In addition, as land endowment increases, second-period income and self-insurance capacity rise. Beyond some critical land endowment level, the indifference locus will begin to slope downward as shown. The dashed line in Fig. 3.2 portrays the shift in the educational investment

---

[13] For Fig. 3.2, other endowments are held at some constant level, and all households are assumed to face an identical risk distribution, technologies, etc.

[14] Note that because of the fixed costs of educational investment, small amounts of educational investment will never be chosen.

indifference locus as agricultural productivity increases from α_0 to α_1. The increase in agricultural productivity will in general decrease the amount of financial wealth needed for a household to engage in education, as shown. The decrease and the shift in the indifference locus are relatively larger for households with larger amounts of land. We are now in a position to discuss the impact of agrarian structure on educational investment in this model.

Landownership inequality ($\tilde{G}_{it}^T$) will thus have several critical effects on the nature of the relationship among growth, human capital accumulation, and income distribution. To keep matters simple, assume that all households have the same initial endowment of education, that they all have an initial money endowment of S^* (shown in Fig. 3.2), and that the per-capita land stock, T^*, is distributed in an egalitarian fashion (i.e. all households would have an initial land endowment of T^*). Under this egalitarian scenario, as exogenous agricultural growth pushes agricultural total factor productivity to α_1, all households would invest in human capital. Inequality in human capital asset distribution ($\tilde{G}_{it}^H$) would remain unchanged, and there would be no change in overall income inequality.

In contrast to this egalitarian scenario, growth will have unequalizing effects when there is inequality in the initial landownership distribution. First, note that landownership inequality means that some households will find themselves with endowments above T^* (say between T^* and T^{*+}), and others below that amount (between T^{*-} and T^*). Following agricultural productivity growth to α_1, wealthier households will accumulate human capital and experience relatively large income growth driven by both their larger, now more productive land holdings and their ability to reap the high returns to human capital. In contrast to the egalitarian scenario, both human capital asset inequality and income inequality increase with growth. Note further that aggregate human capital accumulation is suppressed, suggesting that the returns to the unequally held human capital remain high.[15] Finally, note that non-agricultural growth that boosts returns to human capital may also result in unequal human capital accumulation that deepens inequality and affects human capital decisions. As in the latter case, agrarian structure will condition the income distribution consequences of growth. In summary, we see that in a world of imperfect financial (capital and insurance) markets, the distribution of land may indirectly influence the distribution of income by conditioning the inequality in the distribution of human capital, as well as the amounts and scarcity price of human capital. The reach of agrarian structure can thus extend well beyond the agricultural sector itself.

While there has been little direct empirical examination of this proposition, its implications are entirely consistent with the corpus of work assembled by Birdsall *et al.* (1995) that emphasizes the consistently low and unequal rates of human capital accumulation in Brazil (where agrarian structure is highly unequal) versus East Asian countries like Korea and Taiwan that grew from an egalitarian agrarian structure along a growth-with-equity path marked by extremely high rates of human capital accumulation.

---

[15] Bourguignon (1998) emphasizes the importance of this general equilibrium quantity effect in his analysis of inequality in Taiwan.

3.3. ECONOMETRIC ANALYSIS OF THE IMPACT OF AGRARIAN STRUCTURE ON THE INCOME DISTRIBUTION CONSEQUENCES OF GROWTH

The analysis in the previous section hypothesizes four linkages between landownership inequality and income inequality:

1. *Conventional, but self-dampening level effect*: a given level of landownership inequality will have an effect on the initial level of income inequality. However, this direct level effect is dampened over time as the share of agricultural income in GDP falls.

2. *Persistent but spurious legacy effect*: to the extent that a high level of agrarian inequality spills over and creates an unequal distribution of industrial assets that persists over time, the statistical relationship between income inequality and agrarian structure may continue. While such a persistent effect seems unlikely, it would be a spurious reflection of this past relationship between agrarian structure and initial industrial asset distribution rather than an indication of a direct agrarian structure effect that could be exploited to impact current income inequality.

3. *Exclusionary agrarian growth effect*: there is historical, empirical, and theoretical evidence that landownership distribution can become less equal as growth occurs. Again, while the evidence is still tentative, such exclusionary effects seem most likely to emerge in environments of high initial asset inequality. Less equal landownership distributions are themselves more likely to result in reduced labour absorption and hence a lower reservation wage/living standard floor for the entire economy. Together, these considerations suggest that high levels of initial landownership inequality may translate into agrarian growth that deepens income inequality over what it otherwise would be. While the aggregate inequality effects of a given level of agricultural inequality will diminish over time, this exclusionary growth hypothesis suggests that this dampening effect is offset by increasing agricultural inequality.

4. *Unequal human capital accumulation effect*: at high levels of landownership inequality, both agricultural and non-agricultural growth may result in unequal human capital accumulation that deepens inequality in the distribution of human capital and overall income inequality. As with the second hypothesis, the impact of growth on income distribution is conditioned by agrarian structure. By conditioning the income distribution consequences of non-agricultural growth, agrarian structure may have real and durable effects on aggregate income inequality.

While each of these hypotheses could potentially be explored with direct structural models, the approach here will be to specify a simple, reduced form framework that permits us to identify the conditioning effect of landownership inequality on inequality trends. Because effects 3 and 4 are hypothesized to operate through the growth-generating process, interactions between agrarian structure and rates of agricultural and overall economic growth will be used to try to separate these effects from the level effects. Estimation will be carried out using flexible 'mixed effects' methods that recognize both the panel structure of the data and the possibility that an identical treatment (e.g. economic growth) may have heterogeneous effects at different points in a country's economic history.

3.3.1. *Panel Data on Income and Agrarian Inequality*

Table 3.1 displays descriptive statistics from the available data, which are composed of 210 observations from sixty-four countries. The primary constraint to expanding the data coverage has been the shortage of information on agrarian structure or landownership inequality. Deininger and Olinto (1999) describe in more detail the creation of this landownership inequality information drawn primarily from Food and Agricultural Organization (FAO) sources. The income inequality data have been taken from the Deininger–Squire (1996) dataset, and the growth rates and other data have

Table 3.1. *Descriptive statistics for variables used in analysis*

	Africa	Asia	Latin America	Eastern Europe	OECD and others
Income Gini					
Minimum value	33.0	28.3	39.2	32.0	23.1
Median	42.5	37.7	50.0	40.8	31.9
Maximum value	62.9	62.3	60.0	44.0	56.0
Initial GDP per capita (1965)					
Minimum value	147.6	104.6	365.2	246.6	285.8
Median	235.8	299.8	568.2	329.6	1997.0
Maximum value	390.2	693.0	1854.4	683.6	3156.0
Ag share (%)					
Minimum value	19.1	4.7	2.4	7.0	1.2
Median	31.7	27.7	11.9	15.3	4.3
Maximum value	56.7	59.0	26.0	30.1	41.1
GDP growth					
Minimum value	−0.5	−2.4	−4.6	−3.1	−0.5
Median	2.7	4.9	4.3	4.0	3.0
Maximum value	7.1	10.9	9.5	12.9	11.1
Ag GDP growth					
Minimum value	−1.3	−2.8	−30.9	0.1	−8.9
Median	2.9	3.8	1.7	5.9	0.3
Maximum value	6.1	10.1	8.4	10.1	8.8
Initial land inequality (1965)					
Minimum value	39.7	36.8	60.7	54.9	33.8
Median	49.3	56.0	82.1	64.6	55.2
Maximum value	80.4	76.5	92.3	67.6	85.3
Number of countries	10	14	16	4	20
Total observations	15	55	49	9	82

Source: Derived from data from Deininger and Olinto (1999).

been taken from the Penn World Tables and World Bank sources. While the expanded World Institute for Development Economics Research (WIDER) World Inequality Database offers income inequality measures beyond those found in the Deininger–Squire dataset, its additional information does not make more observations available for the analysis because of the limited amount of landownership information.

As can be seen in Table 3.1, the data display significant variation along all dimensions. Income Ginis range from a low of 23 to a high of 63. The agricultural share of GDP in the sample ranges from 59 per cent down to 1 per cent, while agrarian inequality (measured by the Gini coefficient for the landownership distribution) ranges from 37 to 92. The dataset's biggest weakness is that African and East European economies are poorly represented. Data are available for only ten African countries (with less than two observations per country) and only nine East European countries (two observations per country). In contrast there are observations for some fifteen to twenty countries for each of Latin America, Asia, and the Organization of Economic Cooperation and Development (OECD), with an average of four observations per country.

3.3.2. *Mixed Effects or Random Coefficients Estimation*

The essence of the argument put forward here is that landownership inequality may condition the impact of growth on income inequality. Mixed effects models (see Laird and Ware 1982, and the estimation techniques put forward by Pinheiro and Bates 1995) provide an empirically open and flexible way to approach this issue. Let us begin with the following Kuznets model of the relationship between growth and income inequality:

$$G_{it} = \beta_{0i} + \beta_{1i}\dot{y}_{it} + \varepsilon_{it}, \tag{3.7}$$

where $\dot{y}_{it}$ is the annualized rates of growth for GDP over the 5-years leading up to time t, in country, i. Note that the coefficients are subscripted, indicating that they potentially differ for each country depending on observed and unobserved factors. As a first window on the heterogeneous regression process, we can consider each coefficient to be composed of an average population effect and a random component:

$$G_{it} = [\beta_{00} + \beta_{01}y_{i0} + \beta_{01}y_{i0}^2 + v_{i0}] + [\beta_{10} + \beta_{11}y_{i0} + v_{i1}]\dot{y}_{it} + \varepsilon_{it}, \tag{3.8}$$

where y_{i0} is the log of the country i's initial level of GDP, and the β_{m0} ($m = 0, 1$) are composed of a conditional mean effect (for instance, $\beta_{10} + \beta_{11}y_{i0}$), plus a random, country-specific deviations-from-the-average effect (the v_{im}). Regression (3.7) and (3.8) is a Kuznets relationship in the sense that it permits an inverted-U-shaped relationship, since the intercept is hypothesized to shift with initial GDP, and the impact of growth on inequality can also change with the level of initial GDP. Note that this model is more general than the classic cross-sectional inequality analysis (e.g. Ahluwalia 1976), as it exploits the panel data to estimate the impact of growth on inequality, controlling for the initial level of inequality, which may itself be influenced by initial income levels. We assume that the v_{im} are distributed with mean zero and

M. Carter

covariance matrix Ω. Another way to express this model is as a random coefficients formulation:

$$\beta_{0i} \sim ([\beta_{00} + \beta_{01} y_{i0} + \beta_{01} y_{i0}^2], \nu_{i0}) \tag{3.9a}$$

$$\beta_{1i} \sim ([\beta_{10} + \beta_{11} y_{i0}], \omega_1), \tag{3.9b}$$

where ω_m is the mth diagonal element of Ω. Among other things, the degree of variation in the ν_{im} will give us a measure of the degree of heterogeneity in the regression. The challenge is to see how much of the heterogeneity in this basic Kuznets regression can be explained by agrarian structure and landownership inequality.

Table 3.2. *Mixed effect estimates*

	Kuznets model	Agrarian level effects model	Exclusionary growth model
Level of inequality			
Population average effect	−72	−23	−29
	[62]	[66]	[66]
Std dev of random effect, ν_i	8.6	8.1	8.0
Initial log GDP	41.3**	21	22
	[19]	[21]	[21]
(Initial log GDP)^2	−3.6**	−2.0	2.1
	1.5	[1.6]	[1.6]
Initial land inequality, G_0^T	—	0.17**	0.20**
		[0.08]	[0.08]
Dampening effect, $\phi^A G_0^T$	—	0.002*	0.002**
		[0.001]	[0.001]
GDP growth, $\dot{y}$			
Population average effect	−0.82	−0.01	0.65
	[1.1]	[1.1]	[1.2]
Std dev of random effect, ν_i	0.02	0.013	0.014
Initial GDP (log)	0.18	0.05	0.04
	[0.17]	[0.17]	[0.17]
Initial land inequality, G_0^T	—		−0.01
			[0.01]
Weighted ag output growth, $\phi^A \dot{y}^A$			
Population average effect	—	−0.004	−0.01
	—	[0.005]	[0.02]
Std dev of random effect, ν_i	—	0.008	0.01
Initial land inequality, G_0^T	—		0.0002
			[0.0003]
Likelihood ratio test	—	14.4**	21.2**
(p-value)	—	(0.02)	(0.00003)

Note: Figures in square brackets are estimated standard errors. * and ** indicate statistical significance at the 10% and 5% levels, respectively.

Source: Derived from data from Deininger and Olinto (1999).

The first column of Table 3.2 presents the results of the mixed effects estimation of the Kuznets model. Interestingly, the expected value of the intercept follows a significant Kuznets inverted-U pattern, first increasing and then decreasing with initial income levels. However, consistent with the more recent literature that has seen the Kuznets relationship dissipate in the face of repeated observations on individual countries, the coefficient relating the impact of economic growth to income inequality is not significant. More surprisingly, the standard deviation of the random component of this term is also small. A large value of this term would indicate the presence of heterogeneous, but strong country-specific relationships between growth and income inequality. We now ask whether the pattern of income inequality can be better explained by bringing in variables that capture the hypothesized linkages between agrarian structure and income inequality. We do this in two stages. First, we introduce variables that capture the level effect of agrarian structure on inequality, generalizing (3.8) as follows:

$$G_{it} = [\beta_{00} + \beta_{01}y_{0i} + \beta_{02}y_{0i}^2 + \beta_{31}G_{i0}^T + \beta_4\phi_{it}^A G_i^T + v_{i0}]$$
$$+ [\beta_{10} + \beta_{11}y_{0i} + v_{i1}]\dot{y}_{it} + [\beta_{20} + v_{i2}]\phi_{it}^A \dot{y}_{it}^A + \varepsilon_{it}. \tag{3.10}$$

In addition to introducing the terms representing the potentially self-dampening level effect in the constant term, we also introduce a new variable, the (share-weighted) lagged rate of growth of agricultural output ($\phi^A\dot{y}^A$) as another factor that may independently influence the level of income inequality. This term should pick up any intrinsically unequalizing (or equalizing) effects of agricultural growth. Equation (3.10) will be called the 'agrarian level effects model'.

The second generalization of (3.8) is found by specifying the growth coefficients as functions of the initial level of landownership inequality:

$$G_{it} = [\beta_{00} + \beta_{01}y_{0i} + \beta_{02}y_{0i}^2 + \beta_{31}G_{i0}^T + \beta_4\phi_{it}^A G_i^T + v_{i0}]$$
$$+ [\beta_{10} + \beta_{11}y_{0i} + \beta_{21}G_{i0}^T + v_{i1}]\dot{y}_{it}$$
$$+ [\beta_{20} + \beta_{21}G_{i0}^T + v_{i2}]\phi_{it}^A\dot{y}_{it}^A + \varepsilon_{it}, \tag{3.11}$$

where the level of initial landownership inequality is represented as before. The term $\beta_{12}G_{i0}^T$ captures the human capital inequality effect of landownership inequality that makes general economic growth less equalizing. The term $\beta_{21}G_{i0}^T$ captures the hypothesis that agricultural growth will itself be less equalizing if landownership inequality is high. Equation (3.11) will be called the 'exclusionary growth model'.

Table 3.2 also presents the estimation results for the agrarian level effects and exclusionary growth models. Several interesting results emerge from the level effects model. First, the agrarian structure level effects variables are relatively large and statistically significant. The variables are scaled such that an agrarian economy ($\phi_{it}^A = 50$ per cent) with Latin American levels of agrarian inequality ($G_{i0}^T = 80$) will have its Gini boosted by 21 points compared to a completely egalitarian agrarian economy. As the agricultural economy wanes in importance and ϕ_{it}^A falls to zero, the agrarian inequality effect dampens down to 13.5 points, a still surprisingly strong number. This persistent effect suggests either a spurious relationship induced by a link between agrarian and initial industrial asset inequality, or a relationship between agrarian structure and other factors excluded from (3.10). Somewhat unexpectedly, the presence of the agrarian structure level variables in (3.10) halves the size and eliminates the statistical significance of the initial GDP variables.

A final noteworthy feature of the estimated agrarian level effects model is the coefficient of the weighted lagged agricultural growth term. While the average population level for this coefficient is not significantly different from zero, its point estimate is of a size such that a heavily agricultural economy ($\phi_{it}^A = 50$ per cent) that has sustained rapid agricultural growth for 5 years (5 per cent) would experience a 2-point drop in the income inequality Gini coefficient. While this result is not significant, the standard deviation of the estimated random component of this coefficient is twice the size of the underlying population average effect. The same agricultural country with a coefficient one standard deviation above the average would experience a 6-point drop in its income Gini, while a country one standard deviation above would have a 2-point *rise* in its Gini following 5 years of rapid growth.

The exclusionary growth model lets us see whether any of this variation in the estimated coefficient of the agricultural growth variable and other features of the level effects model are influenced by the inclusion of agrarian structure as a factor that shifts the mean coefficients of the growth variables. Unfortunately, as examination of Table 3.2 shows, none of these new factors are individually statistically significant. The level effects coefficients remain significant, but otherwise it proves impossible to gauge precisely any effect of agrarian structure on the income distribution consequences of agricultural or overall economic growth. The results remain provocative. The likelihood ratio test statistics reported at the bottom of Table 3.2 show that it is impossible to accept the parameter restrictions implied by moving from the exclusionary growth model to the level effects model (the test has a p-value below 0.001), and (less surprisingly) it is impossible to accept the restrictions implied by moving from the level effects model to the Kuznets model (the test has a p-value of 0.02). The implication is that the significant explanatory power has been added by conditioning the growth effects on agrarian inequality. However, given limitations in the data (and perhaps in the modelling techniques), it proves impossible to identify what those effects are.

3.4. POLICY IMPLICATIONS INSIDE AND OUTSIDE AGRICULTURE

While unequal landownership has a role to play in explaining historically high levels of income inequality, this chapter begins by asking whether agrarian structure plays any role in explaining contemporary trends in increasing income inequality. Using a Gini decomposition framework to structure the analysis and drawing on a variety of theoretical, historical, and econometric evidence, this chapter identifies four linkages or pathways between agrarian structure and income inequality:

(1) the conventional level effect
(2) the legacy effect
(3) the exclusionary agrarian growth effect
(4) the unequal human capital accumulation effect.

The first of these effects is shown to be self-dampening, and, unless unequal agrarian structure leaves behind a durable legacy of unequally distributed industrial capital assets (effect 2), the statistical relationship between agrarian structure and income inequality should disappear in the industrializing economy. Using panel data to estimate a mixed effects model of income inequality, this chapter finds significant evidence of both the self-dampening level and legacy effects. However, the policy implications of these findings are modest. The first of these effects supports the notion that a major agrarian asset redistribution in largely agrarian economies could have a major impact on the level of income inequality, reducing the Gini by an estimated 8 points. However, no such impacts would be expected in more industrialized economies. While the econometric estimates indicate a large, persistent legacy effect in these economies, this effect likely represents the crystallization of past agrarian inequality into industrial inequality. Contemporary manipulation of the agricultural economy would do nothing to erase that legacy.

While neither of these first two effects is likely to have anything to do with contemporary trends in income distribution, the second two effects are intrinsically dynamic. They both speak to ways in which agrarian structure conditions the income distribution consequences of both agricultural and non-agricultural growth and thus potentially have a role to play in explaining current income distribution trends. While there is some theoretical and empirical evidence in support of these effects, this chapter's econometric analysis has been unable to identify precisely the dynamic impacts of agrarian structure on trends in income inequality. Likelihood ratio tests do indicate that the variables meant to capture these effects add significantly to the explanatory power of the income inequality model. However, none of the individual effects are statistically significant.

While precise identification of these effects and their quantitative significance will have to depend on future research efforts, the available theoretical evidence offers insights on the policy implications of these effects. From a theoretical perspective, both the exclusionary agrarian growth effect and the unequal human capital accumulation effect are rooted in missing financial markets. Put differently, agrarian structure can condition the income distribution consequences of growth because missing financial markets create a linkage between the assets that a household already has and the new investments that it can undertake. Policymakers interested in modifying the income distribution consequences of agrarian structure thus have two choices:

(1) modify the existing agrarian asset distribution
(2) modify the conditions that make the asset distribution matter.

The first of these policy approaches corresponds to the conventional set of land reform ideas, though the motivation suggested here may be as much to enhance the human capital accumulation of rural households as to influence directly the distribution of agricultural income. Interestingly, the second policy approach may have nothing to do with agriculture at all. If agrarian structure has its deepest effects when landless and near-landless rural households cannot afford to finance educational investment given the costs of education and imperfections in financial markets, then policy that subsidizes education or makes financial markets function for the rural poor could actually break the linkage between agrarian structure and income distribution. If this were done, agrarian asset redistribution would be of minor consequence at least in terms of its conditioning of the effects of non-agricultural growth.

Finally, it is worth noting that in some ways these two policy approaches are less far apart than the preceding discussion makes them seem. Current calls to achieve agrarian asset redistribution through market-based methods (e.g. see Deininger 2001) are likely to work only if the financial market access problems of the rural poor are resolved (see Carter and Barham 1996). While it would be nice to have firmer evidence about the payoffs to such policies, there seems little doubt that a policy priority must be to make markets work better for the less well-off in rural areas so that they can position both themselves and their children to participate in the benefits of future economic growth.

REFERENCES

Ahluwalia, M. (1976). Inequality, poverty and development. *Journal of Development Economics* 3, 307–42.

Atkinson, A. B. (1997). Bringing income distribution in from the cold. *Economic Journal* 107(2), 197–321.

Barrett, C. B. (1996). On price risk and the inverse farm size–productivity relationship. *Journal of Development Economics* 51(2), 193–216.

——and M. R. Carter (1999). Microeconomically coherent agricultural policy reform in Africa. In Joanne Paulson (ed.), *The Role of the State in Key Markets*. Macmillan: Basingstoke.

Binswanger, H., and M. Rosenzweig (1986). Behavioral and material determinants of production relations in agriculture. *Journal of Development Studies*, 22(3), 503–39.

——, G. Feder, and K. Deininger (1996). Power, distortions and reform in agricultural land relations. In J. Behrman and T. N. Srinivasan (eds.), *Handbook of Development Economics III*. North Holland: London.

Birdsall, N., D. Ross, and R. Sabot (1995). Inequality and growth reconsidered: Lessons from East Asia. *World Bank Economic Review* 9(3), 477–508.

Bourguignon, F. (1998). Education and distribution in the process of economic development: The case of Taiwan, 1979–1995. DELTA Working Paper.

Bowles, S. (1985). The production process in competitive economies: Walrasian, neo-Hobbesian and Marxian models. *American Economic Review* 75(1), 16–36.

Carter, M. R. (1988). Equilibrium credit rationing of small farm agriculture. *Journal of Development Economics* 28(1), 83–103.

——(1997). Environment, technology and the social articulation of risk in West African agriculture. *Economic Development and Cultural Change* 45(2), 557–90.

——and B. Barham (1996). Level playing fields and laissez faire: Post-liberal development strategy in inegalitarian agrarian economies. *World Development* 24(7), 1,133–50.

——, ——, and D. Mesbah (1996). Agro-export booms and the rural poor in Chile, Paraguay and Guatemala. *Latin American Research Review* 31(1), 33–65.

——and F. Zimmerman (2000). The dynamic costs and persistence of asset inequality in an agrarian economy. *Journal of Development Economics* 63(2), 265–302.

——,Y. Yao, and K. Deininger (2000). A theory of property rights reform with embedded social safety nets. Mimeo.

Castillo, L., and D. Lehman (1983). Agrarian reform and structural change in Chile, 1965–1979. In A. K. Ghose (ed.), *Agrarian Reform in Contemporary Developing Countries*. St Martin's Press: New York.

Chenery, H., and M. Syrquin (1973). *Patterns of Development, 1950–1970*. Oxford University Press: Oxford.

Chiu, W. H. (1998). Income inequality, human capital accumulation and economic performance. *Economic Journal* 108(1), 44–59.

Collier, W., Soentoro, G. Wiradi, and Makali (1976). Agricultural technology and institutional change in Java. *Food Research Institute Studies* 13, 169–94.

Deininger, K. (2001). Making negotiated land reform work: Initial experience from Brazil, Colombia and South Africa. In A. de Janvry, J.-P. Platteau, and E. Sadoulet (eds.), *Land Access, Rural Poverty and Public Action*. Oxford University Press: Oxford.

—— and L. Squire (1996). A new data set measuring income inequality. *World Bank Economic Review* 10(3), 565–91.

——, and —— (1998). New ways of looking at old issues. *Journal of Development Economics* 57(2), 259–87.

—— and P. Olinto (1999). Is broad asset growth good for growth?: Panel evidence from 62 countries. Mimeo, World Bank, Washington, DC.

de Janvry, A., and E. Sadoulet (1993). Relinking agrarian growth with poverty reduction. In M. Lipton and J. van der Gaag (eds.), *Including the Poor*. World Bank, Washington, DC.

——, and —— (1996). Growth, inequality and poverty in Latin America: A Causal Analysis, 1970–1994. Mimeo, University of California, Berkeley.

Eswaran, M., and A. Kotwal (1986). Access to capital and agrarian production organization. *Economic Journal* 96, 482–98.

Fields, G. (1980). *Poverty, Inequality and Development*. Cambridge University Press: Cambridge.

Jorgenson, D. (1961). The development of a dual economy. *Economic Journal* 71(2), 309–34.

Kelly, A., J. G. Williamson, and R. Cheetham (1973). *Dualistic Economic Development*. University of Chicago Press: Chicago.

Kuznets, S. (1955). Economic growth and income inequality. *American Economic Review* 45(1), 1–28.

Lachmann, R. (1987). *From Manor to Market: Structural Change in England, 1536–1640*. University of Wisconsin Press: Madison, WI.

Laird, N., and J. Ware (1982). Random effects models for longitudinal data. *Biometrics* 38, 963–74.

Lewis, W. A. (1953). Economic development with unlimited supplies of labour. *Manchester School of Economic and Social Studies Working Papers* 22(1), 139–91.

Li, H., L. Squire, and H. Zou (1998). Explaining international and intertemporal variation in income inequality. *Economic Journal* 108, 26–43.

Lipton, M. (1993). Limits of price policy for agriculture: Which way for the World Bank? *Development Policy Review* 5(2), 197–214.

Lodoño, J. L., and M. Székely (1997). Persistent poverty and excess inequality: Latin America, 1970–1995. InterAmerican Development Bank Working Paper 357, IDB, Washington, DC.

Lundberg, M., and L. Squire (1998). New evidence on inequality, poverty and growth. World Bank Working Papers. World Bank: Washington, DC.

Lunqvist, L. (1994). Economic underdevelopment: The case of a missing market for human capital. *Journal of Development Economics* 40(2), 219–39.

Pinheiro, J. C., and D. M. Bates (1995). Mixed effects models methods and classes for *S* and *Splus*. Mimeo, University of Wisconsin, Department of Statistics: Madison, WI.

Ravallion, M., and G. Dattp (1995). Growth and poverty in rural India. Background paper for World Development Report 1995. World Bank, World Development Report Office: Washington, DC.

Scott, J., and B. Kerklievett (1975). How traditional rural patrons loss legitimacy. *Cultures et Développement* Summer, 501–40.

Sheehan, J., and E. Iglesias (1998). Kinds and causes of inequality in Latin America. In N. Birdsall and R. Sabot (eds.), *Inequality-Reducing Growth in Latin America*. Johns Hopkins: Baltimore, MD.

Taylor, L. (1979). *Macromodels for Developing Countries*. McGraw-Hill: New York.

Williams, R. (1985). *Export Agriculture and the Crisis in Central America*. University of North Carolina Press: Chapel Hill, NC.

Zimmerman, F., and M. R. Carter (2003). Asset smoothing, consumption smoothing and the dynamics of inequality under risk and subsistence constraints. *Journal of Development Economics* 71(2), 233–60.

4

Does Educational Achievement Help
Explain Income Inequality?

DANIELE CHECCHI

4.1. THE ISSUE

In the literature on the relationship between income inequality and output growth, several authors claim that greater income inequality reduces growth.[1] The empirical evidence indicates that one standard deviation decrease in income inequality raises the annual growth rate of product per capita by 0.5–0.8 percentage points. However, there is no consensus about the underlying causal mechanism. On one side, a political economy mechanism calls for a role for redistributive policies: greater income inequality generates increased social pressure and social instability, and this creates an adverse environment for investment in physical capital. On the other side, greater income inequality and greater poverty inhibit access to schooling and investment in human capital, thus reducing the potential for growth. Both explanations do not stand up to a deeper scrutiny. The political mechanism hinges on the disincentive effect created by fiscal redistribution, which is not confirmed by the data (Perotti 1996). The liquidity constraint explanation requires that the access to education be prevented by lack of financial resources, which is hardly the case in countries where public education is nearly cost-free at the compulsory level.[2]

On the whole, this literature seems unable to provide conclusive results for the very same reasons that the contribution of Kuznets (1955) never achieved the status of a stylized fact in economics: it is impossible to identify a common pattern of development among countries throughout the world because social structures evolve differently

The author wishes to thank the participants in the workshop on Inequality, Growth, and Poverty under the Washington Consensus (UNU/WIDER, Helsinki, July 1999) for their comments on an earlier version of this chapter. He also thanks Meghnad Desai and David Soskice for very helpful discussions. Additional thanks to the audiences at seminars held at the Wissenschaftszentrum (Berlin), the London School of Economics, the SASE Conference (London, June 2000), the University of Pisa, and the University of Piacenza for their feedback. Luca Flabbi provided excellent research assistance. Finally, the financial support of the Ministry of University (MURST fondi ex-40%) is gratefully acknowledged.

[1] Good surveys of this literature can be found in Benabou (1996a), Bourguignon (1996), Aghion et al. (1999), and Barro (1999).

[2] Some empirical evidence in support of these propositions is offered in Bourguignon (1994), Checchi (1999), and Filmer and Pritchett (1998).

(according to historical heritage, religion, ethnic composition, and cultural traditions).[3] While we largely share the opinion on the impossibility to identify a unique model for a 'social structure of accumulation', we still believe that there is something to be learnt from generalizing single country experiences. In this respect, the causal relationships governing aggregate educational choices have yet to be understood. The theoretical literature makes many simplifying assumptions, the main one of which is that income inequality and educational choices are perfectly correlated and that the resulting earning distribution replicates educational choices. This allows the identification of an intergenerational equilibrium in income and education distributions. Since the two variables are perfectly correlated, the distribution of incomes and the distribution of human capital are shaped by the same factors. In many models, the same barriers (the absence of financial markets for education financing, the cultural poverty of the environment, the inefficiency of tax administration) prevent investment in human capital by part of the population, who subsequently earns less income.[4] Whenever this phenomenon persists across generations (by inheritance or family cultural background effects), the same social groups remain trapped at low levels of education and low levels of income for more than one generation. Thus, within the logic of formal models, illiterate people and the poor are synonymous. But in reality things are far more complicated. Educational choices are also influenced by the public provision of schools, the prohibition of child labour, and the availablity of opportunities in the labour market.[5] Likewise, income distribution is influenced by labour legislation, trade union coverage, and fiscal policies in addition to educational achievements (see Chapters 8 and 9).[6]

However, the distribution of incomes and the distribution of educational attainments are obviously related. On one hand, income inequality may prevent access to education when education is too costly for the family: the more skewed the income distribution, the higher the population share excluded from schooling and the higher the inequality in educational achievements. In this respect, we have a self-perpetuating poverty trap that can only be avoided by easing access to education.[7] On the other hand, improved access to education raises the earning opportunity of the lowest strata and, other things being constant, reduces earnings inequality. As long as total income is proportional to labour income, we can expect a positive correlation between the distribution of educational

---

[3] This is the explanation put forward by Brandolini and Rossi (1998) to account for different relationships between inequality and growth in subgroups of countries.

[4] For example, Galor and Zeira (1993), Banerjee and Newman (1993), and Piketty (1997) consider financial market imperfection, while Benabou (1996a) takes into account the role of social capital, and Perotti (1993) points to the stage of development and the level of available resources.

[5] For example, in rural economies the output gains of child labour are the main obstacle to schooling among children. See the Zambian case described by Skyt Nielsen (1999), the Bangladesh case analysed by Ravallion and Wodon (1999) and the Indian case discussed by Weiner (1991).

[6] See Gottschalk and Smeeding (1997) and Bardone et al. (1998) for the determinants of earnings distribution in Organization for Economic Cooperation and Development (OECD) economies. Globalization and the effect on wage inequality are discussed in Borjas and Ramey (1995), Sachs and Shatz (1996), and Feenstra and Hanson (1996).

[7] Checchi (1999) shows that income inequality effectively reduces school enrolment, mainly at secondary level. Similar results are in Flug et al. (1998). From a formal point of view, this corresponds to the case where *current* income inequality affects the *rate of change* of inequality in educational achievement.

achievements and the distribution of incomes in the population. But the 'other things being constant' assumption is rather crucial here, since we have to take into account the general equilibrium consequences of these changes. Consider, for example, the case of skill-biased technological change. Many authors agree that this is one of the potential reasons for the boost in the college 'premium', at least in the United States. With a time lag, this has produced an increase in college enrolments despite the rise in tuitions. Until the supply of new college graduates depresses the premium, we will observe growing income inequality, accompanied by a reduction in inequality in educational achievement.[8]

Therefore, we cannot predict a priori the sign of the relationship between educational achievements and income inequality. For this reason, in this chapter we intend to investigate the empirical determinants of aggregate income inequality and, more specifically, the relative contribution of education to measured income inequality. In our opinion, this is crucial for two considerations. First, from a theoretical point of view, it is important to understand the plausibility of studying intergenerational equilibria under stationary distributions of income and human capital in the population. Second, and far more important, from a policy point of view we want to understand whether urging countries (or people) to increase their educational achievements is going to exacerbate, moderate, or have little influence on the subsequent earnings distribution.

The chapter is organized as follows. Section 4.2 reviews the literature on income inequality determinants, Section 4.3 provides empirical evidence, and Section 4.4 concludes. Appendix 4.1 indicates data sources and discusses data reliability.

4.2. THE EXISTING LITERATURE

There is a growing literature on the current trends in income inequality at world level.[9] Rising income inequality occurred initially in Anglo–Saxon countries, but now is affecting most industrialized nations.[10] Among the potential causes of this phenomenon, the reduction of the redistributive role of the state, the decline in union presence in the workplace, the increased competition at international level, technological progress, and all possible combinations of these are often indicated. (These explanations are sometimes referred to as 'the transatlantic consensus'.) However, the experiences at national level are very diversified, and it is quite hazardous to draw general conclusions. Apart from the Kuznets (1955) hypothesis on the existence of a non-linear relationship between output per capita and income inequality, we do not find much progress in the statistical explanation of the observed inequality. In particular, little work has been undertaken so far seeking to test alternative explanations of the evidence on income distribution and even less concerning the relationship between educational attainment

---

[8] Freeman (1986) has shown the existence of a similar phenomenon during the 1960s for engineers in the United States and has provided a 'cob-web' model for the dynamics of this phenomenon. For more recent evidence, see Murphy *et al.* (1998).

[9] See Atkinson (1999), Cornia (1999), and the references therein.

[10] Milanovic (1999) has computed an increase of 3 Gini points in world income inequality from 1988 and 1993, mainly attributable to between-country inequality.

and income inequality. This is surprising, given the fact that compulsory education is publicly and freely provided in almost all countries of the world.

The existing literature on the effects of educational attainments on income inequality mainly focuses on the two first moments of income distribution, namely, the average educational attainment and the dispersion of schooling in the population. For the first, Barro (1999) suggests that the relationship between income inequality and output growth is negative for poor countries and positive for rich countries.[11] He runs conditional convergence regressions on the income inequality (from the Deininger and Squire 1996, dataset) measured 5 years earlier in order to exclude the case of reverse causation. Then he moves this regressor to the left-hand side and studies the determinants of income inequality. He puts forward some evidence on the existence of an inverted U-shaped relationship between output per capita and income inequality (with a turning point around US$1636). He controls for educational achievement by introducing average educational attainments at three levels (primary, secondary, and tertiary).[12] But his results are difficult to interpret in this respect, because of the contemporaneous presence of different information on the distribution of educational achievements (namely, the contribution of average human capital and its distribution across population subgroups).

A similar strategy is followed by O'Neil (1995), who decomposes output growth over 1967–85 into a 'quantity' component (as measured by enrolment rates) and a 'price' component (as measured by relative stocks of human capital). His analysis suggests that, while there is convergence among countries in the level of educational achievement, the price effect works in the opposite direction.[13] In the same line of research, Deininger and Squire (1998) show that initial inequality in assets (land) is relevant in predicting both income growth and changes in income inequality.[14] Since land inequality also reduces average years of education in their regressions, they explain this evidence by referring to the liquidity constraints on access to education. As a consequence, income inequality and educational attainments are positively correlated because of the presence of a third conditioning variable (wealth inequality). However, while asset (or income) inequality may reduce the creation of new human capital (the 'flow' represented by new school leavers), we see no good reason to suppose it might depreciate existing human capital (the 'stock' represented by the average educational attainment of the population). In a related paper, Li et al. (1998) interpret the evidence that the effect of (initial-period) average secondary school years on income inequality is significant as a proxy for a political effect: the more political freedom there is, the more

[11] Perotti produced some evidence pointing in the same direction as discussant of Benabou (1996b).

[12] 'The panel also includes the average years of school attainment for people older than 15, classified over three educational levels: primary, secondary, and higher. The results are that primary schooling is negatively and significantly related to inequality, secondary school is negatively (but not significantly) related to inequality, and higher education is positively and significantly related to inequality' (Barro 1999: 26).

[13] 'The results in Table 4.2 also show that, for both developed countries and Europe, the rise in the return to education experienced over the last two decades has caused incomes to diverge substantially, as those countries that are better endowed with skilled labor reap the benefit of the rising premium' (O'Neil 1995: 1295).

[14] 'Low initial inequality is thus doubly beneficial. It is associated with higher aggregate growth, the benefits of which accrue disproportionately to the poor' (Deininger and Squire 1998: 261).

informed society is, the more difficult it will be for the rich to appropriate extra resources. Gradstein and Milanovic (2000) provide additional evidence on the potential existence of links between political inclusion and income equality. However, it is not clear which is the direction of causation: whether extended franchise supports more redistributive policies, or whether less unequal societies strengthen democracy. Finally, Breen and García-Peñalosa (1999) find that greater income inequality is positively associated with higher income volatility, as measured by standard deviation in output growth rates, and they show that this finding is robust even if one controls for previous variables.[15]

All these papers recognize the existence of a distributional aspect in the relationship between income inequality and educational inequality, but they rely mainly on average attainments. In contrast, the issue of education distribution is central in the paper by Lopez *et al.* (1998).[16] They demonstrate that human capital, as measured by average educational attainment, is statistically non-significant in output-growth regressions unless one does not control for the distribution of human capital ('who gets what') or for openness to international trade ('what to do with education'). They explain their evidence (on twelve countries over 1970–94) through reference to the absence of tradability in human capital that makes price equalization impossible and can produce shortages in human capital during physical capital accumulation. Along the same lines is the argument by Higgins and Williamson (1999), who predict the Gini index of income inequality using output per worker (linear and quadratic, in accordance with the hypothesis of Kuznets) and cohort-size effects (large mature working-age cohorts are associated with lower aggregate inequality because of relative excess supply). However, as they explicitly recognize, this approach neglects the endogeneity of educational choices. Let us suppose that a society is undergoing a transitional phase, in which the average educational requirement is rising, such that the younger cohorts are more well educated than the older ones. Other things being constant, the smaller the size of the more educated cohort, the lower the recorded inequality in incomes. It is therefore rather possible that, through reliance on age-composition variables, the authors were actually capturing educational changes.[17]

At any rate, the two measures for educational achievement (average educational attainment and some measure of the dispersion of attainment) are intertwined. Both Ram (1990) and Londoño (1996) claim the existence of an inverted U-shaped relationship between educational achievement and educational inequality, and they locate the turning point at 6.8 average years of education. However, they do not provide a sound theoretical argument to explain this occurrence, nor do they show whether this relationship might hold for alternative measures of dispersion or concentration.

---

[15] They suggest that this could be due to the fact that firms offer an implicit contract to risk-averse workers. When the environment becomes more uncertain, the cost of this implicit insurance rises, and wages are consequently reduced, thus increasing income inequality.

[16] Galor and Tsiddon (1997) offer another theoretical paper focusing on educational inequality as a source of technological progress (and output growth).

[17] It is true that they control for secondary enrolment rates, but, as we have already argued above, this variable measures the flow and not the distribution of the stock of human capital.

What do we learn from this mainly empirical literature? Income inequality is clearly related to the stage of development in accordance with some sort of Kuznets relationship. It may also reflect the skill level of the population, as proxied by average educational attainment. The evidence on the role played by the distribution of schooling is weaker, and it is still unclear how mean attainment and dispersion jointly contribute to shape income distribution. In addition, in all previous work, we find no measure related to labour market institutions (such as the presence of unions, unemployment benefits, or the minimum wage). In the sequel, we will analyse the determinants of income inequality, making use of average educational achievement and dispersion in the population, as well as some measure of the quality/quantity of the resources invested in education.

4.3. EMPIRICAL ANALYSIS

Starting from enrolment rates and making appropriate assumptions about the distribution of educational achievements at some point in time and about mortality rates, Barro and Lee (1996) obtained (using a method similar to the permanent inventory method used to estimate the stock of physical capital) estimates of the average years of education among the population for each level of education. Let us illustrate this with an example. Consider a population in which each age cohort grows at a constant rate n and in which the probability of death is constant across ages and equal to δ. If we define k as the life expectancy in the population[18] and $\text{Pop}_{t,j}$ as the population aged j at time t, the entire population is given by

$$
\begin{aligned}
\text{Pop}_t &= \text{Pop}_{t,k} + \text{Pop}_{t,k-1} + \cdots + \text{Pop}_{t,0} \\
&= \text{Pop}_{t-k,0}(1-\delta)^k + \text{Pop}_{t-k,0}(1-\delta)^{k-1}(1+n) + \cdots + \text{Pop}_{t-k,0}(1+n)^k \\
&= \text{Pop}_{t-k,0}\sum_{i=0}^{k}(1-\delta)^{k-i}(1+n)^i.
\end{aligned}
$$

Suppose that schooling consists of one year and dropout rates are zero (such that enrolment rates coincide with graduation rates). Under this assumption, if we indicate by π_t the percentage of the population born at t that achieves education, we obtain the number of people with education as

$$
\begin{aligned}
\text{Pop}_t^{\text{educated}} &= \pi_{t-k}\text{Pop}_{t,k} + \pi_{t-k+1}\text{Pop}_{t,k-1} + \cdots + \pi_t\text{Pop}_{t,0} \\
&= \text{Pop}_{t-k,0}\sum_{i=0}^{k}\pi_{t-i}(1-\delta)^{k-i}(1+n)^i.
\end{aligned}
$$

---

[18] This can be determined as $k : (1-\delta)^k \approx 0$.

Therefore, under the previous assumptions, the current population share with education is given by

$$HC_t = \frac{\text{Pop}_t^{\text{educated}}}{\text{Pop}_t} = \frac{\pi_{t-k}\text{Pop}_{t,k} + \pi_{t-k+1}\text{Pop}_{t,k-1} + \cdots + \pi_t\text{Pop}_{t,0}}{\text{Pop}_{t,k} + \text{Pop}_{t,k-1} + \cdots + \text{Pop}_{t,0}}$$

$$= \frac{\sum_{i=0}^{k}\pi_{t-k+i}(1-\delta)^{k-i}(1+n)^i}{\sum_{i=0}^{k}(1-\delta)^{k-i}(1+n)^i} = \frac{\sum_{i=0}^{k}\pi_{t-k+i}\left(\frac{1-\delta}{1+n}\right)^{k-i}}{\sum_{i=0}^{k}\left(\frac{1-\delta}{1+n}\right)^{k-i}}$$

$$= \sum_{i=0}^{k}\pi_{t-k+i}\frac{\omega^{k-i}}{\sum_{j=1}^{k}\omega^{k-j}}$$

$$= \sum_{i=0}^{k}\pi_{t-k+i}\,\omega^{k-i}\left[\frac{1-\omega}{1-\omega^{k+1}}\right], \qquad \omega+\left(\frac{1-\delta}{1+n}\right)<1, \tag{4.1}$$

which is a weighed average of past enrolment rates (with declining weights, as in an Almon's polynomial). In the particular case of constant enrolment rates (that is, $\pi_i = \pi, \forall i$), Eq. (4.1) collapses to $HC = \pi$.[19] Repeated applications of Eq. (4.1) yield

$$HC_t = (\omega HC_{t-1} + \pi_t)\left[\frac{1-\omega}{1-\omega^{k+1}}\right] = (\omega HC_{t-1} + \pi_t)\Omega, \quad \Omega < 1. \tag{4.2}$$

If we now indicate the population share with some primary education as HC_{pt} and the enrolment rate for primary education as P_{pt}, both measured at time t, it is easy to understand why the former variable can be thought of as the integral of the latter (using the decline rate $\mu = 1 - \omega$ as a discount factor). In symbols

$$HC_{pt} = \Omega\Big\{[HC_{p0}\cdot(1-\mu)+P_{p1}]\cdot(1-\mu)+P_{p2}\Big\}(1-\mu)+ \cdots$$

$$= \Omega\left[HC_{p0}\cdot(1-\mu)^t + \sum_{i=1}^{t}P_{pi}\cdot(1-\mu)^{t-i}\right], \tag{4.3}$$

where HC_{p0} is the (estimated) population share with primary education at a given year of reference (usually a census year), and μ represents the (constant) decline rate of an age cohort in the population. The use of a continuous time representation yields

$$HC_{pt} = \Omega\left[HC_{p0}\cdot(1-\mu)^t + \int_0^t P_p(s)\cdot exp(-\mu\cdot s)ds\right]. \tag{4.4}$$

[19] With educational cycles lasting more than 1 year and having positive dropout rates, things are more complicated, but the logic of the argument holds unchanged. Indicating by λ_t the age-cohort share enrolling

Should the growth rate of the population or the mortality rate not remain constant over the years, the above derivations do not correspond exactly to the theoretical value implied by Eq. (4.4). By multiplying HC_p by the number of years required to complete primary education, we obtain the average number of years of primary education for the population. When we possess this piece of information for each level of education, we have an approximation of the distribution of the human capital stock in a country. The calculation is only an approximation because in many cases an attained educational level, say, a secondary degree, may actually be acquired after a longer than average period of study (because of repetition); in addition, we could encounter cases of people who have attended school without attaining any certificate (because they drop out). Even if the information on dropout rates is available, we may not know when individuals leave a course of study; therefore, we cannot integrate this information in the computation of the average stock of human capital. Once we have the rough distribution of educational achievement in the population, it is possible for us to calculate several measures of inequality, among which the Gini concentration index of the distribution of attained education is one of the easiest to compute. If only subgroup averages are known, the general definition of the index is modified accordingly:

$$G = \frac{1}{2n^2 \cdot \mu} \sum_{i=1}^{N} \sum_{j=1}^{N} |n_i - n_j| = \frac{1}{2\mu} \sum_{k=1}^{M} \sum_{h=1}^{M} |\bar{n}_k - \bar{n}_h| \cdot HC_k \cdot HC_h, \qquad (4.5)$$

where N is the population size, n_i is the number of years of schooling of individual i, μ is the average years of schooling in the population, M is the number of subgroups, and $\bar{n}_h$ is the (average) educational attainment in subgroup h. In the case of educational attainments, Barro and Lee (1996) provide us with the available information on three educational levels. This allows us to divide the population into four subgroups: higher education (a share HC_h has attained n_h years of education), secondary education (HC_s has with n_s years), primary education (a share HC_p has with n_p years), and a residual group without education ($HC_n = 1 - HC_h - HC_s - HC_p$, for which zero education is assumed).[20] By construction, the average population attainment is given by

$$\mu = \overline{HC} = HC_p \cdot n_p + HC_s \cdot n_s + HC_h \cdot n_h, \qquad (4.6)$$

in a school level lasting n years (say, primary school starting at the age of m and lasting n years) and subject to a (constant) dropout rate y, then the enrolment rate would be

$$\pi_t = \{\lambda_{t-n}(1-\delta)^{m+n}(1+n)^{k-m-n}(1-\gamma)^n$$
$$+\lambda_{t-n+1}(1-\delta)^{m+n-1}(1+n)^{k-m-n+1}(1-\gamma)^{n-1} + \cdots$$
$$+\lambda_t(1-\delta)^m(1+n)^{k-m}\}/\{(1-\delta)^{m+n}(1+n)^{k-m-n}(1-\gamma)^n$$
$$+(1-\delta)^{m+n-1}(1+n)^{k-m-n+1}(1-\gamma)^{n-1} + \cdots$$
$$+(1-\delta)^m(1+n)^{k-m}\}$$

which is a weighted average of the enrolments at the first year, taking into account the decline due to dropouts.

[20] Barro and Lee (1996) make a distinction between 'attained' and 'completed' educational levels. Given the high correlation between the two series, we have preferred to adopt the former variable because there are fewer missing observations for it.

and the Gini index of educational attainments is computed as follows:

$$G_{ed} = \{HC_h \cdot n_h \cdot (HC_s + HC_p + HC_n) + HC_s \cdot n_s \cdot (-HC_h + HC_p + HC_n)$$

$$+ HC_p \cdot n_p \cdot (-HC_h - HC_s + HC_n)\}/\overline{HC}$$

$$= HC_n + \frac{HC_hHC_s(n_h - n_s) + HC_hHC_p(n_h - n_p) + HC_sHC_p(n_s - n_p)}{\overline{HC}}.$$

$$(4.7)$$

Starting from the original Barro and Lee (1996) dataset, we have extended the observations up to 1995. We therefore have information about educational achievements in the population for 149 countries at 5-year intervals over the period 1960–95. Overall, these data cover three-fourths of the 210 countries listed by the World Bank (1998), but account for 86.3 per cent of the world population (in 1990). However, missing values have reduced the potential number of observations from 1192 to 848 cases, corresponding to 117 countries (with an average of 7.2 observations per country). Descriptive statistics on these variables appear in Table 4.1 at world aggregate level, in Table 4.2 with a temporal disaggregation, and in Table 4.3 with temporal and regional disaggregations; additional information on the data sources is contained in Appendix 4.1.

Table 4.1. *Descriptive statistics*

Variable	Variable name	Weight = population			Observations
		Mean	Median	Standard deviation	
Population without education	HC_n	40.4%	43.1%	0.278	883
Population with primary education	HC_p	33.8%	32.3%	0.172	902
Population with secondary education	HC_s	19.8%	17.2%	0.143	916
Population with higher education	HC_h	5.6%	2.5%	0.077	919
Average duration, primary education	n_p	5.35	5.10	1.153	869
Average duration, secondary education	$n_s - n_p$	4.59	4.58	0.824	929
Average duration, higher education	$n_h - n_s$	3.49	3.33	0.791	898
Average years of education	μ	4.66	3.89	2.757	848
Gini: educational attainment inequality	Ginied	49.32	51.74	23.261	848
Gini: income inequality	Gini	38.01	36.85	8.239	546

Source: See Appendix 4.1.

Table 4.2. *Mean values (weight = population) across years*

Variable	1960	1965	1970	1975	1980	1985	1990	1995
Population without education, %	46.3	46.7	44.1	44.6	43.1	38.6	33.5	35.5
Population with primary education, %	38.1	37.1	37.4	34.8	31.2	32.6	33.2	32.3
Population with secondary education, %	12.5	12.7	14.0	16.2	20.4	22.5	25.3	22.9
Population with higher education, %	2.5	2.8	3.5	4.4	5.4	6.3	8.1	9.0
Average duration, primary education	4.9	5.0	5.1	5.0	5.2	5.3	5.4	6.4
Average duration, secondary education	4.5	4.5	4.6	4.6	4.5	4.5	4.6	4.8
Average duration, higher education	3.2	3.8	3.4	3.6	3.5	3.4	3.4	3.7
Average years of education	4.3	3.7	3.9	3.9	4.3	4.8	5.4	5.9
Gini: educational attainment inequality	44.9	53.6	52.4	53.7	52.0	48.3	44.3	47.0
Gini: income inequality	42.0	36.6	37.1	36.5	37.7	37.7	38.4	39.3

Source: See Appendix 4.1.

Table 4.3. *Population weight mean values of selected educational variables by region, 1960–95*

Variable	1960	1965	1970	1975	1980	1985	1990	1995
OECD countries								
Average years of education	6.75	6.98	7.46	7.65	8.59	8.66	9.00	8.81
Gini: educational attainment inequality	20.68	21.41	21.26	22.64	20.75	20.72	20.98	24.21
Gini: income inequality	39.55	37.27	38.01	36.87	35.87	36.20	36.35	37.36
North Africa and the Middle East								
Average years of education	1.03	1.12	1.36	1.57	2.14	2.77	3.48	4.90
Gini: educational attainment inequality	85.95	86.03	83.38	83.21	77.70	71.00	64.82	52.71
Gini: income inequality	49.05	46.87	49.59	49.29	41.37	47.40	38.72	35.30
Sub-Saharan Africa								
Average years of education	1.01	1.65	1.61	1.66	1.96	2.14	2.32	2.74
Gini: educational attainment inequality	82.47	74.39	74.83	72.79	67.08	64.33	63.08	75.35
Gini: income inequality	51.86	50.76	56.22	44.31	42.47	46.24	52.75	44.98

Table 4.3. (*Continued*)

Variable	1960	1965	1970	1975	1980	1985	1990	1995
South Asia								
Average years of education	0.91	1.37	1.74	2.08	2.45	2.81	3.20	4.23
Gini: educational attainment inequality	86.23	79.67	77.99	76.14	76.71	72.78	69.08	61.49
Gini: income inequality	38.90	37.40	36.74	38.37	38.22	38.64	35.52	30.02
East Asia and the Pacific								
Average years of education	3.72	3.96	4.34	4.71	5.35	5.82	6.31	6.43
Gini: educational attainment inequality	50.64	49.02	41.24	39.11	35.33	31.86	31.44	39.27
Gini: income inequality	40.19	37.51	36.41	39.65	39.18	39.88	40.02	38.38
Latin America and the Caribbean								
Average years of education	3.06	2.99	3.37	3.47	3.97	4.13	4.74	6.17
Gini: educational attainment inequality	49.70	50.75	47.68	45.05	44.27	44.23	39.08	43.22
Gini: income inequality	52.22	49.93	53.99	53.77	52.31	54.66	54.63	56.05
Formerly centrally planned economies								
Average years of education	3.92	4.83	5.28	3.61	3.68	4.96	6.09	8.17
Gini: educational attainment inequality	33.37	35.72	32.20	56.04	52.86	44.69	35.15	23.12
Gini: income inequality	—	30.52	27.83	26.72	32.06	30.50	33.37	41.53

Source: See Appendix 4.1.

In the most recent year of observation (1995), we find that one-third of the world population is illiterate; one-third has primary education, and the remaining one-third have secondary schooling or more. During the time span under consideration in this chapter, the average number of years of education rose from 4.3 to 5.8 at the world level, although this rise was accompanied by growing gaps in the same variable computed at regional level. The population share composed of illiterate people or people with primary education exhibited a declining trend, with some reversal at the end of the period, and there was a similar trend in the index of inequality of educational achievement. But the global picture varied by region: while educational inequality declined in North Africa, South Asia, and the formerly planned economies, it decreased during the first three decades, but rose thereafter in other regions (especially in sub-Saharan Africa). Inequality in terms of years of schooling remained almost constant at low levels in the OECD countries, despite the increase in the average educational attainment. It is therefore difficult to trace out a single trend at world level, especially because there seems to be a difference among countries in the rates of change, as well as in the levels of the variables.

Since we are interested in the relationship between educational achievement and income distribution, we now add the dynamics of income inequality to the picture.

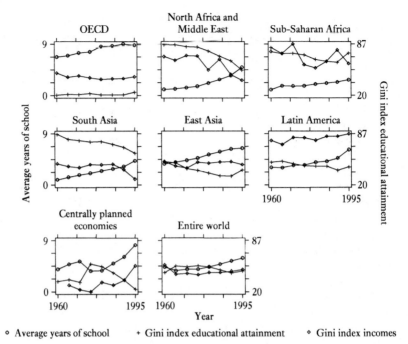

Figure 4.1. *Educational achievements and income inequality by main region 1960–95*

Here, we rely on the dataset of Deininger and Squire (1996) and on the larger 'world income inequality database' (WIID) collected by World Institute for Development Economics Research (WIDER), both of which contain a substantial amount of information on inequality measures collected from secondary sources. Among these measures, the Gini index on income inequality is the most readily available.[21] In the present case, we have information on 546 observations, corresponding to 113 countries (with an average of 4.8 observations per country). If we restrict our selection to the subset in which there is information about both income and education inequality, we have 477 observations for ninety-seven countries (with an average of 4.9 observations per country; Appendix 4.1 contains a list of the countries). Table 4.2 reports the population-weighted average for this measure computed on all available information in the dataset.[22] We notice that, despite a declining trend in educational inequality (reversed only during the 1990s), income inequality at world level started rising after 1975. Figure 4.1 (which graphs the data reported in Table 4.3) seems to indicate that this is mainly attributable to the OECD, the Latin American countries, and the formerly centrally planned economies.

[21] See Appendix 4.1 for a discussion of the changes made in the original (Deininger and Squire and WIID) datasets, including the 1995 update of the observations.

[22] Given that the Gini index is not decomposable by population subgroup, the trend in the population-weighted average has to be viewed with caution. See Milanovic (1999) for a more accurate picture based on population surveys (albeit with observations only over 2 years, 1988 and 1993).

So that we can make more precise statements, let us now consider what we may expect from theoretical models. If we adopt a standard version of the theory of human capital investment, initially proposed by Becker (1964) and subsequently taken up by Mincer (1974) to estimate the returns to education, the (log)incomes and years of education are linearly related. In fact, when a Mincer–Becker theory of earnings applies, individual earnings would be determined as

$$\log(y_i) = \alpha + \beta \cdot n_i + \text{individual characteristics (gender, age, experience, etc.)} + \varepsilon_i, \quad (4.8)$$

where y_i is the earning capacity of individual, i, n_i is the educational attainment of individual, i (measured in years of schooling), β is the (percentage) rate of return to education, α is the earning of an individual without formal education, ε_i is an error term assumed to be identically independently distributed (i.i.d.). If we assume that the *individual characteristics* are idiosyncratic in the population and orthogonal with acquired education, population subgroups differ only in terms of average educational achievement (namely, the within-group variance is constant).[23] We therefore expect there to be a relationship between the distribution of educational achievements and the distribution of actual incomes. However, the things are not so simple. Inserting Eq. (4.8) into Eq. (4.7) and ignoring the (average) individual characteristics, we obtain the Gini index of log-income inequality as

$$G_{\text{log-income}} = \{(HC_h \cdot \beta \cdot n_h \cdot (HC_s + HC_p + HC_n) + HC_s \cdot \beta \cdot n_s$$
$$\times (-HC_h + HC_p + HC_n) + HC_p \cdot \beta \cdot n_p$$
$$\times (-HC_h - HC_s + HC_n)\} / \{\alpha + \beta \cdot \overline{HC}\} \quad (4.9)$$

or more synthetically:

$$G_{\text{log-income}} = \frac{\overline{HC}}{(\alpha/\beta) + \overline{HC}} \cdot G_{ed}(\overline{HC}) = f(\overline{HC}). \quad (4.10)$$

Equation (4.10) suggests that, at a given average in educational achievements, the inequality in education and the inequality in (log)earnings are linearly related. If incomes are proportional to earnings, this also applies to inequality in (log)incomes. However, since the inequality in education is negatively related to average education, the actual relationship is non-linear. The situation is rendered more complicated by the fact that we do not possess individual data allowing the calculation of inequality measures for (log)incomes. Rather, we are forced to rely on aggregate measures based on actual incomes. Once more, the relationship between the inequality measures obtained from the actual values of the variables and the corresponding measures computed based on the logarithms is not easily ascertained. However, it can be formally demonstrated that—under mild assumptions about the distribution of education in

---

[23] Actually, Mincer (1996) shows that between-group variance in earnings distribution in the United States remained nearly constant during 1970–90, whereas the within-group variance expanded after the 1980s.

D. Checchi

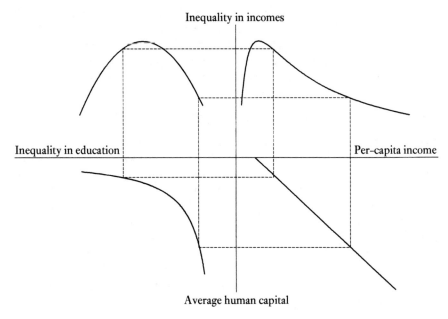

Figure 4.2. *Theoretical relationships between per capita income, income inequality, inequality in education, and average human capital*

the population and the general assumption that the rate of return to education is constant—the relationship between the Gini index of actual incomes and the average years of education initially rises and then declines.[24] When the assumptions hold, income inequality, education inequality, and average educational inequality are strictly related, as shown in Fig. 4.2, where we have also added a fourth variable, the output per capita, in order to control for an exogenous driving force.

Starting from the lower right-hand quadrant, we assume that an increase in per-capita income is associated with an increase in the average educational attainment. By construction, this yields a consequent decline in educational inequality (lower left quadrant). If the relationship between average educational attainment and income inequality is non-linear, this necessarily implies a non-linear relationship between income inequality and education inequality (upper left quadrant). By the same token, we also obtain an inverted U-shaped relationship between income inequality and per capita income, in the Kuznets tradition (upper right quadrant). The graph tells us a story about the transition from an uneducated population to an actual level of schooling. When only the elite attends schools, the average level of human capital development among the population is low, whereas the inequality in educational achievements and in incomes is high. A lowering of the access barriers to education leads to an initial

---

[24] See Checchi (2000).

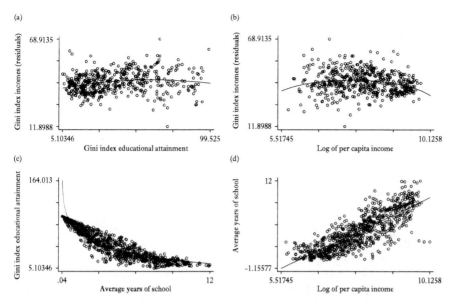

Figure 4.3. *Empirical relationships between pairs of variables influencing educational inequality: (a) inequality in incomes and inequality in education; (b) inequality in incomes and per capita income; (c) inequality in education and average human capital; (d) average human capital and per capita income*

increase and then to a decline in both inequality measures, and this is accompanied by a rise in average educational attainments.

A first inspection of our dataset indicates that this story may have some plausibility. Figure 4.3 gathers together all the available observations, whereby income inequality is measured by regression residuals on regional dummies and year-related dummies in order to compensate for trends in the variables and regional disparities. In addition to a mildly non-linear relationship between inequality in actual incomes and inequality in education (see the upper left quadrant), a similar relationship emerges between the former variable and (the log of) GDP per capita, in line with the Kuznets tradition (upper right quadrant). Without concerning ourselves too much about the direction of the causal relationship, we also find evidence of a strict positive correlation between output per capita and educational achievement (lower right quadrant). Finally, almost by construction, we find an inversely proportional relationship between inequality in education and average educational achievement (lower left quadrant).

However, the dispersion of single observations suggests that many other forces are at work. We should not forget that the validity of the story of Fig. 4.2 is conditional on the assumption that individual incomes are determined according to Becker's theory of human capital investment and that returns to education are constant and are, moreover, identical throughout the population. In reality, we know that earnings distribution is shaped by many other factors, including technology, unemployment rates, minimum wages, age composition, the existence of labour unions, and so on. Were it certain that these factors remained constant during our sample period, we could consider them country specific fixed effects. The problem is that there is no guarantee that they remained constant, especially if we take into account the transformation in public policies induced by the 'transatlantic consensus' (Atkinson 1999).

As a consequence, instead of pretending to predict the shape and the evolution of income distribution worldwide, we follow in the sequel the less ambitious aim of discovering whether the average educational achievement and the distribution of educational attainment have played any role in determining income inequality. We have already mentioned the fact that other authors (Londoño 1996; Deininger and Squire 1998; Barro 1999) have shown that average educational achievement is one of the determinants of actual income inequality. To this result, we now add an examination of the effect on income inequality of the distribution of educational achievement in the population.

In order to take into account the simultaneous effects of all the variables, we resort to multivariate regressions. We take our dataset as an unbalanced panel with a potential dimension of 752 observations (ninety-four countries times 8 observations per country), which we reduce to 454 observations because of missing data on one or the other variable. Table 4.4 shows estimates of actual income inequality using fixed effects. In this table we start with two alternative specifications of the relationship between income inequality and output per capita, without taking into account educational factors (first and second columns). Both specifications reject the hypothesis of

Table 4.4. *Estimates of the determinants of income inequality (94 countries, 454 observations, dependent variable = Gini index) 1960–95*

Intercepts	46.953	47.401	49.283	59.164	57.491	48.163
	(29.91)	(31.75)	(15.76)	(12.17)	(11.67)	(15.26)
GDP	0.000	−0.001			0.000	−0.001
	(−0.77)	(−2.39)			(−1.86)	(−2.64)
GDP^2	−0.000					
	(−0.16)					
1/GDP		−423.050				
		(−0.23)				
Ginied			−0.182	−0.310	−0.279	−0.069
			(−1.45)	(−2.31)	(−2.08)	(−0.53)
$Ginied^2$			0.002	0.002	0.002	0.000
			(1.48)	(1.95)	(2.03)	(0.32)
h_c				−1.470	−1.134	
				(−2.64)	(−1.94)	
$1/h_c$						2.364
						(2.84)
Years	Yes	Yes	Yes	Yes	Yes	Yes
R^2 (within)	0.066	0.066	0.056	0.075	0.084	0.095

Notes: Estimation was carried out with a fixed effect procedure; *t*-statistics in parentheses.

Source: See Appendix 4.1.

a non-linear relationship between income inequality and per capita output. The two measures are negatively correlated, with a rather low elasticity (-0.049 at sample means). This implies that, in order for the Gini index of income inequality to be reduced by 1 point, income per capita has to rise by US\$2311 (at 1985 international prices). If we replace per capita income by educational variables (third and fourth columns), we notice an increase in explanatory power only if we consider average educational achievement. This is not surprising given the high correlation of the latter measure with per capita income. Both average educational achievement and educational inequality are significant, but the relationship between the two measures of inequality is opposed to the theoretical expectation (being U-shaped and not inverted U-shaped). We consider gross-domestic product (GDP) per capita and educational variables together in the fifth column. Here, we find that output per capita has a low negative impact, as does average human capital, though with a higher effect: an average increase of one year of education in the population lowers the Gini index of income inequality by more than 1 point. The sixth column offers an alternative (hyperbolic) specification of the functional relationship relating income inequality and average human capital: given the non-linear relationship existing between the Gini index of educational inequality, the variable $1/h_c$ seems able to capture all the explanatory power contained in the educational distribution variable.

However, the explanatory contribution of the distribution of educational achievement is rather unstable. If we include repeated cross-sectional estimates (as in Table 4.5), we find that the average educational achievement and the Gini index of educational inequality (in level and squared level) are statistically significant in five of eight cases, but now the non-linear relationship is of the inverted U-shaped type (which is in line with human capital investment theory). One potential reason for this instability is that omitted variables might contribute to a reversion in the trend in income inequality.

In Fig. 4.4 we have graphed the coefficients of yearly dummies obtained in the regressions reported in the fifth columns of Tables 4.4 (and Checchi: 2000, table A1). These coefficients (normalized by the coefficient of the initial year) measure a shift in the intercepts of the regressions, thus capturing part of the variance that is left unexplained by the estimated model and that is year specific. For the first half of the sample (until 1975), we witness a growing pressure for the compression of income distribution (on the order of 1 point in the Gini index every 5 years), whereas this effect disappears during the 1980s. In the 1990s the phenomenon works in the opposite direction, favouring widening income disparity.

Regional dummies (used in the estimates of random effects reported in table A1 of Checchi: 2000) indicate that the greatest inequality was registered in Latin America and sub-Saharan Africa, where inequality indexes were 6 percentage points higher than they were in the OECD countries (which represent the reference case).[25]

---

[25] Londoño (1996) compares the theoretical achievement in education associated with the stage of development (as measured by the level of GDP per capita) and estimates that populations in the Latin American countries lack about two average years of education. Mexico and Brazil account for most of this shortage in educational achievement. Similar conclusions are obtained in IDB (1998).

Table 4.5. *Estimates of the determinants of income inequality on yearly cross-sections, 1960–95*

	1960	1965	1970	1975	1980	1985	1990	1995
Countries	40	47	60	53	55	57	65	24
Dependent variable	Gini	Gini	Gini	Gini	Gini	Gini	Gini	Gini
Intercepts	46.943	40.760	32.317	52.368	37.297	37.560	49.381	19.402
	(4.49)	(3.73)	(2.91)	(6.26)	(3.24)	(3.53)	(2.94)	(0.64)
k/y	2.294	3.595	4.943	2.358	3.926	2.507	0.795	−1.497
	(2.28)	(2.56)	(4.94)	(4.22)	(3.48)	(2.30)	(0.83)	(−0.61)
GDP	0.000	0.000	0.001	0.000	−0.001	−0.001	−0.001	−0.001
	(0.05)	(0.28)	(1.22)	(−0.56)	(−1.98)	(−2.08)	(−1.82)	(−1.97)
Ginied	0.118	0.194	0.574	−0.012	0.291	0.294	0.375	1.150
	(0.56)	(0.60)	(1.92)	(−0.05)	(1.08)	(1.15)	(0.94)	(2.34)
Ginied^2	−0.002	−0.002	−0.006	−0.001	−0.004	−0.003	−0.006	−0.013
	(−0.94)	(−0.76)	(−2.26)	(−0.50)	(−1.72)	(−1.39)	(−1.49)	(−2.44)
h_c	−1.457	−1.980	−2.967	−2.493	−1.052	−0.719	−1.532	2.275
	(−0.98)	(−1.47)	(−3.02)	(−3.09)	(−1.20)	(−0.80)	(−1.28)	(0.67)
R^2	0.263	0.23	0.568	0.498	0.538	0.45	0.38	0.446

Note: Robust standard error estimates; t-statistics in parentheses.

Source: See Appendix 4.1.

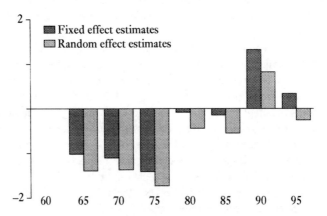

Figure 4.4. *Values of the estimated coefficient of the temporal dummy variables*

Conversely, the distribution was more egalitarian in the currently (or previously) centrally planned economies, where the Gini index was 12 percentage points lower than it was in the OECD, and in South Asia, North Africa, and the Middle East.

Since by definition yearly/regional dummies capture unexplained components, we do not have reliable explanations for these effects that do not refer to per capita income or educational achievement. Nevertheless, we have experimented with two additional variables that may capture some of the differences among countries or years. The first one is the physical capital/output ratio. On theoretical grounds, if physical and human capital are substitutes in the aggregate production function, an increase in the former raises the productivity of the latter. Therefore, *ceteris paribus*, we will obtain higher returns to education whenever physical capital accumulation becomes more intensive. Thus, we can expect greater income inequality whenever and wherever there is intensive investment in physical capital. This variable is introduced in Table 4.5 (and also in table A2 in Checchi: 2000) (which reproduces information in Table 4.4, though the number of observations is reduced because of missing information). This variable is not very significant in the fixed effect estimates, but has a positive and significant sign in the repeated cross-sectional estimates (up to 1985). Other things being constant, countries characterized by higher accumulation in physical capital also exhibit higher income inequality: passing from an average k/y ratio of 2 in South Asia to 3 in the OECD countries raises the Gini index of income inequality by 2 (up to 5) points. However, it is insignificant in more recent years.

The second variable we take into account is the amount of public resources invested in education. If the technology for human capital formation includes invested resources, we can expect increased human capital per unit of time spent in school whenever education expenditure is raised. The resources invested in education should include both public and private expenditure for the management of educational institutions. In the absence of reliable information about private expenditure, we can use the ratio of government educational expenditure to GDP. An undesirable feature of introducing new controls is the increase in the number of missing observations. In the first column of Table 4.6, we have reproduced the fifth column of Table 4.4 to facilitate comparison. Using the same specification, we restrict the number of cases to applicable observations for the capital/output ratio (second column), and then we introduce the capital/output ratio (third column). We observe that an increase in capital accumulation raises income inequality (though with an elasticity which is quite low); all the other variables preserve their signs and significance. We now proceed to consider the ratio of (current + capital) government expenditure on education to GDP (variable edgvsh).[26] The fourth column reduces the sample to country/year observations corresponding to non-missing values for the edgvsh variable, whereas the fifth column introduces the edgvsh variable; the k/y variable is dropped in the sixth column, which makes full use of the available sample. Even in this case, we observe that countries characterized by higher public expenditure on education exhibit higher income inequality. It is obvious that countries with higher educational achievements spend more on education. However, given the fact that we are controlling for average educational achievement (variable h_c) and the distribution of educational achievement (variable $Gini_{ed}$), the additional effect could be taken as evidence that the 'quality' of human capital incorporated in the same number of years of schooling is higher, thus generating more dispersion in earnings. In this specification, however, the capital/output ratio loses significance.

[26] This variable is taken from UNESCO (1998). It is missing for 1960 and 1965, and there is a sample mean of 4.25% (standard deviation: 1.86).

Table 4.6. *Estimates of the determinants of income inequality: Fixed effects using educational expenditure, 1960–95*

Countries	94	76	76	69	69	75
Observations	454	401	401	241	241	256
Dependent variable	Gini	Gini	Gini	Gini	Gini	Gini
Intercepts	57.491	66.599	65.054	65.538	66.066	68.070
	(11.67)	(12.93)	(12.20)	(6.69)	(6.82)	(7.20)
GDP	0.000	−0.001	−0.001	−0.001	−0.001	−0.001
	(−1.86)	(−2.31)	(−2.36)	(−3.25)	(−3.47)	(−2.95)
Ginied	−0.279	−0.529	−0.515	−0.614	−0.718	−0.648
	(−2.08)	(−3.64)	(−3.53)	(−3.07)	(−3.53)	(−3.10)
Ginied^2	0.002	0.005	0.005	0.008	0.009	0.007
	(2.03)	(3.59)	(3.44)	(4.21)	(4.67)	(3.95)
h_c	−1.134	−1.977	−2.059	−1.419	−1.523	−1.921
	(−1.94)	(−3.18)	(−3.29)	(−1.70)	(−1.85)	(−2.43)
k/y			0.791	0.570	0.030	
			(1.12)	(0.60)	(0.03)	
edgvsh					0.979	0.902
					(2.22)	(2.04)
Years	Yes	Yes	Yes	Yes	Yes	Yes
R^2(within)	0.084	0.137	0.141	0.194	0.218	0.169

Note: t-statistics in parentheses.

Source: See Appendix 4.1.

Summing up, we have found that per capita income and average years of education in the population negatively affect income inequality. Some additional explanatory contribution is provided by the distribution of educational attainments in the population, and this variable exhibits a non-linear relationship with income inequality. Higher investment in physical capital (as proxied by capital/output ratio) or in human capital formation (as proxied by the ratio of educational expenditure to gross output) contributes to higher income inequality. These results are robust to alternative specifications, and we therefore go back to our initial specification, which is provided in the fifth column of Table 4.4 and reproduced here for simplicity (yearly dummies not shown):

$$\text{Gini}_{\text{income}} = 57.49 - 0.004 \cdot \text{gdp} - 0.279 \cdot \text{Gini}_{\text{educ}} + 0.002 \cdot \text{Gini}_{\text{educ}}^2 - 1.13 \cdot \overline{HC}.$$
$$\quad \; {\scriptstyle (11.6)} \qquad {\scriptstyle (1.86)} \qquad\qquad {\scriptstyle (2.08)} \qquad\qquad {\scriptstyle (2.03)} \qquad\qquad {\scriptstyle (1.94)}$$

$$(4.11)$$

If we take into account that, on the same sample, fixed effect regression yields (again, yearly dummies are not shown here)

$$\text{Gini}_{\text{educ}} = 71.37 - 6.77 \cdot \overline{HC}, \qquad\qquad (4.12)$$
$$\qquad\quad {\scriptstyle (43.3)} \quad {\scriptstyle (22.84)}$$

and if we replace Eq. (4.12) into Eq. (4.11), we get

$$\text{Gini}_{\text{income}} = 37.72 - 0.004 \cdot \text{gdp} - 1.18 \cdot \overline{HC} + 0.091 \cdot \overline{HC^2}. \qquad (4.13)$$

Equation (4.13) tells us that, for a given level of per capita income, income inequality has a U-shaped relationship with the average years of education in the population, with a turning point around 6.48 years. For all countries below this threshold, the two variables are negatively correlated, while the two become positively correlated above this threshold. Using the regional averages reported in Table 4.3, we can say that additional education promotes inequality in the OECD countries (and very recently also in the formerly planned economies), whereas it is beneficial with respect to inequality in the other regions of the world.

We now examine whether these results help us account more accurately for the temporal evolution of income inequality. In Fig. 4.5 we make use of Eq. (4.11) to predict the potential evolution that we would have observed if the educational achievement (in terms of both average years and distribution) would have remained at the 1975 levels. We notice that income inequality would have been higher in only two regions, North Africa and South Asia, thus suggesting that the increase in educational achievement and the reduction in educational inequality have effectively helped to reduce income inequality in these two regions. For all the other regions we do not record significant differences between a prediction based on observed educational values and a prediction based on 1975 values for the same variables.

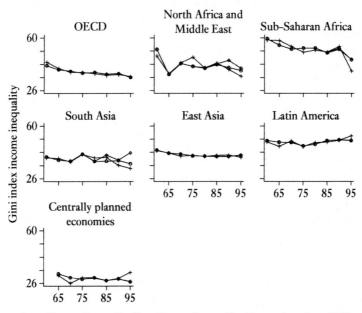

+ Actual inequality   o Predicted inequality   ◇ Pred.ineq.education=1975

Figure 4.5. *Share of total income inequality explained by educational achievements*

The other measure we can provide for the contribution of educational variables in explaining income inequality is obtained by calculating the increase in the explained variance. In Table 4.7 we show the variation in the (multiple) correlation coefficient R^2 that we obtain when we insert the educational variables. Thus, the table compares the models reported in the second and fifth columns of Table 4.4 at regional and yearly levels. At the world level, the table suggests that the contribution of educational achievement in the explanation of the total variance in income inequality ranges between 3 and 16 per cent (the last year looking rather exceptional). Keeping in mind the picture obtained in Fig. 4.4, it seems that the contribution of education is higher during years when income inequality is either declining (1970–5) or increasing (1985–95, especially in the case of the OECD countries). Regional variations have to be viewed with caution because of the limited degrees of freedom; nevertheless, we notice a rising trend in the relative contribution of education to growing income inequality.

A final perspective on the relevance of educational achievement in predicting income inequality can be obtained by manipulating Eq. (4.10), which can be rearranged as

$$\frac{\alpha}{\alpha + \beta \overline{HC}} = 1 - \frac{G_{\log - \text{income}}}{G_{\text{ed}}}. \tag{4.14}$$

Equation (4.14) tells us that 1 minus the ratio between the inequality in (log)incomes and the inequality in education can provide a rough estimate of the ratio between the income of an uneducated person and the income of a person with average education. The problem is that we do not have information on individual earnings (or incomes), and we therefore cannot compute the Gini index of logarithms of these variables, as required in Eq. (4.10). However, using simulations based on the observed distribution of educational achievement in the sample, we have computed the Gini index on both incomes and log-incomes. The two measures are proportionally related, with the

Table 4.7. *Additional variance explained by educational variables: Random effect estimates*

	1960	1965	1970	1975	1980	1985	1990	1995
Whole sample, %	4.2	4.4	16.3	11.0	7.0	3.4	6.3	31.2
Observations	*40*	*47*	*60*	*53*	*55*	*57*	*65*	*24*
OECD, %	12.2	12.4	33.4	5.8	24.7	29.3	34.6	45.4
Observations	*13*	*16*	*19*	*21*	*21*	*18*	*18*	*7*
Sub-Saharan Africa, %			15.4			79.1	28.2	
Observations			*9*			*7*	*10*	
East Asia, %		56.6	8.0	2.5	15.1	15.0	20.3	
Observations		*8*	*8*	*8*	*7*	*8*	*8*	
Latin America, %	23.6	62.0	35.5	54.1	25.2	33.7	18.8	51.1
Observations	*13*	*12*	*17*	*12*	*13*	*15*	*19*	*9*

Note: The figures are calculated as $[R^2_{\text{including educational variables}} - R^2_{\text{excluding educational variables}}]$.

Source: See Appendix 4.1.

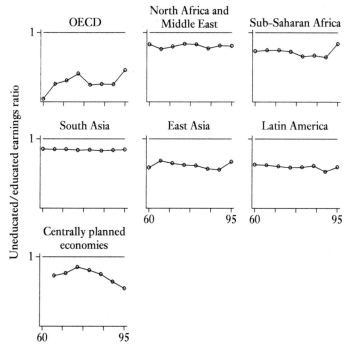

Figure 4.6. *Region/year averages of the population weighed uneducated/educated earnings ratio*

goodness of the fit declining with the rate of return, β, assumed in the simulation. Using this result, we have computed an (estimated) Gini index of log-income that allows us to obtain the measure proposed in Eq. (4.14). This is depicted in Fig. 4.6. From the dynamics of this indicator at regional level, we notice that the educational premium is higher in the OECD countries (mainly because they have a higher average educational achievement), followed by Asia and Latin America. In all cases but one, this premium has been declining in recent years. In contrast, the return to education seems to be rising in the formerly planned economies.

4.4 CONCLUSIONS

Our plan in this chapter has been to measure the inequality in educational achievement by constructing a Gini index of educational attainment. We have then used the proposed measure to analyse the relationship between inequality in incomes and inequality in educational achievement (in terms of both the average attainments and the concentration of educational achievement). Though theoretical considerations based on the theory of human capital investment suggest that we should expect a non-linear relationship between these two measures of inequality, we have seen that the actual data indicate that average years of education have a stronger negative impact

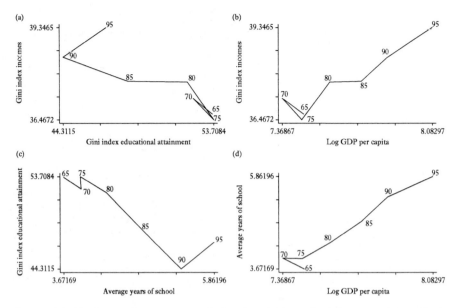

Figure 4.7. *World inequality in incomes and education: (a) inequality in incomes and inequality in education; (b) inequality in incomes and per capita income; (c) inequality in education and average human capital; (d) average human capital and per capita income (means − weights = population)*

on measured income inequality. Multivariate regressions also demonstrate that, if we take into account the negative correlation between average educational achievement and the dispersion of educational achievement, the relationship between income inequality and average years of schooling is U-shaped, with a lower turning point at 6.5 years. Obviously, income inequality is also negatively related to per capita income; other things being constant, countries characterized by higher accumulation or greater government expenditure on education experience higher-income inequality. In relative terms, we find that education contributes a portion of the variance enclosed between 3 and 16 per cent in explaining income inequality, though the fraction is higher and shows a rising trend in developed countries.

Figure 4.7 replicates Fig. 4.3 with the addition of the weighted mean values for each time unit of observation.[27] Looking at the lower left panel, we see that the world has experienced what can be called an 'educational cycle' during the post-war period. By investing public resources in education and lowering access barriers to education, various governments were able to increase the average schooling by 2.2 years and to reduce the Gini index of educational inequality by about 9 percentage points (mainly during 1965–90). This effort was eased by a (median) growth in gross domestic product per capita of 60.9 per cent over this period (lower right panel).

---

[27] Notice that we have suppressed the initial observation (1960) to facilitate the reading of the graph. (The values are, however, reported in Table 4.2.)

Despite these changes, mean income inequality has risen rather steadily at world level, showing an increase of 2.7 points in the Gini index of income inequality (upper right panel). However, while income inequality and educational inequality seem to have been loosely related during the initial subperiod (indicatively until 1980), in more recent years further expansion in schooling among the world population has been accompanied by a widening in the dispersion in income distribution. The observations referring to 1995 reflect a possible further change in the process: while average educational achievement continues to rise (with an additional jump of a half year), inequality in educational achievement, instead of declining, rises by almost 3 points. Both variations are accompanied by a further increase in income inequality of 1 point. The causes of this change are not immediately clear, but we can get an intuition by going to regional level, as in Fig. 4.8, which reports the relationship between income inequality and educational inequality.

In this case we notice that at least three separate patterns can be identified in the 'educational cycle' at world level. North Africa and South Asia exhibit the first pattern. Most of the countries in these regions started from a quite low initial base of educational attainment (around 1 year of average schooling in North Africa and South Asia in the 1960s), but were quite effective in improving the situation, more than quadrupling this average. These are not the only regions in which we find that education has the effect of reducing inequality (see Fig. 4.5).

A second pattern is represented by East Asia and sub-Saharan Africa, which initially followed the first pattern, though at a slower speed (the average years of schooling increased from 3.7 to 6.4 and from 1.0 to 2.7, respectively, during 1960–95). The 'leap forward' in educational attainment in these countries seems to have been insufficient to modify basic social structures (in contrast to the successful countries in the first group). Inequality in education initially declined, but after the 1970s there was a trend reversal, and this was accompanied by an increase in income inequality.

Finally, the third group is formed by the Latin American countries and the (formerly or currently) centrally planned economies. Both sets of countries were characterized by high initial levels of education (3.1 and 3.9 years on average, respectively, in 1960); nonetheless, they were able to raise the average significantly (to 6.2 and 8.2 years, respectively, by 1995). Educational inequality declined, but income inequality rose substantially, as indicated by the Gini index: 6 additional points in Latin America and more than 10 points in the planned economies.

The OECD countries represent a story on their own. The only group with average educational attainments above the threshold of 6.5 years, these countries experienced a widening in educational differentials during the entire sample period that was accompanied, after 1975, by rising income inequality.

A general lesson emerges from this evidence: increased access to education reduces income inequality only if two conditions are met. First, the initial level of educational attainment must be sufficiently low; second, the average educational attainment must be raised sufficiently rapidly. A potential explanation of these results is offered by the interaction between the supply and the demand of human capital,

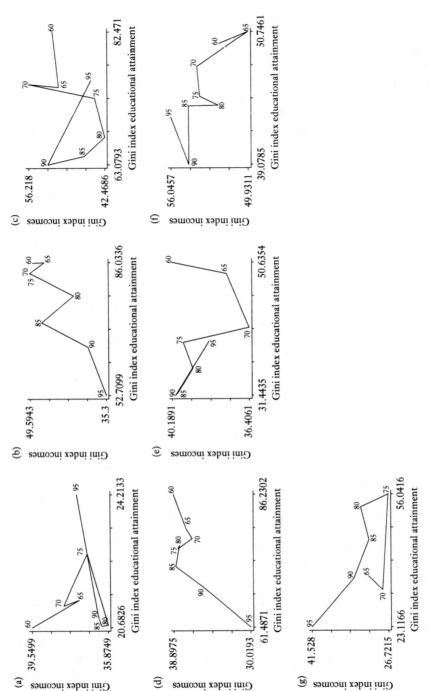

Figure 4.8. *Dynamics of inequality in incomes and education in selected regions: (a) OECD countries; (b) North Africa and Middle East; (c) sub-Saharan Africa; (d) South Asian countries; (e) East Asia and the Pacific; (f) Latin America and the Caribbean; (g) former centrally planned economies (means – weights = population.)*

that is, the educational choices of the population and job creation by firms.[28] When the average educational level in the population is low, there are very few highly educated people who are likely to obtain high salaries. At the same time, there are no incentives for the creation of new jobs for skilled workers since firms are constrained by factor demand. However, when more and more educated people begin entering the labour market, the speed of technological innovation increases, followed by the creation of more skilled jobs. More people earn higher wages, and as a consequence income inequality starts declining. When the bulk of the labour force has at least a primary level of education, leaps in technology (such as in information technology and telecommunications) are possible because the more sophisticated tasks can now be accomplished by skilled workers. The rise in the productivity of these workers is reflected in their remuneration, thus inducing a trend reversal in income inequality. In this way, we replicate the non-linear relationship between average educational attainment and income inequality, which is also conditioned by the level of technical development.

APPENDIX 4.1: DATA SOURCES

We have taken seriously the recommendation of Atkinson and Brandolini (1999). Data on income inequality are from Deininger and Squire (1996)[29] and WIID, downloadable at www.wider.unu.edu/wiid.[30] Overall, we have 546 observations on 113 countries (with an average of 4.8 observations per country).[31] While there are no significant differences in Gini indexes when the recipient unit is the (equivalized) household or the individual, we find an average difference of 6.47 percentage points when the same measure is based on gross incomes instead of net incomes. We could have introduced a dummy variable controlling for the income definition (as in Deininger and Squire 1998), but in this case we would have dispensed with all observations in which this information was absent. For this reason, we have preferred to augment the measures based on the net incomes by the average difference.[32]

Data on physical capital stocks are from Nehru and Dhareshwar (1993). Data on per capita income and educational achievements are from Barro and Lee (1993, 1994, 1996, 1997).[33] In particular, the data on the estimated length of schooling,

---

[28] On the relationship between the availability of skills and job creation, see Agemoglu (1995, 1996).

[29] Downloaded on 22 October 1998. Among these, 349 observations are labelled 'high quality' (average = 38.79), and 153 observations are labelled 'low quality' (average = 45.87).

[30] In addition, twelve observations (average = 35.05) on OECD countries are from Brandolini (1998), and twenty-five (average = 43.54) are from World Bank (1998). Finally, seven observations (average = 37.65) are from Honkkila (1998).

[31] The number of observations is reduced to 471 (corresponding to ninety-seven countries, with an average of 4.9 observations per country) if we restrict the cases to those with non-missing data on educational variables.

[32] A similar correction has been applied to Gini measures based on rural samples (five observations) that were on average higher than the national coverage samples by 8.94 points.

[33] Barro and Lee (1994) is in turn based on Summers and Heston (1991).

$n_p i = p,s,h$, have been obtained by dividing the average years of schooling for a given level of education by the population share which has completed this level of education using the definitions of Barro and Lee (1996):[34]

$$n_p = \frac{\text{pyr25}}{\text{pri25} + \text{sec25} + \text{high25}}, \quad n_s = \frac{\text{syr25}}{\text{sec25} + \text{high25}}, \quad n_h = \frac{\text{hyr25}}{\text{high25}}.$$

Where possible, the series have been updated to 1995 using World Bank (1998) and UNESCO (1998). Data on average years of schooling for 1995 have been estimated based on the corresponding enrolment rates for the previous three decades.

The list of ninety-seven countries for which we have non-missing observations on inequality in incomes and inequality in educational achievements is as follows (the number of available observations is given in brackets):

Sub-Saharan Africa

Botswana (3), Cameroon (1), Central African Republic (1), Gambia (1), Ghana (3), Guinea-Bissau (1), Kenya (7), Lesotho (1), Liberia (1), Malawi (4), Mauritius (3), Niger (1), Rwanda (1), Senegal (3), Sierra Leone (3), South Africa (6), Sudan (2), Tanzania (6), Uganda (3), Zambia (4), Zimbabwe (2).

North Africa and Middle East

Algeria (2), Egypt (3), Tunisia (7), Iran (3), Israel (5), Jordan (3), North Yemen (1), Cyprus (1).

East Asia and the Pacific

Hong Kong (7), Indonesia (7), Japan (7), Korea (7), Malaysia (7), Philippines (7), Singapore (6), Taiwan (7), Thailand (7), Fiji (3).

South Asia

Bangladesh (7), India (7), Nepal (3), Pakistan (7), Sri Lanka (7).

Latin America and the Caribbean

Barbados (4), Reunion (1), Costa Rica (8), Dominica (4), El Salvador (6), Guatemala (4), Honduras (4), Jamaica (7), Mexico (8), Nicaragua (1), Panama (6), Trinidad and Tobago (5), Argentina (6), Bolivia (3), Brazil (7), Chile (7), Colombia (8), Ecuador (4), Guyana (2), Paraguay (3), Peru (6), Uruguay (7), Venezuela (7).

OECD

Australia (8), Austria (4), Belgium (6), Canada (8), Denmark (6), Finland (8), France (8), (West) Germany (8), Greece (6), Ireland (5), Italy (6), Netherlands (7), New Zealand (7), Norway (7), Portugal (3), Spain (6), Sweden (7), Switzerland (2), Turkey (6), United Kingdom (8), United States (8).

Centrally Planned Economies (formerly)

China (4), Cuba (3), Czechoslovakia (7), Hungary (7), Yugoslavia (6), Bulgaria (7), Romania (1), (former) Soviet Union (5).

---

[34] This procedure yields unreasonable values for n_p for a few observations. In these cases, these values have been replaced with the corresponding values computed based on either the population over 15 years of age or the legal duration of primary education (as measured in 1965: variable *durp* in the original Barro–Lee dataset).

REFERENCES

Agemoglu, D. (1995). Reward structures and the allocation of talent. *European Economic Review* 1, 17–34.

—— (1996). Changes in unemployment and wage inequality: An alternative theory and some evidence. CEPR Working Papers 1459.

Aghion, P., E. Caroli, and C. Gracia-Peñalosa (1999). Inequality and economic growth: The perspective of new growth theories. *Journal of Economic Literature* 37(4), 1615–60.

Atkinson, A. B. (1999). Is rising inequality inevitable?: A critique of the transatlantic consensus. WIDER Annual Lectures 3. UNU/WIDER: Helsinki.

—— and A. Brandolini (1999). Promise and pitfalls in the use of secondary data-set: A case study of OECD income inequality. Mimeo.

Banerjee, A., and A. Newman (1993). Occupational choice and the process of development. *Journal of Political Economy* 101(2), 274–98.

Bardone, L., M. Gittleman, and M. Keese (1998). Causes and consequences of earnings inequality in OECD countries. *Lavoro e Relazioni Industriali* 2, 13–60.

Barro, R. (1999). Inequality, growth and investment. NBER Working Papers 7038.

—— and J. W. Lee (1993). International comparisons of educational attainment. *Journal of Monetary Economics* 32(3), 363–94.

—— and —— (1994). Data set for a panel of 138 countries. World Bank, Washington DC.

—— and —— (1996). International measures of schooling years and schooling quality. *American Economic Review Papers and Proceedings* 86(2), 218–23.

—— and —— (1997). Schooling quality in a cross-section of countries. NBER Working Papers 6198.

Becker, G. (1964). *Human Capital: A Theoretical and Empirical Analysis with Special Reference to Education*. University of Chicago Press, Chicago.

Benabou, R. (1996a). Inequality and growth. In B. Bernanke and J. Rotemberg (eds), *NBER Macroeconomic Annual 1996*. MIT Press: Cambridge MA.

—— (1996b). Equity and efficiency in human capital investment: The local connection. *Review of Economic Studies* 63, 237–64.

Borjas, G., and V. Ramey (1995). Foreign competition, market power and wage inequality. *Quarterly Journal of Economics*, 1075–110.

Bourguignon, F. (1994). Growth, distribution and human resources. In G. Ranis (ed.), *En Route to Modern Growth*. Johns Hopkins University Press: Baltimore.

—— (1996). Equity and economic growth: Permanent questions and changing answers? *Delta Documents de Travail* 96(15).

Brandolini, A. (1998). A bird's-eye view of long-run changes in income inequality. Mimeo.

—— and N. Rossi (1998). Income distribution and growth in industrial countries. In V. Tanzi and K. Chu (eds.), *Income Distribution and High Quality Growth*. MIT Press: Cambridge, MA.

Breen, R., and C. García-Peñalosa (1999). Income inequality and macroeconomic volatility: An empirical investigation. Mimeo

Checchi, D. (1999). Inequality in incomes and access to education: A cross-country analysis (1960–90). WIDER Working Papers 158. UNU/WIDER: Helsinki.

—— (2000). Does educational achievement help to explain income inequality? WIDER Working Papers 208. UNU/WIDER: Helsinki.

Cornia, G. A. (1999). Liberalization, globalization and income distribution. WIDER Working Papers 157. UNU/WIDER: Helsinki.

Deininger, K., and L. Squire (1996). A new data set measuring income inequality. *World Bank Economic Review* 10(3), 565–91.

Deininger, K., and L. Squire (1998). New ways of looking at old issues: Inequality and growth. *Journal of Development Economics* 57, 259–87.

Feenstra, R., and G. Hanson (1996). Globalization, outsourcing and wage inequality. *American Economic Review* 86(2), 240–51.

Filmer, D., and L. Pritchett (1998). The effect of household wealth on educational attainment: Demographic and health survey evidence. World Bank Policy Research Working Papers, 1980.

Flug, K., A. Spilimbergo, and E. Wachtenheim (1998). Investment in education: Do economic volatility and credit constraints matter? *Journal of Development Economics* 55, 465–81.

Freeman, R. (1986). Demand for education. In O. Ashenfelter and R. Layard (eds.), *Handbook of Labour Economics*. North Holland: New York.

Galor, O., and D. Tsiddon (1997). The distribution of human capital and economic growth. *Journal of Economic Growth* 2, 93–124.

——and J. Zeira. (1993). Income distribution and macroeconomics. *Review of Economic Studies* 60, 35–52.

Gottschalk, P., and T. Smeeding (1997). Cross-national comparisons of earnings and income inequality. *Journal of Economic Literature* 35, 633–87.

Gradstein, M., and B. Milanovic (2000). Does liberté = égalité?: A survey of the empirical evidence on the links between political democracy and income inequality. Mimeo.

Higgins, M., and J. Williamson (1999). Explaining inequality the world round: Cohortsize, Kuznets curve, and openness. Mimeo, June.

Honkkila, J. (1998). Investment in education and its effect on income. Mimeo, UNU/WIDER: Helsinki.

IDB (Inter-American Development Bank) (1998). *Facing Up to Inequality in Latin America: 1998–99 Report*. Johns Hopkins University Press: Baltimore.

Justman, M., and M. Gradstein (1999). The democratization of political elites and the decline in inequality in modern economic growth. In E. Brezia and P. Temin (eds.), *Elites, Minorities and Economic Growth*. Elsevier: Amsterdam.

Kuznets, S. (1955). Economic growth and income inequality. *American Economic Review* 45, 1–28.

Li, H., L. Squire, and H. Zou (1998). Explaining international and intertemporal variations in income inequality. *Economic Journal* 108, 26–43.

Londoño, J. L. (1996). *Inequality and Poverty in Latin America during the Last Four Decades*. World Bank: Washington, DC.

Lopez, R., V. Thomas, and Y. Wang (1998). Addressing the education puzzle: The distribution of education and economic reform. World Bank Policy Research Working Papers 2031.

Milanovic, B. (1999). True world income distribution, 1988 and 1993. World Bank Policy Research Working Papers 2244.

Mincer, J. (1974). *Schooling, Experience and Earnings*. NBER: New York.

——(1996). Changes in wage inequality, 1970–1990. NBER Working Papers 5823.

Murphy, K., C. Riddel, and P. Romer (1998). Wages, skills and technology in the United States and Canada. Mimeo.

Nehru, V., and A. Dhareshwar (1993). A new database on physical capital stock: Sources, methodology and results. *Rivista de Analisis Economico* 8(1), 37–59.

O'Neil, D. (1995). Education and income growth: Implications for cross-country inequality. *Journal of Political Economy* 103(6), 1289–99.

Perotti, R. (1993). Political equilibrium, income distribution and growth. *Review of Economic Studies* 60, 755–76.

——(1996). Growth, income distribution and democracy: What the data say. *Journal of Economic Growth* 1(2), 149–87.

Piketty, T. (1997). The dynamics of the wealth distribution and the interest rate with credit rationing. *Review of Economic Studies* 64(2), 173–89.

Ram, R. (1990). Educational expansion and schooling inequality: International evidence and some implications. *Review of Economics and Statistics* 266–73.

Ravallion, M., and Q. Wodon (1999). Does child labor displace schooling?: Evidence on behavioral responses to an enrolment subsidy. World Bank Policy Research Working Papers 2116.

Sachs, D., and H. Shatz (1996). US trade with developing countries and wage inequality. *American Economic Review* 86(2), 234–9.

Skyt Nielsen, H. (1999). Child labor and school attendance: Two joint decisions. Mimeo.

Summers, R., and A. Heston (1991). The penn world table (mark 5): An expanded set of international comparisons 1950–1988. *Quarterly Journal of Economics* 56(2), 327–68.

UNESCO (1998). *Statistical Yearbook*. Oxford University Press: New York.

Weiner, M. (1991). *The Child and the State in India*. Oxford University Press: New Delhi.

World Bank (1998). *World Bank Data on CD-ROM*. World Bank: Washington, DC.

5

Rural and Urban Income Inequality and Poverty: Does Convergence between Sectors Offset Divergence within Them?

ROBERT EASTWOOD AND MICHAEL LIPTON

5.1. INTRODUCTION AND SUMMARY

5.1.1. *The OTI Hypothesis, Adjustment, and Urban Bias*

This chapter explores recent trends in developing and transitional economies in rural–urban, rural, and urban inequality of income and poverty risk, and the offsetting trends in inequality hypothesis (OTI). OTI claims that underlying the overall inequality trend has been a tendency for rising *intra*sectoral inequality to be offset by falling rural–urban inequality.

After 1980, developing countries experienced much more 'adjustment', in particular price liberalization, than previously. Price liberalization reduces price distortions against tradables. Such distortions, in developing countries, are usually, often substantially, harmful to agriculture (Krueger *et al.* 1995). Hence correcting these distortions should have reduced urban–rural inequality. Opposing factors, some associated with liberalization or adjustment, include:

1. Urban people, being better educated, can exploit economic opportunities following price liberalization.
2. Demographic trends—faster urban fertility transition, plus the selective town-ward movement of young people, educated people, and in Asia and Africa males (Eastwood and Lipton 1999)—may have improved the relative earning power of urban people.
3. Urban and formal activity, most regulated to begin with, had most to gain from deregulation.
4. The successes of poverty reduction in 1970–87 left behind a hard core of low-income, immobile, often regionally and ethnically specific rural groups,

We gratefully acknowledge helpful comments from Tony Addison, Giovanni Andrea Cornia, and participants at the World Institute for Development Economics Research (WIDER) seminar in Helsinki in July 1999, and research assistance from Lidia Cabral and Milasoa Cherel-Robson.

which, as in China, have proved weak in reaping 'spread effects' from national growth.

5. There may be persistent urban bias: allocative outcomes, and political dispositions, in developing countries such that rural shares in many sorts of endowment (investment, health, education, public spending) fall well below both efficiency and equity optima (Lipton 1977). Such political dispositions—being normally unaffected by adjustment in prices or foreign trade regimes—would offset any pro-rural effects by pro-urban changes in other policies, such as location of public investments and schools.[1]

6. Rural–urban inequality might be pushed up by the continuing global downtrend in relative farm prices.

The limited data, reviewed below, refute OTI with the possible, partial exception of Latin America. First, the data show no *overall* tendency for within-country rural–urban inequality to increase or decrease since the 1980s. Second, while modest national and regional tendencies exist, they do not, on the whole, offset trends in overall inequality. Urban–rural ratios of both mean consumption and poverty risk have commonly risen alongside total inequality (often sharply, with rapid but unbalanced change: growth in China, decline in Russia), or fallen alongside total inequality, either as in Zambia when economic decline rendered artificial protection for urban incomes unsustainable, or as in Indonesia alongside labour-intensive growth. And some countries, such as India, have seen rural–urban ratios and total inequality both almost trendless.

Changing urban–rural ratios of poverty or per-person consumption need not imply changing urban bias. They may be caused by exogenous changes in relative returns to urban activities, plus entry or exit barriers. However, rural–urban inequality trends in 'human development' indicators (literacy, longevity, etc.) *do* suggest rising urban bias (Eastwood and Lipton 2000).

5.1.2. *Trends in Average Rural and Urban Outcomes: Why Worry?*

First, rural–urban differences in mean consumption or poverty are not merely reflections of differences in other characteristics such as literacy. Even given these, rural people still tend to be poorer (de Haan and Lipton 1999). Moreover, rural residence may itself reduce educational levels, for example, because school provision is worse.

Second, the absence of any general downward trend in rural–urban ratios of welfare indicators in developing and transitional countries contradicts long-run expectations. These ratios are generally far above unity, yet are close to or below unity in Organization for Economic Cooperation and Development (OECD): one expects increasing information, education, capital and labour mobility, and political representation to induce falls in arbitrary and persistent rural disadvantage. However, this need not be stimulated by the adjustment processes that have underpinned

[1] For evidence, see Eastwood and Lipton (2000).

income-distribution change since the late 1970s. These processes did reduce some anti-rural price distortions, but may have increased other anti-rural distortions, especially given a roughly constant urban policy bias. Moreover, market-friendly adjustment has usually been accompanied by all-round cuts in public expenditure during initial stabilization, and sometimes by a further push towards smaller government later; but, to enable rural–urban disparities to fall, new market opportunities may need to be accompanied by measures that help rural people to exploit them, not by all-round cuts.

Third, our finding of non-convergent rural and urban welfare does not merely reflect productivity trends. Indeed, at first sight, it contradicts the tendency in 1970–85 towards a fall in nonfarm/farm nominal[2] ratios of labour productivity. These were around 1.5 in now-developed countries during early modern growth (usually in the nineteenth century), but about 3 in the early 1970s in Asia and Latin America, and in Africa around 6. The possible inefficiency of ratios so far above unity—since they appear to exist also at the margin, and to be mirrored by nonfarm–farm ratios of average and marginal gross domestic product (GDP) per unit of capital well *below* unity—led to the urban bias hypothesis (Lipton 1977). However, nonfarm–farm ratios of average GDP per worker in 1970–85 fell, often dramatically, in most developing countries (Bourguignon and Morrison 1998), despite the falling world trend (around 0.4–0.5 per cent per year) of farm relative to nonfarm prices. The absence of correspondingly dramatic national—or *any* 'third world-wide'—convergence of rural and urban welfare indicators is therefore surprising, especially given the rising proportion of rural income derived from nonfarm activity (which still typically generates higher income per worker than farming, even if less so than in 1985 than in 1970).

Fourth, trends in rural–urban disparities matter, even if rapid growth temporarily ensures that everybody's economic welfare is increasing. First, an uptrend is often *itself* inefficient. For example, after rural–urban inequality in primary-school provision per person has risen past a certain point, an extra rural place is at once cheaper, more educationally productive, and more contributory to gross national product (GNP) than an extra urban place. Second, an uptrend is often a sign of inefficiency. If the unskilled urban wage keeps rising relative to the rural, why is this trend not reversed as labour moves from village to town, and capital (and employers) from town to village? Third, high or rising rural–urban inequality may damage subsequent economic growth. The balance of evidence strongly supports a negative impact from overall inequality (Bénabou 1996; Kanbur and Lustig 1999), but this is controversial, perhaps because different types of inequality have opposite effects on growth. Inequality of earnings that rewards effort, or provision of growth-constraining skills in income-elastic supply, is likely to be, at least up to a point, pro-growth. Inequality of ascribed income, or income due to ascribed wealth—income or wealth accruing because of, say, inheritance, priestly status, or positioning to seize monopoly rent or

---

[2] The gross domestic product (GDP) shares below are measured at current prices. This is appropriate in seeking 'the productivity counterpart of welfare change': it is nominal, not constant-price, trends in a sector's GDP share that correspond to time-trends in incomes received by factors in that sector.

to undertake political lobbying—rewards its beneficiaries, not as achievers, but with a tax on the incentives payable to achievers; hence it is anti-growth. Rural–urban or other spatial inequality is likely to be ascribed rather than attained. Rural–urban (and farm–nonfarm) inequalities are generally far less in OECD than in developing or transitional countries; one would expect the reduction of such inequalities to be a concomitant of development, and they may well also accelerate it.

5.2. RURAL–URBAN AND INTRASECTORAL CONTRIBUTIONS TO CHANGES IN THE OVERALL INEQUALITY OF CONSUMPTION OR INCOME

5.2.1. *Overview*

Data limitations compel a piecemeal approach. Many countries, especially in Africa, have few useful data. For many others, we have Gini coefficients, national, rural, and urban, at more than one date, but no information on sectoral mean income (or consumption, per household, per equivalent adult, or per capita—this qualifier should be understood in much of what follows). Data on the urban share of population are usually available. Our hypotheses are that (a) in the 1980s and 1990s rural–urban mean income or consumption inequality has fallen (partly in response to adjustment policies) and intrasector inequality has risen (OTI); and (b) this represents a change from the 1960s and 1970s, in which these inequalities generally changed little.

Data limitations mean that our conclusions on OTI are tentative. Nevertheless, the two regions for which our data are best—Latin America and Asia—offer an intriguing contrast. OTI has some success in Latin America in the three countries with evidence extending into the 1990s. It fits the largest country, Brazil, over 1980–95, thanks to a sharp narrowing of rural–urban inequality during 1990–5, and Honduras over 1989–93. In Chile too, the rural–urban gap narrows while rural inequality rises, but here urban inequality falls. Conversely, OTI does badly in Asia: while intrasectoral inequality tends to rise in the 1980s and 1990s, there is no offsetting fall in rural–urban inequality. Indeed, in contrast to Latin America, the rural–urban gap rises in the four Asian countries with evidence for the 1990s (Table 5.3), and in three of them, including China, the rise is rapid.

How can we judge the OTI hypothesis in a particular case? We ideally want trend data from 1960 to the present on rural–urban relative mean income together with urban and rural inequality indices. To go beyond qualitative statements so as to identify the quantitative impact of inter- and intrasectoral inequality change on over-all inequality requires more data and raises conceptual difficulties set out below. To anticipate, even if inequality can be decomposed into inter- and intrasectoral compo-nents (not the case with the most commonly available index, the Gini), its *change* has a component due to changes in the sectoral proportions of the population, so that pop-ulation share data are needed as well. Even if the minimum data needed to judge the OTI hypothesis are not available, trends in relative sectoral mean income or sectoral inequality trends are helpful and are reported. The decompositions to be discussed are all atheoretical, so causal interpretation is perilous. For instance, to say in respect of the dynamic decomposition of the change in the Theil-L that X per cent of the change is *caused* by a change in rural–urban inequality, Y per cent by a change in intrasectoral inequality, and $(100 - X - Y)$ per cent by demographic change would be accurate only if these changes were themselves exogenous and independent. Independence is a strong assumption. Not only does it neglect feedback from (for instance) urban–rural inequality to rural–urban migration, but it requires of rural–urban migration that the migrant group (a) leave rural inequality unaffected on departure, (b) leave urban inequality unaffected on arrival, and (c) leave relative urban mean income unaffected. We know that the education and earning-power of the typical rural–urban migrant is above that of the typical villager but below that of the typical townsperson, so that typical migration tends to lower mean urban *and* rural income, with ambivalent effects both on their ratio and on sectoral inequalities. So (a)–(c) above might conceivably not be too inaccurate in some cases. Nevertheless, a large demographic component in an inequality disaggregation requires extreme caution in interpretation.

5.2.2. *Rural–Urban Inequality Decompositions—Analytics*

Can we decompose inequality changes into components arising from changes in intersectoral (rural–urban) inequality and in intrasectoral (urban and rural) inequality? The commonest measures of inequality are the Gini, Theil-L, and Theil-T. These give different weight to inequality at different parts of the distribution, the Theil-L being most sensitive to low-end inequality changes (e.g. Ferreira and Litchfield 1999). The measures also differ in their decomposability into population subgroup components. The worst is the Gini: while inter- and intrasectoral components can be identified, they are not independent. Worse, there is a residual component reflecting the overlap between incomes in different subgroups (Lambert and Aronson 1993).[3]

The Theil-L and -T indices are the sums of deviations of log individual incomes from log mean income divided by population, unweighted and weighted by individual income relative to the mean respectively. Both are decomposable without leaving a residual, so, with v and u representing sectoral income and population shares,

$$T = T_{\text{BETWEEN}} + T_{\text{WITHIN}} = T_{\text{BETWEEN}} + (v_U T_U + v_R T_R) \tag{5.1}$$

$$L = L_{\text{BETWEEN}} + L_{\text{WITHIN}} = L_{\text{BETWEEN}} + (n_U L_U + n_R L_R). \tag{5.2}$$

---

[3] Specifically: $G = (n_R.n_U.(m_U - m_R)/m) + (n_U.v_U.G_U + n_R.v_R.G_R) + R$, which we could write as $G = G_{\text{BETWEEN}} + G_{\text{WITHIN}} + R$, where n_U, n_R are population shares, v_U, v_R shares in national income, m_U, m_R sectoral mean incomes (we assume $m_U > m_R$), and G_U and G_R are the sectoral Ginis. G_{BETWEEN} is what the overall Gini would be if sectoral incomes were equally distributed, G_{WITHIN} is intrasectoral inequality, and R is the 'overlapping' residual. The interdependence of the inter- and intrasectoral components arises because of the presence of the income share terms in the expression for G_{WITHIN}. So, even with no overlapping ($R = 0$), G_{WITHIN} is *not* what G would be if intersectoral inequality were eliminated, since equalizing sectoral mean incomes would change the weights on G_U and G_R.

The 'between' terms have a natural interpretation in each case: they are what overall inequality would be if *intra*sectoral inequality were eliminated by redistribution. An attractive feature of the Theil-L is that a similar interpretation holds also for the 'within' term: it is what overall inequality would be if income were transferred from the urban sector to the rural sector, scaling down urban incomes and scaling up rural incomes, so that sectoral mean incomes were equalized.[4] The independence of the between and within components in the case of the Theil-L means that we can clearly separate the 'rural–urban' from the 'intrasectoral' part of changes, as well as of levels, in total inequality. The change in L between two dates can, to first order, be written (m_U, m_R are sectoral mean incomes; m is national mean income)

$$\Delta L = [n_U \Delta L_U + n_R \Delta L_R] + [(v_U - n_U)\, \Delta \ln(m_U/m_R)] + [(L_U - L_R) + (m_U/m - \ln(m_U/m)) + (m_R/m - \ln(m_R/m))]\Delta n_U. \quad (5.3)$$

The first and second square-bracketed terms are the contributions of intra- and inter-sectoral inequality changes, respectively; the third reflects demographic change. The first component of this change, $(L_U - L_R)\,\Delta n_U$, indicates how much overall inequality is increased by the rising population share Δn_U (due to migration, say) in the normally more unequal urban sector. The remaining terms represent a sort of Kuznets component, since they underlie the standard explanation of the Kuznets 'inverted-U' hypothesis of the relation between development and inequality (Robinson 1976; Anand and Kanbur 1993); since in the absence of intrasectoral inequality 100 per cent urbanization or ruralization implies zero inequality, population movement towards the numerically smaller sector must (at least initially) be inequality-increasing, unless sectoral mean incomes are equal.[5]

How useful are static decompositions alone? Take the case of the Theil-L. The difficulty is that if, say, the between component has risen and the within component has fallen in Eq. (5.2), one does not know from this alone what has happened to the underlying intra- and intersectoral inequalities. It might be all demography, since changed population proportions will alter both the between and within components even if the two sectoral Theils and relative mean sectoral income are unchanged. However, if one is only interested in qualitative effects, one can look at what has happened to the three underlying inequalities—but then, of course, the static decompositions as such have not helped. The informational requirements of static decompositions at two dates are the same as those for the dynamic decomposition between those dates, so there is little reason not to compute the dynamic decomposition; we add this where only static decompositions have been reported.[6]

---

[4] Using income shares as weights in the 'within' term for the Theil-T makes this term dependent on the 'between' term, as for the Gini. So the Theil-T is termed *weakly* decomposable, and the Theil-L *strongly* decomposable (Mukherjee and Shorrocks 1982).

[5] The Kuznets component captures this effect; other things being equal, urbanization will first raise L and then eventually lower it—if $(m_U - m_R)$ is small (namely, if $\ln(1 + (m_i - m)/m)$ is approximated by $(m_i - m)/m$ for $i = U, R$); crossover can be shown to occur when urban and rural populations are equal.

[6] Similar points apply to the Gini, with further complications due to the residual term in (5.1), and the presence of income shares in the coefficients in the expression for G_{WITHIN}. For example, a change in

5.2.3. Rural–Urban Inequality Decompositions: Evidence

Tables 5.1–5.3 show, respectively, dynamic decompositions of the Theil-L for countries for which this is possible; inter- and intrasectoral inequality data otherwise; and summary findings.[7]

Eastern Europe and the FSU

Lundberg and Squire (1999) (henceforth LS) show a roughly constant median expenditure Gini from the 1960s to the 1980s and a rise from 0.248 to 0.301 in the 1990s. Recent additions to the Deininger–Squire (1996) data set suggest very large rises in some former Soviet Union (FSU) countries, as do Cornia and Addison with Kiiski (Chapter 2, this volume). We have found no estimates of how much of these rises is due to changes in rural–urban inequality,[8] although Milanovic (1998: 57) reports that from 1987/8 to 1993/4 farmers relative to workers became worse off in nine out of ten countries with data. The exception was Romania, the only case for which we have evidence on urban–rural inequality and sectoral Ginis (Table 5.2). Indeed, for 1989–93 intersectoral inequality fell, but rises in both sectoral Ginis together with rural–urban migration meant that the aggregate Gini rose.

Latin America and the Caribbean

Londoño and Szekely (1997) pool data for the region, to describe the evolution of inequality during 1970–95. They distinguish:

(1) stability and growth with falling inequality in the 1970s—the regional income-per-head Gini fell from 0.58 in 1970 to 0.54 in 1982;
(2) stagnation and rising inequality in the 1980s, the Gini rising back to 0.58 by 1990;
(3) growth without changing inequality over 1990–5.[9]

On the OTI hypothesis, we have good evidence for Brazil and Chile, accounting for 34 and 3 per cent of regional population respectively, fair evidence for Honduras in

---

G_{WITHIN} might be *entirely* due to a change in urban–rural inequality (with sectoral Ginis and population shares not changing). So static decompositions of the Gini are hard to interpret and even harder to compare. Again, it makes sense to pay most attention to the underlying inequalities; to insist on accounting for change in the aggregate Gini involves artificial (and usually insoluble) difficulties, not present with the Theil-L. Unfortunately, researchers have historically calculated (from unavailable primary data) Ginis rather than Theils, creating 'lock-in' for current attempts to look at long-term trends.

[7] Full sources for the data in the tables are to be found in the appendix to Eastwood and Lipton (2000), available from the authors or at the WIDER website (www.wider.unu.edu).

[8] Analysts have tended to place little emphasis on the urban–rural divide. Milanovic (1998) stresses (a) rising wage inequality associated with a shift of workers from the state sector to the high-inequality private sector, and (b) the effect of a shift away from wage income to self-employment and property income, each unequally distributed.

[9] Expenditure-per-person Ginis for this region seem to be lower by about 0.10 than income-per-person Ginis (see Lundberg and Squire, 1999: table 1).

Table 5.1. *Urban–rural dynamic disaggregations of the Theil-L*

Country	L(0)	L(1)	% within	LU(0)	LU(1)	LR(0)	LR(1)	rel M(0)	rel M(1)	NU(0)	NU(1)	ΔL	%ΔL	% Within	Between	Demog
China 1988–95	0.258	0.378	61.8	0.22	0.23	0.16	0.15	2.05	2.47	0.26	0.32	0.120	46.51	38.6	7.7	0.20
Indonesia 1987–93	0.228	0.239	77.7					2.00	2.06			0.011	4.82	−1.36	1.84	4.50
Thailand 1988–92	0.365	0.478	82.7					2.90	3.62			0.113	30.96	11.55	19.22	0.2
Philippines 1965–71	0.190	0.200	83.0	0.21	0.16	0.14	0.16	2.52	2.07	0.30	0.30	0.010	5.26	3.50	1.76	0.00
Philippines 1971–85	0.200	0.150	80.0	0.16	0.15	0.16	0.11	2.07	2.11	0.30	0.38	−0.050	−25.00	−24.50	−3.33	2.78
Philippines 1985–91	0.150	0.170	83.0	0.15	0.17	0.11	0.11	2.11	2.17	0.38	0.50	0.020	13.33	12.28	2.04	−1.02
Chile 1987–94	0.527	0.485	95.0	0.53	0.47	0.35	0.40	2.06	1.91	0.80	0.83	−0.042	−7.98	−6.60	−1.20	−0.10
Brazil 1981–90	0.614	0.705	83.0	0.54	0.62	0.44	0.53	3.00	3.23	0.71	0.74	0.091	14.82	14.20	1.70	−1.00
Brazil 1990–5	0.705	0.66	88.6	0.62	0.6	0.53	0.53	3.23	2.88	0.74	0.78	−0.045	−6.40	−2.21	−2.75	−1.43
Brazil 1981–95	0.614	0.66	83.0	0.54	0.6	0.44	0.53	3.00	2.88	0.71	0.78	0.046	7.49	10.37	−1.06	−1.83
Ghana 1988–92	0.209	0.187	93.3	0.185/ 0.202	0.214/ 0.189	0.194	0.179	1.74/ 1.14	1.27/ 1.09	0.082/ 0.263	0.071/ 0.281	−0.022	−10.53	−5.20	−7.45	2.13

Note: '0', '1' refer to beginning and end of period; L, LU, LR = total urban, rural Theil-L; relM = relative urban income or expenditure; NU = urban population share. For Ghana Theils and urban population shares are Accra/other cities, relative means are 'Accra to rural/other cities to rural'. Elaboration: The first block of three data columns shows overall inequality at the beginning and end of the period, together with the percentage of intrasectoral inequality at the beginning; the next block of eight columns shows beginning and end values of intrasectoral, intraurban, intrarural, and urban–rural inequalities and urban population shares; the final block of five columns shows the change in overall inequality, absolute and as a percentage of initial inequality, and the breakdown of the percentage change into contributions from intersectoral, intrasectoral, and demographic components.

Source: Eastwood and Lipton (2000).

Table 5.2. *Inter- and intrasectoral income/expenditure inequality*

Country		T	TU	TR	MU/MR	NU	Gini	Gini(U)	Gini(R)
FSU/EE									
Romania	1989				1.083	46.2	0.210	0.192	0.226
	1993				1.018	54.4	0.225	0.211	0.241
Latin America									
Colombia	1978				×		0.545	0.516	0.526
	1988				1.26×		0.512	0.485	0.469
Costa Rica	1971								0.370
	1974							0.452	
	1982							0.415	0.398
	1984							0.484	0.406
Honduras[c]	1989						0.540	0.450	0.480
	1990				3.67/2.09				
	1993				2.37/1.71		0.540	0.530	0.510
Mexico[a]	1984	0.394	0.284	0.282					
	1989	0.506	0.354	0.290					
	1992	0.502	0.349	0.280					
Peru	1986						0.428	0.320[b]	
	1991						0.390	0.370[b]	
	1991							0.353	0.371
	1994						0.449	0.350	0.367
Uruguay	1981							0.436	
	1984								0.397
	1987								0.391
	1989							0.424	
South Asia/China									
India	1963/4				1.77			0.365	0.290
	1973/4				1.29			0.315	0.283
	1983				1.42			0.334	0.301
	1989/90				1.38			0.356	0.282
	1997				1.31			0.361	0.301
Bangladesh	1984				1.33	0.117	0.255	0.295	0.243
	1989				1.49	0.135	0.279	0.318	0.260
	1996				1.80	0.165	0.310	0.360	0.264
China	1978				2.37		0.317	0.160	0.212
	1983				1.70		0.284	0.150	0.246
	1988				2.05		0.382	0.230	0.301
	1991				2.18		n.a.	0.240	0.307
	1995				2.47		0.430	0.280	0.340
Pakistan	1979				1.61		0.370	0.400	0.320
	1985/6				1.55		0.360	0.350	0.330
	1990/1				1.26		0.410	0.390	0.410
Sri Lanka[a]	1970	0.184	0.2295	0.1661	1.45				
	1981	0.168	0.2163	0.1503	1.38				
	1985/6				1.47	0.208	0.320	0.357	0.299
	1990/1				1.33	0.209	0.297	0.354	0.276

Country		T	TU	TR	MU/MR	NU	Gini	Gini(U)	Gini(R)
East Asia									
Indonesia	1984				1.71		0.324	0.334	0.293
	1990				1.65		0.331	0.347	0.264
Korea	1966						0.340	0.400	0.200
	1969						0.340	0.380	0.190
	1972						0.330	0.380	0.220
	1975						0.380	0.460	0.210
	1978						0.380	0.430	0.210
	1981						0.360	0.410	0.180
	1984						0.380	0.430	0.150
	1987						0.380	0.420	0.120
	1990						0.400	0.440	
	1993						0.390	0.410	
Thailand	1962						0.410	0.360	0.360
	1969	0.322	0.338	0.253	2.73	0.109	0.420	0.440	0.390
	1975	0.298	0.272	0.258	2.27	0.132	0.420	0.410	0.400
	1981	0.335	0.308	0.290	2.09	0.133	0.440	0.430	0.420
	1986						0.470	0.460	0.450
Malaysia	1957						0.450	0.440	0.410
	1970				2.14		0.510	0.480	0.450
	1973						0.510	0.490	0.450
	1976						0.520	0.490	0.470
	1979						0.500	0.480	0.470
	1984						0.480	0.440	0.420
	1987						0.460	0.430	0.420
	1990				1.71		0.450		
	1995						0.460		
Philippines	1957				2.45		0.480	0.440	0.380
	1961				2.47		0.500	0.520	0.400
	1965				2.52	0.30	0.510	0.510	0.420
	1971				2.08	0.30	0.490	0.450	0.460
	1975				1.75				
	1985				2.11	0.38	0.450	0.440	0.380
	1988							0.420	0.380
	1991				2.17	0.50	0.480	0.470	0.390
Middle East/ North Africa									
Jordan	1986/7						0.361	0.362	0.319
	1992						0.432	0.435	0.384
Morocco	1984/5						0.391	0.405	0.317
	1990/1						0.392	0.382	0.312
Sub-Saharan Africa									
Cote d'Ivoire	1985				1.81				
	1988				1.64				
Lesotho	1986/7						0.570	0.570	0.550
	1993						0.570	0.580	0.550
Madagascar	1962							0.500	0.290
	1980							0.487	0.435

Table 5.2. (*Continued*)

Country		T	TU	TR	MU/MR	NU	Gini	Gini(U)	Gini(R)
Malawi	1968/9							0.620	0.203
	1984/5							0.621	0.453
Tanzania	1991						0.570	0.460	0.600
	1993				?/1.67		0.410	0.420	0.350
	1995				3.04/1.90		>0.410	?	0.520
Uganda	1989						0.368	0.371	0.364
	1992						0.383	0.439	0.353

Notes: As Table 5.1. T = Theil(L) except Mexico and Sri Lanka where T=Theil(T).
[a] '×' is unknown. From the World Bank PA we can deduce only that relative urban mean income per capita *grew* by 26% in the decade 1978–88.
[b] Lima only.
[c] The pairs of numbers given in the MU/MR column refer to relative mean incomes (or expenditures) of, respectively, capital city to rural, and urban to rural.

Source: Eastwood and Lipton (2000).

the 1990s, and otherwise only a few urban and rural Ginis from Deininger and Squire, and some Theils from Panuco–Laguette and Szekely (1996).[10]

To summarize, our evidence on Brazil and Chile suggests similar patterns in the two countries, with probable OTI for the 1980s and 1990s *as a whole*; also, the Brazilian evidence suggests that the break at the end of the 1980s identified by Londoño and Szekely was also associated with changes in the behaviour of the sectoral components of inequality. Between 1990 and 1995 there were (a) a sharp enough fall in rural–urban inequality to outweigh its rise in the 1980s, and (b) an end to rising intrasectoral inequality, with urban inequality starting to fall. These trends are perhaps associated with reduced inflation after 1992. Honduras fits OTI in the 1990s, rising urban and rural inequality being offset by a narrowing rural–urban gap. Nevertheless, Table 5.2 shows no uniform trends in either urban or rural inequality after 1980.

Brazil 1981–95.[11]   Between 1981 and 1990 high Brazilian inequality (of gross income per head) rose further: the Gini from 0.571 to 0.607 (Londoño and Szekely 1997), the Theil–L from 0.614 to 0.705. Rising intrasectoral inequality accounts for 96 per cent of the rise in the Theil–L; 11.5 per cent comes from rising intersectoral inequality (the

[10] Summary of Gini data in Deininger and Squire. Argentina: GU rises from 1972 through 1989; Colombia: GU declines in 1970s, rises a little in 1980s; GR data not consistent; Costa Rica: GU falls from 1974 to 1982 and rises sharply during 1982–4; GR rises slowly during 1971–84; Paraguay: GU falls during 1983–90; Peru: GU rises during 1986–91, falls during 1991–4; GR falls a little during 1991–4; Uruguay: GU (capital) shows slow decline in 1980s; GR no trend in 1980s. These numbers tell us only that there is no clear pattern in the rural and urban Ginis. The urban Ginis roughly follow the regional Gini in Colombia, Costa Rica, and Peru, but not in Argentina, Paraguay, or Uruguay. Since we have no data on urban–rural inequality, no static decompositions of the total Ginis are possible. The Theils for Mexico suggest a pattern similar to that of Peru.

[11] Ferreira and Litchfield (1999); Litchfield (personal communication); Table 5.1.

Table 5.3. *Inter- and intrasectoral inequality: Summary*

Country	R-70s	R-80s	R-90s	U-70s	U-80s	U-90s	UR-70s	UR-80s	UR-90s	OTI?
FSU/EE										
Romania			+			++			−1	Yes
Latin America										
Brazil	+++	0			++	−		+2	−7	Yes
Chile	+	+			−	−		−	2	Partial
Colombia	−				−			+2		No
Honduras			++			+6+			−43/−13	Yes
Mexico	0				++					?
Peru			0		+++					?
South Asia/China										
India	0	0	0	0	0	0	0	0	−1	Slight
Bangladesh	+	0			+	++		+3	+4	No
China		++	++		++	++		−3	+6	78–83, Yes
										78–95, No
Pakistan		++			0			−2		Yes
Sri Lanka	0	−		0	0		−1	−1		No
East Asia										
Indonesia	−	0		0	0			−1	+1	?
Korea	−	− − −		0	+	− − −				
Thailand	+	++		0	++		−6	+	18	No
Malaysia	0	− −		0	− −		−2	−2		No
Philippines	−	0		0	+		+1	+1		No
Middle East/North Africa										
Jordan		+++			+++					?
Morocco		0			−					?
Sub-Saharan Africa										
Cote d'Ivoire								−3		?
Ghana		−			++/−			−12/−1		No
Lesotho			0			0				?
Madagascar	++			0						?
Malawi	++	+		0	0					?
Tanzania			0			−?			+6?	No
Uganda			− −			+7+			+?	No

Notes: Gini changes: One '+' for 0.003/yr to 0.006/yr, two '+' for 0.006 to 0.009, etc; same for minuses. 0 is between −0.003 and +0.003; for very sharp changes, we use +N+ to stand for N plusses. UR gives per annum changes in m_U as percent of m_R '/' shows numbers for capital and other urban respectively. Within-cell alignment indicates period within decade. Indications marked '?' for Tanzania and Uganda are very tentative.

Source: Eastwood and Lipton (2000).

ratio of urban income to rural income rose from 3.00 to 3.23 in the period) and minus 7 per cent comes from demographic change (comprising plus 4 per cent associated with migration towards the more unequal urban sector and minus 10 per cent with the Kuznets effect—in this case, migration is towards the smaller sector; urbanization in Brazil was already 71 per cent in 1981).

Between 1990 and 1995 inequality fell (the Theil from 0.705 to 0.660). Both the intra- and intersectoral components contributed. However, this was not a simple redressal of the 1981–90 changes. Changing intrasectoral inequality contributed proportionally far less than in 1981–90 (rural inequality did not fall at all), while rural–urban inequality fell sharply (relative mean income fell from 3.23 to 2.88). Demographic change continued to lower inequality by the Kuznets effect.

The asymmetry between the subperiods means that, for the whole period 1981–95, the evidence fits the OTI hypothesis quite well (Table 5.3). Overall inequality rose by 7.5 per cent, with rises of 11 and 20 per cent in urban and rural sectors offset by a 4 per cent fall in intersectoral inequality together with continuing Kuznetsian equalization by migration. However, since OTI fails in each subperiod and significant adjustment began only in 1992, the Brazilian case *does not* support the theory that adjustment causes OTI. In considering the macroeconomic correlates of the inequality trends of the 1980s, Ferreira and Litchfield find that inflation (rather than unemployment or GDP growth) is the variable most closely associated with inequality. The first half of the 1990s lends support to their view: adjustment eliminated hyperinflation and overall, inter-, and intrasectoral inequality all fell.

Ferreira and Litchfield perform dynamic disaggregations of the Theil-L by age and gender of household head, region, and education. Only for the urban–rural and education disaggregations does the unexplained (intrasector) component account for less than 100 per cent of the total change. For education, it is the Kuznets effect (a tendency of population shares in different educational categories to become more equal) that accounts for most of the explained component (about 30 per cent of the total inequality rise).

Chile 1987–94.[12]   Chile's inequality trend since 1980 follows Brazil (and aggregate Latin America), albeit at a lower level, except for a rather earlier peak in the Gini at about 1987.[13] We have no evidence on the intra- and intersectoral components during the period of rising inequality. In 1987, within-sector inequality accounted for 93 per cent of total inequality. Over 1987–94, the Theil-L for income per equivalized adult fell from 0.527 to 0.485; about 15 per cent of the fall was attributable to a fall in intersectoral inequality and almost all of the remainder to a fall in intrasectoral inequality. In Chile, the net fall in intrasectoral inequality (in contrast with Brazil) can be traced to the urban sector alone, where inequality fell enough to swamp rising rural inequality. Behind a very small demographic contribution lie offsetting effects just like those in Brazil—urbanization raises inequality inasmuch as the urban sector is more unequal but lowers inequality by the Kuznets effect.

So Chile provides only partial support for the OTI hypothesis, essentially because in the recovery period urban inequality was falling. Litchfield and Ferreira find that, as in Brazil, the educational partition is informative. Demographic change is again unequalizing, as population shares in different subgroups (educational categories)

---

[12] Ferreira and Litchfield (1999); Table 5.1.
[13] The aggregate data in Deininger and Squire suggest the 1987 peak; Ferreira and Litchfield show a fall from 1987–90 and little change post-1990. Londoño and Szekely find a continuing fall over 1990–4; one difference between these studies is that Ferreira and Litchfield use income per equivalent adult while Londoño and Szekely use income per adult.

become more equal, but this is swamped by an important convergence in subgroup income means together with equalizing within-subgroup change.

Honduras 1989–93.[14] This fits the Londoño–Szekely characterization, with the income per person Gini roughly constant.[15] Both urban and rural inequality rose, while intersectoral inequality fell, mean income in the capital falling by 35 per cent, and mean income in the urban sector falling by 19 per cent, relative to mean rural income. These trends are consistent with the OTI hypothesis. Noteworthy are the fall in the relative urban–rural wage by 20 per cent and the relative public–private sector wage by 17 per cent in the period and a 60 per cent real devaluation over 1988–92;[16] prima facie, a link from adjustment to, at least, the intersectoral component of the hypothesis seems plausible here.

South Asia and China

LS suggest a seesaw regional pattern, with inequality falling between the 1960s and the 1970s, rising in the 1980s, and falling back in the 1990s. The two Asian giants present a stark contrast. India (with 36 per cent of the regional population) experienced almost no movement in either intersectoral or intrasectoral indices of inequality. China (47 per cent) showed sharp movements in all the indices, appearing to reflect the sequence of policy reform. The OTI hypothesis finds support in this region only in Pakistan in the 1980s and for China during 1978–83. Otherwise rural–urban and intrasectoral inequality move together—up in China after 1983 and in Bangladesh and down in Sri Lanka.

China 1978–95. The relative income data and Ginis in Table 5.2 reflect the changing focus of economic reform in the country since 1978. From 1978 to 1983, with egalitarian quasi-privatization of farmland and some reduction of price and quota extraction from agriculture, urban–rural inequality fell sharply (relative urban income fell by 28 per cent); urban inequality also fell a little. Despite land reform, the regionally very skewed growth in cereals yields (and the growth of less labour-intensive rural nonfarm enterprises) meant that rural inequality rose—but not by enough to prevent the overall Gini falling by about 10 per cent. Post-1983, the focus of reform shifted to the urban sector, with aggregate enterprise wages tied more closely to labour productivity and greater freedom given to enterprises to vary wages among employees (Zhang 1997: 6); throughout 1983–95 we observe substantial rises in total, intra-, and intersectoral inequalities.[17]

Zhang's analysis of the Theil-L over 1988–95 shows (a) a remarkable rise by global standards of 46.5 per cent in total inequality, and (b) that 83 per cent of this

[14] World Bank 13317-HO (1994: table 2).
[15] The poverty assessment (World Bank 13317-HO 1994: 64) notes that property income is excluded.
[16] World Bank 13317-HO (1994: table C-4 and statistical appendix).
[17] See Zhang (1997) for a range of inequality disaggregations, both by population subgroup and by income source.

rise is within-group and virtually all of the rest is between-group. The Ginis tell us that inequality was rising fast in both sectors during this period, although faster in the urban sector. OTI is clearly refuted for the period as a whole. This may seem unsurprising in an economy where central decisions have had so great an influence both on the initial conditions and on the sequencing of reforms. Nevertheless, Chinese experience shows that not all adjustment or liberalization narrows the urban–rural gap: the unequalizing effects of industrial liberalization have clearly outweighed the earlier equalizing effects of agricultural liberalization.

India 1963–97. There is a mass of data, and comparative analysis of regions is informative (Datt and Ravallion 1996), but compared to many countries inequality has changed little since 1973 (Jha, Chapter 12, this volume). Rural–urban inequality clearly fell in 1963–73, after which a slow rise to a peak around 1983 was matched by a similar slow (and non-monotonic) fall over 1990–7. Urban inequality has risen slowly throughout, and rural inequality has hardly changed, although there may be a shallow trough centred on 1990, the year that the reform process began. Does OTI work here? There is some evidence for slight OTI post-1990, but the extent of year-to-year fluctuation evident in Jha (Chapter 12, this volume: Table 12.4) suggests caution.

Bangladesh 1984–96. The data in Table 5.2, based on Wodon (1999), reveal trend increases through the period in rural–urban inequality (a rise in relative urban income of 35 per cent), intrasectoral inequalities, and overall inequality. Wodon's data permit disaggregations of the Gini *a la* Aronson/Lambert (footnote 3), given below:

Year	G	G_B	G_W	R
1983/94	0.255	0.033	0.187 (0.004 + 0.182)	0.036
1988/9	0.310	0.098	0.178 (0.016 + 0.162)	0.034

The bracketed terms give the disaggregation into urban and rural contributions respectively. Intersectoral and urban inequality both rose significantly; namely, the OTI hypothesis is rejected. The fall in R presumably reflects reduced overlapping as the urban and rural means diverge. What is not clear (and what a Theil disaggregation would reveal) is the effect of migration: rural–urban migration has been significant in the period and both components of its impact on the Theil would be inequality-increasing.

Sri Lanka 1970–91. Glewwe (1986) shows a fall in the Theil-L and each of its components between 1970 and 1981. Together with the World Bank Poverty Assessment (PA 13431-CE; henceforth PAs are referenced by their codes alone), this also shows that the ratio of mean urban to rural consumption returned to its 1970 level during the first half of the 1980s. The PA also permits a Lambert/Aronson disaggregation of the consumption per person Gini over 1985/6 to 1990/1, as follows (in the brackets, the first component is the sum of the urban and estate sector contributions).

Year	G	G_B	G_W	R
1985/6	0.320	0.072	0.164 (0.022 + 0.142)	0.084
1990/1	0.297	0.051	0.155 (0.020 + 0.135)	0.092

Demographic change is insignificant in this case, making interpretation easier: the fall in the Gini reflects falls in rural–urban inequality and rural inequality, urban inequality being hardly changed. In sharp contrast to Bangladesh, urban consumption per person in Sri Lanka fell during 1986–91 (by some 5 per cent). So, as regards rural–urban inequality during adjustment, one might view the urban sector as the motor, pulling mean sectoral consumptions apart in Bangladesh (and stimulating migration) with positive responses to incentives in the employment-intensive urban garment industry, but pushing the sectoral means together as urban income fell in Sri Lanka.

Pakistan 1979–91. Changes in overall, rural, and probably rural–urban inequality in Pakistan in 1979–85/6 were well within the range of measurement error plus harvest-related shocks (Table 5.2). Alongside the significant fall in the urban Gini, these changes—during very modest adjustment—support neither OTI nor a major adjustment impact on distribution overall. From 1985–6 to 1990–1, however, OTI works: alongside more rapid adjustment, there were substantial annual falls in rural–urban inequality only partly offset by very substantial rises in the urban and (even more) rural Ginis.

East Asia (other than China)

LS suggest, for the region, that inequality was roughly constant from the 1960s to the 1980s—at roughly South Asian levels—but that there was a discernible increase between the 1980s and the 1990s (see also Ahuja *et al.* 1997). We find no evidence for the OTI hypothesis. Where inequality has changed rapidly (in Thailand over 1988–92), there is a parallel with China and Bangladesh, with the urban sector pulling away from the rural sector and intrasectoral inequality rising too.

Indonesia 1976–95. Deininger and Squire report observations every 2–3 years for urban and rural Ginis of expenditure per household and the national Gini of expenditure per person, from the same national source, for 1976–90. These indicate (a) rises in all three Ginis during 1976–8; and (b) post-1978, a steady fall in the rural Gini; a U-shaped pattern for the urban Gini and the overall Gini, the floor being at about 1986[18] (on this see also Chapter 2).

For 1987–93, the data in Akita *et al.* (1999) allow a dynamic decomposition of the Theil-L, reported in Table 5.1. This indicates a 5 per cent rise in inequality, and is 'anti-OTI': a small rise in the rural–urban gap is mostly offset by a small fall in intrasectoral inequality,[19] leaving demography to account statistically for almost all of the

---

[18] Akita *et al.* (1999) suggest that urban inequality may have started to fall again during 1990–3.

[19] With the fall in rural–urban inequality over 1984–90, this implies that the rural–urban ratio hardly changed over 1984–93.

128 R. Eastwood and M. Lipton

rise in overall inequality. Urbanization rose from 26 to 32 per cent and, since migration was towards the smaller and more unequal sector, both demographic components were unequalizing.

Korea 1966–93. The Ginis show rises in total and urban inequality between the 1960s and 1970s, no significant changes in either since then, but secular decline in rural inequality post-1972.

Thailand 1962–92. The gross income/household Gini in Thailand rose continuously in the period, accelerating around 1980 and by 1992 reaching a level (0.536) atypically high for the region (PA 15689-TH, 10).[20] During 1975–81—not a period of adjustment—the OTI hypothesis fits: a fall in rural–urban inequality was outweighed by rises in sectoral inequalities (Table 5.2). Thereafter all three components of inequality rose through to 1988 at least. The dynamic disaggregation in Table 5.1 shows that intrasectoral inequality increase also contributed to the huge (31 per cent) rise in the Theil-L over 1988–92, but we cannot say how this was divided between urban and rural components. What is striking is the large rise in rural–urban inequality, 73 per cent, between 1981 and 1992 (see also Chapter 16). This is reflected in the dynamic disaggregation of the inequality change over 1988–92: the marginal contribution of raised urban–rural inequality far exceeds the average, supporting 'eye evidence' of an emerging super-rich Bangkok elite. In Thailand, therefore, OTI fits the pre-adjustment period 1975–81, but is rejected for 1981–92, especially 1988–92, when inequality rose fastest. Thailand provides evidence against a recent OTI 'takeover' that might make worsening inequality surprising, or likely to self-correct. On the contrary, as in China and Bangladesh, so in Thailand: recently rising overall Asian inequality is in substantial part associated with rising rural–urban inequality. In China and Thailand, a main explanation is probably that, in recent growth, largely rural regions of 'core poverty'—north and western China, northeastern Thailand— are being left behind.

Malaysia 1970–90. The Ginis in Table 5.2 suggest falling total, intersectoral, and urban inequality in the period overall. The exception is a small rise in total inequality in the 1970s, associated with a temporary rise in rural inequality. Gradual liberalization after 1980 was accompanied by the Bhumiputra policy; this policy favoured a lower income group, so would be expected to have reduced inequality overall and by component.

Philippines 1957–91. From the mid-1950s to the mid-1980s, Table 5.2 suggests: (a) inverted-U patterns for rural, urban, and total inequality; and (b) from the mid-1960s to the mid-1970s a sharp narrowing of the urban–rural gap. Latterly, all components of inequality seem to have turned upwards, the floor for intersectoral inequality having been reached in about 1975 and the sectoral and aggregate floors in about 1988.

---

[20] Isra Sarntisart (Chapter 16, this volume) reports a slight fall in the overall Gini during 1992–6.

For 1971–91, Table 5.1 reports dynamic disaggregations for 1971–85 and 1985–91 (Estudillo 1997), but these appear inconsistent,[21] and the choice of subperiods suppresses the substantial fluctuation in intersectoral inequality in the 1970s (Table 5.2). It would be misleading to conclude, from the disaggregations, that intrasectoral inequality change was most of the story.

Middle East and North Africa

LS suggest steady, significant decline in median Ginis since the 1970s. We can say almost nothing about urban–rural disaggregation of inequality. Moroccan Ginis for 1984/85 and 1990/91 hint at flat inequality overall and a slight fall in urban inequality—alongside a good deal of adjustment, as in Jordan, which however then experienced sharp rises in total urban and rural expenditure-per-person Ginis. Among factors which might account for the contrast is relatively high gender inequality of economic opportunity in Jordan.

Sub-Saharan Africa

LS find a sharp rise in the median Gini (from 0.422 to 0.489) between the 1960s and the 1970s, reversed in the 1980s, with a perceptible rise between the 1980s and the 1990s. We have complete evidence for two dates on the rural–urban inequality breakdown only for Ghana (Table 5.1), together with partial evidence for five other countries (Tables 5.2 and 5.3). A test of the OTI hypothesis requires reliable evidence from the 1990s, and we have this only for Ghana, where OTI is not supported. In Tanzania and Uganda rural–urban inequality may have widened in the early 1990s. The case of Ghana (like Honduras) suggests that 'capital city versus the rest' is sometimes as interesting a disaggregation as 'urban versus rural'.

Ghana 1988–92.   This period saw structural adjustment, partly associated with the economic recovery programme adopted in 1983. The disaggregations of the Theil-L are based on a three-way division into Accra/other cities/rural; nonetheless 93 per cent of inequality is in the unexplained intrasectoral component.

In the period inequality fell by 10.5 per cent, of which 7.5 per cent was intersectoral, 5.2 per cent intrasectoral, and −2.1 per cent demographic. So the marginal intersectoral component was far larger than the average, due to the sharp fall in relative per-capita expenditure in Accra, which bore the brunt, under structural adjustment, of reduced public-sector employment because alternative employment opportunities proved especially inadequate to the volume of workers displaced. Thus not only did relative mean expenditure fall in Accra, but its population share fell, while

---

[21] The contribution of intersectoral inequality change during 1971–85 is shown as negative, which in view of the *rise* in relative urban income (and the fact that it exceeds +1) is impossible in view of Eq. (5.3) of this chapter.

that of other cities increased (by more). As regards the intrasectoral component, inequality unsurprisingly rose in Accra but this was outweighed by falls in the other two areas.

5.3. CHANGING RURAL–URBAN POVERTY RATIOS AND 'URBAN BIAS'

5.3.1. *Introduction*

This section examines trends in rural and urban poverty indices and, in particular, in rural/urban ratios. Although poverty and inequality indicators are linked, the former are of independent interest for several reasons. First, policy should concern itself more with poverty than with inequality as such: for instance, transfers among the better-off that reduce inequality without touching poverty should be of second-order concern. Second, a sustained difference between rural and urban poverty risk indicates—if long-term differences in the innate characteristics of rural and urban inhabitants are excluded—both arbitrary inequality associated with accident of birth-place, and barriers to rural–urban migration and urban–rural capital flow. Furthermore, higher relative rural poverty may indicate urban bias, in that identifiable changes in policies or institutional structures might both reduce the rural–urban imbalance and raise efficiency.

How is relative rural poverty linked to inter- and intrasectoral inequalities? It tends to fall if (a) rural–urban inequality falls, (b) urban inequality rises, and (c) rural inequality falls.[22] So there is no neat link to the OTI hypothesis. Nevertheless, it is useful to consider what is happening to these three inequality measures in a given case.

Analysing comparative trends in rural and urban poverty helps us to assess an influential current 'development narrative' about the linkage between macroeconomic policy, urban bias, and poverty reduction. This is well exemplified by the World Bank's Madagascar PA (PA 14044-MAG: 11–12):

(I)n the mid 1970s . . . interventionist economic policies (were) characterized by widespread nationalization, extensive price and marketing controls which were particularly severe in the agricultural sector, extremely high tariffs, high taxation of agricultural exports, a chronically overvalued exchange rate, and a public investment programme that gave priority to large capital-intensive projects with low returns, while neglecting investments in . . . rural infrastructure and the social sectors. These policies favoured urban over rural areas, where most of the poor live . . . . The legacy . . . has been a relative decline of agriculture . . . which provides a livelihood for the majority of the country's poor . . . and public expenditure programmes that for several decades have neglected . . . areas . . . from which the poor are major beneficiaries . . . . Not surprisingly, not only did poverty increase in this period but so did inequality . . . . (From 1987) the government took measures to stabilize the macroeconomic situation and to reform the economy . . . .These measures had several positive effects. There was

[22] Paradoxes can arise, especially for the incidence measure of poverty. For example, if individuals are bunched just below the poverty line in only one sector, then a small rise in everybody's income in that sector can greatly reduce poverty incidence; the same rise in the other sector would achieve little.

an economic recovery...domestic terms of trade (moved) in favour of the rural sector. Liberalization resulted in an expansion of nontraditional agricultural exports.... However, the deterioration in rural infrastructure prevented a recovery of traditional agriculture and (following protests in 1991) the stabilization and reform programmes were derailed (and GDP per person fell through 1994).

Few would deny that poverty reduction in many countries has been impeded by interventionism inimical to progress in the agro-rural economy; and that such policies reflected urban bias and contributed to overall (not just rural–urban) inequality. Yet many would see the above account as only half the story. As regards agricultural development, if poor farmers are to show high supply responsiveness to new market incentives, the state must not only slash its direct production and price regulation, but also boost some expenditures: to spread access to land, knowledge and human capital; to support agricultural research and its application; and to reduce rural risk and insecurity, through measures ranging from water management, through nutrition and health programmes, to rural roads. As regards political economy, simply moving from a dirigiste to a market-oriented economy does little to reduce the pro-urban power biases that have prevented adequate public focus on, and spending for, rural development. Unless those biases are reduced, there is little prospect for the shifts in public expenditure, required to make the post-reform dispensation more amenable to poverty reduction (by rural focus and hence growth and equalization) than was the old. The non-sustainability of some adjustment programmes (as in Madagascar above), and the limited gains to the poor from adjustment even in the quite frequent cases where it improved economic performance, are probably inherent in the one-sided nature of the reforms.

5.3.2. *Choice of Poverty Variable*

We discuss changes in two indicators: incidence, H (the proportion of population below the poverty line)[23] and the poverty-gap index (PGI—incidence times depth, the poor's mean proportionate shortfall below the poverty line). Few countries have surveys sufficiently far apart for trends in relative (rural–urban) poverty to be estimated. Moreover, governments or agencies often either refuse to release grouped poverty data or allow access only at prohibitive cost. We concur with Stiglitz (1999) that, as a rule, 'information obtained at public expense should be publicly available'.

We prefer to measure relative rural poverty using PGI rather than H: the choice matters, since the rural poor typically lie further below the poverty line than the urban poor. The PGI, intrinsically to be preferred to H because it takes intensity into account, measures both (a) the 'burden of poverty', equal to the cost-per-head of its elimination, if transfers are perfectly targeted and there are no transactions or incentive costs, and (b) a person's risk of poverty times the intensity of poverty if that risk materializes.

---

[23] Sensitivity tests, especially to variations in the poverty line (dominance tests: fn. 1), are sometimes carried out. See sources cited here, and on measurement issues Ravallion (1993) and Lipton and Ravallion (1995). International comparisons of poverty levels are risky. Trend comparisons, however, are feasible, especially where dominance tests have been done.

Table 5.4. *Changes in poverty and their decomposition into growth and distribution components*

Country and period	Poverty incidence change (initial–final) (Growth component, inequality component, residual)			Poverty gap index change (initial–final) (Growth component, inequality component, residual)		The ratio of rural to urban poverty, initial → final
	Rural	Urban	National	Rural	Urban	
West Asia						
Jordan, 1986/7–92	+17.3 (12.5, 1.4, 3.4)	+10.4 (7.1, −2.1, 5.4)	+11.9 (8.3, −1.3, 5.0)			7.5 → 28.71 [a]
Southeast Asia						
China, 1978–90	−21.5 (33.0–11.5)	−4.0 (4.4–0.4)		−7.53 (12.8–5.3)	−1.67 (3.5–1.8)	3.87 → 2.37 I
Indonesia, 1984–90	−19.1 (45.7–26.6) (−15.28, −2.42, −1.44)	−4.64 (15.9–11.2) (−6.26, 2.53, −0.91)		(−5.52, −2.24, 0.23)	(−1.54, 0.20, −0.33)	3.66 → 2.94 PGI [b]
Malaysia, 1973–89	−36.0 (55.3–19.3)	−30.5 (44.8–14.3)	−30.5 (44.8–14.3)			1.23 → 1.35 I
Philippines, 1961–88	−11 (64–53)	−28 (51–23)	−22 (59–37)			1.25 → 2.30 I
1985–8	−6.6 (69.4–62.8)	−7.3 (56.8–49.5)		−4.7 (27.3–22.6)	−4.6 (21.6–17.0)	1.22 → 1.27 I
						1.26 → 1.33 PGI
South Asia						
Bangladesh 1984–90	−0.9 (53.8–52.9) (−2.50, 1.60, 0.00)	−7.3 (40.9–33.6) (−10.8, 3.6, −0.1)		−0.4 (15.0–14.6) (−1.0, 0.6, 0.0)	−3.0 (11.4–8.4) (−3.9, 1.3, −0.4)	1.32 → 1.57 I
						1.32 → 1.74 PGI
India, 1957/8–89/90	−20.9 (55.2–34.3)	−14.4 (47.8–33.4)		−11.2 (19.0–7.8)	−7.4 (16.0–8.5)	1.16 → 1.03 I
						1.19 → 0.92 PGI
1989/90–97	−0.1 (34.3–34.2)	−5.5 (33.4–27.9)		+0.3 (7.8–8.1)	−1.3 (8.5–7.2)	1.03 → 1.23 I
						0.92 → 1.13 PGI
Sri Lanka, 1985–6/90–1	−7.3 (31.7–24.4) {Estate: −1.7 (14.3–12.6)}	+1.9 (16.4–18.3)		−2.4 (7.7–5.3) {Estate: −0.8 (1.4–0.6)}	+0.7 (3.5–4.1)	1.93 → 1.33 I
						2.20 → 1.27 PGI
Latin America						
Colombia, 1977–92	−7.2 (38.4–31.2)	−4.1 (12.1–8.0)		−3.1 (16.6–13.5)	−2.2 (4.6–2.4)	3.17 → 3.90 I
1978–92	−5.3	−4.1		−2.8	−2.1	3.61 → 5.62 PGI
Extreme poverty line	(0.4, −6.5, 0.8)	(−1.2, −2.2, −0.7)		(0.4, −3.1, −0.05)	(−0.5, −1.7, 0.1)	
Ecuador, 1990–4	−38.0 (85.0–47.0)	−22.7 (47.7–25.0)				1.78 → 1.88 I
Guatemala, 1980–86/7	−7.2 (79.2–72.0)	+13.7 (40.7–54.4)	+2.2 (65.4–67.6)			1.95 → 1.33 I
	−4.0 (83.7–79.7)	+13.3 (47.0–60.3)	+2.1 (71.9–73.2)			1.78 → 1.32 I
Honduras, 1989–93	−7 (56.1–39.7)	+4 (51–55)	−2 (55–53)			1.10 → 0.72 I

Africa	Cote d'Ivoire, 1985–8					
	15.0 (41.6–56.6)	15.2 (13.8–29.0)	15.9 (30.0–45.9)	5.0 (13.8–18.8)	2.7 (4.2–6.9)	3.01 → 1.95 I 3.3 → 2.7 PGI
Ghana, 1987–8/91–2	−8.0 (41.9–33.9)	−0.9 (27.4–26.5)	−5.4 (36.9–31.5)			1.53 → 1.28 I
Kenya, 1992–4	+0.4 (46.3–46.7)	−0.3 (29.3–28.9)				1.59 → 1.62 I
Nigeria, 1985–92	−0.7 (16.1–15.4)	+6.0 (4.9–10.9)				3.29 → 1.41 I
Zambia, 1991–6	−4.2 (79.1–74.9)	+6.8 (27.2–34.0)	+4.3 (55.5–59.8)	−12.3 (50.1–37.8)	+1.9 (9.5–11.4)[a]	2.91 → 2.20 I 5.27 → 3.32 PGI
Transitional Romania, 1989–93	+17.5 (5.9–23.4)	+15.8 (1.2–17.0)	+16.3 (3.7–20.20)			4.92 → 1.38 I

Note: The first row of the table indicates how the data are presented. Gaps in the cells indicate data unavailability. Example: in the rural sector in Colombia between 1977 and 1992, poverty incidence fell by 7.2%, from 38.4% to 31.2%, a growth/inequality disaggregation is not available.

[a] I = Incidence.

[b] PGI = Poverty gap index.

Source: Eastwood and Lipton (2000).

Table 5.4 shows national changes in rural, urban, and national *H* and PGI. Only in Bangladesh, Colombia, Indonesia, and Jordan can we decompose such changes into effects of (a) growth of the group's mean income, (b) changed distribution within the group (namely, rural or urban), and (c) a residual.[24] The data shortage, especially for long periods and for Africa and transitional countries, is striking; many surveys do not publish even 1 year's mean rural and urban income, let alone urban and rural trends in poverty.

The following discussion goes beyond the few countries with PGI trends in Table 5.4. Where only headcount trends can be compared between urban and rural sectors, there are sometimes hints about sectoral PGIs. If not, inferences on rural and urban poverty trends from *H* are only weaker. We also consider information for countries not shown in Table 5.4.

5.3.3. *Evidence on Trends in Rural–Urban Poverty Ratios*

While we prefer the PGI to *H* in assessing trends in relative rural poverty, Table 5.4 shows that relative rural incidence moves in the same direction where both measures are available.[25] Table 5.4 shows that, of the four countries where changes in incidence and/or PGI of urban and rural poverty can be decomposed into growth, distribution, and residual effects, differential growth effects drive changes in relative rural poverty in Jordan, Indonesia, and Bangladesh; only in Colombia do distribution changes play the main role. Also, combining Table 5.4 (last column of numbers) with the tables in Section 5.2, we see that in *almost* every case rural–urban inequality rises (falls) alongside relative rural poverty.

Asia

The picture is diverse, but overall there is no convergence between urban and rural poverty. We must pay special attention to China and India, which are home to over half the world's 'dollar-poor'; both seem incompatible with any plausible OTI story.

China. Food poverty fell from 28.0 per cent in 1978 by 9.2 per cent in 1985 to 8.6 per cent in 1990; urban from 4.4 per cent in 1978 to 0.4 per cent in both 1985 and 1990;

---

[24] (a) The published decompositions of change in *H* and PGI are into the effect of mean income growth and of shifts in the fitted Lorenz curve. There is inevitably a residual in this case. (b) For some countries we have informal indications of the extent to which changes in the urban–rural poverty ratios are associated with changes in intrasectoral distributions as against changes in sectoral means.

[25] In Table 5.4 India appears to be an exception over the complete period 1957/8–97, though not over the subperiods before and after reforms: both the PGI ratio and the incidence ratio fell in 1957/8–1989/90, and then rose in 1997; rural–urban PGI converged in 1958–97, yet poverty incidences appear to have diverged. That, however, is an oddity due to the fact that we are presenting the longest available and comparable series, and the end-year 1997 is exceptional in that the rural/urban PGI ratio showed a sudden fall to 1.13, namely, below the 1957/8 level of 1.19. But the ratio was 1.20 in 1995–6 and 1.23 in both 1993/4 and 1994/5 (Jha, Chapter 12, this volume: Table 12.4), that is, on these data there was a slight rural–urban PGI divergence over the whole period from 1957/8 in PGI, as in incidence. Note also that 1989–90—with the rural PGI suddenly plummeting for just 1 year, to only 92 per cent of the urban ratio—is unique; rural PGI is over 100% of urban in all other years (Jha, Chapter 12, this volume: Table 12.4).

rural from 33 per cent by 11.9 per cent to 11.5 per cent.[26] Meanwhile the urban population share rose from 17.9 per cent to 26.4 per cent.[27] Thus both urban and rural poverty fell; urbanization also reduced national poverty incidence.[28] Rural poverty fell in 1977–84 alongside rapid, egalitarian, and essentially individual land reform, declining price repression of agriculture, and major technical progress in rice and wheat; yet even then urban poverty fell faster.

More recently, the ratio between urban and rural mean income rose from 1.7 in 1983 to 2.2 in 1995 (on this, see also Table 2.5 in Chapter 2); both the level and the rise are more, if differentials and changes in the cost of living and in subsidies are allowed for (World Bank 1997: 16). This must have raised rural–urban poverty ratios, and was reinforced by rising rural inequality after 1983, as township and village enterprises replaced agriculture as the engine of rural growth, and backward areas fell further behind (Howes 1993; Gang *et al.* 1996). In 1985–93, after urban poverty had fallen almost to zero (on the national poverty line; it was about 2 per cent on the dollar-a-day line) rural poverty almost stopped falling. (Local studies, cited in the PA and the STICERD study, Howes 1993, etc., suggest that sectoral PGI and *H* showed similar trends.)

China's urban/rural poverty ratios are linked to high and rising regional inequality. Since 1984 growth has been much faster where there was little poverty left to eliminate—the urban SE coastal belt and its fast-urbanizing rural hinterland. Hence urban/rural poverty ratios have widened, and—except for very sharp falls during 1993–6—poverty has fallen only slowly (Gang *et al.* 1996), the more so because rural inequality is rising due to regional divergence; greater risks to decollectivized farmers, for example, from market volatility; specialization within agriculture; and rapid growth of nonfarm income, which accrues disproportionately to better-off people (Howes 1993; Howes and Hussain 1994). Rises in the urban–rural gap and rural inequality may *both* reflect increased urban bias: high rural inequality may favour urban residents by raising rural–urban flows of tradables, skills, and savings.[29]

India has substantial rural–urban (and regional) differences in mean income and poverty, close to the norm for developing countries, but well below China. Between 1957–8 and 1997, the typical townsperson's risk of falling below the (locally price-adjusted) national poverty line fell by 58 per cent, and the typical villager's by 48 per cent, of its previous level, implying overall divergence (Table 5.4; on the PGI, see fn. 1).

There are three periods. From the mid-1950s to the mid-1970s, real (purchasing power parity (PPP)) GDP and mean consumption per person and overall poverty

---

[26] National poverty is on the same line as in 1994, that is, 11.4%: World Bank (1998: 64).

[27] World Bank (1992) *China: Poverty Assessment*: ix 23, 146–7.

[28] This is an arithmetical statement, implied by lower urban poverty rates plus urbanization. It does not imply that the poor are urbanized; that urbanizers thus reduced their risk of poverty; or that rural poverty was reduced because urbanization moderated the pressure on land. Empirically, all three statements are, in this case, probably correct.

[29] Some 100 million Chinese 'floating migrants' work in the towns but are registered as rural. They lack most urban entitlements and subsidies, and are seldom if ever surveyed as urban. So data shortages prevent firm conclusions about their poverty. But they are probably intermediate between registered urban and settled rural people in both incidence and speed of decline since the mid-1980s.

stagnated, as did both rural and urban poverty incidence and hence the ratio between them (though with huge fluctuations, greater in rural areas). From the mid-1970s to around 1990, incidences and PGIs converged as both urban and rural poverty fell: the rural/urban incidence ratio was around 1.2 in the mid-1970s and below 1.1 around 1990, while the PGI ratio fell from close to 1.3 to barely above unity. Post-1990, adjustment saw urban poverty falling, rural poverty trendless, and hence poverty risks diverging: in 1992, with a spotty harvest accompanying economic sluggishness due to stabilization, the incidence ratio rose sharply to 1.3 and the PGI ratio to over 1.2. By 1997, despite even faster growth in mean rural than urban consumption, urban and rural poverty had again diverged—indeed, urban poverty over the reform period fell sharply, while rural poverty appears not to have budged (Table 5.4, Appendix 5.1 sources; and Jha, Chapter 12, this volume: Table 12.4).

Can we be sure that adjustment in India has been associated with a rise in relative rural poverty (in contrast to Africa) and a fall in the elasticity of rural poverty to mean consumption? Sampling error aside, Deaton and Tarozzi (2000) suggest that in 1989/90–1993–4 National Sample Survey (NSS) overestimated inflation, especially in rural areas: this leads to faster estimated poverty decline and no clear conclusion about rural–urban poverty divergence. However, the longer data set to 1997 now available strengthens the inference that the rural–urban poverty gap widened and rural poverty fell little over the whole adjustment period. Srinivasan (1999) argues that (a) this may be due to the far slower pace of reform in agriculture (and in rural financial markets) than elsewhere, not to reform itself; (b) rural poverty appears to have done worst in the least-reforming states of Uttar Pradesh, Bihar, Orissa, and Rajasthan, and to have fallen elsewhere, though less than in urban areas.

Indonesia, before the financial crisis of 1997, experienced very fast falls in poverty, fastest in rural areas, especially during the rapid progress with high-yielding rice varieties in the 1980s. The 1984 and 1990 surveys, after price adjustment,[30] show that during 1984–90 rural PGI fell by 59 per cent and urban PGI by 48 per cent (*H* fell by 42 and 29 per cent, respectively).[31] In *Bangladesh*, however, in the same period, the urban PGI fell by 26 per cent (*H* by 24 per cent) and rural PGI by only 3 per cent (*H* by 2 per cent) (Table 5.4). In *Pakistan* during 1984/85–1990/91 rural poverty incidence, at best, fell no faster than urban (de Haan and Lipton 1998). Urban and rural poverty converged between in *Sri Lanka* (1985/6–91),[32] but diverged in *Malaysia* (1973–89), the *Philippines* (1961–88 and 1985–8), *Thailand*[33] (1988–92), and (in sharp economic contraction) *Jordan* (1986/7–92). For Asia overall, these data,

---

[30] Official comparisons substantially overstate the extent to which urban prices exceed rural (thus overstating urban relative to rural *H* and PGI) and somewhat understate poverty overall (at the national line) (Ravallion and Huppi 1991).

[31] Firdausy (1994) for the whole 1980–90 period, shows rural and urban *H* falling at similar rates (respectively from 33.5% to 16.0% and from 36.7% to 17.3%), but uses the flawed official price series.

[32] The data for Sri Lanka, however, exclude the eastern and some northern areas affected by civil war.

[33] Incidence fell from 1988 to 1992 in municipal areas from 6.4% to 2.4%, in (semi-urban) 'sanitary districts' from 28.6% to 16.8%, and in villages from 25.5% to 15.5%. PGI fell, respectively, from 5.5% to 3.4%, from 8.6% to 5.1%, and from 7.5% to 4.0%. PA, p. 65.

mostly for 1984–94, show, if anything, some rural–urban poverty divergence. This parallels mean income divergence (Section 5.2).

Africa

The region's uniquely high urban–rural gaps in welfare indicators, including poverty, around 1960–85—due largely to structures of outlays, prices, and institutions associated with urban bias—probably declined in 1985–95.[34] Some of the inefficiencies became unaffordable as some of the underpinnings of urban bias were cut away by adjustments, or rather cuts, enforced less by international institutions than by fiscal and foreign exchange crisis and economic decline. Cuts in public-sector jobs, and rises in food prices due to devaluation, impinged more on urban than on rural areas. Reduced public spending, increased health or school charges, etc. affected the rural areas less, because they had enjoyed much smaller per-person flows of such resources in the first place.

Thus in *Nigeria* in 1988–92, urban incidence more than doubled (to 10.9 per cent) while rural incidence fell slightly (to 15.4 per cent). The number of extreme poor in urban areas soared—from 1.5 to 4.3 million—and also rose in rural areas, from 8.6 to 9.6 million (World Bank, Nigeria PA 14733-UNI 1996: #2.14; de Haan *et al.* 1997).

Zambia's story is telling: 1991–6 was a period of negative growth. Yet rural poverty fell, partly because the brunt of adjustment had to lie in the urban sector which had benefited from most subsidization and artificial public employment, and partly because of substantial rises in rural equality as input and milling subsidies (benefiting mainly surplus farmers) were phased out (World Bank Zambia PA 12985-ZA 1994; McCulloch and Baulch 1999).

The phasing in *Ghana* was different: the urban–rural ratio of mean income in 1973, at 1.5, was much lower than the African norm (cf. Kenya's 3–4), and imploded to unity or less in 1973–83 as urban income contracted in 'one of the most spectacular declines in economic fortune that any country has known'. Yet by 1987 rural headcount poverty was well above urban (respectively, 42 and 27 per cent). In the recovery of 1987–92 the rural–urban mean income ratio rose again (Canagarajah *et al.* 1998). Hence the big fall in the ratio of rural to urban poverty (Table 5.4) reflects the big rise in inequality within the cities, especially Accra, and perhaps a fall in rural inequality, in the recovery years. *Kenya's* phasing is intermediate, with 1992–4 neither as unfavourable as in Zambia nor as recovery-oriented as in Ghana, but there is still a mild fall in relative rural poverty.

Côte d'Ivoire 1985–8 saw economic adjustment, followed by 'abandonment of the effort...a period of destabilization' (Grootaert *et al.* 1996: xiii). While both urban and rural poverty increased, relative rural poverty fell (as did rural–urban inequality: Table 5.2). This mirrors Ghana's experience, signalling overall economic contraction

---

[34] That is not because urban power weakened, or rural pressures became less weak and diffuse. Given unaltered power-balances, it is likely that the urban state—compelled to correct price bias against rural people (and especially deficit farmers who delivered nothing to the cities), and thus to cut the ratio of urban to rural poverty—will gradually offset such effects by increasing public expenditure bias towards the towns.

that hit the towns harder. However, in both cases the capital city élites probably escaped. In Côte d'Ivoire, mean income in Abidjan (in sharp contrast to other towns) fell no more than in rural areas. In Ghana—although in Accra mean income fell more than in rural areas—the big rise in inequality suggests that income falls were concentrated among the poor.

Latin America

A review[35] (Costa Rica PA: Annexes: 33, table 2) estimates trends in poverty incidence in 1980–90. It rose for the ten countries together, from 16.8 to 23.6 per cent in urban areas, and only from 45.1 to 52.5 per cent in rural areas, suggesting[36] an odds ratio converging towards unity. However, we found only five countries with clearly comparable surveys in the World Bank screened database. Of these, all but Honduras show a fall in relative rural poverty (Table 5.4).[37]

Transitionals

Only Romania has data in the framework of Table 5.4, but three points relate to urban–rural poverty trends. PAs from two Asian transitionals (Laos and Mongolia) show rural poverty slightly below urban; very equal rural distribution, without the huge regional inequalities characterizing China, outweighed the effects of extractive policies. However, in 1993 the rural headcount below the national poverty line in Vietnam was 57.2 per cent, as against 25.9 per cent in the urban areas (World Bank 1998: 66).

Of ten 'European' transitionals reviewed by Milanovic (1995), mean rural income (or expenditure) fell during the transition, relative to urban, in eight and stayed unchanged in two. In Poland, farmers—historically the group with the highest poverty incidence—saw it rise from 11 per cent in 1987–9 to 27 per cent during 1991–4, much faster than other groups (Milanovic 1998: 94). Yet, given the substantial rise in urban inequality, urban poverty may have outpaced rural in the few transitionals (Romania, Albania, Armenia) that undertook radically egalitarian private distribution of formerly collective and/or state lands. In Romania in 1989–93 rural poverty incidence tripled (to over 23 per cent), but urban incidence exploded, from

---

[35] Costa Rica PA, Annexes: 33, Table 2. The headcount trends 1980–90 are Argentina, metro 3.0–6.4%, rural 11.5–23.4% (1989); Bolivia, urban 34.1–54.0%, rural 81.3–76.2%; Brazil, urban 23.9–33.2%, rural 55.0–62.1%; Chile, urban 15.9–9.9%, rural 34.0–10.4%; Colombia, urban 13.0–8.0%, rural 68.4–40.6%; Costa Rica, urban 9.9–3.5%, rural 16.3–3.2%; El Salvador, urban 23.6–41.5%, rural 50.6–51.4%; Guatemala, urban 35.7–50.9%, rural 52.7–76.5%; Honduras, urban 38.8–54.5%, rural 70.6–82.6%; Mexico, urban 9.4–14.1%, rural 19.7–26.9%.

[36] Weakly; different national poverty lines were used, making aggregation problematic.

[37] However, first, the data for one of the countries (Bolivia) show initial rural poverty incidence below urban (probably because of an inappropriately high urban–rural cost-of-living differential) and rising at almost exactly the same modest rate; second, if poverty trend data for Chile were available, they would probably show convergence between the two good surveys of 1987 and 1992, since rural and urban mean income converged and low-end inequality in both sectors fell at roughly similar rates (Ferreira and Litchfield 1998).

1 to 17 per cent. Even in some transitionals with largely unreformed collective or state farms (notably the Ukraine) tiny family plots have provided more support for low-income groups in rural than in urban areas.

However, given the small scale of agricultural reform or development in Russia and most other transitional economies and the divergence of urban from rural mean incomes, most rural and urban PGIs (and headcounts) have probably diverged, though more research is needed.

Global overview

There is no evidence for a global decline in relative rural poverty, either since adjustment or in the longer term. In several African countries it has declined from a high level associated with rural price repression and urban job protection that proved increasingly unaffordable. In South and East Asia, notably in China and India, and (despite limited evidence) in the transitionals, relative rural poverty has, if anything, risen. For Latin America the evidence is mixed and inconclusive. Globally, the impact of changes in intrasectoral distribution on relative rural poverty seems at least as important as that of differential sectoral growth.

How does the relative rural poverty story relate to the message of Section 5.2? In Asia and the transitionals (except in Indonesia) we see no convergence between rural and urban poverty *or* mean income. Elsewhere the stories differ slightly. Latin America shows some convergence in mean income, but no general reduction in relative rural poverty, perhaps because rising rural inequality affected the lowest tercile especially. Relative rural poverty falls in Africa, but the overall distribution data in Section 5.2 are not good enough to allow this to be linked to a trend in any one component of inequality.

REFERENCES

Ahuja, V. *et al.* (1997). Everyone's miracle? Revisiting poverty and inequality in East Asia. World Bank Directions in Development Series. World Bank: Washington DC.

Akita, T., R. Lukman, and Y. Yamada (1999). Inequality in the distribution of household expenditures in Indonesia: A theil decomposition analysis. *The Developing Economies* 37(2), 197–221.

Anand, S., and S. M. H. Kanbur (1993). The Kuznets process and the inequality-development relationship. *Journal of Development Economics* 40(1), 25–52.

Bénabou, R. (1996). Inequality and growth. *NBER Macroeconomics Annual: Vol.11*. MIT Press: Cambridge, MA.

Bourguignon, F., and C. Morrison (1998). Inequality and development: The role of dualism. *Journal of Development Economics* 57, 233–57.

Canagarajah, S., D. Mazumdar, and Y. Xiao (1998). The structure and determinants of inequality and poverty reduction in Ghana, 1988–92. World Bank Working Paper, WPS1900 Series. World Bank: Washington, DC.

Datt, G., and M. Ravallion (1996). Why have some Indian states done better than others at reducing rural poverty? World Bank Poverty Analysis and Policy Division Working Paper 1594. World Bank: Washington, DC.

Deaton, A., and A. Tarozzi (2000). Prices and poverty in India. Princeton University Working Paper 196. Princeton University: Princeton NJ.

de Haan, A., and M. Lipton (1998). Poverty in emerging Asia: Progress, setbacks, and log-jams. *Asian Development Review* 16(2), 135–76.

—— *et al.* (1997). *The Role of Government and Public Policy Alleviation in Sub-Saharan Africa.* African Economic Research Consortium, Nairobi.

Deininger, K., and L. Squire (1996). A new data set measuring income inequality. *World Bank Economic Review* 10(3).

Eastwood, R. K., and M. Lipton (1999). The impact of changes in human fertility on poverty. *Journal of Development Studies* 36(1), 1–30.

—— and —— (2000). Rural–urban dimensions of inequality change. WIDER Working Paper 200. UNU/WIDER: Helsinki.

Estudillo, J. P. (1997). Income inequality in the Phillipines, 1961–91. *The Developing Economies* XXXV-1.

Ferreira, F. H. G., and J. A. Litchfield (1998). Calm after the storms: Income distribution in Chile. 1987–94. PREM Policy Research Paper 1960. World Bank: Washington, DC.

—— and —— (1999). Education or inflation? The roles of structural factors and macroeconomic instability in explaining Brazilian inequality in the 1980s. STICERD Discussion Paper DARP 4. London School of Economics: London.

Firdausy, C. M. (1994). Urban poverty in Indonesia: Trends, issues and policies. *Asian Development Review* 12(1), 68–89.

Gang, F., D. Perkins, and L. Sabin (1996). China's economic performance and prospects. Mimeo, Paper for the Asian Development Bank's Emerging Asia Project, ADB: Manila.

Glewwe, P. (1986). Income distribution in Sri Lanka. *Journal of Development Economics* 45.

Grootaert, C., L. Demery, and R. Kanbur (1996). *Analyzing Poverty and Policy Reform: The Experience of Cote d'Ivoire.* Avebury, Aldershot.

Howes, S. (1993). *Income Inequality in Urban China in the 1980s: Levels, Trends and Determinants.* STICERD, London School of Economics: London.

—— and A. Hussain (1994). Regional growth and inequality in rural China. STICERD Programme of Research into Economic Transformation and Public Finance 11. London School of Economics: London.

Kanbur, R., and N. Lustig (1999). Why is inequality back on the agenda? Annual World Bank Conference on Development Economics, 28–29 April, World Bank, Washington, DC.

Krueger, A., A. Valdes, and M. Schiff (1995). Agricultural incentives in developing countries: Measuring the effect of sectoral and economy-wide policies. In G. Peters (ed.), *Agricultural Economics.* Elgar: Aldershot.

Lambert, P. J., and J. R. Aronson (1993). Inequality decomposition analysis and the Gini coefficient revisited. *Economic Journal* 103, 1221–7.

Lipton, M. (1977). *Why Poor People Stay Poor: Urban Bias and World Development.* Temple Smith and Harvard University Press: Cambridge, MA.

—— and M. Ravallion (1995). Poverty and policy. In J. Behrman and T. N. Srivanasan (eds), *Handbook of Development Economics,* Volume III. Elsevier: Amsterdam.

Londoño, J.-L., and M. Székely (1997). Persistent poverty and excess inequality: Latin America 1970–95. Office of the Chief Economist Working Paper 357. Inter-American Development Bank: Washingtond, DC.

Lundberg, M., and L. Squire (1999). Growth and inequality: Extracting the lessons for policymakers. Mimeo; May, World Bank: Washington, DC.

McCulloch, N., and R. Baulch (1999). Poverty, inequality and growth in Zambia. Mimeo; 2 June, Institute of development Studies: Brighton.

Milanovic, B. (1995). Poverty, inequality and social policy in transition economies. Mimeo.

——(1998). Income, inequality and poverty during the transition from planned to market economy. World Bank Regional and Sectoral Studies. World Bank: Washington, DC.

Mukherjee, D., and A. F. Shorrocks (1982). A decomposition analysis of the trend in UK income inequality. *Economic Journal* 92, 886–902.

Panuco-Laguette, H., and M. Székely (1996). Income distribution and poverty in Mexico. In V. Bulmer-Thomas (ed.), *The New Economic Model in Latin America and its Impact on Income Distribution and Poverty*. Macmillan: Basingstoke.

Ravallion, M. (1993). *Poverty Comparisons (Fundamentals of Pure and Applied Economics Series)* vol. 56. Harwood Academic Press: Chur.

——and M. Huppi (1991). Measuring changes in poverty: A methodological case study of Indonesia during an adjustment period. *World Bank Economic Review* 5, 57–84.

Robinson, S. (1976). A note on the U-hypothesis relating income inequality and economic development. *American Economic Review* 66, 437–40.

Srinivasan, T. N. (1999). Poverty and reforms in India. Paper presented at NBER-NCAER Conference on Reform, 13–15 December 1999, New Delhi.

Stiglitz, J. E. (1999). On liberty, the right to know and public discourse: The role of transparency in public life. In M. Gibney (ed.), *Globalizing Rights: 1999 Oxford Amnesty Lectures*. Oxford University Press: Oxford.

Wodon, Q. T. (1999). Micro determinants of consumption, poverty, growth, and inequality in Bangladesh. World Bank Working Papers WPS 2076. World Bank: Washington, DC.

World Bank (1997). *China 2020: Sharing Rising Incomes*. World Bank: Washington, DC.

——(1998). *World Development Indicators*. World Bank: Washington, DC.

——(various). *Poverty Assessment* (PAs): Belarus, 15380-BY (1996). Brazil (2 vols.), 14323-BR (1995). Colombia (2 vols.): 12673-CO (1994). Congo 16043-COB (1997). Cote d'Ivoire 15640-IV (1997). Costa Rica (1997). Ecuador 14533-EC (1995). Guatemala 12313-GU (1995). Hashemite Kingdom of Jordan (2 vols.) 126750-JO, (1994). Honduras 13317-HO (1994). India 16483-IN (1997). Lao PDR 13992-LA (1995). Lesotho 13171-LSO (1995). Madagascar (2 vols.) 14044-MAG (1996). Mauritania 12182-MAU (1994). Mongolia 15723-MOG (1996). Nicaragua (2 vols.) 14038-NI (1995). Nigeria 14733-UNI (1996). Paraguay 12293-PA (1994). Philippines 14933-PH (1995). Romania 16462-RO (1997). Russia 14110-RU (1995). Sri Lanka 13431-CE (1995). Tanzania 14982-TA (1996). Togo 15526-TO (1996). Thailand 15689-TH (1996). Uganda 12029-UG (1993). Vietnam 13442-VN (1995). Zambia 12985-ZA (1994).

Zhang, P. (1997). Income Distribution during the Transition in China. WIDER Working Paper 138. UNU/WIDER: Helsinki.

PART III

RECENT FACTORS INFLUENCING THE DISTRIBUTION OF INCOME

6

Globalization, Technology, and Income Inequality: A Critical Analysis*

AJIT SINGH AND RAHUL DHUMALE

6.1. INTRODUCTION

This study provides a critical analysis of some widely accepted explanations for the significant changes in income distribution, which have occurred in many advanced countries during the last two decades. The subject has attracted a great deal of attention from economists. However, much of this vast literature emphasizes the role of globalization and technology, either singly or together, as the primary influence(s) on income distribution during this period, in industrial economies. The study assesses the validity of these propositions and provides an alternative analytical and policy perspective. It also considers whether these globalization and/or technology theses can be applied to developing countries.

An analysis of the relationship between income inequality, globalization, and technological change raises complex theoretical, empirical, and policy questions. There are disputes about facts as well as the evidential value of some of the facts, which are adduced in support of particular theories. At the analytical level, there are not only distinct approaches from the various (labour, international) fields of economics to these questions but also within international economics, there are diverse schools of thought.

It is not the purpose of this study to provide yet another survey of the literature. This would be a duplication of effort—several excellent surveys already exist.[1] Our main objective is to review the principal issues in the continuing debate on the subject, to assess what conclusions have been reached, how robust these conclusions are, to outline some fresh issues which require research, and importantly to provide an alternative

* This is a revised and shortened version of the paper 'Trade, Technology, Institutions and Social Norms: A Perspective on the Determinants of Income Inequality', presented at the WIDER workshop on 'Rising Income Inequality and Poverty Reduction: Are They Compatible?' in Helsinki in December 1999. The authors are grateful to the workshop participants, and particularly to Giovanni Andrea Cornia for his detailed and helpful comments. Their intellectual debt to him and to Tony Atkinson is reflected in the study. However, the usual disclaimer applies.

[1] See for example Burtless (1995), Gottschalk and Smeeding (1997), and Slaughter and Swagel (1997) for recent reviews of the literature. See also Atkinson and Bourguignon (2000).

analytical and policy perspective on these questions. The study concentrates relatively more on advanced than on developing countries. This is not because the question of income distribution is any less significant for the latter group of countries than for the former—indeed quite the contrary. The main reason for this focus is not only that greater and more reliable information is available for advanced countries but also that a wider (though admittedly rather contentious) literature exists for this group.

The study is organized as follows. Section 6.2 outlines the main stylized facts about inequality of income distribution and other unfavourable labour market tendencies (high unemployment and deindustrialization), which have come to characterize industrial economies during the 1980s and 1990s; it also reviews the relevant characteristics of North–South trade in manufactured products. Section 6.3 outlines the nature of the 'Transatlantic Consensus', which has emerged in this area, notwithstanding serious methodological differences between trade and labour economists. This consensus gives a unified explanation for increased income inequality in the United States and of high unemployment in Europe within the same conceptual framework. Section 6.4 provides a critique of the consensus and suggests an alternative perspective on income inequality, unemployment, and deindustrialization in advanced countries. Sections 6.5 and 6.6 assess the extent to which changes in income inequality in developing countries can be attributed to globalization, technology, and financial liberalization. Section 6.7 sums up the discussion and outlines policy conclusions, which are substantially different than those that follow from the Transatlantic Consensus.

6.2. ADVERSE LABOUR MARKET OUTCOMES IN THE NORTH AND TRADE WITH THE SOUTH: STYLIZED FACTS

6.2.1. *Adverse Labour Market Outcomes*

Although the focus of this study is to examine the effects of globalization (mainly in the form of reduction in trade barriers) and technology on income distribution, it is important to appreciate that in popular perception trade with the South is being held responsible not only for increased inequality and wage dispersion in advanced countries but also for other important labour market outcomes. The latter include specifically deindustrialization and very high overall unemployment, which has afflicted industrial countries over the last quarter century. These two variables are also briefly considered here, not least because as we shall see later, they also influence income distribution.

These misgivings of the general public have been given powerful intellectual backing by Adrian Wood's (1994) influential treatise. The Wood study reached the conclusion that trade with the Third World during the 1980s and 1990s has been a major contributor to all the observed unfavourable labour market tendencies in the North: (a) deindustrialization; (b) high unemployment, and (c) growing income inequality. Wood estimated that Southern competition resulted in a net reduction of

12 per cent in manufacturing employment in the North during the period studied (1980s and early 1990s). Further, to the extent such competition-induced labour saving technical progress in advanced countries, this probably led to additional job losses of equal magnitude. He also assembled a considerable array of evidence to suggest tentatively that increased inequality between skilled and unskilled labour in the North, particularly in the United States, has largely been a result of southern competition rather than arising from technical change. Wood (1998), however, goes on to suggest that whilst skills-biased technical progress does have a significant influence on labour market inequality, it is only globalization that can account for the increase in the rate of change of observed income inequality in the recent period. Wood has received important analytical support for his conclusions from some, but by no means all, leading trade economists (notably Leamer 1998, 2000). This issue will be taken up further in Section 6.3 below.

Table 6.1 reports unemployment rates in industrial countries and indicates the alarming increase in these rates since 1973, which marks the end of the so-called Golden Age (1950–73) of economic development in these countries. Particularly striking in this table are the figures for Germany. For the 10 years before 1973 (the last decade of the Golden Age), the average unemployment rate in West Germany was only slightly over 1 per cent. However, during the last 10 years the average unemployment rate has climbed to 9 per cent. Although the latter figure is to some extent an overstatement as it includes East Germany, nevertheless the difference is still quite dramatic. As for deindustrialization, manufacturing employment in G7 countries fell by 15 per cent on average during 1970–93. The extent of changes ranged from −45.7 per cent in the United Kingdom to a positive figure of 3.6 per cent in Canada. Thus, in the United Kingdom the manufacturing labour force was literally halved over this 15-year period, representing massive deindustrialization[2] (see UNCTAD 1995).

Table 6.1. *Standardized unemployment rate in industrialized countries, 1964–99 (average annual percentage changes)*

Country	1964–73	1974–9	1980–9	1990–9
United States	4.5	6.7	7.3	5.8
Japan	1.2	1.9	2.5	3.0
Germany	1.1	3.2	7.0	9.0
United Kingdom	3.0	5.0	9.0	7.3
Total of G7 countries	3.1	5.0	6.9	7.1
Total EU 15	2.7	4.7	9.0	10.3
Total OECD	3.0	4.9	7.2	7.4

Source: OECD (1995a).

[2] However, there has importantly been a trend increase in UK productivity growth. For a fuller analysis of UK deindustrialization and its comparison with the United States, see Howes and Singh (2000) and Singh (1987, 1989). See also Kitson and Michie (1996), and Rowthorn and Ramaswamy (1997).

Comprehensive information on income inequality and wage dispersion in the North during the 1980s is given in Table 6.2. The table reports data on both market and disposable income distribution in as comparable a form as possible for a large number of industrial countries.[3]

Table 6.2. *Changes in market and disposable income inequality in industrial countries, 1980s*

Country	Years, change	Market income inequality	Disposable income inequality
United Kingdom	1981–91	+++	++++
United States	1980–93	+++	+++
Sweden	1980–93	++	+++
Australia	1980–1, 1989–90	+	+
Denmark	1981–90	+	+
New Zealand	1981–9	+	+
Japan	1981–90	+	+
Netherlands	1981–9	+	+
Norway	1982–9, 1985–92	+	+
Belgium	1985–92	+	+
Canada	1980–92	+	0
Israel	1979–92	+	0
Finland	1981–92	+++	0
France	1979–89	0	0
Portugal	1980–90	0	0
Spain	1980–90	n.a.	0
Ireland	1980–7	+	0
West Germany	1983–90	+	0
Italy	1977–91	—	—

Note: Degree of change is coded as follows:

Designation	Interpretation	Rate of change in Gini (%)
—	Small decline	−5 or more
0	Zero	−4–+4
+	Small increase	+5–10
++	Moderate increase	10–15
+++	Large increase	16–29
++++	Extremely large increase	30 or more

Source: Gottschalk and Smeeding (1997).

[3] In the nature of the data on income distribution, such international comparisons can never be quite exact as the definition of income may differ between countries; different adjustments may be made for household size. Comparison in terms of trends is more reliable than levels, but even trends may be affected. See further Gottschalk and Smeeding (1997) and Atkinson (2000).

There is an enormous amount of information in this table, but the relevant points for our purposes together with those from other data not presented here may be summarized as follows (on this see also Chapters 2 and 9):

1. Most countries in the stated periods recorded either some increase in inequality of market income or no change at all. However, in the case of disposable income, there were many countries, which show no change in inequality despite the fact that there was a worsening of market income distribution.

2. The highest increase in income inequality during the 1980s has been reported for the United Kingdom. The Gini coefficient for the UK disposable income increased by a massive 30 per cent. In fact during this period, the UK market income inequality rose less than inequality in disposable income.

3. Sweden, normally a country with relatively equal incomes, also experienced a large rise in the Gini coefficient for disposable income. This increase was also greater than that for the market income in Sweden.

4. The Organization for Economic Co-operation and Development (OECD 1995*b*) provided information on earnings dispersion for industrial countries between 1975 and 1990. These data (not presented here) suggested that although dispersion as measured by the ratio of the ninetieth percentile to the tenth percentile was increasing in advanced countries, this was not true for all countries. Germany was a notable exception. Moreover, the timing and the extent of the increase in dispersion were far from being uniform between countries.

5. Another important aspect of growing inequality, which has received particular attention in the United States, is the increasing gap since 1970 between skilled and unskilled workers. Slaughter and Swagel (1997) suggest that in the United States relative wages of less skilled workers have fallen steeply since the late 1970s. Between 1979 and 1988 the average wage of a college graduate relative to the wage of a high school graduate rose by 20 per cent; the average weekly earnings of males in their forties to those of males in their twenties rose by 25 per cent, thus putting a premium on experience. This growing inequality reverses a trend of previous decades (by some estimates going back as far as the 1910s) towards greater income equality between the more skilled and the less skilled. At the same time, the average real wage in the United States has grown only slowly since the early 1970s and the real wage for unskilled workers has actually fallen.

6. It will be seen to be highly significant for subsequent analysis that the data on measures of income inequality for the 1990s do not conform to the pattern observed in the 1980s. Thus in Chapter 9 Atkinson reports that unlike in the 1980s, when there was an enormous increase in the Gini coefficient for disposable income in the United Kingdom, during 1990–7 it hardly changed at all. Indeed, the OECD (1996) found that in the first half of the 1990s, there was no evidence of a general increase in earnings inequality in OECD countries; of the sixteen countries studied, it rose in half and fell in half. Similarly, Katz (1999) observes that the US wage structure (measured in terms of real hourly wages of the ninetieth, fiftieth, and tenth per centile of workers)

widened between 1980 and the early 1990s, but narrowed between 1996 and 1998. There has also been rapid real wage growth since 1996.

7. In Chapter 9, Atkinson rightly emphasizes another point in relation to the observed changes in income inequality, which is significant. He suggests that it is not correct to speak about long-term trends in income inequality since what the data show, not only for the United Kingdom but also for other countries, are periodic episodes of increasing, decreasing, or constant inequality.

6.2.2. *North–South Trade in Manufactures*[4]

These unfavourable developments in northern labour markets occurred at the same time as a major spurt in imports from developing to industrial country markets. An important part of Wood's empirical case for suggesting that trade is the main cause of all the adverse outcomes in the post-1980 period for northern workers rests on the close negative correlation between changes in manufacturing imports as a proportion of the gross domestic product (GDP) and manufacturing employment share for a cross-section of industrial countries. Further, he puts a great deal of weight on coincidence of the timing of the two phenomena in his rejection of technical change rather than trade as the main causal factor. In assessing the strength of Wood's analysis, it is therefore necessary to examine the nature, pattern, and volume of North–South trade in manufactures in recent decades.

The relevant points, which emerge from the analysis of the North–South manufacturing trade during the last three decades, may be summarized as follows:

1. It is indeed true that the volume of manufacturing imports from the South to the North rose at a rapid average rate of 12 per cent per annum between 1970 and 1990, but the starting volume was quite low. Consequently, the total imports from developing countries, including China, in the early 1990s constitute only 2 per cent of the combined GDP of the OECD countries (World Bank 1995). Many economists therefore find it difficult to see how such large changes in unemployment or income inequality in advanced countries can be attributed to this marginal volume of trade with developing countries (see, however, below).

2. The North's manufacturing exports to the South have invariably been greater than its corresponding imports throughout the period. The data indicates that advanced countries enjoyed a surplus of nearly US$100 billion in 1993 (measured in 1985 prices) in their manufacturing trade with developing countries. This amounted to about 1 per cent of the North's combined GDP in that year, which significantly was much the same figure as that recorded 20 years earlier in 1974.

3. The pattern of changes in North–South manufacturing trade balance is of significance. There are three distinct phases in the evolution of this balance. During the first phase, 1970–82, the North's trade balance with the South rose; it declined in the second between 1982–9 and started to rise again in the third phase in the 1990s. The proximate causes of this evolution lay in the great surge of petrodollar borrowings and spending by

---

[4] Unless indicated otherwise, the data used in this subsection comes from UNCTAD (1995).

developing countries in the 1970s; the debt crises in the 1980s, which greatly reduced southern imports from advanced countries; and the post-1989 period when economic revival in developing countries again lead to increased imports from the North.

4. An analysis of changes in manufacturing employment in industrial countries suggests that these were much more closely related to recessions in these countries (1973–4, 1980–2, 1990–1) and to a reduction in exports to developing countries in the 1980s, rather than to rising manufacturing imports from the latter. It is therefore not surprising that there is very little correspondence between timing of unemployment surges in advanced countries and either that of the growth of imports or of changes in trade balance. UNCTAD (1995) observes: 'Not only was the growth of manufactured imports from the South actually faster in the 1970s than in the 1980s, but also the most important influence on the trade balance in the 1980s came through a decline in northern exports due to unfavourable economic conditions in the South.'

5. Finally, it is important to note that there have been previous surges of imports into advanced countries of similar magnitudes as those observed during the 1970s and 1980s without leading to adverse labour market consequences. Data on import penetration by low-wage developing countries into industrial country markets between 1970 and 1992 and corresponding information for the period 1958–75 on import penetration by the then low-wage (where wages were less than half those of the United States) countries of Italy and Japan of the European Economic Commission (EEC) and US manufacture markets indicate that the import penetration of industrial country markets during the two periods (1958–75 and 1975–92) was on a roughly comparable scale. However, this earlier fast penetration of US and EEC markets by Japan and Italy did not result in either mass unemployment in Europe or stagnant real wages and increasing income inequality in the United States. Indeed, during 1960–73, average US wages rose at 2 per cent per annum and the country had a better employment record than it has achieved subsequently. Howes and Singh (2000) argue that the main reason for the stagnation of average real wages in the United States between 1973 and 1996 is that the economy in the post-1973 period has been expanding at a lower long-term rate than before. Between 1960 and 1973, the US GDP grew at an annual rate of 4 per cent compared with 2.3 per cent since 1973.

6.3. THE TRANSATLANTIC CONSENSUS

As indicated in the Introduction, studies to estimate the effects of trade on income distribution are methodologically contentious with trade economists using rather different methods than labour economists to study the same phenomenon. There are, moreover, important methodological differences between the trade economists themselves—see for example Krugman (2000) and Leamer (2000).[5] Nevertheless as

[5] For a discussion of the methodological issues see Singh and Dhumale (2000), the longer working paper version of this present study. To save space this discussion has not been included in the present chapter. However, it is important to note that a main issue between the trade and labour economists is whether prices or quantities are the chief channel through which international trade affects wage inequality. See the reference to the relevant literature in Singh and Dhumale (2000).

noted by Atkinson in Chapter 9, there is a remarkable degree of consensus among scholars on both sides of the Atlantic concerning one central issue. The increased income inequality in the United States and the United Kindgom as well as mass unemployment in continental Europe are both ascribed to a single uniform cause: a shift of demand away from unskilled towards skilled workers. In the United States and the United Kingdom, because of their flexible labour markets, this shift leads to increasing inequality. In continental Europe, on the other hand, with rigid labour markets, the same causal factor results in large increases in unemployment, as the relative wages of skilled and unskilled workers do not change.

This is of course a straightforward demand–supply model, although analysts disagree about the reasons for the rise in the relative demand for skilled workers. Some, like Wood, attribute it largely to trade with low-wage developing countries. Others, probably the large majority of mainstream economists (including both specialists in trade and labour markets), contrary to Wood, put far greater emphasis on technology and relatively little on trade.

Despite the Transatlantic Consensus, this model has serious limitations as an adequate explanation for the observed changes in income distribution in advanced countries during the last two decades. These shortcomings may be summarized as follows:

1. At a theoretical level Davis (1998a,b) has pointed out that the predictions of mass unemployment in Europe and income inequality in the United States do not follow from the two-factor, two-goods, two-countries model normally used in the theory of international trade. To capture the essential elements of the Transatlantic Consensus at a theoretical level, at least a three-country model is needed, which can examine the implications of trade between Europe, the United States, and the newly industrializing countries. However, a general equilibrium analysis of such a model does not yield the predictions postulated in the consensus.

2. At an empirical level the trade story is not convincing either as earnings dispersion has increased not only in the traded sector but also in the far bigger non-traded sector. This suggests some common forces at work other than trade. Moreover, as Krugman (2000) and others have pointed out, despite the relative rise in skills premiums in the 1980s, the demand for skilled workers rose rather than fell in most sectors of the economy. This again points towards a non-trade explanation, indeed, in the direction of a broad-based skill-biased technical progress.

3. Importantly the available information on income inequality for the 1990s creates difficulties with both the trade and technology explanations for the Transatlantic Consensus model (TCM). The 1990s data do not confirm the pattern of increasing inequality observed for the 1980s. In many countries, income inequality has not worsened despite growing imports from developing countries. Further in both the United States and the United Kingdom, the wages of the bottom decile relative to the median wage have increased, thus undermining the very basis of TCM.

4. Katz (1999) provides a useful analysis of the college/high school wage premium in the United States in terms of the variations in the relative supply of and the relative

demand for college and high school equivalents for successive decades since 1940 (see Table 6.3). One important point that emerges from this table is the growth of relative demand for college graduates in the 1990s has fallen considerably compared not just with the 1980s but also with the earlier decades, starting in the 1950s. This evidence creates additional difficulties for the skill-biased technology hypothesis. If the latter hypothesis was valid for the last two decades, the data should indicate a trend increase in the rate of growth of relative demand for college graduates in the 1980s and the 1990s, which Katz's figures do not.[6]

There are two types of further evidence, which are also incompatible with the skill-biased technical progress hypothesis. First, there are data for the United States and the United Kingdom to indicate that wage differentials have not only increased in individual industries, but also within individual, narrowly defined occupational groups. To suggest that increased earning inequality for lawyers, doctors, accountants, cooks, waiters, and so on is all due to skill-biased technical change brought about by a general purpose technology such as information technology (IT) is not plausible. Second, the male earnings distribution data for the United States in the 1990s

Table 6.3. *Growth of college/high school relative wage, supply, demand, selected periods, 1940–98*

Ten-year periods	Relative wage	Relative supply	Relative demand
1940–50	−1.86	2.35	−0.25
1950–60	0.83	2.91	4.08
1960–70	0.69	2.55	3.52
1970–80	−0.74	4.99	3.95
1980–90	1.51	2.53	4.65
1990–8	0.36	2.25	2.76
Longer periods			
1940–70	−0.11	2.61	2.45
1970–98	0.38	3.33	3.86
1940–60	−0.51	2.63	1.92
1960–80	−0.02	3.77	3.74
1980–98	1.00	2.41	3.81

Note: The relative wage measure is the log college/high school wage differential. The relative supply and demand measures are for college equivalents (college graduates plus half of those with some college) and high school equivalents (those with 12 or fewer years of schooling and half of those with some college). The implied relative demand changes assume an aggregate elasticity of substitution between college equivalents and high school equivalents of 1.4. The relative supply measure adjusts for changes in the age–sex composition of the pools of college and high school equivalents; see Autor *et al.* (1998) for details.

Original source: Autor *et al.* (1998). Updated by Katz (1999).

[6] In a different form, the technology hypothesis can still survive even if there is no observed break in trend for the skill premium in the 1980s. See further Murphy *et al.* (1998).

indicate that while the wages of the bottom decile have improved relative to the median, the latter has declined in relation to the earnings of the top decile. However, in France the top decile to the median ratio was the same in 1996 as in 1974; the bottom decile to the median ratio rose slightly over this period, arguably due to the French minimum wage protection for low-paid workers. However, as there are no such legal limits to incomes at the upper end of the distribution, this might be expected to be market determined. It would be difficult in that case to attribute the observed changes at the top end of the male earnings distribution in the two countries to a general skill-biased technological change, which affected all industrial countries (Atkinson 2000). Another limitation of the TCM is that it ignores capital market variables altogether. These clearly affect income distribution both theoretically and at an empirical level.

To sum up, the TCM, despite its wide acceptance, is deeply flawed—even under its own narrow tenets. Neither trade nor technology explanations are compatible with some important data for advanced countries, particularly for the 1990s. The consensus also has rather weak theoretical foundations.

6.4. BEYOND THE TRANSATLANTIC CONSENSUS

A very important limitation of the literature on trade and technology reviewed above is that it provides at best a bivariate explanation of changes in income distribution; the analysis is almost entirely in terms of either trade or technology or a combination of the two. However, economists know that income distribution is subject to many influences other than just technology and trade. The most important of the additional variables include levels of employment and unemployment and macroeconomic conditions in general, deindustrialization, the strength of the trade unions, minimum wage legislation, terms of trade, and exchange rates. There are both theoretical reasons as well as empirical evidence to indicate the relevance of each of these additional variables for examining changes in income distribution. To illustrate, Burtless (1995) found that changes in the unemployment rate accounted for about 20 per cent of the increase in earnings inequality of the US males between 1954 and 1986. At the theoretical level, both competitive and segmented labour market models can be used to explain why when there is full employment there is a relative increase in earnings at the lower end of the distribution, and why increased unemployment and the reduced demand for labour has the opposite effect.

With respect to unionization, Card (1992) suggested that a fifth of the increase in the variance of wages of the adult male population in the United States could be attributed to this variable. Deindustrialization can cause an increase in earning inequality, quite independently of the unionization effect, as structural change in the course of economic development leads to a reduction in the relatively well-paid manufacturing jobs and an increase in the less well-paid service jobs (see further Harrison and Bluestone 1990).

At an empirical level in order to assess the relative explanatory power of these variables in accounting for the observed changes in income distribution, it is necessary to carry out a multivariate analysis. Galbraith (1998) provides one such study for recent changes in income distribution in the United States. His results indicate that most (90 per cent) of the US wage dispersion variation in this period can be explained by macroeconomic variables such as unemployment rates, movements in terms of trade and exchange rates, and changes in minimum wages. Neither trade nor technology figures directly in the analysis; these would, however, have indirect effects through variables such as exchange rate changes included in the regression equation. Galbraith's analysis of inequality in the US wage structure over the longer period (1920–92) suggests that a single variable—change in the unemployment rate—explains 70 per cent of the variation in interindustry wage dispersion. His results provide a rough rule of thumb; when unemployment averages about 5.5 per cent, there is no change in inequality; a rate higher than this leads to a rise in inequality whereas an unemployment figure of less than 5 per cent reduces inequality. Analogous to the concept of nonaccelerating inflation rate of unemployment (NAIRU), Galbraith suggests that an unemployment rate of 5.5 per cent should be called the 'ethical rate of unemployment'.

Many economists draw attention to the specific case of Canada, which did not experience the same increase in income inequality in the 1980s as those recorded in the United States (see Table 6.2). This is despite the fact that the United States and Canada are close trading partners, have similar levels of per capita incomes, and both belong to the North American Free Trade Agreement (NAFTA). It is suggested by the adherents of the Transatlantic Consensus that the reason for the lower increase in inequality in Canada in the 1980s was the relatively greater growth in the supply of college-educated labour in Canada than in the United States. This was made possible by the fact that in Canada university education is subsidized by the government, unlike in the United States. However, McFail (2000) in her recent comprehensive multivariate analysis of changes in income distribution in Canada in the 1980s finds that the most important influences on earnings inequality were the level of unemployment and decline in unionization. The author reports that this finding is robust to various measurement choices, including gender, income concept, and work status. Other significant variables were deindustrialization and increased supply of male college-educated workers. McFail found trade and technology to be insignificant determinants of income inequality.

Apart from the important role of macroeconomic factors and labour market institutions the analysis of income distribution in advanced countries will be seriously incomplete without reference to changing social norms. As noted earlier, a significant stylized fact concerning income distributions in these countries is the increasing share of the top decile in the United States and the United Kingdom but not in France. It will be argued below, in agreement with Atkinson (2000, as well as Chapter 9 of this volume), that changing social norms are a necessary explanation of the observed changes at the top end of the income distribution within and between industrial countries. Economists are often uncomfortable with non-economic explanations. It is therefore important to observe that social norms such as that of fairness have a long and respectable pedigree in labour economics—Pigou (1920), Hicks (1963), Phelps Brown (1997). More recently, in a series of path-breaking contributions Professor Fehr and his colleagues (e.g. see Fehr and Gächter 2000) have presented analyses and empirical evidence to suggest the critical significance of the norms of fairness in all areas of economics.

Atkinson (2000, as well as Chapter 9 of this volume) argues that as a consequence of the changes in the social norms, workers have moved from cooperative, solidaristic wages to individual wage determination in accordance with their own productivity. Apart from providing an alternative theoretical rationale for social norms, Singh and Dhumale (2000) supplement Atkinson's analysis by giving an historical account of the process by which the social norms came to be changed during the last two decades compared with the period before. This issue is important from a policy perspective since it gives us an indication of how such norms may be altered again, this time in the egalitarian direction.

Singh and Dhumale trace the historical evolution of social norms concerning income inequality with changing economic circumstances and power relations. They argue that the outstanding economic performance of advanced countries in the Golden Age (1950–73) was not simply a statistical artefact or an accidental occurrence but was made possible by the adoption of a new model of economic development in these countries in the post-Second World War period. This model, which differed significantly from the one that prevailed in these countries in the pre-war period, emphasized cooperation both at the national level between government, employees, and business as well as at the international level (between nation states). This cooperative economic environment of the Golden Age led to high rates of investment and productivity growth, and with relatively equal income distribution, also to high rates of consumption. The latter justified the initial investment and encouraged further capital formation in a positive feed-back loop. This model of a social market economy was, however, undermined by its own success, and after nearly 25 years of more or less full employment, it fell victim to the economic shocks of the 1970s.[7]

In the event, the Golden Age model of social market economy was abandoned in the late 1970s and early 1980s in favour of the Reagan/Thatcher model of market supremacy. This evolution of a new economic model also involved significant changes in social norms towards acceptance of far more unequal income distribution than before. The new model involved huge institutional changes such as deunionization, deregulation, privatization, and other components of market supremacy. These institutional and related changes in social norms were more readily embraced in the United States and the United Kingdom than by the continental economies. This is the reason why in countries such as France and Germany, there continue to be much narrower differentials between pays of workers and managers, whereas in the Anglo-Saxon countries the enormous increase in such differentials since the Golden

---

[7] This is a highly condensed version of the argument put forward in a long essay (Glyn *et al.* 1990). See also Kindleburger (1992) and Eichengreen (1994).

Age has become commonplace. As seen earlier, it also explains why, while being market determined, the French incomes in the top decile have not increased relative to those of the middle decile while they have risen appreciably in the United States and the United Kingdom.

6.5. TRADE, TECHNOLOGY, AND INEQUALITY IN DEVELOPING COUNTRIES

How do globalization and technology affect income inequality in developing countries? Are the effects analogous to these expected or observed for advanced countries? Our earlier analysis of globalization and income inequality in advanced countries has considered the concept of globalization as essentially being synonymous with free trade, in line with much of the literature on this issue. However, in economic terms, globalization also refers importantly to free capital movements. The latter have assumed great significance in the 1980s and the 1990s for income inequality in many developing countries, particularly in Asia and Latin America. The question of the relationship between capital account liberalization and income distribution deserves special consideration and will be considered separately in the next section. The present section will parallel the discussion for advanced countries and examine the effects of globalization only in the sense of free trade, as well as those of technology, on recent changes in income distribution in developing countries.

In an influential contribution Sachs and Warner (1995) have argued that openness[8] to the world economy (in the sense of trade liberalization and reduced distortions) benefits developing countries through two distinct channels: it raises their growth rates[9] and leads to a convergence of their per capita incomes with the higher per capita incomes of developed countries—in other words, openness leads to beta convergence. In other contributions, Ben-David (1993, 1996) has suggested that countries or regions that integrate through trade liberalization display lower intercountry or interregional income inequality than those which do not; namely, liberalization leads to gamma convergence between countries. Although the author's examples are taken from advanced countries, his general argument is clearly relevant and important for developing countries.

The theoretical foundation for the above studies is the factor-price equalization (FPE) theorem. The latter, however, can only provide a comparative static analysis of the convergence question. Leamer and Levinson (1995) have modified the FPE theorem and given it dynamic content: their factor-price convergence (FPC) theorem suggests that as economies open up and there is freer trade between them, there would be a tendency for factor prices between countries to converge. Both FPE and FPC

---

[8] Sachs and Warner (1995) do not consider capital account liberalization in their empirical application of openness.
[9] The question of the relationship between openness and economic growth will not be considered here. Their relationship has been examined critically in Singh (1997a), Ocampo and Taylor (1998), and Rodriguez and Rodrik (1999) among others.

theorems are, however, valid only under highly restrictive assumptions with respect, among other things, to technology, factor number, and goods, intercountry differences in tastes, and whether or not there are factor intensity reversals. Bhagwati (1994) has argued that FPE is a theoretical curiosum, not applicable to the real world. Indeed, there are many theoretical models, both within and outside the neoclassical tradition, which predict divergence rather than either beta or gamma convergence between trading countries.[10]

Empirical evidence on the question of convergence between developed and developing countries is not very kind to the Sachs and Warner hypothesis. Detailed analysis in UNCTAD 1997 shows that except for a few Asian developing countries (including importantly, however, populous ones like China), there has been divergence rather than convergence between rich and poor countries during the last two decades. Per capita incomes in a majority of developing countries have been falling further behind those of advanced countries for a much longer period. Further, Pieper (1997) suggests that among developing countries themselves differences in total factor productivity growth rates have increased since globalization began in about the mid-1980s.

Slaughter (1997) has challenged the basic statistical methodology of Ben-David's empirical analysis (referred to above) suggesting convergence among countries, which integrate through freer trade. Slaughter uses the superior difference-in-differences method and re-examines the same instances of integration investigated by Ben-David (1993). Slaughter's contribution comes to a clear opposite conclusion: trade liberalization did not lead to convergence in any of the cases studied; on the contrary, it appears to have led to income divergence between countries in the samples.

Further evidence in relation to developing countries on the distributional consequences of globalization comes from Latin America as well as from middle-income countries elsewhere. This evidence suggests that, contrary to what may have been expected on the basis of the Stolper–Samuelson theorem, as well as contrary to the experience of East Asian countries when they liberalized their trade regimes in the 1950s and 1960s, trade liberalization in Latin America in the recent period has not led to reduced wage dispersion between skilled and unskilled workers. For example, in Mexico, Lustig (1998) shows that between 1984 and 1994 wages of skilled workers increased by more than 15 per cent while those of unskilled workers fell by a similar margin.[11] The World Bank (2000) reports that individual country studies for Chile, Columbia, Turkey, and Venezuela also indicate a similar pattern: the skill premia increased in all of these countries.

Wood (1997) has argued that this evidence is compatible with the predictions of a Hecksher–Ohlin model applied to middle-income countries. It is suggested that these countries have a comparative advantage in medium-skill industries. Free trade with low-skill and low-income countries leads to unskilled workers being squeezed out by competition, lowering wages, and employment in these sectors. The expansion

---

[10] See for example Kaldor (1978), Baldwin (1992), and Ventura (1997).

[11] For other studies of wage distribution in Mexico after liberalization, see Harrison and Hanson (1999) and Robertson (2000).

in exports of medium technological goods leads to the observed skill premium in middle-income developing economies.

Although this is a plausible interpretation of some of the facts mentioned earlier, the World Bank (2000) suggests that it is not compatible with the whole of the available evidence. The Bank favours a skill-biased technology interpretation of the observed changes. It provides further bits and pieces of evidence in support of its case. First, despite the rise in the relative wages of skilled labour, the employment of skilled workers has increased. Second, this pattern is observed in all industries rather than there being just increases in certain sectors and declines in others as some trade models predict. The Bank also suggests that 'there is evidence that the pattern of shifts towards more skill-intensive employment in the industrial world in the 1970s and 1980s is being matched by a similar, later shift in the developing world'.[12]

Thus the balance of evidence so far would appear to favour technology over globalization as the more important determinant of income inequality in developing countries. It will, however, be appreciated that this evidence is not strong. The technology story cannot, for example, adequately explain some other striking facts in relation to the evolution of income distribution in developing countries in the recent period. With respect to Mexico, for example, Birdsall (2000) points out that, following the end of the debt crisis, economic growth resumed in Mexico in the 1990s, but most of these gains went to the richest 10 per cent; incomes actually fell for the remaining households. It would be difficult to attribute this phenomenon entirely to skill-biased technical progress. Moreover, the superiority of technology over trade as an explanation for income inequality in developing countries has not considered the free capital movements aspect of globalization. Nor has it considered any of the many other factors (apart from just technology and trade) that may effect income distribution in these countries. It is to these issues that we now turn.

6.6. FINANCIAL LIBERALIZATION AND OTHER FACTORS

In orthodox economic analysis, free capital movement between countries should, in principle, have similar benefits as those of free trade: indeed the former may be regarded as a form of intertemporal trade. International Monetary Fund (IMF 1998) notes 'the same arguments that create a presumption in favour of current account convertibility to promote trade in different goods at a point in time create a presumption in favour of capital account convertibility to promote trade in the same goods at different points in time'.[13] Thus capital account liberalization should lead to a more efficient intertemporal allocation of resources between countries.

A large number of middle-income countries in Asia and Latin America, with encouragement from the Bretton Woods institutions, undertook capital account liberalization in the 1990s. From the mid-1980s, many of these countries were already moving towards liberalization of their financial systems internally, leading to financial

---

[12] *World Development Report 2000/2001* (p. 71).   [13] IMF (1998: 29).

derepression and higher market determined rates of real interest. There was also a huge expansion of the stock markets in developing countries. This internal liberalization of the financial system was gradually supplemented by permitting foreign portfolio capital inflows as well as freer international capital movements generally.[14]

Critics of capital account liberalization argue that, at a theoretical level, the conventional view above ignores crucial aspects of the problem. They suggest that free trade in goods is a fundamentally different concept from that of free movements of capital. Unlike the former, the latter are intrinsically subject to asymmetric information, agency problems, adverse selection, and moral hazard. The critics also emphasize the impact of speculation on asset prices and its implications for systemic instability. Consequently, they regard financial markets as being particularly prone to contagion, herd behaviour, coordination failures, and multiple equilibria.[15]

Capital account liberalization in developing countries has been invariably accompanied by financial crisis and economic instability (see further Demirguc-Kunt and Detragiache 1998). In the cases of Mexico in 1994–95, of Indonesia, Thailand, Korea, and Malaysia in 1997–98, of Brazil and Russia in 1998–89, these crises resulted in 'virtual meltdowns' of the affected economies. There were devastating losses of output and employment leading to hugely adverse distributional consequences. Nobody claims today that such crises will not happen in developing countries in the future.[16]

Apart from the financial crisis, liberalization of the financial system may also have other unfavourable effects on income distribution. Increases in real interest rates benefits lenders and rentiers at the expense of borrowers, including notably the government. A large part of the government budgets in many middle-income countries now goes towards interest payments rather than being used for social expenditure. Moreover, the very fast expansion of the financial sector in real terms, namely in terms of the capital stock and the number of people employed, in developing countries may have led to greater inequality than before despite the increase in employment opportunities in this sector. Financial sector salaries and rewards tend to be extremely high for those at the top end of the distribution. It is difficult to justify such rewards wholly in terms of skill-biased technical progress. They are more compatible with changing social norms and the demonstration effect of the North on the South.

Thus financial liberalization rather than trade is likely to have been a greater influence on the recent evolution of income distribution in developing countries. However, this deliberate concentration on globalization (in the form of either free trade or free capital movement) and technology in this essay does not in any way imply that there are not other factors, which are any less important. Milberg (1997), for example, has emphasized that labour market institutions and employment growth have been more important determinants of income distribution in developing countries than trade. There are also country-specific factors, which cannot be overlooked. These may be illustrated by considering the case of China, which has recorded an appreciable increase in income inequality since the mid-1980s. Students of the Chinese economy

---

[14] See further Singh (1997*a*); Singh and Weisse (1998).

[15] For a fuller discussion see Stiglitz (1994), Singh (1997*b*), and Singh and Zammit (2000).

[16] These issues have been discussed more fully in Singh (1998, 1999) and Singh and Weisse (1998).

attribute this to the growing role of the markets, decentralization, and diminishing fiscal ability of the central authorities to ameliorate regional income inequalities.[17] However, the role of changing social norms typified by Deng's famous slogan 'its glorious to be rich' is also likely to have been important in changing people's perceptions and making increased inequality socially acceptable.

To sum up, both globalization (particularly in the form of financial liberalization) and technology are likely to have influenced the recent evolution of income distribution in developing countries. Available empirical evidence, however, does not allow us to determine the relative importance of these factors either in relation to each other or more importantly with respect to the other kinds of factors outlined above. More varied case studies as well as multivariate analyses are required for an assessment of the relative influence of the various factors. Such empirical work is particularly important for devising appropriate policy response to the challenge of adverse trend changes in income distribution experienced by many developed and developing countries in the last two decades.

6.7. CONCLUSION AND POLICY IMPLICATIONS

There is a large and growing literature on changes in income distribution in advanced countries during the last two decades. Most of the contributions attribute these changes either to globalization (specifically in the form of trade liberalization with low-wage developing countries) or to skill-biased technology, or to a combination of the two. These two factors are thought to have led to reduced relative demand for unskilled labour and to an increase in that for skilled workers. This has resulted in increased income inequality in the United States and the United Kingdom (because of the greater labour market flexibility in these two countries) and in mass unemployment in continental European countries (owing to their rigid labour markets). This study challenges these conclusions on both analytical and empirical grounds. Evidence and analysis here suggests that with respect to developed countries neither trade nor technology is necessarily the most important factor in causing increased income inequality in the recent period. Although there is still considerable theoretical controversy surrounding this issue, there is robust empirical evidence to indicate that the concentration on these two factors to the exclusion of other is not justified. The study has highlighted the role of social norms, economic institutions, and growth of output and employment, in causing the observed changes in income distribution.

With respect to developing countries, the study suggests that there is not sufficient empirical evidence for establishing robust conclusions. Available data indicate that globalization (in the form of financial liberalization rather than trade) and technology are both likely to be significant factors in accounting for the increased inequality in developing countries during the last two decades. However, there is no reason to believe that the contribution of the other relevant factors (e.g. social norms, labour market institutions such as unions and minimum wages, macroeconomic conditions)

---

[17] See further Khan and Riskin (1999).

are likely to be any less important in explaining the observed distributional changes in poor countries.

Turning to policy, in advanced countries, the main proposal of most scholars in this field, whether they believe trade or technology to be the principle factor in causing increased income inequality, is to emphasize increased training and education of the workforce. This would enable workers to keep up with the new technology, as well as to maintain and enhance competitiveness.

The analysis of this study, however, leads to a rather different policy perspective.[18] This perspective, in addition to measures to increase unionization and improve minimum wages, would emphasize faster economic growth and full employment, as being important in themselves as well as leading to more equal income distribution. In other chapters, one of us has suggested that the main constraints in fast growth of the world economy lie today on the demand rather than the supply side.[19] The world economy expanded at a rate of nearly 5 per cent per annum during the Golden Age, but has only grown at a rate of a little over 2 per cent in the subsequent quarter century, despite the availability of new information technology. This technology is regarded by scholars of technical change as being at par with the two or three most important technological revolutions of the last two centuries, for example, the steam engine and electricity. The full potential of this technology is not, however, being realized, mainly because of constraints on the rate of growth of world demand. The analyses of Singh (1999), and Howes and Singh (2000), indicate that the demand constraint is not just a technical question of simply changing monetary and fiscal policies in leading economies, but is a deeply institutional barrier. To ensure faster, non-inflationary growth on a sustained basis would require new cooperative institutions at both the national and international levels, suitably adapted in the light of the experience of the Golden Age. The political processes involved in achieving this institutional renewal should also help change the social norms towards greater equality.

REFERENCES

Atkinson, A. B. (2000). The changing distribution of income: Evidence and explanations. *German Economic Review* 1, 3–18.

—— and F. Bourguignon (2000). *Handbook of Income Distribution*. Elsevier: Amsterdam.

Autor, D., L. Katz, and A. Krueger (1998). Computing inequality: Have computers changed the labour market? *Quarterly Journal of Economics* 113, 1169–213.

Baldwin, R. (1992). Measurable dynamic gains from trade. *Journal of Political Economy* 100(1), 162–74.

Ben-David, D. (1993). Equalizing exchange: Trade liberalization and income convergence. *Quarterly Journal of Economics* 108, 653–79.

—— (1996). Trade and convergence among countries. *Journal of International Economics* 40, 279–89.

---

[18] The following discussion is based on Singh (2001).

[19] See Singh (1995, 1997a, 1999). See also Howes and Singh (2000).

Bhagwati, J. (1994). Free trade: Old and new challenges. *The Economic Journal* 104(423), 231–46.

Birdsall, N. (2000). Inequality within nations is the danger. Letter to the Editor of the *Financial Times*, London, 16 February.

Burtless, G. (1995). International trade and the rise in earnings inequality. *Journal of Economic Literature* 33, 800–16.

Card, D. (1992). The effect of unions on the distribution of wages: Redistribution or Relabelling?. NBER Working Paper 4195, National Bureau of Economic Research: Cambridge, MA.

Davis, D. R. (1998a). Does European unemployment prop US American wages? National labour markets and global trade. *American Economic Review* 88, 478–94.

—— (1998b). Technology, unemployment and relative wages in a global economy. *European Economic Review* 42, 1613–33.

Demirguc-Kunt, A., and E. Detragiache (1998). The determinants of banking crises from industrial and developing countries. World Bank Policy Research Working Paper 1828. World Bank: Washington, DC.

Eichengreen, B. (1994). Institutions and economic growth: Europe after World War II. In N. Crafts and G. Toniolo (eds.), *Economic Growth in Europe Since 1945*. Cambridge University Press: Cambridge.

Fehr, E., and S. Gächter (2000). Fairness and retaliation: The economics of reciprocity. *Journal of Economic Perspectives* Summer, 159–91.

Galbraith, J. K. (1998). *Created Unequal: The Crisis in American Pay*. The Free Press: New York.

Glyn, A., A. Hughes, A. Lipietz, and A. Singh (1990). The rise and fall of the Golden Age. In S. Marglin and J. Schor (eds.), *The Golden Age of Capitalism: Reinterpretation of Postwar Experience*. Clarendon Press: Oxford.

Gottschalk, P., and T. Smeeding (1997). Cross national comparisons of earnings and income inequality. *Journal of Economic Literature* 35(2), 633–87.

Harrison, A., and G. Hanson (1999). Who gains from trade reform? some remaining puzzles. *Journal of Development Economics* 59, 125–54.

Harrison, B., and B. Bluestone (1990). Wage polarization in the US and the flexibility debate. *Cambridge Journal of Economics* 14, 351–73.

Hicks, J. R. (1963). *The Theory of Wages*. Oxford University Press: Oxford.

Howes, C., and A. Singh (2000). *Competitiveness Matters: Industry and Economic Performance in the US*. University of Michigan Press: Ann Arbor.

IMF (1998). Capital account liberalization: Theoretical and practical aspects. *IMF Occasional Paper* 172. IMF: Washington, DC.

Kaldor, N. (1978). The effects of devaluation on trade in manufactures. In N. Kaldor (ed.), *Further Essays on Applied Economics*. Duckworth: London.

Katz, L. (1999). Technology, change, computerization and the wage structure. Paper prepared for the conference organized by the University of California on Understanding the Digital Economy: Data, Tools and Research, 25–26 May, Washington, DC.

Khan A. and C. Riskin (1999). Income distribution and poverty in China in the era of globalization (draft).

Kindelberger, C. P. (1992). Why did the Golden Age last so long?. In F. Cairncross and A. Cairncross (eds.), *The Legacy of the Golden Age: The 1960s and Their Economic Consequences*. Routledge: London.

Kitson, M., and J. Michie (1996). Britain's industrial performance since 1960: Underinvestment and relative decline. *Economic Journal* 106, 196–212.

Krugman, P. (2000). Technology, trade and factor prices. *Journal of International Economics* 50, 51–71.

Leamer, E. (1998). In search of Stolper-Samuelson linkages between international trade and lower wages. In S. Collins (ed.), *Imports, Exports and the American Worker*. Brookings Institutional Press: Washington, DC.

—— (2000). What's the use of factor contents? *Journal of International Economics* 50(1), 17–51.

—— and J. Levinson (1995). International trade theory: The evidence. In R. W. Jones and P. B. Kenen (eds.), *Handbook of International Economics*, Vol. 3., Elsevier: Amsterdam.

Lustig, N. (1998). From structuralism to neostructuralism: The search for a heterodox paradigm. In P. Meller (ed.), *The Latin American Development Debate*. West View: Boulder.

McFail, F. (2000). What caused earning inequality to increase in Canada during the 1980s? *Cambridge Journal of Economics* 24(2), 153–76.

Milberg, W. (1997). *The revival of trade and growth theories: Implications for income inequality in developing countries*. New School for Social Research: New York.

Murphy, K. M., W. C. Riddell, and P. M. Romer (1998). Wages, skills and technology in the United States and Canada. In E. Helpman (ed.), *General Purpose Technologies*. MIT Press: Cambridge, MA.

Ocampo, J., and L. Taylor (1998). Trade liberalization in developing economies: Modest benefits but problems with productivity growth, macro prices and income distribution. *Economic Journal* 108, 1523–46.

OECD (1995a). *Historical Statistics*. OECD: Paris.

—— (1995b). *The OECD Jobs Study: Implementing the Strategy*. OECD: Paris.

—— (1996). *Employment Outlook*. OECD: Paris.

Phelps Brown, E. H. (1977). *The Inequality of Pay*. Oxford University Press: Oxford.

Pieper, U. (1997). *Openness and Structural Dynamics of Productivity and Employment in Developing Countries: A Case of Deindustrialization?* New School for Social Research: New York.

Pigou, A. C. (1920). *Economics of Welfare*. Macmillan: London.

Robertson, R. (2000). Trade liberalization and wage inequality: Lessons from the Mexican experience. *World Economy* 23(6), 827–49.

Rodriguez, F., and D. Rodrik (1999). Trade policy and economic growth: A skeptic's guide to the cross-national evidence. NBER Working Paper 7081. National Bureau of Economic Research: Cambridge, MA.

Rowthorn, R., and R. Ramaswamy (1997). Deindustrialization: Its causes and consequences. *Economic Issues* 10. IMF: Washington, DC.

Sachs, J., and A. Warner (1995). Economic reforms and the process of global integration. *Brookings Papers on Economic Activity* 1, 1–118.

Singh, A. (1987). Manufacturing and deindustrialization. In *The New Palgrave: A Dictionary of Economics*. Macmillan: London.

—— (1989). Third world competition and deindustrialization in advanced countries. *Cambridge Journal of Economics* 13, 103–20.

—— (1995). Institutional requirements for full employment in advanced economies. *International Labour Review* 135(4–5).

—— (1997a). Liberalization and globalization: An unhealthy euphoria. In J. Michie and J. Grieve Smith (eds.), *Employment and Economic Performance*. Oxford University Press: Oxford.

—— (1997*b*). Financial liberalization, the stock market and economic development. *Economic Journal* 107, 771–82.

—— (1998). Financial crisis in East Asia: The end of the Asian Model? ILO Discussion Paper 24. ILO: Geneva.

—— (1999). Global unemployment, growth and labour market rigidities: A commentary. In *Perspectives on Globalization and Employment*. UNDP: New York.

—— (2001). Income inequality in advanced economies: A critical examination of the trade and technology theories and an alternative perspective. CBR Working Paper Series 219. Centre for Business Research, University of Cambridge.

—— and B. Weisse (1998). Emerging stock markets, portfolio capital flows and long-term economic growth: Micro and macroeconomic perspectives. *World Development* 26(4), 607–22.

—— and R. Dhumale (2000). Globalization, technology, and income inequality: A critical analysis. WIDER Working Paper 210. UNU/WIDER: Helsinki.

—— and A. Zammit, (2000). International capital flows: Identifying the gender dimension. *World Development* 28(7), 1249–68.

Slaughter, M. (1997). Per capita income convergence and the role of international trade. *American Economic Review* 87(2), 194–204.

—— and P. Swagel (1997). Does globalization lower wages and export jobs? *IMF Economic Issues* 11. IMF: Washington, DC.

Stiglitz, J. (1994). The role of the state in financial markets. In *Proceedings of the World Bank Annual Conference on Development Economics*. World Bank: Washington, DC.

UNCTAD (1995). *Trade and Development Report*. UNCTAD: Geneva.

Ventura, J. (1997). Growth and interdependence. *Quarterly Journal of Economics* 112(1), 57–84.

Wood, A. (1994). *North–South Trade, Employment and Inequality: Changing Fortunes in a Skill-Driven World*. Claredon Press: Oxford.

—— (1997). Openness and wage inequality in developing countries: The Latin American challenge to East Asia conventional wisdom. *World Bank Economic Review* 11(1), 33–57.

—— (1998). Globalization and the rise in labour market inequalities. *The Economic Journal* 108, 1463–82.

World Bank (1995). *World Development Report*. World Bank: Washington, DC.

—— (2000). *World Development Report*. World Bank: Washington, DC.

7

External Liberalization, Economic Performance, and Distribution in Latin America and Elsewhere

LANCE TAYLOR

7.1. INTRODUCTION

As seen from the year 2000, economic policy in developing and post-socialist economies during the preceding 10–15 years had one dominating theme. Packages aimed at liberalizing the balance of payments, on both current and capital accounts, showed up throughout Latin America, Eastern Europe, Asia, and even in parts of Africa. Together with large but highly volatile foreign capital movements (often but not always in connection with privatization of state enterprises), this wave of external deregulation was the central feature of 'globalization' for the non-industrialized world.

In two recent research projects, the implications of external liberalization have been investigated through the use of quantified narrative histories for a number of countries, based on a methodology developed by the present author to decompose and analyse changes over time in effective demand, productivity growth, employment, and the sectoral/functional income distribution. The studies appear in collections edited by Ganuza *et al.* (2001) and Taylor (2000). The former concentrates on countries in Latin America and the Caribbean, while the latter includes papers on Argentina, Colombia, Cuba, India, South Korea (hereafter simply 'Korea'), Mexico, Russia, Turkey, and Zimbabwe. After a summary of the results of the projects and possible interpretations, the next step taken here is to develop a model of the likely effects of liberalization. The decomposition methodologies are then presented, and used to check the outcomes that the model generates—there is substantial overlap between observed phenomena and its projections. This discussion leads naturally to policy alternatives and suggestions about the future course of the liberalization process.

7.2. VIEWS ABOUT LIBERALIZATION

Liberalization arrived abruptly. Stabilization and structural adjustment efforts through the mid-1980s had concentrated on fiscal and monetary restraint and realignment of exchange rates. Then in the late 1980s and early 1990s came drastic reductions in trade restrictions and domestic and external financial liberalization, almost simultaneously in most countries. Complementary policies included deregulation of domestic financial markets, tax systems, and labour markets. All these changes are very recent. It will take time before their full effects on growth, employment, income distribution, and poverty can be fully assessed. But external liberalization marks such a dramatic switch in development policy away from traditional regimes of widespread state controls and import-substituting industrialization that one would expect large consequences.

The old policy model had been criticized for failing to promote efficient and competitive industrial production, for creating insufficient employment, and for failing to reduce income inequality. Its rapid abolition raises a new set of fundamental questions. Will the liberalization of trade and capital flows help countries meet social goals such as reductions in inequality and poverty, better provision of health and education, and social security? Will a world system in which national economies are highly integrated in commodity and capital markets (in terms of both increased transactions flows and tendencies towards price equalization) attain these goals of its own accord? Can social policies be deployed to ease the task?

The main official justification for the reforms was stated in terms of visible increases in economic efficiency and output growth that they were supposed to bring. Governments and international institutions promoting them were less explicit about their distributional consequences. The predominant view is that liberalization is likely to lead to better economic performance, at least in the medium to long run. Even if there are adverse transitional impacts, they can be cushioned by social policies, and in any case after some time they will be outweighed by more rapid income growth.

This conclusion is fundamentally based on supply-side arguments. The purpose of trade reform is to switch production from non-tradable goods and inefficient import-substitutes towards exportable goods in which poor countries should have comparative advantage. Presumed full employment of all resources (labour included) enables such a switch to be made painlessly. Opening the capital account is supposed to bring financial inflows that will stimulate investment and productivity growth. In a typical mainstream syllogism, Londoño and Szekely (1998) postulate that equity is positively related to growth and investment. These in turn are asserted to be positively related to structural reforms, so the conclusion is that liberalization supports low-income groups.

A second position is more radical in that its proponents such as Sen (1999) argue that social policies *should* be deployed to help the poorest, on the implicit assumption that the forces determining the income distribution, the extent of poverty, and social relationships are largely independent of liberalization, globalization, and market processes more generally.

Finally, others argue that while there may be supply-side benefits from trade and capital market reforms one should not overlook aggregate demand, its potentially unfavorable interactions with distribution, and the impact of capital inflows on relative prices. The import-substitution model relied on expansion of internal markets with rising real wages as part of the strategy. Under the new regime, controlling

wage costs has come to centre stage. So long as there is enough productivity growth
and no substantial displacement of workers, wage restraint need not be a problem
because output expansion could create space for real income growth. But if wage
levels are seriously reduced and/or workers with high consumption propensities lose
their jobs, contraction of domestic demand could cut labour income in sectors that
produce for the local market. Income inequality could rise if displaced unskilled
workers end up in informal service sector activities for which there is a declining
demand.

Rising capital inflows following liberalization tend to lead to real exchange rate
appreciation, offsetting liberalization's incentives for traded goods production and
forcing greater reductions in real wage costs. Appreciation in turn may be linked to
high real interest rates, which add to production costs and penalize capital formation.
Higher rates may also draw in more external capital, setting off a high interest
rate/strong exchange rate spiral. Via the banking system, capital inflows feed into
international reserves and domestic credit expansion. On the positive side, more credit
may stimulate aggregate spending through increased domestic investment. However,
credit expansion can also trigger a consumption boom (with purchases heavily
weighted toward imports) or a speculative asset price bubble (typically in equity
and/or real estate). The demand expansion may prove to be short-lived if the
consequent widening of the external balance is unsustainable or if capital flees the
economy when the bubble begins to deflate. Lack of prudential financial regulation
makes the latter outcome all the more likely.

The thrust of these observations is that the effects of balance of payments liberalization on growth, employment, and income distribution emerge from a complex set
of forces involving both the supply and the demand sides of the economy. Income
redistribution and major shifts in relative prices are endogenous to the process. Nor is
social policy a panacea for rising inequality and distributional tensions. Only a few
countries such as Korea in 1998–99 and Chile and Colombia through much of the
1990s took advantage of strong fiscal positions to introduce large-scale programs to
offset some of liberalization's adverse distributional effects. Elsewhere, they were
simply allowed to cascade through the system.

The bottom line is that there can be no facile conclusions about liberalization,
or about how its consequences can be contained. To date, social costs in many countries have outweighed the benefits, and this situation may persist for an extended
period of time.

7.3. THE APPROACH OF THE COUNTRY PAPERS

The authors of the country studies in the two projects largely adhere to the third,
'structuralist' worldview mentioned above. Structuralism is not accepted in all circles.
But the strength of the chapters is that their shared methodological stance eases the
task of cross-country comparisons and points to coherent policy conclusions. Their
analyses in-depth are able to support generalizations about likely outcomes of the
globalization/liberalization policy mix in diverse national circumstances.

How did the authors separate effects of specific policy changes from other factors, such as external shocks and other policy initiatives? They addressed this standard problem in economic analysis with a mixture of the following approaches:

1. Well-informed country 'narratives' discussing policy changes and observed outcomes in a before-and-after approach. The country stories started with a basic set of questions and hypotheses and a simple analytical framework suggesting possible channels of causation as outlined below. Authors subdivided their period of analysis into 'episodes' with relatively homogeneous policy packages and economic circumstances. They could then trace the effects of liberalization from one episode through another.
2. Still within the realm of 'before and after', the decomposition analyses of aggregate demand, the factoral income distribution, employment, and productivity growth mentioned above were applied wherever data availability made them possible. They give essential comparative information on changes in output, employment, and inequality that actually took place.
3. Counterfactual policy simulations ('with and without') were incorporated in some case studies, based on country-specific models.

7.4. INITIAL SUMMARY OF RESULTS

An immediate conclusion is that the effects of globalization and liberalization have not been uniformly favourable. In a classification that is overly simplistic but still suggestive, changes in growth rates and the primary income distribution for the countries included in the studies can be summarized in the following fashion:

Effect on growth	Distributional impacts		
	Favourable	Neutral	Unfavourable
Positive	Chile (post-1990)	Peru Uruguay	Argentina (until 1997–98) Chile (until 1990) Dominican Republic El Salvador Mexico (post-1995)
Neutral	Costa Rica	Brazil Cuba Turkey	India Korea Mexico (until 1995)
Negative		Colombia	Argentina (post-1997–98) Jamaica Paraguay Russia Zimbabwe

The general impression given by the matrix is a tilt towards the southeast—slower growth and deterioration in the primary income distribution. Just two countries had a clear distributional improvement, and only Chile after 1990 managed to combine high growth with decreasing inequality (in contrast to increasing inequality over the preceding liberal 15 years). Stable or more rapid growth on a sustained basis was observed in a few small, open economies that benefited from capital inflows and a somewhat illiberal policy orientation discussed subsequently. Two-thirds of the countries had rising inequality, and the five towards the extreme southeast (with Argentina late in the decade as a possible exception) to a greater or lesser extent were 'disasters' (on this see also Chapter 2).

7.5. A MODEL OF LIBERALIZATION

Along with the aggregate outcomes just summarized, liberalization had strong differential effects on prices and quantities in different sectors. For many but not all countries, an appropriate disaggregation of the non-financial, price/quantity side of the economy focuses on traded and non-traded goods. The key relative price is the real exchange rate or ratio of traded to non-traded goods price indexes. In more populous, less intrinsically open economies one also has to consider other price ratios such as the agricultural terms of trade (India, Turkey) or the relative price of energy products (Russia). In sub-Saharan African countries such as Zimbabwe as well as in primary product exporters in Latin America and the Caribbean, the terms of trade between an urban-industrial and rural-agricultural sector come to the fore. In all cases, a mixture of price and quantity adjustments to liberalization is evident. Since it is broadly applicable, the traded/non-traded separation is explored in the discussion to follow. Direct effects of removing barriers to trade and capital movements show up first in the traded (or tradable) goods sector but spillovers in both directions with non-traded goods have been immediate and substantial—Amadeo and Pero (2000) and Ros (1999) point out the major connections in similar fashions.

The framework is a 'fix-price/flex-price' model *à la* Hicks (1965) and many others. Traded goods are assumed to be produced under imperfect competition. The simplest model involves a discriminating monopolist manufacturing goods that can both be exported and sold at home, as in Ocampo and Taylor (1998). Households at home buy both domestically made and imported consumer goods. Before liberalization, firms have established mark-up rates over variable costs in both their markets—the levels will depend on the relevant elasticities. Variable cost is determined by the market prices and productivity levels of unskilled labour and intermediate imports; skilled labour and physical capital are fixed factors in the short run. The traded goods price level P_t follows from the domestic mark-up over variable cost.

With stable mark-up rates, traded goods comprise a Hicksian 'fix-price' sector, with a level of output X_t determined by effective demand. The level of production of non-traded goods is also determined by demand, but the sector may well have decreasing returns to unskilled labour in the short run. Higher production X_n is made possible by greater unskilled employment (or labour demand) L_n^d. However, cost-minimizing producers will hire extra workers only at a lower real product wage w/P_n, where w is the unskilled nominal wage (fixed in the short run but subject to adjustment over time as discussed subsequently) and P_n is the price of non-traded goods. In other words, a higher price-wage ratio P_n/w is associated with greater non-traded goods production and employment, and (if there are decreasing returns) reduced labour productivity. If P_n/w is free to vary, then non-traded goods aggregate into a 'flex-price' sector. With stable mark-up rates in the traded goods sector, the intersectoral price ratio P_t/P_n will fall as P_n/w rises, that is to say, a rising price of non-traded goods is associated with real appreciation as measured by the ratio of traded to non-traded goods price indexes (a commonly used proxy is the ratio of wholesale to retail price levels).

In a number of countries, an important component of the non-traded sector comprises the finance, insurance, and real estate (FIRE) subsectors. As argued below, both the national interest rate i and the level of financial activity have tended to increase with liberalization—higher values of i and P_n/w go hand-in-hand, with distributional consequences to be discussed below.

Figure 7.1 gives a graphical presentation of the model.[1] The key quadrant lies in the extreme northeast. It shows how prices and output in the two sectors are determined. Along the schedule for 'non-traded goods equilibrium', a higher traded goods output level X_t is assumed to generate additional demand for non-traded goods. As it is met by an increase in supply, the non-traded price-wage ratio P_n/w will rise. In the market for traded goods, depending on income effects a higher level of P_n/w can be associated with either higher or lower demand. The 'Traded goods equilibrium' schedule illustrates the former case—demand for X_t is stimulated by an increase in P_n/w. As drawn in the figure, the short-run macro equilibrium defined by the intersection of the two curves is stable.

This equilibrium helps determine the status of several markets in the economy. For example, unskilled labour demand in the non-traded sector (L_n^d) is determined in the northwest quadrant. Employment in the traded goods sector is shown in the second quadrant from the top on the right. A lower employment level in traded goods liberates labour that can be used in the other sector, as shown in the second quadrant from the top on the left. As the figure is drawn, labour supply L_n^s exceeds demand L_n^d in the non-traded sector; that is to say, there is open or disguised unemployment as measured by the difference $L_n^s - L_n^d$. Finally, in the extreme southeast quadrant, bigger trade deficits are associated with higher levels of X_t and P_n/w.

7.6. EFFECTS OF LIBERALIZATION

As indicated above, in many developing economies both current and capital accounts of the balance of payments were liberalized nearly simultaneously in the late 1980s or early 1990s. Given this history, one has to consider the two policy shifts together. However, for analytical clarity it is useful to dissect them one at a time. In addition, effects of other reforms have to be considered as well, in particular domestic financial, tax, and labour market deregulation. We begin with the capital account, followed by the current account, to end with some comments regarding the other sets of reforms.

---

[1] See Taylor (1991) for an algebraic treatment of linkages like those described in the text in models closely related to the one illustrated in Fig. 7.1.

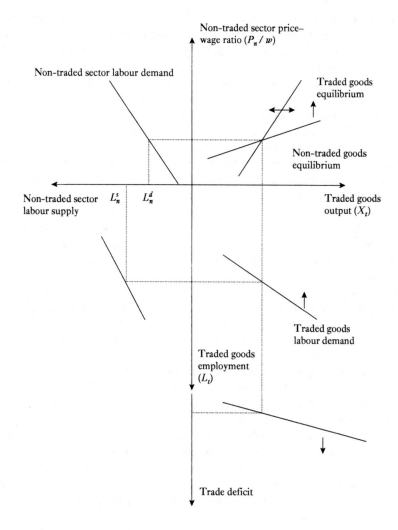

Figure 7.1. *Initial equilibrium positions in traded and non-traded goods, markets, and probable shifts after current and capital account liberalization*

7.6.1. *Capital Account Liberalization*

Countries liberalized their capital accounts for several apparent reasons—to accommodate to external political pressures (Korea and many others), to find sources of finance for growing fiscal deficits (Turkey, Russia), or to bring in foreign exchange to finance the imports needed to hold down prices of traded goods in exchange rate-based inflation stabilization programmes (Argentina, Brazil, Mexico). Whatever the rationale, when they removed restrictions on capital movements, most countries received a surge of inflows from abroad. They came in subject to the accounting restriction that an economy's *net* foreign asset position (total holdings of external assets minus total external liabilities) can only change gradually over time through a deficit or surplus on the current account. Hence, when external liabilities increased as foreigners acquired securities issued by national governments or firms, external assets had to jump up as well. The new assets typically showed up on the balance sheets of financial institutions, including larger international reserves of the central bank. Unless the bank made a concerted effort to 'sterilize' the inflows (selling government bonds from its portfolio to 'mop up liquidity', for example), they set off a domestic credit boom. In poorly regulated financial systems, there was a high risk of a classic mania-panic-crash sequence along Kindleberger (1996) lines—the famous crises in Latin America's Southern Cone around 1980 were only the first of many such disasters.

When the credit expansion was allowed to work itself through, interest rates could be low. However, other factors entered to push both levels of and the spread between borrowing and lending rates upwards. One source of widening spreads is related to asset price booms in housing and stock markets, which forced rates to rise on interest-bearing securities such as government debt. Another source playing a role at times originated from central banks trying to sterilize capital inflows, and so pushing up rates as well. Finally, in non-competitive financial markets, local institutions often found it easy to raise spreads. High local returns pulled more capital inflows, worsening the overall disequilibrium. Unsurprisingly, exchange rate movements complicated the story. In many countries, the exchange rate was used as a 'nominal anchor' in anti-inflation programmes. Its nominal level was devalued at a rate less than the rate of inflation, leading to real appreciation. In several cases, the effect was rapid, with traded goods variable costs in dollar terms jumping upwards immediately after the rate was frozen.

The same outcome also showed up via another channel. As countries removed capital controls and adopted 'floating' rates, they lost a degree of freedom in policy formulation. From standard macroeconomic theory we know that in a closed economy the market for bonds will be in equilibrium if the money market clears as well. When proper accounting restrictions (including a fixed level of net foreign assets in the short run) are imposed on portfolio choice in an open economy, this theorem continues to apply (Taylor 1999). That is, an open economy has just one independent 'asset market' relationship, say an excess supply function for bonds of the form

$$B - B^{\mathrm{d}}\,[i, i^*, (\varepsilon/e)] = 0.$$

In this equation, B and B^{d} are bond supply and demand, respectively. The latter depends positively on the domestic interest rate i, and negatively on the foreign rate and i^* on expected depreciation ε as normalized by the current spot rate e.[2] Total bond supply B will change slowly over time as new paper is issued to cover corporate and (especially) fiscal deficits.

For given expectations, the formula suggests that the interest rate and spot exchange rate will be related inversely. If, for the reasons mentioned above, the domestic rate i tended to rise, then the exchange rate would appreciate or fall. Or, the other way `round, if the exchange rate strengthened over time, then interest rates would be pushed upwards. This tendency would be amplified if real appreciation stimulated aggregate demand in the short run—the other side of the coin of the well-known possibility that devaluation can be contractionary in developing economies (Krugman and Taylor 1978). Abandoning capital controls made the exchange rate/interest rate trade-off far more difficult to manage. Some countries did succeed in keeping their exchange rates relatively weak, but they were in a minority.

Summarizing, capital account liberalization combined with a boom in external inflows could easily provoke 'excessive' credit expansion. Paradoxically, the credit boom could be associated with relatively high interest rates and a strong local currency. These were not the most secure foundations for liberalization of the current account, the topic we take up next.

7.6.2. Current Account Liberalization

Current account deregulation basically took the form of transformation of import quota restrictions (where they were important) to tariffs, and then consolidation of tariff rates into a fairly narrow band, for example, between 0 and 20 per cent. With a few exceptions, export subsidies were also removed. There were visible effects on the level and composition of effective demand, and on patterns of employment and labour productivity.

Demand composition typically shifted in the direction of imports, especially when there was real exchange appreciation. In many cases, national savings rates also declined. This shift can partly be attributed to an increased supply of imports at low prices (increasing household spending, aided by credit expansion following financial liberalization), and partly to a profit squeeze (falling retained earnings) in industries producing traded goods. The fall in private savings sometimes was partially offset by rising government savings where fiscal policy became more restrictive. Many countries showed 'stop-go' cycles in government tax and spending behaviour.

Especially when it went together with real appreciation, current account liberalization pushed traded goods producers towards workplace reorganization (including greater reliance on foreign outsourcing) and down-sizing. If, as assumed above, unskilled labour is an important component of variable cost, then such workers would bear the brunt of such adjustments via job losses. In other words, traded goods

---

[2] Scaling the expected change in the exchange rate by its current level puts the quantity ε/e—the expected rate of return from capital gains on foreign securities—on a comparable footing with the two interest rates.

enterprises that stayed in operation had to cut costs by generating labour productivity growth. Depending on demand conditions, their total employment levels could easily fall. The upshot of these effects often took the form of increased inequality between groups of workers, in particular between the skilled and unskilled. This outcome is at odds with widely discussed predictions of the Stolper and Samuelson (1941) theorem, according to which trade liberalization should lead to an increase in the remuneration of the relatively abundant production factor in low and middle income countries (unskilled labour) with respect to the scarce factor (capital or skilled labour). Of course, besides considering exchange rate and capital flow effects on remunerations, the model just presented departs from the standard Heckscher–Ohlin trade theory framework underlying Stolper–Samuelson by working with more than two production factors and allowing for open unemployment, factor immobility, and product market imperfections. These considerations along with changes in the sectoral composition of output, as emphasized in Fig. 7.1, are important factors in determining the distributive effects of trade liberalization (Wood 1997). With liberalization stimulating productivity increases leading to a reduction of labour demand from modern, traded-goods production, primary income differentials widened between workers in such sectors and those employed in non-traded, informal activities (e.g. informal services) and the unemployed.

7.7. GRAPHICAL ILLUSTRATION OF THE EFFECTS OF LIBERALIZATION

It is easy to trace through the implications of these changes in Fig. 7.1, beginning with the traded goods equilibrium schedule in the northeast quadrant. The sector was subject to several conflicting forces:

- By switching demand towards imports, current account liberalization tended to reduce output X_t. This demand loss was strengthened by real appreciation and weakened or even reversed by devaluation. Removal of export subsidies hurt manufacturing and raw materials sectors in some cases.
- Domestic credit expansion and a falling saving rate stimulated demand for both sectors, although high interest rates may have held back spending on luxury manufactured items such as consumer durables and cars (in countries where they were produced). Income generation via FIRE activity helped stimulate the non-traded sector.

The outcome is that the shift in the traded goods equilibrium schedule was ambiguous, as shown by the double-headed arrow in the diagram. The contractionary forces just mentioned did not impinge directly on non-traded goods; as shown, the corresponding market equilibrium schedule shifted upwards. The likely results after both schedules adjusted were a higher non-traded price-wage ratio P_n/w, a fall in the intersectoral terms-of-trade P_t/P_n, and an ambiguous change in X_t. In some cases (notably Cuba, Russia, and Zimbabwe), the increase in the 'flex-price' P_n was associated with an inflationary process shifting the income distribution away from wages and towards public revenues or profits. The outcome was a reduction in effective demand through 'forced saving' by wage-earners with high propensities to consume, as analysed by Keynes and contemporaries in the 1920s and Kaldor after the Second World War.[3]

Turning to employment and productivity changes, new jobs were typically created in the non-traded sector; namely, L_n^d went up along the demand schedule in the northwest quadrant. With overall decreasing returns in the sector, its real wage w/P_n and labour productivity level X_n/L_n^d could be expected to fall.

In the traded goods sector, higher labour productivity meant that the labour demand schedule in the middle quadrant on the right moved towards the origin. Regardless of what happened to their overall level of activity, traded goods producers generated fewer jobs per unit of output. Reading through the lower quadrant on the left, L_n^s or unskilled labour supply in non-traded goods tended to rise. The effect on overall unemployment $(L_n^s - L_n^d)$ was unclear. Wage dynamics appeared to be driven by institutional circumstances in partly segmented labour markets, with details differing country by country. In many cases, stable or rising unemployment and unresponsive wages caused the overall income distribution to become more concentrated. The differential between skilled and unskilled wage rates tended to rise. The final curve that shifted was the one setting the trade deficit in the extreme southeast quadrant. Higher import demand and (typically) lagging exports meant that it moved away from the origin—for a given output level, the deficit went up. The corresponding increase in 'required' capital inflows fed into the shifts in the capital account discussed above.

7.7.1. *Other Reforms*

When assessing the effects hypothesized above in real country contexts, one has to take account of other measures that were implemented simultaneously in many places and which compounded the effects discussed above. We briefly mention three other major areas of liberalization.

Domestic financial sector deregulation

The effects of capital account liberalization have to be understood in conjunction with the domestic financial sector reforms that also took place in many countries before or around 1990. The lifting of interest-rate ceilings, lowering of reserve requirements, and easing of entry for new banks and other financial institutions were conducive to private credit expansion fuelled by foreign capital inflows. With inadequate bank regulation and supervision in most countries, these changes in regulatory policy exacerbated the risk of banking crises along the lines described above (Vos 1995: 179–220).

---

[3] See Taylor (1991) for references and further discussion.

Labour market liberalization

Typically, only small changes have occurred in this area. However, distributional outcomes can be strongly influenced by the degree of wage rigidity and labour market segmentation. In most cases institutional wage setting in modern sector firms continues to prevail (as assumed above), as well as regulations stipulating high severance payments in case of dismissal of employees. Strongly segmented labour markets are still a main characteristic in many countries. The bargaining power of organized labour may well have declined, reducing the political space for real wage adjustments.

Tax reforms

Broadly speaking, countries moved towards taxation of consumption through valued-added taxes and away from direct taxation, roughly a shift away from taxing the wealthy and towards lower and middle income groups. Substantial lowering of marginal rates on income and corporate taxes has been common.

7.8. DECOMPOSITION TECHNIQUES

To trace through the sorts of changes described by the model in detail, the first step is to examine how major economic aggregates shift over time. To this end, the country chapters deploy several simple time series decomposition techniques. The essentials are outlined in this section, beginning with effective demand and going on to employment, productivity growth, and the functional income distribution.

7.8.1. *Effective Demand*

Over the liberalization period, there have been substantial changes in demand-side parameters such as import coefficients and savings rates along with jumps in flows such as annual exports, investment, etc. It is illuminating to look at how output has responded to these shifts, using a simple decomposition of demand 'injections' (investment, government spending, exports) versus 'leakages' (saving, taxes, imports). The key point is that in macroeconomic equilibrium, totals of injections and leakages must be equal. Broadly following Godley (1999) this fact can be used to set up a decomposition methodology for effective demand. At the one-sector level, aggregate supply (X) can be defined as the sum of private incomes (Y_P), net taxes (T), and imports (M):

$$X = Y_P + T + M. \tag{7.1}$$

The aggregate supply and demand balance can be written as

$$X = C_P + I_P + G + E, \tag{7.2}$$

namely, the sum of private consumption, private investment, government spending, and exports. Leakage parameters can be defined relative to aggregate output, yielding the private savings rate as $s_P = (Y_P - C)/X$, the import propensity as $m = M/X$, and the tax rate as $t = T/X$. From this one gets a typical Keynesian income multiplier function:

$$X = \frac{1}{s_P + t + m}(I_P + G + E), \tag{7.3}$$

which can also be written as

$$X = \frac{s_P}{(s_P+t+m)} \cdot \frac{I_P}{s_P} + \frac{t}{(s_P+t+m)} \cdot \frac{G}{t} + \frac{m}{(s_P+t+m)} \cdot \frac{E}{m}, \tag{7.4}$$

in which I_P/s_P, G/t, and E/m can be interpreted as the direct 'own' multiplier effects (or 'stances') on output of private investment, government spending, and export injections with their overall impact scaled by the corresponding 'leakages' (savings, tax, and import propensities respectively).

The country chapters use Eq. (7.4) in several ways. The simplest is a diagram of stances and total supply over time. In Mexico before 1994, for example, I_P/s_P was substantially higher than X, as the private sector pumped demand into the system, while $(E/m) < X$ meant that high import levels were cutting into demand. The roles of the private and foreign sectors reversed sharply after the devaluation of 1994–5. Another representation involves the levels of $(I_P - s_P X)$, $(G - mX)$, and $(E - mX)$, which from (7.4) must sum to zero. Both such diagrams are helpful in identifying expansionary and contractionary factors in effective demand. Several papers apply discrete-time 'first differencing' techniques to (7.4) along the lines presented below. These show the contributions of shifting weights versus shifting multiplier impacts in determining X.

From the above equation system one can also derive the economy's real financial balance as

$$\Delta P + \Delta Z + \Delta A = (I_P - s_P X) + (G - tX) + (E - mX) = 0, \tag{7.5}$$

where ΔP, ΔZ, and ΔA stand, respectively, for the net change in financial claims against the private sector, in government debt, and in foreign assets. In continuous time, we have $dP/dt = I_P - s_P X$, $dZ/dt = G - tX$, and $dA/dt = E - mX$.

A couple of points can be made here. First, claims against an institutional entity (the private sector, government, or rest of the world) are growing when its stance with respect to X exceeds X itself. So when $E < mX$, net foreign assets of the home economy are declining, while $G > tX$ means that its government is running up debt. A contractionary stance of the rest of the world requires some other sector to be increasing liabilities or lowering assets, for example, the public sector when $G > tX$. Because it is true that $dP/dt + dZ/dt + dA/dt = 0$, such offsetting effects are unavoidable.

Second, stock/flow disequilibrium problems threaten when ratios such as P/X, Z/X, or $-A/X$ (or P/Y_P, Z/tX, or $-A/E$) become 'too large.' Then the component expressions in (7.1) and the accumulation flows in (7.2) have to shift to bring the system back towards financial 'stock-flow' or 'stock–stock' equilibrium. Such adjustments can be quite painful.

Costs associated with the accumulation of net lending over time may imply important income redistribution effects between private and public domestic agents and the rest of the world. When taking such asset-related income transfers into account, we get the more familiar macroeconomic balances linked to expenditures and savings out of the disposable income of each institution, rather than from total supply as implied by Eq. (7.5) above, namely,

$$\Delta D_p + \Delta D_g - (\Delta F_p + \Delta F_g) = (I_P - s_P X - iD_g + ei^* F_p) + (G - tX + iD_g + ei^* F_g)$$
$$+ (E - mX - ei^* F) = 0, \qquad (7.6)$$

where D_p, D_g, and $F (= F_g + F_p)$ stand for, respectively, the stock of net private sector debt, net government debt, and net external liabilities, as accumulated through the financing of the three gaps (in parentheses on the right-hand side) 'after transfers' over time. The level of $-F$ is the 'after transfer' counterpart of net foreign assets A. The parameters i, i^*, and e in Eq. (7.6) stand for the domestic interest rate, foreign interest rate, and the nominal exchange rate. The formula permits detailed study of shifting patterns of effective demand.

7.8.2. *Employment Decompositions*

Next, we take up decompositions of employment shifts. To save algebra, the formulas are presented in continuous time. That is, they are *not* set up in terms of discrete changes of the variables that they contain, even though this is how the data are always presented. With enough patience in writing down discrete-time first difference expansions, the right- and left-hand sides of all the decomposition expressions that follow can be made equal by balancing beginning- and end-of-period terms—see Pieper (2000) for examples. Such refinement is omitted here in the interest of ease of presentation.

In terms of notation, we consider changes from time $t - 1$ to t, or from time zero to time one. The difference operator is Δ, namely, $\Delta X = X_t - X_{t-1}$, and we set $\hat{X} = \Delta X / X_{t-1}$ to indicate a growth rate. Let P be the population, E the economically active population, L the total of people employed, and U the total unemployed or $U = E - L$. The participation rate is $\varepsilon = E/P$ and the unemployment rate is $v = U/E$. The employment rate is $L/E = 1 - v = \lambda/\varepsilon$ with $\lambda = L/P$ as the employed share of the population. Evidently, we have $E = L + U$. Dividing by P lets this expression be rewritten as $\varepsilon = \lambda + \varepsilon v$. Taking first differences and a bit of algebra show that

$$0 = (1 - v)(\hat{\lambda} - \hat{\varepsilon}) + v\hat{v} = -(1 - v)\hat{\varepsilon} + v\hat{v} + (1 - v)\hat{\lambda}. \qquad (7.7)$$

The first expression basically states that changes in the rates of employment and unemployment must sum to zero. The second further decomposes this condition in terms of the participation rate ε, the unemployment rate v, and the employed share of the population λ. In turn, the employment ratio, $\lambda = L/P$, provides a useful tool to analyse job growth across sectors. Let L_i be employment in sector i, with $L = \Sigma L_i$.

Let X_i be real output in sector i, and $x_i = X_i/P$ or sectoral output per capita. The labour/output ratio in sector i can be written as $b_i = L_i/X_i$, and let $\lambda_i = L_i/P$. Then we have $\lambda = \Sigma(L_i/X_i)(X_i/P) = \Sigma b_i x_i$. Taking first differences gives

$$\hat{\lambda} = \Sigma\lambda_i(\hat{x}_i + \hat{b}_i) = \Sigma\lambda_i(\hat{x}_i - \hat{\rho}_i), \tag{7.8}$$

so that the growth rate of the overall employment ratio is determined as a weighted average across sectors of differences between growth rates of output levels per capita and labour productivity (with productivity defined as $\rho_i = X_i/L_i$, and $\hat{\rho}_i = -\hat{b}_i$). Combined with (7.7), Eq. (7.8) provides a framework in which sources of job creation can usefully be explored. In expanding sectors (relative to population growth), productivity increases do not necessarily mean that employment declines. Under liberalization, the interaction of non-traded and traded translate into reduced employment; in slow-growing or shrinking sectors, higher productivity sectors can be traced in this fashion, along with the behaviour of sectors acting as 'sources' or 'sinks' for labour (agriculture has played both roles recently, in different countries).

7.8.3. *Labour Productivity Growth*

Formalizing a suggestion by Syrquin (1986), one can also decompose growth of overall labour productivity $\rho = X/L = \Sigma X_i/\Sigma L_i$. The first difference decomposition is

$$\hat{\rho} = \Sigma[(X_i/X)\hat{X}_i - (L_i/L)\hat{L}_i]$$

$$= \Sigma(L_i/L)\hat{\rho}_i + \Sigma[(X_i/X) - (L_i/L)]\hat{X}_i$$

$$= \Sigma(X_i/X)\hat{\rho}_i + \Sigma[(X_i/X) - (L_i/L)]\hat{L}_i. \tag{7.9}$$

The first line decomposes overall productivity growth into movements in output and employment, weighted by sectoral shares of these two variables. As discussed above, a common pattern under liberalization involved slow output growth and positive productivity growth in traded goods sectors, and faster output growth but low or negative productivity growth in non-tradeds. Across sectors, the outcome was fairly slow productivity growth overall. The second and third lines show how overall productivity change can be written as a weighted average of sectoral productivity shifts plus a 'correction' term involving weighted reallocations of output or employment across sectors. The reallocation weights $[(X_i/X) - (L_i/L)]$ reflect differing productivity levels in different sectors. An output or employment loss in a low productivity sector (agriculture, for example, with a negative value of $[(X_i/X) - (L_i/L)]$) will add to overall productivity growth, as will an employment or output gain in a sector with a relatively high output/labour ratio. In the country studies, such reallocation effects were observed everywhere, but were economically important in only a few cases.

7.8.4. *Capital and Labour Productivity and Real Earnings*

Assuming two labour skill or ascriptive classes, total value-added nationally or in a sector can be written out as $PX = \Pi + w_1L_1 + w_2L_2$, where P is an output price index, w_1 and w_2 are wage levels for the two sorts of labour, and Π stands for other payment flows (profits in a broad sense, perhaps self-employment income, etc.). Let $\theta_i = w_iL_i/PX$. The first difference version of the decomposition of payments is then

$$0 = (1 - \theta_i - \theta_2)(\hat{\Pi} - \hat{P} - \hat{X}) + \sum \theta_i[(\hat{w}_i - \hat{P}) - (\hat{X} - \hat{L}_i)]. \qquad (7.10)$$

If a breakdown of value-added by components is available, (7.10) provides a useful means to think about productivity and payment shifts. If $\Pi = rPK$, where r is the profit rate and K the level of capital stock, then $\hat{\Pi} - \hat{P} - \hat{X} = \hat{r} + \hat{K} - \hat{X}$. With a rising capital/output ratio, a falling profit rate would be needed to open room for real (product) wage growth $\hat{w}_i - \hat{P}$ for labour type i to equal or exceed its productivity growth rate $\hat{X}_i - \hat{L}_i$. In practice under liberalization, such trends in favour of wage incomes were not observed. In the labour market itself, moderate wage and high productivity growth for skilled workers tended to combine with low or negative productivity and wage growth for the unskilled to maintain the equality in (7.10).

7.8.5. *Structure of Costs*

Finally, it makes sense to extend the foregoing breakdown to consider the costs of producing total supply. Equation (7.1) above can be restated in nominal terms as

$$PX = \pi PX + iD_p + wbX + T + ep^*M,$$

where π is the share of profits in total output. In a variation on (7.1), interest on private sector debt iD_p is (realistically) treated as a component of costs of production rather than as a transfer between sectors as is the usual practice in the national income accounts. Let the debt/output ratio be $\delta = D_p/PX$, the real import/output ratio $a = M/X$, and the cost of imports $z = ep^*/P$. Then a decomposition of the unit cost of output takes the form

$$1 = \pi + i\delta + \omega b + za. \qquad (7.11)$$

Although the country papers did not use this precise formula, it can be used to say something about changes that were typically observed. Beginning at the far right, the real import cost z tended to fall due to appreciation of the exchange rate while the import share rose—an ambiguous effect. Both the real wage ω and the overall labour/output ratio were stable or declined; namely, b did not rise outside specific sectoral labour sinks. The effect of these changes on income accruing to capital could easily be favourable. Thus, the (real) interest rate i usually rose as did the volume of credit relative to output, δ—the FIRE sector was the main beneficiary. As already noted, π or the share of 'pure' profits in income may well have risen as well.

Table 7.1. *Growth, employment, and inequality*

Country	Periods	Characterization	Growth	RER	Employment rate	Real wages	Overall primary incomes (labour force)	Skilled/ unskilled	Traded/ non-traded	Formal/ Informal
							Income inequality		Employment structure	
Argentina	1991–4	Plan Conv, Expansion I	8.9	+	+	++	+	+		+
	1995	Tequila effect	−4.6	+	−	−−	+	+		+
	1996–7	Expansion II	6.5	+	−	+	+	+		+
Bolivia	1980–5	Destabilization	−1.6	+	−	−				
	1986–9	Stabilization	1.6	−	−	+	+	+		
	1990–7	Post-liberalization	4.2	−	+	+/−	+	+	0/−	+
Brazil	1982–6	Pre-reform period	4.4	+	+	+	0	−	−	+
	1987–91	Liberalization	−0.3	−	0	−	0	0	−	+
	1992–4	Post-liberalization I	5.4	−	−	+	0	+	+	−
	1994–7	Post-liberalization II	3.2	+	−	+	0	−	−	0
Chile	1970–4	Demand expansion, hyperinfl.	1.0	+	+	−	+	−	+	
	1976–81	Liberalization	9.4	+	+	++	+	+	−	
	1985–9	Readjustment	8.4	−	++	++	+	+	−	
	1990–7	Free trade agreements	9.4	+	+	++	−	−	−	
Colombia	1992–5	Liberalization and boom	5.2	+	+	++	+	+	−	+
	1995–8	Stagnation	1.4	+	−	+	+	+	−	−
Costa Rica	1985–91	Trade lib. (CA)	3.7	+	+	−		+	−	+
	1992–8	Further opening	4.3	0	+	+		+	−	+
Cuba	1989–93	Opening forex market	−8.5	++	+/0	−−	+		+	−
	1994–8	Fiscal adj, flexib. own-account act.	4.4	−/+	−/0	+	−		−	−

Country	Period	Description								
Dominican Rep.	1991–8	Post-liberalization	6.1	++	+	+	+	+	–	+
Ecuador	1988–91	Pre-reform	2.6	–	+/–	–	+	+	–	–
	1992–8	Stab. & liberalization	2.7	++	–/+	+	+	+	0	–
El Salvador	1980–2	BoP Crisis	–9.5	+	–	–	–	+		
	1983–9	War Economy	1.3	++	–	–	–	+		
	1990–5	BoP and Financial Liberalization	6.0	++	+	0/–	+	–		
	1996–8	Demand Contraction	3.0	+	0/–	0/–	0/+	–		
Guatemala	1987–92	BoP liberalization	3.9	–	–	–		+	+	–
	1992–7	BoP cum dom. fin. lib.	4.0	+	+	+		+	+	–
Jamaica	1980–9	Pre-liberalisation	1.6	+	+	+		+	–	++
	1990–2	Financial liberalisation	1.2	+	+	–		+	–	++
	1993–8	Trade liberalisation	–0.7	+	–	+		+	–	+
Mexico	1988–94	Trade and financial liberalization	3.9	++	+/–	+	+	+	+	+
	1994–5	Peso crisis and NAFTA	–6.2	––	––	–––	+	+	–	+
	1996–8	Post-crisis	5.8	+	+	+	+	+	–	+
Paraguay	1988–91	Trade & exchange rate reform	3.8	–	+/0	+	+	+	+	+
	1992–4	MERCOSUR	3.6	+	0	+	+	+	–	–
	1995–8	Financial reform	2.0	+	–	+/0	+	+	–	+
Peru	1986–90	Hyperinflation	–1.1	++	–	––	–/0	+	–	–
	1991–8	BoP liberalization	4.9	+/0	+	++	+	+	+	+
Uruguay	1986–90	Pre-MERCOSUR	2.5	–	0	+	0/–	+	+/0	0
	1990–7	MERCOSUR	4.1	+	–	+/–	+/0	+	–	0/–
India	1986–91	Pre-reform period	5.9	+/–	+	+	+	+	–	–
	1992–6	Liberalization	5.3	–/+	+	–		+	–	–
Korea	1980–8	Lib., depreciation, boom	9.4	+/–/+	+	++ (6.0)	++	–	–	++
	1988–93	Appreciation, slowing growth	7.2	–	0	++ (9.4)	+	0/–	+	+
	1993–7	Capital account liberalization	7.5	+/–	+/0	++ (5.4)	0	0	+	+
	1997–8	Financial crisis	–5.8	––	––	–– (–9.3)	–	++	–	–

Table 7.1 (*Continued*)

Country	Periods	Characterization	Growth	RER	Employment rate	Real wages	Income inequality		Employment structure	
							Overall primary incomes (labour force)	Skilled / unskilled	Traded/ non-traded	Formal/ Informal
Russia	1990–2	Declining growth	−9.8	−	−−	−−−	−−−	−−	0/−	0
	1992–4	Lib. of current account	−10.7	++	−−	+/−	−	+	+	−−
	1994–7	Convertibility, capital acct. lib.	−2.2	++	−−	−−/+	0	+	−/+	−−
	1998	Crisis	−4.6	−	−	−−/+	−	−	0/−	0
Turkey	1980–8	Exp. promotion and trade lib.	5.4	−−	++	−	−−	+	+	−
	1989–93	Unregulated fin. liberalization	4.8	++	+	++	+	++	−	−−
	1994	Financial crisis	−5.5	−−	+/0	−−	−	++	−	−
	1995–7	Post-crisis adjustment	7.2	+/0	+	+/0	−	++	−	−
Zimbabwe	1986–0	Pre-liberalization period	5.2	−	+	+	+	+	+/0	+/0
	1991–2	Transition and drought	−1.8	+	0/−	−−	−	+	−−	−
	1993–7	Post-liberalization period	3.6	−	0	−	−	+	−	−

Notes: ++ = strong increase; + = increase; +/0 = slight increase; 0 = no change; 0/− = slight decrease, almost stable; − = decrease; −− = strong decrease; +/−/+ = fluctuating trend (stop-go).

Growth = annual rate of GDP.

RER = real exchange rate (+ = real appreciation).

Employment rate = change in employed as share of EAP (+ = rise in employment or decrease in unemployment).

Real wages = change in average wage rate.

Inequality = refers to per worker primary income (wages, other) (+ = rising inequality) change in ratio earnings of skilled and unskilled workers.

Source: Ganuza *et al.* (2001) and Taylor (2000).

Table 7.2. *Aggregate demand decomposition*

Demand decomposition			Aggregate demand	Direct Multiplier Effects			Effect of Leakages			Decomposition of effective sources of change in aggregate demand (see terms at bottom of table)		
Country	Periods	Characterization		I/s	G/t	E/m	s	t	m	Private spending ('investment'-'savings')	Government spending ('government'-'tax')	External demand ('exports'-'imports')
Argentina	1990-4	Private consumption boom	9.6	+	n.a.	-	+/-	n.a.	-			
	1995-6	Private demand contraction	0.5	-	n.a.	-	+	n.a.	+			
	1996-7	Private demand (C,I) recovery	10.1	+	+/0	-	0	-	-			
Bolivia	1980-5	Private consumption and govt led	-1.5	+	-	+/-	++	0	+/-	+	-/+	+
	1986-9	Export led	2.1	-/+	0	+	-	0	0	-	-/+	-/+
	1990-7	Export led	4.8	+	+	+	-	0	-	-/+	0	-/+
Brazil	1982-6	Govt. and export led	-0.9	0	+	+	-	0	+			
	1987-91	Govt. led	3.0	-	+	+	-	-	-			
	1992-4	Private cons. and govt. led	0.9	+	+	-	0	-	-			
	1994-7	Private investment and consumption	5.2	+	-	-	+	0	-			
Chile	1970-4	Private and gov. cons.	1.0	-	+	-	-	0/-	+/0	0.2	2.7	-1.9
	1976-81	Cons. squeeze, exports	9.4	0	+	-	0/-	-	+	7.4	1.6	0.4
	1985-9	Investment, exports	8.4	++	+/0	++	+/0	+/0	+	5.8	0.2	2.4
	1990-7	Investment, exports	9.4	++	+/0	++	-	+/0	+	6.5	0.2	2.7
Colombia	1990-2	Export and govt. led	2.2	-	++	+	++	0	-	-9.2	3.9	5.3
	1992-5	Private consumption boom	9.6	-	+	+	++	-	-	4.6	1.7	0.5
	1995-8	Private exp. contraction	1.5	-	+/-	+	0	0	-	-2.0	3.6	1.0
Costa Rica	1985-91	Export led	5.7	+	+	++	-	++	-	1.7	0.7	3.3
	1992-8	Export led	6.5	+	+	++	+/0	+	-	0.4	0.7	5.4
Cuba	1989-93	Private demand squeeze	-13.7	-	-	+	-	+	-	-61.6	6.9	13.4
	1994-8	Publ. exp and export recovery	7.0	++	++	+	++	-	-	52.8	-41.1	6.4

Table 7.2. *(Continued)*

Demand decomposition			Aggregate demand	Direct Multiplier Effects			Effect of Leakages			Decomposition of effective sources of change in aggregate demand (see terms at bottom of table)		
Country	Periods	Characterization		I/s	G/t	E/m	s	t	m	Private spending ('investment'-'savings')	Government spending ('government'-'tax')	External demand ('exports'-'imports')
Dominican Rep.	1991–7	Private demand and export led	8.8	+	+	+	–	0	–	4.7	1.2	2.9
Ecuador	1988–91	Private demand	4.4	+	0/–	–	+	–	0			
	1992–8	Export led	2.9	–	0	++	–	0	0			
El Salvador	1990–5	Investment and export	41.7	++	–	+	+	––	––			
	1996–7	Export	6.7	––	++	++	––	+	–			
Guatemala	1986–91	Consumption led	3.4	+	+/0	0	+/0	0/–	–	2.8	0.8	–0.3
	1991–8	Consumption led	5.0	+/0	+/–/+	+	+	–	–	3.0	0.8	1.1
Jamaica	1980–9	Private consumption led	2.0	+	–	0	++	–	0			
	1990–2	Export led	8.1	–	–	+	–	+	–			
	1993–8	Private dem. and export contraction	–3.1	+/–/+	+	–	+	+	+			
Mexico	1988–94	Consumption boom	5.5	++	+/0	–	++	0	––			
	1994–5	Crisis and cons. squeeze	–7.8	––	0	++	–	+	+			
	1996–8	Investment recovery	8.3	+	+/0	0	–	0	–			
Paraguay	1988–91	Private demand expansion	6.7	+	+	0/–	–/+	0	–			
	1992–4	Private demand expansion	10.8	+	–	0/–	++	0	–			
	1995–8	Private dem. and export contraction	–0.6	+	+	–	+	0/–	+			
Peru	1986–90	Collapse private demand	–1.9	++	+		+	+	+	2.7	–1.3	–3.4
	1991–7	Private demand recovery	5.6	++	+	–/0	–	–	–	5.1	1.1	–0.6

		Growth		tax	imports	investment	government	exports			
Uruguay	1986–90	Export led, priv. demand squeeze	2.9	−	−/+/−−	+	0	0	0	0.7	0.6	2.7
	1990–4	Private demand expansion	8.4	++	+/0	+/0	++	−/+	−−	8.2	1.0	−1.0
	1994–7	Private demand and exports	4.4	−/+	−	+	+/0	0/−	−−	2.5	0.0	1.7
India	1986–91	Pre-reform period	5.4	0	++	−	−	−	−			
	1992–6	Liberalization	7.5	−	+	+	+	+/−	−−			
Korea	1980–8	Lib., depreciation, boom	8.3	+/0	−	−	+	0/−	+			
	1988–93	Appreciation, slowing growth	6.9	+	0	−	0	0/−	0			
	1993–7	Capital account liberalization	9.6	++	0	0/−	0/−	+/0	−			
Russia	1990–2	Declining growth	2.4	−−	++	+/0	+	n.a.	−−			
	1992–4	Lib. of current account	−19.2	−−	+	−	++	+	−−			
	1994–7	Convertibility, capital acct. lib.	−3.0	−−	+	−	++	+	−−			
Turkey	1980–8	Exp. promotion and trade lib.	6.2	+	−−	−	−	+/−	−			
	1989–93	Unregulated fin. liberalization	5.2	+	++	++	+	+/0	−−			
	1994	Financial crisis	−4.9	+	−	−−	−	−−	−−			
	1995–7	Post-crisis adjustment	10.1	+	+/0	−−	+/0	+	−−			
Zimbabwe	1986–90	Pre-liberalization period	5.5	+	+	+	+	−	−−			
	1993–7	Post-liberalization period	4.6	+	−	++	0	+	−			

Notes: ++ = strong increase; + = increase; almost stable; +/0 = slight increase, almost stable; 0 = no change; 0/− = slight decrease, almost stable; − = decrease; −− = strong decrease; +/−/+ = fluctuating trend (stop–go).

Aggregate demand = GDP + Imports (numbers refer to annual rates of growth).

Decomposition aggregate demand.

Decomposition of change in aggregate demand.

$$X^* = \beta X / X0 = -\Delta s\,(A0/\gamma X0) - \Delta t\,(A0/\gamma X0) - \Delta m\,(A0/\gamma X0) + \Delta I\,(\alpha 0/\gamma X0) + \Delta G\,(\alpha 0/\gamma X0) + \Delta E\,(\alpha 0/\gamma X0),$$

$$\underset{\text{tax}}{} \quad \underset{\text{imports}}{} \quad \underset{\text{investment}}{} \quad \underset{\text{government}}{} \quad \underset{\text{exports}}{}$$

where $A0 = I_0 + G_0 + E_0$
$\alpha_0 = s_0 + t_0 + m_0$
$\gamma = \alpha_0\,(s_0 + t_0 + m_0)$.

Source: Ganuza *et al.* (2001) and Taylor (2000).

Table 7.3. *Productivity and employment*

Country	Periods	Characterization	Productivity growth			Sector reallocation effects	Labour supply decomposition		
			Overall	T	NT	Employment	Participation rate	Unemployment rate	Employment rate
Argentina	1990–4	Plan Conv, Expansion I	7.8	n.a.	n.a.	negative	+	++	– –
	1995–6	Tequila effect	2.7	n.a.	n.a.	negative	+	++	0/–
	1996–7	Expansion II	1.2	n.a.	n.a.	small	+	–	+/0
Bolivia	1980–92	Destabilization/stabilization	–3.0	–3.2	–3.2				
	1992–7	Post-liberalization	1.0	1.0	0.8				
Brazil	1982–6	Pre-reform period	0.7	2.0	–0.4		+	–	+
	1987–91	Liberalization	–4.0	–2.4	–5.1		0	0	0
	1992–4	Post-liberalization I	4.4	2.4	4.6		+	+	–
	1994–7	Post-liberalization II	0.9	4.4	–1.2		0	+	–
Chile	1970–4	Demand expansion, hyperinfl.	0.8	0.1	1.3	small	–	+	+/0
	1976–81	Liberalization	2.6	3.7	1.9	small (–)	+	+	+
	1985–9	Readjustment	0.1	–1.2	0.9	small (–)	+	–	+
	1990–7	Free trade agreements	3.9	4.8	3.5	small (–)	+/0	–	+/0
Colombia	1992–5	Liberalization and boom	2.6	2.7	2.9	small			
	1995–8	Stagnation	2.0	2.8	1.9	small			
Costa Rica	1987–91	Trade lib.	1.5	2.3	0.9	small	–	–/0	–/0
	1992–8	Further opening	0.6	3.0	–1.0	small	+	–/0	+
Cuba	1989–93	Opening forex market	–8.3	–13.7	–5.0	0	–	+	+/0
	1994–8	Fiscal adj, flexib. own-account act.	4.1	11.1	0.1	0	–	–	–/0
Dominican Rep.	1991–6	Post-liberalization	3.5	5.7	2.3	small	–	–	+
Ecuador	1992–7	Post-reform	0.1	1.3	–0.9	large (away from NT)	0	–	+
El Salvador	1991–5	BoP and financial liberalization	14.3	–0.6	31.3	large			
	1995–6	Demand contract	9.6	4.4	14.0	small			
Guatemala	1987–92	BoP liberalization	0.4	–0.4	1.1	large	0		
	1992–7	BoP cum dom. financial lib.	0.3	–1.3	0.8	large	0/–		
Jamaica	1980–9	Pre-liberalisation	3.2	1.7	0.9	small	0		+

Country	Period	Description				Reallocation			
	1990–2	Financial liberalisation	3.7	1.2	2.1	small	0	–	+
	1993–8	Trade liberalisation	–1.0	0.5	–1.6	small	+	+	–
Mexico	1988–93	Financial liberalization	0.6	6.0	–0.5	small			
	1994–7	Peso crisis, NAFTA, adjustm.	–0.8	–0.2	–2.1	small			
Paraguay	1982–2	Trade and exchange rate reform	–0.4	1.2	–2.5	large (away from T)	+	+/–	+
	1992–7	MERCOSUR and fin. liberalization	–5.7	–2.1	–8.7	large (away from T)	+	–/0	+
Peru	1986–90	High inflation period	0.7	1.1	0.6		–	+	–
	1991–8	BoP liberalization	0.6	1.1	0.5		+	–	+
Uruguay	1986–90	Pre-MERCOSUR	0.4	–0.7	0.6		+	+	–
	1990–4	MERCOSUR (I)	3.8	0.0	2.2		+	–/0	–/0
	1994–7	MERCOSUR (II)	2.7	6.5	2.4		+	+	+
India	1986–91	Pre-reform period	3.8	n.a.	n.a.	none	+	–	+/0
	1992–6	Liberalization	2.5	n.a.	n.a.	negative	+	+/0	0/–
Korea	1980–8	Lib, depreciation, boom	6.4	n.a.	n.a.	large	++	–	+
	1988–93	Appreciation, slowing growth	4.8	n.a.	n.a.	large	++	0	+
	1993–7	Capital account liberalization	5.3	n.a.	n.a.	small	+	0/–	+
	1997–8	Financial crisis	n.a.	n.a.	n.a.	negative	–	++	–
Russia	1990–2	Declining growth	–7.5	–9.5	–5.5	negative	+/0	++	–
	1992–4	Lib. of current account	–8.5	–11.0	–6.0	negative	–	++	–
	1994–7	Convertibility, capital acct. lib.	–1.0	9.0	–5.5	none	–	++	–
	1998	Crisis	–3.0	–3.0	–4.0	negative	0	+	+
Turkey	1980–8	Exp. promotion and trade lib.	2.6	–2.1	8.3	small	+	–	++
	1989–93	Unregulated fin. liberalization	1.7	1.2	2.3	none	+	–	+
	1994	Financial crisis	–7.5	–13.1	–0.6	negative	0	0/–	+/0
	1995–7	Post-crisis adjustment	3.5	3.2	3.9	none	+	–	+
Zimbabwe	1986–90	Pre-liberalization period	1.5	1.2	1.6	none	+/0	–	+
	1991–2	Transition and drought	–3.0	–6.8	–0.2	negative	0	+	0/–
	1993–7	Post-liberalization period	0.9	–1.0	2.4	negative	+/0	0	0

Notes: Productivity growth = annual rate of change of productivity (Q/L).

T = traded goods sectors.

NT = non-traded goods sectors.

Reallocation effect.

Source: Ganuza *et al.* (2001) and Taylor (2000).

7.9. SUMMARY OF LIBERALIZATION'S OUTCOMES

To trace through all the changes described in previous sections, the first step is to examine how major economic aggregates shifted over time. Tables 7.1–7.3 give overviews of the main country findings regarding growth, employment, productivity, inequality, sources of effective demand, and overall macroeconomic performance. Their periodization is based on the policy 'episodes' identified by the country authors in their chapters.

7.9.1. *Growth and Macroperformance*

Apart from years of overt crisis, most countries achieved moderate growth rates of gross domestic product (GDP) in the 1990s. As already observed, Russia and not quite so disastrously Jamaica, Paraguay, and Zimbabwe were the main losers. Except in Argentina before 1997–8, Chile, the Dominican Republic, India, and Korea prior to its crisis, rates of growth of household per capita income were negative or modestly positive. Towards the end of the decade, growth had tapered off in many countries due to emerging domestic financial crises (Paraguay, Colombia, Ecuador) or external events. Adverse foreign shocks included the impacts of the Asian crisis on capital flows to Russia and Brazil (with spillover effects on Argentina), and falling export earnings for most primary exporting economies due to plummeting commodity prices.

Capital inflows increased substantially to most countries (in some cases, only prior to their respective crises). As discussed above, incoming foreign capital tended to be associated with increases in international reserves, domestic credit expansion, and real appreciation. Stronger exchange rates were generally associated with higher interest rates and increasing interest spreads. Capital inflows, credit creation, and real appreciation together stimulated aggregate demand to increase more rapidly than GDP, with consequent widening of the current account deficit.

7.9.2. *Income Inequality*

Inequality of primary incomes increased in most countries. Virtually without exception wage differentials between skilled and unskilled workers rose with liberalization, reflecting employment reallocation as suggested in Fig. 7.1. Relative to the economically active population (following the standard definition), the unemployment rate was stable or tended to rise, again consistently with Fig. 7.1. Excess labour was absorbed in the non-traded, informal trade, and services sectors (Bolivia, Colombia, Ecuador, India, Peru, Russia) or where traditional agriculture served as a sponge for the labour market (Costa Rica, Guatemala, Mexico).

Primary income inequality seemed to increase for several reasons. In Argentina productivity increases in the traded goods sector affected all skill levels. With greater wage rigidity for unskilled workers, there was a reduction in earnings inequality in the sector. Increasing overall inequality was due to rising income concentration in the non-traded sector along with greater skill-intensity of new investment and to the rise of unemployment in traded goods. In contrast, in Mexico reorganization of manufacturing production was found to be a major source of greater skill demand in manufacturing, pushing up wage inequality in the traded goods sector with many of the displaced workers absorbed by agriculture (at least until 1994). As already indicated, in other cases productivity growth in traded goods pushed up skill differentials in that sector along with the gap between formal and informal sector workers.

In Colombia, primary inequality increased as people with low skill levels lost jobs and suffered real wage reductions—labour demand appeared insensitive to the wage cuts. In India, poverty and inequality both went up, in part because of policy-induced increases in food prices and cutbacks in public expenditure. These initiatives were subsequently reversed, as policy responded to the political reaction that followed.

Tracing the distributional effects of two decades of liberalization in Korea is not easy. Through the 1980s, unemployment decreased, the wage share increased, wage inequality (Gini coefficient and the ratio of average wages in the top and bottom deciles) declined, skill premiums fell, and the wage differential between large and small enterprises went down. Rising wage and falling profit shares put distributional pressure on the traditional growth model, which had been led by investment demand supported by high corporate and household saving rates and a fiscal surplus. A transition towards growth led by consumption from wage income is as yet incomplete.

The favorable distributional trends petered out in the early 1990s, in part because of increased subcontracting by the chaebol (conglomerate firms) to domestic suppliers with lower wage and productivity levels, in Korea's version of the shifts depicted in Fig. 7.1. When the crisis hit, the International Monetary Fund (IMF) imposed an outlandishly intense austerity package that lasted through mid-1998. The unemployment rate rose by five percentage points and the real wage fell by 9 per cent. Excepting the top decile, which benefited from higher interest rates on its assets, average household incomes fell across the board, with the greatest reductions (on the order of 20 per cent) in the bottom deciles. Government spending on social support was increased in 1998, and following relaxation of the IMF's demand restraints there was strong output growth (partly led by domestic demand) in 1999. Whether the crisis will provoke a long-term trend towards increasing inequality in Korea remains to be seen.

One last example of distributional deterioration is in Russia. Prior to its demise, the Soviet system had two main proto-classes, the nomenklatura in charge of the party/state governing apparatus and the rest of the population. The nomenklatura were the clear gainers from the transition, as in connection with the criminal 'mafia' they seized control of the major productive assets in a blatantly rigged privatization process, and engaged in massive capital flight. The capital outflow largely offset any current account improvement from higher world prices or volumes of energy exports, leaving the economy in a difficult external position.

Employment increased in relatively successfully adjusting sectors such as energy, FIRE, and public administration, and was held fairly stable elsewhere. As in Cuba after its external shock, job protection combined with falling output and real wage reduction due to forced saving led to negative apparent productivity growth in virtually all sectors. The only Russians (the so-called 'new Russians') whose real earnings rose were people in upper income strata who benefited from forced saving and the rapid, corrupt privatization. In less than a decade, the Gini coefficient literally doubled, from around 0.3 to 0.6. Around four-fifths of the population are now poor or very poor according to the official poverty lines.

Only in a handful of economies is the distributional picture not mostly gloomy. In El Salvador and Costa Rica, rapid employment growth of unskilled workers, particularly in export sectors, offset widening between group (skill) differentials. In Chile, overall labour market tightening probably was the main factor behind a reduction in wage differentials in the 1990s.[4] In Brazil, elimination of hyperinflation and labour demand shifts towards the unskilled have been factors underlying the dampening of primary income differentials. Earnings trends have also been influenced by minimum wage policies, such as in Ecuador where upward adjustments in the minimum wage allowed for a temporary decline in wage inequality (1992–5), despite an overall rising trend (1990–8).

7.9.3. *Sources of Effective Demand*

As noted in connection with Fig. 7.1, real exchange rate (RER) appreciation has been a central characteristic of the post-liberalization period in most countries. Trade expansion and diversification stimulated growth only where depreciation occurred or the currency was kept weak (Bolivia, Chile, Colombia 1990–92, Korea and Russia post-1998, Mexico post-1995, Uruguay 1986–90). Similar observations hold for small Latin American countries with credible incentive systems for non-traditional exports (Dominican Republic, Chile, Costa Rica, El Salvador, and Uruguay via MERCOSUR).

These observations are of interest because one of the principal justifications for external liberalization was its anticipated effect on trade performance. Due to efficiency gains induced by freer trade, 'export-led' growth was supposed to be an immediate consequence. It did not happen, at least in terms of effective demand generation in most of the countries in Table 7.2. As the detailed studies demonstrate, exports did tend to rise with liberalization but import leakages went up as well, especially when the local currency appreciated in real terms. Trade therefore held back or added weakly to effective demand. Growth stimulus from trade was present, but much less strongly than originally supposed by advocates of liberalization.[5]

The public sector's contribution to demand varied across countries. It was positive in Chile and Costa Rica, in Columbia due to increases in social spending, in Cuba as it recovered from external shocks in 1994–8, in India where the consolidated government deficit has supported demand for many years, and in Russia as plummeting demand was at least slowed by the fact that government spending did not decrease

---

[4] It should be recalled that liberalization began in Chile in the 1970s and inequality increased considerably up to the end of the 1980s.

[5] By way of clarification, *effects* of changes in saving, tax, and import parameters are reported with positive signs in the tables. For example, the saving rate dropped sharply in Mexico in 1988–94, strongly stimulating aggregate demand.

quite so rapidly as receipts from a failing taxation system. Elsewhere, government's impact on demand was broadly neutral. Positive or 'stop-go' public sector demand effects are a surprising outcome, given the rhetoric about downsizing the state that accompanied the drive towards liberalization.

Without strong contributions from the foreign and public sectors, private sector demand growth emerged as the major driving force in several countries. In particular, import-led consumption booms following trade and financial liberalization were the rule rather than the exception. They were triggered by both cheapening of imported traded goods (import liberalization and real exchange rate appreciation) and expansion of domestic credit supply (fomented by the surge in capital flows and domestic financial liberalization). Private savings rates fell in consequence. Fewer cases were observed in which domestic demand was driven by expanding private investment, but it did occur in Argentina, Chile, and Korea in the 1990s. The rapid reduction in demand in Russia was provoked by an investment collapse in an economy that had historically been driven by high rates of accumulation. In Mexico late in the decade, higher private capital formation could give hope for a brighter future were it not for a setback due to global instability in 1998–9.

7.9.4. *Productivity and Employment Growth*

With Korea prior to its crisis as a notable exception, only modest aggregate productivity increases were observed. Where data are available, they are broadly consistent with greater observed productivity growth in traded than non-traded sectors. As observed above, the change in aggregate productivity is result of the sum of productivity changes by sectors (weighted by sectoral output shares) plus a positive reallocation effect if labour moves from low- to high-productivity sectors. Findings from the country studies indicate that within-sector productivity shifts and output growth rates largely determined the aggregate outcomes. However, in some cases there was a negative reallocation effect as workers moved towards low-productivity non-traded goods sectors. In Guatemala, Mexico, and Ecuador these sectors served as important 'employers of last resort'.

With Cuba and Russia as exceptions, the share of the economically active population (or the 'participation rate') increased under liberalization. With the exception of Turkey, the unemployed as a proportion of the economically active went up as well, especially after crises and/or later in the decade. Given the modest growth of GDP noted previously, a lackluster employment performance under liberalization is scarcely surprising.

7.10. POLICY ALTERNATIVES

The usual caveats about policy prescriptions apply. Given the diversity of country experiences just reported, it is risky to generalize about lessons and conclusions. Of course, diversity of outcomes is a result in itself. It negates general sweeping statements about whether the reforms have been exclusively beneficial or exclusively costly in terms of growth, employment, and equity. If one is to sing a sad song, however, the evidence certainly shows that in the post-liberalization era few if any of the countries considered seem to have found a sustainable growth path. Employment growth has generally been slow to dismal and rising primary income disparity (in some cases over and above already high levels of inequality) has been the rule. Better performances such as those in Mexico and Korea after their financial crises (as of the year 2000, 3 years of sustained growth in Mexico and one in Korea) were associated with avoiding the macro price mixture of a strong real exchange rate and high domestic interest rates. Post-crisis effective demand was led by the foreign sector in Mexico and by private consumption and investment spending in Korea, suggesting that each recovering country may have its own particular demand path.

Similar conclusions apply to the handful of Latin American economies that combined adequate growth with improvement or stability of indexes of inequality. Their better performances were associated with a policy mix that combined (a) avoiding a macro price mixture of real exchange rate appreciation and high domestic interest rates, (b) maintaining a system of well-directed export incentives whether put in place at the national level or as part of regional integration agreements, and (c) having a system of capital controls and prudential financial regulation able to contain the negative consequences of capital surges. In some cases, cross-border financial flows were extremely important; for example, emigrant remittances in El Salvador are more than 10 per cent of GDP.

For the other countries, the news is less good. Turkey and Argentina continue to wander in a slow growth, falling employment, and increasing inequality wilderness. India's growth and equity performance has not improved with liberalization, and despite a strong effort on the social policy front, Colombia's is worse. In part because of an explicit effort to cushion the liberalization shock, Cuba's growth and equity performances are mediocre. Jamaica's, Zimbabwe's, and especially Russia's are disasters.

Of the three views regarding liberalization mentioned at the outset, the first 'market friendly' narrative is hard to discern in the countries analysed here. In line with the second view, some might argue that their distributional deterioration was *not* the result of liberalization and globalization but they would have to strain to make the case. For most of the countries, it is difficult to refute the third view that liberalization and deteriorating growth and equity performances can easily go hand-in-hand.

Finally, fundamental questions arise regarding social coherence and social policy. The mainstream view of liberalization emphasizes its likely positive effects on economic performance. Adverse transitional impacts can in principle be smoothed by social policies, and in any case after some time 'a rising tide lifts all boats' (except for, is as sometimes added, the ones that sink). The much more disquieting possibility is that liberalization can unleash dynamic forces leading not only to an unimpressive aggregate economic performance but also to long-term slow employment expansion and increasing income concentration. In principle, governments could put countervailing social policies into place. In practice, they probably lack the capacity to do so because of their own fiscal and administrative limitations.

Such constraints on social policy and burden-sharing can be reduced by investment in the capability of the state, as experience in now industrialized countries demonstrated in the nineteenth century and again after the Second World War in the construction of welfare states (Polanyi 1944). But an explicit political decision would be needed before such investments could be undertaken. It would be comparable in scope to the one that led to the worldwide spread of liberalization in the first place. Nevertheless, for the countries considered here, the initial outcomes of liberalization suggest that a 'double movement' á la Polanyi, first towards and then away from an extreme liberal policy stance, could be forthcoming in the not-so-distant future. Inadequate social performance of any economic policy line leads ultimately to its reversal as society organizes to protect its own.

REFERENCES

Amadeo, E. J., and V. Pero (2000). Adjustment, stabilization, and the structure of employment in Brazil. *Journal of Development Studies* 36(4), 120–48.

Ganuza, E., P. de Barros, L. Taylor, and R. Vos (eds.) (2001). *Liberalización, Equidad y Pobreza. América Latina y el Caribe en los Noventa*. Ediciones Universidad de Buenos Aires: Buenos Aires.

Godley, W. (1999). *Seven Unsustainable Processes*. Jerome Levy Economics Institute: Annandale-on-Hudon, NY.

Hicks, J. R. (1965). *Capital and Growth*. Clarendon Press: Oxford.

Kindleberger, C. P. (1996). *Manias, Panics and Crashes*, 3rd edn. John Wiley & Sons: New York.

Krugman, P., and L. Taylor (1978). Contractionary effects of devaluation. *Journal of International Economics* 8, 445–56

Londoño, J. L., and M. Székely (1998). Sorpresas distributivas después de una Década de Reformas. *Pensamiento Iberoamericano-Revista de Económica Política* (Special Issue).

Ocampo, J. A., and L. Taylor (1998). Trade liberalization in developing economies: Modest benefits but problems with productivity growth, macro prices and income distribution. *Economic Journal* 108, 1523–46.

Pieper, U. (2000). Openness and structural dynamics of productivity and employment in developing countries: A case of deindustrialization? ILO Employment and Training Papers 14, ILO: Geneva.

Polanyi, K. (1944). *The Great Transformation*. Rinehart: New York.

Ros, J. (1999). La Liberalization de la Balanza de Pagos en Mexico: Efectos en el Crecimiento, el Empleo y la Desigualdad Salarial. Paper presented at UNDP-CEPAL-IDB conference on the Effects of Balance of Payments Liberalization on Employment, Distribution, Poverty and Growth, Rio de Janeiro, February.

Sen, A. (1999). *Development as Freedom*. Alfred A. Knopf: New York.

Stolper, W. F., and P. A. Samuelson (1941). Protection and real wages. *Review of Economic Studies* 9, 58–73

Syrquin, M. (1986). Productivity growth and factor reallocation. In H. B. Chenery, S. Robinson, and M. Syrquin (eds.), *Industrialization and Growth*. Oxford University Press: New York.

Taylor, L. (1991). *Income Distribution, Inflation, and Growth*. MIT Press: Cambridge, MA.

Taylor, L. (1999). The exchange rate is indeterminate in the portfolio balance and Mundell–Fleming models—each has one fewer independent equation than people usually think. Mimeo, New School for Social Research: New York.

Taylor, L. (ed.) (2000). *External Liberalization, Economic Performance, and Social Policy.* Oxford University Press: New York.

Vos, R. (1995). Financial liberalization, growth and adjustment: Some lessons from developing countries. In S. Griffith-Jones and Z. Drábek (eds.), *Financial Reform in Central and Eastern Europe.* Macmillan: London.

Wood, A. (1997). Openness and wage inequality in developing countries: the Latin American challenge to East Asian conventional wisdom. *World Bank Economic Review* 11, 33–57.

8

Labour Market Institutions and Income Inequality: What are the New Insights after the Washington Consensus?

ROLPH VAN DER HOEVEN AND CATHERINE SAGET

8.1. INTRODUCTION

This chapter looks at some of the labour market outcomes of the recent economic reforms. The extent to which labour market institutions affect the relationship between reform policies and inequality remains controversial. Some see labour market institutions as a hindrance to more efficient development and growth, while others argue that without proper labour market institutions an economy cannot progress. It should be recalled that labour market policies, regulations, and institutions have at least three goals: improving allocative efficiency (matching supply and demand); improving dynamic efficiency (increasing the quality of the labour force); and improving or maintaining a sense of equity and social justice among labour force participants.[1] These different goals will inform the discussion throughout the chapter, which is organized as follows: Section 8.2 touches briefly on some theoretical aspects of labour markets and reform policies. Section 8.3 reviews trends in labour market changes in terms of informalization of employment, wage shares in national income, and wage inequality. Section 8.4 reviews some general trends in labour market policies which have typically been implemented under the Washington Consensus, namely, a decline in minimum wages, shifts in the bargaining power of unions, and a reduction in employment protection. Section 8.5 concludes.

8.2. LABOUR MARKETS AND ECONOMIC REFORM: SOME THEORETICAL CONSIDERATIONS

In the short run, the impact of economic reforms on labour markets depends on the stabilization effects of macroeconomic and exchange rate policies (van der Hoeven 1987;

Observations by Ricardo Infante, Victor Tokman, and Ajit Ghose from the International Labour Organization (ILO), as well as by Giovanni Andrea Cornia, Tony Atkinson, Tony Addison, other participants at the World Institute for Development Economics Research (WIDER) project meetings and two anonymous referees, are gratefully acknowledged.

[1] This is further developed in van der Hoeven and Taylor (2000) and van der Hoeven (2001).

Horton *et al.* 1994).[2] Stabilization involves a reduction in domestic final demand through restrictive monetary policies, budget deficit reduction, and exchange rate policies. The assumption is that the labour market functions in such a way that it can absorb the decline in demand.

It is often argued that, if wages are flexible, the labour market works well. Therefore the labour market institutions which reduce wage flexibility should be modified to help increase adjustments in the labour markets. Yet, such an interpretation suffers from serious flaws. First, it ignores the fact that real wages are not only a cost factor, but are also an important determinant of aggregate demand. Thus, wage reduction when the economy is below full capacity (as is often the case in countries where stabilization policies are implemented) will not lead to full employment. Second, the increased imports caused by a rise in wage inequality (reflecting a shift in the wage–profit relationship in favour of profits) will put renewed pressure on the balance of payments which will necessitate a further spell of stabilization policies. Despite these uncertainties about the allocative function of the labour market, policies to improve its allocative efficiency dominate the reform process. Yet, in the long run, it is not the allocative efficiency of the labour market, which will allow reform efforts to be translated into a renewal of growth, but rather the dynamic efficiency of labour market policies.

One main component of structural adjustment is the set of policies to change the composition of national production in favour of the production of tradable products (export products and import-competing products). The change in production in favour of tradables requires a reallocation of labour from the non-tradable to the tradable sector. Although various labour market instruments can be used to achieve this, many studies emphasize the importance of increased wage differentials between the tradable and non-tradable sectors to achieve reallocation in favour of tradable production. In due course the movements of supply and demand are then assumed to reduce the sectoral wage differentials once more.

But changes in sectoral output depend on more factors than well-functioning labour markets. Infrastructural changes, the development of new capacity, credit, and so on are all important elements in determining sectoral output shifts. Hence, the reallocative function of labour market policies is heavily mortgaged on a large number of other policies and changes in institutions.

The relationship of these other sets of policies with the labour market is more complex because they go beyond the view that the labour market can function as an allocative mechanism and attribute to it the more significant role of raising dynamic efficiency. The interplay between the short-run and long-run affects of labour market policies becomes very important. For instance, growing unemployment, declining wages, and retreating government expenditures have serious impacts on human capital formation, and can affect seriously the longer term dynamic function of the labour market (Buffie 1994).

---

[2] Some paragraphs in this section draw on van der Hoeven and Taylor (2000).

In the short term, the allocative function of the labour market prevails in the mind of the policy-maker, and many of the existing labour market measures are not regarded as 'macroeconomically compatible' (Toye 1995). This then leads to such recommendations that minimum wage laws be abolished, that the practice of making wage settlements binding for whole sectors be reconsidered, that dismissal regulations be repealed, and so on. Also trade unions come frequently to be seen as a 'hindrance factor' in the achievement of stabilization policies. Yet, many of these labour market policies have been adopted not only with the purpose of increasing the allocative function of the labour market, but also to indirectly improve its dynamic efficiency by building up human capital, and improving equity and social stability. These contrasting views of the role of the labour market often give rise to the emanation of conflicting policy recommendations from different members of the same government, with one side emphasizing the allocative function of the labour market and another its dynamic and equity function.

8.3. RISING INEQUALITY WITHIN LABOUR MARKET TRENDS

This section provides a broad overview of trends of inequality in the labour markets in terms of employment, the wage share in national income, and wage inequality.[3]

8.3.1. *Changes in Employment Patterns*

In Africa, the percentage of the labour force working in formal sector jobs has fallen since the introduction of reform programmes (Table 8.1). This is mainly due to a decline in the number of workers in state enterprises and the inability of the economic and social system to generate new formal sector jobs to accommodate the retrenched workers. Industrial and formal service employment has barely increased

Table 8.1. *Sub-Saharan Africa: Evolution of the share of employment in the formal sector during structural adjustment,*[a] *1990–5*

	1990	1995
Kenya	18.0	16.9[b]
Uganda	17.2	13.3
Tanzania	9.2	8.1
Zambia	20.7	18.0[b]
Zimbabwe	28.9	25.3

[a] % of the active population.
[b] 1994.

Source: van der Hoeven and van der Geest (1999).

---

[3] For more specific country analyses on adjustment and labour market issues, the reader is referred to, for example, van der Geest and van der Hoeven (1999), Khan (1993), and Toye (1995).

(van der Hoeven and van der Geest 1999). The aim of the reform programme was to create conditions for rapid formal sector growth, and deep policy changes were introduced to this end. Exchange rates were devalued, currencies became (almost) fully convertible, and budget deficits have decreased. In most countries per-capita growth became positive. However, despite all these policy changes, the recovery in Africa has not yet translated into perceptible job creation. Of course, policy reform takes time and reform programmes were in many cases stretched from an initial duration of 2 or 3 years to 5 years or longer. Nevertheless, results have been very slow in appearing and this has put pressure on the reform process. International markets have sensed this ambivalence of the African adjustment programmes. Despite Africa's wealth in terms of primary commodities, climatic conditions, and low labour costs (following successive currency devaluations), the foreign domestic investment needed for structural change and employment creation did not materialize. This has made the short-term costs of policy reform even more difficult to manage.

The employment experience in East and South Asia has differed substantially from that of the African region. In East Asia there has been sustained growth of formal sector employment in most countries, resulting in increases in manufacturing employment. In contrast, in South Asia there are indications that employment has rapidly expanded in the informal sector (see ILO 1996 for more details). Finally, in Latin America the transitional costs of liberalization have been high. As Lee (1996: 489) points out, 'The experience of Chile in the early 1980s illustrates the severe effects of overshooting in terms of stabilization policy. Output contracted by 23 per cent in 1982–93 and unemployment remained above 23 per cent for 5 years. Similarly the Mexican crisis of 1994–5 illustrated the devastating effect of wrong monetary and exchange rate policies'.

Output growth recovered in Latin America in the 1990s, with almost all countries showing positive gross domestic product (GDP) growth rates. However, as the GDP growth rate remained well below that of the labour force, the rise of formal sector employment remained limited. Growth in formal sector jobs is correlated with high economic growth, irrespective of the type of labour market regulations prevailing (ILO 1995). In effect, in most countries in Latin America one detects an increase in the number of workers in the informal sector (Table 8.2).

8.3.2. *Changes in Wage Shares*

An increase in wage and income inequality is another phenomenon which has been observed in many countries (on this, see Chapter 2). The reform process in many countries has caused a decline in the wage share and thus weakened the position of workers. Table 8.3 provides the wage share in manufacturing industries for a large number of developing countries. For twenty of twenty-six countries the wage share declined between the early 1980s and the early 1990s, and in those countries where the share increased the increase was slight. (East and Southeast Asian countries exhibited the most favourable trends in the wage share.) The shift towards profits has led to changes in consumption patterns and life styles and added to inequities (see ILO 1996; Pieper 1998).

Table 8.2. *Share of informal employment in the total,*[a] *in Latin America, 1990–7*

	1990	1991	1992	1993	1994	1995	1996	1997
Latin America	51.6	52.4	53.0	53.9	54.9	56.1	57.4	57.7
Argentina	47.5	48.6	49.6	50.8	52.5	53.3	53.6	53.8
Brazil	52.0	53.2	54.3	55.5	56.5	57.6	59.3	60.4
Chile	49.9	49.9	49.7	49.9	51.6	51.2	50.9	51.3
Colombia	55.2	55.7	55.8	55.4	54.8	54.8	54.6	54.7
Mexico	55.5	55.8	56.0	57.0	57.0	59.4	60.2	59.4
Paraguay	61.4	62.0	62.2	62.5	68.9	65.5	67.9	59.4
Uruguay (Montevideo only)	36.3	36.7	36.6	37.0	37.9	37.7	37.9	37.1
Venezuela	38.8	38.3	37.4	38.4	44.8	46.9	47.7	48.1

[a] As a % of the non-agricultural labour force.

Source: ILO (1997*a*).

This decline in the wage share is partly explained by what some call the 'ratchet effect'. As it has been well established (Pastor 1985), after an economic shock or a financial crisis, the wage share in national income tends to decrease. Some authors argued that the decline in the wage share following the economic shocks of the 1980s was in effect the consequence of its artificially high level before the crisis. Thus, they partly blamed labour for the build-up of distributed distortions leading to the crisis. However, further research has established that only in a minority of cases were the financial crises determined by the prior excessively high level of wages and labour shares. In most cases the crises were generated by external events or the rent-seeking behaviour of capital owners. Since many countries have undergone more than one crisis, the decline of the wage share during a crisis and the partial recovery following it has led to secular decline in the wage share. Based on a large sample of countries, Diwan (1999) reports an average drop in the wage share equal to 5.5 percentage points of GDP during crisis periods but to only a rise of 2.5 percentage points during recovery. Given that most countries have undergone more than one crisis, the cumulative drop in the wage share over the last 30 years is estimated at 4.1 per cent of GDP. From the 1970s to the 1990s, the drop of the wage share in Latin America was especially high at 6.7 per cent of GDP.

Amsden and van der Hoeven (1996) therefore conclude that 'forcing firms to restructure under the highly contractionary (and destabilizing) conditions of the 1980s stymies rather than stimulates change', and 'import liberalization, except for imports destined directly or indirectly for use in manufactured exports, was not generally an important means of reducing anti-export bias'. Based upon a large sample of developing countries, they argue (p. 522) that, 'Given what appears to have been an absence of thorough-going industrial restructuring in most non-Asian developing countries in the 1980s, the decade's decline in real wages and its fall in wage share of value added suggest that what mainly happened in the manufacturing sector was a distribution of income from labour to capital.' They express the fear that 'lower wages

Table 8.3. *Share of wages in value added*[a] *in selected developing countries, 1975–80, 1985–92*

	1975–80	1980–5	1985–92
Argentina	21.4	19.2	19.1
Brazil	20.6	22.1	20.6
Chile	16.4	17.9	15.4
Colombia	20.1	19.4	15.4
Mexico	36.7	27.8	19.6
Panama	29.8	31.7	35.7
Peru	15.2	17.7	16.0
Venezuela	27.2	28.5	22.2
India	48.2	49.0	45.2
Pakistan	23.5	19.6	19.9
Sri Lanka	29.5	23.8	17.2
Hong Kong	52.4	54.3	56.9
Republic of Korea	27.0	27.2	27.6
Singapore	32.5	34.1	31.4
Indonesia	19.7	18.7	21.1
Malaysia	26.5	29.4	27.5
Thailand	23.5	22.8	25.5
Philippines	22.3	23.4	23.3
Ghana	19.2	16.0	13.8
Kenya	41.1	44.2	42.6
Zambia	26.2	26.4	25.8
Zimbabwe	43.7	42.6	33.3
Egypt	53.5	59.4	41.5
Morocco	53.6	51.0	39.2
Tunisia	48.5	45.7	41.4
Turkey	34.6	24.8	19.2

[a] Total remuneration of labour as a percentage of value added in manufacturing.

Source: Karshenas (1998).

rather than higher productivity may have to bear the burden of creating competitiveness in the 1990s as a result of unsuccessful restructuring in the 1980s'.

8.3.3. *Wage Inequality*

Another related phenomenon observed during periods of economic reform is the increase in wage inequality. This outcome contradicts the prediction of mainstream trade theory about the impact of adjustment and trade liberalization, as the latter supposedly favours the production and export of goods making use of the production factors of which a country is well-endowed, this being unskilled labour in most developing countries (Berry *et al.* 1997). However, the evidence often does not support these theoretical outcomes. ILO (1996) indicates, for example, that in most countries that underwent structural adjustment programmes in the 1980s, wage dispersion increased as real wages fell (Table 8.4). The measure of dispersion is the coefficient of variation, which is the standard deviation of wages in the manufacturing sector divided by the overall manufacturing wage.

'[I]nformation on wage inequality in developing countries is sparse and mixed', argues the World Bank (1995). 'Evidence from East Asia supports the view that greater openness in countries with an abundance of unskilled labour benefits this type of labour', but 'even for these countries . . . the picture of relative wages is more complex, reflecting the interplay of the increase in relative demand for unskilled labour and the supply of skilled labour'. For Africa 'greater openness and policy changes in the 1980s are associated with recovery in growth and some reduction in poverty, but with an increase in equality in some cases'. 'The generally favourable verdict on East Asia in the 1960s and 1970s has been brought into question by analysis of experience in Latin

Table 8.4. *Changes in wage dispersion and real wages in manufacturing, 1975–9 to 1987–91*

	Wage dispersion	Real wage[a]
Singapore	−12.5	58.5
Taiwan (China)	−9.8	151.5
India	−9.3	−2.5
Republic of Korea	−8.2	116.9
Indonesia	4.7	−22
Philippines	7.4	12.5
Sri Lanka	8.2	−10.2
Pakistan	14.7	17.9
Malaysia	19.8	2.8
Thailand	49.2	29.5
Mauritius	−25.1	−37.3
Zimbabwe	−8.8	−32.2
South Africa	6.9	−7.4
Kenya	17.2	−40.4
Tanzania	38.0	−83.1
Colombia	−5.3	−31.5
Uruguay	1.8	−3.9
Mexico	15.1	−44.5
Guatemala	25.3	−41.2
Peru	26.5	32.7
Argentina	26.5	−29.1
Panama	27.2	−17.1
Brazil	34.2	−15.5
Chile	55.4	−16.6

[a] The value of the real wage is partly determined by exchange rate variations since it is expressed in constant US dollars, hence, these figures may not always be consistent with the trends reported by national sources.

Source: ILO (1996).

America in the 1980s', the World Bank (1995: 61) continues, 'In some countries increased openness has been associated with widening wage differentials'.

The facts thus seem to be clear. Driven by differences in earnings between skilled and unskilled workers, wage inequality has increased everywhere except in Southeast Asia. Different conclusions may be drawn about this growing inequality in wages, however. One conclusion is that liberalization has not advanced sufficiently and that domestic labour market constraints have inhibited the markets from profiting from liberalization (World Bank 1997). Yet, one might also conclude that the liberalization process has been influenced by other mechanisms that are not explained by mainstream trade theory. Alternative explanations for increased inequality introduce more than two categories of labour (namely, no education, basic education, and higher education) and argue that, for successful export production, at least basic education is necessary among the workforce (Berry et al. 1997: 14; Owens and Wood 1997). Other explanations are that manufacturing tends to be dominated by large formal-sector companies, which pay higher wages and which have weak linkages to the small-scale sector (so that globalization accentuates the disadvantage of small-scale producers), or that trade liberalization makes it easier to import capital goods (especially if exchange rates are overvalued), and this increases productivity and raises the demand for skilled labour (UNDP 1997).

8.4. CHANGES IN LABOUR MARKET POLICY

In a survey of the literature on income inequality and earnings in industrialized countries, Gottschalk and Smeeding (1997) come to the following stylized conclusions about these countries (see Chapter 6: Table 6.2):

1. At any given time, there are wide differences between advanced countries in the level of earnings, and nations with centralized wage bargaining (e.g. Sweden and Germany) have greater earnings equality than nations with less centralized bargaining (e.g. the United States and Canada).
2. Almost all industrialized countries experienced some increase in wage inequality among prime-aged males during the 1980s, but the differences in the trends were large. Wage inequality increased the most in the United States and the United Kingdom and the least in the Nordic countries.
3. The increased demand for skilled workers, coupled with differences among countries in the increase in the supply of skilled workers, explains a large part of the differences in the trends in returns to education and experience.
4. Institutional constraints on wage inequality also seem to matter. The rise in relative unemployment rates among the least skilled in some, but not all, countries with centralized wage-setting institutions suggests that such constraints were at least partially responsible for limiting the rise in inequality.

Gottschalk and Smeeding explain the rapid rise in earnings inequality in the United States in terms of a variety of structural shifts in the economy, such as changes in industrial structure, foreign trade, immigration, skill-based technical change, and the weakening of institutions that influence wage setting (such as a fall in real minimum wages and a decline in unionization). Real minimum wages fell by 44 per cent in the United States during the 1980s. Although the decline in the minimum wage cannot explain the increase in wage inequality due to the rapid rise of top wages, most of the change in inequality in the United States reflects declines at the bottom of the distribution (on this, see Chapter 9). Studies have found that the decline in real minimum wages accounted for roughly 30 per cent of the increase in the dispersion in wage rates. In turn, at the theoretical level, the impact of unionization on wage dispersion is ambiguous since unions can contribute to the wage gap between union-ized and non-unionized workers by negotiating more favourable contracts for their members. However, in the United States, it is estimated that the decline in unioniza-tion accounts for roughly 20 per cent of the increase in male earnings dispersion. Although some double counting may occur when one adds up the effect of the lower real minimum wages and the effect of the decline in unionization, studies *do* confirm that these two labour market changes explain a large part, possibly up to 50 per cent, of the increase in the dispersion of wage earnings in the United States.

Several other industrialized countries also experienced a rise in wage inequality. Looking for common features and differences between the United States and European countries, Gottschalk and Smeeding argue that differences in wage-setting institutions may well account for some of the differences in the growth in inequality (on this see also Chapters 2 and 9): 'There is certainly a prima facie case that countries with high union coverage on centralized wage setting were able to limit the growth in inequality', they write (1997: 653).

It is of interest to try to verify whether changes in labour market institutions in developing countries have had a similarly large impact on the growing wage disparity in these countries. In the following subsections, we therefore review some of the changes in labour market institutions in developing countries (minimum wages, unionization and bargaining, and employment protection) and try to understand how these have interacted with the various indicators of inequality on the labour markets, employment status, wage share, and wage distribution which we reviewed earlier.[4]

8.4.1. *Minimum Wages*

The policy reforms of the 1980s and 1990s led to a decline in real minimum wages in many countries. In southern Africa the real minimum wage in the mid-1990s was 60 per cent of its level in the early 1980s (Table 8.5). In Latin America, the real minimum wage had fallen by the early 1990s to about 70 per cent of the 1980s level,

---

[4] Forteza and Rama (2000) also addressed the issue of the impact of labour market institutions such as the level of minimum wages, the cost of mandated benefits, the strength of trade unions, and the size of public employment on growth. Forteza and Rama found that growth performance is not affected by the level of minimum wages and non-wage costs. However, these authors assume that labour market institutions did not change structurally between 1980 and 1996; our study shows that crucial changes happened in terms of trade-union density, level of the minimum wage, etc. and that the assumption of unchanged labour market institutions during the periods of reform in the 1980s and 1990s cannot be sustained.

and by the end of the 1990s it was still at a lower level than in 1980s in all but five cases. This trend varied among countries, but only Colombia, Costa Rica, and Paraguay managed to sustain their minimum wages in relation to their 1980 values. While the real minimum wage increased in Chile in the 1990s, by the end of the decade it had barely recovered its 1980s level (Table 8.6).

Table 8.5. *Index of real minimum wages in three African countries, 1987–94 (1982 = 100)*

	1987	1988	1989	1990	1991	1992	1993	1994
Kenya	85.0	—	78.0	85.0	74.0	64.0	59.0	55.0
Uganda	33.3	92.7	61.9	75.1	78.1	65.6	—	—
Zimbabwe	—	—	—	89.5	84.6	63.8	—	—

Source: van der Hoeven and van der Geest (1999).

Table 8.6. *Index of urban real minimum wages in Latin America 1990–7 (1980 = 100)*

	1990	1991	1992	1993	1994	1995	1996	1997	Growth rate 1990–7
Argentina[a]	40.2	52.9	45.3	70.0	81.1	78.4	78.3	78.0	9.9
Bolivia[a]	16.1	26.3	26.4	28.8	31.7	31.1	31.3	32.2	10.4
Brazil[a]	55.4	64.8	56.5	63.9	60.8	67.1	68.9	73.2	4.1
Chile[a]	73.3	79.9	83.4	87.5	90.8	94.8	98.8	102.3	4.9
Colombia[a]	105.7	103.5	101.8	104.6	102.8	102.4	101.5	103.8	−0.3
Costa Rica[b]	127.2	123.3	125.4	130.6	134.6	129.9	130.3	135.0	0.9
Ecuador[a]	33.9	30.9	33.0	37.8	41.1	49.5	52.3	50.5	5.9
El Salvador[b]	33.9	34.6	29.2	35.9	37.3	36.8	33.5	32.0	−0.8
Guatemala[b]	108.7	99.5	87.5	78.4	74.7	89.3	88.4	80.9	−4.1
Haiti	71.4	67.0	56.8	50.2	39.0	—	—	—	—
Honduras[b]	81.9	83.5	100.1	100.9	82.8	80.2	79.5	78.3	−0.6
Mexico[a]	42.0	39.6	38.3	37.8	37.7	33.3	30.5	30.1	−4.6
Panama[b]	98.4	97.1	95.5	107.2	105.8	105.6	111.4	110.0	1.6
Paraguay[a]	132.1	125.7	114.7	110.2	113.2	112.8	103.6	107.0	−3.0
Peru[a]	—	14.9	15.6	12.1	14.4	14.7	15.2	26.7	3.2
Dominican Republic[a]	65.2	78.6	74.7	72.7	73.1	80.3	78.0	—	—
Uruguay[a]	68.8	62.9	60.0	51.5	46.0	42.9	41.7	40.8	−7.2
Venezuela[a]	55.2	61.5	70.2	50.8	52.7	53.7	45.9	39.9	−4.5
Average[c]	68.4	69.3	67.5	68.4	67.8	70.8	69.9	70.0	0.3

[a] National minimum wage.
[b] Lowest industrial minimum wage.
[c] Arithmetic average.

Source: ILO (1997a).

The minimum wage and the level of employment

The theoretical literature on the minimum wage argues that the introduction of a minimum wage has a negative effect on employment. This argument, however, is based on a static model of pure and perfect competition which assumes homogeneity of goods and workers, perfect information, and many small suppliers and buyers. If one of these hypotheses is relaxed (e.g. workers are heterogeneous or paid an efficiency wage, or if there are few employers) or if dynamic considerations are introduced (e.g. the minimum wage affects household labour supply or aggregate demand), the impact of the minimum wage on employment cannot be predicted.

We therefore analysed the effect of the minimum wage on the level of employment on a dataset of thirty developing countries.[5] The main objective is to determine the relationship between changes in employment and changes in the ratio of minimum to average wages (which proxies the relative price of unskilled labour). We therefore regressed on time series data the changes in the ratio of employment to population on the following variables: changes in the ratio of minimum to average wages, growth of the real average wage, changes in the terms of trade, GDP growth, and changes in educational levels:

$$\text{DLNEMPO} = \beta_0 + \beta_1 \text{ GDP} + \beta_2 \text{ REGIONAL DUMMIES} + \beta_3 \text{ DLNREALW}$$
$$+ \beta_4 \text{ DLNOVER} + \beta_5 \text{ DTRADE} + \beta_6 \text{ DLNEDUC} + \varepsilon,$$

where DLNEMPO is the log annual change in the ratio of employment to population, GDP is the rate of growth of GDP while DLNREALW, DLNOVER, and DLNEDUC are respectively the log annual change in real average wage in manufacturing, the ratio of minimum to average wage, and the percentage of GDP spent on education. Finally, DTRADE represents changes in trade volume from 1 year to the next. The results of the regression are reported in Table 8.7.

The results in Table 8.7 suggest that, other things being equal, the minimum wage level has no significant effect on the level of employment. The results also show that GDP growth is positively correlated with employment growth when controlling for other factors. The effect of other variables is much more unstable, as in the case of an increase in the average manufacturing wage which appears to have a negative but weakly significant impact on the level of employment. Restricting the analysis to manufacturing employment or excluding specific geographic areas like Africa leads to the same conclusion. Overall, the fit of the regression is low. Other empirical studies (e.g. Bell 1997 on Mexico) also failed to find evidence of a negative effect on employment following the introduction of a low minimum wage.

The above conclusions are, however, weakened by the fact that the above equation is affected by the endogeneity of GDP growth and mean wages. If its results are to be interpreted in a causal sense, these two variables must both be exogenous, but in most macromodels GDP is dependent on the employment rate while wages and employment are jointly determined. Identifying causal links is, thus, complicated and the

---

[5] This paragraph draws on Saget (2001).

Table 8.7. *Results of the ordinary least squares (OLS) regression of changes in employment levels*

Variables	Specification 1	Specification 2	Specification 3
DGDPCAP	0.004**(0.001)	0.005**(0.002)	0.005*(0.003)
Africa	−0.074** (0.032)	0.078**(0.038)	0.069 (0.052)
East Asia	−0.082**(0.034)	0.026 (0.040)	0.015 (0.054)
North Africa	0.007 (0.027)	—	—
Latin America	−0.068 **(0.031)	0.027(0.038)	0.036 (0.056)
DLNOVER	—	−0.051 (−107)	0.003 (0.179)
DLNWAGE	—	−0.156 (0.104)	−0.026 (0.112)
DTRADE	—	—	−0.000 (0.000)
DLNEDUC	—	—	−0.036 (0.108)
R^2	0.071	0.141	0.05
Observations	218	60	48

Notes: The symbols are explained in the main text. The dependent variable is the log change in employment. Robust standard errors are given in parentheses (White estimator). ** indicates that the coefficient is significant at the 5% level and * at the 10% level. The changes over time refer to the years for which information was available between 1980 and 1999.

Source: Authors' calculations.

results in Table 8.7 are therefore to be considered as tentative both because of the simultaneity problem just indicated and because of the difficulties in accounting for the indirect effects of minimum wages on informality, wage inequality, and other variables that, in turn, affect the overall employment rate and that are discussed hereafter in this chapter.[6]

The minimum wage and the informality of employment

ILO (1997*a*) finds that, in 1995, the minimum wage in high-minimum-wage Latin American countries stood at 43 per cent of the industrial wage and 75 per cent of the wage of informal enterprises, while in low-minimum-wage countries it stood at 38 per cent of the industrial wage and 63 per cent of the wage in informal enterprises. In theory, the minimum wage should cover all people working in the formal sector, but there are quite a few exceptions. In countries with high minimum wages, 22 per cent of the wage earners in the formal sector were receiving wages below the minimum wage. For countries with a low minimum wage, the figure was 12 per cent.

It has been argued that the existence of a minimum wage results in greater informal employment, but ILO (1997*a*) finds that the real minimum wage has fallen so much that this is not the case in most countries: '[I]ncreases in the minimum wages up to a certain level (two-thirds of the wages of unskilled workers) will not produce substantial increases in informality'. 'However, increases above that point are associated with an increase of 0.6 percentage points [in the share of] workers in

---

[6] We would like to thank an anonymous referee for attracting our attention to the problem of endogeneity of GDP growth and mean wages.

the informal sector.' Among the poorest 20 per cent of households, ILO finds no correlation between unemployment and the ratio of the minimum wage in urban informal sector wages.

Did changes in the minimum wage play any role in explaining changes in the relative size of the informal economy? This explanation was put forward during the 1980s in several studies. Is it still valid given the relatively low value of the minimum wage in most countries? To reply to these questions, we constructed a dataset on the informal sector and other related variables with observations for nine countries: Bolivia, Colombia, Paraguay, Brazil, Chile, Costa Rica, Mexico, Peru, and Venezuela. The datasets include changes in the real value of the minimum wage, changes in real average wage in manufacturing, and the share of informal employment in total from 1990 to 1997.

For all countries in the sample—except Colombia, Paraguay, and Costa Rica—the value of the minimum wage is lower during the 1990s than the 1980 value, often much lower (e.g. Bolivia, Mexico, and Peru). For half of the countries in the sample, Bolivia, Brazil, Chile, and to a lesser extent also for Costa Rica, we observe, however, that the minimum wage tends to increase in real terms during the 1990s. As to the informal sector, the data show that the share of informal employment in total employment increased in all countries during the first half of the 1990s and then decreased in a number of countries, including Bolivia, Colombia, Paraguay, and Chile. In Peru and Mexico, informal employment also declined as a share of total employment, but the decrease was not substantial or sustained over time.

Obviously factors other than changes in the minimum wages (such as changes in domestic demand and exports as well as changes in living standards) explain variations in the share of informal employment. The following equation was therefore tested:

$$\text{DLNINFORMAL} = \text{EMPO} = \beta_0 + \beta_1 D \text{ GDP/CAP} + \beta_2 D \text{ MW/AW} + \varepsilon,$$

where DLNINFORMAL EMPO is the annual change in the log of the share of the informal economy in the total, D GDP/CAP represents yearly changes in GDP per capita and D MW/AW measures yearly changes in the ratio of the minimum wage to the average wage. The changes in GDP per capita are assumed to measure the incentives associated with the supply of labour to the informal economy, while on the labour-demand side, the difference between the growth rates in the real minimum wage and average wage represent shifts in the flexibility of the labour market for unskilled labour relative to more skilled labour.[7] The above regression was carried out on a cross section of first differences over time or growth rates.[8] Its results, summarized in Table 8.7, suggest that increases in per capita GDP tend to

---

[7] GDP per capita is also a demand-side variable.

[8] Amongst the subsample for which none of the variables of interest were missing, all observations related to Chile 1993 were deleted due to changes in the way average wage is calculated for that year. An outlier, Bolivia 1991, where the minimum wage increased by 75% in real terms, while remaining at a low value with respect to both its value in 1980 and its value with respect to the average wage, was excluded from the analysis. The number of remaining observations is fifty-eight.

Table 8.8. *Results of the regression of the share of informal employment in total employment*

	Coefficient	SE	t
D MW/AW	0.0013573	0.0389661	0.035
D GDP/CAP	−44.45848	12.33605	−3.604
Constant	3.635627	0.6984937	5.205

Notes: The symbols are explained in the main text. This is the result of the OLS regression of changes in the share of informal economy in total employment on changes in the ratio of the minimum to the average wage and changes in GDP ratio on fifty-eight observations. $F(2,55) = 6.49$; $Prob > F = 0.0029$; adjusted $R^2 = 0.1691$.

Source: Authors' calculations.

reduce urban informal employment significantly. In contrast, the difference between the rate of growth of minimum and average wage seems to have no significant impact on the share of informal employment. In other words, when the minimum wage increases more than the average wage, that is to say, when the price of unskilled labour increases with respect to more skilled labour, employment does not become more informal.

Results in Table 8.8 tend to support the view that the wage rigidity due to the introduction of minimum wages was not the main cause of the informalization of employment in Latin American economies in the 1990s. The expansion of the informal economy seems to have its roots in the lack of growth and in macroeconomic problems, rather than in the level of the minimum wage. This is not to say that the minimum wage could not play a role in creating more informal employment, but given the low level of minimum wages prevailing in most Latin American countries in the 1990s, modest changes in their level cannot explain a rise in informal employment. As a matter of fact, the minimum wage is well below 30 per cent of average manufacturing wage in Mexico for most of the period under consideration, around 20 per cent of average in Bolivia and Brazil, while the ratio for Chile and Colombia was below 40 per cent.

The minimum wage and wage inequality

In order to examine the role of the minimum wage in explaining trends in wage inequality, we use time series data for Mexico in the 1990s. The example of Mexico was chosen because of the availability of time-series data and the importance of wage employment in that country. Evidence on the role of the minimum wage in explaining the level of wage inequality is available for at least two industrialized countries. A study by Lee (1999) concluded that most of the growth in inequality in the lower categories of the US-wage distribution is attributable to erosion of the real value of the minimum wage during the 1980s. The impact of the minimum wage on low-level wages was also confirmed by data on the Netherlands (see Teulings *et al.* 1998). To our knowledge, there is no study that investigates the effect of the minimum wage on wage inequality in developing countries.

To test the impact of the introduction of a minimum wage on wage inequality, we relied on United Nations Industrial Development Organization (UNIDO) wage data at the three-digit industry level for 1984–98 (fewer years were available at the four-digit industry level).[9] The inequality index chosen is the ratio of the lowest to the highest wage. This indicator suffers from a number of limitations, including the fact it is based on the comparison between low and high wages, while the minimum wage probably affects only the lower tail of the distribution rather than the upper tail of the distribution.[10]

Second column of Table 8.9 shows that the ratio of the average wage in the lowest three-digit-level industries to that of the highest oscillated between 26 per cent in 1996 and 41 per cent in 1991. The data provide evidence of an irregular decrease in equality from the mid-1980s to 1991, followed by an almost continuous increase in inequality from 1991 onwards. The next two columns of the table also show that the

Table 8.9. *Ratio of the lowest to the highest paid three-digit-level industries (L/H) and ratio of the minimum to the lowest wage (MW/LW) in 1984–98*

	L/H wage	Minimum	Maximum	MW/LW
1984	0.37	Clothing apparel	Rubber products	0.38
1985	0.34	Clothing apparel	Rubber products	0.39
1986	0.36	Clothing apparel	Rubber products	0.38
1987	0.38	Clothing apparel	Rubber products	0.37
1988	0.37	Clothing apparel	Rubber products	0.35
1989	0.39	Clothing apparel	Rubber products	0.30
1990	0.41	Clothing apparel	Rubber products	0.24
1991	0.40	Clothing apparel	Other chemicals	0.24
1992	0.36	Clothing apparel	Other chemicals	0.23
1993	0.36	Clothing apparel	Other chemicals	0.22
1994	0.34	Wood products, except furniture	Tobacco	0.22
1995	0.26	Wood products, except furniture	Other chemicals	0.26
1996	0.28	Wood products, except furniture	Other chemicals	0.27
1997	0.29	Wood products, except furniture	Iron and steel	—
1998	0.28	Wood products, except furniture	Iron and steel	—

Source: UNIDO database.

[9] UNIDO wage data on Mexico excludes the maquiladoras sector, a very low-paid assembly sector. This exclusion is due to the way wage data are gathered in the country. Data on maquiladoras are available from the Mexico Industrial Census, which is carried out every 5 years.

[10] Another shortcoming of this indicator is that it is based on between-sectors inequality, rather than within-sector inequality, while there are indications in the literature that a lot of the increase in wage inequality happened within sectors (Ghose 2001).

lowest and the highest wage industries changed over time, especially the former. Finally, the last column provides information on the ratio of the minimum wage to the average wage in the lowest paid industry. Such ratio decreases from 38 per cent in 1984 to 22 per cent in 1994 before slightly increasing again in 1996 and 1997. The minimum wage thus represents a small share of the average wage which means that in the formal sector the minimum wage is not binding (though it might play some role in the informal sector) and that it cannot therefore explain much of the recent increase in the wage inequality observed on UNIDO data.

Since we are concerned that the residuals in our time-series model are serially correlated, we estimated the following simultaneous equations:

$$\text{Wage inequality}_t = \beta \, \text{YEAR} + \eta X_t + v_t$$
$$v_t = \rho v_{t-1} + \varepsilon,$$

where Wage inequality$_t$ is the wage-inequality index discussed above in the year t, YEAR is a time trend, and X_t represents all other time-dependent factors which could affect wage inequality such as the average wage, educational shifts, and trade patterns; ρ is the time dependency, and α, β, η, and ρ are the coefficients to be estimated. The results of this Cochrane–Orcutt regression on our wage-inequality index are shown in Table 8.10.[11] Changes in wage inequality are related to the share of exports in GDP, GDP growth, average wage growth (AW), and enrolment rates in secondary education. The illiteracy rate was dropped from the regression as its inclusion led to no results. All variables are normalized to a base of 100 for 1984. There was no time trend identified in the estimation and the results presented exclude the variable YEAR.

Table 8.10. *Results of the Cochrane–Orcutt regression on an index of wage inequality*

	Coefficient	SE	t
Secondary education	−1.193	0.253	−4.71
AW	−0.863	0.214	−4.04
GDP growth	0.087	0.198	0.44
X/GDP	−0.459	0.096	−4.95
Constant	15.65	1.254	12.47
Time dependent ρ	−0.111	0.184	−61

Note: The dependent variable is the log of the ratio of the lowest to the highest wage in the three-digit-level category. The Durbin–Watson statistic was calculated for the inequality equation and was estimated to be 1.9472. As the 5% critical values are 0.632 and 2.030, the hypothesis of no autocorrelation is not rejected. Adjusted $R^2 = 0.9051$.

Source: See text.

[11] The analysis, which was carried out on fourteen observations, shows that the probability of all coefficients being non-significant is zero ($F(4, 9) = 31.99$).

The regression results are interesting in several regards. First, changes in the average wage seem to play a strong role in explaining changes in inequality (the coefficient on the variables measuring the log of average wage is significant and negative); thus a rise in the average wage is associated with a rise in inequality. This result could be interpreted as follows: the average wage increases when top wages increase, and this is associated with a rise in inequality. Second, an increase in secondary education enrolment rates raises wage inequality, as indeed, over the period under consideration, labour demand was biased towards higher skills while the supply of skilled workers lagged behind. All this would suggest that wage inequality in Mexico rose because of a faster increase in top wages in relation to the average. Third, other things being equal, a higher share of export in GDP tends to increase wage inequality. The dramatic reform of trade policy and the opening up to foreign investment introduced in Mexico in 1985 thus seems to have had a negative impact on wage inequality. This finding goes against the conventional wisdom for developing countries, but confirms the results of other studies on Mexico. For instance, Harrison and Hanson (1999) showed that trade openness is associated with a rise in wage inequality in Mexico. The study presents evidence that foreign direct investment (FDI) and the increasing share of export and technological change played an important role in explaining the rise in observed wage inequality, but is silent on the impact of declining minimum wage. Finally, no effect of GDP growth could be identified in the estimation.

Our results support the conclusion that the minimum wage was too low to counteract the above factors or to have a strong impact on the level of wage inequality. We emphasize the fact these results were found for a country, where the level of the minimum to the average wage varied from 22 to 34 per cent for the period under consideration, hence a relatively low level.

It would be interesting to carry out the same analysis for other countries with different levels of the minimum wage. Obviously, the finding that government could use the minimum wage as an instrument to reduce wage inequality is more relevant for countries where wage employment is developed, as in Mexico, than in countries with limited wage employment.

8.4.2. *Changes in Bargaining Power*

Adjustment and liberalization are leading to more intense competition and are generating pressures to reduce wages and labour standards around the world as the bargaining position of labour is being weakened. As ILO (1996) has pointed out, the underlying reasons for this are, first, that the demand for labour becomes more elastic when the labour market becomes more exposed to foreign competition and, second, that the capacity of governments to regulate labour markets is weakening in the face of heightened international competition. However, it is not yet clear how strong these forces are, especially given the fact that in many countries the part of the labour market which is exposed to foreign competition is very small (in industrialized countries, where 70 per cent of workers are engaged in service industries, and in developing countries, where workers in tradable industries are still a minority in the labour force).

Yet, one notices a general decline in trade-union membership (ILO 1997b). The decline is not uniform, but appears to be occurring irrespective of the type of industrial relation system prevailing. Substantial declines have been witnessed in some African and Latin American countries (Table 8.11), where most of the labour force is not covered by collective agreements.

In the literature, there are divergent opinions on the effects of globalization on the role of social partners and, particularly, on unionization. Some observers see a high unionization rate as indicative of labour market distortions; it may occur that significant labour market distortions require governments to maintain a high degree of external protection, leading to slower growth and slower employment creation (World Bank 1995). However, ILO (1996, 1997b) and Rodrik (1997) argue that undertaking adjustment and liberalization through the destruction of trade unions is very short-sighted and counterproductive in the long run because trade unions contribute to social cohesion, which is necessary if globalization is to be successful.

Rodrik (1997: 25) argues furthermore that 'the efficiency benefits are reaped only to the extent that employment expands in industries in which artificially high wages

Table 8.11. *Trade-union density and collective bargaining coverage rates in selected countries*

	Trade-union density (non-agricultural)	Change, trade-union density (%)	Collective bargaining coverage rate
Ghana	26.0	—	25.0
Kenya	17.0	−60.0	35.0
Mauritius	26.0	−25.0	40.0
Nigeria	17.0	—	40.0
Swaziland	19.0	—	25.0
Uganda	4.0	—	25.0
Zambia	13.0	−33.0	30.0
Zimbabwe	14.0	+20.0	25.0
China	55.0	−8.0	15.0
India	5.0	−18.0	2.0
Malaysia	12.0	−13.0	2.0
Philippines	23.0	+24.0	4.0
Taiwan (China)	28.0	−8.0	4.0
Thailand	3.0	−7.0	27.0
Argentina	25.0	−50.0	73.0
Bolivia	16.0	—	11.0
Chile	16.0	+37.0	13.0
Honduras	5.0	—	13.0
Panama	14.0	—	16.0
Uruguay	12.0	−14.0	27.0

Source: ILO (1997b).

previously kept employment below efficient levels', and 'the first order effects of trade appears to have been a redistribution of the enterprise surplus towards employers rather than the employment of that surplus' (as shown by Amsden and van der Hoeven 1996, to have been the case in many developing countries in the 1980s). Adjustment and liberalization should also aim at increasing social cohesion. New forms of collective bargaining that include a greater focus on responsibility for wage adjustments and employment creation at the central, sectoral, and plant levels, as ILO (1995) carefully argues, can contribute greatly towards improved social cohesion.

'Liberalized trading regimes...have so far been associated with the reduction of workers' rights and the concentration of wealth', Weeks (1999) observes for Latin America. If this is to change, a healthy labour movement is required to ensure effective collective bargaining.

Cortazar *et al.* (1998) describe labour relations in Latin America as confrontational, with a non-encompassing elite, which could find agreement with labour unions in protected industries; however, with the opening up of the economy, this has become impossible. The authors therefore suggest that collective bargaining should be decentralized and that the severance process and severance payments should be reformed to foster more flexibility. These recommendations run counter to recent experiences in small European countries where centralized, national-level agreements on wages, social security, disability benefits, and unemployment compensation have permitted the unions to adopt positions favouring more job flexibility, while maintaining employment and income security. Emphasizing decentralized wage bargaining and abolishing job exit options through the maintenance of a system of social security for workers will increase feelings of insecurity and block processes of change. Schultz (1998) also argues that centralized wage bargaining, if combined with a system of non-adversarial labour relations, can influence decision-making so as to help reduce real wages during periods of economic shock.

Recent research (ILO 2000) indicates that there is a strong inverse relationship between consumer price inflation and the *coordination* of collective bargaining. In countries with a low degree of coordination in collective bargaining consumer price inflation was over 250 per cent in 1990–8, while in countries with a moderate degree of coordination average inflation was around 25 per cent, and in countries with a high degree of coordination average inflation was below 5 per cent. Furthermore, the correlation between income inequality and coordination in collective bargaining has been found to be negative (significant at the 1 per cent level). Countries with a high degree of coordination in collective bargaining had an average Gini ratio slightly below 0.3, while countries with a low degree of coordination had an average Gini ratio over 0.45.

8.4.3. *Employment Protection*

Little research has been carried out on the effects of employment protection on unemployment and poverty rates. Research in Organization for Economic Cooperation and Development (OECD) countries on the relevant effects on employment is

Table 8.12. *Legal labour protection regimes in Latin America*

	Dismissal	Temporary contracts
Argentina	I	P
Brazil	P	R
Mexico	R	R
Colombia	I/R	P
Chile	P	I
Peru	R	P
Uruguay	P	I

Notes: P = permissive, I = intermediate, R = restrictive.
Source: Marshall (1994).

mainly inconclusive (Bertola 1990), although some have found that protection reduces short-term unemployment, but may increase long-run unemployment among certain groups (Nickell 1997). However, most research in the OECD is tied to investigations relying on weak evidence (which is further weakened by the rapid decline in unemployment in 1999–2000 that resulted from the favourable macroeconomic situation rather than from the effect of protection on poverty and inequality). A study by Esping-Andersen (1999) finds that liberalizing measures have increased the vulnerability of poorer groups.

A cross-country study using panel data finds a negative relationship between employment protection and employment rates in the countries of Latin America (Marquez and Pages 1998). However, when GDP per capita is added as a control variable, the relationship is no longer found to be significant, as lower GDP is positively correlated with lower employment/population rates.

Although most policy discourse points to the need to change the regulations regarding job dismissal and to employ more flexible contracts, a major study (Marshall 1994; see also Table 8.12) finds that differences among labour protection regimes are not reflected in the comparative performance in manufacturing in Latin American countries.

8.5. CAN LABOUR MARKET POLICIES REDUCE INEQUALITY?

Most economic reform programmes call for flexibility in the labour market in order for reform programmes to become more effective. However, we need to be cautious about the way regulations are perceived in developing countries. Amadeo and Camargo (1997) point out that it is important to distinguish between written rules and the actual practice of regulation. Their research indicates that, although, judged by the law, the Brazilian labour market can be qualified as very regulated, the actual practice is such that it is less regulated than the French or German labour market. A similar finding has also been reported by Banuri and Amadeo (1991).

In many countries the de facto flexibility in the labour market has increased with growing informal-sector employment, declining minimum wages, and widening wage disparity except in some high-growth countries. However, despite this observed trend, poverty rates have remained substantial, and economic growth has not been vigorous. One might therefore argue that the emphasis on the allocative function of the labour market during the reform process—which has resulted in greater flexibility and inequality in the labour market—should not be the preferred policy instrument for fostering growth and reducing poverty but that other functions of the labour market, namely the dynamic function, the equity function, and the social cohesion function, deserve more attention.

The dynamic function of the labour market is enhanced by greater investment in human capital, improvements in aptitudes, and the development of more innovative skills at lower school level and of complex problem-solving techniques at higher school level, as well as more workplace training and lifelong learning. Squeezing education budgets and subjecting workers to precarious contracts do not help improve the dynamic function of the labour market. Longer-term contracts and established and well-negotiated roles for employment protection can provide a better climate for improvements in productivity.

Equity can be enhanced through the establishment of well-functioning minimum wage mechanisms. In most developing countries, real minimum wages have declined and lost any relevance. Yet, minimum wages can provide stability, foster the commitment of workers, represent an incentive to raise productivity, and help reduce poverty. Thus, rather than regarding minimum wages as a bottleneck in the operation of the labour market, one should regard them as tools (for instance, for taking account of various groups, such as youth, so as not to price them out of the labour market).

Many have considered centralized wage-setting as a hamper on the allocative function of the labour market. Yet, the evidence is overwhelming that centralized wage-setting has favoured lower inequality and lower inflation rates (if it is the outcome of a genuine collective bargaining process). Hence, rather than abolish or block the creation of centralized wage-setting, as suggested by many proponents of the Washington Consensus, policies should seek to strengthen the relevant institutions.

Reform programmes have often discarded efforts to promote social dialogue, as these have been found cumbersome and time consuming and are sometimes considered as caving in to interest groups (van der Hoeven and van der Geest 1999). Although there is now some discussion about this (Stiglitz 2000), the institutions necessary to promote constructive social dialogue and smooth out potential conflicts and redistributive issues (which are inherent in each reform programme) still do not exist in most countries. The establishment of these institutions needs to become an aim in the reform process.

In sum, this chapter has argued that labour market policies other than those emphasizing allocative efficiency should be pursued much more vigorously in reform policy. Labour-market policies, especially the dynamic, equity, and social cohesion elements, are an important component of redistributive and growth policies. Once the process of redistribution and growth has been initiated, it becomes easier to deal with the allocative aspects of labour-market policies that were so much heralded by the Washington Consensus. By focusing narrowly on the *allocative* aspect of the labour market, the Washington Consensus seriously compromised the options for equitable and pro-poor development policies in the 1990s.

REFERENCES

Amadeo, E. J., and J. M. Camargo (1997). Brazil: Regulation and flexibility in the labour market. In S. Edwards and N. C. Lustig (eds.), *Labor Markets in Latin America*. Brookings Institution Press: Washington, DC.

Amsden, A., and R. van der Hoeven (1996). Manufacturing output, employment and real wages in the 1980s: Labour's loss until century's end. *Journal of Development Studies* 32(4), 506–30.

Banuri, T., and E. J. Amadeo (1991). Worlds within the third world: Labour market institutions in Asia and Latin America. In T. Banuri (ed.), *Economic Liberalization: No Panacea*. Clarendon Press: Oxford.

Bell, L. A. (1997). The impact of minimum wages in Mexico and Colombia. *Journal of Labour Economics* 15(3), 102–35.

Berry, A., *et al.* (1997). Globalization, adjustment, inequality and poverty. Mimeo, Department of Economics, University of Toronto: Toronto.

Bertola, G. (1990). Job security, employment and wages. *European Economic Review* 34, 851–86.

Buffie, E. (1994). The long-run consequences of short-run stabilization policy. In S. Horton, R. Kanbur, and D. Mazumdar (eds.), *Labour Markets in an Era of Adjustment*. World Bank: Washington, DC.

Cortazar, R., N. C. Lustig, and R. H. Sabot (1998). Economic policy and labour market dynamics. In N. Birdsall, C. Graham, and R. H. Sabot (eds.), *Beyond Tradeoffs: Market Reforms and Equitable Growth in Latin America*. Brookings Institution Press: Washington, DC.

Diwan, I. (1999). Labour shares and financial crises. Mimeo, World Bank: Washington, DC.

Esping-Andersen, G. (1999). *Social Foundations of Post-Industrial Economics*. Oxford University Press: Oxford.

Forteza, A., and M. Rama (2000). The labour market 'rigidity' and the success of economic reforms across more than one hundred countries. World Bank Working Paper 2521. World Bank: Washington, DC.

Ghose, A. K. (2001). Global economic inequality and international trade. Employment Paper 2001/12. ILO: Geneva.

Gottschalk, P., and T. M. Smeeding (1997). Cross-national comparisons of earnings and income inequality. *Journal of Economic Literature* 35(June), 633–87.

Harrison, A., and G. Hanson (1999). Who gains from trade reform?: Some remaining puzzles. *Journal of Development Studies* 59, 125–56.

Horton, S., R. Kanbur, and D. Mazumdar (1994). *Labour Markets in an Era of Adjustment*. World Bank: Washington, DC.

ILO (1995). *The Employment Challenge in Latin America and the Caribbean.* ILO Regional Office for the Americas: Lima.

—— (1996). *World Employment 1996/97.* ILO: Geneva.

—— (1997*a*). *1996 Labour Overview: Latin America and the Caribbean.* ILO Regional Office for the Americas: Lima.

—— (1997*b*). *World Labour Report, 1997/98.* ILO: Geneva.

—— (2000). *Organization, Bargaining and Social Dialogue in a Globalizing World.* ILO: Geneva.

Karshenas, M. (1988). Labour markets and the diversity of adjustment experiences. SOAS Working Papers 78. Department of Economics. University of London.

Khan, A. (1993). *Structural Adjustment and Income Distribution: Issues and Experiences.* ILO: Geneva.

Lee, D. S. (1999). Wage inequality in the United States during the 1980s: Rising dispersion or falling minimum wage? *Quarterly Journal of Economics* 114(3), 977–1023.

Lee, E. (1996). Globalization and employment: Is anxiety justified? *International Labour Review* 135(5).

Marquez, G., and N. Pages (1998). Ties that bind employment protection and labour market outcomes in Latin America. IADB Working Papers 373. Inter-American Development Bank: Washington, DC.

Marshall, A. (1994). Economic consequences of labour protection regimes in Latin America. *International Labour Review* 133(1).

Nickell, S. (1997). Unemployment and labor market rigidities: Europe versus North America. *Journal of Economic Perspectives* 11(3), 55–74.

Owens, T., and A. Wood (1997). Export-oriented industrialization through primary processing. *World Development* 25(May–September).

Pastor, M. (1985). The effect of IMF programmes in the third world: Debate and evidence from Latin America. Mimeo, University of Pennsylvania: Philadelphia.

Pieper, U. (1998). Openness and the tructural dynamics of productivity and employment in developing countries: A case of deindustrialization. Employment and Training Papers 8. ILO: Geneva.

Robinson, S. (1991). Macroeconomic, financial variables and computable general equilibrium models. *World Development* 19(11), 1509–26.

Rodrik, D. (1997). *Has Globalization Gone too Far?* Institute for International Economics: Washington, DC.

Saget, C. (2001). Poverty reduction and employment in developing countries: Do minimum wages help? *International Labour Review* 140(3), 237–69.

Schultz, T. P. (1998). Labor market reforms: Issues, evidence and prospects. Paper prepared for the conference. Economic Policy Reform: What We Know and What We Need to Know (September). Center for Research on Economic Development and Policy Reform, Stanford University: Stanford, CA.

Stiglitz, J. (2000). *Democratic Development as the Fruits of Labor.* Industrial Relations Association: Boston.

Teulings, C. N., E. H. Vogels, and J. van Dieten (1998). *Minimum loon, arbeidsmarkt en inkomensverdeling.* SDU: The Hague.

Toye, J. (1995). *Structural Adjustment and Employment Policy.* ILO: Geneva.

UNDP (1997). *Human Development Report.* Oxford University Press: New York.

van der Geest, W., and R. van der Hoeven (1999). *Adjustment, Employment and Missing Labour Market Institutions in Africa.* James Curry: London.

van der Hoeven, R. (1987). External shocks and stabilization policies: Spreading the load. *International Labour Review* 126(2).

van der Hoeven, R. (2001). Labour markets and income inequality: What are the new insights after the Washington consensus? WIDER Working Paper 201. UNU/WIDER: Helsinki.

—— and W. van der Geest (1999). The missing institutions of Africa's adjusted labour markets. In W. van der Geest and R. van der Hoeven (eds.), *Adjustment, Employment and Missing Labour Market Institutions in Africa*. James Curry: London.

—— and L. Taylor (2000). Structural adjustment, labour markets and employment: Some considerations for sensible people. *Journal of Development Studies* 36(4), 57–65.

Weeks, J. (1999). Wages, employment and workers rights in Latin America 1970–1998. *International Labour Review* 138(2).

World Bank (1995). *World Development Report*. Oxford University Press: New York.

——(1997). *Global Economic Prospects and the Developing Countries*. World Bank: Washington, DC.

9

Increased Income Inequality in OECD Countries and the Redistributive Impact of the Government Budget

ANTHONY B. ATKINSON

9.1. INTRODUCTION

The recent rise in inequality in the distribution of disposable income in many, although not all, countries has led to a search for explanations, particularly since for much of the post-war period falling inequality has been the norm. In Organization for Economic Cooperation and Development (OECD) countries, on which I concentrate here, the cause has been identified as rising wage dispersion, coupled with persistent unemployment in Europe. Indeed the distribution of income is often treated as synonymous with the distribution of earnings. However, a number of factors need to be brought into any explanation of the extent and timing of changes in the income distribution (Atkinson 1997, 2000), including movements in factor shares, changes in real interest rates, and the impact of the government budget. The last of these is the element on which I focus in this chapter. It is of particular importance given the emphasis placed on the budgetary pressures, which have been generated by demographic and other shifts increasing dependency ratios. What is the role of the government budget, particularly taxes and transfers, in explaining the evolution of the distribution of disposable income? Do differences in welfare states across countries explain the differing evolution of the final (post-transfer post-tax) distribution? Have active policy changes contributed to offsetting rising market inequality or have they engendered rising final inequality? To the extent that changes in demographic structure, such as the ageing of the population, have intensified budgetary pressures, have governments been forced to cut back on the generosity of their welfare states?

The first section of the chapter reviews the statistical evidence available from official and other sources about the redistributive impact of the government budget, taking five OECD countries where there is a time series of studies covering the 1980s and the 1990s. These studies are not comparable across countries, differing in their coverage,

I am grateful to Giovanni Andrea Cornia, Raghbendra Jha, participants in the July 1999 meeting at World Institute for Development, Economics Research (WIDER) in Helsinki, and the referees for very helpful comments on earlier drafts of this study.

but the contrasts across countries are highly suggestive. As already noted by Fritzell (1993), the equalizing effect of welfare state redistribution did not decrease in all countries. At the same time, these findings need to be interpreted in the light of an analytical framework, and this is the subject of Section 9.2. To this end, I set out a simple framework within which we can explore the distributional implications of different responses to changes in economic conditions and the different elements—on both supply and demand side—influencing the choice of response. Can we separate the effects of automatic policy responses and active policy changes? What is the benchmark by which we should judge cutbacks in social protection? How do different formulae for sharing the burden of adjustment to external shocks affect the Gini coefficient for disposable income? The actual policy changes observed in the five European countries and the United States are summarized in Section 9.3, where I take unemployment benefits and personal income taxation as two case studies. What changes have been made in policy structures and parameters over the 1980s and 1990s? What (if anything) was said in advance about their likely redistributive impact? What can be concluded about the actual impact? The final part of the chapter summarizes the main conclusions, both analytical and empirical.

9.2. REDISTRIBUTIVE IMPACT OF THE GOVERNMENT BUDGET IN SELECTED OECD COUNTRIES

The distribution of the tax burden, and of the benefits from government spending, have long been an important subject in public finance (on this, see also Chapter 10). One of the landmark studies of the tax burden in the United States is that by Musgrave *et al.* (1951), later followed by Musgrave *et al.* (1974). The same year saw also the publication of the celebrated *Who Bears the Tax Burden?* by Pechman and Okner (1974), to which Pechman published sequels (1985 and 1990). For 1980, using a range of incidence assumptions, Pechman found that 'Because the degree of progressivity or regressivity is relatively small under any of the incidence assumptions, it is clear that the tax system has very little effect on the distribution of income. However, the system of transfer payments is highly progressive and has a major effect on the income distribution' (Pechman 1985: 4–5).

In other countries, too, it has been found that taxes as a whole have relatively little redistributive impact, and that it is transfers, which make the government budget significantly progressive. In the United Kingdom, the official statistics now published annually in *Economic Trends* (e.g. Office for National Statistics 1998) indicate that the addition of cash benefits to market income reduces recorded inequality substantially, but that taxes have only a modest effect, the reduction in overall inequality associated with direct taxation being offset by the indirect taxes.

The overall impact of the government budget depends on the combined effects of taxes and expenditure. A progressive transfer system financed by a proportional tax is progressive overall. Moreover, personal taxation may dampen down disequalizing changes in the market distribution, even where the tax system is purely proportional. A simple example may help illustrate this point and set the scene for the following analysis. Suppose that there is a group, making up a proportion p of the population, who have zero market income, referred to for convenience as 'pensioners'. They receive a state transfer, b, financed by a proportional tax at rate t on the income of the rest, $1 - p$, of the population. The transfer is revenue-neutral in the sense that the sum of market incomes is equal to the sum of post-tax post-transfer 'net' incomes. The Lorenz curves for market incomes (solid line) and net incomes (dashed line) are drawn in Fig. 9.1. Suppose now that there is an increase in inequality in the market incomes of the non-pensioner population, leaving the mean unaffected, so that the same tax t finances the same state transfer. A given increase in the Gini coefficient for market income translates into an increase in the inequality of disposable income of $(1 - t)$ as much. In terms of Fig. 9.1, the outward shift in the dashed line is scaled down by the factor $(1 - t)$. With a tax rate of 50 per cent, an increase of market inequality of 5 percentage points corresponds to an increase of 2.5 points in disposable income inequality.

9.2.1. *Observed Changes in the 1980s and 1990s*

It is the changes over time that are my concern here. In Figs 9.2–9.6, I have assembled estimates of the overall degree of inequality (measured by the Gini coefficient) before and after redistribution for five selected OECD countries (on this point see also Chapter 2). The selection is determined largely by the availability of a long time series of estimates of the redistributive impact of the government budget, but the countries have in common a rise in the inequality of market incomes between 1980 and the mid-1990s. In Canada and in West Germany, the Gini coefficient for market income increased by some 5 percentage points; in the United Kingdom by around 7 points; in Sweden by 10 percentage points; and in Finland (from 1981) by more than 10 points.

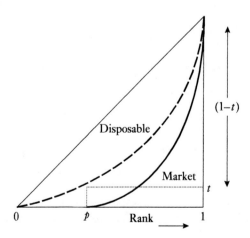

Figure 9.1. *Pensioner–worker example: market income and net income*

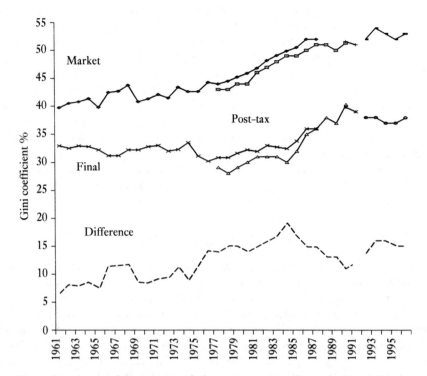

Figure 9.2. *Impact of the government budget on income inequality in the United Kingdom*
1961–96

Source: First series (from 1961)—distribution (not equivalized) among households of original income
and final income; 1961–75—from Royal Commission on the Distribution of Income and Wealth, 1977,
pages 247 and 251; 1976—from *Economic Trends*, January 1982, page 105 (for 1976), December 1982,
page 112 (for 1977–81), November 1983, page 87 (for 1982), December 1984, page 95 (for 1983), July
1986, page 103 (for 1984), July 1987, page 103 (for 1985), and May 1990 (for 1986, 1987). Second
series (from 1977)—distribution among households of equivalized original income and post-tax
income. There are breaks in the series in 1990, 1992, and 1996/7 (although a figure is given for this
year on the previous basis); *Economic Trends*, April 1998, page 58 (for 1977, 1979, 1981, 1983, 1985,
1987, 1989, 1991, 1993–4 to 1996–7), December 1994, page 65 (for 1978, 1980, 1982, 1984, 1986, 1988,
1992), and January 1993, page 159 (for 1990).

Reference is also made to the United States, where the rise in market income inequality
from 1980 to 1993 receives a +++ rating ('large increase') from Gottschalk and
Smeeding (1997: table 4). These six countries include the five studied by Fritzell
(1993) in his comparison of market and disposable income inequality; the results here
differ from his based on annual series, rather than 2 datapoints, and in extending to
the 1990s.

The series go back to the 1970s (Sweden and Canada) or the 1960s (Finland, West
Germany, and the United Kingdom). My main focus is on the 1980s and 1990s, but it

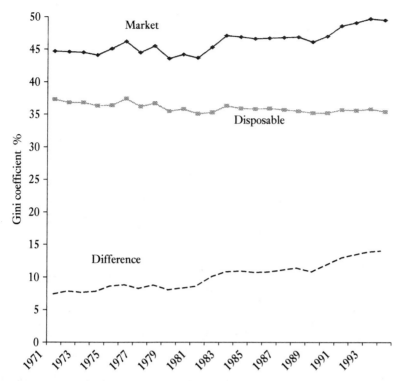

Figure 9.3. *Impact of the government budget on income inequality in Canada 1971–94*
Source: Statistics Canada (1996: table 6).

is helpful to keep in perspective the longer run trends. In a number of countries, the 1960s and 1970s were periods of declining inequality in disposable income. Long time series are therefore of especial value. At the same time, the reader should bear in mind that statistics at different dates may be defined in different ways or need to be interpreted differently. I have tried to show the major breaks in the series, but even a consistently defined series may have a different significance as economies and societies evolve. Moreover, these studies suffer from well-known limitations: the problem of determining the incidence of taxes and transfers, the shortcomings of a snapshot picture (not allowing for redistribution over the life cycle), and the need to allow for other dimensions of redistribution (such as that by gender). These caveats should be borne very much in mind when considering the evidence presented below.

9.2.2. *United Kingdom*

The *Economic Trends* estimates for the United Kingdom, shown in Fig. 9.2, are built up from calculations for each household in a sample survey. Households have incomes from market sources (earnings, self-employment income, rent, dividends, interest, and

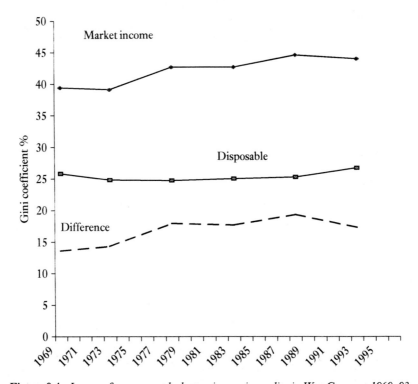

Figure 9.4. *Impact of government budget on income inequality in West Germany 1969–93*

Source: 1969–88 from Becker and Hauser (1997: tables 4 and 6); 1993 from Hauser (1999: tables 4 and 5); the distribution refers to equivalized household income, and excludes households with foreign heads.

private transfers). Arithmetically, we add cash benefits and subtract direct taxes to arrive at disposable income. If we further subtract indirect taxes, this gives post-tax income (shown from 1977 in Fig. 9.2). Finally, the official estimates add benefits from government spending on health, education, housing, and transport subsidies to give final income (shown up to 1987).[1] The results suggest that inequality of market income varied cyclically, but the predominant impression is of a long-run steady rise in the Gini coefficient for market income since the mid-1960s. In the 20 years from 1965 to 1984, the Gini coefficient increased from 40 to 50 per cent. Even more striking is the fact that the coefficient for final income showed scarcely any rise over this period. The redistributive impact of cash transfers, other benefits, and taxation increased enough to offset the more unequal market incomes.

After 1984, the story is quite different. Inequality in market income continued to rise, but between 1984 and 1990 the Gini coefficient for post-tax income increased much more sharply. Measured in terms of the difference between the two coefficients (the dashed

---

[1] It might be expected that the Gini coefficient for final income would be less than that for post-tax income; however, the two series differ also in the definition of income. The first (up to 1987) relates to total income, not adjusted for household size; the second (from 1977) is based on equivalized household income.

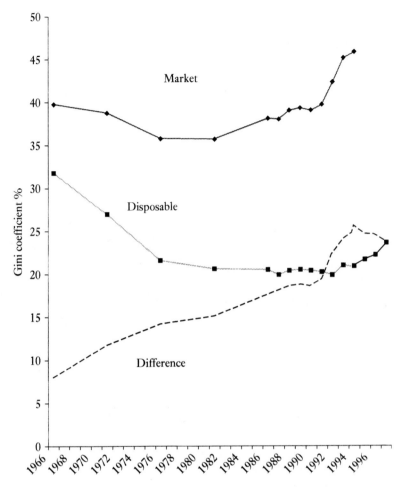

Figure 9.5. *Impact of the government budget in Finland 1966–97*
Source: Uusitalo (1998: table 2).

line), the redistributive contribution of transfers and taxes fell from 19 percentage points (the difference between the two Gini coefficients in 1984) to 11 percentage points in 1990. The reduction in redistributive impact was attributable to a smaller impact of cash transfers (minus 5 percentage points), less progressive direct taxes (minus 1 percentage point), and more regressive indirect taxes (minus 2 percentage points).

9.2.3. *Canada*

The United Kingdom experience is in sharp contrast with that of Canada shown in Fig. 9.3. The coverage of the estimates is different, in that the post-budget figures refer to disposable income, such as income after direct taxes but before indirect taxes and before government in-kind benefits. This may affect the comparison not only of

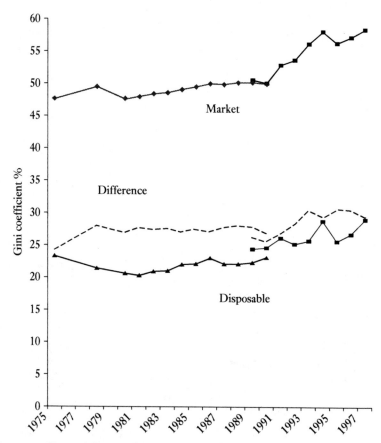

Figure 9.6. *Impact of the government budget in Sweden 1975–97*
Source: Statistics Sweden (1999: 3, table 2).

levels but also of *trends*. However, the difference in trends from the United Kingdom is so striking that this cannot be explained solely by definitions. As has been noted by Brandolini, in Canada 'the Gini coefficient of incomes after taxes was much the same... over the entire period. This... was particularly remarkable when contrasted with the dynamics of the distribution of incomes before public redistribution [which] was marked by two episodes of sharp rise of inequality' (1998: 20). Over the period 1980–94 as a whole, the Gini coefficient for market income rose by some 5 percentage points, whereas that for disposable income in 1994 was not significantly higher than 15 years earlier. The difference between the two series (dashed line) rose in line with the market income series.

9.2.4. *West Germany*

The series for West Germany in Fig. 9.4 has some likeness to that in Canada up to 1988, in that inequality of market incomes increased substantially after 1973, but this was not accompanied by an equivalent rise in inequality of disposable income. More recently, between 1988 and 1993, there was a slight decline in market inequality but a 1.5 percentage point increase in the Gini coefficient for disposable income. The difference curve slopes down. According to Hauser (1999: 14), this reflects inroads into social protection in recent years, but its modest size should be noted (the estimated standard error of the Gini coefficient is 0.6 of a percentage point). Overall, as Hauser comments (my translation) 'The German tax and transfer system reduces the inequality of market income quite considerably. . . . the German social security system, despite the increasingly unfavourable conditions, has largely reached its goals from 1973 to 1993'. (1999: 18)

9.2.5. *Finland*

The picture for Finland in the 1980s and 1990s in Fig. 9.5 contains elements of similarity with both Canada and the United Kingdom, but attention should be drawn first to the impressive earlier record of reduced inequality in both market and disposable income (see Uusitalo 1989, 1999). The Gini coefficient for market incomes fell by nearly 5 percentage points between 1966 and 1976, and that for disposable income by twice as much, the redistributive impact of taxes and transfers intensifying the fall in inequality (see the dashed difference line). From 1981 to 1994 the Gini coefficient for market income rose by 10 percentage points, particularly after 1990 with the economic difficulties faced at that time, the unemployment rate reaching 16 per cent in 1994. This was, however, offset by the government budget to the extent that inequality in disposable income did not increase. As is brought out by Uusitalo (1999), the main contributors were transfer payments; the redistributive impact of taxation did not increase in line with the inequality of market income, and actually fell after 1989. Since 1994, moreover, the picture has changed as a result of policy measures cutting the redistributive impact of transfers, which have led inequality of disposable income to rise more than that of market income. As summarized by Uusitalo, the story of the 1990s in Finland was that

during the deepest recession in the OECD-area in the 1990s, income inequality did not change, since redistribution of cash transfers compensated the growing inequality of factor incomes. After the recession, during years when economic growth has been among the highest in the OECD-area, income inequality has increased, because redistribution of cash transfers has declined, while factor income inequality has continued to grow. (Uusitalo 1998: 4)

As a result of the 1994–7 upturn in inequality, Finland can be said to have a U-shaped pattern like that in the United Kingdom. There is, however, little resemblance in either the timing or the shape of the U. In the United Kingdom, the left hand arm of the U is relatively flat. In Finland, there was a pronounced downward trend followed by a decade of stability; and the right-hand arm is both more recent and, so far, modest in size. Both countries have lopsided U-shapes, but on different sides.

9.2.6. *Sweden*

The position in a second Nordic country, Sweden, is shown in Fig. 9.6. In this case, a U-shape is again visible for disposable income, with the Gini coefficient rising along with that for market income since 1980. Before commenting on the impact of the budget, we should note that the Swedish case illustrates the need to interpret the observations in the light of social and economic change. The Statistics Sweden series has a rather different household definition from that in the other studies quoted here, in that young adults who live at home with their parents are treated as separate households. This may be expected to affect not only the level but also the trend in inequality measurement. Second, the Statistics Sweden figures, which are in part based on income tax records, include realized capital gains (not included in many other countries). Temporary tax changes in Sweden in 1994 caused many better-off households to realize capital gains in that year, causing the 'spike' in measured inequality in that year (see Fig. 9.6). There was also a concentration of capital gains in 1997.[2] The finance ministry has produced alternative estimates excluding young adults living with their parents and smoothing real capital income (namely, also adjusting capital income for inflation). Their results are summarized as showing 'a weak increase in income inequality during the 1990s' (Ministry of Finance 1999: 7).

Bearing in mind these qualifications, we can see that over the 1980s the 'difference' line is fairly flat, indicating that the (modest) rise in market inequality in that decade had been accompanied by a rise in disposable income inequality. In the 1990s the redistributive difference increased, in that the rise in disposable income inequality was definitely less than the increase in market inequality. According to Jansson (2000: table 13), the Gini coefficient for factor income inequality rose by 5.4 percentage points between 1991 and 1997, whereas that for disposable income increased by 3.2 points, the difference mainly reflecting the transfer system. The total redistributive effect is of course large. The redistributional achievements of the Swedish welfare state have been described by Björklund *et al.* (1995)[3] and Björklund (1998), who examine the impact not just on annual incomes but also on long-run incomes of cohorts. The latter calculations (see Björklund and Palme 1999) seek to separate redistribution over the life cycle from that of lifetime income, an important issue, which I do not discuss here.

9.3. THE GOVERNMENT BUDGET IN PRINCIPLE AND POLICY REACTION TO DEMOGRAPHIC SHIFTS

The observed changes in the 1980s and 1990s immediately raise the question as to how far we can separate automatic and discretionary changes in redistributive policy. Is it

---

[2] The Gini coefficient including capital gains was 29.0%, compared with 26.0% when they are excluded, whereas for 1996 the difference was only 1.4% (Statistics Sweden 1999: table 4).

[3] In comparing their findings with those in Fig. 9.6, it should be noted that their sample includes people aged between 25 and 64 (and the members of their households), and that before tax pay includes pensions, sick pay, unemployment benefits, and parents allowance. The estimates therefore exclude the impact of growing unemployment (see Agell *et al.* 1996: 177).

the case that progressive tax/transfer policy automatically dampens the response to adverse movements in market inequality? Does a larger increase in inequality in disposable income than in market income mean that there must have been discretionary policy changes reducing the redistributive role of the budget? In order to address these questions, we need an analytical framework.

9.3.1. *Policy Responses*

The simple example used at the start of Section 9.1 suggests that a flat rate benefit/proportional tax system would be automatically equalizing in the face of exogenous shocks. This example is, however, a special one in the sense that, by assumption, the previous tax and benefit policy remained feasible after the shift. This may be seen from the government budget constraint:

$$bp = t\,(1 - p)\,\mu,\tag{9.1}$$

where μ is the mean market wage (assumed to be the only market source of income) of the non-pensioner population, so that the overall mean income is $(1 - p)\,\mu$. A redistribution of market income that leaves the mean unchanged is therefore consistent with constant t and b.

In general this is not the case. Suppose that there is an increase in the proportion of pensioners (a demographic shift), drawn proportionately from all earnings ranges, so that the relative distribution of market wages remains unchanged. Per head of the total population, average income falls, and hence the tax base per head of population falls. To preserve budget neutrality, either the tax rate has to rise or the benefit per person has to be reduced. Suppose that the tax rate is held constant and benefits fall relative to overall mean income as p rises. In terms of Fig. 9.1, the lower part of the Lorenz curve rotates clockwise, and the Gini coefficient for disposable income increases on this account. The net of tax wage is unchanged for each worker, but the working population is now a smaller fraction of the total. This shrinking of the working population means that we have to go further down the earnings range to reach the top x per cent of the total population, so that with a constant tax rate the upper part of the Lorenz curve also moves outwards. We should expect the demographic shift, coupled with a 'constant tax rate' policy, to cause a rise in inequality of disposable income, as well as in market income.

Suppose now that the government raises the tax rate in response to the increased need to pay pensions and that the benefit is maintained in relation to overall average income. I refer to this as 'sharing the burden', since the benefit is reduced in absolute terms, in line with the fall in the overall average income, and, from the budget constraint (9.1), the tax rate rises in proportion to p, so that net wages are also reduced. For the moment, it is assumed that there is no behavioural response to these changes in taxes and benefits. The fact that the benefit is reduced proportionally with average income means that the slope of the Lorenz curve remains unchanged at the lower end; at the same time, if the benefit is less than the lowest net of tax wage, the Lorenz curve beyond the pre-shift value of p is lower than before; and among the working population the slope at the end can be seen to rise. In this situation too, therefore, we would expect to observe an increase in inequality of disposable income, even if more muted than in the first case, as a result of the demographic shift and the associated policy response.

The 'sharing the burden' policy means that benefit entitlement falls in relation to the average wage, which would be the reference point in a (gross) earnings replacement scheme. A third possible situation is where the pension is maintained as a proportion of the average wage ('no scheme adjustment'), which means that the tax rate has to rise proportionately to the dependency ratio $p/(1-p)$. If, say, p has risen from a fifth to a third, the tax rate has to double, compared with a two-thirds rise in the 'sharing the burden' case. The Lorenz curve now shifts upwards at the bottom, and there could be a fall in the Gini coefficient for disposable income. By continuity, we can see that a policy, which cuts benefit entitlements by less than the fall in average income, could mean that the demographic shift, plus policy response, left unchanged the Gini coefficient for disposable income. This warns that it is not always easy to read across from policy parameters to the impact on measured distributions.

9.3.2. *Incidence*

Changes in taxes and benefits may be expected to lead to behavioural change. The rise of inequality in market incomes may in part be due to the existence and growth of transfer programmes. This brings me to the issue of incidence. Some of the possible implications may be seen by extending the analytical framework already described. At the simplest level, the rise in the tax rate may reduce the level of wage income. Suppose that the working population reduce their hours of work, a change which may take many forms (e.g. ceasing a second job, slower return to work after family responsibilities, putting in less effort). In the government budget constraint, μ now becomes a declining function of t (assuming that the substitution effect outweighs the income effect). In the second and third situations described above, the benefit level will be lower than predicted on the basis of constant μ. The range of choices open to the government is now shown by the heavy curved line in Fig. 9.7 rather than by the straight line. Also drawn is the social indifference curve, indicating a policy choice, E. The effect of a rise in the scale of the dependent population is that the benefit level possible at any tax rate falls (see the dashed line in Fig. 9.7), and that the slope at any tax rate is reduced, making benefit cuts more attractive to the government.[4]

---

[4] Introduction of incentive considerations also affects the evaluation of the redistributional outcome. A reduction of work effort by the working population reduces their cash income, but has offsetting advantages in terms of increased leisure, home production, and so on. It is not therefore appropriate to measure their welfare simply by their cash income. The correct adjustment depends on the underlying model of behaviour. A simple case is that used by Atkinson and Bourguignon (1990), where the cost of effort is assumed to be a fixed proportion, $1-\delta$, of net earnings (where $0<\delta<1$). The distribution is then evaluated in terms of benefits and δ times net earnings.

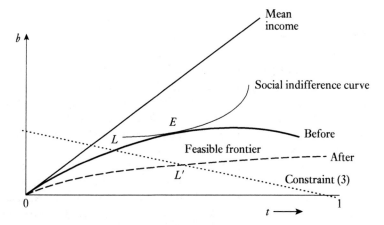

Figure 9.7. *Policy options open to a government to adjust to the distributive impact of demographic shift*

A second form of behavioural adjustment is withdrawal from the labour force. Through early retirement, for example, the size of the dependent population, p, may become a function of the tax and benefit parameters. To take a simple example, suppose that the participation decision is based on a comparison of net income in work and the benefit level. There is then a critical wage, w^*, defined by

$$\delta w^* (1 - t) = b. \tag{9.2}$$

If we assume that the wage, w, that a person can command is related to their rank in the skill distribution $F(w)$, where $0 \le F \le 1$, there will be a proportion, $F^* = F(w^*)$, who do not participate. The proportion F^* rises with the tax rate and falls if benefits are cut. It is possible that $F^* = 0$, in that no one has potential wages of w^* or lower. Indeed, a government may take this as a constraint on the choice of tax and benefit parameters. For such a 'limited' welfare state, there is the constraint imposed from the supply side that

$$b < \delta (1 - t) w_{min}, \tag{9.3}$$

where w_{min} is the lowest wage. Such a constraint is shown in Fig. 9.7, the choice in this case being L (for 'limited').

9.3.3. *Policy Choices*

So far I have discussed the menu of choices open to the government in the event of a demographic shift. How could we in fact expect governments to react? As we have seen, inaction is not an option. We cannot take 'no change' as the policy reference point, since this will not, in general, allow the budget to be balanced.[5] What then are the main considerations? We may distinguish two sides of the equation. The first—which has received most attention—is the cost side. As is clear from the government budget constraint in Fig. 9.7, at any given tax rate benefits are lower, and a lower level of social welfare can be attained. We might expect there to be some sharing of the burden, in the sense that would be implied by moving to a lower social indifference curve in the 'normal' case, but the slope also worsens, inducing a move round the frontier towards lower benefits and taxes. It is possible that the tax rate would actually be cut. However, it is also possible that the tax rate will rise. In the case where the welfare state is limited by (9.3), we will see a fall in b, as L moves to L', but there will also be a rise in t. With a lower benefit, the tax rate can be raised without violating the constraint, so that there is a degree of burden-sharing.

Whereas attention tends to concentrate on the cost side, the demand side of the government policy choice is also important. A rise in the dependent population certainly increases the cost, but it also increases the value attached to providing adequate benefits. Taking both sides into account, it is possible that a rise in the dependency ratio would lead a country to extend its welfare state. Whether it would do so depends on the nature of social objectives. If the government is solely concerned with the welfare of the worst-off—a Rawlsian objective—then the number of people in this target category does not enter the social calculus. In this respect, however, the Rawlsian objective differs from social welfare functions that give positive weight to all of the population. If the weight is uniform, then there is no motive for redistribution. But even the most conservative of governments typically has some degree of concern for the poor. Suppose that we have what may be called 'charitable conservatism', where distributional concern is represented by attaching a higher social marginal valuation of income for the retired population (not the voluntarily unemployed). In this case, the size of the target population enters the equation on the demand side: a doubling of the dependency ratio doubles the desirability of a more extensive transfer. In terms of Fig. 9.7, there has been a shift in the social indifference contours. This has to be set in the balance with the increased cost. There are pressures in both directions.

Policy responses in recent decades may also have been affected by shifts in government objectives. Just to give an example, it is possible that a perception that the elderly on average are better off has led to a fall in the weight attached to their incomes according to the charitable conservative position. This shift in objectives may offset the opposite pressure to give more weight to this group, as it has become a larger fraction of the population. Or earlier governments had more extensive redistributive

---

[5] An unbalanced budget, financed through government borrowing, is also a possibility, but again this constitutes a 'policy change', which has distributional implications.

ambitions, where there was concern not just with the least advantaged but also with the relative distribution among those higher up the scale. There has been a switch to the less ambitious charitable conservative position. Changed objectives may also take the form of greater weight attached to cutting the size of the government budget. The fiscal criteria adopted by European governments at Maastricht are an example. We may be observing policy changes driven, not by demographic shifts, but by new political agendas.

The explanation of such shifting agendas takes us into the field of public choice, or political economy. The literature suggests a variety of possible explanations. A voting model indicates that we need to consider the preferences of the electorate, and the mechanisms by which their concerns and interests are translated into action. They may be influenced by the ideology of politicians and by the attempt of these actors to obtain and retain political power. Moving beyond strictly electoral models, we have to recognize that the civil servants administering public policy may themselves have objectives, which they are anxious to pursue. In the fields of taxation and social security, there are active pressure groups and lobbies. Viewed in an international context, the behaviour of national governments may be influenced by what is happening in other countries. Tax reform is contagious: 'The US example raised the profile of comprehensive tax reform as an issue in public discussion in Canada' (Dodge and Sargent 1988: 51). The actual nature of policy responses is the subject of the next section.

9.4. POLICY CHANGES IN REDISTRIBUTIVE TAXES AND TRANSFERS: CASE STUDIES OF UNEMPLOYMENT BENEFIT AND PERSONAL TAXATION

What have been the actual policy responses? In this section, I consider some of the changes in redistributive policies that have taken place in OECD countries over the 1980s and 1990s, taking unemployment benefits and personal taxation as examples. These are only part of the redistributive process, but there are policy areas which have received a great deal of attention. I look in detail at the six countries identified in Section 9.1.

One approach to the policy responses might be to consider the aggregate expenditure on transfers and the aggregate receipts of the government. These are illustrated in Fig. 9.8, which shows the changes between 1974 and 1979 and 1990 and 1995. Social transfers increased relative to gross domestic product (GDP) in all five countries (Germany is not included since the period spans reunification). The increase was particularly large in Finland, where it doubled, and in Sweden. Canada and the United Kingdom show a rather similar increase. On the tax side, the picture is more mixed. There were again large increases in Finland and Sweden, and a sizeable increase in Canada, but there was a fall in the United Kingdom.

Aggregate spending has been used in a number of studies. Political scientists have investigated the relation between the political complexion of governments and welfare spending—see for example Maravall (1997: appendix 3) and Castles (1998: chapter 5). The relationship between aggregate transfers and poverty rates has been

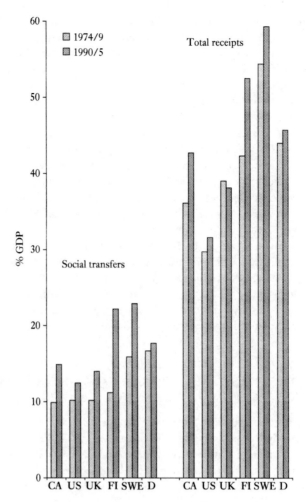

Figure 9.8. *Social transfers and total government receipts as a percentage of GDP*
Source: OECD (1997a: tables 6.3 and 6.6).

investigated—see for example Atkinson *et al.* (1995: chapter 7). It is, however, clear
that any such relations have to be interpreted with care. As the 'sharing the burden'
example shows, a rise in total transfers relative to gross national product (GNP) may
be the result of demographic shifts, and not correspond to any policy decision to
improve benefits. Aggregate figures are the outcome of a number of factors. I therefore turn to the other end of the scale, looking at the micropolicy parameters: levels
of benefit, eligibility conditions, duration, tax rates, tax base, and so on. Changes in
microparameters, too, need to be interpreted with care, and I discuss issues of
interpretation in the final part of the section.

9.4.1. *Unemployment Compensation*

In the past, the response to increased need for unemployment compensation has been to cutback on benefits. The situation in Germany in the early 1930s (public insurance was introduced in 1927) has been described by Schmid *et al.*:

The system was unable to cope with its first test, the depression of the early 1930s. It had already come under pressure by the end of the 1920s as a result of increasing deficits, which... were an occasion for constant changes: increases in contributions, exclusion from coverage, reductions in the level and duration of benefits, and finally even a means test (incompatible with insurance principles)... At the end of the Weimar Republic only 11 percent of the unemployed were receiving benefits'. (Schmid *et al.* 1992: 73)

Has the increased unemployment of the latter part of the twentieth century led to a similar reaction?

United Kingdom

In the United Kingdom, the response to rising unemployment in the 1980s was indeed to restrict benefit generosity and entitlement. The replacement rate, already low by European standards, was significantly reduced by such measures as the abolition of the earnings-related supplement, leaving only a flat rate benefit. Atkinson and Micklewright (1989) list seventeen distinct changes in unemployment insurance between 1979 and 1988, the majority of which reduced the level or coverage of benefit. In the 1990s there has been the replacement of national insurance benefit by a jobseeker's allowance in 1996, restricting insurance benefit to 6 months.

United States

In the United States, a range of measures were taken by the federal government in the 1980s to reduce the value and coverage of unemployment benefit. These included the taxation of benefits, partially from 1979 and fully from 1986, and the requirement that states repay with interest federal loans to their trust funds, which caused states in turn to tighten eligibility to unemployment insurance and to reduce benefits. The Federal General Accounting Office reported that, during 1981–7, no fewer than forty-four states adopted tighter eligibility standards or stricter disqualification provisions.[6]

Canada

In Canada, the Unemployment Insurance Act 1971 had increased significantly the coverage and generosity of benefits (Card and Riddell 1993), but a series of subsequent changes 'have been in the direction of a more restrictive or less generous programme'

---

[6] *Monthly Labor Review*, September 1995: 35.

(OECD 1996: 78). In 1977 the minimum number of weeks required to qualify was increased, and this was further tightened in 1979 for new entrants and repeat claimants. In 1979, the replacement rate was lowered to 60 per cent (from 67 per cent). In 1990, the entry requirements were further increased, and benefit durations reduced. In 1993, the replacement rate was further reduced to 57 per cent (and in 1994 to 55 per cent except for low-income claimants with dependants), and those leaving jobs voluntarily became ineligible for unemployment insurance. Changes made in 1996, replacing unemployment insurance by employment insurance, reduced the replacement rate for repeat claimants, clawed back through the income tax system some of the benefit to those with high incomes, and capped the maximum duration at 45 weeks. The OECD note that the ratio of beneficiaries to unemployed, which was 83 per cent in 1989/90, had fallen to 42 per cent by 1996, although not all of this fall should be attributed to programme changes (OECD 1998c: 93).

On the other hand, it is often argued that continental European countries have not followed the Anglo-Saxon route in recent years: 'The majority of European countries have made only marginal changes to their labour market institutions in the 1990s' (Siebert 1997: 53).

Germany

In Germany, in 1994, for instance, the replacement rates were reduced by 3 percentage points, which could be regarded as marginal, since the replacement rate under unemployment insurance remained 60 per cent (or 67 per cent for beneficiaries with children). Stricter criteria were introduced in April 1997 concerning the conditions under which the unemployed can refuse a job offer on the grounds that it does not correspond to previous wages, but the OECD report that the labour office had had difficulties in enforcing these measures (OECD 1998a: 107).

Finland

In Finland, there have been a series of changes, not all in the same direction.[7] There was a major reform of unemployment compensation in 1985 (OECD 1995: 57). The previously flat rate unemployment insurance system became earnings-related; the benefits were significantly raised; and the eligibility widened. Benefits became taxable. From January 1994, first-time jobseekers and those who have exhausted unemployment compensation coverage became eligible to an indefinite, flat rate, means-tested labour market support benefit; and unemployment assistance became limited in duration, but no longer means-tested. This pattern of benefit improvement was reversed in September 1995, when the government launched an employment programme, which included restrictions on the coverage or duration of benefit. Beginning in 1997, the period of employment required to qualify for unemployment benefit was extended from 6 to 10 months, limiting the capacity of people to move from unemployment

---

[7] For discussion of changes in all four Nordic countries, see Kautto *et al.* (1999).

insurance to subsidized job programmes and then back to unemployment insurance, since the subsidized jobs do not usually last beyond 6 months (OECD 1997). The effect was to phase down unemployment compensation. The sanctions for voluntary unemployment were increased from the beginning of 1998 (MISSOC 1998: 62–3), as were the requirements for job search. The total effect of these measures was in the direction of reducing benefit receipt, but the modest scale should be noted. The OECD for example found 'progress to be largely insufficient' (OECD 1998*b*: 56) towards meeting the objectives of the OECD *Jobs Strategy*.

Sweden

Equally, in Sweden it would be wrong to suggest that all changes were in the same direction. It is true that the fiscal consolidation measures initiated in 1994 embodied reductions in the replacement rate, and less than complete indexation of benefit parameters, but replacement rates were later restored, and an offsetting proposal to introduce an upper limit on the duration of benefit was repealed (OECD 1998: 72). Changes in unemployment compensation have, therefore, gone in the directions of both increased and reduced generosity, with the latter predominating in the three Anglo-Saxon countries.

9.4.2. Personal Taxation

In contrast to the proportional tax considered in the simple analytical framework, we now need to separate the level of personal taxation from its structure. A rising average tax rate may coexist with a lower degree of progression. The OECD *Jobs Study*, using data up to 1991/2, concluded that the tax rate had increased in many countries, but pointed out that there had been a rearrangement of the tax burden, via reduced progression: 'There were large reductions in the schedule rates of tax in... Germany, Norway, Sweden, the United Kingdom, and the United States. These reductions, however, were mainly targeted on the higher income groups' (OECD 1994: 241). On the other hand, summarizing the experience of ten OECD countries, Messere (1998: 11) concluded that 'there was a sharp decline in top tax rates between 1985 and 1994, together with a reduction in the number of rates. This does not, however, entail a loss of overall progressivity of income tax systems among most of the ten countries, because of the offsetting progressivity of the base-widening as well as increases in tax thresholds'.

Looking now in more detail at the six countries identified in Section 9.1, we find that there have indeed been significant changes in the structure of personal income taxation. Just to give one index, the average number of tax brackets (for four of the countries) fell from more than 10 to slightly over 4 (Messere 1998: 13).

United Kingdom

In the United Kingdom, the investment income surcharge, payable at a rate of 15 per cent on investment income in excess of a threshold, was abolished with effect from 1984. The changes in rate structure in the 1988 Budget were undoubtedly a major step in the direction of making the system less progressive. The structure of a basic rate of 27 per cent, followed by graduated rates from 40 to 60 per cent, was replaced by a two-rate structure of 25 and 40 per cent. The subsequent introduction of reduced rate bands has moderated the effect, but the system remains much less progressive at the top. This was not the only substantial change in the personal tax system, where the period saw also the move to independent taxation of husbands and wives, and a reduction in the deductibility of interest payments for house purchase. It is not easy to predict the distributional impact of such changes, but the calculations of Redmond *et al.* (1998: fig. 3.2) suggest that the 1996/7 income tax system, compared to that in 1978/9 indexed by price increases, was considerably less progressive, particularly at the top decile.

United States

Tax reform in the United States has been widely documented. The Tax Reform Act of 1986 was described by Pechman as 'the most significant piece of tax legislation enacted since the income tax was converted to a mass tax during World War II' (1990: 11–12). The changes in rate structure were indeed dramatic, replacing the fourteen rates going from 11 to 50 per cent by a two-rate structure of 15 and 28 per cent (with an intermediate 33 per cent arising from the phasing-out of the benefit from the personal exemptions and lower rate bands). This 'collapse of the rate structure' was seen by Musgrave as 'a giant step towards the principle of a flat rate tax' (1987: 65). The change in income tax rates was accompanied by tax based broadening (full taxation of capital gains, curtailment of deductions, lengthening depreciation periods—see Sunley and Stotsky (1998: 407)) and by a shift in taxation from individuals to corporations. This latter switch was taken into account by Pechman (1990) in his estimates of the distributional impact. Assuming that corporate income taxes are borne by capital income, he finds (Pechman 1990: table 3) that the changes in the United States since 1980—of which the most important is the 1986 act—have reduced the tax burden for the bottom 3 deciles, increased the burden for the next 6 deciles, and reduced it for the top 10 per cent. The tax rate for the top 1 per cent in 1988 was far below that in 1970: 'The inescapable conclusion from these figures is that the well-to-do in our society had very large reductions in tax rates in recent years, while the tax rates at the low and middle income levels have not changed much' (Pechman 1990: 4).

The most significant subsequent legislation in the early 1990s was the Omnibus Budget Reconciliation Act of 1993, which was directed at reducing the deficit but also was concerned with progressivity with the creation of two new marginal income tax rates at the top end (36 and 39.6 per cent) and the expansion of the earned income tax credit, bringing in low-income workers without children.

Canada

In Canada, the Government in 1988 simplified the federal income tax structure in a similar way, replacing the ten-bracket schedule, from 6 to 34 per cent, by three rates of 17, 26, and 29 per cent. This was accompanied by base-broadening measures, with the elimination of deductions and the conversion of deductions to credits of the same value to all taxpayers. The elimination of tax preferences previously benefiting high incomes had the effect of increasing effective, as opposed to nominal, progressivity and the overall effect may have been increased redistribution. According to Dodge and Sargent, 'there is a modest shift in the share of federal tax payable from lower to higher income groups' (1988: 58). To the federal tax has to be added provincial income tax, and Bird *et al.* note that 'since 1987, the provinces have taken up the slack, pushing the top marginal rates to well over 50 per cent again for most provinces' (1998: 73).

Germany

In Germany, a substantial reform of personal income taxation was carried out in the period 1986–90. The basic tax allowance was increased and the child tax allowance reintroduced. The marginal tax rates were flattened to become a linear function of income. This resulted in lower marginal rates at all levels, particularly in the upper middle part, and less at the very top (the top rate was reduced only from 56 to 53 per cent). Such a pattern of reduction meant that the average tax rate was reduced by about the same absolute number of percentage points from around DM70,000. The tax base was broadened, but there was a sizeable reduction in tax revenue. Subsequently, however, according to the OECD, 'In the wake of German reunification, the supply-side strategy of progressive income tax relief implemented since 1986 gave way to comprehensive tax increases' (OECD 1994*a*: 95). In 1997, proposals for a further wide-ranging reform of personal and corporate tax systems was rejected, with much of the disagreement centring on the distributional implications (OECD 1998*a*: 69).

Finland

In Finland, a process of tax reform was implemented in the late 1980s. Marginal rates were reduced, the highest personal income tax rate levied by the central government falling from 51 to 39 per cent. The aim was, however, to combine the rate changes with broadening of the tax base (such as higher taxation of fringe benefits and lower deductibility of interest payments), so as to leave the average effective tax rates in different income classes unchanged (OECD 1989: 87). It was estimated that the non-taxability of certain incomes had previously reduced the redistributive role of taxation (Aarnio 1989). From January 1993, individual capital income was taxed at a flat rate of 25 per cent, as under the Nordic system of dual income taxation (Sørensen 1994; Nielsen and Sørensen 1997).

Sweden

In the case of Sweden, the Government announced in 1988 the introduction of a comprehensive tax reform starting in 1991.[8] This reform—billed as the 'tax reform of

---

[8] There had been a 'minor' tax reform in 1981, implemented between 1983 and 1986, which lowered the top rate of income tax (to 70%) and sought to offset the distributional impact by a progressive child benefit, which was higher for the third and subsequent children in a family—see Björklund *et al.* (1995).

A. B. Atkinson

the century' (Agell *et al.* 1996, 1998)—involved a substantial reduction in top marginal tax rates, from around 75 to 50 per cent (depending on local tax rates). This was in part financed by a broadening of the income tax base (e.g. in the coverage of non-cash benefits), and by a broadening of the coverage of the value-added tax. Capital income became taxable under a dual income tax at a flat central government rate of 30 per cent. Net transfers to families with children were increased via child and housing allowances. The 1991 tax reform was presented as not affecting the degree of redistribution: 'According to its proponents, the reform would avoid the classical goal conflict between efficiency and income distribution. In spite of drastic marginal tax cuts, high-income earners were not supposed to gain relatively to other groups' (Agell *et al.* 1996: 644–5). According to the OECD, the reform 'was neutral with respect to overall income equality' (1996*a*: 70).

Subsequent to the tax reform of 1991, there were further tax adjustments, directed in part at dealing with the underfinancing of the reform. In 1994, the incoming government announced a series of fiscal consolidation measures including reduced replacement rates (see previously), lower child allowances, and the top tax rate was raised to 25 per cent plus an average local tax rate close to 32 per cent (OECD 1998: 71). This still represents a considerable reduction on the earlier top rates.

9.4.3. *Evaluation of the Overall Impact*

In broad terms, there appear to be similarities in the general direction of change in policy parameters, but there are significant differences in its extent and in some cases countries have gone in different directions. We have moreover to allow for the possible differences in the impact of policy parameter changes on the individual citizen. Even modest or symbolic cuts may have dramatic implications on individuals. Politicians are very aware of this, and debate about policy reform is often heavily influenced by calculations of the impact in individual cases. Calculations for 'representative individuals' are widely used in policy analysis. An example is provided by the OECD calculations of the replacement rates for the unemployed, shown for 1981 and 1991 in Fig. 9.9 for the six countries. The replacement rate is a summary measure of benefit entitlements, based on an average for eighteen cases (crossing three family situations by three unemployment durations by two earnings levels). The replacement rate rose in Canada, Sweden, and Finland; it was broadly constant in Germany and fell in the United Kingdom and the United States. (It should be borne in mind that a number of the changes described above came after 1991.)

Such hypothetical calculations make some allowance for variety of individual circumstances, but there are nonetheless serious limitations with any such indicator. There is no real alternative to the use of sample surveys of households, which reflect the full diversity of their circumstances: for example, that households may have several members and may have income from sources other than employment. Such complexity means that the impact of reductions in benefits on the overall distribution of household incomes cannot be straightforwardly deduced. While there is some presumption that recipients are to be found in the lower part of the distribution, this is

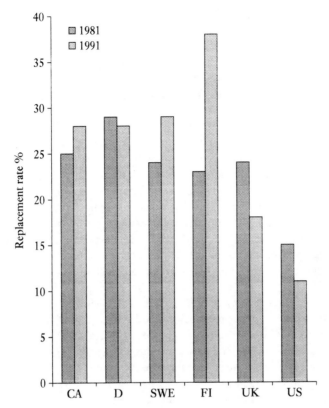

Figure 9.9. *Evolution of replacement rates for unemployed 1981–91*
Source: OECD (1994: table 8.B.1).

not inevitably the case, since they may have partners who are employed and may have other sources of income.

The second essential ingredient in a distributional analysis is that it include the full range of policies. My case studies of unemployment and personal income taxation are only part of the story. Reforms of benefits and taxation have been accompanied by other measures, which have redistributive implications, and we need to look at the total impact. Just to give one instance, the thrust of policy in a number of countries has been to combine reductions in unemployment benefit with active labour market policies. If the active measures lower unemployment, then the distribution of market income will improve and there will be less need for redistribution. Moreover, there are interactions between different policies, as is illustrated by an example affecting the two areas considered here: the imposition of income taxation on benefits received, a policy change made in the United Kingdom, depends on the structure of income tax rates.

There have been interesting studies of the distributional effects of policy reforms in individual countries, which combine the two features emphasized above: based on simulations of policy changes using representative samples of households. In Sweden, Björklund *et al.* (1995: 263) used the HINK annual income survey provided by Statistics Sweden to examine pre- and post-distributions under the old and new tax rules following the 1991 Swedish tax reform. Their summary of the effect of the 1991 tax and benefit reform on the overall income distribution is that 'a decreased equalising effect due to decreased income tax progressivity and lower overall average income tax rates was offset by increased horizontal equity of income taxes and increased child and housing allowances'.

At the same time, they point out that this result of counteracting forces could still mean that subgroups of the population were differentially affected. The taxation of earned income had become less redistributive, so that in this respect there were similarities with, for example, the United Kingdom. The flat tax on capital may have reduced tax avoidance by the wealthy, increasing the redistributive impact. Child and housing allowances were more important, increasing redistribution for those with two or more children. This underlines the dangers in seeking to make summary statements about the degree of redistribution and points to the need to take account of differences apart from income and for a life-time as well as a snapshot picture.

The Swedish study just cited focused on the 1991 tax reform and subsequent measures. In the United Kingdom, Redmond *et al.* (1998: table 4.3) have examined the total effect of all tax and benefit changes over the period 1978/9 to 1996/7. They estimate that the 1996/97 tax and benefit system, compared with that in 1978/9 indexed in line with per capita GDP, raised the net tax burden for all decile groups except the top, with large losses in the bottom three decile groups. The Gini coefficient would have been lower by about 5 percentage points with the 1978/9 system. Ideally, we would be able to compare such studies across countries, contrasting, on a systematic basis, the distributional impact of policy reforms in different countries. However, as far as I know, no such cross-country study exists. There are comparisons of changes in the overall level of taxation in different countries; there are comparisons across countries of the extent of redistribution at a point in time (see, e.g., Wagstaff *et al.* 1999). But there is no systematic set of comparisons of the distributional effect of the changes in policy in different countries over the 1980s and 1990s. In order to carry out such research, we need policy simulation models for different countries on a comparable basis. In the European Union, the EUROMOD project is bringing together microdata for all member states, which will allow analysis of the distributional impact of policy changes on a parallel basis in member states as well as in the Union as a whole (see Sutherland 1997). This will be subject to the same limitations as national tax benefit models in that some features of policy reforms are not easily modelled; for example, those directed at base broadening are less easily incorporated than changes in the rate structure. But it will offer a first step.

9.5. SUMMARY OF CONCLUSIONS

In this chapter, I have examined the redistributive impact of the government budget in five OECD countries over the period from the 1980s (or earlier) to the mid-1990s. I began with the evidence in terms of inequality of market income and disposable income. The countries have all seen a rise in the inequality of market income between 1980 and the mid-1990s, but the experience with regard to the distribution of disposable income differed both across countries and across time. Different governments appear to have made different choices. Canada and the United Kingdom are two good examples. In Canada, over the period studied, there was no apparent increase in the inequality of disposable income, the government budget offsetting the rise in market income inequality. In the United Kingdom, up to the mid-1980s the redistributive impact of the government budget increased by enough to offset the more unequal market incomes, but after 1984, the story is quite different: between 1984 and 1990 the redistributive contribution of transfers and taxes fell sharply, reflecting a definite policy change. In Finland, redistribution was effective in preventing rising inequality in disposable income when the inequality of market income rose abruptly in the early 1990s, but there was a subsequent change in redistributive policy, which has been scaled back since 1994. In Sweden, on the other hand, the government budget has operated throughout the 1990s to moderate the rise in market income inequality.

In order to interpret this diversity of outcomes, an analytical framework is necessary and this has been the subject of Section 9.2. Using a simple theoretical model, I argued that we cannot distinguish 'automatic' from 'discretionary' policy responses, since inaction is not, in general, consistent with budget balance. The theoretical analysis shows that there can be a range of different policy reactions. Depending on the policy choice, a demographic shift could lead to a rise or fall in the Gini coefficient for disposable income, or leave it unchanged. This warns that it is not always easy to read across from policy parameters to the impact on measured distributions. The choice made by governments will reflect a balancing of cost considerations and redistributive objectives. This balance will be affected by demographic and other shifts. Here attention has tended to focus on the cost side, with increased dependency making the trade-off less favourable to social transfers, but the demand side of the government policy choice is also important, and a rise in the size of the dependent population can increase the value attached to providing adequate benefits. Taking both sides into account, it is possible that a rise in the dependency ratio would lead a country to extend its welfare state. Whether it would do so depends on the nature of social objectives, and here we may have observed shifts over the period in question.

In Section 9.3 I have given a summary of actual government policy responses in the six OECD countries. Taking unemployment benefit and personal income taxation as case studies, we have seen that the changes to policy parameters differed in extent and even in direction. Reduced progression in tax rates has been pursued in all countries, but in some there have been reversals and in a number it has been accompanied by base broadening, which has offset the overall redistributive effect. The United Kingdom stands out as having had the most substantial and sustained reduction in income tax progressivity. Benefit levels and coverage have been cut, but in some countries the adjustment is modest in extent. The Anglo–Saxon countries, Canada, the United Kingdom, and the United States, have significantly reduced the generosity and coverage of their unemployment benefit programmes, but the changes in the Continental European countries have been more modest. These differences undoubtedly in part reflect differences

A. B. Atkinson

in policy choices by governments faced with similar external changes, but differences across countries have also arisen on account of changed circumstances which apply to specific countries. Germany, faced with the domestic agenda of reunification, may have responded differently from the United Kingdom. Finland and Sweden may have made fiscal adjustments as a result of their accession to the European Union. These examples underline the richness of the story that needs to be told, a story that defies a simple summary.

REFERENCES

Aarnio, L. (1989). Reform of income taxation in Finland. *Bank of Finland Bulletin* 63.

Agell, J., P. Englund, and J. Södersten (1996). Tax reform of the century: The Swedish experiment. *National Tax Journal* 49, 643–64.

——, ——, and —— (1998). *Incentives and Redistribution in the Welfare State*. Macmillan: London.

Atkinson, A. B. (1997). Bringing income distribution in from the cold. *Economic Journal* 107, 297–321.

—— (2000). The changing distribution of income: Evidence and explanations. In K. W. Rothschild Lecture, *German Economic Review* 1, 3–18.

—— and J. Micklewright (1989). Turning the screw: Benefits for the unemployed 1979–1988. In A. Dilnot and I. Walker (eds.), *The Economics of Social Security*. Oxford University Press: Oxford.

—— and F. Bourguignon (1990). The design of direct taxation and family benefits. *Journal of Public Economics* 41, 3–29.

——, L. Rainwater, and T. Smeeding (1995). *Income Distribution in OECD Countries*. OECD: Paris.

Becker, I., and R. Hauser (1997). Abgaben- und Transfersystem wirkt Polarisierungstendenzen entgegen. *EVS-Projekt Arbeitspapier* 12, Frankfurt University.

Bird, R. M., D. B. Perry, and T. A. Wilson (1998). Canada. In K. Messere (ed.), *The Tax System in Industrialized Countries*. Oxford University Press: Oxford.

Björklund, A. (1998). Income distribution in Sweden: What is the achievement of the welfare state? *Swedish Economic Policy Review* 5, 39–80.

—— and M. Palme (1999). Income redistribution within the life cycle versus between individuals: Empirical evidence using Swedish panel data. Mimeo, Sofi: Stockholm.

——, ——, and I. Svensson (1995). Tax reforms and income distribution: An assessment using different income concepts. *Swedish Economic Policy Review* 2, 229–66.

Brandolini, A. (1998). A bird's eye view of long-run changes in income inequality. Mimeo, Banca d'Italia: Rome.

Card, D., and W. C. Riddell (1993). A comparative analysis of unemployment in Canada and the United States. In D. Card and R. B. Freeman (eds.), *Small Differences That Matter*. University of Chicago Press: Chicago.

Castles, F. G. (1998). *Comparative Public Policy*. Edward Elgar: Cheltenham.

Dodge, D. A., and J. H. Sargent (1988). Canada. In J. A. Pechman (ed.), *World Tax Reform*. The Brookings Institution: Washington, DC.

Fritzell, J. (1993). Income inequality trends in the 1980s: A five-country comparison. *Acta Sociologica* 36, 47–62.

Gottschalk, P., and T. M. Smeeding (1997). Cross-national comparisons of earnings and income inequality. *Journal of Economic Literature* 35, 633–87.

Hauser, R. (1999). Personelle Primär- und Sekundärverteilung der Einkommen unter dem Einfluss sich ärnderner wirtschaftlicher und sozialpolitischer Rahmenbedingungen—eine empirische Analyse auf der Basis der Einkommens- und Verbrauchstichproben 1973–1993. *Allgemeines Statistisches Archiv* 83, 88–110.

Jansson, K. (2000). Inkomstfördelninge under 1990-talet. Mimeo, SCB, Örebro.

Kautto, M., M. Heikkilä, B. Hvinden, S. Marklund, and N. Ploug (1999). *Nordic Social Policy*. Routledge: London.

Maravall, J. M. (1997). *Regimes, Politics and Markets*. Oxford University Press: Oxford.

Messere, K. (ed.) (1998). *The Tax System in Industrialized Countries*. Oxford University Press: Oxford.

Ministry of Finance (1999). *Government Budget Bill 1999: Report on Income Distribution*. Ministry of Finance, Stockholm.

MISSOC (Mutual Information System on Social Protection in the Member States of the European Union) (1998). *Social Protection in the Member States of the Union*, EC DG-V: Brussels.

Musgrave, R. A. (1987). Short of euphoria. *Journal of Economic Perspectives* 59–71.

——, J. J. Carroll, L. D. Cook, and L. Frane (1951). Distribution of tax payments by income groups: A case study for 1948. *National Tax Journal* 4, 1–53.

——, K. E. Case, and H. Leonard (1974). The distribution of fiscal burdens and benefits. *Public Finance Quarterly* 2, 259–311.

Nielsen, S. B., and P. B. Sørensen (1997). On the optimality of the Nordic system of dual income taxation. *Journal of Public Economics* 63, 311–29.

OECD (1989). *OECD Economic Surveys: Finland 1989*. OECD: Paris.

——(1994). *The Jobs Study*. OECD: Paris.

——(1994a). *OECD Economic Surveys: Germany 1994*. OECD: Paris.

——(1995). *OECD Economic Surveys: Finland 1995*. OECD: Paris.

——(1996). *OECD Economic Surveys: Canada 1996*. OECD: Paris.

——(1996a). *OECD Economic Surveys: Sweden 1997*. OECD: Paris.

——(1997). *OECD Economic Surveys: Finland 1997*. OECD: Paris.

——(1997a). *Historical Statistics: 1960–1995*. OECD: Paris.

——(1998). *OECD Economic Surveys: Sweden 1998*. OECD: Paris.

——(1998a). *OECD Economic Surveys: Germany 1998*. OECD: Paris.

——(1998b). *OECD Economic Surveys: Finland 1998*. OECD: Paris.

——(1998c). *OECD Economic Surveys: Canada 1998*. OECD: Paris.

Office for National Statistics (1998). The effects of taxes and benefits on household income. *Economic Trends* 533, 33–67.

Pechman, J. A. (1985). *Who Paid the Taxes, 1966–85?* (with revised tables). The Brookings Institution: Washington, DC.

——(1990). The future of the income tax. *American Economic Review* 80, 1–20.

——and B. A. Okner (1974). *Who Bears the Tax Burden?* The Brookings Institution: Washington, DC.

Redmond, G., H. Sutherland, and M. Wilson (1998). *The Arithmetic of Tax and Social Security Reform*. Cambridge University Press: Cambridge.

Royal Commission on the Distribution of Income and Wealth (1977). *Report No.5 Third Report on the Standing Reference* Cmnd. 6999. HMSO: London.

Schmid, G., B. Reissert, and G. Bruche (1992). *Unemployment Insurance and Active Labour Market Policy*. Wayne State University Press: Detroit.

Siebert, H. (1997). Labour market rigidities: At the root of unemployment in Europe. *Journal of Economic Perspectives* 11(3), 37–54.

Sørensen, P. B. (1994). From the global income tax to the dual income tax: Recent tax reforms in the Nordic countries. *International Tax and Public Finance* 1, 57–79.

Statistics Canada (1996). *Income After Tax, Distributions by Size in Canada 1994.* Statistics Canada: Ottawa.

Statistics Sweden (1999). *Income Distribution Survey in 1997.* Statistiska meddelanden, Stockholm.

Sunley, E. M., and J. G. Stotsky (1998). The United States. In K. Messere (ed.), *The Tax System in Industrialized Countries.* Oxford University Press: Oxford.

Sutherland, H. (1997). The EUROMOD preparatory study: A summary report. Department of Applied Economics, University of Cambridge.

Uusitalo, H. (1989). *Income Distribution in Finland.* Central Statistical Office of Finland: Helsinki.

——(1998). *Changes in Income Distribution During a Deep Recession and After.* STAKES: Helsinki.

——(1999). *Changes in Income Distribution During a Deep Recession and After.* STAKES: Helsinki.

Wagstaff, A., *et al.* (25 authors) (1999). Redistributive effect, progressivity and differential tax treatment: Personal income taxes in twelve OECD Countries. *Journal of Public Economics* 72, 73–98.

10

Income Distribution and Tax and Government Social-Spending Policies in Developing Countries

KE-YOUNG CHU, HAMID DAVOODI, AND
SANJEEV GUPTA

10.1. INTRODUCTION

For many developing countries, widespread poverty and the small income share of the poor have been a source of particular concern. Increasing international economic interdependence, uncertainties arising from this interdependence, and some evidence of widening income disparities in recent decades (see Chapter 2) have further heightened the economic profession's interest in income distribution, its changes, and the underlying factors. The evidence of widening income disparities also has heightened the economic profession's interest in the role of fiscal policy as a redistributive instrument in the short run and in the long run, as well as in the progressivity (or the lack) of tax and transfer policies. At the same time, questions have been raised on the effectiveness of tax and transfer policies as a redistributive tool.

Assigning a more activist role to tax and transfer policies in developing and transition countries often gives rise to many challenges. The interaction between the progressivity of tax and transfer policies and income distribution is complicated by a set of factors that are unique to these countries, which, in general, have a number of weak fiscal features: a low tax-to-gross domestic product (GDP) ratio, reflecting poor governance, weak tax administration, and widespread tax evasion; the predominance of indirect taxes and a limited menu of capital and wealth taxes; and a limited role of

The authors wish to thank Giovanni Andrea Cornia, John Norregaard, Vito Tanzi, Gustavo Yamada, and Chi-Wa Yuen for helpful comments, and Randa Sab and Erwin Tiongson for efficient research assistance. An earlier version of this study was presented at a World Institute for Development Economics Research (WIDER) conference on 'Rising Income Inequality and Poverty Reduction: Are They Compatible?' held in Helsinki, 16–18 July 1999. The views expressed are those of the authors and do not necessarily represent those of the International Monetary Fund (IMF).

formal cash transfer and social protection policies.[1] These features cast doubt on the ability of tax policy to redistribute income.[2]

Noting that the poor rarely pay income taxes in many developing countries and that education and health spending and other in-kind transfers account for a large share of the budget, many have argued that the expenditure side of the budget should be a primary redistributive tool (Tanzi 1974, 1998; Harberger 1998). The major contribution of tax policy as a redistributive instrument should be to raise the revenues needed to finance efficient pro-poor and other essential government expenditures, and to avoid generating horizontal inequities. To this end, tax systems should have broad bases, limited exemptions, and low rates. This view has formed a basis for an agreement among many researchers and policy-makers on the relative role of tax and expenditure policies in income redistribution in developing and transition countries.

As regards income distribution and the role of fiscal and other economic policies in developing and transition countries, a number of questions arise: How do these countries differ in income distribution—both among themselves and from industrial countries? Is income distribution in these countries becoming more unequal? What is the redistributive role of tax, transfer, and other expenditure policies? Unfortunately, the limited availability of high-quality data for developing countries prevents a rigorous analysis of these questions. While numerous studies have focused on income distribution in individual countries and, to some extent, on international comparison of income distribution, scarce high-quality data have limited studies of long-term changes in, and international comparison of, income distribution in developing countries.

This chapter provides an overview of the changes in income distribution in developing and transition countries in recent decades, and assesses the incidence of taxes and government expenditures in these countries. For the overview of income distribution, this chapter relies largely on a set of newly available 'high-quality' income-distribution data.[3] For the assessment of tax and government expenditure incidence, it relies on existing incidence studies on individual countries.

The chapter is organized as follows. Section 10.3 provides a survey of the studies on the incidence of taxes and expenditures, paying a particular attention to the incidence of government spending on education and health, reviewing the available evidence for a large number of developing countries. Section 10.4 also offers a brief overview of the changes in income distribution in developing countries from the 1970s through the 1990s. Section 10.3 provides a selective review of the literature. Section 10.4 discusses possible underlying factors, including the role of social spending policies. Section 10.5 concludes.

---

[1] Alesina (1999) discusses the role of poor governance and the vicious cycle of low tax-to-GDP ratio and tax evasion.

[2] See Tanzi (1998), who notes these and other practical problems involved in administering a progressive tax system in developing countries.

[3] Deininger and Squire (1996). The paper also examines the WIDER database, which includes before-tax and after-tax Gini coefficients for a same set of developing and transition countries.

10.2. THE ROLE OF TAXES AND SOCIAL SPENDING

The analysis of income distribution and distributional implications of taxes and government spending is subject to many conceptual and practical difficulties. Should income or consumption be used? How should the benefit of government spending be valued? The difficulties are particularly severe for developing and transition countries. Income distribution data for these countries are expanding, but still are not adequate. Internationally comparable data on before-tax *and* after-tax household incomes for same countries are virtually nonexistent. The available data do not allow an assessment of the long-term evolution of income distribution for a large number of developing countries.

Subject to the above caveats and based on Gini data compiled for twenty-two countries by Deininger and Squire, before-tax Gini coefficients in developing and transition economies range widely, between 0.25 and 0.52, averaging 0.38; by contrast, after-tax Gini coefficients range between 0.25 and 0.45, averaging 0.34. The difference of 4 percentage points between the two averages does not necessarily suggest the redistributive impact of taxes. The two samples comprise two different sets of countries. This small difference between the before- and after-tax Gini coefficients for developing countries contrast with a large reduction in Gini coefficients industrial countries achieve through redistributive tax and government transfer programmes (see Chapter 9). The World Institute for Development Economics Research (WIDER) world income inequality database (WIID) and the Gini coefficients reported in tax incidence studies also support the conclusion that, on average, the taxes do not significantly reduce Gini coefficients of developing and transition economies.

10.3. SELECTIVE LITERATURE SURVEY

Income distribution has many aspects. The distribution of market incomes is an important aspect of income distribution. The distribution of disposable incomes is another. One could also look at the distribution of disposable incomes together with government in-kind transfers, such as education and health services. More broadly, one could analyse the distribution of disposable incomes and all government services, including defence, justice, and infrastructure services. In a country with a large-scale provision of free public education and health care, this last measure of income distribution could be substantially different from that of disposable incomes. Even in a country where markets play a dominant role, the distribution of income based on the first and last measures could be substantially different.

There are many factors that affect the distributions of market and disposable incomes. These factors include the distribution of physical, financial, and human capital; rates of returns to these forms of capital; and formal and informal institutions. Taxes and transfers affect the difference between market and disposable incomes in the short run, but they can also affect the distribution of market incomes over time. Some taxes can affect individuals' work efforts. Excessively high-tax rates can drive economic activities out of the formal sector or out of a country. Government social-spending policies have distributional implications not only because social spending can offer immediate benefits (e.g. health and education services), but they also affect the distribution of earning capacities of individuals and households, and thus help shape the distribution of market incomes over time. Some social expenditures (e.g. expenditures on primary schooling) can affect income distribution with a long time lag.

10.3.1. *Recent Tax Incidence Studies*

This section discusses five surveys of tax incidence studies of developing countries: Bird and De Wulf (1973); De Wulf (1975); and subsequent surveys by McLure (1977) and Shah and Whalley (1990, 1991).[4]

Bird and De Wulf—covering twenty-nine studies on seventeen Latin American countries—conclude that tax systems in these countries were often ineffective as redistributive tools. They note that only four of twenty-nine studies suggest a mild redistributive impact of the tax system, whereas the remaining studies suggest 'rough proportionality or even regressivity over most income classes' (Bird and De Wulf 1973: 671).[5] Although De Wulf (1975), in a subsequent survey of sixty-six studies covering twenty-three countries, concludes that the tax system in developing countries tends to be progressive (and the degree of progressivity varies from steep to moderate), he reverses himself in a subsequent survey by noting that it is 'difficult . . . not to conclude that tax systems in LDCs must be *regressive*'. Underlying his reasoning is the relative dominance of consumption taxes, which he assumes to be mostly regressive.

McLure (1977), in a survey of seven studies on the tax burden faced by the urban poor in developing countries, notes that tax rates for urban households are *progressive* but not smooth. For example, although the effective tax rates for the urban rich (top 2–5 per cent of urban households) are at least twice those of the urban poor (bottom 40 per cent of urban households), the fourth urban quintile and the urban poor face similar effective tax rates. He concludes that, because policy decisions are made at the margin, a tax incidence analysis would be more useful to policy-makers if it focused on the distributional implications of *changes* in tax systems rather than on the incidence of an existing tax system.

Shah and Whalley (1990, 1991), in a brief survey of seven tax incidence studies, conclude that, with some exceptions, the overall tax system is broadly progressive.

---

[4] Any study of tax incidence confronts a number of problems, including the coverage of incomes and taxes, assumptions about the shifting of the tax burden and its measurement, estimation of *counterfactual* before-tax income distribution, behavioural responses of individuals, and the time horizon of the analysis. These problems make cross-country comparisons of tax incidence and even intertemporal within-country comparisons difficult, and more so when a country's major tax reform has made the task of reaching a firm conclusion regarding tax incidence difficult.

[5] These conclusions are based primarily on the calculation (and visual inspection) of average effective tax rates by income class whenever reported in a study and some notion of departures from proportionality.

Regarding individual taxes, they find excises, personal income taxes (PITs), and urban property taxes to be progressive; sales and import duties to be regressive; corporate taxes to vary, depending on assumptions used; and general indirect taxes to have a U-shaped incidence pattern.[6]

Some methodological improvements in measuring the incidence of taxes have been made since the surveys by Bird and De Wulf (1973) and De Wulf (1975). Fully specified computable general equilibrium models have gradually replaced various (forward or backward) shifting assumptions featured in a large number of studies surveyed by Bird and De Wulf (1973) and Shah and Whalley (1990, 1991), although in some cases the results of judgemental studies were close to general equilibrium simulations.

General equilibrium analysis seems to add an interesting dimension that was absent in partial equilibrium studies. For example, personal and company taxes in Kenya are found to be progressive on the basis of a general equilibrium analysis (Mwega 1986), but to be regressive on the basis of a partial equilibrium analysis (Westlake 1973). Similarly, indirect taxes in the Philippines are found to be broadly neutral, but only after taking into account their general equilibrium effects (Devarajan and Hossein 1998). Mostly, however, tax incidence studies still visually inspect the effective tax rates by income group and present a judgement of the degree of progressivity. Certain methodological difficulties, dating back to the surveys of Bird and De Wulf (1973), continue to persist. For example, income concepts used in incidence studies continue to vary widely, from taxable income (Chowdhury 1988) and gross income (Bolkowiak *et al.* 1996), to permanent income (Gil-Diaz 1982). In addition, there are significant differences in taxes studied, units of analysis, and underlying assumptions.

For a better understanding of the state of knowledge on the incidence of taxes in developing countries, this chapter offers the results of a systematic survey of all tax incidence studies conducted since the surveys of Bird and De Wulf (1973) and De Wulf (1975). The intention of the survey[7] is to record the following crucial features for each study: the country and period covered, concept of income used, taxes included, unit of analysis (e.g. individuals or households), coverage (e.g. all individuals, wage earners, or pensioners), measure of tax progressivity, and the study's conclusion about the tax incidence.

Table 10.1 suggests the following: as regards overall tax systems or both direct and indirect taxes in nineteen countries studied, only thirteen of thirty-six cases are progressive, seven are proportional, seven are regressive, and the rest have mixed findings or insignificant effects. As regards income tax systems in eight countries,

---

[6] These conclusions are based on studies that rely on a standard tax incidence analysis with shifting assumptions that in general determine the outcome of the incidence studies. Typically, the burden of PITs and payroll taxes is assumed to be borne by the taxed income recipient, whereas that of indirect taxes is assumed to be shifted forward to consumers of taxed commodities. Incidence of corporate taxes is controversial, however. In an earlier study, Whalley (1984) shows how a tax system can be made to appear sharply progressive or sharply regressive by changing a number of shifting assumptions.

[7] The detailed bibliographical references of the studies surveyed in this chapter are given in Chu *et al.* (2000: table 10).

Table 10.1. *Summary results of tax incidence studies on developing countries; 1971–5 and 1991–5*

Countries studied		All taxes	Direct taxes	Income	Payroll	Indirect taxes
Frequency		36	3	14	5	5
PP		1				
P		12	1	12		2
Prop		7	1			1
Insig		1			2	
Mixed		8	1	1		2
R		7			3	
RR				1		
Periods studied						
1971–5	Colombia	PP				
	Mexico	P				
	Korea	Prop				
	Jamaica	Mixed				
	India			P–		
1976–80	Mexico	P				
	Pakistan	P				
	Korea	Prop				
	Korea	R				
	India			P–		
	India					P
1981–5	Korea	Prop				
	Jamaica	Mixed				
	Korea	R				
	India			P–		
	Bangladesh			Mixed		
	Jamaica			RR		
	India					P, Prop
	Jamaica					Prop
1986–90	Jamaica	P				
	Philippines	Prop				
	Philippines	Mixed				
	Korea	R				
	Hungary			P–		
	Hungary				R	
	Poland				R	
	Peru					Mixed ()
1991–5	Guatemala	P				
	Jamaica	Insig				
	Poland		Mixed			
	Bulgaria			P		
	Hungary			P–		
	India			P–		
	Bulgaria				Insig	
	Poland					Mixed

Notes: PP = strongly progressive; P = progressive; P– = decline in progressivity; Prop = proportional; Mixed = mixed; R = regressive; RR = strongly regressive; Insig = insignificant effect; ( ) = selective taxes studied.

Source: Calculated from the data in Chu *et al.* (2000: table 10).

twelve of the fourteen cases are progressive, one is regressive, and one has mixed findings. In the five cases of payroll taxes in three countries, three cases are regressive, and two cases have insignificant effects. Finally, eight studies report a decline of the progressivity of direct taxes over time. Some studies, not reported in the table, suggest that indirect taxes may not be as regressive as assumed in the surveys of Bird and De Wulf (1973) and De Wulf (1975).[8]

10.3.2. *Benefit Incidence of Government Spending*

In an exhaustive survey of some 25 years ago, McLure (1974) defines *expenditure* incidence as 'how government spending affects private incomes' and *benefit* incidence[9] as 'who receives benefit of government services'.[10] Benefit incidence analysis is meaningful only if they can be interpreted properly, given its limitations. The concepts of targeting and progressivity, commonly used to interpret such data and used in this chapter, need to be defined as follows;[11] government spending is considered to be well (poorly) targeted if the poorest quintile's share of benefits from such spending is larger (smaller) than the richest quintile.[12] This means that the poorest 20 per cent benefit more than the richest 20 per cent, in absolute terms. In addition, government spending is considered to be progressive (regressive) if the benefits to the poorest quintile are larger (smaller) than the benefits to the richest quintile, *relative* to their income or expenditure. With progressive (regressive) spending, benefits represent a smaller (larger) fraction of income or expenditure at higher income or expenditure quintiles.

These definitions imply that if spending is well targeted, it will be progressive, but progressive spending may not be well targeted. It also implies that if spending is poorly targeted, it may be progressive or regressive. Targeting an expenditure well is a much more demanding objective than making it progressive.

Benefit incidence of government education spending

Thirty-one of the fifty-five studies for twenty-five developing countries for which central government spending data are available on 'all education' (primary, secondary,

---

[8] For example, value-added taxes (VATs) have a progressive incidence in four African countries. Sahn and Younger (1998) provide no explanation for this nonconventional finding. See Bird and De Miller (1989); Shikha and Srinivasan (1989); and Shah and Whalley (1990 and 1991).

[9] This section draws on Davoodi *et al.* (2003).

[10] There are three methods of measuring the incidence of public expenditure: the individual's own valuation of public goods; expenditure incidence analysis; and benefit incidence analysis. The first approach involves eliciting the prices that individuals are willing to pay for public goods (Aaron and McGuire 1970). This is a demanding task, because of the well-known problems associated with the provision of public goods (e.g. free-riding, non-rivalry). The other two methods attempt to circumvent these problems by making various assumptions about the 'ultimate' beneficiaries of publicly financed goods and services. Identification of the 'ultimate' beneficiaries of government spending under any of the three approaches is also a problem that is shared with the identification of the tax burden under tax incidence analysis, because benefits of government spending can be shifted just as much as tax burden can.

[11] These definitions are used, among others, by Selden and Wasylenko (1992).

[12] For analytical convenience, the poor are assumed to be in the bottom quintile and the rich in the top quintile.

Table 10.2. *Summary results of studies on the incidence of social expenditures in developing countries, 1974–95*

	Targeting				Progressivity			
	All	Primary	Seconday	Tertiary	All	Primary	Secondary	Tertiary
Education								
Targeting	55	54	54	52				
Good	22	42	23	0				
Poor	33	12	31	52				
Incidence					31	37	26	11
Progressive					31	37	26	6
Regressive					0	0	0	5
Health								
Targeting	38							
Good	21							
Poor	17							
Incidence					30			
Progressive					30			
Regressive					0			
Transfers								
Targeting	14							
Good	4							
Poor	9							
Inconclusive	1							
Incidence					15			
Progressive					14			
Regressive					0			
Inconclusive					1			

Sources: Davoodi *et al.* (2003); central government data.

and tertiary education) find government educational spending to be progressive (Table 10.2).[13] Spending on education, on average, is poorly targeted in thirty-three studies; there are regional differences, however. Education spending is well targeted in Asia and Latin America, but poorly targeted in sub-Saharan Africa, the Middle East, and transition economies.[14] Sub-Saharan Africa's record stands out among the latter economies: the poorest quintile receives the least (13 per cent of benefits), and the richest quintile receives the most (32 per cent of benefits). In all regions, government spending on primary education is well targeted, but there are notable differences across the regions. The poorest quintile in sub-Saharan Africa receives from government primary education spending slightly more than the richest quintile, whereas the poorest quintile in Latin America receives more than four times the richest quintile. Government

[13] This pattern holds regardless of whether benefits are expressed as per cent of income or expenditure.
[14] The coverage of the Middle East is too narrow as Tunisia is the only country with data in this region.

secondary education spending, on average, is well targeted in Asia and Latin America but poorly targeted in sub-Saharan Africa, the Middle East, and transition countries. Government tertiary education spending mostly benefits the richest quintile in all regions. Sub-Saharan Africa stands out in this respect. The poorest quintile receives 4.5 per cent of benefits from government tertiary education spending, whereas the richest quintile receives as much as 59 per cent.

The data compiled by Davoodi *et al.* (2003) also allow an analysis of the changes in benefit incidence over time. The available data indicate that the poor's share of the benefits from education spending has increased relative to the richest quintile. Of the eleven countries for which benefit incidence data for education are available, eight countries show improvements for the poorest quintile while three countries show a deterioration.[15]

Benefit incidence of government health spending

Table 10.2 indicates that twenty-one of thirty-eight studies find government health spending to be well targeted, and all thirty available studies find government health spending to be progressive. Government spending on 'all health' (comprising expenditures on health centres, hospitals, and hospital inpatients and outpatients) for a sample of fourteen developing countries are progressive over the period 1974–95 for which data are available.[16] Much like the benefit incidence of government education spending, there is a striking diversity in the degree of progressivity among countries.

Government spending on health, on average, is well targeted in a sample of twenty-nine developing and transition economies over the period 1978–95. Sub-Saharan Africa and transition economies are the only areas in which government health spending is poorly targeted. In contrast, the poorest quintiles in Asia and Latin America receive, respectively, 1.5 and 3 times as much in benefits as the richest quintiles.[17] Benefit incidence of health spending has changed over time. Of the ten countries for which data at two points in time are available for health spending, the poorest quintile's share of benefits has increased relative to the rich in five countries but has decreased in another five. Similarly, changes in incidence for subcategories of health spending do not follow a uniform pattern.

---

[15] Using the two latest incidence data for each country, changes in benefit incidence are measured as changes in the ratio of $Q1$ to $Q5$, where $Q1$ and $Q5$ have been defined previously in Chu *et al.* (2002). As for categories of education, there are more countries showing improvements than deterioration for government primary education and tertiary education spending, but there are as many cases of improvement as deterioration for government secondary education spending.

[16] This pattern holds regardless of whether benefits are expressed as per cent of income or expenditure.

[17] Spending on each subcategory of health spending is, on average, well targeted except for spending on hospital outpatients. Sub-Saharan Africa and transition countries are the only regions in which each subcategory of health spending is poorly targeted, thus mirroring the pattern observed at the level of total health expenditure.

Benefit incidence: Other government expenditures

Table 10.2 offers a summary of the results for selected transfers. As in the case of 'other government expenditures', transfers are not well targeted in many countries. Not surprisingly, the well-targeted programmes include a number of expenditure items that involve some targeting mechanism, such as food stamps (Jamaica) or self-targeted food subsidies (Tunisia). In Sri Lanka's (Edirisinghe 1987), although both universal and targeted programmes are found to be progressive, the food stamp programme in fact resulted in a greater degree of progressivity and a better targeting. Universal food subsidies in the sample are poorly targeted, with upper-income quintiles obtaining more benefits in absolute terms (e.g. Tunisia).

A number of housing expenditures are poorly targeted (four of six cases), as well as pension and social security benefits (Chile, Costa Rica, and Uruguay). However, a better targeting is sometimes achieved when pensions are combined with pro–poor family allowances and other benefits (e.g., see Milanovic 1995). Meanwhile, residential utilities are often poorly targeted, except for new investments in Colombia from 1970 to 1974.

A limited number of studies allow for meaningful comparisons over time. They generally show that there has been some improvement in progressivity and targeting over time. For example, in Chile (Aninat *et al.* 1999), the share of cash transfers received by the poorest quintile increased from 33 per cent in 1992 to 40 per cent in 1996. The redistributive impact of cash transfers, along with social spending, was seen to have compensated for some deterioration in the distribution of income during this period. In Colombia, pro–poor investments from 1970 to 1974 resulted in a larger percentage of households in the poorest quintile with access to public utility services (electricity, water and sewage, and street lighting). In Costa Rica, the share of pension benefits received by the poorest quintile increased from 6 per cent in 1986 to 9 per cent in 1992, although this is still somewhat lower than their 1983 share (10 per cent).

10.4. ROLE OF TAXES AND GOVERNMENT SOCIAL SPENDING POLICY

On the basis of the available data, the average Gini coefficient for the sample countries was stable during the 1970s and 1980s.[18] The average remained at 44 per cent for the nineteen countries. The average Gini coefficient for the 10 sample countries increased only slightly, from 32 to 34 per cent, during the 1980s and 1990s. The stable average

[18] For changes in Gini coefficients from the 1970s to the 1980s, consistent data are available for only nineteen countries. For changes from the 1980s to the 1990s, data are available for ten countries. The discussion of income distribution in this chapter is based on the high-quality data compiled by Deininger and Squire (1996). Estimates of before-tax and after-tax Gini coefficients and quintile income shares in the 1990s are available only for twenty developing (and transition) countries. In general, these estimates are based on household incomes including government cash transfers. For a considerable number of countries, however, the estimates are based on consumption data. Unlike the income data used for tax or expenditure incidence studies in individual countries, the Deininger and Squire data have been compiled on the basis of a common methodology and are intertemporally and internationally comparable.

Gini coefficient during the 1970s and the 1980s, however, masks considerable changes in the coefficients for some countries. For example, during the 1970s and 1980s, the Gini coefficient for Thailand increased by 4 percentage points, while the Gini coefficient for Turkey declined by 7 percentage points. During the 1980s and 1990s, Thailand and two transition countries (Bulgaria and Hungary) experienced a large increase in the Gini coefficient.

On the basis of the averages, data are not clear about the distributive role of taxes. From the 1970s to the 1980s, the tax burden, on average, increased slightly, with no notable change in the composition of direct and indirect taxes. From the 1980s to the 1990s, neither the average tax burden nor the tax composition changed significantly.

10.4.1. *Overview*

From the 1970s to the 1980s, five countries significantly reduced Gini coefficients (one of them on the basis of after-tax income), but five other countries significantly increased Gini coefficients (all on the basis of before-tax incomes) (Table 10.3).

The countries that significantly reduced Gini coefficients are Trinidad and Tobago, Turkey, the Philippines, Indonesia, and Malaysia. Indonesia and Malaysia achieved sustained high economic growth, pursued with strong poverty reduction and equity objectives. Malaysia and the Philippines had broadly progressive and well-targeted educational and health programmes. Indonesia had progressive and well-targeted (albeit increasingly less effective) education programmes, although its health programmes were poorly targeted. Moreover, Indonesia and Malaysia raised their tax-to-GDP ratio, by increasing direct taxes but reducing indirect taxes as a ratio to GDP. In particular, both countries reduced international taxes significantly.

The countries that significantly increased Gini coefficients are Bangladesh, Singapore, Thailand, Sri Lanka, and Guatemala. Of these, government education and health spending incidence studies are available only for Bangladesh, which had poorly targeted primary, secondary, and tertiary education programmes, although its health programme was considered progressive and well targeted. Singapore achieved a high-economic growth, but Guatemala's growth was low. The deterioration in Thailand's Gini coefficient is notable: that country's high-economic growth reduced poverty, but was regionally unbalanced, and the returns to education expenditures differed significantly among schooling levels and occupations (Ahuja *et al.* 1997).

From the 1980s to the 1990s, only two countries significantly reduced their Gini coefficients (Jamaica and Mauritius), but nine countries significantly increased theirs, sharing the widespread experiences of industrial, developing, and transition countries. No public spending incidence analysis is available for Mauritius, but available studies suggest that Jamaica's foodstamp programme was progressive and well targeted, although its tax system was considered to have either a highly regressive (income tax) or mixed or insignificant (overall tax system) incidence. Moreover, Jamaica's agricultural production responded strongly to the introduction of market-oriented reforms of the 1980s (Handa and King 1997). Of the nine countries for which

Table 10.3. *Changes in the tax burden and structure in nineteen developing countries between 1970s and 1990s (percentage points of GDP)*

		Tax type					Changes in income distribution
		All	Direct	Indirect			
				All	Domestic goods	International goods	
Average	All	1.6	1.0	0.5	0.6	−0.1	
	b	1.5	0.9	0.6	0.8	−0.2	
	a	2.1	1.4	0.4	0.1	0.3	
Trinidad and Tobago	b	5.9	6.4	−0.4	−0.3	−0.1	iid
Turkey	b	−1.9	0.4	−2.1	−0.7	−1.4	iid
Philippines	b	0.0	0.0	−0.1	0.7	−0.7	iid
Malaysia	a	1.9	2.3	−0.4	0.6	−0.9	iid
Indonesia	b	2.8	3.0	−0.5	0.2	−0.7	
Costa Rica	b	3.4	−0.2	1.7	−0.1	1.8	
Jamaica	b	3.8	0.0	5.0	5.5	−0.5	
Mexico	a	4.0	3.4	−0.4	−0.7	0.3	
Panama	b	0.1	0.6	0.1	0.6	−0.5	
Korea, R.	b	1.7	0.4	1.1	0.7	0.4	
Colombia	b	0.0	−0.7	0.9	1.2	−0.3	
India	b	2.5	1.0	1.8	0.2	1.5	
Pakistan	a	2.1	0.6	1.6	0.9	0.6	
Venezuela	a	0.1	−0.5	0.6	−0.4	1.0	
Bangladesh	b	1.1	0.2	1.0	0.1	0.9	did
Singapore	b	0.6	0.9	−0.7	0.4	−1.1	did
Thailand	b	1.6	0.9	0.6	1.0	−0.4	did
Sri Lanka	b	1.8	0.3	1.3	1.9	−0.6	did
Guatemala	b	−1.3	0.0	−0.9	0.3	−1.1	did

Notes: a = after-tax income data used; b = before-tax income data used; iid = improvement in income distribution; did = deterioration in income distribution.

Sources: Authors' calculations on International Monetary Fund (IMF), International Financial Statistics, and Government Finance Statistics databases.

income distribution deteriorated, China, Poland, Bulgaria, Romania, and Hungary were in the transition and in general achieved a low economic growth. Poland, Bulgaria, and Hungary experienced a large decline in their tax-to-GDP ratio. Of the other four, Hong Kong and Thailand achieved a high economic growth, but Jordan and Nigeria experienced a low economic growth. No public spending incidence study is available for Jordan, Nigeria, Hong Kong Special Administrative Region of the People's Republic of China (SAR), China, or Thailand (Table 10.4).

The increase in income inequality observed for the sample countries reflects, to a considerable extent, the increase in inequality in several transition countries included

Table 10.4. *Changes in the tax burden and structure between the 1980s and 1990s in ten developing countries (percentage points of GDP)*

		Tax type					Changes in income distribution
		All	Direct	Indirect			
				All	Domestic goods	International goods	
Average	All	−1.0	−0.3	−0.3	−0.1	−0.2	
	b	−2.4	−1.0	−0.3	−0.3	0.0	
	a	0.4	0.3	−0.3	0.2	−0.5	
Mauritius	a	−0.3	0.0	−1.2	1.2	−2.4	iid
Pakistan	b	0.5	0.4	0.1	0.3	−0.3	
India	a	−0.1	0.6	−0.7	−0.7	0.0	
Colombia	b	1.8	2.4	1.4	1.8	−0.4	
Peru	a	1.1	−0.1	−0.5	0.9	−1.4	
Jordan	a	6.5	1.1	4.9	3.9	1.0	did
Poland[a]	b	−4.4	−0.3	−1.1	−1.0	−0.1	did
Thailand	b	2.8	2.3	0.1	0.3	−0.2	did
Bulgaria[a]	b	−12.6	−9.6	−1.8	−3.0	1.2	did
Hungary[a]	a	−5.1	0.0	−4.2	−4.4	0.2	did

Notes: a = after-tax income data used; b = before-tax income data used; iid = improvement in income distribution; did = deterioration in income distribution.
[a] Denotes transition economies.
Sources: IMF, International Financial Statistics, and Government Finance Statistics databases.

in the sample. However, even if the transition countries were removed from the sample, the upward trend in Gini coefficients would be notable, with many market-oriented developing countries sharing a similar experience with industrial countries (see Chapters 2 and 9).

The role of changes in the tax system in this deterioration is not obvious. On average, these countries did not change their tax structure significantly, although many transition countries, which experienced an increase in their Gini coefficients, also suffered from a substantial reduction in their tax revenue. None of the eight developing countries whose tax reforms were studied in a recent World Bank report has a pre-reform schedule of progressive tax rates successfully generating a progressive distribution of tax burdens (Thirsk 1997). In general, tax reforms in developing countries have been aimed at increasing revenues with a degree of efficiency and with some attention to equity; rarely have they been aimed specifically at improving equity.

Developing countries in general have been expanding primary and secondary school enrolment rates through public education programmes. Transfer programmes often have taken more of the form of untargeted food, fuel, fertilizer, and other subsidies than of cash transfers, such as unemployment benefits and pensions, which are largely limited to public-sector employees. Transition economies started the transition to the market in the early 1990s with expansive social programmes and generally high levels of social indicators. The subsequent compression of output has forced many of them to reduce social spending. As a result, many of the transition economies experienced a deterioration in social indicators.

The results of an econometric estimation of Gini equations for some eighty-five developing and transition economies (not shown for reasons of space; see Chu *et al.* 2000) provide some evidence of the effects of the tax regime and the secondary school enrolment on income distribution.[19] In particular, an increase in the ratio of direct to indirect tax revenues and an increase in the secondary school enrolment rate both reduce the Gini coefficient. This is consistent with the literature survey, which indicated the progressivity of direct taxes and of education expenditure, including secondary education expenditure. The small magnitude of the effect of tax policy does not suggest the active use of tax policy for redistribution; however, country-specific analyses might suggest otherwise. A number of reasons have been offered to explain increases in before-tax income inequality in the context of industrial countries (Freeman 1995; Tanzi 1998; Atkinson 1999). Two of them might be applicable to developing countries. To start with, the opening up of low-income developing countries (e.g. China and India) to foreign direct investment and trade tends to reduce the wages of unskilled workers in middle-income developing countries (e.g. Thailand), which are competing with low-income countries. In addition, with globalization, developing countries gradually adapt their traditional income–equalizing social norms to those tolerating a higher degree of income inequality.

Among the countries that defied this broad trend were those that had progressive and well-targeted education and health programmes that increased the earnings potential of low-income workers and some countries that achieved a sustained high-economic growth, although not all high-growth countries achieved a reduction in inequality. It is worth noting the difficulties in comparing before-tax and after-tax income inequality in developing countries. Unlike for industrial countries, for which separate Gini coefficient estimates are available for before-tax, before-transfer 'market incomes', and after-tax and after-transfer 'disposable incomes', Gini coefficients for developing countries are available only for *either* before-tax (but after-transfer) *or* after-tax (and after-transfer) incomes. Both types of Gini coefficients are available only for two countries on a common methodology. Data are not available for before-tax and before-transfer Gini coefficient estimates and after-tax and after-transfer Gini coefficient estimates. However, the relatively small cash transfer programmes in developing countries suggest that the two types of Gini coefficients for developing countries would not differ, on average, as substantially as in industrial countries.

10.4.2. *Selected Country Experiences*

The remainder of this section discusses the nature of tax reforms and social expenditure policy and their distributional implications in Hungary, Indonesia, and Thailand,

---

[19] The regression results are reported in Chu *et al.* (2000).

Table 10.5. *Changes in Gini coefficient, tax structure, and secondary school enrolment in selected developing countries, 1970–80s and 1980–90s*

		% point change in Gini		Change in DT/IT (%)		Change in secondary school enrolment (%)	
		1970s–80s	1980s–90s	1970s–80s	1980s–90s	1970s–80s	1980s–90s
Large decline in Gini							
Turkey	b	−7		151		128	
Trinidad and Tobago	b	−7		136		149	
Philippines	b	−3		100		116	
Malaysia	b	−3		153		118	
Indonesia	a	−3		147		190	
Large increase in Gini							
Singapore	b	4		125		115	
Thailand	b	4		138		112	
Sri Lanka	b	6		90		131	
Guatemala	b	9		119		146	
Large decline in Gini							
Mauritius	a		−3		105		116
Large increase in Gini							
Poland	b		4		103		117
Thailand	b		4		172		148
Bulgaria	b		5		59		91
Hungary	a		9		124		122

Notes: a = after-tax Gini cofficient; b = before-tax Gini coefficent; DT = direct taxes; IT = indirect taxes.

Sources: Deininger and Squire (1996) and IMF, International Financial Statistics, and Government Finance Statistics databases.

three of the countries that experienced a large change in the Gini coefficient. All of these countries increased the ratio of direct and indirect taxes and expanded secondary school enrolment. However, their achievements in income distribution diverged. While Indonesia reduced its Gini coefficients, Thailand and Hungary experienced an increase in their Gini coefficients (Table 10.5).

Hungary

During the 1980s and 1990s, Hungary's transition to a market-oriented society resulted in major structural change in its economy. While modestly increasing both the ratio of direct to indirect taxes (by 24 per cent) and the secondary school enrolment rate (by 22 per cent), Hungary suffered a 9-percentage-point increase in the after-tax Gini.

The changes in the tax system and social protection programmes discussed below had direct implications for the after-tax (and after-transfer) Gini. The changes in education programmes probably influenced the before-tax Gini, which is not reported in this chapter, and, thereby, the after-tax Gini. The reform of the Hungarian tax system began with the establishment of PIT and value-added tax (VAT) in 1988, followed by the introduction of a modern corporate tax in 1992. Since then, the attempt has been to improve the efficiency of the tax system by adjusting marginal tax rates and brackets for personal and corporate taxes as well as by reducing tax exemptions. A broadening of the VAT base through rate rationalization and extension of coverage has accompanied this. The Hungarian tax system now relies more on direct and broad-based consumption taxes than in 1988. Some 40 per cent of the revenue in 1998 accrued from personal taxes, corporate taxes, and VATs compared with 30 per cent in 1990.

Adjustments to the tax system have been made almost every year in the past decade. In 1988, the PIT consisted of eleven brackets, and the tax rates ranged from 20 to 60 per cent; by 1999, there were three brackets ranging between 20 and 40 per cent. The general profit tax was 50 per cent in 1988, but was reduced to 20 per cent of the corporate income in 1997. In 1988, the VAT comprised three rates: 0, 15, and 25 per cent. The zero rate applied to most food products, fuels, pharmaceuticals, household heating, and exports; the 15 per cent rate was levied on most services; and the 25 per cent rate applied to about 40 per cent of consumer expenditures. A major change was effected to the VAT rate structure in 1993; 80 per cent of food products and household heating were subjected to the lower rate of 10 per cent, and all public services began to be taxed at 25 per cent. In 1998, the 10 per cent rate was increased to 12 per cent and zero-rating confined to pharmaceuticals and exports. Financial, education, health, and postal services are still tax-exempt.

Like other transition economies, Hungary started the transition to the market with expansive social welfare programmes, including state-provided health and education services. The education system, which produced a secondary education enrolment rate of some 80 per cent, enjoyed a pupil–teacher ratio that was even lower than in industrial countries. From the mid-1980s to the mid-1990s, the large reduction of untargeted price subsidies was compensated for by an increase in cash benefits to vulnerable groups, including old-age pensioners, families with children, and the unemployed.

Indonesia

During the 1970s and 1980s, Indonesia achieved sustained economic growth, improved income distribution, and reduced poverty. Indonesia also made progress in improving the tax system and in expanding education programmes. Between the 1970s and the 1980s, the after-tax Gini coefficient declined by 3 percentage points; the ratio of direct to indirect taxes increased by 50 per cent, although this ratio declined subsequently, and the secondary school enrolment rate almost doubled. It appears that both tax and social-spending policies had reinforced each other in reducing the after-tax Gini. Indonesia's tax reform during the 1980s was aimed at increasing revenues and enhancing the efficiency and simplicity of the tax system but without causing an adverse impact on the poor. The 1983 tax-reform package aimed at broadening the base of the income taxes, but reducing their rates. It also included a VAT and a luxury sales tax, which were implemented in 1985. Subsequent reforms broadened the property tax. The VAT, from which unprocessed foodstuffs, certain farm products, and services were exempted, was extended later to wholesale trade and other services. The result was a broader-based, more equitable tax system.

Since then, the attempt has been to improve the efficiency of the tax system by Indonesia expanded social programmes largely on the strength of its sustained economic growth. Without a considerable increase in social expenditures as per cent of GDP, social indicators improved. From the 1970s to the 1980s, the secondary school enrolment rate almost doubled. Significant improvements in school enrolments among the lower-income groups took place in the late 1970s. Indonesia had achieved nearly universal primary education by the late 1980s, although there were concerns that the improvements were achieved at the expense of the quality of education.

Thailand

Thailand is a high-growth country that reduced poverty substantially. For the proportion of people below the poverty line, the head-count index has fallen from about 23 per cent in 1981 to about 13 per cent in 1992 (World Bank 1996). More recently, in response to the financial crisis, Thailand expanded social safety net programmes. During the 1970s and 1990s, however, Thailand experienced a large increase in the before-tax Gini (see Chapter 16). It is unclear why the increase in the Gini occurred, in spite of a large expansion of secondary school enrolment. Between the 1980s and the 1990s, the Gini coefficient increased by 4 percentage points while the secondary school enrolment rate increased by 48 per cent. It is also unclear how the changes in the tax system have changed the after-tax Gini, which is not reported. The ratio of direct to indirect taxes increased by 72 per cent. This expansion of direct taxes should have, *ceteris paribus*, tended to reduce the after-tax Gini. As discussed below, however, the tax system has been changed frequently, in response to fiscal needs, while other factors contributed to a steep rise in the pre-tax Gini (see Chapter 16).

Thailand's changing direction on tax reforms has often been triggered by macro-economic imbalances. During the 1973–6 period, for example, indirect tax rates were reduced to alleviate the burden of higher inflation and lower real GDP growth that followed the oil shock of 1973–4. The ensuing deficit spending in the next 2 years, which was intended to counteract slower real income growth, necessitated higher revenues. As a result, a series of tax rate increases were instituted during the 1977–9 period, followed by income tax rate reductions between 1980 and 1986, in the aftermath of the oil shock of 1979–80.

The burden of higher taxes in the 1977–9 period seems to have fallen mostly on indirect taxes that tend to be regressive; in the 1970s, indirect taxes, for example, made up almost 80 per cent of all taxes. Reduction in tax rates in the 1980–6 period led to a decline in the buoyancy of PITs that may have contributed to the increase in after-tax income inequality, since for a given income increase, the average effective tax rate did not increase in the 1980s as much as it did in the 1970s. The tax structure is complex and has been characterized by 'base erosion resulting from special allowances, high standard deductions, and by failure to tax fringe benefits and non-neutrality in the tax treatment of different income sources on different transactions' (Tanzi and Shome 1992). In 1989, Thailand carried out further tax reforms aimed at simplification, neutrality, and revenue generation. The number of PIT brackets were reduced from eleven to six and a greater number of low-income tax payers were left out of the income tax net. No attempt was made to reduce expense deductions and allowances for business incomes.

In the early 1990s, Thailand introduced another series of tax reforms. VAT was introduced in 1992 at a rate of 7 per cent, which replaced an inefficient and complex business tax with twenty-one rates ranging from 0.10 to 50 per cent; the number of PIT brackets was further reduced from six to four; the top PIT rate was reduced from 50 to 37 per cent, and more incomes became subject to the lower tax rates. These tax simplifications, other things being equal, would not necessarily lead to a deterioration in income inequality. While the ratio of direct to indirect taxes rose by 70 per cent from the 1980s to the 1990s, given the observed increase in income inequality in the 1990s, these reforms have not reversed the rise in income inequality, nor the legacy of tax reforms of the earlier decades.

Social spending does not seem to have had much effect on income inequality, although the secondary school enrolment rate increased substantially. Government spending on transfer programmes (in kind and cash) as well as employment generation programmes constitute a small portion of government expenditure (about 1.6 per cent during the 1990–5 period), and various programmes are not well targeted towards regions with high incidence of poverty and inequality. Despite the increase in income inequality, government spending on education and health has remained steady in the last two decades at about 19 and 7 per cent of total expenditures, respectively. There is no benefit incidence study of government transfer programmes or social spending that can be used for analysing the incidence structure of the past spending.

10.5. SUMMARY AND CONCLUSIONS

The available data indicate that, before the effects of redistributive tax and transfer programmes, income inequality in developing countries is, *on average*, lower than in industrial countries. While industrial countries improve income distribution effectively through taxes and transfers, most developing countries do not have adequate redistributive programmes to achieve a greater post-tax, post-transfer income equality comparative to those of industrial countries.

According to the data compiled by Deininger and Squire (1996), before-tax (but after-transfer) Gini coefficients for developing and transition countries are, on average, lower than 'market-income' Gini coefficients compiled by the Organization for Economic Cooperation and Development (OECD) for industrial countries. For the 1990s, the former average was 0.38; the latter average was 0.44. However, there are indications that the tax programmes in developing and transition countries are not as

Table 10.6. *Changes in income inequality due to taxation: Selected studies on developing and transition economies*

Country	Year	Gini coefficient		Difference	Type of tax	Source
		Before-tax	After-tax			
Bulgaria	1989	24.5	25.6	1.1	Payroll	Milanovic (1994)
Chile	1996	48.8	49.6	0.8	Direct and indirect	Engel *et al.* (1998)
Czechoslovakia	1988	26.9	26.0	−0.9	Payroll	Milanovic (1994)
Egypt	1958–9	44.5	43.0	−1.5	Direct and indirect	El-Edel (1979)
Egypt	1964–5	43.1	41.8	−1.3	Direct and indirect	El-Edel (1979)
Egypt	1974–5	43.1	42.2	−0.9	Direct and indirect	El-Edel (1979)
Hungary	1989	30.4	31.6	1.2	Payroll	Milanovic (1994)
Hungary	1989	24.8	23.3	−1.5	Direct personal	Milanovic (1994)
Poland	1989	33.5	34.5	1.0	Payroll	Milanovic (1994)
Ukraine	1989	26.5	25.8	−0.7	Direct	Kakwani (1996)
Ukraine	1991	21.8	21.2	−0.6	Direct	Kakwani (1996)
Ukraine	1992	23.4	22.6	−0.8	Direct	Kakwani (1996)
Yugoslavia	1989	38.7	38.1	−0.6	Payroll	Milanovic (1994)
Yugoslavia	1989	37.9	37.9	0.0	Direct personal	Milanovic (1994)
Average		33.4	33.1	−0.3		

Source: Compilation by the authors on the basis of the studies indicated in the table.

effective in reducing income inequality in industrial countries (Table 10.6). The before-tax and after-tax Gini measures for two separate groups of developing countries average, respectively, 0.38 and 0.34. Likewise, the difference does not exceed 4 points between the two Ginis for two transition countries for which comparable data are available.

Existing studies on tax and transfer incidence support the argument that their redistributive effects are not as large as in industrial countries. Studies of tax incidence suggest that their redistributive effects are minor in developing (and transition) countries. The tax structure in developing countries is dominated by indirect taxes, with only a limited menu of capital and wealth taxes. In general, their weak tax administration in these countries gives rise to tax evasion, a marked difference between de jure and de facto tax regimes, and a low tax-to-GDP ratio. They have only limited formal cash transfer and social protection programmes. These features cast doubt on the ability of tax (and transfer) policies in developing countries to redistribute income effectively. Corruption and poor governance also limit the effectiveness of taxes and transfers as redistributive instruments. The survey of tax incidence studies carried out in this chapter shows that only thirteen of the thirty-six overall tax systems studies were found to be progressive, the rest were either proportional or regressive. Over time, the progressivity has declined in several developing countries following the introduction of recent tax reforms. It should be noted, however, that the survey has found thirteen tax systems to be progressive. In particular, most income taxes were progressive.

Education, health, and transfer programmes in developing countries, in general, had a progressive incidence but many were *not* well targeted. All primary and secondary education programmes, but only half of the tertiary education programmes, assessed had a progressive incidence. Their targeting, however, was less effective. While all health programmes were progressive, only half of them were well targeted. Overall, while fourteen of the fifteen transfer programmes were progressive, nine of them were not well targeted. The welfare impact of progressive government spending programmes is, however, not easy to assess because their effectiveness matters crucially. Government expenditure on an ineffective primary education programme might be more a cash transfer to teachers than a benefit to school children.

From the 1980s to the 1990s, many developing and transition countries have experienced an increase in income inequality based on both before-tax and after-tax measures. Indeed, the tax and transfer policies in developing and transition economies were not sufficiently effective in limiting the increase in after-tax and after-transfer Gini coefficients and, as indicated in the before last paragraph, the decline in progressivity of tax systems may have in some cases contributed to the rise in after-tax income inequality (on this, compare the findings of Chapter 9 discussing redistributive trends in OECD countries). Industrial countries experienced a large increase in market-income Gini coefficients. Relative to developing and transition countries, however, industrial countries successfully used their taxes and transfers to limit the increase in disposable income Gini coefficients.

While many global and country-specific factors might be contributing to the widespread increases in income inequality, it appears that sound economic and social policies help to either limit a deterioration of income distribution or achieve its improvement. High economic growth, alone, does not appear to ensure an improvement in income distribution. Possible factors underlying these changes are the impact of opening up to international trade of low-income developing countries on wage rates in middle-income developing countries and changes in social norms. Indeed, the opening of low-income countries might have an adverse effect on the wages of unskilled workers in middle-income developing countries. Yet, countries that pursued sound macroeconomic and structural policies, including sound social policies, improved their income distribution, in spite of the limited equity objectives of their tax reforms. For example, Jamaica and Indonesia improved income distribution in spite of the limited equity orientation of their tax reform efforts.

The use of tax instruments for redistribution remains an interesting issue that needs to be further explored. The survey finds income taxes to have progressive incidence. Should developing countries actively promote their expansion? Alternatively, should the developing countries promote an increase in tax revenue and use the revenue to expand well-targeted social programmes? This question would be difficult to answer without considering individual countries' specific circumstances, such as the nature of their tax regime and tax administration. Countries that have capacity to increase tax revenue with a degree of progressivity without causing disincentive effects on work efforts would enrich their redistributive policy instruments. The preliminary econometric evidence in this regard, however, seems to suggest that the magnitude of the effect might be small (Chu *et al.* 2000). If the progressivity of the tax system were achieved at the cost of revenue, relative to the case of a neutral tax regime, the gains in redistribution on the tax side could be more than offset by lost opportunities to use progressive expenditure policy instruments.

REFERENCES

Aaron, H., and M. C. McGuire (1970). Public goods and income distribution. *Econometrica* 38(6), 907–20.

Ahuja, V., B. Bidani, F. Ferreira, and M. Walton (1997). *Everyone's Miracle? Rising Poverty and Inequality in East Asia*. World Bank: Washington, DC.

Alesina, A. (1999). Too large and too small governments. In V. Tanzi, K.-Y. Chu, and S. Gupta (eds.), *Economic Policy and Equity*. IMF: Washington, DC.

Aninat, E., A. Bauer, and K. Cowan (1999). Addressing equity issues in policymaking: Lessons from the Chilean experience. In V. Tanzi, K.-Y. Chu, and S. Gupta (eds.), *Economic Policy and Equity*. IMF: Washington, DC.

Atkinson, A. B. (1999). Equity issues in a globalizing world: The experience of OECD countries. In V. Tanzi, K.-Y. Chu, and S. Gupta (eds.), *Economic Policy and Equity*. IMF: Washington, DC.

Bird, R. M., and B. D. Miller (1989). The incidence of indirect taxes on low-income households in Jamaica. *Economic Development and Cultural Change* 37, 393–409.

—— and L. De Wulf (1973). Taxation and income distribution in Latin America: A critical review of empirical studies. *IMF Staff Papers* 20(3), 639–82.

Bolkowiak, I., *et al.* (1996). Tax burden on gross incomes of households. Institute of Finance Working Papers 49. Institute of Finance: Warsaw.

Chowdhury, N. (1988). Income tax incidence in Bangladesh, 1980–84. *Bangladesh Development Studies* 16, 81–97.

Chu, K.-Y., H. R. Davoodi, and S. Gupta (2000). Income distribution and tax, and government social spending policies in developing countries. WIDER Working Paper 214. UNU/WIDER: Helsinki.

Davoodi, H. R., E. R. Tiongson, and S. S. Asawanuchit (2003). How useful are benefit incidence analysis of public education and health spending? IMF Working Papers 03/227.

Deininger, K., and L. Squire (1996). A new data set for measuring income inequality. *World Bank Economic Review* 10, 565–92.

Devarajan, S., and S. Hossain (1998). The combined incidence of taxes and public expenditures in the Philippines. *World Development* 26, 963–77.

De Wulf, L. (1975). Fiscal incidence in developing countries: Survey and critique. *IMF Staff Papers* 22(1), 61–131.

Edirisinghe, N. (1987). The food stamp scheme in Sri Lanka: Costs, benefits, and options for modification. *International Food Policy Research Institute Research Report* 58. IFPRI: Washington, DC.

El-Edel, M. R. A. (1979). Impact of taxation on income distribution: An exploratory attempt to estimate tax incidence in Egypt. Income distribution project conference paper. Princeton University: Princeton, NJ.

Engel, E., A. Galetovic, and C. E. Raddatz (1998). Taxation and income distribution in Chile: Some unpleasant redistributive arithmetic. NBER Working Papers 6828. National Bureau of Economic Research: Cambridge, MA.

Freeman, R. B. (1995). Are your wages set in Beijing. *Journal of Economic Perspectives* 9(3), 15–32.

Gil-Diaz, F. (1982). The incidence of taxes in Mexico, a before and after comparison. Mimeo.

Handa, S., and D. King (1997). Structural adjustment policies, income distribution and poverty: A review of the Jamaican experience. *World Development* 25(6), 915–30.

Harberger, A. C. (1998). Monetary and fiscal policy for equitable economic growth. In V. Tanzi and K.-Y. Chu (eds.), *Income Distribution and High Quality Growth*. MIT Press: Cambridge, MA.

Kakwani, N. (1996). Income inequality, welfare and poverty in Ukraine. University of New South Wales School of Economics Discussion Papers 94. University of New South Wales: Sydney.

McLure, C. E. (1974). On the theory and methodology of estimating benefit and expenditure incidence. Program of Development Studies. William Marsh Rice University: Houston.

—— (1977). Taxation and the urban poor in developing countries. *World Development* 5(3), 169–88.

Milanovic, B. (1994). Cash social transfers, direct taxes, and income distribution in late socialism. *Journal of Comparative Economics* 18(April), 175–97.

—— (1995). Impact of cash and in-kind transfers in eastern Europe and Russia. In D. van de Walle and K. Nead (eds.), *Public Spending and the Poor*. Johns Hopkins University Press: Baltimore.

Mwega, F. M. (1986). Incidence of taxes and transfers in Kenya: a general equilibrium analysis. *Eastern African Economic Review* 2 (June), 6–13.

Sahn, D., and S. Younger (1998). Poverty and fiscal policy: Microeconomic evidence. Mimeo, Cornell University.

Selden, T. M., and M. J. Wasylenko (1992). Benefit incidence analysis in developing countries. World Bank Policy Research Working Papers 1015. World Bank: Washington, DC.

Shah, A., and J. Whalley (1990). An alternative view of tax incidence analysis for developing countries. PRE Working Papers 462. World Bank: Washington, DC.

—— and —— (1991). The redistributive impact of taxation in developing countries. In J. Khalilzadeh-Shirazi and A. Shah (eds.), *Tax Policy in Developing Countries*. A World Bank Symposium. World Bank: Washington, DC.

Shikha, J., and P. V. Srinivasan (1989). Indirect taxes in India: an incidence analysis. *Economic and Political Weekly* 24(April), 811–30.

Tanzi, V. (1974). Redistributing income through the budget in Latin America. *Banco Nazionale del Lavoro Quarterly Review* 27(108), 65–87.

—— (1998). Fundamental determinants of inequality and the role of government. IMF Working Papers 178. IMF: Washington, DC.

—— and P. Shome (1992). The role of taxation in the development of east Asian economies. In T. Ito and A. O. Krueger (eds.), *The Political Economy of Tax Reform*. University of Chicago Press: Chicago and London.

Thirsk, W. (1997). Overview: The substance and process of tax reform in eight developing countries. In W. Thirsk (ed.), *Tax Reform in Developing Countries*. World Bank: Washington, DC.

Westlake, M. J. (1973). Tax evasion, tax incidence and the distribution of income in Kenya. *Eastern Africa Economic Review* 5(1), 1–27.

Whalley, J. (1984). Regression or progression: The taxing question of incidence analysis. *Canadian Journal of Economics* 17(4), 654–82.

World Bank (1996). *Poverty Reduction and the World Bank: Progress and Challenges in the 1990s*. World Bank: Washington, DC.

11

The Impact of Adjustment-Related Social Funds on Income Distribution and Poverty

GIOVANNI ANDREA CORNIA AND SANJAY G. REDDY

11.1. INTRODUCTION

Most poverty and inequality has deep-rooted causes that can be removed only by structural (and often slow) interventions such as land redistribution, educational expansion, the modernization of the tax system, and changes in the institutional structure of credit and property markets. However, apart from these deep-seated phenomena, it is now increasingly evident that structural adjustment, premature financial liberalization, and uncontrolled globalization can exacerbate poverty by inducing protracted recessions and macroeconomic instability. For example, the eruption of the Asian economic crisis in the late 1990s brought to the fore the large social impact of ill-designed macroeconomic policies.

One of the dominant responses to these policy-induced problems on the part of the institutions that have pressed for these policy changes has been the establishment of temporary social safety nets. The most popular type of such temporary social safety nets are known as 'social funds'. Social funds have become a prime policy choice for offsetting the social impact of policy reform. Indeed, the strengthening of adjustment-related social safety nets—as opposed to the development of permanent social protection systems or the introduction of policy measures with a milder distributive impact—has been one of the pillars of the dominant approach to policy reform.

It is accordingly paramount to assess the extent to which social funds constitute an effective antidote to policy reform-induced increases in poverty and inequality. It is difficult, however, to assess their record. This is not least because during their comparatively brief existence, their objectives, main activities, target population, funding patterns, and institutional structure have continuously evolved. Their impact also varies in relation to the strength of the social protection systems inherited from the prereform era, and to the impact of adjustment policies themselves, which in turn

The authors are grateful for the comments made on a prior version of this chapter by two anonymous referees and by the participants to the WIDER project meeting held in Helsinki in July 1999.

have enjoyed varying degrees of success in different country settings. Finally, systematic data on social funds performance is still relatively difficult to find.[1]

Despite these methodological difficulties, there is enough evidence today for an assessment of social fund performance to be made. This chapter argues that most of them played a minor role in containing the social costs arising from liberalization policies and in reducing the number of unemployed, 'adjustment poor' and 'chronic poor'. In addition, the emphasis placed on short-term social funds may have diverted resources and the attention of policy-makers from the extension and reform of standing social security arrangements that may more effectively address both chronic and adjustment-induced poverty.

11.2. THE HISTORICAL CONTEXT LEADING TO THE MASS INTRODUCTION OF SOCIAL FUNDS

As noted throughout this book, the 1980s and 1990s can be described as 'decades of policy reform'. The widespread balance of payments crises of 1981–4, the debt crisis of the mid-1980s, the simultaneous shift of the World Bank to structural adjustment lending, and the wave of restructuring and privatization programmes introduced in the formerly planned economies of Europe were the main factors leading to a rapid increase in stabilization and structural adjustment programmes. A rough idea of the intensity of this effort can be grasped from the number of adjustment programmes carried out with the assistance of the Bretton Woods Institutions during this period; while in the 1970s the number of countries initiating programmes with the support of the International Monetary Fund (IMF) averaged about ten per year, it increased from nineteen to thirty-three between 1980 and 1985 (Cornia *et al.* 1987: 49). As a result, in the 1980s, the Latin American countries undertook an average of six adjustment programmes with the assistance of the World Bank and IMF, while Jamaica, Mexico, and Costa Rica undertook between nine and fourteen each. Likewise, in the 1980s, the African nations initiated an average of seven adjustment programmes, with Senegal, Kenya, Mauritius, and Cote d'Ivoire undertaking between twelve and fifteen (Jespersen 1992: Table 1.2). The effort at policy reform accelerated in the 1990s with the onset of the transition and the explosion of the 'Asian crisis'.

The poverty, distributive, and growth impact of these reform programmes remains controversial. During the first half of the 1980s, adjustment focused mainly on restoring macroeconomic balance, as the Bretton Woods Institutions expected that this would lead to a rapid resumption of growth and poverty alleviation. It soon became apparent, however, that resumption of growth would take longer than initially expected, that adjustment caused at least a temporary increase in poverty and inequality and that, in the interim, measures were needed to offset these social costs (World Bank 1986). In 1990, the World Bank (1990: 23) formally acknowledged the need to develop special

---

[1] This gap is being belatedly and gradually being remedied through studies such as the 'Social Funds 2000 Impact Evaluation'; see World Bank (1998*a*).

measures for social protection to accompany an unaltered approach to adjustment. The 'social funds' were the most prominent measure of this kind.

Beginning in 1986, a few developing countries started introducing semi-autonomous and fast-disbursing social funds aimed at compensating the adjustment poor by means of short-term income maintenance and social expenditure programmes. With persistent stagnation, some of these programmes became semi-permanent. This is the phase that saw the development of the first sizeable emergency social funds of Ghana and Bolivia. At a later stage, the distinction between adjustment poor and chronic poor started to be blurred and the scope of social funds was enlarged so as to address also the problems of the 'chronic poor' who, despite the adjustment reforms, were still being bypassed by growth.

In a third phase, the social funds increasingly shifted from compensatory to promotive measures, so as to incorporate the poor into the production process by increasing their human and physical assets. During this period emergency social funds began to evolve into social investment funds which effected, by and large, a programmatic shift from the objective of income generation as a means of compensating for macroeconomic shocks to that of the providing social services in a more efficient and responsive manner.

Since the early- to mid-1980s a growing part of the literature on inequality focused on the distributive consequences of policy reforms bringing about the liberalization of the domestic and international markets. The theoretical literature in this field comes to ambiguous conclusions. The distributive impact of policy reform is indeterminate, as it varies with the quality of existing institutions, human capabilities, and physical infrastructure, the degree of diversification of the economy, the size, degree of export orientation and labour intensity of the tradable sector, the elasticity of supply responses, and the policy mix. However, the empirical literature reviewed in UNCTAD (1997), Kanbur (1998), Kanbur and Lustig (1999), Chapter 2, and several other chapters of this volume suggests that inequality rose over the last 20 years in about two-thirds of the countries with adequate time-series data. To what extent have social funds offset the distributive and poverty impact of the increases in inequality associated with policy reforms? And how do they compare with the standard transfer programmes (e.g. those analysed in Chapter 10 by Chu *et al.*)? To answer these questions we review the evidence on the scale and structure of social funds.

11.3. ADJUSTMENT-RELATED SOCIAL FUNDS: SCALE, SCOPE, AND STRUCTURE

Since the first adjustment-related social fund was launched in Bolivia in 1986, their number has burgeoned dramatically, as has their geographical reach. There now exist at least seventy social funds throughout the less-developed and transition countries.[2] Social funds can be found in every major region, with some regions (notably Latin

---

[2] Authors' calculations and personal communication from Soniya Carvalho, World Bank.

America) having become effectively saturated. Social funds are financial intermediaries that channel public funds to subprojects administered by diverse actors. They do so, as will be described below, in a manner that is 'multisectoral' and 'demand-driven', serving in effect like public sector grant-giving foundations that disburse funds for a variety of purposes.

In many contexts, social funds appear to have become the social protection instrument of choice and to have replaced some of the usual social transfers (see Chapter 10). At the end of 1998, social funds accounted for roughly 3 per cent of active World Bank projects, 1 per cent of total financial commitments, and 10 per cent of annual commitments to the social sectors.[3] By May 2001, the World Bank commitments to social funds had risen to over US$3.5 billion covering ninety-eight projects in a total of fifty-eight countries (World Bank 2002). Other external donors have also provided a sizeable amount. The Inter-American Development Bank, for instance, had by 1997 lent over $1.3 billion for social funds in the Americas, ultimately accounting for almost 15 per cent of its annual lending to the social sectors (Bigio 1998). Other donors accounted for 18.4 per cent of total financing, amounting to a total of $801 million through 1996.[4] An illustration of the breadth of donor interest in such a policy tool is provided by Egypt's social fund, which has a total cost of $775 million of which 15.5 per cent is financed by the World Bank with the remainder provided by a patchwork of sixteen donors and the government of Egypt. Social funds have in general been heavily reliant on external funding, averaging 88 per cent in Africa and 72 per cent in Latin America (UNCTAD, 1994; Table 11.1 below).

Social funds first became widespread in Latin America, and subsequently became common in Africa. More recently, however, they have been implemented in a number of Asian countries—notably Cambodia, Jordan, Mongolia, Pakistan, and Thailand—and are being implemented in a number of low-income countries in transition including Albania, Armenia, Georgia, Moldova, Romania, Tajikistan, and Uzbekistan. Their multiplication around the world is an extraordinary example of a genuine institutional innovation that has been rapidly disseminated across countries. Although this is partly due to the supposed applicability of this model to the circumstances of developing countries, it is also due to having become a favourite instrument of officials in multilateral institutions.

As noted in the introduction, social funds have not always been adopted wholesale, but rather have undergone considerable adaptation and innovation as they have been implemented in new settings. As a result, the current generation of social funds bears only a family resemblance to the very earliest ones. Current social funds fall into a number of distinct categories—emergency social funds, social investment funds, and AGETIPs[5]—a form of social fund focusing on infrastructure development, and common in francophone Africa—each representing innovations that have emerged over

---

[3] The latter figure is calculated by dividing the sum of fiscal year 1996 World Bank expenditure on education, health nutrition, and population, and the 'social sectors' as identified in the *World Bank Annual Report 1998*, by the value of social funds approved in fiscal year 1996 as identified in World Bank (1997).

[4] Calculated by the authors on the basis of table 2.1 in Goodman *et al.* (1997).

[5] Aagences d'exécution des travaux d'intérêt public contre le sous emploi.

Adjustment-Related Social Funds

Table 11.1. *Expenditure on SF as percentage of GDP and social expenditure (SE), SE/GDP ratio, real social expenditure per capita for selected countries*

Country (Name of SF, years)	Total amt of SF, in $mn (and % of external funds)	SF per prog. year, as % of GDP[a]	SF per prog. year, as % of SE[a]	SE as % of GDP before and during social funds[b]	Real SE before and during social funds[c]
Bolivia (SEF, 1986–91)	191 (85)[d]	0.72	11.0	Before 6.2[e] during 6.6	Before 96 during 98
Bolivia (FIS, 1990–4)	96 (69)[d]	0.38	4.5	6.3 8.7	92 136
Chile (FOSIS, 1990–4)	77 (43)[d]	0.04	0.3	13.1 13.1	52,500 62,300
Ecuador (several, 1983–90)	180 (n.a.)	0.20	3.8	5.9 5.2	12,300 10,300
El Salvador (FIS, 1990–3)	67 (67)[d]	0.31	9.3	3.7 3.4	158 156
Mexico (PRONASOL, 1989–93)	2500 (0)[d]	0.17	2.7	5.1 6.5	126 171
Nicaragua (FISE, 1990–4)	93 (n.a.)	—	—	n.a. 16.9	— —
Panama (FISE, 1990–3)	32 (62)[d]	0.10	0.6	16.5 16.1	349 396
Cameroon (SDA, 1991–5)	49 (78)[d]	0.11	1.8	6.0 7.7	18,100 19,100
Egypt (SFD, 1991–5)	613 (n.a.)[d]	0.36	2.7	12.8 13.7	144 159
Ghana (PAMSCAD, 1987–92)	80 (94)[d]	0.22	3.8	5.3 6.4	2,850 3,650
Madagascar (SIRP, 1989–93)	41 (88)[d]	0.28	7.5	3.5 3.8	8,930 9,310
Zambia (SRP, 1989–93)	49 (94)[d]	0.28	5.7	5.4 4.9	166 140
Zambia (MPI, 1991–5)	20 (n.a.)[d]	0.12	2.2	4.8 6.5	142 151

[a] Total value of SF (divided by the number of years of operations) and further divided by the average yearly GDP of the period considered.

[b] 'Before' = average social expenditure/GDP ratio over the 2 years preceding the onset of the SFs (social expenditure includes health, education, social security, housing, and other amenities), 'during' = unweighted average during the programme years.

[c] 'Before' = average real social expenditure per capita (in national currency in constant 1987 prices) over the 2 years preceding the onset of the SFs, 'during' = unweighted average during the programme years.

[d] Share of SFs funded with foreign, NGOs, and other resources.

[e] 1983–4.

Source: Cornia (1999) based on data in UNCTAD (1994), Glaessner *et al.* (1994), Marc *et al.* (1995), Reddy (1997), and IMF's *Government of Finance Statistics* 1998.

time so as to incorporate a number of new design features and modified objectives; see Reddy (1997) and Carvalho (1999) for some of the salient differences. Increasingly, the emergency social funds have been supplanted by social investment funds, which are seen as longer-term service delivery mechanisms whose ambit extends beyond the provision of infrastructure to that of general social programmes.[6] Despite this diversity, all social funds share two defining characteristics. They all are multisectoral and demand-driven financial intermediaries, which provide public funds to external actors as a means of furthering social objectives.

The first shared characteristic—that social funds are *meant* to be demand-driven—constitutes a genuine innovation with respect to previous anti-poverty and social service delivery instruments. A social fund is demand-driven if the projects financed by it are proposed by external entities such as Nongovernmental Organizations (NGOs), municipalities, and community organizations, acting on behalf of the potential beneficiaries. The social fund may apply evaluation criteria of its own choosing to sift among these proposals, and it may also assist these external organizations to prepare and submit proposals. Although a demand-driven social fund relies for project proposals on external entities, it may or may not rely upon these organizations to implement the projects. In a traditional supply-driven social programme, in contrast, the programme management identifies and designs projects.

The second shared characteristic—that social funds are generally multisectoral in the sense that they finance activities, which would otherwise fall under the jurisdiction of a variety of ministries—is less innovative but nevertheless distinctive.[7] It is not wholly innovative because previous multisectoral development programmes, such as the so-called integrated rural development programmes, have had a lengthy prior history. The social funds have financed activities ranging from the provision of health, education, and water infrastructure and services, through to peace-building efforts, skills generation, and the provision of microcredit.[8] There is an intrinsic logical and practical link between their multisectoral character and the intent that they should be demand-driven. Relying upon counterparts to present project proposals of their own formulation necessitates openness to a range of possible formats and goals that may be difficult to accommodate within narrow sectoral boundaries. As a result, demand-driven social funds are usually administered by distinct decision-making bodies that are relatively independent of existing ministries.

There is little comparable or systematic evidence on the precise volume of funds spent on the various components of social fund projects. However, a review of World

---

[6] For example, Panama's FES supports programmes for street children, services for the elderly poor, and for abused women run by NGOs and community organizations, while Jamaica's SF funds drug rehabilitation and literacy programmes. Through such broader and more flexible initiatives, SFs are beginning to conform to a larger extent to the conceptual model of 'semi-autonomous public sector foundations'.

[7] UNCTAD (1994) found that of twenty-nine social funds surveyed, twenty-eight were multisectoral (six had four or more types of projects, twenty had three or more types of projects, two had two or more types, and only one had a single type).

[8] Social funds are gradually but continually expanding into new areas. For example, Jamaica's social investment project has a menu of options including the financing of conflict resolution programmes, the creation and rehabilitation of 'integrated community spaces', and drug abuse counseling, all directed at reducing the level of urban violence—see World Bank (1996).

Bank-financed projects reports that roughly one-third of total project cost is allocated to 'economic infrastructure' and a similar proportion to social infrastructure and provision (health, nutrition and population, and education sectors), with the remaining one-third covering activities such as training, environmental interventions, and microfinance (World Bank 1997). The figures for Latin American social funds contained in Grosh (1990) and in Goodman *et al.* (1997) in contrast suggest a rather higher average proportion allocated to social infrastructure and provision (68 and 62 per cent respectively).[9] This difference may reflect continuing regional variation as the African social funds in particular (the AGETIPs) have tended to focus heavily on public works of a general kind.[10]

The rationale of social funds was to recognize and counteract the deleterious impact of structural adjustment, initiated in diverse countries under the pressure of adverse economic circumstances and under the intellectual influence of the Washington Consensus. This was attempted through the financing of a combination of labour-intensive employment generation programmes, social expenditures aimed at counteracting direct fiscal retrenchment in the social sectors, and in certain cases programmes of retraining or direct compensation to those displaced by the adjustment process, especially from public employment.[11] As the social costs and adverse distributional impact of adjustment mounted and became less deniable, social funds—rather than the usual social transfers illustrated in Chapters 9 and 10—became the favoured answer to the question of how these costs were to be reduced.

---

[9] Authors' calculation based on the average value of the sum of 'service provision', and health, education, and water/sewerage infrastructure lines of Reddy (1997: table 6) (derived from Grosh, 1990), and by averaging the social infrastructure line for all funds for which complete data are available in Goodman *et al.* (1997). Note that this calculation generates a conservative estimate of expenditures on social infrastructure and provision as it does not include social assistance amounts, which may be included in the 'other' category in the original tables. There may be differences of definition between the three sources considered in this paragraph, which limit the possibilities for comparison. It is difficult to tell as the definition of categories has not been made explicit in all of the sources.

[10] For suggestive evidence see Marc *et al.* (1995: table A.3). In Senegal AGETIP I and Senegal AGETIP II, for instance, 'labor intensive works' take up between seventy and eighty-four of overall expenditures. It is not possible to distinguish the social from economic infrastructure components of 'labor intensive works' (e.g. schools versus roads). Descriptive evidence suggests, however, that the AGETIPs have placed no special priority on the former.

[11] A somewhat incoherent distinction made frequently in this period was between the so-called 'new poor' and the so-called 'old poor'. The 'new poor' (really the 'newly poorer') refers to individuals such as retrenched civil servants made poorer by the adjustment process though they may not have fallen below the poverty line. The old poor in contrast refers to those who may or may not have been negatively affected by the adjustment process, but were already below the poverty line. As a result, not all of the newly poorer are in fact poor and not all of the newly poorer are in fact new to poverty. The distinction between new poor and old poor is therefore quite misleading. Nevertheless, it has been widely used in the literature on social funds. A significant debate has taken place as to whether social funds should be targeted at the new poor or the old poor. In any event, it is likely that social funds failed to reach the new poor. For example, evidence shows that in the case of the Bolivian emergency social fund, of the very large number of tin miners who lost their jobs during the adjustment process, a very small percentage (likely less than 2 per cent) came to be employed on its projects. Admittedly, 'The ESF did not target the ex-employees of the public sector who are generally considered to have been the persons most directly affected by Bolivia's structural adjustment programme' (Newman *et al.* 1992; Jorgensen *et al.* 1992).

The political rationale for using social funds to mitigate the social costs of adjustment was to make the bitter pill of adjustment easier to swallow. This consideration was an explicit one and is evinced in many documents and discussions of early interventions of this kind. It is well-known that the first social fund (in Bolivia) was initiated in large part as a result of the forceful conviction of a World Bank consultant who was an ex-politician (a British member of parliament) who argued that it was necessary to undertake 'highly visible action' to mitigate the social costs of adjustment in order to make the latter more politically palatable.[12] The often close link between social fund management and the executive branch of governments owes its origin in part to the perceived need for the national political leadership to be able to claim credit for social fund achievements. One version of this argument, which has been influentially made, is that social funds help to create new coalitions for reform composed of those benefiting from the fund, who may well be distinct from those injured by the adjustment process. The former, if sufficiently numerous, can aid the political viability of the reform package even if it continues to harm others.[13] A less cynical version of this argument noted by Cornia (1999) is that 'if the government was not able to generate enough popular support for the economic reforms, it would not have been able to sustain any adjustment programme, without which the poor would have suffered even more because of a likely return to unsound macro policies'.

As the purpose of this chapter is to examine the ability of social funds to offset the poverty and inequality impact of adjustment, it is only necessary to mention briefly the other objectives upon which they have increasingly focused. Indeed, the compensatory role of social funds is today scarcely mentioned, although their pivotal role in the multilateral response to the Asian crisis testifies that they still are seen as potentially playing this role.[14] That the emergency response role of social funds is of continued importance is also testified to by the reliance upon them as mechanisms with which to respond to natural disaster and post-conflict reconstruction needs. Social funds are increasingly conceived as an intermediate and long-term service delivery instrument, which is more efficient than traditional means of service delivery through established ministries, through their employment of an ostensibly more participatory, decentralized, and demand-responsive approach. In this connection, they have been seen as everything from a 'beachhead' for the 'modernization of the state' (through the demonstration effect they have on ineffectual state bureaucracies) to a 'training ground in the democratic process' (Beneria and Mendoza 1995). These diverse claims, which are themselves controversial and call for more systematic evaluation, are not all taken up here (for independent evaluations see Goodman *et al.* 1997; Reddy, 1997; Tendler and Serrano 1999).

---

[12] See Marshall (1992) in Jorgensen *et al.* (1992).

[13] See Graham (1994). It is not clear how this argument can be reconciled with our knowledge of the small numbers of people affected by social funds (see next section) unless the argument rests on there being a powerful symbolic appeal to the creation of social funds.

[14] See in particular the 'social investment fund' component of the $300 million 'social investment project' for Thailand proposed by the World Bank (1998*b*).

11.4. EFFECTS ON INCOMES, INCOME DISTRIBUTION, AND POVERTY: MACROPERSPECTIVE

Have the resources assigned to social funds been adequate to contend with the scale of social costs entailed by policy reform, and the social needs in developing countries? Real programme expenditures in this area are difficult to enumerate on a strictly comparable basis. However, some rough comparisons are possible. It appears that the scale of social funds has varied substantially, from 6 to 85 million US dollars in the case of Africa, and from 40 million to 2.5 billion dollars in the case of Latin America (Table 11.1) (Marc *et al.* 1995: Annex 1, Table A.5).

If the expenditure on social funds is examined as a percentage of gross domestic product (GDP), their small scale is even more evident. Of the countries included in Table 11.1, in no case do social fund resources per programme year rise above 1 per cent of GDP, a figure smaller than the already small expenditures on income transfers and social programmes discussed in the previous chapter. Their scale in relation to GDP appears to have been somewhat lower in Africa (between 0.1 and 0.4 per cent per programme year) than in Latin America (between 0.4 and 1 per cent). As a share of social expenditure, social funds have accounted from 0.3 per cent in the case of Chile to 11 per cent in the case of Bolivia's emergency social fund, in the sample shown in Table 11.2. It can be observed that in Africa this share has more narrowly ranged between 1.7 and 7.4 per cent.

It is interesting to note that during the years of the social funds, total social expenditure (either as a percentage of GDP or on a per capita basis) declined in four cases (Panama, Ecuador, El Salvador, and Zambia) out of 12 in Table 11.1, rose by an amount less than or equal to the expenditure on social funds in two cases (Bolivia and Madagascar (it is conceivable that some diversion from regular social expenditure to social funds might have occurred here), and rose in the remaining six. This muddy picture suggests that the claim that social funds arrested the decline in aggregate social expenditure during the reform period is difficult to sustain. This result is even starker when the initial year of the comparison is allowed to vary. When the comparison is carried out in relation to a suitable preadjustment period (e.g. 1979–81, which preceded the mass of adjustment programmes), rather than the relatively depressed interval 1987–9, it no longer appears that the social funds have in fact offset the fall in social expenditure as a percentage of GDP or indeed of social expenditure per capita (Tables 11.1 and 11.2). In this broader comparison, in 10 cases out of the fourteen included in Table 11.2, the additional expenditure failed to compensate for the initial fall in social expenditure or was not able to arrest its declining trend. This point takes on even more importance in light of the fact that the needs of the populations of the countries concerned are likely to have been heightened by their declining incomes and increased insecurity as a result of the adjustment process.

A third way to assess the scale of social funds might consist in comparing their yearly expenditure with the increase in the poverty gap over the years in questions entailed by stabilization or policy reform. This measure would best capture the extent to which social funds were able to compensate the poverty and inequality effect of

Table 11.2. *SE/GDP ratio and SE per capita in constant prices pre-crisis/adjustment, 2 years before the launch of SFs and during SFs*

Country (SFs name, years)	SE/GDP pre-crisis and adjustment[a]	SE/GDP 2 years prior SF[a]	SE/GDP during SF[a]	SE per capita pre-crisis and adjustment[b]	SE per capita 2 years prior SF[b]	SE per capita during SF[b]
Bolivia (FSE, 1986–91)	6.0 (1978–80)	6.2 (1983–4)	6.6 (1986–91)	111 (1978–80)	96 (1983–4)	98 (1986–91)
Bolivia (FIS, 1990–4)	6.0 (1978–80)	6.3 (1988–9)	8.7 (1990–4)	111 (1978–80)	92 (1983–4)	136 (1990–4)
Chile (FOSIS, 1990–4)	19.3 (1980–2)	13.1 (1988–9)	13.1 (1990–4)	65800 (1980–2)	52500 (1988–9)	62300 (1990–4)
Ecuador (several, 1983–90)	5.9 (1980–2)	5.7 (1981–2)	5.2 (1983–90)	12300 (1980–2)	12000 (1981–2)	10300 (1983–90)
El Salvador (FIS, 1990–3)	6.1 (1980–2)	3.7 (1988–9)	3.4 (1990–3)	284 (1980–2)	158 (1988–9)	156 (1990–3)
Mexico (PRONASOL, 1989–93)	7.5 (1980–2)	5.1 (1987–8)	6.5 (1989–93)	208 (1980–2)	126 (1987–8)	171 (1989–93)
Nicaragua[c] (FISE, 1990–4)	3.9 (1978–80)	—	16.9 (1990–4)	— (1978–80)	—	— (1990–4)
Panama (FSE, 1990–3)	14.8 (1985–7)	16.5 (1988–9)	16.1 (1990–3)	377 (1985–7)	349 (1988–9)	396 (1990–3)
Cameroon (SDA, 1991–5)	6.8 (1985–7)	6.0 (1989–90)	7.7 (1991–5)	25700 (1985–7)	18100 (1989–90)	19100 (1991–5)
Egypt (SFD, 1991–4)	16.7 (1981–3)	12.8 (1989–90)	13.7 (1991–4)	156 (1981–3)	144 (1989–90)	159 (1991–4)
Ghana (PAMSCAD, 1987–92)	6.4 (1977–8)	5.3 (1985–6)	6.4 (1987–92)	4130 (1977–8)	2850 (1985–6)	3650 (1987–92)
Madagascar (SIRP, 1989–93)	—	3.5 (1988)	3.8 (1989–93)	—	8930 (1988)	9310 (1989–93)
Zambia (SRP, 1989–93)	9.5 (1976–82)	5.4 (1987–8)	4.9 (1989–93)	358 (1976–82)	166 (1987–8)	140 (1989–93)
Zambia (MPI, 1991–5)	9.5 (1976–82)	4.8 (1989–90)	5.8 (1991–5)	358 (1976–82)	142 (1989–90)	151 (1991–5)

[a] In percentages.

[b] Social expenditure per capita in constant 1987 local currency units.

[c] For Nicaragua comparisons are made difficult as in 1990–1 a new currency and a large devaluation were introduced, and the war ended.

Source: Cornia (1999); IMF (various) Government of Finance Statistics; IMF (1997); World Bank World Development Indicators (1998).

Table 11.3. *Maximum possible average expenditure per poor person by social funds in selected countries*

Social fund	Amount (US$)
Bolivia, FSE	9
Bolivia, FIS	7
Chile, FOSIS	30
Dom. Republic, PROCOMUN	7
Ecuador, FISE	6
El salvador, FIS	11
Ghana, PAMSCAD	19.5
Guatemala, FONAPAZ	3
Guatemala, FIS	3
Haiti, FAES	3
Honduras, FHIS	7
Madagascar, SIRP	7.5
Mexico, PRONASOL	135
Nicaragua, FISE	11
Peru, FONCODES	11
Panama, FES	16
Senegal, SF	3.5
Uruguay, PRIS/FAS	62
Zambia, SRF/SMI	< 1
Zimbabwe, SF	< 1

Sources: Graham (1994), Stewart and van der Geest (1995), Goodman *et al.* (1997).

adjustment. However, information on the increase in the poverty gap during the relevant period for the countries that have introduced social funds is generally not available. Conclusions about the adequacy of the funds allocated would depend, in addition, on the precision of their targeting which, as it will be noted later, has often been poor.

Other indicators of the scale of social funds are also instructive. For instance, their absolute level of annual disbursements per poor person are generally small. Table 11.3 shows that these vary from less than $1 (Zimbabwe and Zambia) to an exceptional $135 (Mexico's Pronasol), and averages less than $18 per poor person, a figure that weakens the credibility of the somewhat grandiose claim that social funds could effectively cushion the poor from the adverse consequences of adjustment.

Similarly, Table 11.4 shows that the employment created per year by social funds in Latin America as a fraction of the labour force varied from 0.1 to 1 per cent; that is, values that cannot impact perceptibly poverty or inequality. It is also reported that in Honduras (1990–5) social fund-generated employment amounted to 7 per cent of the unemployed, in Peru (1991–5) to 2.7 per cent, and in El Salvador (1990 onwards) to 2.5 per cent (Tendler 2000). It is difficult to view these levels of impact on employment as sizable, or as likely to serve a meaningful compensatory function under the social strains generated by crisis and orthodox adjustment.

Table 11.4. *Employment creation in Latin American SFs*

Social fund	Social fund employment as a fraction of labour force (%)
Bolivia, FES	1.0
Bolivia, FIS	0.1
Chile, FOSIS	'negligible'
Ecuador, FISE	0.2
El salvador, FIS	0.3
Guatemala, FIS	0.3
Haiti, FAES	0.3
Honduras, FHIS	0.8
Nicaragua, FISE	0.6
Peru, FONCODES	0.2
Panama, FES	0.2

Source: Goodman *et al.* (1997).

Finally, social funds meant to compensate for the social costs of adjustment have often been very slow to begin functioning, seriously prejudicing their ability to achieve their proclaimed short-term goals. Ghana's PAMSCAD, the first major effort in Africa to mitigate the social costs of adjustment through compensatory action, was notoriously slow to begin to operate, casting much doubt on its value. Tendler and Serrano (1999) also report that many traditional social programmes appear to have disbursed funds more rapidly than social funds, contrary to a common conception. This may in large part be due precisely to the attempt of the latter to be participatory and demand-driven. Of course this does not suggest that participation is an undesirable goal—only that social funds or other institutional mechanisms that attempt to instantiate it may not be the most suitable vehicles for providing emergency compensation to the poor because their administrative structures take time to establish and because counterparts take time to organize themselves and to identify and formulate projects. Whether or not social funds are a viable instrument of long-term service delivery, they are patently inadequate as compensatory devices for short-term shocks. A more suitable institutional arrangement to contend with such shocks would be standing social protection institutions capable of expanding the supply of social protection services when required at low marginal costs.

11.5. EFFECTS ON INCOMES, INCOME DISTRIBUTION, AND POVERTY: MICROPERSPECTIVES

It has been argued above that, in general, social funds have not disposed of the aggregate resources necessary to meet their proclaimed poverty and equity objectives. However, if they had had larger resources, would it have been possible for them to meet these objectives? Are social funds in fact more efficient and equitable per unit of

Table 11.5. *Costs of employment generation in selected SFs*

Social fund	Total cost per person-day of employment (US$)
Senegal, AGETIP	18.3
Madagascar, EMSAP	3.0
Guinea Bissau, SIRP	19.1
Ghana, PAPSCA	8.4
Bolivia, ESF	9.8
Bolivia, FIS	41.3
Nicaragua, FISE	30.0
El Salvador, FIS	20.7
Haiti, FAES	3.5

Note: Where there were discrepancies between the figures implicit in these different sources, the authors used the most reasonable estimates based on regional comparisons and internal consistency of data. In order to generate comparable data estimates, it was assumed that a person-year contains 12 person-months and 300 person-days.

Sources: Authors' compilation based on Jorgensen *et al.* (1992), Glaessner *et al.* (1994), Marc *et al.* (1995), and Goodman *et al.* (1997).

expenditure than traditional anti-poverty instruments, as frequently argued? After almost one and a half decades, the data with which to answer these questions remain limited.[15] However, it is now possible with some confidence to make some preliminary judgements in this regard.

11.5.1. *Transfer and Cost Efficiency*

A widespread claim on behalf of social funds has been that unit costs of the infrastructure and services that they provide are lower than under traditional governmental programmes. There is little direct documentary evidence for this claim, however. In any event, it is usually overlooked that a proper accounting of costs should include both the costs undertaken by the counterpart and those of the social fund itself. Including counterpart costs would tend substantially to increase unit cost estimates for social funds. A recent study by the semi-independent Operations Evaluation Department of the World Bank (World Bank 2002: Annex H) offers the first systematic evaluation of the unit costs of infrastructure and social service delivery through social funds and alternative means. Strikingly, it provides no evidence to

---

[15] By far the best publicly documented social fund remains the first, the Bolivian emergency social fund (see Jorgensen *et al.* 1992). Elementary data on such fundamental matters as unit costs, the distribution of economic status of beneficiaries, and the composition of expenditures remain generally lacking. Efforts to fill these gaping lacunae would enable a more realistic assessment of the claims made on their behalf and a more comprehensive assessment of the value of social funds.

G. A. Cornia and S. Reddy

support the claim that social funds have lower unit costs. The unit costs reported in the study present a mixed picture that offers no basis for this inference. Other evidence is provided by the costs of generating employment through social funds and other means (see Table 11.5).

Although these costs are difficult to interpret as they include all programme costs, including those for administration and materials, and are based on conversion of costs at market exchange rates, they are often relatively high (averaging $17 per person-day of employment), and do not appear to compare favourably to those of traditional supply-driven employment generation schemes. For instance India's supply-driven Jawahar Rozgar Yojana scheme has a cost of roughly $1.5 per person-day of employment created.[16] In turn, indirect evidence of the cost efficiency of social funds service delivery is, however, available in the form of the reported administrative costs of some of these funds. Table 11.6 summarizes this data.

Glaessner *et al.* (1994) report that the administrative costs of most social investment funds in Latin America amounted to '8 to 13 per cent of the annual commitments once they reached a relatively high level of activity'. The internal comparison of the administrative costs of different funds is complicated by the use of different accounting conventions (Cisneros 1993; quoted in Glaessner *et al.* 1994). Nevertheless, it does seem that their administrative costs may be relatively low as compared to traditional governmental ministries and agencies. This evidence must be interpreted with great caution, however. Social funds administrative costs do not include the direct and opportunity costs to counterparts of executing projects. The administrative costs of

Table 11.6. *Reported administrative costs as a share of expenditure in selected SFs*

Social fund	Percentage
Bolivia, ESF	5.5
Bolivia, SIF	9
Honduras, FHIS	8–14
Honduras, ESF	9
Haiti, ESF	10
Guatemala, SIF	10
Senegal, AGETIP	5
Zambia, SRF	12
Sao Tome, SIF	15
Guinea Bissau, SIRP	26

Sources: Grosh (1990), ILO (1992), Jayarajah *et al.* (1996), Stewart and van der Geest (1995), UNCTAD (1994), Marc *et al.* (1995), and Glaessner *et al.* (1994).

[16] Authors' calculation based on figure reported in the Government of India Economic Survey for 1998–9.

traditional approaches to delivering social services in final form to communities cannot therefore be straightforwardly compared with those of social funds, the work of which may consist only in promoting, selecting, and financing subprojects, but not in executing them.

11.5.2. *Targeting Efficiency*

The appropriate targeting of benefits is a central issue in designing and evaluating any programme meant to benefit the poor. The goals of ensuring that as many intended beneficiaries as possible are reached (minimizing errors of exclusion or F-errors), and that as few unintended beneficiaries as possible are reached (minimizing errors of inclusion or E-errors), are paramount.[17] The goal of targeting benefits effectively is closely connected with the more general goal of achieving equity in the distribution of benefits. An efficient and equitable anti-poverty programme will both reach as many of the poor as possible (minimize F-errors) and benefit as few of the non-poor as possible (minimize E-errors).

Social funds may suffer from errors of exclusion, which are sizable for a number of reasons. First, even if they have the alleviation of poverty as their sole objective (which the AGETIPs for instance typically do not) their resources may simply be insufficient. Second, even if they were to have sufficient resources to reach the poor, the ability of their administrators to sort among project proposals according to the extent of deprivation of the proposed beneficiaries may be limited due to incomplete information. Third, poor communities may be less capable than less deprived ones of effectively identifying viable projects and articulating their demands. The last problem is particular to so-called 'demand-driven' programmes such as social funds. It is likely that both the first and third problems have been especially severe for social funds.

In practice, the quality of targeting of social funds has been mixed. Bolivia's emergency social fund has been by far the best documented one in this respect. It was found that employees in positions generated by the fund were overwhelmingly 'prime age' (20–65 years), married (71 per cent), male (99 per cent), and largely the sole income earners in their families (62 per cent). Ninety-three per cent of workers in one survey reported themselves as heads of household, and received 90 per cent of their income from the fund. Finally, statistical estimates suggest that only 13.5 per cent of the fund workers were drawn from the two lowest family income deciles. However, 77 per cent of workers appear to have been drawn from the bottom 40 per cent of the distribution of individual income, and almost half from the lowest three income deciles (Jorgensen *et al.* 1992; Stewart and van der Geest 1995). Thus, in Bolivia's fund employment generation can be concluded to have been weakly targeted in income terms, in that it reached the moderately poor, but failed to reach the truly disadvantaged. However, the fund was a massive failure in attaining gender equity.

---

[17] The terms F-errors and E-errors are used by Cornia and Stewart (1993), to describe errors of exclusion '(F)ailing beneficiaries', and errors of inclusion '(E)xcess benefits', respectively. Besley and Kanbur (1988) and Sen (1994) use alternative terminology ('Type I' and 'Type II' errors) to describe the same concepts.

The recent study by the Operations Evaluation Department of the World Bank (World Bank 2002: 14) offers damaging evidence regarding the targeting efficiency of the Bolivian fund and of the social funds for Armenia, Honduras, Nicaragua, Peru, and Zambia. Figures produced in the report show that for all these countries the distribution of the benefits among beneficiaries was strictly proportional. When targeting of poor areas rather than poor households is used as the criterion, the picture is almost identical, with the exception that one country (Peru) appears to be successful at targeting on this basis. It is striking that the only available quantitative evidence on social fund targeting openly contradicts the claim about the targeting and redistributive characteristics of this kind of income transfer.

Other studies confirm the unfavourable benefit incidence of the monies disbursed by social funds. It has been reported that in Honduras' demand–driven social investment fund municipalities with a higher poverty incidence received only $5.40 per head, whereas those with lowest incidence received $56.40. Most cases are far less extreme, however, if still unbalanced. For example, in El Salvador's social investment fund 26 per cent of resources went to the five (out of fourteen) poorest provinces, 46 per cent to the four richest (1990–5). In a study of beneficiaries, it was estimated that 60 per cent of the beneficiaries of Fondo de Inversión Social (FIS) projects were poor and that 40 per cent were non–poor (Goodman et al. 1997). Pradhan et al. (1998) find on the basis of a careful study of preintervention household-level data that better-off households are more likely to be beneficiaries of social funds investments in health, water, and sanitation. A number of such examples can be readily listed, although there are also examples of seemingly more successful targeting such as Ecuador's Emergency Social Investment Fund (FISE), in which only 3 per cent of loans went to the top 40 per cent of the municipalities (Goodman et al. 1997).

Regional imbalance is also frequently observed. Both Senegal's DIRE and AGETIP and Ghana's Programme of Action to Mitigate the Social Consequences of Adjustment (PAMSCAD) were significantly urban-biased. Almost two-thirds of the expenditures of Senegal's AGETIP were located in the capital city and one other district (Goodman et al. 1997). In general, AGETIPs appear to have been significantly urban biased. Other illustrative examples of heavy urban bias among AGETIPs include Chad's Social Development Action Project (PADS), the Guinea-Bissau Social and Infrastructure Project (SIRP), and Gambia's GAMWORKS (Marc et al., 1995; and authors' fieldwork). Draper (1996) found that the Economic and Social Assistance Fund (FAES) in Haiti allocated 69 per cent of all financial commitments and 73 per cent of projects to three of nine (more accessible by road and better-off) departments containing 53 per cent of the population. The case evidence makes it difficult to conclude that social funds are successfully targeted at the poor and can help in correcting the inequality of market income.

Little rigorous evidence on exclusion errors of individual social funds is available. However, some idea of the magnitude of such errors of exclusion can be gained by assessing the maximum number of individuals who could be reached by social funds under the best-case scenario, as compared with the actual numbers of the poor in adjusting countries. It can be seen that such proportion has been small. Proportions of the population estimated to have been reached in different countries range from 0.3 per cent of the population in Ghana, and 0.5 per cent in Egypt to 13 per cent in Honduras, 19 per cent in Bolivia, and 27 per cent in Mexico (UNCTAD 1994).[18] As mentioned earlier, these unsatisfactory results are due to the low resources of social funds in relation to needs, as well as from inadequate information about where the poor are, and the low capacity of the poor to voice demands effectively.

The problem of the differential capacity of communities to successfully formulate and present projects to social funds has been widely documented under Bolivia's SEF, in Brazil, Honduras, and Nicaragua, among other places (Reddy 1997; Tendler 2000). Even where communities do successfully present project proposals, it is possible that these are priorities of community leaders or NGOs rather than genuinely of communities themselves. In Ghana's PAMSCAD (community initiatives project), which was intended to play the role of a demand-driven social fund, 'district-level officials often submitted project lists to central authorities for funding while ignoring project requests at the village level' (Kingsbury 1994). Beneficiary assessments of social funds have also systematically found that projects are disproportionally initiated and led by prominent local persons. For example, such an assessment in Zambia found that fifty-eight of sixty subprojects were initiated by one or two prominent local individuals (Owen and van Domelen 1998). A further index of the extent to which social funds are not truly demand-driven is the striking degree of ignorance of the existence of social funds, their functioning, and local responsibilities, which is prevalent even in communities containing subprojects (Owen and van Domeler 1998).

The problem of low capacities of the poor to formulate and present successful projects has been addressed by social funds in recent years. Their managers have sometimes tried to deal with this problem by consciously intervening to upgrade these skills and assist representatives of the poor in this process. Peru's Fondo Nacional de Compensación y Descardlo Social (FONCODES), Bolivia's FIS, and El Salvador's fund are said to have used active promotion of projects among communities as a means of reaching the poor (Goodman *et al.* 1997). Nicaragua's European Solar Industry Foundation (ESIF), for example, initiated such a programme when this deficiency became clear.[19] Bolivia's Social Equity Forum (SEF), an outreach unit, was established to help people prepare projects but was eventually changed into a programming department, concerned with attaining a particular mix of projects. Such activity appears at least in some instances to have been successful.

Another approach to the equity problems of demand-driven social funds has been to construct 'hybrid' programmes in which targeted supply-driven components complement demand-driven activities. Thus, Chile's Fondo de Solidaridad e Inversión

---

[18] These figures may include double counting due to individuals being 'reached' by more than one subproject. The definition of 'reached' is unclear as is that of 'beneficiary'. Fergany (1994), for instance, complains of the 'extremely vague' character of the definition of 'beneficiaries' by the Egyptian SFD, which leads to one-fifth of the population being officially claimed as such.

[19] In the early stages of the ESIF, procedures were apparently so unrealistic that even government social welfare agencies were unprepared to produce project proposals at the speed and in the manner required (Fergany 1994).

Social (FOSIS) has a bank of its own projects developed according to equity criteria alongside those received from communities. Similarly, Peru's FONCODES has launched a massive school desk manufacturing programme for which it intentionally contracts only from small vendors, in addition to its demand-driven component (Grinspun 1995).

The idea of a social safety net being demand-driven may be a mirage in the sense that, to ease the administrative burden of selection, project managers often only choose projects that conform to a number of predetermined project types. Beneria and Mendoza (1995) found that this was the case in Honduras and wrote in this regard that 'in reality, the poor have to comply to a pre-established menu of projects if they wish to benefit from ESIF funds'. The variety of problems besetting the demand-driven mechanism of social funds makes it evident that they would be hard pressed to disburse funds both quickly and well. Indeed, in instances where such funds have been lauded for their quick response to emergency needs, this has been only because of their relaxation of their usual requirements, by becoming in particular more supply-than demand-driven (e.g. see World Bank 2000).

A final serious obstacle to social funds reaching the poor is the insistence on receiving counterpart contributions for subprojects. In fact contributions by communities have perversely come to be described in much social fund literature as an indicator of a community's commitment in regard to a subproject, and thereby as a sine qua non for 'participation' (for instance, see Narayan and Ebbe 1998). Although these contributions may in principle be reduced or waived for the very poor, they are often set at a substantial level (e.g. 25 per cent of costs in the case of the Zambian social fund). Even worse, in some cases (Zambia, for instance) communities willing to make bigger contributions score higher in the selection process. Further, contributions are usually required on an 'up front' basis prior to subproject implementation. Narayan and Ebbe (1998) report that 62 per cent of World Bank-sponsored social fund projects require a 'community contribution' in money, land labour, or materials prior to implementation. Alton (1999) finds on the basis of a survey of World Bank project documents a consistent discrepancy between social fund target user contribution levels and actual levels, suggesting that the insistence on such contributions runs in to real constraints of poor people's ability to provide them.

11.5.3. *Long-run Benefits of Social Funds*

Do social funds generate short- or long-range benefits? Clearly, this depends on the nature of the projects involved. The early social funds, which had focused on employment generation, must be judged primarily on their short-run achievements, as it is upon these that they had focused. However, the social investment funds and to a lesser extent the AGETIPs ought to have been examined with the criterion of whether they have produced longer range benefits for the poor, through their investments in social infrastructure. Morley (2000), for example, argues that 'the funds deliver government services to poor communities that never had them before...and they build simple social infrastructure quite efficiently at low cost. They improve the living conditions of the poor even if the measured income of the poor does not go very much up'. However, as noted above there is *no* concrete evidence that social funds' costs of delivering such infrastructure are in fact lower than those of traditional delivery systems.[20] Some analysts have raised questions of whether social funds have made adequate provision for the recurrent costs entailed by social investments; see, for example, the survey of such concerns in Reddy (1997). Later generations of social funds seem to have addressed this concern by requiring commitments by communities or government agencies to undertake such commitments for the future; see Narayan and Ebbe (1998). There may of course be other reasons that social funds are an instrument of more efficient service delivery than traditional mechanisms, such as that the 'demand-driven' approach of social funds may have enabled them to finance the development of forms of social infrastructure most desired by communities. There is, unfortunately, little evidence to permit the rigorous evaluation of this proposition.

Claims that social funds are an instrument for 'demonstrating' pathways of modernization of the traditional state apparatus are probably also highly overstated. It is almost impossible to find documented instances of the vaunted 'demonstration effect'. Additionally, although the participatory approach of social funds is surely an essential element of any appropriate strategy of provision of social services in developing countries, for the reasons adduced above it cannot be the only element. In addition to the errors of exclusion, which they would necessarily entail (due to the differential propensity of communities to engage in self-organization and articulation), there are further inherent limitations to the applicability of this approach, associated with the limited capabilities of local counterparts and communities, and asymmetries of information and incentives. Local counterparts may lack in the capability, and in some instances the incentive, to efficiently provide services to local communities or act to protect a monopolistic role or special interest.

Social funds may be an important long-run instrument, within a larger repertoire of options for delivering income transfers or social services to the poor, and thereby for combating inequality and reducing poverty. However, there is little evidence to support this claim. Moreover, this role for social funds is very different from that originally ascribed to them—to be a 'cushion' with which to reduce the social costs of adjustment.

11.6. CONCLUSIONS AND RECOMMENDATIONS

Social funds have been presented as capable of much larger tasks than they have in fact been able to fulfil. Why then have they been so alluring to decision-makers? The answer lies in the heady mixture of their political symbolism, the ease with which they are seen as 'offering convincing and simple explanations for the causes of certain problems and providing appealing blueprints for action' (Tendler 2000), reflecting a general

---

[20] For instance, Walker *et al.* (1999) find that although unit costs of Honduras' FHIS are 'very reasonable' compared with the industry norms, those for new water projects are 'three times that which is normally expected in other programmes'.

scepticism of the role of the state and a belief that policy reforms that cause damage to some can still be 'beneficial for all' if suitable compensation is offered.

Notwithstanding the visibility and appeal they enjoyed with national and international decision-makers, social funds played a minor role in reducing the number of adjustment poor and chronic poor, and in reversing the adverse distributive and poverty shifts entailed by economic stabilization and liberalization. The number of jobs added to the economy was generally less than a meagre 1 per cent of total employment. In addition, social funds often allocated their expenditures not to the poorest groups and activities with high social benefits but rather to programmes that required little preparation and were perceived as having large demonstration effects. The targeting effectiveness of social funds has been lower than that of traditional income transfer programmes.

Greater impact on poverty and inequality would have required much larger resources, more permanent relief structures established prior to crisis, improved planning and targeting, and limited reliance on demand-driven mechanisms. Social funds should be viewed at best as a partial corrective to the social costs and inequality generated by policy reform. A more substantial impact on adjustment-induced poverty and inequality would have required a different approach to the policy reform process itself. In its absence, however, social protection would have been more effectively delivered by permanent social security arrangements providing universal but modest insurance against both individual and collective risks. Such social security arrangements (which contrast with the ad hoc and limited social funds) exist in a number of developing countries, as will be discussed. Our most important conclusion is that poverty reduction requires a combination of measures, including a macroeconomic policy designed with attention to its distributive and social impact, sustained investments in social programmes, and the development of flexible but permanent and universal social protection systems that are well integrated into a nationwide social and economic development framework. Our critical examination of the worldwide experience of social funds in the context of adjustment-induced increases in poverty and inequality leads to the following more detailed conclusions as well. To start with, alternative policy reform programmes ensuring macroeconomic stability while avoiding large distributional dislocations and social costs must be identified and employed (examples of such alternative approaches can be observed in countries as different as China, Malaysia, India, and Mauritius). The experience reviewed in this volume indicates that the social costs associated in many cases with the introduction of Washington Consensus-type reform packages were almost never significantly reduced by the introduction of social funds. In addition, the reform–related cuts in social expenditure were reversed by the launch of social funds only in a small number of cases, and years later. Few organizational changes have been effected so far at the IMF to meet this challenge, mobilize adequate funds, or modify the orthodox position on key adjustment policies that have been shown to have adverse consequences for poverty and inequality. In turn, it is too soon to determine whether the changes underway at the World Bank in this area are leading to alternative macroeoconomic and sectoral policies with more favourable effects on poverty and inequality.

Second, it is essential to develop during normal times permanent and cost-effective social security systems. Prior to the introduction of the social funds, several developing countries had developed a variety of social insurance arrangements including employment-based safety nets, targeted transfers, food subsidies, and nutrition interventions (Cornia 1999). Employment-based safety nets can effectively reach needy but able people of working age and permit the achievement of distributive and poverty alleviation objectives over the short-run while contributing to the growth of productivity and poverty alleviation over the long term by speeding up the creation of public infrastructure. India's Jawahar Rozgar Yojana and Chile's Minimum Employment Programme are some of the most successful examples of permanent, large-scale, and affordable public work schemes that were flexibly increased or decreased to meet changes in needs and that covered far greater numbers of poor persons than social funds could have been able to do.

Some middle-income countries had also achieved extensive coverage of social insurance against the risks of unemployment, sickness, invalidity, old age, and occupational injury. In addition, as shown by the experience of Kerala and Tamil Nadu, low-income countries have also been able to develop low-cost, non-contributory, state-funded insurance arrangements providing coverage against key risks of immiseration arising from old age, sickness, injury, and widowhood also in low-income rural settings (Guhan 1992, 1995). Finally, many countries had developed transfer schemes aiming at guaranteeing access by the poor to basic items. In urban South Asia the transfer took the form of targeted rations sold to low-income people at 'fair price' shops while generalized wheat or tortilla subsidies were available in Brazil, Egypt, and Mexico. While generalized food subsidies suffered from several problems, subsidies targeted by broad criteria (e.g. the distribution of inferior commodities disfavoured by the non-poor, programmes limited to poor areas, schoolchildren, nursing mothers, and so on) and direct nutritional interventions constituted cost-effective transfers. Such systems, once in place, provide effective standing protections for the poor and can be readily expanded to protect the newly poor during downturns or sharp price adjustments.

Permanent but flexible cost-efficient arrangements of this type are more likely to contain the social costs of severe crises than hastily arranged temporary social funds with a 'demand-driven' orientation. Social protection arrangements should be introduced prior to the launch of major policy reform programmes—and not years after these have been in operation—both because of the human costs generated by such delay and because increases in poverty, inequality, and unemployment which may occur in the aftermath of policy reform can become self-reinforcing and difficult to reverse, due to the loss of the capabilities of individuals and communities that often results. Creating permanent and yet flexible social safety nets along the lines mentioned above should thus be a priority of governments, the Bretton Woods Institutions, and the International Labour Organization (ILO). Ad hoc social funds should be established mainly in the case of exceptional contingencies, such as when sharply rising social demands entail an overly rapid expansion of existing social arrangements that would limit their ability to protect the poor.

Third, during periods of crisis and policy reform, there is no substitute for the allocation of adequate resources to social protection. It would be virtually impossible to achieve nationwide social protection objectives with the resources allocated to social funds in recent years. In countries committed to fighting poverty, the social protection systems alluded to above absorbed substantially larger resources (2–5 per cent of GDP, excluding pensions) than those assigned so far to social funds. Their ability to expand quickly when necessary in order to meet social needs depended on a permanent structure of experienced staff, a sound portfolios of projects, clear management rules, adequate allocation of domestic resources, supply-driven execution, and, with the exception of food subsidies, fairly efficient targeting.

Finally, the targeting of social protection programmes should aim not only at reducing programme leakage but also at minimizing the exclusion of the poor. Where demand-driven programmes exist they should be combined with supply-driven programmes explicitly aiming at reaching the poorest.

All in all, countries faced by the need for significant policy changes will do well to learn from the chequered experience with social funds and to invest in comprehensive social security arrangements, which can lessen the human and distributive toll of such changes, as well as, more fundamentally, to pursue creative alternative approaches to achieving economic stabilization and policy reform. Such change is unlikely to be the result of shifting intellectual currents alone. It will also be the outcome of social demands, political interests, and institutional imagination.

REFERENCES

Alton, G. (1999). Social funds performance: A review. Mimeo. World Bank: Washington, DC.

Beneria, L., and B. Mendoza (1995). Structural adjustment and social emergency funds: The cases of Honduras, Mexico and Nicaragua. *European Journal of Development Research* 7(1), 53–76.

Besley, T., and R. Kanbur (1988). Food subsidies and poverty alleviation. *Economic Journal* 98 (September) 701–19.

Bigio, A. G. (1998). *Social Funds and Reaching the Poor: Experiences and Future Directions*. World Bank: Washington, DC.

Carvalho, S. (1999). Social funds: Guidelines for design and implementation. Mimeo. World Bank: Washington, DC.

Cisneros, R. (1993). Los Fondes Sociales en Latino América y el Caribe: Análisis Comparativo de 16 Esperiencias' (draft). Latin America and the Caribbean Department, World Bank: Washington, DC.

Cornia, G. A. (1999). Social funds in stabilization and adjustment programmes. WIDER Research for Action 48, UNU/WIDER: Helsinki.

——and F. Stewart (1993). Two errors of targeting. UNICEF Innocenti Occasional Papers 36. UNICEF International Child Development Centre: Florence.

——, ——, and R. Jolly (1987). *Adjustment with a Human Face: Protecting the Vulnerable and Promoting Growth*. Clarendon Press: Oxford.

Draper, M. (1996). Social investment funds study: Country case report: Haiti. Mimeo. Inter-American Development Bank: Washington, DC.

Fergany, N. (1994). On the impact of economic restructuring on human development and proposed strategies to alleviate poverty: The case of Egypt. Mimeo. UNRISD: Geneva.

Glaessner, P., *et al.* (1994). Poverty alleviation and social investment funds: The Latin American experience. World Bank Discussion Paper 261. World Bank: Washington, DC.

Goodman, M., *et al.* (1997). *Social Investment Funds in Latin America: Past Performance and Future Role*. Inter-American Development Bank: Washington, DC.

Graham, C. (1994). *Safety Nets, Politics, and the Poor: Transition to Market Economies*. The Brookings Institute: Washington, DC.

Grinspun, A. J. (1995). Social Funds: Fertile Ground for South-South Cooperation. UNDP Cooperation South, May.

Grosh, M. E. (1990). What should social funds finance? portfolio mix, targeting, and efficiency criteria. View from LATHR 3, Human Resource Division, Latin America and Caribbean Technical Department, World Bank: Washington, DC.

Guhan, S. (1992). Social security for the unorganized poor: A feasible blueprint for India. UNDP and Indira Gandhi Institute of Development Research Discussion Paper: Bombay.

——(1995). 'Social Security Options for Developing Countries'. In J. Figueredo and Z. Shaheed (eds.), *Reducing Poverty through Labour Market Policies: A Contribution to the World Summit for Social Development*. International Institute for Labour Studies: Geneva.

ILO (1992). Stabilization, structural adjustment and social policies in Costa Rica: The role of compensatory programmes. Interdepartmental Project on Structural Adjustment Occasional Paper 1. ILO: Geneva.

IMF (various issues). *Government of Finance Statistics*. IMF: Washington, DC.

——(1997). *International Financial Statistics*. IMF: Washington, DC.

Jayarajah, C., W. Branson, and B. Sen (1996). *Social Dimensions of Adjustment: World Bank Experience, 1980–93*. World Bank: Washington, DC.

Jespersen, E. (1992). External shocks, adjustment policies and economic and social performance. In G. A. Cornia, R. van der Hoeven, and T. Mkandawire (eds.), *Africa's Recovery in the 1990s: From Stagnation and Adjustment to Human Development*. Macmillan: Basingstoke.

Jorgensen, S., M. Grosh, and M. Schacter (1992). *Bolivia's Answer to Poverty, Economic Crisis, and Adjustment: The Emergency Social Fund*. World Bank: Washington, DC.

Kanbur, R. (1998). Income distribution and development. Mimeo. Washington, DC.

——and N. Lustig (1999). Why is inequality back on the agenda? Paper presented at the Annual Bank Conference on Development Economics, 28–30 April, World Bank: Washington, DC.

Kingsbury, D. (1994). Compensatory social programmes and structural adjustment: A review of experience, AID Evaluation Special Study 72. US Agency for International Development: Arlington.

Marc, A., *et al.* (1995). Social action programmes and social funds: A review of adjustment and implementation in sub-Saharan Africa. World Bank Discussion Papers 275. World Bank: Washington, DC.

Marshall, K. (1992). The genesis and early debates. In Jorgensen *et al.* (eds.), *Bolivia's Answer to Poverty, Economic Crisis, and Adjustment: The Emergency Social Fund*. World Bank: Washington, DC.

Morley, S. (2000). Distribution and growth in Latin America in an era of structural reform. Paper presented at the Conference on Poverty and Inequality in Developing Countries: A Policy Dialogue on the Effects of Globalization, 30 November–1 December, OECD Development Centre: Paris.

Narayan, D., and K. Ebbe (1998). *Design of Social Funds: Participation, Demand Orientation, and Local Organizational Capacity*. World Bank: Washington, DC.

294 *G. A. Cornia and S. Reddy*

Newman, J., *et al.* (1992). How did workers benefit? In Jorgensen *et al.* (eds.), *Bolivia's Answer to Poverty, Economic Crisis, and Adjustment: The Emergency Social Fund*. World Bank: Washington, DC.

Owen, D., and J. van Domelen (1998). Getting an Earful: A Review of Beneficiary Assessments of social funds. Mimeo. Human Development Network, World Bank: Washington, DC.

Pradhan, M., L. Rawlings, and G. Ridder (1998). The Bolivian social investment fund: An analysis of baseline data for impact evaluation. *World Bank Economic Review* 12(3), 457–82.

Reddy, S. (1997). Social funds in developing countries: Recent experiences and lessons. Office of Evaluation Policy and Planning: UNICEF Staff Working Paper EPP-EVL-98-002. UNICEF: New York.

Sala-I-Martin, X. (2002). The disturbing 'Rise' of Global Income Inequality, NBER Working Paper 8904. National Bureau of Economic Research: Cambridge, MA.

Sen, A. (1994). The political economy of targeting. Mimeo, Annual World Bank Conference on Development Economics, World Bank: Washington, DC.

Stewart, F., and W. van der Geest (1995). Adjustment and social funds: Political panacea or effective poverty reduction? Employment Department Papers 2, ILO: Geneva.

Tendler, J. (2000). Why are social funds so popular? In S. Yusuf, W. Wu, and S. Everett (eds.), *Local Dynamics in the Era of Globalization*. Oxford University Press: Oxford.

Tendler, J., and R. Serrano (1999). The rise of social funds: What are they a model of? Mimeo. Department of Urban Studies and Planning, MIT: Cambridge, MA.

UNCTAD (1994). Recent developments in social funds and safety nets: Background note by the UNCTAD Secretariat UNCTAD/PA/2. Standing Committee on Poverty Alleviation, Intergovernmental Group of Experts on Poverty Alleviation, Item 3 of the Provisional Agenda, Geneva, 24 January. United Nations: New York.

——(1997). *Trade and Development Report*. UNCTAD: Geneva.

Virak, Y. (2000). A reflection on the social funds in Cambodia. Available at http://aric.adb.org/.

Walker, I., *et al.* (1999). Ex-post evaluation of the Honduran social investment fund. Mimeo, World Bank: Washington, DC.

World Bank (1986). *Financing Adjustment with Growth in Sub-Saharan Africa, 1986–90*. World Bank: Washington, DC.

——(1990). *World Development Report 1990: Poverty*. Oxford University Press: New York.

——(1996). *Infrastructure Notes*, December. World Bank: Washington, DC.

——(1997). *Portfolio Improvement Programme: Review of the Social Funds Portfolio*. World Bank: Washington, DC.

——(1998a). Social funds 2000 impact evaluation: Updated midstream issues paper. Mimeo. World Bank: Washington, DC.

——(1998b). *Project Appraisal Document Report* No. 17785TH. World Bank: Washington, DC.

——(1999). *Participation Sourcebook*. World Bank: Washington, DC.

——(2000). Coping with natural disasters: Role of social funds. Available at http://wbln0018.worldbank.org/HDNet/HDdocs.nsf.

——(2002). *Social Funds: Assessing Effectiveness*. World Bank: Washington, DC.

PART IV

COUNTRY CASE STUDIES

12

Reducing Poverty and Inequality in India: Has Liberalization Helped?

RAGHBENDRA JHA

12.1. INTRODUCTION

The ultimate aim of economic growth must be the betterment of the living conditions of the poor. Economic growth that does not lead to sharp and sustained reductions in poverty may create more problems than it solves. Similarly, if rapid growth is achieved at the expense of a worsening in the distribution of resources, it ultimately becomes unsustainable, since it engenders social tensions. Indeed, it is possible to imagine a situation in which economic growth leads to such exacerbation of inequality that poverty actually rises.

In India, the accepted wisdom is that the trend rate of economic growth was low and stable for a considerable period. A break was achieved through the process of trade and investment liberalization and economic reforms begun in 1991.[1] This led to a sharp rise in the trend rate of economic growth. An important question that arises here is how has this economic growth affected levels of inequality and poverty in India? This study is designed to arrive at some tentative conclusions on this important issue.

The approach to liberalization in India (the Delhi Consensus) has some clear differences with the standard approach (the Washington Consensus). Of particular importance are differences in the basic philosophy of liberalization. India has opted for gradual and controlled liberalization and downplayed the stress on the speed of reforms emphasized by the Washington Consensus. In addition, there are differences in detail. Thus, apart from the International Monetary Fund (IMF) funds received in 1991, reliance on foreign bilateral or multilateral public capital inflows has been very limited. Consequently, after the reforms, policy-makers have been facing a hard government budget constraint, but not a threatening external payments situation.

For very helpful comments on two earlier drafts, the author is grateful to Giovanni Andrea Cornia. Conversations with Gianni Vaggi, Michael Lipton, Tony Addison, and Tony Atkinson have helped improve the chapter. Raghav Gaiha and Martin Ravallion generously provided copies of their work in this area. The author's student, Ibotombi Longjam, extended invaluable research assistance. The responsibility for all opinions and any errors is the author's alone.

[1] Some have argued that growth picked up in the mid-1980s as a sequel to the reforms initiated then. Nevertheless, 1991 still marks a watershed year for economic reforms in India.

The Delhi Consensus has emphasized the slow liberalization of trade and very gradual privatization and avoided capital account liberalization. This prudent approach has sidestepped major shocks, and the changes in inequality consequent upon these reforms have been modest by the standards of, say, the transition economies. Rural inequality has risen at a slower pace than have urban and overall inequality. The rise in inequality has been the result of three factors:

(1) a shift in earnings from labour to capital income;
(2) the rapid growth of the services sector, particularly the FIRE sector,[2] with a consequent explosion in demand for skilled workers; and
(3) a drop in the rate of labour absorption during the reform period. There has also been an increase in regional inequality, especially in the incidence of rural poverty. This rise in inequality has implied that, despite better growth, poverty reduction has been sluggish.

The plan of this chapter is as follows. Section 12.2 outlines salient aspects of the economic performance of the Indian economy since the 1950s and provides a brief overview of the economic reforms initiated. Section 12.3 analyses trends in aggregate inequality and poverty and suggests possible explanations. Section 12.4 outlines the major characteristics of poverty and inequality at the level of individual states. Section 12.5 concludes.

12.2. SALIENT ECONOMIC PERFORMANCE ASPECTS AND RECENT POLICY REFORMS

Three broad phases[3] can be identified in the development of the Indian economy. During the first phase (1951–63) the rate of growth of gross domestic product (GDP) was low. The industrial economy was in its infancy, and feudal structures such as the Zamindari[4] were being dismantled. Slightly higher economic growth was typical during the second phase (1964–90) primarily because of the boost in agriculture consequent upon the Green Revolution and a more mature industrial base. The third phase, post-1991, has been characterized by much higher growth rates, though this growth is not propelled by the agricultural sector. Table 12.1 provides a summary of the behaviour of key macroeconomic aggregates for these periods.

The real GDP of the Indian economy has grown by about 4 per cent per annum on a trend basis over the nearly 50 years since 1950–1. In per capita terms, this would mean a growth rate of about 2 per cent per annum, which would then imply that per capita output grew by a factor of about 2.5 over the period 1950–99.

In consonance with international experience, economic growth in India has been characterized by considerable transformation in the sectoral composition of aggregate

[2] FIRE refers to banking, financial institutions, insurance, and real estate.

[3] This periodization also characterizes the development of inequality and poverty, as discussed in Section 12.3. There are important problems of comparability (discussed in footnote 16) of the consumption data for 1999–2000; hence, in the analysis we confine ourselves to the period until 1997.

[4] Zamindari is a landlord–serf type of agriculture tenure arrangement, whereby most of the land belongs to a landlord, and peasants pay the landlord for the right to till the soil and harvest crops.

Table 12.1. *Key national account aggregates (at 1980–1 prices; yearly percentage changes)*

	Mean growth				GDP share		
	RGDP	PFCE	GFCE	Per capita NNP	Agriculture	Manufactures	Services
1951–63 (Phase I)	3.8	3.4	6.8	1.6	53.50	17.43	29.07
1964–90 (Phase II)	4.3	3.8	5.8	1.8	40.92	24.22	34.82
1991–7 (Phase III)[a]	5.0	5.2	3.2	3.8	31.53	25.65	42.82
1992–7	5.0	4.5	5.0	4.7	31.35	25.35	43.29
1997–2001[b]	5.3			3.3	23.90	22.06	54.04

Notes: RGDP = real GDP (at 1980–1 prices). PFCE = private final consumption expenditure. GFCE = government final consumption expenditure. NNP = net national product.
[a] Phase III figures are given in two stages: one including and the other excluding the 'crisis year', 1991.
[b] = Computed from *Economic Survey, 2000–01*, Government of India and *Handbook of Statistics on the Indian Economy 2001*, Reserve Bank of India.
Source: See text.

output (Table 12.1). The share of agriculture in value added remained steady until about 1971 and then started to decline. Agricultural productivity was virtually stagnant and quite volatile (in per capita terms) until about 1974. Since around 1975 it has shown an almost steady growth of slightly above 1 per cent per annum. The share of manufacturing has grown very slowly, reaching a plateau of about 20 per cent in 1996. It is widely believed (Jha and Sahni 1993) that total factor productivity growth in the manufacturing sector has been sluggish. The share of services has increased quite quickly, with two phases of rapid expansion. The years following the nationalization of banks in 1969 saw a rapid expansion in bank penetration, particularly in rural areas. The financial liberalization begun in 1991 and the rapid development of industries in the field of information technology have had beneficial effects on productivity and the growth of output in the services sector.

Fluctuations in the growth rate of GDP were until recently driven mostly by the vagaries of the monsoon. Good rainfall would lead to better harvests and better GDP performance.[5] However, since the 1980s, as a result of the shift in the sectoral composition of output, the economy has become less dependent on the monsoons, and GDP growth was positive in 1987 and 1991 despite poor rains. Changes in employment patterns have been sluggish in comparison to the shift in the sectoral composition of output. Agriculture still accounts for the bulk of employment (Table 12.2). Even as late as 1993–4, about 70 per cent of the population was dependent for work on agriculture in rural areas. In urban areas, the figure was 8 per cent. Since the rural population accounts for about three quarters of the total population, a large majority of India's population is still dependent on agriculture for their livelihoods.

Table 12.3 presents evidence on the rate of unemployment (the number of people unemployed per 1000 persons in the work force) using three different time concepts. The first concept refers to usual status (US) and indicates the extent of unemployment

[5] The GDP growth rate was negative in the drought years of 1957–8, 1965–6, 1972–3, and 1979–80.

Table 12.2. *Household distribution by employment (%)*

	Rural				Urban			
	Agriculture	Industry	Service	Other	Agriculture	Industry	Service	Other
1983	77.3	10.0	12.7	—	16.5	31.0	52.5	—
1987–8	70.7	11.8	13.6	3.9	7.5	31.2	52.9	8.2
1993–4	71.0	10.9	14.8	3.4	7.7	29.6	54.2	8.6

Notes: 'Other' represents households which had no income from economic activity. For 1983, agriculture includes 'other'.

Source: Government of India (1996a).

Table 12.3. *All-India unemployment rates*

	Male				Female			
	US	US (adj.)	CWS	CDS	US	US (adj.)	CWS	CDS
Rural								
1993–4	2.0	1.4	3.0	5.6	1.4	0.8	3.0	5.6
1987–8	2.8	1.8	4.2	4.6	3.5	2.4	4.4	6.7
1983	2.1	1.4	3.7	7.5	1.4	0.7	4.3	9.0
1977–8	2.2	1.3	3.6	7.1	5.5	2.0	4.1	9.2
1972–3	—	1.2	3.0	6.8	—	0.5	5.5	11.2
Urban								
1993–4	4.5	4.0	5.2	6.7	8.3	6.2	8.4	10.5
1987–8	6.1	5.2	6.6	8.8	8.5	6.2	9.2	12.0
1983	5.9	5.1	6.7	9.2	6.9	4.9	7.5	11.0
1977–8	6.5	5.4	7.1	9.4	17.8	12.4	10.9	14.5
1972–3	—	4.8	6.0	8.0	—	6.0	9.2	13.7

Notes: US: usual status; US (adj.) US adjusted for subsidiary activity; CWS: current weekly status; CDS: current daily status.

Source: Government of India (1996a).

'for a relatively longer period during the reference period of 365 days' and measures the magnitude of chronic unemployment. Some of those who are unemployed according to this criterion may be working in a subsidiary capacity. When the unemployment rate excludes those employed in a subsidiary capacity, the corresponding figures are reported in the column 'US adjusted'. The second concept of unemployment refers to the current weekly status (CWS) and indicates the number unemployed (per 1000) during the average week of the survey year. It includes those who are chronically unemployed, as well as those who, among the usually employed category, are intermittently unemployed due to seasonal fluctuations in labour demand. Finally, the current daily status (CDS) gives this same information for an average day during the survey year.

Between 1972–3 and 1993–4 the chronic unemployment rate among males varied between 2 per cent and 2.8 per cent in rural India and between 4.5 per cent and 6.5 per cent in urban India. These figures might appear low in comparison to those in developed countries, but, as several authors have argued, the poor, who depend almost exclusively on labour income, can ill afford to remain unemployed on a regular basis. Their poverty is reflected by their earnings rather than by their unemployment status. As we move from the usual status to the weekly or daily status, the unemployment rate rises substantially because of extensions in coverage. In 1993–4, it was 6 per cent in the rural sector among both males and females and 7 per cent (11 per cent) for the urban male (urban female) population on a daily status basis, indicating large seasonal or intermittent unemployment. There is no clear trend in the unemployment rates over the last two decades[6] except that there was a drop[7] between 1987–8 and 1993–4. Fluctuations in unemployment are more severe for females than they are for males.

Indian economic reforms, which began in 1990–1, were an amalgam of macro-economic stabilization and structural adjustment and were initiated after a severe macroeconomic crisis. The contours of this crisis and the response to it have been well studied (Joshi and Little 1996). Therefore, only brief comments are made on these now. In the early months of 1991 there was a steep drop in foreign exchange reserves (to about US$1 billion, or two weeks' imports). India's credit rating was sharply downgraded, and private foreign lending was cut off. Industrial growth was sluggish. Inflation at 12 per cent (high by Indian standards) and rising, high fiscal and current account deficits[8] (at 10 and 3 per cent of GDP, respectively) and a heavy and growing burden of domestic and external debt, as well as falling real investments, were signs of deep-rooted structural malaise. However, it was recognized that these problems were transitory and were occurring against the background of the relatively healthy economic performance in the latter half of the 1980s. Thus, the World Bank (1996) observes:

India did not have the inflation, external debt, and social inequities so severe as in Latin America—and was thus able to stabilize the economy more rapidly and at lower social cost. Unlike former centrally planned economies in Eastern Europe and elsewhere, and while extremely regulated, India already had an ubiquitous private sector, all the institutions of a free market economy, and a relatively well-developed financial sector. India was thus able to avoid the costly industrial and financial closures and restructuring, so frequent and so painful in most of the former socialist economies of Eastern Europe and Central Asia, and which have considerably delayed the supply responses to reforms.

However, this also meant that, once the basic economic crisis had been tackled, the pressures to develop a consensus to advance and deepen structural reforms would be

---

[6] Mundle and Tulasidhar (1998) argue that recent economic reforms have not changed unemployment very much and that changes in unemployment cannot account for a significant portion of the increase in poverty in the immediate aftermath of the reforms.

[7] There is evidence (see Section 12.3.5) suggesting that there has been a slowdown in the rate of growth of employment generation in the post-reform period.

[8] Throughout this chapter, fiscal deficit refers to the combined fiscal deficits of central and state governments.

reduced,[9] and subsequent economic reforms would be gradual and not sweeping. The justification given for this is that India's economic crisis was not as serious as that of the transition economies and that there is a need to attain political consensus on economic reforms in a large and varied democracy. The essential contours of the economic reform programme were as follows.

12.2.1. *Fiscal Consolidation and Stabilization*

Fiscal consolidation and stabilization were seen as preconditions for successful reforms and assigned the highest priority, especially during the initial phase of the reform programme. Some reduction in the fiscal deficit was achieved by systemic improvements, such as the abolition of export subsidies in 1991–2, the partial restructuring of the fertilizer subsidy in 1992–3, and the phasing out of budgetary support to loss-making public sector enterprises. But this was accompanied by sharp reductions in capital expenditures and the transfers to the state governments. The state governments were unable to cut their recurrent expenditures and responded by decreasing their own capital expenditures, so that the expenditure pattern of both central and state governments was irrevocably biased in favour of non-capital (or revenue) expenditures from about 1987.

12.2.2. *Industrial Policy and Foreign Investment*

Industrial policy was subjected to a complete overhaul. Several barriers to entry into industries were removed. Industrial licensing was abolished except for a small number of small-scale sectoral units. The parallel, but separate controls over investment and expansion by larger industrial houses through the monopolies and restrictive trade practices act were abolished. The companies act was streamlined. The list of industries reserved for the public sector was drastically reduced.

There was also a radical restructuring of the public policy towards foreign investment. Earlier, India's policy towards foreign investment had been very selective and had been perceived by foreigners as unfriendly. Equity participation was limited to about 40 per cent, except in selected high technology or export-oriented sectors. With the beginning of reforms, the foreign investment limit was raised to 51 per cent and then still further a little later. Foreign investment is now permitted in a much larger number of sectors. The Foreign Investment Promotion Board has been set up to facilitate foreign direct investment in India. India has entered into bilateral and multilateral investment guarantee schemes.

12.2.3. *Trade and Exchange Rate Policies*

Trade policies were substantially liberalized for all except final consumer goods. The complex import control regime for imports of raw materials and intermediate and capital goods was virtually dismantled. Baggage allowances for international travellers

---

[9] This is reflected, for example, in a reluctance to tackle the fresh fiscal crisis that has emerged. See Jha (1999).

were raised. Quantitative restrictions on imports and customs duties were lowered. However, tariffs in India are still high by Asian standards. The exchange rate regime has undergone complete transformation. The highly controlled regime based on a chronically overvalued exchange rate for the rupee was dismantled. Two substantial devaluations were followed by the establishment of a dual and then a unified exchange rate regime. In 1994 the rupee became convertible on the current account. The liberalization of the capital account is still to take place.[10]

12.2.4. *Tax Reform*

Tax reform was undertaken subsequent to the report of a government committee and had the following broad characteristics. To start with, the number of income tax categories was brought down (on this topic, see Chapter 10). The top marginal rate of personal tax, which had been 56 per cent in 1991, came down to as low as 30 per cent.[11] The number of exemptions was lowered, although significant progress needs to be made on this front.[12] Stronger incentives for saving were provided by redefining the base of the wealth tax (which earlier included all personal assets) to exclude all productive assets including financial assets. In addition, corporate tax rates, which (in 1991) had been 51.75 per cent for a publicly listed company and 57.5 per cent for closely held companies, were unified at 46 per cent. Corporate taxes were further lowered.

Finally, excise duties on manufactured goods had hitherto been charged at varying rates on different commodities, and most of these duties had been specific rather than *ad valorem*. There had been an abundance of exemptions and interpretations of the tax laws. Indirect tax procedures were now simplified, and most duties were made *ad valorem*. The 'Modvat' system of tax credit for taxes paid on inputs was extended to include key sectors like textiles and petroleum. The number of excise rates was more than halved. A beginning was made with respect to the taxation of services. The longer term objective of the government is to move to a full-scale VAT. There are some important problems here, not the least of which is the integration of taxes on production (which are under the control of the central government) with taxes on sales (which are under the control of state governments).

12.2.5. *Public Sector Policy*

Under the patronage of the Feldman–Mahalanobis model of development, the public sector in India entered into almost every conceivable area of productive activity.

---

[10] In 1997 the government set up a committee to examine the possibility of making the rupee convertible on the capital account. This committee recommended stiff conditions and a target date of 2000. In the aftermath of the East Asian currency crisis, the enthusiasm for capital account convertibility has considerably waned.

[11] In the budget for 1999–2000, a surcharge of 10 per cent was added to the higher categories of income, raising the effective top marginal tax rate to 33.3 per cent. A 10 per cent surcharge was also levied on corporate taxes.

[12] Agricultural income has never seriously been taxed in India. In the 1999–2000 union budget, dividend income was also made exempt from income taxation. Many perquisites still remain untaxed.

Many public sector enterprises were highly inefficient; indeed, they were little more than guarantors of continuous employment to some workers. In 1997, for example, the Bureau of Public Enterprise calculated that public sector enterprises as a whole, representing a total capital worth of Rs 600 billion, were earning a negative real rate of return. This aggregate picture masked considerable heterogeneity because some public sector enterprises continued to be professionally managed.

Public sector restructuring policy took the form of selective disinvestment rather than privatization *per se*. Initially, the government retained 51 per cent of the equity and, therefore, control over management. This percentage has subsequently been lowered in some areas. Revenues from disinvestment have been used for general budgetary purposes. Public sector undertakings were given the clear signal that their investment plans would have to be financed either by internal resource generation, or through the capital markets. Although the budget constraints of loss-making enterprises have become much harder, the government has not ordered any public sector enterprise to be closed, but has brought public sector undertakings under the purview of the Board of Industrial and Financial Reconstruction to facilitate their restructuring.

12.2.6. *Financial Sector Policy*

The crisis of 1991 brought into the open the full magnitude of the lingering and neglected problems of real sector stagnation and financial sector complacency. The government's response followed the recommendations of the Narasimham Committee—formed in August 1991 against the backdrop of pressure from the IMF to lower the fiscal deficit; see Narasimham (1992).

The first banking reform dealt with regulation. The government's role in banking shifted from the management of credit to supervision and regulation. This carried the risk (moral hazard) that banks which had hitherto been protected were suddenly permitted, at least partially, to set their own credit goals, would, in the competition to lend more, sacrifice prudent norms and face insolvency. A government in the grips of a weak fiscal situation would not be able to bail such banks out in time.

Efforts to improve transparency and reduce transaction costs were undertaken (such as the adoption of modern accounting practices and appropriate definitions of assets and liabilities, the setting up of the Board of Financial Supervision within the Reserve Bank of India, and the development of a reliable financial database). The massive clean-up needed for some public sector banks could not be pursued because the government was the sole stakeholder and privatization was not possible until the banks had become profitable. Banks were recapitalized through the general budget. In May 1989 the call money rate was freed from the ceiling of 10 per cent, and the interest rate ceiling on the rediscounting of commercial bills was withdrawn. In 1994–5 the government agreed to phase out its automatic access to Reserve Bank of India (RBI) financing within 3 years. Commercial banks, as well as public financial institutions, were allowed to issue certificates of deposits as of June 1989 and commercial paper as of 1990, and, as of April 1992, they were permitted to set up their own money market funds. Guidelines were also progressively liberalized.

The development of treasury bills as a money market instrument has deepened the government securities markets. Short-term liquidity management has been conducted through repos, particularly since November 1996. Interbank liabilities were exempted from cash reserve requirements in April 1997 so that repo transactions could take place in a more flexible manner. Banks have been given considerable freedom in setting interest rates. Many anomalous practices in the Bombay Stock Exchange were contained. The creation and empowerment of the Securities and Exchange Board of India—a regulatory body—and the national stock exchange, with on-line trading from a large number of centres throughout the country, were important steps in this regard. Capital controls on foreign direct investment were gradually removed.

12.2.7. *Agricultural Sector Reforms*

Under the Indian Constitution, agriculture is within the purview of the states. Thus, the strategy adopted by the central government of lowering the budget deficit by reducing the transfers to the states has meant that investment (both public and private) in agriculture has stagnated. In contrast, the lowering of the protection for industry and the end of the overvaluation of the rupee have reduced the anti-agriculture bias in India's development strategy. Agricultural exports have become viable, particularly those from the agro-processing industry. All central government restrictions on interstate trade in food grains have been removed, although some state government restrictions remain. The procurement of food grains has registered handsome gains, leading to substantial increases in farm incomes. Agricultural credit markets are a cause of worry. Laxness in loan recovery has made several cooperative banks non-viable.

12.2.8. *Labour Market Reforms*

Indian labour laws provide considerable protection from retrenchment to labour in the organized sector of the economy. These laws have reduced the impact of successes in other policy areas. Flexible labour laws are needed to attract new capital and to make old firms with a history of excess labour more viable. Advocates of economic reform have argued that a successful long-term reform strategy should devote more attention to the sector that is slowest to change. In the Indian case, this is the labour market. Some flexibility has been transmitted through a voluntary retirement scheme, but this is not pervasive, nor is it a substitute for a rational policy towards exit from the workforce.

12.2.9. *Complementary Social Measures*

From the very beginning policy planners recognized that, while market-oriented economic reforms would improve investment and growth prospects, these could not be looked upon as ends in themselves, given India's mammoth and long-standing problems of inequality and poverty. In an important speech the then Finance Minister Manmohan Singh in his speech presenting the 1992–9 union budget remarked that markets can only serve those who are part of the market system. A vast number of people in our country live on the edges of a subsistence economy. We need credible programmes of direct intervention focusing on the needs of these people. We have the responsibility to provide them with quality social services, such as education, health, safe drinking water and roads. In the same way, the development of capital and technology intensive sectors, characterized by long gestation periods, such as transport and communications and energy, will need to be planned with much greater care than ever before. The control of land and water degradation, which threatens the livelihood of millions of poor people in this country, will also require effective government leadership and action.

What the Delhi Consensus hoped to achieve was not less government, but more effective government to implement what the then Prime Minister P. V. Narasimha Rao, borrowing a term used by Cornia *et al.* (1987), called 'reforms with a human face'. The government was aware that the reform and structural adjustment programme would result in a temporary fall in public expenditure and that economic growth did not automatically 'trickle down' to the poor.[13] Hence, a number of programmes directly attacking poverty were initiated. These included the food for work programme begun in 1977, subsidized food supplies through the public distribution system, and concessional loan schemes for on- and off-farm development for small farmers, marginal farmers, and agricultural labourers.

Other ongoing initiatives have concentrated on the creation of rural wage and self-employment programmes through asset endowment rather than on needs-oriented programmes designed to ensure access to basic amenities, such as drinking water, to the poor. The most prominent among these is the Jawahar Rozgar Yojana, which brings together the National Rural Employment Programme and the Rural Landless Employment Guarantee Programme. Among these, the Maharashtra Employment Guarantee Scheme, which derives its success mainly from the strong political commitment of the state government (Hirway and Terhal 1994), is the most well known. In addition, there are the Integrated Rural Development Programme, the Employment Assurance Scheme, the Accelerated Rural Water Supply Programme, and programmes to counter area-specific endemic poverty caused by hostile agro–climatic conditions and the degeneration of the ecosystem (Gaiha 1991).

A national renewal fund was set up in February 1992 to provide assistance to workers becoming redundant following the adjustment programme. This fund was expected to finance the retraining, redeployment, or retrenchment of workers made redundant. Despite budgetary pressures, the financing has been maintained and even enhanced for these social programmes. Operational efficiency has been sought through decentralized programme operation. In 1994, the Indian parliament passed the 73rd Amendment to the Constitution of India, making

---

[13] There is some disagreement about the extent of the increase in poverty during the initial phase of reform and the responsibility of the reforms for this increase. Tendulkar and Jain (1995) and Gupta (1995) attribute some of the increase in rural poverty to the reforms, but Datt and Ravallion (1997) argue that about nine-tenths of the measured deterioration in rural living standards in India in the immediate aftermath of the reforms occurred independent of the reforms.

the panchayats, a village-level organization, directly responsible for implementing poverty-alleviation programmes (Gaiha and Kulkarni 1998).

12.3. TRENDS IN INEQUALITY AND POVERTY IN INDIA

Some evidence on the temporal behaviour of inequality and poverty[14] at the all-India level is presented in Table 12.4. The poverty measures used are all drawn from the Foster–Greer–Thorbecke (1984) class of functions written as

$$P_\alpha = \sum_{y_i < z} [(z-y_i)/z]^\alpha / n,$$

where y_i is the consumption of the ith household or class of household, z is the poverty line, n is the population size, and α is a non-negative parameter. The headcount ratio, H, given by the percentage of the population who are poor, is obtained when $\alpha = 0$. The poverty-gap index (PGI), given by the aggregate income shortfall of the poor as a proportion of the poverty line and normalized by the population size, is given by $\alpha = 1$, and the Foster–Greer–Thorbecke (SPG) measure is obtained when $\alpha = 2$.

Poverty measures are calculated for each of two parametric specifications of the Lorenz curve: The Beta model (BETA) of Kakwani (1980) and the general quadratic (GQL) model of Villasenor and Arnold (1989). Standard tests based on R^2 and log likelihood functions enable us to make a choice between the two functional forms. The computations cover the 13th (1957–8) to the 53rd (1997) Rounds of the National Sample Survey (NSS).[15] Results for 1999–2000 are also

---

[14] The poverty line is taken as per capita consumption worth Rs.49 (Rs.57) at 1973–4 prices for the rural (urban) sector.

[15] The database of the NSS is used here. NSS data in the socio-economic field include details on consumer expenditure, demographic characteristics, labour force statistics, and employment and unemployment particulars. The sample households for consumption inquiries are selected on the basis of probability proportional to population. The sampling design chosen for the surveys is a two-stage stratified sampling, instead of simple random sampling carried out separately for the rural and urban sectors (Government of India 1955). Consumer expenditure relates to domestic consumption of the household only and excludes the homeless population and the population residing in institutions such as prisons and hospitals. NSS does not take into account the expenditure by households for productive purposes. Consumption includes consumption (in value) of goods and services originating from (a) home-grown stock, (b) monetary purchases, (c) receipts in exchange of goods and services, (d) gifts, loans, etc. The food consumed by the employee at the employer's household is not included in the NSS estimates of food consumption of the former. This is done to avoid double counting of the expenditure on food. This procedure involves an underestimation of the consumption (of food, as well as in total) of the employee households which in all likelihood belongs to lower expenditure classes and an overestimation of the consumption of generally richer employer households. As a result, the food grain consumption and calorie intake of the poorer households in general would be underestimated (with implications for estimates of poverty measures based on calorie norms). NSS collects data from sample households with a reference period of a week, a month, or a year preceding the date of inquiry. When the entire sample is considered, the reference period becomes a moving one, as the NSS spreads out the interviews among different households uniformly over the duration of the survey. The moving reference period averages out the seasonal variations of the characteristics at the aggregate level. The dataset, although rich, has some drawbacks. For an assessment of the quality of the NSS dataset, see Dandedkar (1996), Deaton and Paxson (1998), Ghose and Bhattacharya (1994), Minhas (1988, 1991), Murthy and Roy (1975), Subramanian and Deaton (1996), and Ray and Bhattacharya (1992).

Table 12.4. *Selected measures of inequality and poverty, 1957–2000*

	Gini	H	PG	SPG	RMC	Index of RMC	Distribution
Rural							
1957–8	33.74	55.16	19.01	8.77	55.68	103.07	GQL
1963–4	29.01	48.53	13.88	5.49	45.86	84.89	GQL
1968–9	30.70	59.00	18.96	8.19	50.32	93.15	BETA
1973–4	28.30	55.72	17.18	7.13	54.02	100.00	GQL
1977–8	31.20	50.64	15.04	6.06	61.17	113.24	GQL
1983	30.10	45.32	12.65	4.84	61.44	113.74	GQL
1986–7	30.15	38.90	10.02	3.72	66.89	123.82	BETA
1987–8	30.16	39.52	9.67	3.38	66.83	123.71	BETA
1989–90	28.23	34.30	7.80	2.50	67.50	124.95	BETA
1990–1	27.71	36.43	8.64	2.93	66.81	123.68	BETA
1992	29.88	43.47	10.88	3.81	63.84	118.18	BETA
1993–4	28.50	38.70	9.40	3.27	73.00	135.14	BETA
1994–5	29.19	34.22	8.70	2.90	76.50	141.61	BETA
1995–6	28.97	35.44	8.30	2.60	74.70	138.28	BETA
1997	30.11	34.22	8.13	2.57	78.90	146.06	BETA
1999–2000 (30-day recall)	26.22	27.61	5.45	1.61	79.2	146.6	BETA
1999–2000 (7-day recall)	26.23	24.49	4.75	1.42	79.5	147.1	BETA
Rural average							
1963–4 to 1990–1	29.51	45.37	12.65	4.92	60.09	111.24	
1992–7	29.33	37.21	9.08	3.03	73.39	135.85	
Urban							
1957–8	35.90	47.75	15.95	7.00	76.16	109.61	GQL
1963–4	36.54	44.83	13.29	5.17	81.05	116.65	GQL
1968–9	32.90	49.29	15.54	6.54	72.14	103.83	BETA
1973–4	31.50	47.96	13.60	5.22	69.48	100.00	BETA
1977–8	33.70	40.50	11.69	4.50	83.77	120.57	BETA
1983	33.40	35.65	9.52	3.56	87.49	125.92	BETA
1986–7	35.60	34.29	9.10	3.41	93.84	135.06	BETA
1987–8	35.57	35.60	9.30	3.25	90.66	130.48	GQL
1989–90	35.59	33.40	8.51	3.04	93.44	134.48	BETA
1990–1	33.95	32.76	8.51	3.12	91.05	131.04	BETA
1992	35.55	33.70	8.82	3.19	84.70	121.91	BETA
1993–4	34.50	30.03	7.62	2.76	95.00	136.73	BETA
1994–5	33.43	28.40	7.10	2.60	102.30	147.24	BETA
1995–6	35.36	27.30	6.90	2.40	105.60	151.99	BETA
1997	36.12	27.9	7.2	2.5	103.50	148.96	BETA
1999–2000 (30 day recall)	34.40	25.09	5.75	1.86	106.2	152.8	BETA
1999–2000 (7 day recall)	34.25	23.22	5.20	1.67	107.1	154.1	BETA
Urban average							
1963–4 to 1990–1	34.31	39.36	11.01	4.20	84.77	122.00	
1992–7	34.99	29.47	7.53	2.69	98.22	141.36	

Notes: The table shows national results. RMC = real mean consumption in terms of 28th Round prices. Results for the 55th Round of NSS (1999–2000) are not strictly comparable to the earlier rounds; the reasons for this are explained in footnote 22 of the text.

Source: See text.

noted.[16] Table 12.4 also notes movements in the level of real mean consumption in rural and urban areas, as well as the form of the distribution (BETA or GQL) which best fits the data.

This time span can be usefully split up into three subperiods: (a) 1951–63, (b) 1964–90, and (c) 1991 and later. (This last period is considered to begin during the crisis year, 1991, and, alternately, to include or exclude this year and extends to 1997. We exclude the year 1999 for reasons explained in footnote 22.) In the first subperiod, as Table 12.1 indicates, the average rate of growth was low. Mildly redistributive policies, such as the abolition of the zamindari system, were effected, but the incidence of poverty was high. With rapid population growth, the number of the poor increased considerably. The second subperiod was characterized by a controlled and stable policy regime. GDP growth was higher essentially because of the adoption of green revolution-type technologies and a more mature industrial base. Inequality remained stable, so that there was a more rapid drop in the incidence of poverty. However, because of rapid population growth, the absolute number of the poor increased also during this period.

In response to controlled liberalization, in the 1990s there was a modest rise in rural inequality and a more significant rise in urban inequality, and, because growth in this period was characterized by a shift of the population to urban areas (which exhibits higher Gini coefficients than rural areas), there was an increase in aggregate inequality. There was also an increase in regional inequality, of which the most striking aspect was the increase in the variation in the incidence of rural poverty. Despite healthy growth, the rural poverty rate almost stagnated because of the increase in inequality and the sluggish increase in agricultural wages, as well as the rise in prices in the public distribution system consequent upon the reduction of food and fertilizer subsidies and the rise in tradable prices following the devaluation of the rupee. In contrast, the urban poverty rate declined by about 5 percentage points between 1990–1 and 1997. Table 12.5 illustrates the relationship between the salient characteristics of the economy and changes in inequality and poverty. Table 12.6 provides information on food availability.

---

[16] In the 55th Round the NSS made a major deviation from the technique it had used earlier. The basic change was in terms of the reference period used in for questions on consumption. Up to Round 50th, the reference period was uniform for all kinds of consumption in the past thirty days. During the 55th Round, however, the question on consumption of clothing, footwear, education, and institutional health were asked with a reference period of 365 days and that on food consumption for (alternately) 30 and 7 days. It should be noted that several economists had asked for these adjustments. Many had felt that the 7-day recall period for food consumption would give a better indication of actual consumption. Hence, this change in technique should actually be welcomed. However, since the poverty estimates of the earlier rounds were done with the uniformly longer recall period, comparison of poverty estimates becomes difficult unless the results from the earlier Rounds are cast in terms of the new recall period. Unless this is accomplished the results of the 55th Round are unlikely to provide any conclusive indication of the trends in poverty. Some authors, for example, Visaria (2000), wanted to keep the 7-day recall period but argued that the poverty line should be raised to better reflect minimum nutritional norms. However, as Howes and Lanjouw (1998) argue, differences in sample design can be a more serious distortion to poverty estimates than merely differences in recall periods. Others, such as Sen (2000), have argued for a completely new 55th Round with the old reference period so that comparability of data can be maintained. In Table 12.4, I report my calculations for poverty, inequality, and real mean consumption for 1999–2000.

Table 12.5. *Dynamics of inequality and poverty in India under three policy regimes, 1957–97*

	Gini	H	Growth: real wage/real GDP/per capita NNP	Food availability/ agricultural growth	Inflation, CPIAL
Rural					
1957–63	↓ (−4.73)	↓ (−6.63)	n.a./↑/n.a.	↑/n.a.	n.a.
1963–4 to 1989–90	↓ (−0.73)	↓ (−14.23)	n.a./↑/n.a.	↑/↑	n.a.
1990–1 to 1997	↑ (+2.40)	↓ (−2.21)	↑/↑/↑	↑/↑	↓

	G	H	Growth: real wage/real GDP/per capita NNP	Food availability/ industrial growth	Inflation, CPIIIW
Urban					
1957–63	↓ (−0.6)	↓ (−2.92)	n.a.	n.a.	n.a.
1963–4 to 1989–90	↓ (−0.95)	↓ (−11.43)	n.a./↑/n.a.	↑/↑	n.a.
1990–1 to 1997	↑ (+2.17)	↓ (−4.18)	↑/↑/↑	↑/↑	↓

Notes: *G* = Gini. *H* = headcount ratio. NNP = net national product. Inflation refers to percentage changes in the CPIAL (consumer price index for agricultural labourers) and CPIIW (consumer price index for industrial workers). n.a. = data unavailable.

Source: See text.

Table 12.6. *Per capita food availability (metric tonnes per annum)*

	Cereal	Food
1973–4	0.163	0.180
1977–8	0.180	0.199
1982–3	0.166	0.183
1986–7	0.171	0.186
1987–8	0.164	0.178
1989–90	0.192	0.208
1990–1	0.193	0.210
1991–2	0.183	0.197
1993–4	0.193	0.208
1994–5	0.196	0.212
1995–6	0.183	0.197

Source: Reserve Bank of India (1998).

12.3.1. *Inequality and Poverty in the Rural Sector*

As noted, the period until 1963 witnessed a fall in the rural Gini in response to the dismantling of the zamindari and other feudal structures. However, growth rates were so low that real mean consumption declined between 1957–8 and 1963–4. Thus, the moderate distributional improvement achieved during those years was unable to generate a drop in poverty. The poverty rate remained high, and the number of poor rose. From 1963–4 to 1990, inequality remained stable, with the rural Gini falling by only 0.78 points. Inequality (and poverty) increased in response to the brief, but costly war with Pakistan in 1965–6, which was followed by 2 years of poor monsoons and consequent near famine-like conditions in many parts of the country. Inequality began to decline after the onset of land reform in 1969. With inequality almost unchanged, the greater agricultural growth consequent upon the adoption of green revolution-type technologies in some parts of the country led to a considerable drop in poverty (about 14 points in the headcount ratio). The only aberration occurred in 1987–8, when poverty rose as a result of poor harvests (and lower agricultural wages) following a widespread failure of the monsoons.

The post-1991 period provided a major break with the past in rural inequality. The period began with a crisis. Food grain production declined between 1991 and 1992 largely as a result of the increase in the price of fertilizers after a cut in the fertilizer subsidy noted above. Macroeconomic performance started to improve in 1993–4. GDP, NNP per capita, agricultural output, and food availability registered good gains, and the inflation rate fell. This growth, however, exacerbated rural inequality. The Gini was higher in 1997 than it had been at the onset of the economic crisis in 1990–1 (30.1 as compared to 27.7). Poverty initially rose in response to the economic crisis and the liberalization programme undertaken thereafter,[17] but then started to drop very marginally following the successful liberalization of the agricultural sector and substantial increases in the procurement prices for food grains. Although there were modest gains in real mean consumption (from 66.8 in 1990–1 to 78.9 in 1997), growing inequality meant that the drop in poverty was marginal (34.2 in 1997 compared to 36.4 in 1990–1). Given the rapid growth of population in rural areas, the number of the poor in the rural sector went up. Hence, the economic reform programme of the 1990s led to a rise in rural inequality, a very mild drop in rural poverty,[18] and a small increase in real mean consumption. There was some year-to-year fluctuation.

Changes in the real wage in agriculture (graphed in Fig. 12.1) have been a reasonable proxy for the movements in inequality and, particularly, for those in poverty in rural India. Real mean consumption has shown a weak upward trend, and, along with fluctuating real agricultural wages, this indicates the slowly rising importance of (non-agricultural) labour income. Growth in urban real wages seems to have had little impact on rural poverty.

As an explanation of the movements in the real agricultural wage, the following regression had a good fit:

Agwage =	6.2865	+0.307*time	−0.0103*infl	−0.29*dummy	−0.03*ginir	−0.029*hcr
	(1.954)	(4.911)	(−1.45)	(−1.22)	(−0.26)	(−1.1)

$R^2 = 0.96$, DW and LM and F version of chi-squared tests reject serial correlation.

---

[17] Gaiha (1998) notes that the most important cause of the increase in rural poverty, at least initially, was the rise in fertilizer prices. Mundle and Tulasidhar (1998) argue that, besides this, higher food grain prices also contributed.   [18] Rural poverty rose in 1995–6 following an inadequate monsoon.

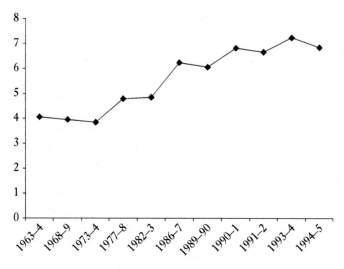

Figure 12.1. *Real agricultural wages (rupees per day)*

Agwage, time, infl, dummy, ginir, and hcr are, respectively, the real agricultural wage, a time trend, inflation in the consumer price index for agricultural labourers (CPIAL), a dummy (with a value of 1 for a bad monsoon year and 0 otherwise), the rural Gini, and the rural headcount ratio. All signs are as expected. Figures in parentheses indicate *t*-values, which show that only the constant and the time trend are significant. On the basis of the likelihood ratio tests, ginir and hcr can be dropped from the regression. The new equation is:

Agwage =	3.7334	+0.37366*time	−0.101*infl	−0.4054*dummy
	(13.2733)	(11.12)	(−1.473)	(−1.875)

Inflation in CPIAL (the Mundle–Tulasidhar effect) has the right sign, but is insignificant, whereas the poor monsoon dummy has the right sign and is significant (at 10 per cent). Hence, real agricultural wages in India seem to be growing along a trend, with fluctuations being caused largely by variations in the monsoons.

12.3.2. *Inequality and Poverty in the Urban Sector*

The urban Gini has always been higher than the rural Gini. During the first period it rose slightly. In the 26-year period from 1963–4 to 1989–90, the urban Gini was almost constant (falling by only 0.95 points). In contrast, in the period between 1990–1 and 1997, the urban Gini went up by 2.17 points. In 1997 it stood at one of the highest values ever in the Indian context: 36.12. Thus, the reforms have led to a perceptible rise in urban inequality. For much of the period between 1957–8 and 1997, urban poverty fell. The only exceptions were the drought years of 1967–9, 1987–8, 1992 (the year immediately after the stabilization programme was put into place), and 1997, when industrial recession set in, mean consumption fell, and inequality and poverty rose. Food availability varied continuously over this period, underscoring its diminished importance as a determinant of urban poverty as compared to rural poverty.

Urban poverty has had a close association with industrial growth, underscoring the fact that, with an almost stable distribution, higher growth means lower poverty. Whenever the industrial growth rate went up, the urban headcount ratio fell—even in 1995–6, when higher industrial growth was associated with lower real GDP and lower agricultural growth. Similarly, whenever the industrial growth rate fell, urban poverty increased or declined more slowly.

12.3.3. *Comparison of Inequality and Poverty in the Rural and Urban Sectors*

Figure 12.2 reports the differences in inequality and poverty between the rural and the urban sectors. The urban sector always has higher inequality and lower poverty than the rural sector. The difference between the Gini coefficients in the two sectors

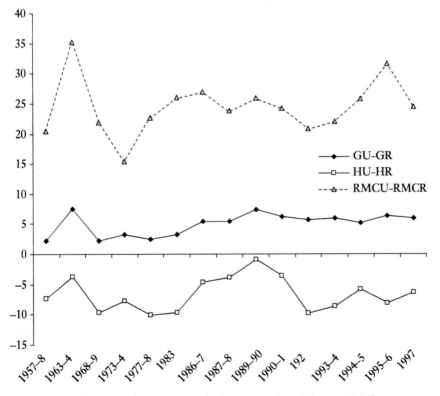

Figure 12.2. *Inequality, poverty, and mean consumption: Urban–rural differences*

rose during the first period because of an increase in urban inequality, the implications of the import-substitution-led industrial growth strategy adopted during the second 5-year plan, and a drop in rural inequality. During 1964–89 this difference diminished and remained below 5 points until 1989–90, but rose during the reform period.

The difference between rural and urban poverty diminished in the first period as rural poverty fell and the industrial sector was still in its infancy. During the second period, the difference remained nearly stable, narrowing somewhat until 1989–90. With the onset of the reforms, urban poverty declined more sharply than did rural poverty, and the gap between the two widened. The association between rural and urban poverty is much closer than the association between urban and rural inequality. The coefficient of correlation between the urban and rural headcount ratios is 0.95 for the entire period and 0.78 for the 1990s, while the corresponding correlation between rural and urban Ginis is only 0.21 for the entire period and 0.67 for the 1990s. The links between inequality and poverty within each sector are weak. The coefficient of correlation between the rural headcount ratio and the rural Gini is 0.5 for the entire period and 0.12 for the 1990s. In the urban sector the Gini coefficient and the headcount ratio showed a correlation of −0.29 for the entire period and −0.12 for the 1990s. Hence, the reforms weakened the association between poverty and inequality within each sector. The variability of inflation for agricultural workers is higher than that for industrial workers (Fig. 12.3) and increased in the 1990s.[19] If utility functions are concave, higher inflation variability would amount to lower

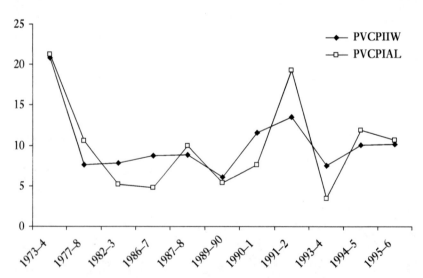

Figure 12.3. *Trends in the consumer price index for industrial workers (CPIIW) and agricultural labourers (CPIAL) (% variations over the previous year)*

[19] Ravallion and Datt (1996, 1999) confirm the deleterious effect of inflation on rural poverty in shorter data series. Nominal wages respond sluggishly to inflation, so that higher inflation leads to lower real earnings and higher poverty in the short run.

expected utility, *ceteris paribus*, and a decline in the welfare of rural households. Except for 1993–4, agricultural workers experienced greater erosion in purchasing power in the 1990s.

12.3.4. *Economic Reforms and Poverty*

There are two broad reasons for the inability of the reforms to make a serious dent in poverty, particularly rural poverty. First, the effectiveness of economic growth in reducing poverty depends considerably on the pattern of this growth (Ravallion and Datt 1996). In the countryside, if growth is primarily concentrated in the non-farm sector, its ability to reduce poverty in places characterized by 'poor' human resources and 'poor' initial development conditions (in absolute terms, as well as relative to urban areas) is limited.

Second, the effectiveness of anti-poverty programmes is crucial. The evidence on the effectiveness of these programmes in India is mixed. Gaiha (1998), Gaiha *et al.* (1998), and Gaiha and Kulkarni (1998) argue that these measures have not been very effective and that economic growth, by itself, is not able to make much of a dent in the core poverty in India.[20] In contrast, building upon a model of the movement in and out of poverty, Paul (1998) argues that the Integrated Rural Development Programme has been quite effective in reducing poverty in rural India. Be that as it may, there remains considerable room for improvement in the design and execution of anti-poverty programmes. The strategy must involve resource mobilization to finance these programmes, which the current fiscal deficit of 10 per cent of GDP makes difficult. The scope and design of the public distribution system (PDS) need to be enhanced so that the system can offer the poor improved access to food. Jha *et al.* (1999*b*) show that the allocation of food grains through the PDS to various states has not been based on demand. Mundle and Tulasidhar (1998) have argued that the targeting and coverage of the PDS have been inadequate, and therefore the system has failed to shield the poor from the rise in food grain prices that has followed the boost in the price of fertilizers and the procurement price for food grains in the aftermath of the reforms.

12.3.5. *Economic Reforms and Inequality*

There is compelling evidence that the reforms have exacerbated inequality. However, the deterioration in India has been less substantial than that in several transition economies. What accounts for the rise in inequality in India? An examination of the share of factor incomes sheds light on this issue. Particularly since 1992–3, as Table 12.7 indicates, the share of operating surpluses (profits) in net domestic product (NDP) has been rising, while that of mixed income has been falling. The share of wage income has been on a mild downward trend. In the organized sector of the economy,

---

[20] Gaiha (1998) argues that a substantial amount of expenditure on anti-poverty programmes is cornered by middlemen or powerful vested interests who control the panchayats and that a coalition of the poor to force social expenditure towards more meaningful ends is necessary if anti-poverty programmes are to succeed.

Table 12.7. *Trends in the factoral distribution of income in India (shares of net domestic product)*
1980–1 to 1995–6

	Total			Organized sector			Unorganized sector		
	Employee compensation	Operating surplus	Mixed income	Private sector	Employee compensation	Operating surplus	Total	Employee compensation	Mixed income
1980–1	36.8	7.7	55.5	12.5	7.1	5.4	70	14.5	55.5
1981–2	36.2	9.4	54.4	12.9	7.1	5.8	68.4	14	54.4
1982–3	37	10.2	52.8	12.9	7.3	5.7	66.6	13.7	52.9
1983–4	37	10	53	13	7.3	5.7	66.6	13.7	52.9
1984–5	38.5	9.9	51.6	13.1	7.6	5.5	65.6	14	51.6
1985–6	38.5	10.3	51.2	12.3	6.9	5.4	65.1	13.9	51.2
1986–7	39.6	10.5	49.9	12.2	7.5	4.6	63.5	13.6	49.9
1987–8	40.2	9.9	49.9	11.8	7.3	4.4	63.6	13.7	49.9
1988–9	38.9	10.7	50.4	11.7	6.7	5	64	13.6	50.4
1989–90	38.7	11.3	50	11.9	6.2	5.7	63.7	13.7	50
1990–1	38.4	11.5	50.1	12.2	6.6	5.6	63.8	13.7	50.1
1991–2	38	12.1	49.9	11.8	6.7	5.1	63.3	13.4	49.9
1992–3	38	11.8	50.2	11.6	6.6	5	63.5	13.3	50.2
1993–4	36.5	14.2	49.3	12.6	6.5	6.1	62.3	13	49.3
1994–5	35.8	15.3	48.9	13.7	6.6	7.1	61.7	12.9	48.8
1995–6	36.8	16.2	47	16.2	7.3	8.9	59.7	12.6	47.1

Source: Author's compilation of various data from the Central Statistical Organization.

these tendencies are even more pronounced. The share of the organized sector in NDP has risen enormously (by about 50 per cent) since 1992. Within this sector, the share of profits has gone up rapidly since 1992, whereas the share of wage income (the compensation of employees) has broadly stagnated. The share of the unorganized sector in NDP has dropped. The share of wages has been stagnating within this sector, and that of mixed income (self-employment and agricultural income) has been declining, indicating a rise in the share of profit.

A possible factor in this trend relates to the labour intensity of the growth pattern of the 1990s. In this regard, Tables 12.8 and 12.9 provide evidence that the economic reforms have been associated with a drop in the rate of labour absorption and with considerable change in output and employment structure. Indeed, as Table 12.9 indicates, the growth of the FIRE sector has outstripped the growth of agriculture during almost every year of the reform period. Since 1996–7 the growth of the FIRE sector has consistently outpaced the growth in manufacturing. It is well known that growth in the FIRE sector creates demand for highly skilled and specialized factors of production and has a substantial speculative component. Facilitating the development of enterprise and investment has led to considerable improvement in profit opportunities, but less so in the case of labour earnings.

The gradual pace of the reforms and the practice of staggering major policy changes have limited the negative effects in terms of a worsening of inequality. Moreover, the lack of flexibility in labour markets, particularly the difficulties associated with the retrenchment of workers, has tended to cushion workers from the unemployment implications of the reforms. It is widely accepted, however, that this has also acted as

Table 12.8. *Annual compound growth in employment, by industry (%)*

	1980–91[a]	1990–4[b]	1994–8[c]
Agriculture, forestry, fishing, and hunting	0.9	−0.4	0.1
Mining and quarrying	1.5	0.5	−2.8
Manufacturing	0.3	0.4	2.0
Electricity, gas, and water supply	2.8	1.1	0.7
Construction	0.5	−0.1	−0.9
Trades, hotels, and restaurants	1.3	0.9	1.1
Transport, storage, and communications	1.1	0.7	−0.2
Financing, insurance, and real estate	4.4	2.4	1.1
Community, social, and personal services	2.2	1.1	0.9
Total	1.6	0.8	0.8

[a] 1 April 1980 to 30 March 1991.
[b] 1 April 1990 to 31 March 1994.
[c] 1 April 1994 to 31 March 1998.
Source: Author's compilation of various data from the Central Statistical Organization.

Table 12.9. *Annual real GDP growth rates in agriculture, manufacturing, and services*

	Agriculture, forestry and logging, fishing, mining, and quarrying	Manufacturing and construction	Transport, communications, trade	Banking and insurance, real estate and ownership of dwellings, business services
1991–2	−2.0	−1.7	2.3	10.5
1992–3	5.8	4.4	6.2	4.6
1993–4	3.6	6.9	12.5	5.6
1994–5	5.3	9.3	9.9	6.1
1995–6	−0.4	12.5	13.3	7.6
1996–7	8.8	6.6	7.7	7.1
1997–8	−1.1	5.6	5.8	11.8

Source: Author's calculations based on various data from the Central Statistical Organization.

a brake on more rapid economic growth. Hence, there has been a tradeoff. Furthermore, since India is a large country, the aggregate indicators may be concealing considerable diversity in regional experiences.[21] This necessitates a more disaggregated analysis of trends in inequality and poverty. Some results at the level of states are, therefore, now reported.

[21] Ravallion (1998) argues similarly in the case of rural China.

12.4. POVERTY AND INEQUALITY AT THE STATE LEVEL

To highlight the regional dimensions of inequality and poverty, the Gini index and *H*, *PG*, and *SPG* have been calculated for fourteen Indian states: Andhra Pradesh, Assam, Bihar, Gujarat, Karnataka, Kerala, Madhya Pradesh, Maharashtra, Orissa, Punjab, Rajasthan, Tamilnadu, Uttar Pradesh, and West Bengal.[22] This analysis reveals a rich variety of experiences at the state level. For example, the rural Gini went up for India as a whole in 1994–5 (51st Round), but the rural Gini actually fell at the state level in Andhra Pradesh, Madhya Pradesh, Orissa, Punjab, Tamilnadu, and West Bengal. The aggregate rural Gini fell in 1995–6 (52nd Round), while the rural Gini rose in Assam, Bihar, Kerala, Madhya Pradesh, Orissa, and Uttar Pradesh. Likewise, the rural headcount ratio has been reduced sharply in Andhra Pradesh and Punjab. In contrast, poverty has worsened in states such as Assam, and its incidence remains disturbingly high in a populous state such as Bihar.

Some states that have had high rates of economic growth and enjoy high per-capita consumption also show low inequality (and poverty levels) compared to states that are lagging behind. For example, the rural Gini for Bihar was 31.65 in the 13th Round (1957–8) and had deteriorated to 38.9 by the 52nd Round (1995–6). Bihar has also had low rates of economic growth and is among the poorest states in India. On the other hand, in Punjab, the richest state[23] in the country, the rural Gini coefficient dropped from 32.2 to 24.4 over the same time period, with poverty falling sharply. Thus, too much inequality seems to be an impediment to economic growth in this case. In specific situations, the cause and effect could work either way. Not only can more equality and less poverty be good for growth, but also high growth may lead to more equality and less poverty. To illuminate the behaviour of inequality at the level of states as a group, a number of panel regressions have been run relating rural and urban Ginis to a host of variables. The best results are as follows:

GINIR =	0.00528*time	+ 0.339*HR	+ 0.2569*RMCR	+ 0.00125*RMCR2
	(3.2752)	(16.1379)	(3.638)	(1.8459)

GINIU =	0.00518*time	+ 0.3434*HU	+ 0.4267*RMCU	− 0.00111*RMCU2
	(3.543)	(16.1367)	(9.076)	(−3.359)

where GINIR, GINIU, HR, HU, RMCR, RMCU, RMCR2, RMCU2 are, respectively, the rural Gini, the urban Gini, the rural headcount ratio, the urban headcount ratio, rural real mean consumption, urban real mean consumption; the square of the

---

[22] The detailed results are not reported here to conserve space. However, they are available from the author.
[23] As a matter of fact, Punjab has a better track record in poverty reduction and mean consumption than even the welfare-oriented states with long periods of socialist rule such as Kerala and West Bengal.

rural real mean consumption, and the square of the urban real mean consumption. The *t*-values (in parentheses) indicate that all coefficients are significant at at least 5 per cent. The random effects model is rejected in favour of the fixed effects model in both cases. In both sectors, inequality has a tendency to rise over time, and this tends to be accompanied by a rise in poverty. In the rural sector, inequality rises monotonically with mean consumption, whereas in the urban sector it may fall after a very large value of real mean consumption is reached.[24] Furthermore, whereas the coefficients on poverty and time are comparable for the two sectors, the coefficient on real consumption is much higher in the urban sector. This underscores our finding that urban growth has been more disequalizing than rural growth. Overall, in the Indian context, there is reason to view growth as tending to increase inequality.

Given these differences among states, it is pertinent to inquire whether there is a long-term convergence in the performance of the states. As a first step in addressing this important question, Figs. 12.4 and 12.5 report the time paths of the coefficients of the cross-state variations of rural and urban inequality and poverty. In neither sector is there a tendency for this diversity to diminish. Indeed, with the onset of reforms, the divergence among states in respect of the incidence of urban and, to a greater extent, rural poverty seems to have increased. To assess formally the relative dynamics of the different states, two modern tests of convergence (the ranks test and the levels test) were carried out.

The Kendall index of rank concordance was computed to track the mobility of the states in respect of real mean consumption, the Gini coefficient, and *H* (see Boyle and McCarthy 1997; and Jha *et al.* 1999*a,b*). Defining a coefficient of concordance,

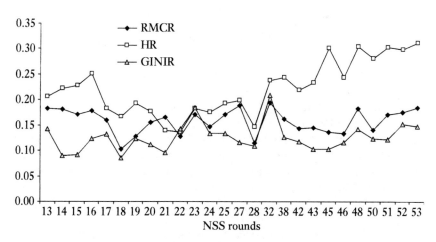

Figure 12.4. *Evolution over time of the coefficients of variation in rural mean consumption, inequality, and poverty across Indian states*

---

[24] This follows from the small value of the coefficient of RMCU2 in comparison to that for RMCU.

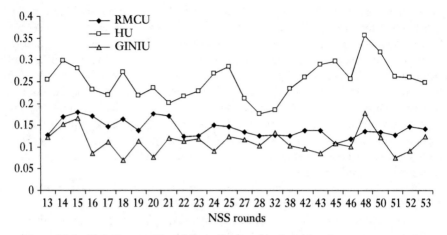

Figure 12.5. *Evolution over time of the coefficients of variation in urban mean consumption, inequality, and poverty across Indian states*

W, as an index of the divergence of the actual agreement of ranks from the maximum possible (perfect) agreement, W is calculated as

$$W = s/\{(1/12)(k^2)N(N^2 - 1)\},$$

where $s =$ the sum of the squares of the observed deviations from the means of R_j (the sums of the ranks obtained by a particular state in different years), that is,

$$s = \left[\sum_j R_j - mean(R_j)\right]^2,$$

where $mean(R_j)$ is the mean of R_j, N is the total number of states, and k is the number of years.

The maximum possible sum of squared deviations is $(1/12)k^2(N^3 - N)$. W varies between 0 and 1 and is computed for the first two sets of rankings (that is, the first 2 years), then for the first 3 years, and so on, until all the years are covered, thus charting the mobility of rankings over time. The probability associated with the occurrence under H_0 (rankings are unrelated to each other) of any value as large as an observed W is determined by computing χ^2 as

$$\chi^2 = s[(1/12)kN(N+1)] = k(N-1)W$$

with $N-1$ degrees of freedom. Jha (2000) presents the results of this test for the rural and urban sectors. In the rural sector the critical value of χ^2 (at 5 per cent) exceeds the computed value only for the first entry for the Gini coefficient. In the urban sector this happens for the first two entries for the Gini. In all other cases, the null hypothesis of no agreements among the ranks is rejected. Hence, by and large, there has been remarkable stability in ranks across these states in regards to these critical welfare-determining variables. The Kendall test statistics for the reform period are reported in Table 12.10 for the rural and urban sectors. Rank convergence obtains in urban mean consumption for some years, but not for other variables.

States may not converge in ranks, but may do so in levels. To check this, the levels test of Evans and Karras (1996), an improvement upon the standard (β-type) tests of convergence, was carried out. This test involves two steps. Consider y_t, the log of any variable of interest. The first step consists in running the following ordinary least squares (OLS) regression:

$$\Delta(y_{nt} - \bar{y}_t) = \delta_n + \rho_n(y_{n,t-1} - \bar{y}_{t-1}) + \sum_{i=1}^{p} \varphi_{ni} \Delta(y_{n,t-i} - \bar{y}_{t-i}) + u_{nt},$$

where n indexes states, and a bar (–) over a variable indicates mean value. ρ_n will be negative if the states converge, 0 otherwise. The φ's are parameters such that all roots of $\Sigma_i \varphi_{ni} L^i$ lie outside the unit circle. Use the standard error of each regression, $\hat{\sigma}_n$, to compute the normalized series:

$$\hat{z}_{nt} \equiv (y_{nt} - \bar{y}_t)/\hat{\sigma}_n.$$

The second step entails using OLS to obtain the estimate, $\hat{\rho}$, and its t-ratio, $\tau(\hat{\rho})$, by estimating

$$\Delta \hat{z}_{nt} = \hat{\delta}_n + \rho \, \hat{z}_{n,t-1} + \sum_{i=1}^{p} \varphi_{ni} \Delta \hat{z}_{n,t-i} + \hat{u}_{nt},$$

Table 12.10. *Rank concordance among states during the reform period (first year, 1991–2)*

Number of rounds	Chi square			
	Gini	H	SPG	Mean consumption
Rural				
2	22.63	24.46	21.97*	23.31
3	34.50	36.94	25.78	35.23
4	43.86	39.69	33.96	36.43
5	37.98	43.88	44.66	29.14
6	37.45	44.01	45.98	32.01
Urban				
2	22.11*	23.31	23.80	22.57*
3	33.51	35.27	36.24	23.57
4	39.00	39.74	40.10	22.66*
5	45.71	48.47	48.60	27.99
6	45.72	49.03	48.06	22.45*

Note: An asterisk (*) indicates acceptance of the null hypothesis at 5%.
Source: See text.

Table 12.11. *Convergence tests in levels*

	RH	RG	RC	UH	UG	UC
Andhra Pradesh	−1.4	−2.12	−2.29	−2.9	−1.9	−2.2
Assam	−1.28	−2.15	−1.83	−2.6	−4.4	−0.21
Bihar	−0.48	−1.39	−1.82	−1.7	0.19	−3.4
Gujarat	−2.26	−2.22	−1.27	−2.9	−2.2	−2.2
Karnataka	−1.72	−3.28	−2.58	−1.1	−2.3	−1.7
Kerala	0.83	−3.06	−1.27	0.05	−2.9	−0.5
Madhya Pradesh	−0.58	−4.3	−1.9	−2.7	−4.2	−4.2
Maharashtra	−2.49	−1.67	−1.4	−2.02	−3.5	−1.9
Orissa	1.42	−2.81	−3.5	−1.7	−4	−1.3
Punjab	−0.37	−1.65	−0.59	−1.6	−1.9	−2.2
Rajasthan	−3.2	−1.59	−4.9	−2.4	−3	−2.2
Tamilnadu	−2.84	−2.47	−2.4	−3.2	−3	−3.9
Uttar Pradesh	−1.15	−2.99	−1.5	−2.2	−2.3	−2.2
West Bengal	−2.06	−2.22	−1.8	−0.49	−1.9	−0.48
t-stat on rho from panel	−3.1	−5.5	−5.4	−4.49	−6.23	−4.87
F-value	3.47	6.97	5.78	5.03	9.06	5.94

Notes: Individual entries denote *t*-values in OLS regression. In each case, the panel *t*-statistic is significant, denoting convergence, and the *F*-value is greater than the critical value, denoting conditional convergence. RH, RG, RC = rural headcount ratio, rural Gini, and rural mean consumption, respectively. UH,UG,UC = urban headcount ratio, urban Gini, and urban real mean consumption, respectively.

Source: See text.

as a panel for $n = 1, 2, \ldots, N$ (states) and $t = 1, 2, \ldots, T$ (time), with $\hat{\delta}_n \equiv \delta_n/\hat{\sigma}_n$ and $\hat{u}_{nt} \equiv u_{nt}/\hat{\sigma}_n$. If $\tau(\hat{\rho})$ exceeds a specified value, one can reject H_0: $\forall n \rho_n = 0$ in favour of H_A: $\forall n \rho_n > 0$. In case H_A is accepted, there is convergence in levels. If H_0 can be rejected, calculate the *F*-ratio:

$$\phi(\hat{\delta}) = \frac{1}{(N-1)} \sum_{n=1}^{N} [\tau(\hat{\delta}_n)]^2.$$

$\tau(\hat{\delta}_n)$ is the *t*-ratio of the estimator of δ_n obtained from the OLS regression for state *n*. If $\phi(\hat{\delta})$ exceeds an appropriately chosen critical value, convergence is conditional. If not, convergence may be absolute. In our case, as Table 12.11 indicates, convergence in each of the categories of poverty, inequality, and mean consumption in both the rural and urban sectors is conditional,[25] and therefore weak. These findings suggest that the ranks of states with respect to indicators of inequality, poverty, and mean consumption are unlikely to change significantly over time. Moreover, they suggest also there is only weak convergence in the levels of the relevant variables. The results of the two convergence tests, therefore, reinforce each other and are in consonance with the

[25] This implies that the values for any state gravitate towards their own respective means rather than the means for all states. For a formal definition of conditional and absolute convergence, see Evans and Karras (1996: 252). Conditional convergence is consistent with the finding of Datt and Ravallion (1998) that 'initial conditions' are important in the evolution of poverty in the states.

results on the behaviour of coefficients of variation. This rising regional inequality is now a matter of concern. Reducing interstate disparities has been an important objective of government policy. The 5-year plans have used public investment and industrial licensing to promote balanced regional development. Transfers from the central government to state governments under both the capital and the current categories through the finance commission and the planning commission are overwhelmingly equalizing in nature. Thus, the 10th Finance Commission (Government of India 1994), the recommendations of which guided federal transfers between 1995 and 2000, advocated the following weight structure for the devolution formula: 20 per cent on the basis of the population of 1971 and 60 per cent on the basis of the inverse of the distance between the per capita income of the state in question from the mean per capita income.[26] With the onset of market-oriented economic reforms, government transfers and investments began to play a diminished role in the economic activity of states, so that regional disparities, which exist because of divergent economic conditions among the various states of India, are exacerbated.

12.5. TENTATIVE CONCLUSIONS

We go back now to the theme of this chapter. Have the economic reforms reduced inequality and poverty in the Indian economy? An answer to this vexed question is not easy, since India has been a late and slow reformer. On the basis of a study of the data up to 1997 the following general statements can be made.

In both the rural and the urban sectors, at the all-India level inequality was higher post-reform than it was at the time of the crisis. Since the Gini coefficient for the urban sector is always higher than that for the rural sector, and since the rapid economic growth of the 1990s implied a shift in the locus of growth from the rural to the urban sector, the reform process was been accompanied by an increase in overall inequality. This rise in inequality is the result of a shift in the distribution of income from wages to profits, a drop in the rate of labour absorption, and rapid growth of the FIRE sector. This has increased the demand and, therefore, the remuneration of skilled labour and specialized factors of production. However, since the reforms have been gradual, and partial and labour still enjoys considerable security of tenure, this deterioration in inequality has been mild compared to of the transition economies or other developing countries.

Poverty rose in the immediate aftermath of the reforms. Growth picked up, but the level of rural poverty remained stubborn (partially because of higher inequality and stagnation in the agricultural real wage), while urban poverty declined moderately. The decline in the crucial area of rural poverty was lower than that[27] during the 1980s and quite unsteady. Rural poverty actually rose in 1995–6, and urban poverty rose in 1997. Gains in real mean consumption were higher in the urban than in the rural sector.

---

[26] The remainder of the weights was for area, index of infrastructure, and tax effort.

[27] The smaller decline in poverty despite higher growth in the 1990s relative to the 1980s was due to a drop in the elasticity of poverty measures with respect to growth. This drop was higher for rural poverty.

Movements in aggregate inequality (and poverty) measures are actually the outcome of the movements in the measures in opposite directions in some states. Indeed, the dispersion of poverty, inequality, and mean consumption has generally increased with the reforms. There is no rank convergence among states in respect of inequality and poverty and only conditional convergence in levels. Thus, there is reason to be concerned about the widening of regional inequality. Overall, growth seems to have increased inequality. In some cases, inequality has constrained growth as states with high Gini coefficients recorded a poor growth performance. This reinforces the view that rapid economic growth remains the best bet for reducing India's immense problems of inequality and poverty. Along with this, efforts must be made to see that the distribution of consumption does not become further skewed. This requires several steps. First, the composition of growth needs to be altered to encourage agricultural as opposed to non-agricultural growth, especially in the poorest areas (Ravallion and Datt 1999). In addition, widespread tax reform is necessary to increase tax revenues, effect more redistribution, and offer support for more rapid economic growth that would enable greater provision for public expenditure for anti-poverty programmes. Also, the efficiency of public expenditure and of the social safety net should be improved. This would call for policies that sustain and enhance social expenditure levels and the more effective targeting of subsidies geared towards the poor. Last, but not the least, is the design of a good social sector policy framework. Several factors are involved, and only a few are mentioned hereafter.

First, as argued in Ferreira et al. (1999) and in Chapter 11, emphasized, society must develop lasting, flexible organizations to protect the poor from the effects of macroeconomic shocks. Second, appropriate safety nets, especially workfare programmes that are well targeted and involve appropriate transfer and credit programmes, need to be developed (Lipton and Ravallion 1995). The relevant expenditures should be protected in real terms even when macroeconomic adjustments must be made. Third, it is important to build up pressure groups of the poor to ensure that enough funds are made available for social programmes and that those in charge of these expenditures are accountable to the people (Gaiha and Kulkarni 1998). Decision-making should be appropriately decentralized to ensure the smooth functioning of the programmes.[28]

REFERENCES

Boadway, R., I. Horiba, and R. Jha (1999). The provision of public services by government-funded decentralized agencies. *Public Choice* 100(3–4), 157–84.

Boyle, G., and T. McCarthy (1997). A simple measure of β convergence. *Oxford Bulletin of Economics and Statistics* 59(2), 257–64.

Cornia, G. A., R. Jolly, and F. Stewart (eds.) (1987). *Adjustment with a Human Face: Protecting the Vulnerable and Promoting Growth*. Clarendon Press: Oxford.

[28] Boadway et al. (1999) discuss some problems in the appropriate design of such institutions.

Dandekar, V. M. (1996). *The Indian Economy: 1947–92: Population, Poverty and Employment*, Vol. 2. Sage Publications: New Delhi.

Datt, G., and M. Ravallion (1997). Macroeconomic crises and poverty monitoring: A case study of India. *Review of Development Economics* 1(2), 135–52.

—— and M. Ravallion (1998). Why have some Indian states done better than others at reducing rural poverty? *Economica* 65(1), 17–38.

Deaton, A., and C. Paxson (1998). Economies of scale, household size and the demand for food. *Journal of Political Economy* 106(5), 897–930.

Deininger, K., and L. Squire (1997). Economic growth and income inequality: Re-examining the links. *Finance and Development*, March.

Evans, P., and G. Karras (1996). Convergence revisited. *Journal of Monetary Economics* 37(2), 249–65.

Ferreira, F., G. Prennushi, and M. Ravallion (1999). Protecting the poor from macroeconomic shocks: An agenda for action in a crisis and beyond. Mimeo, World Bank: Washington, DC.

Fishlow, A. (1995). Inequality, poverty and growth: Where do we stand? Paper presented at the Annual Conference on Development Economics. World Bank: Washington, DC.

Foster, J., J. Greer, and E. Thorbecke (1984). A class of decomposable poverty measures. *Econometrica* 52(3), 761–5.

Gaiha, R. (1991). Poverty alleviation programmes in rural India: An assessment. *Development and Change* 22(1), 117–54.

—— (1998). Food prices and income in India. *Canadian Journal of Development Studies* 20(1), 31–58.

—— and V. Kulkarni (1998). Is growth central to poverty alleviation in India? *Journal of International Affairs* 52(1), 145–80.

—— P. Kaushik, and V. Kulkarni (1998). Jawahar rozgar yojana, panchayats and the rural poor in India. *Asian Survey* 38(10), 928–49.

Ghose, S., and N. Bhattacharya (1994). Effect of reference period on engel elasticities of clothings and other items. *Sarvekshana* 17(3), 35–9.

Government of India (1955). Technical records of sample design, instructions to field workers. National Sample Survey, Ninth Round 27. Government of India: New Delhi.

—— (1994). Report of the Tenth Finance Commission. Ministry of Finance: New Delhi.

—— (1996a). Employment and unemployment in India, 1993–4. National Sample Survey Reports 409, Government of India: New Delhi.

—— (1996b). Level and pattern of consumer expenditure: 5th quinquennial survey (50th Round). National Sample Survey Reports 402. May, Government of India: New Delhi.

Gupta, S. (1995). Economic reform and its impact on the poor. *Economic and Political Weekly* 1(June), 295–313.

Hirway, I., and P. Terhal (1994). *Towards Employment Guarantee in India*. Sage Publications: New Delhi.

Howes, S., and J. Lanjouw (1998). Does sample design matter for poverty rate comparisons? *Review of Income and Wealth* 44(1), 99–109.

Jha, R. (1999). India's public finances: Current position and some suggested reforms. In K. Parikh (ed.), *India Development Report 1999–2000*. Oxford University Press: New Delhi.

—— (2000). Reducing poverty and inequality in India: Has liberalization helped? WIDER Working Paper 204, UNU/WIDER: Helsinki.

—— and B. Sahni (1993). *Industrial Efficiency: An Indian Perspective*. Wiley Eastern: New Delhi.

—— M. Mohanty, S. Chatterjee, and P. Chitkara (1999a). Tax efficiency in selected Indian states. *Empirical Economics* 24(4), 641–54.

Jha, R., K. V. Murthy, H. Nagarajan, and A. Seth (1999*b*). Real consumption levels and the public distribution system in India. *Economic and Political Weekly* 34(15), 919–27.

Joshi, V., and I. Little (1996). *India's Economic Reforms: 1991–2001*. Oxford University Press: New Delhi.

Kakwani, N. (1980). On a class of poverty measures. *Econometrica* 48(2), 437–46.

Lipton, M., and M. Ravallion (1995). Poverty and policy. In J. Behrman and T. Srinivasan (eds.), *Handbook of Development Economics Vol. III*. North Holland: Amsterdam.

Minhas, B. S. (1988). Validation of large-scale sample survey data: case of NSS estimates of household consumption expenditure. *Sankhya* 50B(3), 279–326.

——(1991). On estimating the inadequacy of energy intakes: revealed food consumption behaviour versus nutritional norms, nutritional status of indian people in 1983. *Journal of Development Studies* 28(1), 1–38.

Mundle, S., and V. Tulasidhar (1998). *Adjustment and Distribution: The Indian Experience*. Asian Development Bank: Manila.

Murthy, M. N., and A. S. Roy (1975). Development of the sample design of the Indian national sample survey during its first twenty-five rounds. *Sankhya* 37C(1), 1–42.

Narasimham, M. (1992). *Report of the Committee on the Financial System*. Nabhi Publications: New Delhi.

Paul, S. (1998). The performance of the integrated rural development programme in India: An assessment. *The Developing Economies* 36(2), 117–31.

Ravallion, M. (1998). Does aggregation hide the harmful effects of inequality on growth? *Economics Letters* 61(1), 73–7.

—— and G. Datt (1996). How important to india's poor is the sectoral composition of economic growth? *World Bank Economic Review* 10(1), 1–25.

—— and —— (1999). When is growth pro-poor?: Evidence from the diverse experiences of indian states. Mimeo, World Bank: Washington, DC.

Ray, S. N., and M. G. Bhattacharya (1992). An appraisal of the methodologies and data issues relating to poverty analysis. In G. K. Kadekodi and G. V. S. N. Murthy (eds.), *Poverty in India: Data Base Issues*. Vikas Publishing House: New Delhi.

Reserve Bank of India (1998). *Handbook of Statistics on the Indian Economy*. Reserve Bank of India: Mumbai.

Sen, A. (2000). Estimates of consumer expenditure and its distribution—statistical priorities after NSS 55th round. *Economic and Political Weekly* 4(December), 499–518.

Subramanian, S., and A. Deaton (1996). The demand for food and calories. *Journal of Political Economy* 104(11), 133–62.

Tendulkar, S., and L. Jain (1995). Economic reforms and poverty. *Economic and Political Weekly* 1(June), 373–7.

Villasenor, J., and B. C. Arnold (1989). Elliptical Lorenz curves. *Journal of Econometrics* 40(2), 327–38.

Visaria, P. (2000). Alternative estimates of poverty in India. *Economic Times* 29(June).

World Bank (1996). *India: Five Years of Stabilization and Reform and the Challenges Ahead*. World Bank: Washington, DC.

13

Factor Shares and Resource Booms: Accounting for the Evolution of Venezuelan Inequality

FRANCISCO RODRÍGUEZ

13.1. INTRODUCTION

Arguably, Venezuela is the greatest missed opportunity for development of the post-Second World War period. From 1963 to 1996, Venezuela sold $329 billion of fuel exports to the world, or $20,420 per person.[1] However, by 1997 Venezuela's gross domestic product (GDP) per capita was 8 per cent lower than it had been in 1963. In 1963, Venezuela boasted a democratic political system with stable transitions in government administration and civil and political rights, which were the envy of any other Latin American country. But during the 1990s the system barely survived two military coup attempts, and polls showed that half of Venezuelans had no confidence in the democratic system.[2]

To this economic and political debacle, we will argue, a third dimension must be added: the distributive one. We will show that inequality has significantly worsened during the past 27 years. In particular, the worsening has taken the form not of higher inequality among workers, but of higher inequality between those who own and those who do not own capital. Factor shares have moved decisively against labour during the last three decades, resulting in a transfer of approximately 15 per cent of GDP from labour to capital income. The disappointing performance of the country in terms of aggregate economic indicators hides the fact that an average worker today is roughly half as well off in terms of income as an average worker in 1970. Put together, the macroeconomic, political, and distributive failures make Venezuela one of the great economic and social disasters of the post-war period.

In what follows, we will examine several possible explanations for this change in income inequality. We start by documenting it in Section 13.2. We follow up in

The author thanks Daniel Ortega for excellent research assistance, as well as Luis Marcano, Sanjay Reddy, Giovanni Andrea Cornia, and participants at workshops in Helsinki and the Venezuelan Central Bank for helpful comments. He is also grateful to World Institute for Development Economics Research (WIDER) for financial support. All errors remain his (ir)responsibility.

[1] Evaluated at constant 1995 dollars.   [2] *El Nacional*, 25 October 1988.

Section 13.3 with an attempt to explain the evolution of factor shares on the basis of the evolution in human and physical capital accumulation. Alternative influences on factor shares are examined in Section 13.4. Section 13.5 then discusses in depth the loss of political power by the Venezuelan labour movement and the relationship of this with our main hypothesis. Section 13.6 concludes.

The main thrust of our explanation is as follows: the increase in Venezuela's income inequality can to a great extent be traced back to the decline in the country's physical capital stock and its rigid production processes. Rigid production processes imply low substitutability among factors of production and therefore make it possible for a decline in the physical capital stock leading to increases in the return to capital large enough to produce a substantial rise in capital's share of GDP. In other words, Venezuela's economic collapse, occurring within the context of a rigid production structure, has produced the country's distributive collapse. However, we also find that policies like trade liberalization, contractionary macro policies, and capital account convertibility have made a far from negligible additional contribution to the worsening of Venezuela's income distribution.

13.2. WHAT THE DATA SAY

Figure 13.1 shows the Gini coefficient for Venezuela, calculated from data of the biannual household survey conducted by the Oficina Central de Estadística e Informática (OCEI) from 1971 to 1997.[3] As the questions of this survey pertain only to wage income, this Gini coefficient is purely an index of wage inequality, and it includes no estimate of the contribution to overall inequality of disparities in capital income.

Figure 13.1 shows a Gini coefficient that is relatively trendless over the long run. There appears to be a fall in inequality during the 1970s, a rise during the early 1980s, a subsequent fall during the late 1980s, and a rise during the 1990s. The substantial year-to-year variations in the Gini, however, suggest caution in the search for explanations to these changes.[4] Perhaps the only conclusion that can be drawn from Fig. 13.1 is that there seems to be no major long-run shifts in the distribution of income among workers.

Starting in 1994, the OCEI survey included questions regarding capital income. However, capital income appears to be grossly underestimated in the responses.

---

[3] From 1971 to 1978 the source is UN (1981). For later years the source is our direct calculations using Venezuelan Households Survey data. Although other estimates exist for some years after 1978, all are based on tables from the households survey. An exception is Marcano and Ruprah (1999), whose calculations are similar to ours.

[4] If one looks long enough at Fig. 13.1, one can start to see a tendency for inequality to rise over time, particularly given the fact that the 1997 observation (47.76) is higher than the values for any other year. However, this value must be interpreted with utmost caution, as there were important changes in the design of the survey in 1994 that were also accompanied by a jump of 6.1 points in the Gini coefficient. The key changes were adoption of clustering based on the 1990 census, addition of a large number of new questions, and a substantial reduction in the sample size. See Marcano and Ruprah (1999) for a description of these changes.

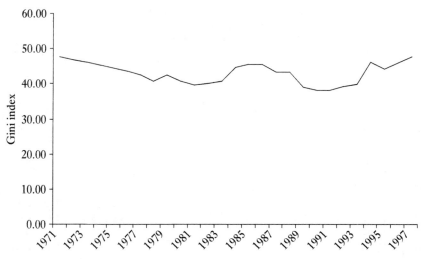

Figure 13.1. *Gini coefficient in labour incomes*

The majority of individuals report very small amounts of capital income. Indeed, if one were to infer from the answers to these surveys the share of capital income in gross national product (GNP), one would find a capital share of 6.6 per cent, substantially lower than the 63 per cent figure in national income statistics. It is apparent that there is a systematic bias towards underreporting income from capital, which may be related to the widespread evasion of capital income taxes in Venezuela or with the difficulties in assessing the income of very wealthy individuals. In Table 13.1, we have calculated the Gini coefficients using the proportion of capital income derived from national accounts statistics to scale up capital income in the OCEI survey responses. The result is a substantially higher Gini coefficient than that which is derived only from labour income: it oscillates between 0.62 and 0.65. Kakwani (1980) decompositions for the years for which data on capital income are available (see Table 13.1) show that the main source of this inequality is a substantial concentration of capital income, the concentration coefficient on capital income being above 0.8.

As discussed above, the distribution of labour income seems almost trendless over the period of study. Venezuela's factorial distribution of income, however, tells another story. Figure 13.2 illustrates the evolution of Venezuela's capital share from 1970 to 1996. The data show a marked increase from the 1970s to the 1980s, accompanied by a sharp jump in 1996, the last year for which there are available data. This jump, to 77.9 per cent, would mean that Venezuela has the third highest capital share among countries in Latin America (on this see also Chapter 2).[5]

This jump in capital share is striking, because the capital share of GDP in Venezuela is affected by the operating surplus of the state oil enterprise. From the 1970s to the 1990s, there was a steady fall in oil's share of GDP. Aggregate capital share statistics

[5] Behind Paraguay (0.81, 1991) and Peru (0.79, 1991).

Table 13.1. *Gini and concentration coefficients*

	Gini in labour incomes	Gini in total incomes	Concentration coefficient		Gini in total income—assumptions		
			Labour income	Capital income	1	2	3
1971	0.47650				0.59356	0.57881	0.61456
1972	0.46846				0.58977	0.57761	0.61161
1973	0.46042				0.59331	0.58401	0.61708
1974	0.45238				0.58241	0.57551	0.60605
1975	0.44434				0.58304	0.57886	0.60813
1976	0.43630				0.57951	0.57796	0.60552
1977	0.42410				0.58221	0.58463	0.61116
1978	0.40720				0.56838	0.57647	0.60067
1979	0.40044				0.56217	0.57263	0.59492
1980	0.38839				0.55601	0.57060	0.59116
1981	0.38078				0.56229	0.57899	0.59853
1982	0.37253				0.57552	0.59396	0.61277
1983	0.38008				0.57855	0.59459	0.61174
1984	0.41135				0.61585	0.62156	0.63832
1985	0.40569				0.61681	0.62404	0.63906
1986	0.40908				0.62531	0.63141	0.64485
1987	0.39776				0.62434	0.63344	0.64503
1988	0.39998				0.62738	0.63580	0.64553
1989	0.38713				0.61265	0.62501	0.63257
1990	0.38093				0.62568	0.63899	0.64490
1991	0.38416				0.61848	0.63134	0.63522
1992	0.37858				0.61813	0.63244	0.63441
1993	0.37523				0.62491	0.63967	0.63973
1994	0.43162	0.65786	0.28235	0.87815	0.65785	0.65785	0.65586
1995	0.41723	0.64674	0.26064	0.86846	0.64673	0.64673	0.64673
1996	0.43147	0.63377	0.25601	0.85071	0.63377	0.63377	0.63377
1997	0.43811	0.62618	0.26366	0.83436	0.62617	0.62617	0.62617

Source: From 1971 to 1978, the Ginis are from UN (1981), with the data for 1972–5 coming from a linear interpolation. After 1978, the Gini in labour incomes is calculated directly from the OCEI Households Survey (the observations are heads of families). The Gini in total incomes is calculated scaling capital income reported in the 1994–7 surveys so that the fraction of capital income equals capital's share in GDP. The ordering in total incomes is then used to calculate the concentration coefficients in capital and labour incomes. The last three rows are then calculated according to the following assumptions. Assumption 1: Concentration coefficients in capital and labour income take their 1994 values for 1971–93. Assumption 2: The concentration coefficient for capital income falls from 0.95 to 0.88 from 1971 to 1994. Assumption 3: The concentration coefficient for labour income's percentage year-to-year changes is equal to that of the labour Ginis.

should therefore be biased against finding a rise in the capital share. The aggregate capital share may thus be underestimating the rise in Venezuela's capital share. Indeed, Fig. 13.2 shows that the rise in the capital share has been higher in the non-oil economy than in the aggregate economy, indicating a transfer of 11 points of GDP from

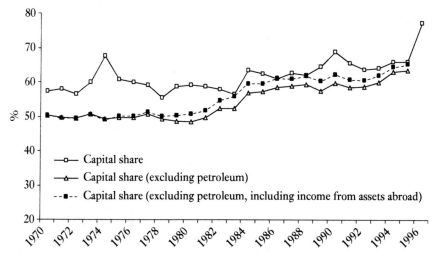

Figure 13.2. *Capital share, 1970–96*

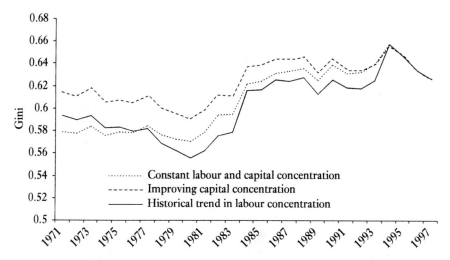

Figure 13.3. *Estimated evolution of Gini coefficient, 1971–97*

labour to capital income between the 1970s and the 1990s. We can use the capital share data to get a rough idea of how the Gini coefficient of total (as opposed to labour) income has evolved in Venezuela since 1971. We do this in Fig. 13.3 and Table 13.1, where we show the evolution of the Gini of total income under three alternative assumptions about the concentration coefficients in capital and labour income. The dotted line shows how income distribution would have evolved if the

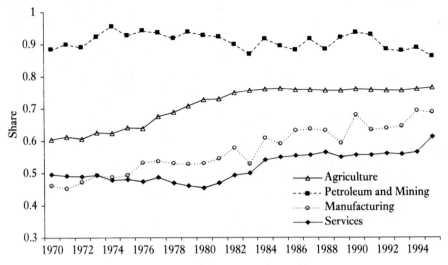

Figure 13.4. *Capital shares by sector, 1970–95*

concentration of capital and labour had been constant from 1971 to 1995. This assumes
that all changes in income distribution are between capital and labour (and not within
these groups). The solid line shows what would have happened if the concentration of
labour income had followed the same trends as the Gini coefficient in labour incomes
from Fig. 13.1.[6] The dashed line shows how income distribution would have evolved
if the concentration of capital had substantially *fallen* during the period of study
(from 0.95 to 0.88). Even under the last optimistic assumption, the deterioration of
income distribution in Venezuela is significant. Indeed, if our calculations are correct,
Venezuela is today one of the most unequal countries in the world, with its 1997 Gini
surpassing that of South Africa (62.3) and Brazil (61.8).

We turn now to a study of the factors that have influenced the distribution of income
between capital and labour. Shifts in the functional distribution of income do not appear
to be a result of sectoral reallocation of resources. Figure 13.4 shows capital shares for
four basic sectors of the Venezuelan economy: agriculture, petroleum and mining,
manufacturing, and services. The upward trend in capital's share of income is present in
all sectors except petroleum and mining (made up almost exclusively of state-owned
enterprises). Curiously, the shift appears to be of roughly the same magnitude among
the sectors, suggesting that it may be the result of economy-wide changes. Indeed,
sectoral reallocations in the Venezuelan economy seem to have contributed, if anything,

---

[6] The concentration coefficient in labour income (used in Fig. 13.3) is based on labour earnings ordered
by rank in the distribution of *total* income, whereas the Gini coefficient in labour incomes (plotted in
Fig. 13.1) orders by rank in the distribution of *labour* income. The solid line in Fig. 13.3 is calculated based
on the assumption that these two share the same movements over time.

Table 13.2. *Manufacturing capital share in large firms*

1960–4	71.1
1965–9	70.4
1970–4	69.0
1975–9	72.1
1980–4	69.8
1985–9	74.5
1990–4	81.2

Source: Rama (1999).

to lowering the capital share, as resources have been moved out of agriculture and into manufacturing.[7]

Another possibility is that rising capital shares may be caused by changes in the form of the ownership of firms. Venezuelan national accounts do not distinguish between corporate and unincorporated (family-owned) enterprises; income from unincorporated enterprises is classified completely as operating surplus. Therefore, shifts of labour from the corporate sector to the unincorporated sector tend to raise the measured capital share even if they have no effect on the real underlying factor distribution of income.

There are two sectoral shifts that could conceivably cause this change in the capital share. One would be a shift from manufacturing and services to agriculture, as the latter is commonly characterized by a higher prevalence of self-ownership. Another would be a shift from the formal to the informal sector, with the informal sector also often characterized by self-employment. Neither of these possible shifts, however, appears to be the underlying cause of changes in the capital share as both the agricultural and informal sectors have declined or remained stable relative to the rest of the economy.[8] Table 13.2 also shows data on the capital share in manufacturing, taken from Rama (1999). The Rama data are based on United Nations Industrial Development Organization's (UNIDO) industrial statistics database, which is put together from plant-level surveys covering relatively large firms, mostly in the formal sector of the economy. Again, even restricted to this sample where self-ownership is nearly absent, we find a consistent rise in capital shares.

Behind this rising capital share is an unprecedented collapse in wage rate that was not accompanied by a fall in the rate of return to capital. Figure 13.5 shows that the wage rate has declined by about 50 per cent over the last 26 years. However, despite

[7] Agriculture tends to display high capital shares because agricultural workers are commonly self-employed, with all their income counting as operating surplus. Venezuelan national accounts statistics do not distinguish the income of corporations from the income of the self-employed.

[8] An alternative way to tackle this issue is by estimating the income of unincorporated enterprises in GDP. We have done this using the coefficients from a regression of capital shares on GDP for ninety-one countries (see Pineda and Rodríguez 1999) and assigning two-thirds of the income of unincorporated enterprises to labour's participation. This calculation gives a similar increase in capital's share, from 0.375 in 1975–80 to 0.458 in 1990–5.

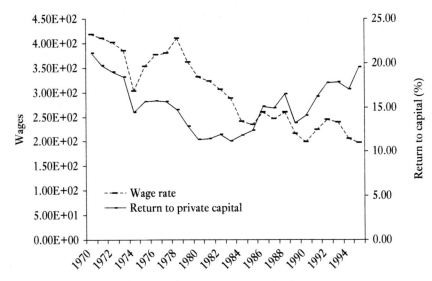

Figure 13.5. *Wages and returns to capital, 1970–95*

substantial swings, the level of the return to capital is roughly the same now as it was at the start of the period.[9]

These data are, furthermore, likely to underestimate the increase in capital's share of income because they do not take into account the income held by Venezuelan nationals in offshore assets. In principle, national accounts statistics on factor income from foreign assets owned by residents should give us an idea of how much capital's total income has risen during the period under study. However, the estimation of net factor income from abroad is often problematic in these statistics, which suffer from gross underreporting. The income on foreign assets reported in GNP statistics is commonly less than 0.5 per cent of GDP.

It is possible to get an alternative estimate of these data through balance of payments statistics. As the current account balance captures the increase in foreign assets held by nationals, we can measure the increase in foreign assets held by *private* nationals as the sum of current account surpluses, plus foreign direct investment, minus the accumulation of publicly held assets (including reserves).[10] Using this procedure, we find that the increase in foreign assets held by Venezuelan nationals was $57.3 billion over the 1970–7 interval. At normal rates of return on international investments, our calculations indicate that the annual income earned by Venezuelans

---

[9] Such a steep fall in the wage rate seems surprising. Did Venezuela not have alternative export industries in which it could have started specializing given low wage rates? Rodríguez and Sachs (1999) have suggested that the wage rates necessary to induce non-traditional exports were substantially lower than equilibrium wages during most of the period under study. The problem is compounded by the fact that the economy's comparative advantage changes over time from more to less capital-intensive production. See Rodríguez and Sachs (1999) for a discussion.

[10] For a discussion of this and other approaches to the estimation of capital flight, see the articles in Lessard and Williamson (1987).

on their holdings of foreign assets in 1997 was \$4.16 billion, or 5 per cent of GDP. In other words, the increase in capital's share of income shown in Fig. 13.2 probably underestimates the actual increase by about 2.5 percentage points of GDP. The capital share inclusive of returns on foreign assets is shown as the broken line in Fig. 13.2.

There is some evidence that the distribution of capital income may itself have become more unequal. Gonzalez and Martínez (1993) have discovered evidence that the concentration of firms increased substantially with trade liberalization in the late 1980s. They find that, in most industries, the number of small and medium firms shrank, and the number of large firms increased substantially. This evidence seems to suggest that income from capital has also become more concentrated.

In the case of the Venezuelan economy, a significant amount of GDP takes the form of oil rents. Therefore, the effective distribution of income may be influenced by what the state does with these rents. The deterioration in the private capital share that we observed above could in principle be offset by a greater progressivity in the distribution of the state's oil rents.

However, this does not seem to have happened in Venezuela. Figure 13.6 shows the evolution of the composition of government spending from 1970 to 1997. The redistributive component of the government budget par excellence is wages and salaries. However, the portion of wages and salaries in the government budget fell from nearly half to less than one-fifth over the period studied. Government purchases of goods and services also fell considerably. The factors that experienced the greatest increase were interest payments on internal and external debt, which rose from just under 2 per cent to over 20 per cent of the government budget, and government subsidies and transfers, which rose from roughly 15 per cent to over 30 per cent. This last component of government

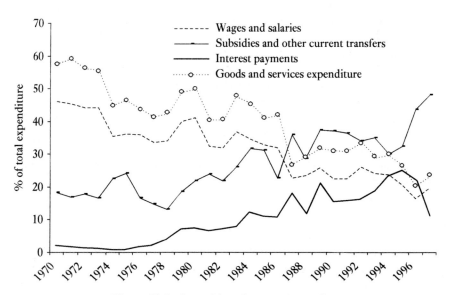

Figure 13.6. *Composition of government spending*

expenditure is made up mainly of subsidies to state and private enterprises. It also includes transfers to social security, but these comprise roughly 1 per cent of government spending.[11] The bulk of subsidies and transfers appears to be taken up by subsidies to state-owned enterprises, government-owned financial institutions, and private enterprise.

In sum, Venezuelan statistics tell a story of a considerably worsening income distribution. They also show that this worsening of income distribution occurred mainly because of a worsening of the distribution between capital and labour.

13.3. FACTOR SHARES, FACTOR PRICES, AND OIL BOOMS

What is behind the trend in the capital share observed in Fig. 13.2? What explains the stable value during the 1970s and the subsequent rise in value during the 1980s? As the capital share is a simple function of the stocks of capital and labour, as well as of their returns, it is natural to divide the above question into two questions: how can we account for the evolution of factor prices? How can we account for the evolution of factor quantities? We attempt to give answers to these questions below.

13.3.1. *The Explanation*

Factor prices

The obvious place to start looking for an understanding of the determination of factor prices is of course the theory of factor markets. According to the theory of competitive factor markets, there is a one-to-one link between factor prices and factor quantities. Relative factor prices should be high when a factor is relatively scarce. This is because the return to capital relative to labour (r/w) reflects the ratio of the marginal products and, given diminishing returns, is an inverse function of the capital–labour ratio (K/L). The higher the amount of capital relative to labour, the lower the equilibrium price of capital relative to labour. As we discuss in more detail below, this relation is not specific to competitive factor markets, but can be generalized to other types of market structures. Figure 13.7 illustrates the intuition for this in a simple diagram. As the capital–labour ratio rises from K_1/L_1 to K_2/L_2, the relative wage rises from w_1/r_1 to w_2/r_2. The greater abundance of capital implies a lower marginal product of capital, which implies a lower rate of return to capital, r.

Can we account for the quantitative magnitude of the movements in capital shares through our approach? To answer this question, note that the capital share can be simply written as

$$\alpha = \frac{rK}{wL + rK} = \frac{1}{1 + \dfrac{wL}{rK}},$$

and is thus related one-to-one with $(w/r)^*(L/K)$. If capital accumulation increases (L/K falls) and (following our argument above) w/r increases, then the movement of factor

---

[11] The author's calculations based on Banco Central de Venezuela (1996: tables VI.5.2 and VI.11.2).

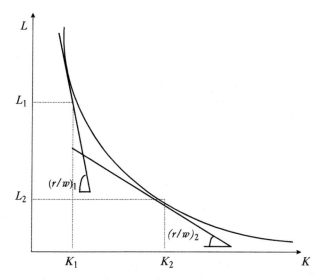

Figure 13.7. *Effects of shifts in capital–labour ratios on relative wages*

shares will depend on the elasticity of substitution between capital and labour. For a Cobb–Douglas specification (where the elasticity of substitution between capital and labour is 1), factor shares are constant and are thus unaffected by capital accumulation. If the elasticity of substitution is greater than 1, then factor prices do not move much with changes in capital–labour ratios, and capital's share is increasing in the capital–labour ratio. If the elasticity of substitution is smaller than 1, then the opposite occurs: factor prices change so much in response to a shift in capital–labour ratios that an increase in the capital stock leads to a fall in capital shares. It thus appears that whether we can account for the movement in capital shares conditional on movements in relative factor quantities depends on the value of the elasticity of substitution between capital and labour.

In the appendix to Rodríguez (2000), we provide a discussion of the empirical evidence relating to the elasticity of substitution between capital and labour in Venezuela. We argue that there is good reason to believe that the elasticity of substitution between capital and labour in Venezuela is substantially below 1, and we estimate a value of $\sigma = 0.57$ using data from Venezuela's *Encuesta Industrial*. However, we emphasize that we can only provide rather crude estimates and that a wide confidence interval should be associated with this estimate.

If we accept that $\sigma < 1$, is Venezuela's pattern of capital shares consistent with the evolution of capital–labour ratios? The answer appears to be 'no', as the capital–labour ratio grew in Venezuela during the 1970s, but has fallen since then. Thus, there should have been a drop in capital's share during the 1970s of approximately the same magnitude as the subsequent rise: something we do not observe.

Figure 13.8 shows more formally why this explanation is unlikely to account for the shifts in factor shares observed in Venezuela during the period under study. It shows

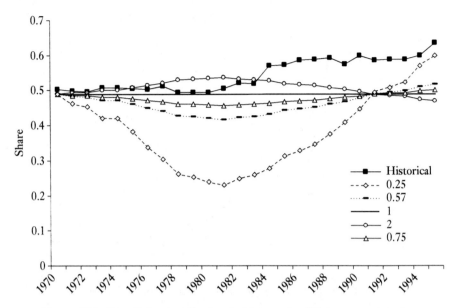

Figure 13.8. *Historical and predicted capital share, under different assumptions about the elasticity of substitution between capital and labour, 1970–95*

the implied capital shares from a constant elasticity of substitution (CES) production function based on the assumption that the relative wage is equal to the relative marginal products and given the capital–labour ratios in Fig. 13.7. As shown in Fig. 13.8, which plots the capital shares implied by five different possible values for the elasticity of substitution between capital and labour, there is a large unexplained residual in factor shares no matter what the assumed elasticity is. In particular, as we have argued above, it is likely that the value of σ for Venezuela is considerably less than 1. For three possible values consistent with this hypothesis plotted in Fig. 13.8 ($\sigma = 0.25$, $\sigma = 0.57$, and $\sigma = 0.75$), including our preferred estimate, capital–labour ratios implied a fall in the capital share that did not occur during the 1970s.

However, it is likely that the underlying data on the capital stock per worker do not capture adequately the factor ratios relevant for analysing capital shares. Table 13.3, on the evolution of human capital (as measured by mean years of schooling between 1960 and 1990), shows that the latter progressed from 2.53 years in 1960 to 4.89 years in 1990. In particular, they seem to have peaked at 5.37 years in 1985 and to have begun to fall subsequently.

These data are consistent with those on primary and secondary school enrolments. Primary school enrolment, which had been rising steadily during the 1980s, fell from a peak of 97 per cent in 1986, to 91 per cent by 1996. Persistence to grade five, which had peaked at 91 per cent in 1989, had fallen to 89 per cent by 1995.[12] If these data

---

[12] Data from World Bank (1999).

Table 13.3. *Mean years of schooling, 1960–90*

	Total	Male	Female
1960	2.53	2.9	2.05
1965	2.63	3.03	2.22
1970	2.92	3.24	2.60
1975	3.76	4.04	3.49
1980	4.93	5.20	4.65
1985	5.36	5.62	5.10
1990	4.89	5.00	4.77

Source: Barro and Lee (1993) with updates provided by Robert Barro.

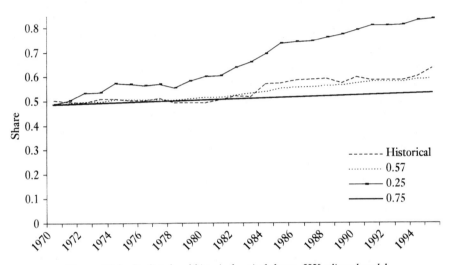

Figure 13.9. *Predicted and historical capital shares, HK adjusted model*

capture correctly the changes in Venezuelan human capital, they suggest that the increase in the capital–labour ratio from 1970 to the early 1980s may not adequately capture the ratio of physical to human capital.

In turn, the ratio of physical to human capital declined steadily from 1970 to 1995 (Rodriquez 2000). This suggests that we may wish to reassess whether the simple facts of capital accumulation can explain what has occurred with capital shares.

Figure 13.9 shows the predicted and historical capital shares for three different values of the elasticity of substitution when the relevant ratio of inputs is that of physical to human capital. For a value of $\sigma = 0.57$, the fit of the model is striking, with the existing ratios of physical to human capital able to account for a substantial part of the observed variation in capital shares.

What does Fig. 13.9 establish? To us, it shows that we can explain the evolution of factor shares *conditional on the evolution of the human-to-physical capital ratio* with an elasticity of substitution of roughly one-half. It therefore leaves open the interesting question of how to account for the evolution of the ratio of human to physical capital, a question that we will address below. But, first, we discuss some criticisms of our approach.

Alternative institutional structures

Several reasonable objections can be levelled at the approach sketched above. Perhaps the first one to jump to mind is the critique of the implicit assumption of competitive factor markets, an assumption that seems to be particularly at odds with much of Venezuelan reality. The active participation of unions and business federations in the bargaining process over wages at the national and firm level and the existence of significant market imperfections and of large monopolistic industrial groups, as well as the significant amount of government regulation in the labour and financial markets during the period studied, would seem to contradict a theory that requires the operation of well-functioning competitive factor markets.

However, our approach is not invalidated by the existence of non-competitive product markets. Our assumption that factor returns reflect marginal products will be true when *factor* markets are competitive, but will not be affected by the degree of competition in product markets. Monopolistic and oligopolistic groups in Venezuelan product markets are a reality, but whether these groups bear substantial market power in factor markets is more questionable, given the existence of a highly competitive informal sector, as well as the importance of migration flows from/to other Latin American countries in response to wage differentials.

Competitive factor markets are a sufficient condition for our approach to be valid, but not a necessary one. What is crucial for our calculations is that the ratio of factor prices be proportionate to the ratio of factor quantities. This is true when there exist competitive factor markets, but is true under alternative market structures also. In particular, wages are equal to the value of marginal products whenever wages are derived from the labour demand curve. Figure 13.10(a) shows that this is the situation in the classical case of competitive factor markets. But Fig. 13.10(b) shows that it is also the situation in an alternative to a competitive theory of factor markets, namely, the theory of monopoly. If wages are set by a monopoly union, then the union will restrict the amount of available labour so as to increase the average wage. It will drive firms to the level *on the labour demand curve* where profits are maximized. Therefore, both wages and employment can be read off the labour demand curve, and wages will reflect marginal products.

Another theory of labour demand—that of monopsony markets, where one large firm manipulates its level of demand to lower the level of wages—would appear to be more problematic for our hypothesis. This case is shown in Fig. 13.10(c), where it is clear that under monopsony the equilibrium wages and quantities cannot be assumed to lie on the demand curve, because the firm has the power to restrict demand so as to push wages to the level on the supply curve that is consistent with profit maximization. However, it can be established that, for the case of a monopsonistic labour market and an isoleastic labour

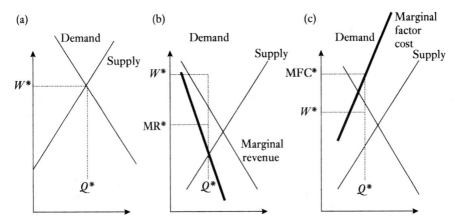

Figure 13.10. *Alternative market structures for the labour market: (a) perfect competition;*
(b) monopoly union; (c) monopsony firm

supply curve, observed factor shares will still reflect the ratio of marginal products.[13] The level of wages will be lower than in the competitive case, but only by a factor of proportionality. Factor shares will also be lower, but the effect of an increase in factor ratios on capital shares will be the same, and our calculations above will remain valid.

A further objection that could be posed against our analysis is that it assumes away institutional influences on the capital share, expressing it purely as the result of market interactions. However, we have not argued in this section that the evolution of capital shares can be totally understood as the outcome of market processes; we have only argued that it can be so understood conditional on existing factor ratios. We will argue that institutional and political factors have an important role in the determination of factor ratios. The objection is, however, correct in that we assume away the effect of changes in market structure on movements in the capital share. An alternative interpretation of the observed behaviour in capital shares would point to the deterioration in labour unions' political clout during the 1980s and the 1990s, which we discuss in depth in Section 13.5. We view such a hypothesis as complementary to ours.

Indeed, it is very difficult to tell the difference between cause and effect when discussing labour's loss of political power. On the one hand, falling labour shares are likely to be at least in part caused by the fall in the capacity of labour to mobilize politically. On the other hand, falling labour shares lead to lower labour incomes and, therefore, to a smaller capacity of labour to mobilize economic resources for the political arena.[14] What we do in this section is to identify one reason behind labour's loss of political power—changes in factor ratios that produced falling labour shares—but we recognize that other causes may have led to the fall in labour's capacity for political

---

[13] This proof is in an unpublished appendix, available from the author upon request.

[14] Pineda and Rodríguez (1999) develop this explanation in detail. They show for a panel of ninety-one countries that capital shares are negatively associated with the capacity of the labour sector to pressure for greater amounts of redistribution and investment in human capital.

mobilization, such as exogenously imposed liberalization policies and the broader ideological loss of direction of the Latin American left.

Factor ratios

We return now to our main argument. We have discussed earlier that, with an elasticity of substitution not too different from 0.5, the observed evolution of capital shares is consistent with the hypothesis that factor prices are proportional to their marginal products, given observed factor ratios. This line of reasoning thus points to the levels of human and physical capital as the variables of interest. If existing patterns in the accumulation of physical and human capital are consistent with the evolution of capital shares, then we should be asking what determines the patterns of human and physical capital accumulation. In particular, why did the ratio of physical to human capital drop so steadily during the 1970–96 period? Analytically, this question can be separated into two distinct questions. The first one regards the evolution of the stock of physical capital per worker. Why did it rise until 1982 and fall during the rest of the 1980s and 1990s? The second one regards the evolution of mean years of schooling shown in Table 13.3. Why did human capital grow steadily during the 1970s and then stabilize and fall during the 1980s? We now attempt to answer these questions.

13.3.2. Patterns of Physical Capital Accumulation

Suppose a country experiences a boom in natural resources. What is likely to be the effect of that boom on the country's patterns of capital accumulation? To answer, we need a model of the interaction of natural resources and economic growth. The standard Ramsey model is not well suited to study an economy with non-renewable natural resources because all factors of production in this model are assumed to be reproducible. A simple way to incorporate natural resources into the Ramsey model would be to consider them as a stock of resources that can be sold at given world prices and exchanged for investment goods. In such a model, one could study the optimal decisions of factor accumulation and resource depletion and derive the macroeconomic implications. Rodríguez and Sachs (1999) present such a model. In their interpretation, the economy is identical to that of a Ramsey model, save for one additional decision: how to deplete an existing natural resource. At every moment in time, the economy must decide how much of the resource to extract and sell in international markets and how much to keep for future use, given a technology of extraction.

   If there are perfect international credit markets, then the optimal decision for the economy is to sell its natural resource internationally and permanently consume the interest on the assets derived from that sale.[15] If this alternative is not open, then the economy will invest the resources internally, generating a boom in production. As it

---

[15] After investing the sum of resources necessary to augment its capital stock so as to jump to the steady-state level, assuming no adjustment costs.

invests them, it forces down the marginal return to capital and therefore provokes a consumption boom, the key feature of which is that it is unsustainable in the long run. Unlike the factors of production of the standard Ramsey model, natural resources cannot be accumulated either exogenously or through savings decisions. Therefore, they cannot grow at a constant rate in a steady state, as capital and labour do. They can, however, allow the economy to enjoy temporarily high levels of consumption during the transition to the long-run steady states. This is what Rodríguez and Sachs term the 'overshooting' result: as the economy grows, if the stock of natural resources is sufficiently large, then the economy surpasses in finite time its long-run steady state level. However, as time passes, the level of income of the economy must converge to its long-run steady state.[16] Therefore, the economy converges from above to its steady state, displaying negative growth rates during the transition to this state. Rodríguez and Sachs use this fact to account for the low growth rates of resource-intensive economies documented by Gelb (1986), Sachs and Warner (1995), and Karl (1997). They also calibrate a dynamic computable general equilibrium model for the Venezuelan economy and show that the economy's growth performance during the boom years is quantitatively accounted for accurately by the overshooting phenomenon.

Figures 15 and 16 in Rodríguez (2000) show the behaviour of the per capita capital stock and investment rates implied by the natural resources model of Rodríguez and Sachs calibrated for the Venezuelan economy in 1972–93. In particular, they show that the boom in capital accumulation can be well accounted for by the overshooting phenomenon: during the early years of the boom the economy accumulates rapidly a capital stock, which is unsustainable in the long run. There is nothing non-optimizing about this behaviour: it is completely optimal to try to enjoy the higher utility, which natural resources can provide while they last. As the boom advances, the marginal product of capital is pushed down sufficiently low to cause disincentives to further investment. This fact, combined with the continuous erosion of the natural resources in per capita terms, leads to a fall in the per capita capital stock. As Fig. 13.9 shows, the predicted trends fit well with the historically observed trends in the Venezuelan economy. Therefore, the pattern in physical capital accumulation is perfectly consistent with the predictions of a theoretical model.

13.3.3. *Patterns of Human Capital Accumulation*

Figure 13.11 plots the time-series of health and educational spending in GNP from 1962 to 1995. These series show levels of social spending which were, generally speaking, rising during the 1960s and 1970s and stable during the 1980s and 1990s. We plot two series for education, one calculated directly from Venezuelan official statistics and another calculated by UNESCO, both of which coincide in the general pattern of stabilization of social spending in GNP from 1980 onwards. Figure 13.11 gives evidence of stabilization in the levels of social spending, but not of a collapse in these levels.

---

[16] With positive population growth, the per capita level of natural resources is zero, and thus its steady state must be the same as that of an economy without natural resources.

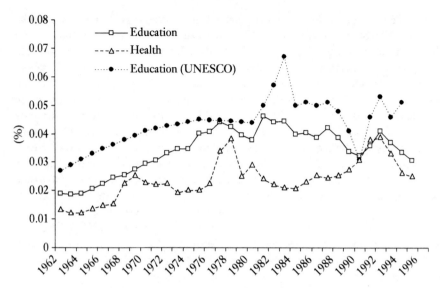

Figure 13.11. *Social spending as a percentage of GNP, 1962–96*

Table 13.4. *Public spending on education by level as a % of GNP*

	Primary and secondary	Tertiary	Non-distributed	Total
1970	2.59	1.12	0.37	4.08
1975	2.21	2.01	0.08	4.30
1980	1.91	2.07	0.24	4.23
1994	2.04	2.40	0.19	4.63

Source: UNESCO Education Spending Data File, available from http://www.unescobkk.org.

However, Table 13.4 shows another side of the process. Despite rising rates of investment in human capital during the 1960s and 1970s, the amount of resources that were being devoted to primary and secondary schooling was actually declining.[17] During this period, the fraction of GNP devoted to tertiary education more than doubled. In other words, spending may have stabilized, but it also became more regressive.

There is sketchy evidence that something similar may have happened in the health sector. Despite the increased spending in health shown in Fig. 13.11, the number of hospitals per 100,000 people fell from 3.2 to 2.8 from 1970 to 1989, and the number of beds per 100,000 people declined from 310 to 247. The percentage of population with safe water rose from 75 to 89 per cent of the total from 1970 to 1989 and then dropped to

[17] The last year for which there are separate data on primary and secondary schooling is 1975. The data show that primary schooling as a share of GDP fell from 1.84 per cent in 1970 to 1.13 per cent in 1975.

79 per cent by 1995, while the percentage with access to sanitation followed a similar pattern. Malnutrition prevalence, as measured by the percentage of children under 5 whose height is less than two standard deviations of the median US population, rose from 4.6 per cent in 1987 to 14.9 per cent in 1997. Therefore, despite constant levels of investment in human capital as a percentage of GNP from the 1970s on, indicators of health performance have weakened considerably, suggesting that health service provision has become increasingly inadequate. This inefficiency could arise, as in the education sector, because higher amounts of spending are being deviated towards upper income groups. They could also arise because of increased rent-seeking in the health sector. Whatever the reason, what is clear for our purposes is that there was a collapse in the levels of effective investment in human capital that fuelled the decline in human capital observed during the late 1980s. An alternative hypothesis is that much of the fall in the stock of human capital was driven by the effect of macroeconomic policies. Lustig (1999) and Behrman *et al.* (1999) have recently found that macroeconomic crises have long-run impacts on the stock of human capital. In particular, strong macroeconomic contractions raise levels of malnutrition and lead to substantially lower school enrolment rates. The result can be negative long-lived or even permanent effects on the stock of human capital.

Feedback effects may exist from the deterioration in the capital share to investment in human capital. Given the high correlation between ownership of human and of physical capital, it may well be the case that those who own the most human capital also own the most physical capital. However, higher investment in human capital— especially in primary education—would lead to an expansion of the human capital of individuals who have little human capital. This could have a strong negative effect on the value of the human capital of those who already have high levels of human capital. Therefore, these elites would see their interest in restricting the ownership of human capital, and a higher share of *physical* capital in GDP may give them the upper hand in the political process by raising the economic resources that they have to influence politics. Such an interpretation would be consistent with the pattern of deterioration in human capital accumulation (more investment in tertiary, less on secondary and primary), as well as the increase in the labour Gini coefficients observed in the late 1990s.

In sum, a mix of economic and political factors seems to account for the evolution of the observed factor ratios. On the economic side, a great part of the trends in physical capital accumulation appear to be a natural consequence of the resource boom. But this cannot explain the whole story without appealing to the behaviour of human capital accumulation. The stock of human capital grew steadily until the mid-1980s and has fallen since; this fall appears to be linked to the waning capacity of the political system to keep up a sufficiently high level of progressive human capital accumulation, perhaps due to changes in the political clout of the groups with an interest in human capital accumulation.

13.4. OTHER INFLUENCES ON INCOME DISTRIBUTION

In the previous section, we argue that the evolution of the factorial distribution of income could be well understood by the changes in the patterns of accumulation of human and physical capital. But even in the most favourable scenario for our hypothesis, there is a substantial amount of residual inequality left unexplained, which is in part due to the factors discussed subsequently.

13.4.1. *1980–7: Macro Policy and Capital Flight*

The early 1980s saw a shift in macroeconomic policy regimes from the expansionary approach of the 1970s towards a highly contractionary stance. Whether this shift was warranted or not is an unsettled issue: supporters argue that it was necessary to restrain growing inflation, whereas opponents counter that a continuation of the improvement in income distribution of the 1970s could make growing wages consistent with a stable aggregate demand.[18] The natural by-product of the induced recession was a fall in the availability of profitable investment opportunities (note the falling profit rate during the early 1980s in Fig. 13.5). Given the low level of the real interest rate (except for a short attempt at financial liberalization, interest rates were controlled at real negative levels until 1989), this substantially reduced the incentives to maintain assets in domestic currency. Persistent budget deficits also fuelled rational expectations of devaluations, which further reduced expected returns to bolívar-denominated assets.

The result of the combination of these factors was a high incentive to move deposits to offshore bank accounts. Indeed, half of Venezuela's capital flight for the 1970–95 period occurred between 1979 and 1983. During those 4 years, capital flight summed to \$28.2 billion, or 37 per cent of fuel exports. It is clear from Fig. 13.2 that the increase in the component of capital's share of GNP deriving from income on foreign assets occurred mostly during this period. Thus, it appears that a non-negligible part of the deterioration of Venezuela's income distribution can be attributed to the combination of persistent devaluations, low real interest rates, and low profit rates that was maintained during the regime of capital account convertibility of the 1980s.

A relatively inegalitarian consequence of the buildup of foreign assets held by Venezuelan nationals is the flipside: the accumulation of foreign debt held by the Venezuelan government. Estimated at \$35.5 billion, Venezuela's external debt is smaller then the \$57.3 billion held by Venezuelan nationals. However, the limited capacity of the Venezuelan state to tax assets held by Venezuelans abroad implies that the burden of the repayment of the Venezuelan external debt falls principally on those who do not own foreign assets. From the policy standpoint, a number of interpretations of this outcome are possible. The Washington Consensus view is that low real interest rates lead to capital flight; the recommended solution to this dilemma is to engineer monetary-induced contractions and high real interest rates. This was indeed the solution followed by Venezuelan administrations from 1989 on. However, recessions tend to lower profit rates, inducing capital flight, and high *nominal* interest rates can cause high budget deficits. These two reasons are at least part of the explanation why capital inflows did not permanently resume in the post-1989 period despite high real interest rates.

---

[18] Gumersindo Rodríguez (1981) and Juan Pablo Pérez Alfonso (1976) are two examples of the different positions in this debate.

A non-Washington Consensus view of this policy dilemma is that the trade-off between economic expansion (through low interest rates) and capital account balance (through the interest-parity condition) holds *only as long* as capital account convertibility is in place. If there are restrictions on capital outflows, a country can choose a monetary policy that is consistent with domestic expansion without worrying about the consequences to the capital account.[19]

The fact that a good number of countries (among which South Korea, Chile, and Malaysia) were able to maintain capital account convertibility restrictions during the post-war period and engineer a sustained process of economic growth illustrates the fact that these restrictions can be a useful instrument in maintaining domestic economic growth financed with domestic investment. Rodrik (1997) has recently shown that countries with capital account restrictions do not seem to pay a cost in terms of economic growth and may actually enjoy substantial benefits in terms of reduced volatility. Indeed, the sole fact that a capital-scarce developing country systematically becomes a capital exporter is indicative of the existence of market failures under which free capital markets are unlikely to lead to optimal outcomes. The non-Washington Consensus view would imply that, if Venezuela had been willing to impose restrictions on capital account convertibility during the 1980s, it could also have averted a significant part of the deterioration of its distribution of income.

13.4.2. *Trade Reform*

Trade policies can have distributive effects because of their impact on relative prices. If an economy liberalizes international trade, then the possibility of importing some goods at lower prices should make the internal prices of import-competing goods fall. The conventional economics wisdom asserts that, in labour-abundant economies such as Venezuela, trade liberalization should lead to a drop in the relative price of import-competing capital-intensive goods and therefore to a rise in real wage rates. Trade liberalization should thus lower capital's share of income. This conventional wisdom has been questioned in a number of studies that have failed to find an effect of trade liberalization on factor shares in developing countries. If anything, these studies tend to find that income distribution deteriorates in many developing countries as a result of greater openness.[20]

Collected trade taxes over imports (a crude measure of commercial protection) rose during the late 1980s, followed by a modest drop after liberalization. In turn, the ratio of prices of imported goods to the wholesale prices of nationally produced goods shows a decline from 1987. The fact that trade liberalization coincided with an increase in the capital share is suggestive that traditional, Stolper–Samuelson effects may not be present in the Venezuelan case. Rodrik (1997) and Reddy and Dube (1999) have

---

[19] A traditional view is that this dilemma can be solved when exchange rates are flexible, as the rate of devaluation will adjust to ensure that the no-arbitrage condition holds. Even though this is true in theory, as Calvo and Reinhart (1999) have recently pointed out, it is seldom true in practice, given that devaluations are used by agents as signals of policymakers' credibility.

[20] See Harrison and Revenga (1995) and further references in Reddy and Dube (1999).

suggested that trade may have an effect on income distribution, which goes beyond the conventional Stolper–Samuelson effect. These authors show that, by raising the elasticity of the derived demand for labour, international trade lowers the bargaining power of labour and thus affects equilibrium wages negatively. Therefore, trade liberalization can easily lead to a deterioration of income distribution even in labour-abundant countries. This is indeed consistent with the Venezuelan experience and points again to the reduced bargaining power of labour as a key factor in the evolution of Venezuelan inequality.

13.4.3. *Financial Crises*

An additional factor which appears to have had an effect on Venezuelan inequality was the financial crisis experienced by the country during the mid-1990s. Between 1994 and 1995, a run on the banking sector precipitated one of the worst banking crises in Latin American history. The cost of banking sector bailouts have been estimated at 13 per cent of GDP in 1994 and an additional 4 per cent of GDP in 1995. An effect of the crisis was a total collapse in domestic credit creation. By 1996, the total domestic credit provided by the banking sector had fallen to 19 per cent of GDP from above 30 per cent before the crisis. One could expect two impacts of this on the capital share. First, it would lead firms to substitute away from capital-intensive activities. This reduction in the use of capital would, given the estimates of the elasticity of substitution discussed above, lead to a rise in capital's share. Second, it could lead capital-intensive firms to experience a greater bankruptcy rate, with labour-intensive firms surviving loan-reliant capital-intensive firms. The latter effect would lower capital's share.

The evidence from manufacturing data points to a predominance of the former effect. Table 13.5 shows that, generally, capital intensity is strongly related to size: large firms tend to be very capital-intensive. Table 13.6, in turn, shows that even though there was some movement of production from the more capital-intensive large firms to labour-intensive firms in the aftermath of the banking crisis, it was not substantial. A possible explanation for this is that large capital-intensive firms were also likelier to have access to international credit markets and therefore were able to weather the storm from the collapse in financial intermediation more easily. Indeed, whatever reallocation there was appears to have occurred between medium- and small-sized firms and very

Table 13.5. *Value added per worker in constant 1984 Bs, 1993–6*

	Average	Large	Medium	Small	Very small
1993	2314.09	3214.60	1101.31	902.78	640.67
1994	2168.84	3034.07	1153.40	899.53	602.33
1995	2659.94	3789.34	1387.16	932.71	654.51
1996	2673.86	4150.50	1345.40	944.74	640.89

Source: OCEI (1996).

Table 13.6. *Gross production in manufacturing as % of total, 1993–6*

	Large	Medium	Small	Very small
1993	82.17	5.68	6.51	5.64
1994	81.61	5.75	6.81	5.83
1995	81.11	7.54	6.07	5.27
1996	81.61	5.45	6.25	6.69

Source: OCEI (1996).

Table 13.7. *Capital shares in manufacturing, 1993–6*

	Total	Large	Medium	Small	Very small
1993	0.800	0.824	0.672	0.648	0.625
1994	0.817	0.842	0.734	0.679	0.625
1995	0.847	0.870	0.775	0.695	0.640
1996	0.896	0.913	0.835	0.800	0.764

Source: OCEI (1996).

small firms. However, Table 13.7 shows that the price effects on capital were extremely high: capital shares rose by 5 percentage points on average in 1996, with the rise being largest (12 points) in small firms. Therefore, it appears that the collapse in financial intermediation may have caused a significant rise in the return to capital, leading to a substantial increase in capital shares from 1993 to 1996.

What was the ultimate cause of the 1994–5 financial crisis? The literature on banking crises is far from providing an unambiguous answer to the question of what causes financial crises, and explanations range from self-fulfilling prophecies to high interest rates and financial liberalization. An additional factor may have been present in the Venezuelan case. As pointed out earlier, financial sector liberalization led to a substantial rise in interest rates from 1989 onwards. Indeed, the deposit rate rose to above 30 per cent from 1989 onwards, and the real interest rate became substantially positive in the early 1990s. Meanwhile, the amount of domestic credit in GDP shrank by more than 15 percentage points. It is apparent that higher real interest rates led to a contraction in the amount of credit and to a concentration of investments in high-return, high-risk projects, making the banking sector much more vulnerable to negative aggregate shocks and banking runs.

13.5. LABOUR'S LOSS OF POWER AND THE POLITICAL ECONOMY OF INEQUALITY

The above analysis points repeatedly to the importance of understanding the shifts in the political influence of the Venezuelan labour movement. We have discussed the feedback effects that exist between the deterioration of labour shares and labour's

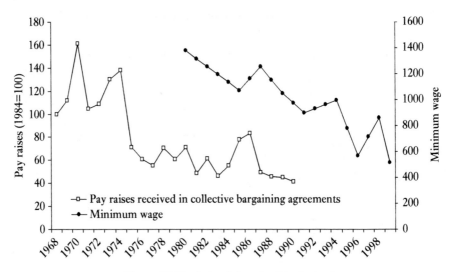

Figure 13.12. *Labour's loss of political power*

political power: lower labour shares can lead to diminished political clout of labour, as a weaker labour movement has a limited capacity to bargain for higher shares of output. Furthermore, many of the policies that may have an impact on inequality—such as trade liberalization—also have a consequent effect on labour's bargaining power, see Fig. 13.12.

The evolution of the Venezuelan labour movement reveals that it became increasingly marginalized as income distribution deteriorated. From the beginning of the democratic period in 1958, the Confederación de Trabajadores de Venezuela (CTV) enjoyed a good relationship with the Acción Democrática (AD) party. AD and, to a lesser extent, the center-right COPEI party followed a corporatist–populist model of government in which bargaining over general levels of wages was carried out at the national level between business and workers' federations, mediated by the government. The favourable relationship between AD and the CTV started to change during the 1970s, when the CTV began to lose representation in AD, and AD's share of CTV delegates dropped from 70 per cent in the 1960s to an average of 46 per cent in the 1970s. At the same time, work stoppages rose from an average of 30 per year during the 1960s to 175 during the 1970s (Roxborough 1995). This trend was somewhat counteracted by the Pérez administration's passage of important labour legislation protecting workers and the generally tight labour markets of the mid-1970s. But the trend towards a loss of power of labour was accentuated during the 1980s.

Indeed, pay raises achieved by workers in collective bargaining contracts declined steadily between 1968 and 1990. Likewise, the real value of the government-mandated minimum wage fell gradually from Bs 1400 per month in 1978 to about Bs 500 in 2000.

In turn, the rate of unionization was 33 per cent in 1975, but had fallen to 22 per cent by 1990 and 17 per cent by 1997 (ILO 1998; also Chapter 8). Meanwhile, the yearly number of officially registered labour disputes grew from less than 200 to 264 by 1994, revealing a labour movement that was increasingly alienated and marginalized from the decision-making process. By the late 1990s, the CTV had been challenged by alternative labour unions, which did not have the traditional linkage to existing parties. These trends strengthen our argument that there has been a mutually reinforcing relationship between the rise in the capital share and labour's loss of bargaining power. It is extremely difficult to sort out cause and effect in this process, however. Did the deterioration in income distribution lead to a lower capacity of labour to exercise political power? Or was labour's falling political clout the cause of increased income distribution?

13.6. CONCLUDING COMMENTS

During the past 25 years, Venezuela has experienced a deterioration in the factorial distribution of income of tremendous proportions. We estimate that labour's share of GDP went down by roughly 15 percentage points during the 1970–96 period. Meanwhile, the distribution of labour income remained somewhat stable.

In this study, we have concentrated on accounting for the increase in Venezuela's capital share. We show that the increase can be traced back to the coupling of a collapse in the ratio of physical to human capital that occurred from the 1970s with a low elasticity of substitution in production between capital and labour. We also argue that other factors can be identified as having a negative influence on inequality, namely, the policy of repeated devaluations of the currency, trade liberalization, and the financial crisis of 1994.

The effects of low elasticities deserve some comment, as they are rather perverse. With low elasticities of substitution, accumulation of a factor of production gives rise to a fall in the rate of return so large as to cause the share of product to decline. This means, for example, that the greater amounts of human capital generated by investment in education and health can actually lead to a decrease in labour's share. It must be clear that this does not necessarily mean that labour will be worse off. Since human capital is an input into the production function, then output will also grow. Labour will have a smaller share of a larger pie.[21] But it is possible to construct perverse scenarios in which the elasticity of substitution is so low that labour is indeed absolutely worse off.

The fact that greater accumulation of human capital leads to a fall in labour's share given low elasticities of substitution implies that sustaining human capital accumulation can be politically very problematic. When investment in human capital raises the stock of human capital, the capital share goes up. The more economic resources in the hands of capital, the greater the political resources capital can muster. Therefore, the power of labour relative to capital can wane precisely as the result of low

---

[21] Another reason why the outcome may favour labour is that, if the investment is financed by a proportional or progressive tax, then labour will pay little of the cost, but appropriate most of the direct benefits.

elasticities of substitution, coupled with human capital accumulation. This increase of the economic and political power of capital can easily help capital lobby for a reduction in the resources that the state devotes to those with less political power.[22]

Low elasticities of substitution are indicative of rigid production processes with few opportunities for changing techniques. They may be due to lack of technological options or strict regulation of the production process. If factor price equalization holds and the economy is perfectly open, then elasticities of substitution are irrelevant: internationally determined factor prices determine the capital share, and an increase in human capital leads, one to one, to an increase in labour's share. However, the Venezuelan economy appears to have been neither open nor subject to the factor price equalization theorem during the period under examination. It rather appears to have been a completely specialized economy, in which factor shares were determined solely by the interaction between capital accumulation and relative rates of return that we have considered in this chapter. It is the coupling of extreme specialization in oil and rigid production processes that can lead to the perverse distributive effects that we have seen. Our study suggests that policy initiatives aimed at improving income distribution in Venezuela must take these structural characteristics of the economy seriously.

Rigid production processes are not independent from industry structure. Production that is highly concentrated in a reduced set of industries is likely to exhibit more rigidities than one with a widely diversified base, because a great part of economy-wide substitution takes the form of substitution among industries. In particular, a broad set of export industries would probably have allowed Venezuela to overcome its problem of low elasticities of substitution. Providing an answer to the question of why Venezuela was unable to diversify its production is outside the scope of this study. It is, however, suggestive that high concentration in energy-intensive industries is precisely the specialization that Venezuela is pushed to by the forces of comparative advantage. In other words, Venezuela's high participation in world trade—given its skewed structure of comparative advantage—may precisely be one of the causes of its low elasticities of substitution.

Low elasticities of substitution are, however, only part of the story. Even after one takes into account the effect of boom–bust cycles on income distribution through changes in factor ratios, one is left with a substantial deterioration of the factorial distribution of income of about 3 percentage points in GDP during the 1980s and 1990s. In Sections 13.4 and 13.5, we argue that these changes can be traced back to policy choices, including trade liberalization, the maintenance of capital account mobility, and contractionary monetary policies, as well as labour's loss of bargaining power. These policy and institutional changes—all favoured by the Washington Consensus view—appear to have considerably exacerbated Venezuela's deterioration in income distribution.

---

[22] Using cross-country panel data, Pineda and Rodríguez (1999) find that labour's power to pressure for redistributive policies and subsidies to human capital accumulation is negatively related to capital's share of income.

REFERENCES

Banco Central de Venezuela (various years). *Anuario de Cuentas Estadísticas*. Banco Central de Venezuela, Caracas.

Barro, R. J., and J.-W. Lee (1993). International comparisons of educational attainment. *Journal of Monetary Economics* 32(3), 363–94.

Behrman, J., S. Duryea, and M. Szekely (1999). Households and economic growth in Latin America and the Caribbean. Mimeo, Inter-American Development Bank: Washington, DC.

Calvo, G., and C. Reinhart (1999). Fear of floating. Mimeo, Centre for International Economics, University of Maryland: College Park.

Gelb, A. H. (1986). Adjustment to windfall gains: A comparative analysis of oil-exporting countries. In J. P. Neary, P. van Wijnbergen, and S. van Wijnbergen (eds.), *Natural Resources and the Macroeconomy*. Basil Blackwell: Oxford.

Gonzalez, R., and M. I. Martínez (1993). *Apertura y Concentración Industrial. Cuadernos de Trabajo*. Centro Gumilla: Caracas.

Harrison, A., and A. Revenga (1995). The effects of trade policy reform: What do we really know? *NBER Working Papers* 5,225, National Bureau of Economic Research: Cambridge, MA.

ILO (1998). *El Trabajo en el Mundo: Relaciones Labor ales, Democracia y Cohesión Social*. ILO: Geneva.

Kakwani, N. (1980). *Income Inequality and Poverty: Methods of Estimation and Policy Applications*. Oxford University Press: New York.

Karl, T. L. (1997). *The Paradox of Plenty: Oil Booms, Venezuela and Other Petro-States*. University of California Press: Berkeley.

Lessard, D. R., and J. Williamson (1987). *Capital Flight and Third World Debt*. Institute for International Economics: Washington, DC.

Lustig, N. (1999). Crisis and the poor: Socially responsible macroeconomics. Presidential address to the Latin American and Caribbean Economics Association, 21–23 October, Santiago Chile.

Marcano, L., and I. Ruprah (1999). Falling apart: Poverty and income inequality in venezuela. Mimeo, Inter-American Development Bank: Washington, DC.

OCEI (1996). *Encuesta Industrial* (www.ocei.gov.ve, Oficina Central de Estadística e Informática).

Pérez Alfonso, J. P. (1976). *Hundiéndonos en el Excremento del Diablo*. Editorial Lisbona: Caracas.

Pineda, J., and F. Rodríguez (1999). The political economy of human capital accumulation. Mimeo, Department of Economics, University of Maryland: College Park, MD.

Rama, M. (1999). *A Labor Market Cross-Country Database*. World Bank: Washington, DC.

Reddy, S., and A. Dube (1999). Liberalization, income distribution and political economy: The bargaining channel and its implications. Mimeo, Harvard University: Cambridge, MA.

Rodríguez, F. (2000). Factors shares and resource booms: Accounting for the evolution of Venezuelan inequality. *WIDER Working Paper* 204, UNU/WIDER: Helsinki.

Rodríguez, G. (1981). *Economía Pública, Planificación y Capitalismo de Estado en Venezuela*. Ediciones Corpoconsult: Caracas.

——and J. D. Sachs (1999). Why do resource abundant economies grow more slowly: A new explanation and an application to Venezuela. *Journal of Economic Growth* 4, 277–303.

Rodrik, D. (1997). *Has Globalization Gone Too Far?* Institute for International Economics: Washington, DC.

Roxborough, I. (1995). The urban working class and labour movements. In L. Bethell (ed.), *Cambridge History of Latin America*, Vol. XI: *Bibliographical Essays*. Cambridge University Press: Cambridge.

Sachs, J., and A. Warner (1995). Natural resource abundance and economic growth. *NBER Working Papers* 5,398, National Bureau of Economic Research: Cambridge, MA.

UN (1981). A survey of national sources of income distribution statistics. *Statistical Papers* M72, United Nations: New York.

World Bank (1999). *World Development Indicators 1999*. World Bank: Washington, DC.

14

The Impact of Financial Liberalization and the Rise of Financial Rents on Income Inequality: The Case of Turkey

A. ERINC YELDAN

14.1. INTRODUCTION

The last two decades have witnessed a fundamental change in the development strategy of most developing economies towards domestic and external liberalization. More recently, however, renewed attention has been placed on the adverse consequences of such public policy changes on income equality and poverty alleviation. United Nations Conference on Trade and Development's (UNCTAD) *1997 Trade and Development Report*, for instance, reveals that, over a sample of 124 countries accounting for 93.6 per cent of the world population, the income share of the richest one-fifth of the world population rose from 69 per cent in 1965 to over 83 per cent in 1990 (UNCTAD 1997: 81). Likewise, the income gap between the richest and the poorest quintiles of the world population widened. The ratio of the average per capita gross national product (GNP) of the richest to the poorest quintile was 31:1 in 1965 but had risen to 60:1 by 1990. Given this evidence, the UNCTAD report presents the following stylized facts about development and income (in)equality during the post-1970 evolution of the global world economy (UNCTAD 1997: 65). First, taken as a whole, the world economy is growing too slowly to alleviate poverty. Second, finance has been gaining over industry, and rentiers over investors. Similarly, capital has gained in comparison to labour, and the share of profits has risen within the functional distribution of income. And finally, the middle class has been under significant pressure as labour markets have become marginalized and the existing wage inequalities between skilled and unskilled labour have intensified.

While the factors behind these changes constitute the topic of active debate,[1] they are acknowledged to be conceptually part of a broader set of developments of the world economy loosely seen as constituting the process of globalization. This process accelerated during the 1970s with the advent of the technological innovations in the

---

[1] See, for example, the contributions by Milanovic (1999), Cornia and Kiiski (1999), Barro (1999), Rodrik (1997, 1998), and Atkinson (1998a,b). See also the 1998, volume 8 issue of *The Economic Journal* for a compilation of the theoretical mechanics of income distribution and technological change.

electronics and telecommunications industries. From the point of view of economic relations, the process of globalization requires two major policy changes: (a) the liberalization of domestic commodity and financial markets (the so-called 'structural adjustment'), and (b) the elimination of all administrative and regulatory norms hindering the free movement of goods and international capital flows. In this sense, economic globalization considers the profitability of capital as the sole objective of economic rationality and labels all kinds of national regulations which limit the owners of capital in their quest for maximization of profit as 'irrational' or 'backward ideology' (Bourdieu 1998).

As a result, the international capital benefiting from the integration of world commodity and financial markets has two strategic targets. First, the reduction of the regulatory powers of national states, and second, the weakening of labour's already limited legal rights to collective bargaining and unionization. Thus, in order to sanctify the power of unfettered market forces in the name of economic efficiency, this 'infernal machine' requires the elimination of all administrative or political barriers which limit the profitability of private capital and necessitates 'a programme for destroying collective structures which may impede the pure market logic' (Bourdieu 1998). The terms 'globalization' and 'financial deregulation' do, in fact, reflect the ideological underpinnings of these overall processes. It is the purpose of this study to investigate and assess the impact of financial rents on income distribution and the overall marginalization of labour incomes in the post-1980 Turkish economy.

Turkey initiated its long process of integration in world commodity and financial markets with the 1980 structural adjustment reforms implemented under the auspices of the International Monetary Fund (IMF) and the World Bank. Since its early inception, the Turkish adjustment programme was hailed as a model by the orthodox international community, and it was supported by generous financial assistance through structural adjustment loans, debt relief, and technical aid.[2] Currently, the Turkish economy can be said to be operating under conditions of a truly open economy: a macroeconomic environment in which its capital account is completely liberalized and the process of financial deregulation is completed. In this setting, many of the instruments of macro and fiscal control have been transformed, and the constraints of macroequilibrium have undergone major structural change.[3] Concurrently, the domestic economy has witnessed drastic changes in the modes of surplus creation and extraction and in the interplay of distribution and accumulation.

The chapter is organized into five sections. The next section gives a broad overview and presents evidence on the patterns of income distribution in Turkey over the last

[2] This financial assistance represented a resource transfer of 4.7 per cent of GDP in 1980. During 1978–80, Turkey alone accounted for nearly 70 per cent of the total volume of debt rescheduled internationally among all developing countries (Celasun and Rodrik 1989). See also Ekinci (1998) for the role of foreign financial assistance in the shaping of the post-1980 adjustments in Turkey.

[3] See Voyvoda and Yeldan (1999), Onaran (1999), Tansel (1999), Boratav et al. (1996), Yeldan (1995), Uygur (1993), Senses (1994), Boratav and Türel (1993), Celasun (1994), and Ozmucur (1986) for analyses of the adjustment patterns and distributional shifts under the Turkish structural adjustment reforms of the 1980s.

three decades. Section 14.3 turns to the evolution of functional categories of income and offers a panorama of the macroeconomic adjustments under post-financial liberalization and the rise of financial rents. Here, of particular importance, is the investigation of the inherent tensions caused by the macroeconomic disequilibria embodied in the process of integration with world markets under conditions of a poorly supervised banking system and underdeveloped and fragile domestic asset markets. Thus, it is found to be analytically convenient to decompose the path of Turkish liberalization after 1980 into two major subperiods partitioned by the strategic step of capital account deregulation which took place in 1989 and was completed by the full integration of the domestic market in global financial markets. The section further studies the patterns of the wage cycle and productivity growth using quantitative filtering techniques, and it reports on the disassociation of labour remunerations from the productivity gains in the real sphere of the economy. Section 14.4 provides a detailed analysis of the rise in public sector deficits and the distributive consequences of the widening fiscal gap. Section 14.5 summarizes and concludes.

14.2. INDICATORS OF INCOME DISTRIBUTION: THE EVIDENCE

Turkey is known to suffer from one of the most skewed income distributions among countries at a comparable level of development. Partly fuelled by the legacy of prolonged import–substitutionist growth patterns, with excessive quota rents and an oligopolistic industrial and banking structure, the economy suffers further from a relatively stagnant and overpopulated agricultural sector, with loose linkages to domestic industry, high rates of immigration due to both economic and political pressures, and unequal opportunities to access education.

With the advent in 1980 of reforms for openness that aimed at commodity trade liberalization and then, in 1989, with the completion of this through financial liberalization, there were renewed orthodox expectations of more equitable forms of distribution of the national product, since, given the signals of efficiency (world) prices, it was thought that import–quota rents would be dissipated and the domestic structure of production would be transformed. It was further argued that, as labour-intensive domestic industries shifted towards export markets, the remuneration of labour would increase in real terms. These orthodox prescriptions failed to function, however, as the economy witnessed sharp changes in the underlying economic polity, with the emergence and administration of new modes and mechanisms of surplus extraction throughout the course of liberalization. First and foremost, the proliberal stance and the integration of the domestic economy with world markets did not lead to a more competitive environment in domestic industry; on the contrary, the concentration rates in most outward–oriented sectors such as food processing, cement, glass production, and ceramics rose sharply. Furthermore, the financing behaviour of corporations did not show significant change, and the banking sector became increasingly disassociated from credit financing and intermediation and evolved towards the financing of the securitization of the domestic debt.

The new outward orientation also opened fresh avenues for wealth accumulation based on a renewed form of rent-seeking, this time towards export promotion subsidies and grants provided by the government. Commercial policies became the leading mechanism for squeezing domestic absorption capacity to generate an exportable surplus for export-oriented manufacturing capital. This exportable surplus was to be obtained through the generation of excess supply by reducing effective domestic demand. This, in turn, necessitated the suppression of wage incomes. This was in stark contrast with the dual role of wages under the import-substitutionist phase both as a cost element and as a source of effective demand. Under the new export orientation, however, as the sources of effective demand would be expected to emerge not from the home market, but from the external economy, wages came to be regarded only as a cost item which needed to be minimized.

Thus, at a more general level, the post-1980 integration process fostered new, intense distributive tensions as the share of non-wage income in national product rose, the marginalization of labour deepened, the existing wage inequalities between skilled and unskilled labour intensified, and the access to social safety nets became increasingly difficult. All of these conditions favoured more adverse consequences in terms of the condition of the poor. Against this evidence on the functional categories of income distribution, there are serious problems in the documentation of these processes as regards the size levels of incomes. Despite the availability of official and independent studies on the size distribution of incomes during the critical years of macroeconomic adjustment, direct comparisons are quite hard to make, as the studies have been subject to significant changes in both coverage and design over the years. Even so, it might be useful to lay down the existing evidence in its entirety and caution the reader against strong conclusions. Table 14.1 summarizes the available dataset from studies on the size distribution of income in Turkey over the last three decades.

Over the broad time horizon, the available Gini coefficients seem to show an overall tendency for the improvement of income distribution in the 1970s, followed by a worsening after the 1980s (on this, see Chapter 2). The rise in the income share of the richest

Table 14.1. *Summary of research on the size distribution of income (percentage of income)*

% of households	SPO (1963)	Bulutay et al. (1968)	SPO (1973)	SIS rural (1973/4)	SIS urban (1978/9)	SIS (1987)	SIS (1994)
1. 20	4.5	3.0	3.5	3.5	6.3	5.2	4.9
2. 20	8.5	7.0	8.0	11.1	12.0	9.6	8.6
3. 20	11.5	10.0	12.5	14.4	13.0	14.1	12.6
4. 20	18.5	20.0	19.5	18.7	21.0	21.1	19.0
5. 20	57.0	60.0	56.5	52.2	47.0	49.9	54.9
Gini coefficient	0.55	0.56	0.51	0.47	0.40	0.43	0.49

Note: Reference year in parentheses.
Sources: SPO (1973); SIS (1987, 1994); Bulutay et al. (1971).

Table 14.2. *Comparison of SIS 1987 versus 1994 surveys of income distribution (percentage of income)*

% of households	1987			1994		
	Turkey	Urban	Rural	Turkey	Urban	Rural
1. 10	1.9	2.2	1.8	1.8	1.9	2.0
2. 10	3.3	3.3	3.4	3.0	2.9	3.6
3. 10	4.3	4.2	4.4	3.9	3.7	4.6
4. 10	5.3	5.1	5.6	4.8	4.5	5.6
5. 10	6.4	6.1	6.8	5.7	5.4	6.7
6. 10	7.7	7.5	8.2	6.9	6.5	8.1
7. 10	9.4	9.2	9.8	8.4	7.9	9.7
8. 10	11.8	11.6	12.2	10.6	10.0	12.1
9. 10	15.9	15.9	16.3	14.4	13.6	16.2
10. 10	34.0	35.0	31.6	40.5	43.6	31.5
Gini coefficient	0.43	0.44	0.42	0.49	0.51	0.41

Source: SIS (1987, 1994).

quintile seems to be a concomitant development, along with the fall of the share of the poorest quintile over the post-1978 time horizon. One becomes more confident in this assessment if attention is focused only on the latest two surveys conducted by the State Institute of Statistics (SIS 1987, 1994). It is clear that, over the 1987–94 period, the SIS data suggest an expansion of the richest quintile at the expense of the other groups, coupled with an overall rise of the Gini index. Given the SIS data, Table 14.2 presents a more detailed assessment of the findings, tabulated at 10 percentage intervals across rural versus urban household income categories.

The overall message of the 1987 and 1994 surveys is that, while the income shares of all nine income groups declined over the period, the share of the richest 10 percentile increased. Within the economy-wide average, the richest 10 percentile raised its share by 6.5 percentage points, from 34 to 40.5 per cent. The polarization of income distribution is more acute in urban households in comparison with the rural sector. The rural economy's Gini coefficient is mostly stable at 0.41, and the worsening of the urban income distribution seems to account for almost all of the economy-wide skewedness in income. In fact, with a Gini coefficient of above 50 per cent in urban centres, the lowest 20 per cent quintile is calculated to receive only 4.8 per cent of national income, in contrast with the share of the richest quintile, which reaches to 57.2 per cent.

The polarization of income is more visible if the comparison is made using purchasing power parity US dollars at constant prices. Such an exercise conducted on the SIS data reveals that the richest quintile consists of 13.9 million individuals with an average gross domestic product (GDP) per capita of $9,878. The per capita income of the top 5 percentile, on the other hand, reaches $22,344 in constant 1997 prices (Table 14.3). Comparing these figures with those for the lowest quintile, the extent of the

Table 14.3. *Average income, richest and poorest quintiles, 1997 (US$)*

Percentile	Number of individuals	Per capita disposable income	Per capita GNP
The richest 20 percentile			
First 5	3,406,030	12,927	22,344
Second 5	3,517,388	4,196	7,252
Third 5	3,562,951	3,193	5,519
Fourth 5	3,421,412	2,770	4,787
Average, top 20	13,907,781	5,726	9,898
The lowest 20 percentile			
First 5	3,013,322	780	1,349
Second 5	2,926,201	694	1,200
Third 5	2,796,454	597	1,032
Fourth 5	2,155,066	465	803
Average, lowest 20	10,891,043	648	1,119

Source: SIS (1994).

income gap becomes more apparent: the lowest 20 percentile consists of 10.9 million individuals, with an average income of only $1119 per head. Among this group, 2.15 million individuals (the poorest 5 per cent) are known to have an income per capita of only $803.

Another facet of this income concentration in the urban sector is the increased wage gap between the skilled/organized and the unskilled/marginal segments of the labour force. Köse and Yeldan (1998) categorize 'informal/marginal' labour as that part of the employed labour force which is not officially registered for any social security coverage and also is not entitled under the 'self employed or employer' status. Based on the State Institute of Statistics Household Labour Survey data, they report that the ratio of marginal labour to total employment in industry increased from 41 per cent in 1980 to 49 per cent in 1994 and stabilized at around 44 per cent after 1995. This form of employment was found to be very extensive in traditional sectors like food processing, textiles and clothing, wood and furniture, and metal products, where small enterprises have greater importance.

Wage data strongly suggest that the substantial improvement in average wages during 1989–93 was almost totally due to what was happening in the organized/formal sector. Wage gaps between large/small and public/private enterprises widened significantly and exceeded the magnitude of the early 1980s. In particular, highly organized mining and electricity/gas workers improved their relative economic positions significantly. In comparison to averages in manufacturing, wages in the clothing industry, on the other hand, eroded by 20 percentage points over the same period, falling below the 1981 level at the start of the liberalization programme (Yentürk 1997; Köse and Yeldan 1998; Boratav *et al.* 2000). Given the extent of polarization indicated by these numbers, it is clear that 'traditional' explanations of income inequality, such as unequal access to education, unequal distribution of assets and land concentration, and the urban-bias do not suffice to provide a coherent portrait of the macroeconomic processes which have given rise to the outcome (see Chapter 1).

Even though easy generalizations can be misleading, one may nevertheless associate the rising income inequality with the broad tendency towards the marginalization of labour due to informal industrial relations, advances in new technologies which favour skill-intensive production patterns, and an unequivocal trend towards the disassociation of the financial sector from the productive sphere of the economy and the concomitant expansion of financial rents. A careful analysis along these lines necessitates a shift of focus towards the functional categories of income and the underlying processes of macro adjustment. The next section turns to these issues.

14.3. MACROECONOMIC ADJUSTMENT UNDER FINANCIAL LIBERALIZATION AND THE RISE OF FINANCIAL RENTS

The Turkish economy experienced two distinct phases along the post-1980 adjustment path. The first covers broadly the period 1981–8, and its main characteristic is structural adjustment with export promotion, albeit under a foreign exchange system of regulated foreign capital inflows. During this period, integration in global markets was achieved mainly through commodity trade liberalization. More importantly, both the exchange rate and direct export subsidies were the main instruments for the promotion of exports and the pursuit of macroeconomic stability. The macroeconomic phases of the post-1980 Turkish economy are sketched in Table 14.4. The table illustrates the various mechanisms of adjustment that have taken place in the spheres of production, distribution, and internationalization.

Three major cycles of adjustment–growth–recession/crisis are evident in Table 14.4. First is the cycle of export orientation, 1981–7, followed by the recession of 1988. The second cycle, 1989–93, was generated by foreign capital inflows following the financial deregulation in 1989 and came to an end with the eruption of the 1994 financial crisis. Lastly, the post-1995 growth was short-circuited by the contagion of the East Asian and Russian crises after 1998. The underlying mode of adjustment in the 1980s was the export orientation of manufacturing industries. During the decade, export revenues increased at an annual rate of 15 per cent, and GNP rose per annum by 4.2 per cent in 1981–2 and by 6.5 per cent between 1983 and 1987. The depreciation of the currency exceeded the rate of domestic inflation for purposes of export promotion and attaining foreign balances, and the Turkish lira was caught in a declining trend in real terms until 1989.

Yet, the underlying feature of the 1981–8 period was the suppression of wages in an attempt to lower production costs and squeeze domestic absorption capacity. Indeed, one of the first measures of the military regime of 1980 was to regulate the labour market through political authoritarianism and the depoliticization and demobilization of the labour force (Cizre-Sakallioglu 1991; Yeldan 1995). With the imposition of the 1982 Constitution and new articles in the 1983 Labour Code, the position of wage labour *vis-à-vis* capital commenced to erode severely throughout the decade.

Table 14.4. *Macroeconomic phases of the Turkish economy, 1980–99*

	Post-crisis adjustment	Export led growth	Exhaustion	Unregulated financial liberalization					Financial crisis	Reinvigoration of short-term foreign capital-led growth			Contagion of world financial crisis	
	1981–2	1983–7	1988	1989	1990	1991	1992	1993	1994	1995	1996	1997	1998	1999.I[a]
I. Production and accumulation (real rate of growth, %)														
GDP	4.2	6.5	2.1	1.2	7.9	1.1	5.9	8.0	−5.5	7.2	7.0	7.5	2.8	−8.5
Fixed investment														
Private sector	25.3	12.3	12.6	1.7	19.4	0.9	4.3	35.0	−9.1	16.9	12.1	11.9	−6.7	−6.7
Public sector	0.2	10.3	−20.2	3.2	8.9	1.8	4.3	3.4	−34.8	−18.8	24.4	28.4	30.0	5.0
Manufacturing industry	−5.1	2.1	−4.8	−14.2	41.6	−4.8	1.1	16.1	−4.7	15.2	2.9	−3.4	−4.8	
As % of GDP														
Savings	17.7	19.5	27.2	22.1	22.0	21.4	21.6	22.7	23.1	22.1	20.0	21.3	21.2	
Investment	18.3	20.9	26.1	22.5	22.6	23.7	23.4	26.3	24.5	24.0	25.0	25.3	25.6	
PSBR	3.7	4.7	4.8	5.2	7.4	10.3	10.6	12.1	7.9	5.2	8.8	7.6	8.7	
Stock of domestic debt		3.5	5.7	6.3	7.0	8.1	11.7	12.8	14.0	14.6	18.8	21.4	22.5	
Interest exp. on dom. debt			2.4	2.2	2.4	2.7	2.8	4.6	6.0	6.2	9.0	7.7	10.9	
II. Distribution and prices														
Inflation rate (CPI)	33.2	39.5	75.4	64.3	60.4	71.1	66.1	71.1	106.3	88.0	80.4	85.7	92.6	73.5
Depreciation of TL/$[b]	45.0	39.7	66.0	49.0	23.0	60.0	65.0	59.0	170.0	54.0	77.0	78.0	76.0	54.7
Real interest rate on GDIs[c]			−5.8	−2.7	24.0	5.3	13.9	9.9	28.6	18.1	31.1	22.1	15.8	32.6

Real wage growth rate (manufacturing)

Private[d]	0.4	−1.5	−5.7	16.1	22.2	20.2	−5.4	−0.1	−30.1	1.4	−1.4	−8.2	3.3
Public	−0.4	−5.9	−7.8	47.5	18.8	37.1	5.8	−0.9	−18.1	−18.0	6.0		
Average mark-up rate, private manufacturing (%)	31.0	32.6	38.0	33.5	38.6	39.1	41.5	43.9	47.0	42.0	39.0		

Wages/manufacturing value added (%)

Private manufacturing	30.0	24.2	20.0	24.0	25.0	27.0	25.0	25.0	20.0	18.0	23.0		
Public manufacturing	27.0	22.2	15.0	20.0	25.0	31.0	37.0	34.0	29.0	20.0	22.0		

III. Internationalization

Man. export, growth[e]	19.7	12.5	14.0	−1.0	11.0	4.0	8.0	4.0	18.0	19.0	7.2	6.7	1.3

As % share of GNP

Imports[f]	14.0	15.9	15.8	14.5	14.6	13.8	14.3	16.2	17.8	20.8	23.6	25.2	22.9
Exports[f]	8.5	10.8	12.8	10.7	8.5	8.9	9.2	8.4	13.8	12.6	17.8	17.1	15.7
Current account[f]	−2.7	−1.9	1.8	0.9	−1.7	0.2	−0.6	−3.6	2.0	−1.4	−1.3	−1.4	1.4
Foreign debt	27.1	37.8	44.8	38.8	32.5	33.6	35.2	37.7	49.6	42.8	46.1	47.8	51.7

[a] Annual % rate of change from the same period of the previous year.

[b] According to the $1.5 + 1 euro basket.

[c] Annual average compounded interest rate on government debt instruments deflated by the CPI.

[d] Private manufacturing labour data pertain to enterprises employing 10 or more workers.

[e] Annual growth rate in manufacturing exports (millions, $).

[f] Inclusive of the luggage trade after 1996.

Sources: State Planning Organization and Undersecretariat of Foreign Trade and Treasury data on main economic indicators and State Institute of Statistics manufacturing industry surveys.

As soon as it assumed power, the military government shut down the major labour union confederations, and trade unions were barred from engaging in political activity and establishing formal and informal links with political parties. With the new Labour Code of 1983, the right to strike was severely restricted and was limited only to collective bargaining disputes. Even then, a strike could be prohibited or postponed, and any dispute could be settled from the outside by a newly formed body called the Supreme Board of Arbitration. Through this body, the state exercised strict control and supervision over labour relations and regulated the evolution of wage demands effectively. Consequently, the share of wage labour in private manufacturing value added receded from 30 per cent to 20 per cent and in public manufacturing from 27 per cent to 15 per cent between 1980 and 1988. In this process, the average mark-up rate (profit margins) in private manufacturing increased from 31 per cent to 38 per cent (Table 14.4).

The other side of this distributional shift was the rise in financial rents. With the advent of the deregulation of domestic financial markets and the liberalization of the capital account, the Turkish economy had completed its integration with global financial markets by 1989. In this setting, the central bank lost its overall control over the exchange rate and the interest rate as instruments of independent policy-making, as these practically turned into exogenous parameters set by the chaotic changes in financial arbitrage in global markets.

Financial liberalization was expected to achieve a more efficient and flexible financial system capable of converting national savings into productive investments at the lowest cost. Contrary to what was expected, however, the reforms were not accompanied by any significant change in the financing behaviour of corporations and did not lead to lower investment costs (Akyüz 1990). The state maintained its dominance in both commodity and asset markets through its complex system of price and fiscal incentives. The real rate of interest, in fact, rose to unprecedented levels, and domestic asset markets, impacted by sudden changes in speculative foreign capital flows, became volatile and uncertain.

Table 14.5 documents the distributional consequences of the post-1980 financial deregulation. The share of interest income in total domestic income rose from close to zero in 1980 to 15.2 per cent by 1998, a figure similar to the total value added of agriculture—a sector that employs 45 per cent of the civilian labour force.

From a longer time perspective, the overall decline of agricultural and wage income is phenomenal. The share of agricultural income has been reduced by almost half in the course of the last three decades. The wage cycle, on the other hand, displayed a rising trend in the 1970s and followed a declining course during the outward orientation of the domestic economy in the 1980s. The income share of non-agricultural wages reached its lowest level in 1986 at 17.1 per cent from the peak of 36.8 per cent realized in 1977. A fall of such magnitude clearly reflected the faltering employment response of domestic industry to significant reductions in real wages. The implication is that the scope for capital–labour substitution has been greatly limited in the productive sectors of the Turkish economy (Celasun 1989: 20). Given this background, it would be illuminating to trace out the dynamics of the real earnings of wage labour

Table 14.5. *The functional distribution of domestic factor income, 1970–98 (percentage)*

	Total domestic factor income	Agriculture	Non-agricultural factor income							
			Total	Wages and salaries			Non-wage income			
				Total	Public sector	Private sector	Total	Income on rent	Interest income	Other factor income
1970	100.00	31.08	68.92	31.15			37.77			
1971	100.00	31.31	68.69	31.33			37.36			
1972	100.00	30.32	69.68	31.57			38.11			
1973	100.00	29.13	70.87	31.56			39.31			
1974	100.00	30.20	69.80	29.77			40.03			
1975	100.00	30.76	69.24	31.51			37.73			
1976	100.00	31.28	68.72	33.11			35.61			
1977	100.00	29.12	70.88	36.81			34.07			
1978	100.00	26.66	73.34	35.19			38.15			
1979	100.00	24.33	75.67	32.79			42.88			
1980	100.00	27.51	72.49	25.27	14.60	10.67	47.22	8.97	0.73	37.52
1981	100.00	25.27	74.73	22.28	11.86	10.42	52.45	8.04	3.54	40.87
1982	100.00	23.52	76.48	20.09	10.17	9.92	56.39	8.13	5.35	42.91
1983	100.00	22.14	77.86	22.02	10.98	11.04	55.84	8.15	5.41	42.28
1984	100.00	22.43	77.57	19.37	9.58	9.79	58.20	7.56	7.68	42.96
1985	100.00	21.17	78.83	17.40	8.49	8.91	61.43	7.78	6.74	46.91
1986	100.00	21.03	78.97	17.08	8.32	8.76	61.89	7.24	7.01	47.64
1987	100.00	19.19	80.81	20.39	9.43	10.96	60.42	6.26	7.80	46.36
1988	100.00	18.58	81.42	20.91	9.10	11.81	60.51	4.80	8.89	46.82
1989	100.00	18.20	81.80	24.07	12.37	11.70	57.73	3.92	5.90	47.91
1990	100.00	19.07	80.93	28.11	15.02	13.09	52.82	3.39	5.79	43.64
1991	100.00	16.35	83.65	33.78	18.27	15.51	49.87	3.76	8.44	37.67
1992	100.00	15.97	84.03	34.42	19.43	14.99	49.61	3.84	7.95	37.82
1993	100.00	16.77	83.23	33.29	19.10	14.19	49.94	3.38	6.97	39.59
1994	100.00	16.70	83.30	27.50	15.47	12.03	55.80	3.23	8.62	43.95
1995	100.00	17.18	82.82	24.56	12.68	11.88	58.26	3.24	11.61	43.41
1996	100.00	18.34	81.66	26.81	12.28	14.53	54.85	3.08	14.71	37.06
1997	100.00	15.73	84.27	29.45	13.50	15.95	54.82	3.10	14.40	37.32
1998	100.00	18.51	81.49	27.44	13.83	13.61	54.05	3.38	15.17	35.50

Sources: 1970–9, Ozmucur (1986); 1980–98, Temel and associates (1999).

against (labour) productivity growth over an extended time horizon. In what follows, recent advances in the business cycle literature are employed, and the variations in the average product of labour and the real wage rate in Turkish industry are decomposed to obtain the underlying long-term trends. Hodrick–Prescott (1980) filtering methods are used to separate out the cyclical variations in productivity growth and wage rates from their respective historical trends. This exercise enables us to isolate the underlying trend paths of the two variables and to make inferences about the evolution of the wage cycle against the long-term productivity patterns in Turkish industry.

Data for our analysis come from the annual manufacturing industry surveys reported by the State Institute of Statistics. For the 'wage rate' series, 'total wage earnings' divided by 'total workers engaged in production' are used. The average labour

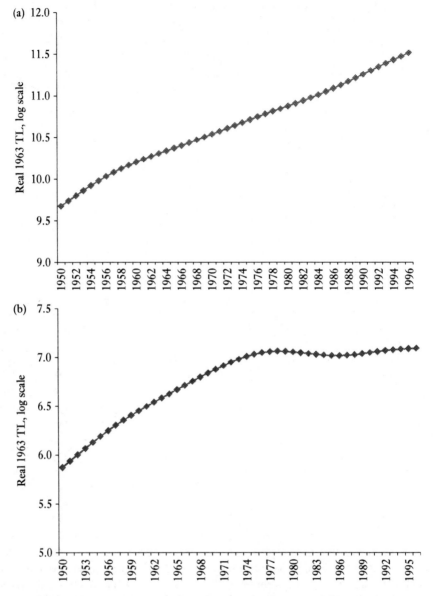

Figure 14.1. *Trends in (a) real average labour productivity and (b) real wages in Turkish manufacturing, 1950–96*

product is derived by dividing 'total value added' by the same labour employment magnitude. Both series are deflated by the wholesale price index and are filtered in logarithmic form. The exercise covers the extended time frame, 1950–96. The results of the filter are portrayed in Figs. 14.1(a) and 14.1(b). The units on the *y*-axis are in real

1963 TL in log scale. In Fig. 14.1(a), we observe the historical long-term trend of the real average labour product in Turkish manufacturing. The trend has a secular upward slope, with an average rate of annual growth of 3.8 per cent for the whole time horizon (1950–96). This is to be contrasted with the trend in the real wage rate portrayed in Fig. 14.1(b). The trend in real wages fluctuates along an increasing path until the mid-1970s, enters a deceleration between 1980 and 1988, and recovers after 1989. The observed recovery in the real wage is clearly the result of post-1989 populism, which enabled sharp increases in real wages between 1989 and 1993, as outlined in Section 14.4. On this record of events, it seems plausible to argue that the post-1989 upswing in manufacturing real wages was, in fact, in line with the real average product of labour as far as the long-term trends of the two series are concerned.[4]

Consequently, the fluctuations in the real wage trend document the periodization of the overall political cycle affecting Turkish labour markets. The fundamental characteristic of this cycle is that it discloses a relatively weak connection between wage remunerations and labour productivity in manufacturing industries. The trend path of real wages clearly signals a break following 1979/80. This is the era when the domestic economy was subjected to a new transformation in terms of foreign competition and integration with global commodity and asset markets. The ongoing wage suppression as manifested by the downswing in the wage cycle indicates that the adjustments in labour markets had served as one of the main mechanisms to bring forth this transformation. Implemented under a military rule which imposed severe restrictions through the Labour Code on collective bargaining and unionization, the cost savings on wage labour were instrumental in extracting an economic surplus which, in turn, was oriented towards export markets via a generous export subsidization programme.

Reading from a different perspective, the sharp contrast in the trend in labour productivity against real wage earnings following the 1980 transformation clearly displays the extent of disassociation between the productive sphere of the domestic economy and its indigenous processes of accumulation and distribution. As the internationalization of commodity and financial markets intensified, the links between the processes of savings generation and the productive use of these funds for capital accumulation—the so-called 'process of intermediation'—were severed. With the complete deregulation of financial transactions and the consequent ascendancy of finance over industry, international capital was able to assume a dominant role so as to act as the sole arbiter, aiming at immediate financial gain rather than at long-term economic development and sustainable growth. As this unbalanced structure failed to generate the necessary accumulation patterns to achieve sustained growth, the impetus for it was exhausted by the end of the decade. The artificial growth path generated through wage suppression and price subsidies reached its economic and political limits by 1988. As summarized in Table 14.4, all economic indicators for 1988 signal a stagflationary macro environment. The rate of GDP growth was only 2.1 per cent, the rate of growth of fixed investments was negative, and the inflation rate accelerated to 75 per cent. Furthermore, the real exchange rate had started to appreciate for the first time since the inception of export orientation.

---

[4] See Boratav (1991) for narrative support for this claim.

Commensurate with these events, we observe real wage earnings entering a period of recovery following the gains of the union movement and also the new wave of populist pressures. As can be seen from the data in Table 14.4, real wages in public manufacturing increased by 47.5 per cent in 1988 and then again by 37.1 per cent in 1991. Similar trends were observed in the private manufacturing sector as real wage costs increased by 16.1 per cent in 1989, 22.2 per cent in 1990, and 20.2 per cent in 1991. Furthermore, the rural economy witnessed a significant improvement in its terms of trade *vis-à-vis* the rest of the economy. This occurred despite an ongoing process of worsening agricultural terms of trade in world markets, a contrasting signal in favour of the rural economy. Finally, beginning in 1989, there was a major shift in public expenditure towards more socially desirable activities. An overall increase in both the share and the level of public salaries and investments in social infrastructure enabled the working masses to attain improved living standards.

14.4. THE RISING FISCAL GAP AND THE ROLE OF THE STATE IN REGULATING THE DISTRIBUTIONAL STRUCTURE

The post-1990 balances in the public sector record an unprecedented rise in the fiscal gap. In contrast, post-1988 populism could evidently be financed by taxing capital incomes and moving towards a fairer tax burden for the working classes. Yet, the strategic preference of the state was the maintenance of its favourable stance towards the evasion of taxable capital incomes and towards surplus transfer because of a lax attitude towards so-called 'unrecorded private transactions'. Consequently, the state apparatus turned into a bastion of privilege as it assumed a regulatory role in the creation and absorption of the economic surplus, and fiscal balances took the major brunt of adjustment. The main macroeconomic policy response to increased wage costs and the shift in the rural terms of trade involved the rapid widening of the fiscal gap and support for the profitability of private capital. As a major indicator of the (functional) distribution of income, for instance, profit margins mark-up rate maintained a rising trend, and, despite the severe jump in real wage costs, reached 47 per cent in 1994, up from 33.5 per cent in 1989. Simultaneous to this development was the rapid rise of the borrowing requirement of the public sector, as the ratio of the PSBR to GDP climbed to 10.3 per cent in 1991 and 12.1 per cent in 1993 (Table 14.4).

Given all this, the widening fiscal deficit and the macroeconomic disequilibria it generated clearly should be understood in the context of the historical role of the state in sustaining capital incomes against the faltering performance of export-led growth patterns along with rapid increases in the costs of wage labour. The fiscal deficit of the Turkish state in the early 1990s does not necessarily imply a chronic problem of bureaucratic mismanagement, but is a reflection of the administrative and socio-economic policies on the part of the public sector that were deemed necessary to sustain the generation of an economic surplus for private capital. The state used its tax and subsidy policies as well as the prices of the goods produced by state enterprises as strategic instruments to this end and financed its fiscal deficits via forced savings by way of price inflation and increased securitization of domestic debt through short-term capital inflows.[5] With this approach, however, the stock of securitized domestic debt rose almost fourfold in the relatively short time span of a decade, from about 6 per cent of GNP in 1989, just when the liberalization of the capital account was completed, to 22 per cent in 1998.

A key characteristic of the Turkish domestic debt was its short-term maturity. As a ratio of the stock of existing debt, annual cumulative domestic borrowings increased over the 1990s and reached 103 per cent in 1993, indicating that each year the state had to resort to new borrowing which exceeded the stock of debt already accumulated. In 1996, this ratio reached 163.5 per cent. Even though the ratio seems to have declined over 1997, provisional indicators for 1998 and 1999 reveal that it again surpassed the 100 per cent threshold.[6] Thus, the public sector has been trapped in a short-term debt spiral, a phenomenon called 'Ponzi-financing'. Under these conditions, and given the fragility of the domestic asset markets, real interest rates rose to very high levels and, as a result, interest payments on the public debt rose from 2 per cent of GNP in 1990 to 4.6 per cent in 1993 and 14.1 per cent by the end of 1999.

On the other hand, the obligation to generate a surplus in the primary budget led to severe retrenchment in the remaining public expenditure items. The major brunt of the adjustment fell on public investment expenditure that was reduced to only 4.6 per cent of total budgetary outlays by the third quarter of 1998. By comparison, the interest payments on the domestic debt reached 1010 per cent of public investments and 481 per cent of social security transfers in the same year. In other words, the Turkish central budget lost in the 1990s all its function as an instrument of social infrastructure development and economic growth, and was transformed into a tool of financial sector development, regulating the distribution of the economic surplus in the domestic asset market in ways which favour the financial rentiers and private capital owners.

The extent of this regulatory role can be more clearly grasped when account is taken of the amount of income taxes generated by capital incomes (Fig. 14.2). By comparing the interest costs of the state and the tax earnings from capital incomes, one can see the extent of the transfer accruing to the rentier classes through the debt management operations of the treasury. As a ratio of GNP, interest payments on domestic debt had exceeded 10 per cent by the end of the decade. However, the tax burden on the incomes of the corporate sector had reached a maximum of only 1.7 per cent over the same period.

It can be seen that capital incomes effectively remain untaxed in Turkey, and as the treasury offered sizable premiums on the market yields of its instruments, it became

---

[5] See, for example, Köse and Yeldan (1998), Yeldan (1996*a*, 1997), and Boratav *et al.* (2000) for a more comprehensive assessment of this argument. Yeldan (1996*b*, 1998), in turn, offers a macroeconomic general equilibrium assessment of the pre-1994 crisis path of the Turkish economy and reports that the fiscal deficits realized between 1991 and 1993 enabled an increase in the real incomes of private industrial capital by as much as 7 per cent per annum.

[6] Data on these indicators can be obtained from the website of the treasury undersecretariat, http://www.treasury.gov.tr.

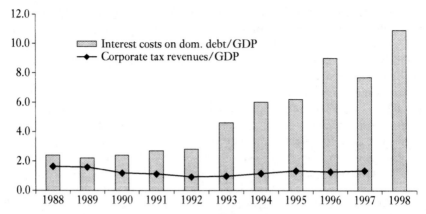

Figure 14.2. *Interest payments on domestic debt and corporate tax revenues (percentage of GNP)*

Source: *Monthly Statistics* (various).

the dominant agent in the financial economy, enabling the banking system to capture significant returns based on the arbitrage of open positions. Consequently, the current mode of domestic debt management through securitization works as a direct income transfer to the commercial banking sector and the rentier classes, with the state playing an active role in regulating this transfer.

The distribution of the government debt instruments shows that in early 1997 more than 92 per cent of the newly securitized deficit was purchased by the banking sector, with the private and public sectors absorbing respectively another 4 and 3 per cent each. Thus, the so-called 'deepening' of the financial system in the Turkish economy has turned into a process of self-fuelled cycles ready to burst. High real interest rates on the GDIs attract speculative short-term funds, and, through the operations of the banking system, these are channelled to the vaults of the treasury. In this manner, the latter was able to bypass the regulations of the central bank, as well as the limits imposed on foreign borrowing. Capital account liberalization has, thus, served the government by enabling banks to engage in extremely profitable short-term borrowing abroad so as to finance the treasury's bond auctions. The major brunt of the costs of this fragile environment, however, has fallen on the productive sphere of the economy, especially the traded sector.

Indeed, throughout the course of these operations, Turkey's banking sector and financial institutions disengaged from investing in production and became the dominant player in manipulating the overall economy. Initially, it was the collapse in public revenue which led to feverish public sector borrowing. The consequent high interest rates on government bonds and Treasury bills set the course for the dominance of finance over the real economy. As a result, the economy is now trapped in a vicious circle: commitment to high interest rates and cheap foreign currency (overvalued TL) against the threat of capital flight leads to further increases in real interest rates. When the adverse impacts on the current account balance become excessively destabilizing, real depreciation seems imminent, which, however, needs to be matched by further upward adjustment in the interest rate if currency substitution or capital flight is to be restrained. This process, as in the case of Mexico in 1994 and the recent crises in East Asia (on this, see Chapter 7), leads to overvaluation of the domestic currency and the cheapening of imports and, thus, to an acceleration of domestic consumption demand at the expense of exports and the real productive industries in general.

Erratic movements in the current account, a rising trade deficit (from 3.5 per cent of GNP in 1985–8 to 6 per cent in 1990–3) and a drastic deterioration in fiscal balances reveal the unsustainable character of the post-1989 populism financed by foreign capital inflows. In the words of Boratav *et al.* (1995):

the post-1990 Turkish experience shows the serious problems confronting a developing economy which decides to move into full external and internal deregulation in the financial system under conditions of high inflation. The specter of capital flight becomes the dominant motive in policy-making and creates commitment to high interest rates and expectations for cheap foreign exchange. The links of these two policy variables with the real sphere of the economy, i.e. investment on physical capital and the current account balance of payments, are deeply severed. Instability in the rates of foreign exchange and interest rates creates feedbacks which lead the economy into further instability.

This prolonged instability reached its climax during the fourth quarter of 1993, when currency appreciation and the consequent current account deficits rose to unprecedented levels. With the sudden drainage of short-term funds in the beginning of January 1994, production capacity contracted, followed by a continued fall in industrial output throughout that year. Together with this contraction, post-1994 crisis management gave rise to significant shifts in income distribution and to an intensification of the ongoing process of the transfer of the economic surplus towards the financial sector and away from wage labour and the industrial sectors. Likewise, dollar-denominated wage costs decreased substantially and enabled export earnings to rise. In this manner, Turkey switched once again to a mode of surplus extraction, whereby the export performance of industrial sectors and the burden of macroeconomic adjustment depended on savings on the wage bill. In fact, the disequilibrium could only have been accommodated by the massive (downward) flexibility displayed in real remunerations of wage labour.

As an overall summary of the dynamics of the post-financial liberalization, Fig. 14.3 characterizes schematically the main mechanisms of macroeconomic regulation in Turkey. Low savings, along with a large fiscal gap, and structural deficiencies in an oligopolistic production structure set the scene portrayed in Fig. 14.3. Low savings generation results directly in disequilibrium in the macroeconomic environment along channel (1). An important addition to the features of the period was the wage explosion and the re-emergence of a populist stance within the background of intensified political struggle. In response to these structural characteristics, we observe that the state assumed an active role in the economic sphere, regulating the distribution of national output.

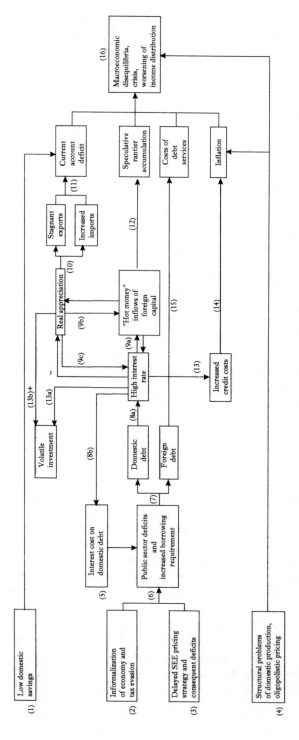

Figure 14.3. *Macroeconomic dynamics of the Turkish economy under full financial liberalization (post-1989)*

Notes: Structural fearutes: (1), (4), wage explosion return to populism; Policy responses: capital account liberalization (3); keeping SEE prices low; First stage outcomes: (2), (6), (7), vicious circle of domestic debt: (8a), (8b), (9c) (13a), (13b); Second stage outcomes: (6), (7), (8a), (8b) repeated, (10) (11) (12), (14) (16).

Vicious circle of capital account liberalization: (9a), (9b), (9c) (13a), (13b); Second stage outcomes: (6), (7), (8a),

The state carried out this task, first, through its enterprise system by way of a mandated policy of delayed price adjustments on intermediate, wage, and capital goods produced by state enterprises (Fig. 14.3, box 3). Second, following the full deregulation of the capital account, the state actively participated in domestic asset markets through the issuance of debt instruments (channels 6 and 7). This, together with the threat of currency substitution in the context of a convertible currency regime, necessitated high interest rates (channels 8a and 8b)—the first vicious circle—and real appreciation (channel 9b). The second vicious circle surrounding channels (9a), (9b), and (9c) is highlighted by the contradictory implications of the three variables involved: short-term capital inflows (hot money), real appreciation, and high real interest rates. Real appreciation was the prime cause of the rise in import volumes and the current account deficits. On the other hand, real appreciation had a direct positive effect on investment demand by reducing the costs of imported capital goods and intermediates (channel 13b). This positive effect was countervailed by the pressures of real interest rates (channel 13a), the result being increased volatility in investment demand. High interest rates gave way to inflationary pressures through the increased costs of credit (channels 8b and 13) and fed a speculative rentier type of accumulation (channel 12), with the consequent worsening in income distribution. The limits of this bonanza of a short-term foreign capital-led growth pattern was the eruption of the financial crisis in 1994 and the continued fragility and the severe disequilibria faced by domestic markets in the late 1990s.

Clearly, the reform fatigue and exhaustion of the 1988 crisis and the unsustainability of the post-1989 growth path which culminated in the crisis in 1994 and the current crises have been characterized by the operation of quite different macro dynamics. Throughout all these episodes, however, in spite of the official stance towards a policy of 'reducing the economic role of the state', we observe continued use of the state's powers as a regulatory agent, overseeing the distributional conflict over the national product.

14.5. CONCLUDING COMMENTS AND OVERALL ASSESSMENT

This chapter has attempted to investigate and assess the impact of financial liberalization and the ongoing rise of financial rents on income distribution in the post-1980 Turkish economy. The data on the size distribution of income and on the long-run dynamics of real wages against labour productivity disclose a worsening in income distribution. They also disclose an overall disengagement of financial institutions from the productive sphere to become the dominant agent in the manipulation of the domestic economy. As financial capital gained supremacy over industry, the links between growth and productivity gains and the channelling of savings to the accumulation of productive capital were severely hampered, with adverse consequences for wage incomes and the working poor. These findings are in stark contrast with the predictions of the standard theory which argues that the expected productivity gains associated with increased liberalization and competition in global commodity and financial markets would translate into increased wages within the labour-intensive sectors in which Turkey was said to hold comparative advantage. Our findings thus underscore that, given the poor vertical integration among industrial sectors typical of peripheral capitalism, the implementation of vigorous export promotion polices and state-led price incentives created sporadic increases in productivity in the 1980s, but failed to generate a sustained increase in economic growth and accumulation.

The Turkish adjustment experience throughout the post-1980 period has been a process in which, in a developing market economy trapped by the needs of its domestic industry to integrate into the world markets and the distributional requirements warranted by this reorientation, the state apparatus became a bastion of privilege, regulating income redistribution within society. The elements of this redistribution involved direct mechanisms to subsidize production and exports, currency depreciation, and wage suppression, as well as indirect mechanisms such as tax evasion on capital incomes and a financial market development strategy that enabled massive income transfers to the rentier class.

REFERENCES

Akyüz, Y. (1990). Financial system and policies in Turkey in the 1980s. In T. Aricanli and D. Rodrik (eds.), *The Political Economy of Turkey*. Macmillan: London.

Atkinson, A. (1998*a*). Equity issues in a globalizing world: The experience of OECD countries. Paper prepared for the Conference on Economic Policy and Equity, June, IMF: Washington, DC.

—— (1998*b*). The changing distribution of income: Evidence and explanations. Mimeo, University of Linz: Linz.

Barro, R. J. (1999). Inequality, growth and investment, NBER Working Papers 7038, National Bureau of Economic Research, Cambridge, MA.

Boratav, K. (1991). *Social Classes and Distribution in the 1980s*. Gerçek Yayinevi, Istanbul, in Turkish.

—— and O. Türel (1993). Turkey. In L. Taylor (ed.), *The Rocky Road to Reform*. MIT Press: Cambridge, MA.

——, ——, and E. Yeldan (1995). The Turkish economy in 1981–92: A balance sheet, problems and prospects. *METU Studies in Development* 22(1), 1–36.

——, ——, and —— (1996). Dilemmas of structural adjustment and environmental policies under instability: Post-1980 Turkey. *World Development* 24(2), 373–93.

——, E. Yeldan, and A. Köse (2000). Globalization, distribution and social policy: Turkey, 1980–1998. Project Papers 20, CEPA-New School: New York.

Bourdieu, P. (1998). The essence of neoliberalism. Le Monde Diplomatique December.

Bulutay, T., S. Timur, and H. Ersel (1971). *Distribution of Income in Turkey, 1968*. Ankara University, Ankara, in Turkish.

Celasun, M. (1989). Income distribution and employment aspects of Turkey's post-1980 adjustment. *METU Studies in Development* 16(3–4), 1–31.

—— (1994). Trade and industrialization in Turkey: Initial conditions, policy and performance in the 1980s. In G. K. Helleiner (ed.), *Trade Policy and Industrialization in Turbulent Times*. Routledge: London.

—— and D. Rodrik (1989). Debt, adjustment and growth: Turkey. In J. Sachs and S. M. Collins (eds.), *Developing Country Debt and Economic Performance, Country Studies*. University of Chicago Press: Chicago.

Cizre-Sakallioglu, Ü. (1991). Labour: The battered community. In M. Heper (ed.), *Strong State and Economic Interest Groups: The Post-1980 Turkish Experience*. de Gruyter: New York.

Cornia, G. A., and S. Kiiski (1999). Trends in income distribution in the post-World War II period: Evidence and interpretation. Paper prepared for the WIDER project meeting Rising Income Inequality and Poverty Reduction: Are They Compatible? July, UNU/WIDER, Helsinki.

Ekinci, N. (1998). Dynamics of growth and crisis in the Turkish economy. *Toplum ve Bilim* 77, in Turkish.

Hodrick, R. J. and E. C. Prescott (1980). Postwar US business cycles: An empirical investigation. Discussion Papers 451. Carnegie-Mellon University: Pittsburgh.

Köse, A. H., and E. Yeldan (1998). Turkish economy in 1990s: An assessment of fiscal policies, labor markets and foreign trade. *New Perspectives on Turkey* 18, 51–78.

Milanovic, B. (1999). True world income distribution, 1988 and 1993: First calculations based on household surveys alone. Mimeo, World Bank: Washington, DC.

Monthly Statistics (various). Undersecretariat of foreign trade and treasury, Turkish prime ministry, Ankara.

Onaran, O. (1999). The effects of structural adjustment policies on the labour market and income distribution in Turkey. Ph.D. thesis, Istanbul Technical University: Istanbul.

Ozmucur, S. (1986). Income distribution in Turkey 1963–85. *Iktisat Dergisi*, 258, 26–32, in Turkish.

Rodrik, D. (1997). *Has Globalization Gone Too Far?* Institute for International Economics: Washington, DC.

——(1998). Globalization, social conflict and economic growth. *The World Economy* 21(2), 143–58.

Senses, F. (1994). Labour market response to structural adjustment and institutional pressures: The Turkish case. *METU Studies in Development* 21(3), 1–26.

SIS (various). *Annual Manufacturing Industry Surveys*. State Institute of Statistics: Ankara.

——(1987). *Household Survey of Income Distribution*. State Institute of Statistics: Ankara.

——(1994). *Household Survey of Income Distribution*. State Institute of Statistics: Ankara.

SPO (1973). Income distribution in Turkey. Mimeo, State Planning Organization: Ankara.

Tansel, A. (1999). Public–private employment choice, wage differentials and gender in Turkey, Discussion Papers 797. Economic Growth Centre, Yale University: New Haven.

Temel, A., and associates (1999). Functional distribution of income in Turkey. Mimeo, State Planning Organization: Ankara.

UNCTAD (1997). *Trade and Development Report*. UNCTAD: Geneva.

Uygur, E. (1993). *Financial Liberalization and Economic Performance of Turkey*. Central Bank of Turkey: Ankara.

Voyvoda, E., and E. Yeldan (1999). Patterns of productivity growth and the real wage cycle in Turkish manufacturing. Discussion Paper 99–11. Department of Economics, Bilkent University: Ankara.

Yeldan, E. (1995). Surplus creation and extraction under structural adjustment: Turkey, 1980–1992. *Review of Radical Political Economics* 27(2), 38–72.

——(1996a). Macroeconomic processes determining the distribution of income in the post-1980 Turkish economy. *Iktisat Dergisi* 359, 26–9, in Turkish.

——(1996b). Evolution of the crisis in the Turkish economy: A general equilibrium investigation 1990–1993. *METU Studies in Development* 23(3), 427–76, in Turkish.

——(1997). The Turkish experience of financial liberalization. *Petrol Is 1995/96 Almanac* 202–18, in Turkish.

——(1998). On structural sources of the 1994 Turkish crisis: A CGE modeling analysis. *International Review of Applied Economics* 12(3), 397–414.

Yentürk, N. (1997). *Wages, Employment and Accumulation in the Turkish Manufacturing Industry*, Friedrich Ebert Stiftung, Istanbul, in Turkish.

15

The Changing Nature of Inequality in South Africa

CAROLYN JENKINS AND LYNNE THOMAS

15.1. INTRODUCTION

Addressing a legacy of extreme racial inequality is one of the chief objectives of South Africa's current government. During the 1960s, legal and administrative restrictions on black labour produced increasing racial inequalities of income; by 1970 the per capita income of whites was 15 times higher than that of blacks.[1] During the 24 years from 1970 to the change of government in 1994, racial disparities in income actually declined as apartheid was eroded in the workplace, although falling inequality *between* races—achieved primarily by a redistribution from whites to blacks—was accompanied by rising inequality *within* race groups. When government was transferred to the majority, deprivation remained characteristic of most black households.

Since the political transition in 1994, policies to address South Africa's inequalities have been pursued. These were set out in the reconstruction and development programme and a variety of legislative initiatives. However, the government's ability to address social problems has been constrained by its commitment both to implement strict fiscal policies and to pursue structural economic reforms (which inevitably have short-term social costs). The underlying theme of economic policy documents like Growth Employment and Redistribution (GEAR) of 1996 (RSA 1996) reflects a view—strongly influenced by neoclassical orthodoxy—that South Africa will be able to overcome permanently the economic legacies of apartheid only through long-term economic growth. What is unclear is whether the growth generated will be sufficient to address inequality—or even begin to make a difference in the medium-term—or whether there are aspects of inequality which require more direct policy responses.

This study reviews the evolution of inequality in South Africa (Section 15.2) and draws together the findings of other authors to highlight the primary sources of changes in the nature of inequality (Section 15.3). The evolution of economic policy

---

[1] The racial classification used in this study is in accordance with South African definitions: Asians, blacks (indigenous people), coloureds (mixed race people), and whites.

and performance is then assessed (Section 15.4), drawing a distinction between the apartheid years and the post-1994 period. The chapter then considers the post-transition policy framework in more detail. Policies targeted at the structural causes of poverty are discussed briefly in Section 15.5. Section 15.6 focuses on the likely impact of the macroeconomic policy framework on the income distribution (unfortunately, at the time of writing data were not yet available to assess the redistributional impact of post-1994 policy in terms of standard measures of inequality). It is argued that changes in labour markets resulting from the breakdown of apartheid in the workplace dominated the observed shifts in the distribution of income during the 1970s and 1980s. However, there is evidence that the shift towards neoliberal orthodoxy is increasingly affecting the income distribution, in line with predictions of other chapters in this volume.

15.2. THE EVOLUTION OF INEQUALITY IN SOUTH AFRICA

15.2.1. *The Context: South Africa in Comparative Perspective*

Early studies of income inequality found that South Africa had the most unequal distribution of income in the world amongst countries where comparable information was available (McGrath 1983; Simkins 1979). South Africa still ranks amongst countries with the most skewed distribution, as is evident from Table 15.1. Table 15.1 presents 1995 per capita gross domestic product (GDP), Gini coefficients, and the human development index[2] for a selection of developing countries. The choice of comparator countries is determined largely by the availability of (reasonably) recent Gini coefficients. In terms of GDP per capita and human development, South Africa compares with Ecuador, Romania, Indonesia, and Peru. However, Gini coefficients show that inequality in South Africa is more typical of highly unequal societies, like Chile and Brazil (where per capita income is considerably higher), or Zimbabwe, which has a similar colonial heritage (but is considerably poorer).

Although South Africa's per capita income is sufficiently high for it to be rated 'upper middle-income' by the World Bank, inequality in the distribution of personal income, compounded by historical underinvestment in human capital (health and education) for the majority of the population, means that poverty is widespread.

15.2.2. *Trends in the Distribution of Income and Poverty in South Africa*

Up until 1970 job reservation for whites ensured their protected employment at high wages and the crowding of the rest of the population into low-skilled, low-paid jobs. The disparity between white and non-white, especially black, wages widened considerably, and by 1970 the per capita income of whites was 15 times higher than that of

---

[2] The human development index is a measure of social development calculated by the UNDP and is based on indicators of GDP per capita, life expectancy, and literacy and school enrolment rates.

Table 15.1. *International indicators of inequality*

	GDP per head (PPP US$ 1995)	Gini coefficient[a]	Human Development Index (1995)
Chile	9930	56.5	0.893
Thailand	7742	46.2	0.838
Brazil	5928	60.1	0.809
Ecuador	4602	46.6	0.767
Romania	4431	28.2	0.767
South Africa	4334	59.3	0.717
Indonesia	3971	36.5	0.679
Peru	3940	46.2	0.729
Philippines	2762	42.9	0.677
Zimbabwe	2135	56.8	0.507
Zambia	986	49.8	0.378
Tanzania	636	38.2	0.358

[a] Based on survey data from various years: Chile 1994; Thailand 1992; Brazil 1995; Ecuador 1994; Romania 1994; South Africa 1993–4; Peru 1996; Indonesia 1996; Philippines 1994; Zimbabwe 1990; Zambia 1996; and Tanzania 1993. Care must be taken in comparing these indicators as surveys may differ in context and coverage.

Sources: UNDP (various); World Bank (1999a).

blacks (Whiteford and McGrath 1999: 1). Monopsonistic employment practices in mining meant that black wages did not rise in nominal terms for about 50 years; black wages in agriculture were also stagnant (Lipton 1985: 44, 388). Some real growth did occur in manufacturing wages, as higher skills are required (Lundahl *et al.* 1992: 299), although blacks tended to occupy lower skilled positions.

After 1970 there was a redistribution of income from whites to blacks. The share of total income accruing to whites (13 per cent of the population in 1991) fell from 71 per cent in 1970 to 61 per cent in 1991, while that of blacks (about 75 per cent of the population in 1991) rose from 20 per cent to 28 per cent over the same period. The remainder went to groups classified as coloureds and Asians. However, for each race group the share of total income accruing to the lowest 40 per cent declined in the two decades to 1991, while the share of the top 10 per cent increased. This was most dramatic for blacks—the share in black household income of the poorest 40 per cent of black households decreased from 12 per cent to 6 per cent, while that of the richest 10 per cent increased from 32 per cent to 47 per cent. Measures of inequality bear this out. Using census data, Whiteford and McGrath (1999: 13) show that the Gini coefficient for household income of the whole population did not change significantly between 1975 and 1991.[3] However, racial Gini coefficients all increased (Table 15.2).

---

[3] The Gini coefficient calculated on a per capita basis was even higher, at 0.71.

Table 15.2. *Gini coefficients: Household income by race, 1975 and 1991; 1990 and 1995*

| | Whiteford and McGrath | | Hirschowitz (12 main urban areas) | |
	1975	1991	1990	1995
Asian	0.45	0.49	0.29	0.46
Black	0.47	0.62	0.35	0.51
Coloured	0.51	0.52	0.37	0.42
White	0.36	0.46	0.50	0.44
Overall	0.68	0.68	0.63	0.55

Sources: Whiteford and McGrath (1999); Hirschowitz (1997).

Table 15.3. *Gini coefficients for different years, 1959–95*

	Gini	Income definition	Recipient	Source
1959	0.52	Income	Person	Cromwell (1977)
1960	0.55	Income	Person	Lachman and Bercuson (1992)
1965	0.58	Income	Person	Jain (1975)
1965	0.56	Income	Person	Lachman and Bercuson (1992)
1965	0.56	Income	Person	Lecaillon (1984)
1965	0.58	Income	Person	Paukert (1973)
1970	0.53	Income	Person	Lachman and Bercuson (1992)
1970	0.71	Income (formal)	Person	Simkins (1979)
1975	0.49	Income	Person	Lachman and Bercuson (1992)
1975	0.68	Income	Household	McGrath (1983)
1976	0.65	Income (formal)	Person	Simkins (1979)
1980	0.50	Income	Person	Lachman and Bercuson (1992)
1980	0.57	Income (formal)	Person	Devereaux (1984)
1985	0.51	Income	Person	Lachman and Bercuson (1992)
1987	0.48	Income	Person	Lachman and Bercuson (1992)
1990	0.63	Income	Urban household	Hirschowitz (1997)
1991	0.68	Income	Household	Whiteford and McGrath (1999)
1993	0.62	Income	Household	World Bank (1996)
1993	0.58	Expenditure	Person	World Bank (1999*b*)
1995	0.55	Income	Urban household	Hirschowitz (1997)
1995	0.59	Income	Household	Hirschowitz (1997)

Source: See fifth column.

Data computed by Hirschowitz (1997) for the twelve main urban areas also show rising inequality for all racial groups, except for whites, and declining overall urban inequality. These coefficients, based on the same definitions of income and the same recipient units, show very strong increases in inequality, especially amongst black households. It, therefore, appears that within-group inequality rose. It is not possible to be certain about what happened to overall inequality over this period. Table 15.3 records calculations of Gini coefficients from a range of different sources.

Table 15.4. *Theil indices of inequality, 1975, 1991*

	1975	1991
Asian	0.20	0.20
Black	0.19	0.34
Coloured	0.25	0.22
White	0.12	0.18
Within-group component	0.14	0.23
Between-group component	0.23	0.16
Total population	0.37	0.39

Source: Whiteford and McGrath (1999: 15).

It is not, at first, clear from these figures whether there is a trend in overall inequality, although comparing like with like allows several observations to be made. The first is that measures of inequality of formal incomes, which tend to be higher than those which take into account all income sources, fell in the 1970s. The second is that calculations made by the same authors (and therefore using the same definitions of income and recipient) tend to indicate a marginal fall in overall inequality in the 1970s and 1980s. The third is that inequality in total income accruing to urban households appears to have fallen in the first half of the 1990s (although urban inequality is generally less than overall inequality). Together, these indicators point to some decline in overall inequality, although the change may be small.

An alternative inequality index provides further support for the argument that within-group inequality rose while overall inequality did not change significantly. The Theil entropy index[4] has an advantage over the Gini coefficient in that it can be additively broken down by subgroup. The advantage of using group-decomposable inequality measures is that inequality between groups, as well as within groups, can be compared. Theil indices calculated by Whiteford and McGrath for 1975 and 1991 are recorded in Table 15.4. They show that inequality within both black and white population groups rose during the 1970s and 1980s. The increased disparity in the black group is particularly high. The within-group component is now the primary contributor to overall inequality,[5] accounting for 38 per cent of total inequality in 1975 and 59 per cent in 1991. By contrast the *between*-group component has fallen, primarily as a result of some redistribution from whites to other groups. Other calculations confirm this finding: racial differentials narrowed even before the change of government in 1994, while inequality within both black and white groups rose (Leibbrandt et al. 1999; Moll 1999).

Apart from the strong racial characteristics evident in the income distribution, several other features of inequality in South Africa have been identified. For instance,

[4] The Theil index defines inequality as the distribution of income per individual (or adult equivalent) over households: $T = (Y_i / Y) \ln (NY_i / Y)$, where $i = 1, \ldots, N$; Y_i / Y is the share of the ith person in total income, and N is the total sample population. The index is equal to zero where perfect equality obtains.

[5] Overall inequality measured in this way appears to have risen slightly.

Table 15.5. *Percentage of households living in poverty, 1991*

	% of households in poverty
Asians	18
Blacks	67
Coloureds	38
Whites	7
Overall (MLL)	49
Overall (75% of MLL)	32
Overall (50% of MLL)	25

Source: Whiteford and McGrath (1999), using 1991 census and various income and expenditure surveys.

rural households tend to be more represented in the lower end of the income distribution; female-headed households on average are poorer than male (Hirschowitz 1997; Budlender 1999). Access to wage-earning opportunities is also crucial. In two different analyses of poverty in South Africa, Budlender (1999) and Seekings (1999) identify *layers* of disadvantage;[6] fewer adults are economically active in poorer households and fewer of those who are economically active find employment. Budlender also notes that access to wage income is highly correlated with other measures of well-being: rural households with little access to basic services have diminished chances of finding income-earning activities.

Calculations of poverty in South Africa indicate high levels of deprivation. Whiteford and McGrath (1999) find that, in 1991, almost half of all households were below the minimum living level (MLL) for (urban) African households.[7] Their calculations also indicate that poverty is highest in the former 'homeland' areas (predominantly rural), where over three quarters of households were below the MLL, and that incidence is highest amongst black households, two-thirds of which were below the MLL. However, they argue that the MLL is generously high (Whiteford and McGrath, 1999: 15). Since their calculations reveal that 7 per cent of whites fall below the same MLL, it is distinctly possible that the MLL overstates the extent of poverty in South Africa. Nevertheless, their estimates of the extent of overall poverty in South Africa using three different poverty lines—the MLL; a poverty line of 75 per cent of the MLL; and one of 50 per cent of the MLL—still show that a significant proportion of households live in circumstances of destitution (Table 15.5).

Compared with similar calculations of the extent of poverty in 1975, it appears that the percentage of households in poverty fell in all racial groups, with the exception of whites. The decline was particularly marked amongst coloured and Asian households.

[6] Budlender's analysis is based on the October Household Survey and the Income and Expenditure Survey of 1995; Seekings's work uses the 1993 SALDRU data.
[7] The MLL is calculated by the Bureau of Market Research.

For black households, the depth of poverty increased between 1975 and 1991, as incomes of the poorest 60 per cent of black households fell (Whiteford and McGrath 1999: 18). These findings provide some confirmation for the view that the redistribution which occurred after 1970 was from whites to Asian, coloured, and the richer black households.

15.3. EXPLAINING THE OBSERVED CHANGES IN INEQUALITY: WAGES AND EMPLOYMENT

While political apartheid ended in the 1990s, economic apartheid had started to crumble during the 1970s. In manufacturing, strong growth during the 1960s had created shortages of skilled and semi-skilled labour (Bell 1985: 24–6), and the removal of discriminatory practices by foreign-owned multinational companies in the 1970s was followed immediately by domestic firms competing for workers. When in the 1970s job reservation on the mines was removed, and the industry was hit by a series of strikes by black miners, the rapidly rising gold price permitted wage increases for the first time since 1911.[8] In 1980 black trade unions were legalized. The net effect of these (and other) changes was an erosion of discriminatory practices against blacks (Knight and McGrath 1987), especially in younger cohorts (Moll 1992). Towards the end of the 1980s some firms began to adopt affirmative action rules—a process which accelerated after the change of government in 1994.

Moll (1999: 2–3) argues that the removal of discrimination in employment practices has three effects. First, the wage gap between black and white workers of equivalent experience and qualification is narrowed. This process is concentrated in the middle of the wage and occupation distribution, where different race groups compete for similar jobs, whereas at the bottom or top of the distribution there is little by way of racial overlap. Second, more blacks are promoted into the most senior occupations, but, because of the relative scarcity of sufficiently skilled black workers, they do not compete away the rents that this group enjoys. At the same time, the demand for semi-skilled blacks is insufficient to draw large numbers out of unskilled positions, so earnings inequality amongst blacks rises. Third, as white unions lose their hold over the semi-skilled occupations, poorly skilled whites fall into lower paid occupations, so that earnings inequality amongst whites rises.

If a process like this does explain the simultaneous fall in racial inequality and rise in within-group inequality, it suggests that inequality in the distribution of income is driven by what happens to wage income. If, as will be argued, the effect of reduced discrimination in the labour market has been reinforced by increasing unemployment, this would underscore the importance of formal sector wages in driving overall inequality.

15.3.1. *The Role of Wage Differentials in Explaining Inequality*

The importance of wage income in determining inequality in South Africa is emphasized in a study by Leibbrandt *et al.* (1996). By decomposing Gini coefficients for

---

[8] Between 1971 and 1975 black wages trebled in the gold mines (Lipton 1985: 388).

black households according to income components,[9] they show, not surprisingly, that wage income contributes most to overall income inequality. This inequality across the population of black households depends *both* on the distribution amongst those that are earning wages *and* on the proportion that have no access to wage income. Leibbrandt *et al.* argue that it is primarily the latter—that is, the extent of unemployment—that contributes to a high Gini coefficient (0.66) for wage income. For the subset of rural black households, their findings are similar. Although remittances and transfers are relatively more important, wage income still contributes significantly to inequality.[10] For rural black households below the household subsistence level (HSL), remittances from family members living away from the household and welfare payments are much more important as an income source—the share of wage income is 23 per cent compared to 63 per cent for those above the HSL—but wages are still the primary source of inequality.

What drives inequality in the distribution of wages has been explained in several recent studies. Fallon and Lucas (1998) argue that racial wage differentials have narrowed since the 1970s, but the precise behaviour of black wages has been subject to conflicting pressures: rising unemployment has exerted downward pressure, but greater freedoms to work and the rise of African trade unionism have offset this. Nevertheless, they find that wage differentials resulting from institutional factors remain high by international standards: Wages paid are still heavily influenced by race and gender, barriers to mobility, and job-related characteristics, like union membership and public versus private sector. At the same time, 'productive differences', such as schooling and years of experience, do also matter.[11]

Moll (1999) traces these factors over time, using 1980 and 1993 data to decompose the white–black earnings gap into 'explained' (productive) components, like education and experience, and 'unexplained' components, like occupational and wage discrimination.[12] He finds that wage discrimination fell from 1980 to 1993, partly due to the improvement of the educational qualifications of blacks, and partly because of decreased labour market discrimination. Occupational discrimination rose, but this was because, although the numbers of blacks in higher occupations rose dramatically, the numbers possessing appropriate qualifications rose even more quickly, which increased the proportion (of those qualified) who were excluded.

Using more recent data, Jensen (1999) also analyses wage differentials and also finds that much of the difference in wages can be attributed to racial differences in the distribution of education, occupation, and urbanization.[13] Like Moll, he finds that

[9] The data used are those from the 1993 SALDRU sample. Income is divided into that from wages, remittances, state transfers, agriculture, capital, and self-employment.

[10] In a study of rural households in the Eastern Transvaal, Sender and Johnston (1995) find that (casual, often unrecorded) women's wages and working conditions on all types of farms are probably the critical determinants of the standards of living of most of the poorest households.

[11] Their findings are based on 1993 SALDRU data.

[12] Data used are the 1980 census and the 1993 SALDRU survey. Moll uses a multinomial logit approach to analyse the gross differential between white and black log wages.

[13] These observable characteristics, particularly education, explain between 50 per cent and 90 per cent of the differences at various parts of the distributions in both sectors.

the racial distribution of occupations is skewed, with Africans underrepresented in technical, professional, and management positions. However, he notes some striking differences across sectors. In the private sector, low levels of education contribute most to relatively low black wages at the bottom end of the distribution, while much of the premium earned by whites in high-wage jobs cannot be explained by observable characteristics. In the public sector, productivity-related characteristics are more important in accounting for wage differentials, although, at the upper end, Africans appear to earn a racial premium beyond what can be accounted for by their observable productivity-related characteristics.

15.3.2. *The Role of Unequal Access to Employment in Explaining Inequality*

The study by Fallon and Lucas (1998) investigates the probability of being unemployed (in the formal economy) across different population groups. They find wide differences in probabilities, which appear to be influenced by both productivity-related and non-productive characteristics, with those who face the greatest risk of unemployment being women, black, or having less (or poorer quality) education. This has important implications for the distribution of income. Seekings (1999) shows that the unemployed are concentrated amongst the poorest households. Kingdon and Knight (1999: 1) and Standing *et al.* (1996: 110) point out that it is not inevitable that unemployment will be associated with poverty; because the poor cannot survive unemployment, in many underdeveloped economies they enter the informal sector and are underemployed. Under these circumstances, employment in the informal sector rather than open unemployment is associated with poverty. Kingdon and Knight contend, however, that South African data do not support this view and that open unemployment is an important source of poverty. They find that the unemployed are the most deprived group and that job search itself is subject to greater impediments if one is poor, black, uneducated, or living in a remote (rural) area.

15.3.3. *Explaining the Changes*

The overwhelming conclusion is that wage income is the most important source of inequality, both racial and geographical. The shift in income from whites to blacks (and Asians) was caused by considerably slower growth of real white per capita incomes from 1970 to 1991—17 per cent for whites compared with 51 per cent for blacks and 103 per cent for Asians. In spite of economic slowdown from the mid-1970s, average non-white wages outside of agriculture rose, because of both occupational mobility and a sharp rise in wages for skilled and semi-skilled blacks and Asians (especially men). After the legalization of black trade unions in 1980, their growing influence on wage setting caused marked increases in black wages across the spectrum from least skilled to highly skilled (Hofmeyr 1999). In other words, the narrowing of racial wage differentials was a result of the removal of discriminatory behaviour in both wage-setting and occupational structures, so that average non-white wages rose sharply to catch up with those of white counterparts. In spite of this, discrimination still accounts for a large portion of remaining racial differentials.

The primary cause of the growing inequality amongst blacks is rising black wages simultaneous with rising black unemployment. Average real wages of blacks in manufacturing, for example, rose 70 per cent between 1972 and 1990, while recorded unemployment rose from under 10 per cent to 25 per cent. Other factors were also at work. There was rapid upward mobility of a small number of educated blacks, and, with economic recession in the 1980s, white unemployment occurred for the first time since the 1920s. At the same time, the growing power of the trade unions resulted in a new form of segmentation in the South African labour market: The main distinctions are now between the unionized and non-unionized parts of the formal sector and between the formal and non-formal sectors (Hofmeyr 1999). Several severe droughts during the 1980s also caused rural incomes to contract, exacerbating inequality between black incomes. The net result implies that much of the redistribution which occurred prior to the change in government was from whites to the richest of the black households. Redistributive policies which have an impact on the poorest households may, therefore, require direct interventions rather than simply the erosion of discriminatory labour market practices which characterized the period 1970–94.

In other words, while the findings of Leibbrandt *et al.* (1996) point to the need for changes in the labour market to drive changes in inequality, it is clear that the policies must go beyond narrow labour market interventions. Short-term policies affecting remittances and transfers and micro-level labour market interventions may help to improve welfare for the poorest, but any improvement in inequality in the longer term must come through creating wage-earning opportunities for poorer households, especially rural black households. Fallon and Lucas (1998) argue that, in the long-term, sound macroeconomic policies will encourage employment-creating growth and competitive pressures are needed to remove discrimination.[14] But, as argued elsewhere (Whiteford and McGrath 1999), growth may not be sufficient to make an acceptable dent in inequality in a reasonable time frame.[15]

It is at least implicit from the above discussion that access to formal sector employment is an important factor in improved levels of income. It would appear, therefore, that policies affecting employment creation play a vital role in reducing inequality and poverty. The following sections review the evolution of the policy framework and economic performance in South Africa. Policy under the African National Congress (ANC)-led government is then assessed more closely, particularly in terms of its likely impact on employment creation and income distribution.

---

[14] Shorter term policies include support for SMEs and land reform targeted at creating productive opportunities in rural areas. Other areas mentioned are promoting education and training for the disadvantaged, encouraging the positive aspects of trade unionism, encouraging labour-intensive techniques in infrastructure projects, and facilitating national tripartite agreements on labour and related issues.

[15] They estimate that, at the current distribution and (real) poverty line, it will take 24 years for the *average* income of the poor to equal the poverty line at an annual real growth rate of 5 per cent, 47 years if growth averages 2.5 per cent a year, and 117 years at an average real growth rate of 1 per cent annually.

15.4. THE EVOLUTION OF ECONOMIC POLICY AND PERFORMANCE

15.4.1. Policy and Performance under the Apartheid Government, 1960–94

The evolution of economic policy

Although the South African economy is not a command economy in any sense in which the word is normally used, the drive towards industrialization from the mid-1920s and the institutionalization of apartheid from the late 1940s meant that by 1960 the South African economy was subject to a comprehensive range of controls. The government was also involved in establishing large parastatal corporations and development finance institutions.

In line with the experience of other non–oil-exporting countries, economic growth slowed in South Africa in the 1970s. At the same time, there was a loss of political direction as both internal dissent and external pressure for change were increasing. Moreover, world ideology was shifting towards neoclassical orthodoxy, and this seemed like an answer to a regime which was contemplating 'reform' without a sense of direction. A series of government-appointed commissions of enquiry recommended wide-ranging reforms, most of them in a more liberal direction.[16] In the mid-1970s, trade reform began with the introduction of export incentives to reduce the anti-export bias. The substitution of tariffs for quantitative restrictions followed in the 1980s, although tariff reduction did not begin until after the change of government. Black trade unions were legalized in 1980, and restrictions on the movement of black labour were eased during the decade. Comprehensive liberalization of monetary and exchange-rate policy was undertaken in the early 1980s. A shift towards market-oriented policy instruments, including positive real interest rates, was initiated; monetary targeting was adopted as the primary means of controlling inflation; the dual exchange-rate system was abolished, although later reinstated during the debt crisis of 1985; and a managed float of the rand was introduced. Commercialization (rather than privatization) of parastatals commenced.

Fiscal policy has generally been comparatively conservative. Until the mid-1970s, the government endeavoured to finance current spending out of current revenue, so that only capital expenditure was financed out of public debt. Although this objective was dropped from 1976, the government initiated a particularly restrictive fiscal policy in an attempt to crush accelerating inflation. This restraint could not be maintained, and from 1981 not only did current spending rise sharply, but also there was an increasing tendency for the authorities to exceed budget estimates—the burden of (domestic) government debt grew as a result.

---

[16] For example, 1973 Reynders (export trade), 1979 Rieckert (black urban affairs), 1980 Wiehahn (labour, including trade unions), 1981 De Lange (education), 1981 Schlebusch (constitutional affairs), 1984 De Kock (monetary policy), 1987 Margo (taxation).

Table 15.6. *Economic performance indicators (per cent per annum)*

	1960–74	1975–84	1985–94
Rate of change in GDP	5.0	2.7	1.0
Rate of inflation	4.2	12.8	13.8
Rate of formal absorption of new jobseekers[a]	80.0	30.0	8.5
Ratio of investment to GDP	26.2	28.5	18.8

[a] There is considerable debate about the rate of formal unemployment, with current estimates ranging from 33 to almost 50 per cent.

Source: Calculated using data from the South African Reserve Bank.

Economic performance: 1960–94

From 1974, South Africa's long-run growth rate began to decline, and the cyclical pattern of economic activity became more unstable (Table 15.6). The slowdown was caused by a combination of external shocks and domestic structural problems, which, amongst other things, reduced the profitability of investment. Labour productivity was falling because of skills shortages, partly the result of historical underinvestment in education. Political unrest, frequently expressed by strikes, was also driving up real unit labour costs. The growth of the capital–labour ratio accelerated (in an attempt to maintain productivity). Consequently, the capital–output ratio rose sharply, causing the profitability of investment to fall (Gelb 1991: 19–23). Insufficiently developed export capacity, together with a high propensity to import investment goods, placed a foreign exchange constraint on growth. This was exacerbated by an overvalued exchange rate and by calls for international sanctions.

Although an increase in the price of gold in the early 1980s helped partially to insulate South Africa from the balance-of-payments crises which were a factor in driving many developing countries into debt, falling world demand contributed to falling production and rising unemployment. The government's almost complete disinterest in stimulating alternative employment for blacks (Thomas 1990: 255), and the deliberate dualism in both agricultural development and skills acquisition made it difficult to absorb new job seekers: Job creation fell from 157,000 annually (1960–74) to 57,000 a year (1974–85).

Financial sanctions imposed in the mid-1980s precipitated a debt crisis, although, unlike other developing countries, debt-service difficulties arose from the structure of foreign debt (predominantly short-term loans) rather than its magnitude. Increasing social conflict, political uncertainty, and tight monetary conditions necessitated by financial sanctions caused private investment to fall. Costs of production rose sharply: of capital, because of a shift in policy towards maintaining positive real interest rates and a weaker currency; of labour, because union pressures saw wage increases outstripping productivity improvements and because of a huge increase in politically motivated strikes, and of raw materials, because of domestic inflation and a weaker currency. The economy stagnated.

15.4.2. *Policy and Performance Since the Political Transition, 1994–9*

The economic policy framework

During the period of negotiation leading up to majority rule, fears were expressed by some commentators that a majority government, dominated by the ANC, would reverse many of the liberalizations that had taken place since the 1970s. In the debate about the post-apartheid economy, two issues were seen to be important: economic growth and the redistribution of resources to the previously disenfranchised majority. The pressures for redistribution in the context of resource constraints were very similar to those faced by most other post-colonial governments in Africa and elsewhere.

Contrary to these expectations, during the new government's first term in office economic policy grew steadily more orthodox, and liberalization was accelerated. The ANC-led government pledged itself to fiscal discipline, aiming to redistribute resources by reorienting rather than increasing expenditure (or taxation). It initially maintained both the finance minister and the central bank governor of the previous regime. It opted for a more neutral trade policy, with a simpler, transparent tariff structure and with tariffs reduced in line with GATT requirements, and it signed an agreement with the WTO in 1994. It abolished exchange controls on non-residents in 1995, and began to relax exchange controls on residents. Its GEAR strategy, released in 1996, committed the government to reducing the fiscal deficit to 3 per cent of GDP in 5 years, to deepening the trade liberalization, to promoting macroeconomic stability, and to injecting greater flexibility into the labour market (RSA 1996). In other words, the ANC-led government adopted a policy package that was almost classically 'Washington Consensus'. The rationale was that this package would enhance investor confidence, through building credibility, and promote growth, job creation, and redistribution.

Much of the policy strategy promised in GEAR has been implemented, although rigidities remain in the labour market, and these are frequently blamed for contributing to the failure of the strategy to create jobs. At present, wage-setting institutions set minimum wage floors and protect the wages of low-paid workers, and new labour legislation has made mandatory the extension of collective agreements to non-parties. In the presence of rapidly falling trade barriers and rising international competition, this could push up unskilled unemployment. Even though its primary objective is dealing with unemployment, especially amongst the less skilled, the government has not opposed trade unions on issues of conditions of employment, in spite of vociferous criticism from the business community.

Economic growth since 1994

With the change of government came the lifting of economic sanctions and a surge in confidence. Average annual growth accelerated to between 2 and 3 per cent (reaching 3.4 per cent in 2000), although this was slower than the GEAR's projected increase. Overall, economic performance has disappointed expectations as to the benefits of liberalization. The slowdown in growth that began in the early 1970s was not quickly

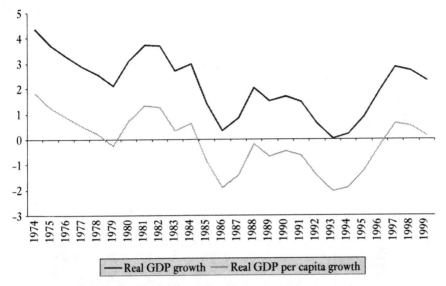

Figure 15.1. *Real economic growth in South Africa, 1974–99 (5-year moving average)*

reversed, and, in per capita terms, real growth was negligible (Fig. 15.1). One important reason for growth being slower than expected has been the series of external shocks to the economy in the form of contagion from emerging market financial crises—although South Africa managed to avoid the depth of financial distress and subsequent recession that these crises caused in several emerging economies. The macroeconomic impact of the GEAR strategy (in terms of employment and growth) should be considered in the context of the external pressures that South Africa has faced.

The growth path is, nevertheless, consistent with that of other countries which have undergone contractionary reform under structural adjustment (see Chapter 1). The policy package, designed to stimulate growth, may have had adverse effects. For example, it is possible that government deficit reduction has reduced rather than stimulated private domestic investment in the short-term, due to the contraction of demand. Structural changes occurring as a result of trade liberalization, the relaxation of exchange controls, and deregulation may have increased uncertainty for investors in the adjustment period. It is even more possible that the tight monetary environment for a sustained period—successful in reducing inflation from over 18 per cent to under 7 per cent per annum—has severely held back growth. Furthermore, the business community has argued that the policy package is being undermined by a lack of flexibility with respect to labour market policy.

Employment and wages

These effects also appear to have had an impact on rate of job creation (Fig. 15.2). Private sector formal employment has contracted steadily since 1990 following a period

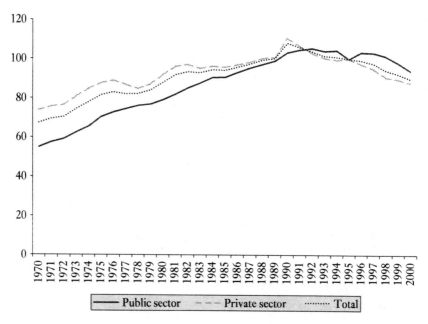

Figure 15.2. *Indices of formal non-agricultural employment, 1970–2000 (1995 = 100)*

of rapid growth in the 1970s and slow growth from the early 1980s (the rate of non-agricultural private sector job creation was below the rate of growth of the labour force for most of the 1980s). This trend has continued, with private non-agricultural employment in 2000 only 90 per cent of the level in 1995. Public sector employment, on the other hand, grew strongly between 1970 and 1990 and then began to drift down after 1990. At the same time, wage indices show that private sector real wages have grown since the beginning of the 1990s, following a period of stagnation in the late 1980s. Real public sector wages have also risen in the 1990s.

The combination of declining formal employment and rising real wages is consistent with the argument that inequality between the employed and unemployed has worsened in recent years: fewer people are now employed, and those in employment receive higher real wages. It is also consistent with the insider–outsider view that trade unions have protected formal wages at the expense of the unemployed.

Sectoral employment indices for the non-agricultural private sector show that manufacturing employment has been in decline since the early 1990s, while service sectors, particularly financial services, have displayed strong and steady growth (Fig. 15.3). Employment in mining has declined significantly since the mid-1980s; by 2000 it was only 70 per cent of what it had been in 1995. Mining and manufacturing have historically been important employers in South Africa, and job-shedding in these sectors appears to be the key to explaining the decline in total private sector employment.

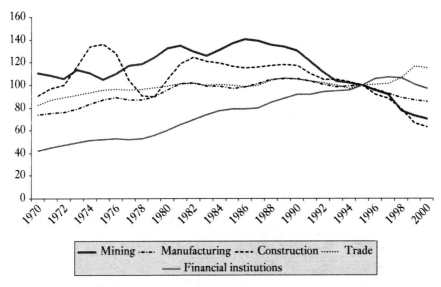

Figure 15.3. *Private-sector employment, sectoral indices, 1970–2000 (1995 = 100)*

The net result is that the service sector is an increasingly important employer in South Africa, even more so if we include government. A contraction of employment in mining and manufacturing has, thus, coincided with the recovery in the rate of economic growth. The possible reasons for this are discussed below.

Unemployment remains South Africa's most pressing problem. While the policy framework is intended to provide a more favourable climate for investment, it is, of course, unable to ensure that the private sector response will be forthcoming, particularly if real interest rates remain high in order to protect foreign exchange reserves. Indeed, private sector investment has not yet shown any significant increase, and the level of foreign direct investment remains low in comparison to other financial flows. At the same time, domestic savings (out of which future domestic investment is financed) are still declining: in 1990 South Africa's gross domestic saving was 19.1 per cent of GDP; by 1999 the ratio had fallen to 14.5 per cent. At present, the government's energy remains concentrated on overcoming the legacy of apartheid. The following sections consider the policy framework in more detail to assess what progress has been made.

15.5. CHANGES IN THE STRUCTURAL CAUSES OF POVERTY AND INEQUALITY SINCE 1994

Traditional explanations of poverty and inequality include a skewed distribution of both real assets and human capital. It is argued that these explain much of the variation in cross-country inequality, although less of its change over time (Cornia 2000: 21). Even so, it is argued, any strategy seeking to alleviate poverty should include policies to improve the access of the poor to social services, especially education, and land.

The equalization of education spending per head across race groups might assist in reducing income disparities over time. However, the evidence that increasing public spending on education raises enrolment rates is weak (see Chapter 4 by Checchi in this volume); it is also possible that more spending will not necessarily raise the quality of education.

15.5.1. *Education and Social Expenditure*

Prior to the 1970s, it was a matter of explicit policy *not* to provide more than a basic education for Africans, who were viewed by the apartheid government as an unskilled workforce. Accompanying this was a strategy of capital-intensive import-substituting industrialization, one aim of which was to provide employment for the small, highly skilled white workforce. As political protests intensified in the 1970s, and as the government began to move proactively towards promoting export diversification, investment in black education rose rapidly from its historically low level, contributing to the improvement in racial income distribution in this period. Despite the increase, however, racial disparities in the quality of education provided by the state remained extreme.

Since 1990 and especially after 1994, spending on education and other social services has started to rise in line with the government's redistributive goals. Table 15.7 records

Table 15.7. *Total government expenditure, as a percentage of* non-interest *expenditure*

	1983–9	1990–3	1994–7	1998–2002
General services and unallocable	12.9	14.3	13.7	14.0
Protection	21.9	21.4	18.0	18.9
Defence	14.9	12.1	7.6	6.8
Public order and safety	7.0	9.3	10.3	12.1
Social services	45.9	48.0	53.9	56.3
Education	20.5	22.3	24.2	26.3
Health	11.1	10.7	11.0	16.6
Social security and welfare	7.0	8.7	12.2	10.7
Housing and community services	5.4	4.6	4.5	2.3
Recreation and culture	1.8	1.6	2.0	0.4
Economic services	19.3	16.4	14.5	10.8
Fuel and energy	0.3	1.1	1.6	0.2
Agriculture, forestry, and fishing	4.2	3.3	2.4	1.9
Mining, manufacturing, and construction	3.7	2.4	1.1	0.1
Transportation and communication	8.9	6.3	6.1	4.7
Other economic services	2.2	3.3	3.2	3.9

Note: Figures for 1998–2002 are estimates.

Sources: Data for 1983–97 are from the South African Reserve Bank; data from 1998 on are from the *Budget Review 2000*, South African Department of Finance and are estimates. Sixty per cent of the national budget is transferred to other levels of general government; this inevitably means that the detailed breakdown of consolidated expenditure is available only with a lag.

the shares of non-interest expenditure averaged over four broad periods from the early 1980s. There has been a marked shift in expenditure towards social services and away from economic services and, to a lesser extent, protection services. Social services now account for more than half of non-interest expenditure, compared with 46 per cent in the early 1980s. Within the social sector, the expenditure shares of education and social security and welfare have both increased over time, and health is planned to receive a larger share in recent budgets. It is also worth noting the shift in expenditure away from defence towards policing and justice—in the context of South Africa's high crime level, improving the safety of the poor will play an important role in improving standards of living.

Expenditure shares are not necessarily an indicator of achievement in addressing poverty. There have been both successes and failures in the strategy to reduce poverty. In the ANC-led government's first term of office, 2.5 million people were given access to tap water as part of the aim of improving the health of the poorest, and 5.5 million households were electrified, providing opportunities for job creation through small-scale cottage industries. At the same time, problems with service delivery meant that the target for building new houses was missed (Standard and Poor's 1999). The most serious delivery failure has been in education, where both availability and standards for the previously disadvantaged majority are yet to show a marked improvement. There appears to be a lack of clear direction in education policy, in a context where radical change is needed, in spite of the increasing share of expenditure, which is high by international standards—evidence that simply spending more money does not necessarily solve problems.

15.5.2. *Land*

Land redistribution is unlikely to play a significant role in the strategy to reduce poverty in South Africa. In spite of a history of dispossession of the indigenous population, the current government is concerned to create a climate of certainty with respect to land tenure. The government allowed for a 3-year period in which claims for land restitution could be lodged—a period which has now expired. A Land Court was established to consider all claims, but there is no evidence to suggest that large-scale redistribution will be the result. Money has been set aside in each budget since 1994 for restitution and land reform, but most urban claims are being handled by blanket payments to claimants of the value of a serviced site in their area of residence. Some land restitution is planned in rural areas, but the focus of rural development is a multi-billion rand programme of finance to small-scale farmers.

Despite its perceived *political* importance, there is evidence to suggest that land redistribution is not an effective way out of poverty, that it reduces poverty by very little, and that a land policy entails both a leakage to the non-poor and imperfect coverage of the poor (Ravallion and Sen 1994: 1). Most of Africa's ultra-poor own or operate significant amounts of farmland, and the problem is one of land quality, remoteness, and fragmentation of land rather than landlessness (Lipton 1988: 54). Even where there is land hunger, as in Zimbabwe, the redistributive process proves complex and, probably most significantly, if not dealt with conclusively soon after the transition to majority rule, a simmering political problem.

15.6. THE IMPACT OF ECONOMIC POLICY SINCE 1994

A growing literature is raising the concern that the shifting of policy in a neoliberal direction may have actually worsened the distribution of income in other developing countries. There are reasons why South Africa's experience may differ from that of many developing countries. Although it now has a fairly orthodox macroeconomic package, the changes to the policy framework have been introduced over 25 years in a phased manner in response to the perceived needs of the economy rather than in pursuit of an ultimate ideologically driven objective. This phased approach, modified by the need of the previous government to ward off political dissent by spreading the benefits of production more widely and the need of the current government to satisfy the aspirations of the newly enfranchised majority, may contribute to an improvement in the distribution of income.

15.6.1. *The Effects of Stabilization: Inflation and Interest Rates*

The poor generally suffer most from high inflation, because they are less able to index their incomes, and the real value of their assets (savings) is eroded. High (and variable) rates of inflation also raise the risks (as well as direct costs) for investors, with implications for employment. However, it has been found that, to the extent that stabilization is contractionary, it tends to be 'disequalizing' in developing countries. Tight monetary policy not only discourages new investment, but also raises the cost of servicing existing debt. Even if firms are not forced to close, they are forced to reduce variable costs (see Chapter 7). The flexibility of low-skilled wages, the readiness of firms to shed labour, and the inadequacy of social safety nets mean that the burden of adjustment frequently falls on those at the bottom of the distribution, especially where the informal sector is small. Moreover, the contractionary impact tends to be greater on wages than on profits.

In South Africa, the tight anti-inflationary stance of the central bank has been criticized by some commentators for undermining the growth and employment objectives of economic policy. However, continued high interest rates have been, in part, a response to external shocks. A key structural weakness in South Africa is the low savings rate. This means that the economy relies heavily on foreign capital inflows, mostly in the form of portfolio investment, to finance the savings–investment gap. High real interest rates have been maintained in order to continue to attract inward flows of capital, or at least to limit the outflows in times of crisis. Thus, while the policy implications of managing the impact of volatile capital flows appear to contradict the goals of growth and employment creation, without access to foreign savings it is unlikely that South Africa could make much progress towards these goals. Table 15.8 shows that real interest rates have been historically high since the election of the ANC-led government. Simultaneously, average annual growth has been at its most rapid since the gold boom period of the early 1980s,[17] although insufficient for an

---

[17] Note that the averages presented in the table mask significant differences in growth on a year-by-year basis.

Table 15.8. *Real interest rates and growth*

	GDP growth	GDP per capita growth	Core consumer price inflation	Real T bill rate[a]	Real long-dated yield[b]
1976–9	2.2	−0.2	10.7	−3.15	−0.28
1980–4	3.0	0.6	12.2	0.39	0.64
1985–9	1.5	−0.7	17.0	−3.22	−0.48
1990–4	0.2	−1.9	14.5	−0.31	0.83
1995–9	2.3	0.1	7.9	6.28	6.87
2000	3.4	1.3	5.3	3.36	7.58

[a] Annual average discount rate on 3-month Treasury bill rate, adjusted using core consumer price inflation rates.
[b] Annual average yield on government bond traded on the bond exchange with maturity of 10 years or more, adjusted using core consumer price inflation rates.
Source: Calculated using data from various years from the South African Reserve Bank and the IMF.

acceleration of per capita income growth. As inflation has fallen, nominal interest rates have fallen by much less, so that real interest rates have generally remained stubbornly high especially when compared to their (negative) level in the early 1990s.

The effects of stabilization on poverty and income distribution are not clear-cut. Lower inflation may be associated with better growth performance in the long run, as lower inflation has a positive impact on domestic savings and investment. Moreover, where lower inflation provides greater protection of the real value of income and savings for the poor, then it is important for reducing poverty. However, as argued above, poverty in South Africa is strongly associated with unemployment. To the extent that high interest rates have retarded employment creation, then the poverty and distributional effects are likely to have been negative, at least in the short-term.[18] Of course, stabilization is not a short-term process, and only by the end of 1999 were market interest rates beginning to fall. Whether this decline will continue, or at least be sustained, is likely to depend to a great extent on the success of the government's inflation targeting strategy, announced in March 2000. At the same time, the credibility of an inflation target is likely to require ongoing restraint in government expenditure, to which the analysis now turns.

15.6.2. *Fiscal Policy*

A worsening of the income distribution as a result of recession may be reinforced by a tight fiscal policy, as cuts in recurrent expenditure reduce public sector employment,

---

[18] It is also worth noting that high real interest rates mean that holders of financial assets have experienced higher than average income growth at the experience of consumers and firms who borrow. This does *not* mean that the holders of financial assets have necessarily gained at the expense of the poor, however, as the poorest in South Africa are effectively excluded from the formal financial sector.

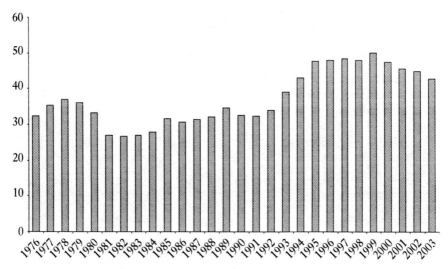

Figure 15.4. *Government debt as a percentage of GDP*
Note: 2001–3 are estimated.

or public services, or both. Even using the fiscus for specifically redistributive objectives has tended to have much smaller effects in developing countries than in industrialized countries. A comprehensive review of studies of the distributional effects of tax and expenditure reforms in nineteen developing countries (see Chapter 10) finds that, in spite of attempts to raise progressivity, many developing countries have experienced an increase in both before-tax and after-tax inequality. The reasons are that weak tax administration makes governments more dependent on indirect taxation, which can be regressive; capital and wealth taxes are limited, and formal cash transfer and social protection programmes are confined. Moreover, corruption limits the effectiveness of taxes and transfers as redistributive instruments. Nevertheless, they find that countries pursuing sound macroeconomic and social policies (like well-targeted health and education programmes) tend to improve their income distribution even if the equity objectives of tax reforms are limited. The scope for redistribution has generally been greater in middle and higher income economies with a pro-poor political economy.

As redistribution through expenditure reform is one objective of the South African government, it is distinctly possible that fiscal policy is contributing to greater racial equality. However, pressure from the servicing of government debt, within the context of reducing the fiscal deficit, has limited the government's ability to promote redistribution through expenditure.[19] Meaningful comparisons of government debt over time are difficult: The data published by the Department of Finance in its annual *Budget Review* are complicated by the inclusion of the debt of the former 'homelands' in total government debt in 1994/5. Bearing this caveat in mind, the debt–GDP ratio since 1976 is presented in Fig. 15.4. Government debt peaked at nearly 50 per cent of GDP

---

[19] In other words, monetary policy may have limited the government's ability to use the budget as a means of redistribution, as high interest rates have raised the cost of servicing an increased public debt.

at the end of fiscal year 1998/9. Since then, it has declined, to 48 per cent in the following year and 46 per cent in fiscal year 2000/1. Privatization proceeds are being used to retire debt in an attempt to reduce the interest burden on the budget. Asset sales together with declining financing requirements mean that debt is expected to fall to around 43 per cent of GDP by the end of 2002/3.

The impact of the debt burden on the budget, in the context of the commitment to reducing the budget deficit, is shown in Table 15.9. The budget deficit as a proportion of GDP peaked at 9 per cent in the last year of the apartheid government. The new government has rapidly decreased the overall deficit in line with its commitments in GEAR, providing additional credibility with the establishment of the medium-term expenditure framework (MTEF) in 1998 as a publicly announced constraint on expenditure over a 3-year horizon.

The decline in the deficit has been achieved through ensuring a primary surplus (the budget balance *excluding* interest payments) in each year since 1995. The debt burden is evident in the share of total expenditure accounted for by interest payments. This rose to 20 per cent in the fiscal year 1998/9, although it is projected to fall to around 18 per cent by 2002/3. Underlying the decline in the deficit are reduced expenditure *and* increased tax revenue. Much of the rise in revenue is due to improvements in tax collection and compliance following the establishment of the semi-autonomous

Table 15.9. *Interest payments and the budget deficit*[a]

	Interest payments as per cent of total expenditure[b]	Overall deficit as per cent of GDP	Primary deficit as per cent of GDP[c]
1990/1	12.4	3.3	−0.8
1991/2	12.4	4.5	0.5
1992/3	12.8	8.3	4
1993/4	13.2	9.1	4.4
1994/5	13.5	5.0	0.1
1995/6	13.6	5.1	−0.1
1996/7	17.7	4.6	−0.7
1997/8	19.0	3.8	−1.8
1998/9	20.3	2.3	−3.4
1999/2000	19.8	2.3	−3.1
2000/1	19.9	1.9	−2.6
2001/2[a]	18.6	2.5	−2.7
2002/3[a]	18.3	2.2	−2.7

[a] Figures for 2001–3 are projections based on the medium-term expenditure framework. These figures are estimates.

[b] Figures for 1990–5 are from the South African Reserve Bank and may not be strictly comparable with later data from the Department of Finance.

[c] A negative number indicates a primary *surplus*.

Sources: Department of Finance (various), *Budget Review*; South African Reserve Bank (various), *Quarterly Bulletin*.

South African Revenue Service (SARS). The early success of SARS and other initiatives in addressing the inherited 'non-compliance' culture has allowed the government some flexibility in expenditure. Nevertheless, the combination of the debt burden and the public commitment to decreasing the deficit has presented a significant constraint on overall expenditure. Despite this, the government has not lost sight of the need for redistribution and the ability of the budget to provide a tool—albeit a limited one in the conservative policy framework—to achieve this goal. This is demonstrated in Table 15.7, where the shift in non-interest expenditure towards social services is evident. This suggests that, as in other middle-income economies with a pro-poor political economy, there is (limited) scope for using fiscal policy to achieve redistribution.

15.6.3. *Trade Liberalization*

To the extent that trade liberalization exposes previously protected firms to competition from more efficient foreign producers, short-term job losses are inevitable as firms adjust. In the longer term, displaced workers should find alternative employment in expanding exporting industries. However, it is possible that opening an economy will lead to technological changes. This is even more likely if greater global integration attracts foreign investment. In this case, the demand for labour might shift from less to more-skilled workers as capital-intensive technology is introduced. Where protection has permitted the payment of higher wages than might have been paid in a more competitive environment, then permanent job losses are possible. Moreover, in an open global economy in which rich countries can subsidize and protect the sectors, like agriculture, where poorer countries might be able to compete, unilateral trade liberalization by poorer countries can have perverse effects. Unfavourable effects on inequality following trade liberalization were observed also in Latin America in the 1990s (Wood 1997).

The combination of falling demand for less-skilled workers as a result of increasing trade openness and the persistence of labour market rigidities in South Africa are likely to have had important implications for inequality. In South Africa, the presence of policies aimed at reducing wage differentials in the formal economy and an informal sector that does not generate significant income-earning opportunities is expected to raise unemployment and overall inequality, even if the dispersion of formal incomes falls.

As shown earlier, a contraction of employment in private sector industry has coincided with the recovery in the rate of economic growth. The historic nurturing of capital-intensive production has meant that many large capital-intensive firms have been able to take advantage of the opportunities created by trade liberalization, even when, in theory, relative prices have moved in favour of labour-intensive production (Harvey and Jenkins 1992). As in other middle-income countries, as trade liberalization has progressed, South African exports have become more capital and skills-intensive.[20]

---

[20] This phenomenon emerged early; 1978 estimates of South Africa's comparative advantage concluded that the country had a comparative advantage in large capital-intensive production (see Holden and Holden 1978).

Standing *et al.* (1996: 39) point out that import-substituting sectors are more labour-intensive than are export-oriented sectors. Tsikata (1998: p.vi, 28) attributes South Africa's 'paradoxical' export structure to comparatively high wages relative to productivity, which reduces the competitiveness of less-skilled labour-intensive exports.[21]

The emphasis on capital-intensive production raises the possibility that manufacturing exports may not generate significant numbers of jobs. The ILO found that employment losses in South Africa were greater in capital-intensive export industries than in import-competing industries between 1994 and 1997 (reported in Nattrass 1999: 16). At the same time, some (but not all) labour-intensive manufacturing sectors have declined. There is, therefore, evidence that South Africa is moving towards more skill-intensive production, with technological change in manufacturing resulting in an increased demand for skilled labour. This is not only consistent with what is predicted in the literature, but it provides support for the explanation advanced earlier for widening within-group inequality between the high-wage, high-skilled workers and the unemployed.

15.6.4. *Financial Liberalization*

Financial liberalization generally leads to the growth of the financial sector and a substantial increase in the rate of return to financial capital. As a result, the share of GDP accruing to non-wage earners increases. Rising real interest rates also generate redistribution from taxed labour and profits income to bondholders as government interest payments rise relative to other spending. This is exacerbated if increasing reliance is placed on indirect taxation and if ownership of government bonds is highly concentrated.

Comprehensive and sustained financial sector reforms in South Africa have led to a strong growth in the size of the sector relative to primary and secondary sectors. Reforms and financial innovation are partly responsible for the decline in personal savings, by making it easier to borrow money to finance consumption (Aron and Muellbauer 1998).[22] This has contributed to the dependence on foreign capital inflows, which in turn has necessitated tight monetary policy. It seems likely that the high real interest rates generated have contributed to an increase in the share of income accruing to the holders of financial assets (see below).

15.6.5. *Labour Institutions*

The erosion of labour institutions may worsen inequality during liberalization (see Chapter 8). It is, therefore, possible that the income distribution would actually deteriorate if trade unions were undermined in South Africa. It is significant that redistribution away from labour and towards profits, rents, and other property income

---

[21] However, she is optimistic that South Africa is able to position itself to compete in niche markets producing high value-added goods, including some that are labour intensive.

[22] Liberalization has not, however, led to the large-scale extension of financial services to the poorest, such that the provision of credit to small-scale entrepreneurs has been dominated by development-oriented institutions.

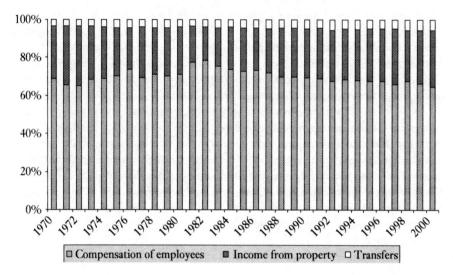

Figure 15.5. *Shares of household income accruing to different factors of production, 1970–2000*

has been a feature of neoliberal reform. Figure 15.5 shows the shares of current household income[23] accruing to labour and capital and arising from transfers. Transfers are typically between 3 and 5 per cent of current household income. However, income from property has risen steadily from 18 per cent of the total in 1981–2 to 29 per cent in 1998 to nearly 30 per cent in 2000; the share of income accruing to labour has fallen 11 percentage points over the period. This shift away from labour to capital occurred *after* the legalization of black unions and during the period of rising union strength. Moreover, it has not been reversed by the change of government in 1994.

There are several implications arising from the shift in shares of income from labour to capital. First, it is consistent with the prediction that structural adjustment, in particular monetary and financial reform, favours the owners of capital, especially financial capital. Second, it is consistent with the prediction that in developing countries recession has a greater impact on wages than it does on profits, as safeguards for labour are weak. Third, it provides some support for the earlier proposition that, across all groups in South Africa, the richest became richer (although it cannot be argued from this evidence that the poor necessarily became poorer). Fourth, it implies that union strength may not be as overwhelming in South Africa as is often claimed.

[23] 'Household' refers to private households (including pension and insurance funds), non-incorporated businesses, and private non-profit organizations providing community services to households. Income from property includes dividend receipts, interest receipts less interest payments, rent receipts less maintenance costs, mortgage interest and consumption of fixed capital, and the profits of non-corporate business enterprises after consumption of fixed capital and inventory valuation adjustment (South African Reserve Bank 1999).

15.7. CONCLUSION

There has been a decline in the dispersion of racial incomes in South Africa since the mid-1970s. This has been accompanied by rising within-group inequality, most markedly amongst blacks, which make up the largest population group. As a result, there has been little overall improvement in aggregate indices of inequality, although formal incomes appear to be more evenly distributed. The problem is growing unemployment, which increases the number of people with no access to formal incomes, the best predictor of poverty.

Changes in structural factors in the 1970s were important in reducing racial inequality: wage and occupational discrimination decreased, and there was some improvement in black education. Later, the legalization of black trade unions assisted in the rapid real growth in non-white formal wages. While trade unions have been successful in reducing the skewness in formal incomes, they have been less successful in preventing redistribution from labour to owners of property. This suggests that the liberalization of markets has been more important than other structural factors in shaping the distribution of income in South Africa in recent years. In other words, labour market reforms through the erosion of apartheid practices in the 1970s were an important force behind the shifting distribution; thereafter, liberalization in other areas of the economy has tended to dominate changes.

The adoption of Washington Consensus policies has been phased rather than occurring as a package for simultaneous implementation. Initially, the changes were accompanied by falling growth and falling employment, but the deepening of liberalization has been simultaneous with more rapid (but still limited) economic growth. This does not imply causation (either when growth was slow or when it was more rapid), but it does indicate that contraction is not an inevitable result of liberalization. Nevertheless, employment is still falling; growth remains insufficient to raise per capita incomes, and some aspects of the package have worsened inequality.

The role of labour policy involves tradeoffs. On the one hand, trade unions play an important role in equalizing formal incomes by defending, in particular, the conditions of employment of workers in the lower and middle ranges of the wage spectrum. On the other, high wages relative to productivity undermine international competitiveness, encouraging the bias towards capital-intensive production which contributes to overall inequality, as increasing numbers are unable to find formal sector jobs.[24] These trade-offs are yet to be fully resolved by government, labour, and business. Job creation is important in shifting people out of poverty. The objective of employment-creating growth is driving the current reform programme. However, growth appears to have been stifled over a long period by sustained tight monetary policy (since the late 1980s) and a climate of uncertainty, as well as by external factors, such as global economic instability in the 1970s, economic isolation in the 1980s, and more recently, contagion effects of emerging economy crises in the 1990s.

---

[24] This does *not* imply that unions are responsible for unemployment. Relatively high formal wages are an exacerbating factor, not a cause.

The government's other priority is the need to redistribute income and wealth. While redistribution is clearly necessary, a fundamental restructuring which shifts resources away from the elite creates a strong impetus to emigrate, particularly among the better educated. This creates a delicate problem for the government. Against the pressure for radical redistribution must be set the need to keep skills and savings within the domestic economy, and to allow sufficient wealth accumulation to attract foreign investors. This will inevitably slow the rate at which redistribution can be achieved.[25]

At present the government's energy is concentrated on overcoming the legacy of apartheid, primarily through a redirection of government spending. The economic policy framework is likely to continue to be comparatively conservative, driven by the need to restructure and liberalize the economy and the need to attract sufficient foreign capital inflows to finance longer term growth. Investing in human resources and providing a policy environment which is, at the very least, not hostile to private investment may well be the optimal solution in the longer run. Slow reform may yet prove to be more sustainable, but it also means that inequality is likely to remain a defining feature of South Africa for many years to come.

REFERENCES

Alesina, A., and D. Rodrik (1994). Distributive policies and economic growth. *Quarterly Journal of Economics* 109(2), 465–90.

Aron, J., and J. Muellbauer (1998). Personal and corporate saving in South Africa: A review of some recent empirical work. *Quarterly Review* 4, Centre for Research into Economics and Finance in Southern Africa, London School of Economics: London.

Bell, T. (1985). Issues in South African unemployment. *South African Journal of Economics* 53(1), 24–38.

Budlender, D. (1999). Patterns of poverty in South Africa. *Development Southern Africa* 16(2), 197–219.

Cornia, G. A. (2000). Inequality and poverty in the era of liberalization and globalization. Paper presented at the United Nations University Millennium Conference, Tokyo, 19–21 January.

Cromwell, J. (1977). The size distribution of income: An international comparison. *Review of Income and Wealth* 23(3).

Department of Finance, Republic of South Africa (various). *Budget Review*, Department of Finance: Pretoria.

Devereaux, S. (1984). South African income distribution, 1900–1980. SALDRU Working Paper 51. University of Cape Town: Cape Town.

Fallon, P., and R. Lucas (1998). South Africa: Labour markets adjustment and inequalities. Informal Discussion Papers on Aspects of the Economy of South Africa 12. Southern Africa Department, World Bank: Washington, DC.

Gelb, S. (1991). South Africa's economic crisis: An overview. In S. Gelb (ed.), *South Africa's Economic Crisis*. David Philip: Cape Town.

---

[25] In the longer run this may be better for the country's economic growth rate, as redistribution of wealth can retard economic growth (Alesina and Rodrik 1994). By contrast, evidence cited elsewhere in this volume states that it is inequality itself that retards growth.

Harvey, C., and C. Jenkins (1992). The unorthodox response of the South African economy to changes in macroeconomic policy. Discussion Papers 300, Institute of Development Studies. University of Sussex: Brighton.

Hirschowitz, R. (1997). *Earning and Spending in South Africa: Selected Findings of the 1995 Income And Expenditure Survey*. Central Statistics Service: Pretoria.

Hofmeyr, J. (1999). Segmentation in the South African labour market. In M. Leibbrandt and N. Nattrass (eds.), *Inequality and the South African Labour Market*. Draft manuscript.

Holden, M., and P. Holden (1978). Effective tariff protection and resource allocation: A non-parametric approach. *Review of Economics and Statistics* 60(2).

Jain, S. (1975). *Size Distribution of Income: A Compilation of Data*. World Bank: Washington, DC.

Jensen, R. (1999). An early assessment of racial wage differentials in post-apartheid South Africa. Mimeo, Harvard University: Cambridge, MA.

Kingdon, G., and J. Knight (1999). Links between unemployment and poverty in South Africa. Mimeo, Centre for the Study of African Economies, University of Oxford: Oxford.

Knight, J., and M. McGrath (1987). The erosion of apartheid in the South African labour market: Measures and mechanisms. Applied Economics Discussion Paper 35. Institute of Economics and Statistics, University of Oxford: Oxford.

Lachman, D., and K. Bercuson (1992). Economic policies for a new South Africa. IMF Occasional Paper 91. IMF: Washington, DC.

Lecaillon, P. (1984). *Income Distribution and Economic Development: An Analytical Survey*. ILO: Geneva.

Leibbrandt, M., C. Woolard, and I. Woolard (1996). The contribution of income components to income inequality in South Africa: A decomposable Gini analysis. Living Standards Measurement Study Working Papers 125. World Bank: Washington, DC.

——H. Bhorat, and I. Woolard (1999). Understanding contemporary household inequality in South Africa. In M. Leibbrandt and N. Nattrass (eds.), *Inequality and the South African Labour Market*. Draft manuscript.

Lipton, M. (1985). *Capitalism and Apartheid, 1910–1984*. Gower: Aldershot.

——(1988). The poor and the poorest: Some interim findings. Discussion Paper 25. World Bank: Washington, DC.

Lundahl, M., P. Fredriksson, and L. Moritz (1992). South Africa 1990: Pressure for change. In M. Lundahl (ed.), *Apartheid in Theory and Practice: An Economic Analysis*. Westview: Boulder.

McGrath, M. (1983). The distribution of personal income in South Africa in selected years over the period from 1945 to 1980. Unpublished Ph.D dissertation, University of Natal: Durban.

——(1984). Inequality in the size distribution of incomes in South Africa, Staff Paper 2. Development Studies Unit, University of Natal: Durban.

Moll, P. (1992). The decline of discrimination against colored people in South Africa, 1970 to 1980. *Journal of Development Economics* 37, 289–307.

——(1999). Discrimination is declining in South Africa but inequality is not. In M. Leibbrandt and N. Nattrass (eds.), *Inequality and the South African Labour Market*. Draft manuscript.

Nattrass, N (1999). Growth, employment and wage-setting institutions in South Africa. Mimeo, University of Cape Town: Cape Town.

Paukert, F. (1973). Income distribution at different levels of development: A survey of evidence. *International Labour Review* 108(2–3), 97–124.

Ravallion, M., and B. Sen (1994). How land-based targeting affects rural poverty. World Bank Policy Research Paper 1270. World Bank: Washington, DC.

RSA (Republic of South Africa) (1996). *Growth, Employment and Redistribution: A Macroeconomic Strategy*. Republic of South Africa Government Printers: Pretoria.

Seekings, J. (1999). Visions of society: Peasants, workers and the unemployed in a changing South Africa. In M. Leibbrandt and N. Nattrass (eds.), *Inequality and the South African Labour Market*. Draft manuscript.

Sender, J., and D. Johnston (1995). A fuzzy snapshot of some poor and invisible women: Farm labourers in South Africa. School of Oriental and African Studies Working Paper Series 56. University of London: London

Simkins, C. (1979). *The Distribution of Personal Income among Income Recipients in South Africa, 1970 and 1976*. University of Natal: Durban.

South African Reserve Bank (various). *Quarterly Bulletin*, South African Reserve Bank: Pretoria.

Standard and Poor's (1999). South Africa. *Standard and Poor's Ratings Direct*, March.

Standing, G., J. Sender, and J. Weeks (1996). *Restructuring the Labour Market: The South African Challenge*. ILO: Geneva.

Thomas, W. (1990). Unemployment and the job creation challenge. In R. Schrire (ed.), *Critical Choices for South Africa: An Agenda for the 1990s*. Oxford University Press: Cape Town.

Tsikata, Y. (1998). Liberalization and trade performance in South Africa. Informal Discussion Papers on Aspects of the Economy of South Africa 13. World Bank: Washington, DC.

UNDP (various). *Human Development Report*. Oxford University Press: New York.

Whiteford, A., and M. McGrath (1999). Income inequality over the apartheid years. In M. Leibbrandt and N. Nattrass (eds.), *Inequality and the South African Labour Market*. Draft manuscript.

Wood, A. (1997). Openness and wage inequality in developing countries: The Latin American challenge to East Asian conventional wisdom. *The World Bank Economic Review* 11(1).

World Bank (1996). *World Development Report 1996: From Plan to Market*. World Bank: Washington, DC.

——(1999a). *World Development Indicators, 1999*. World Bank: Washington, DC.

——(1999b). *World Development Report 1999*. World Bank: Washington, DC.

16

Growth, Structural Change, and Inequality: The Experience of Thailand

ISRA SARNTISART

16.1. INTRODUCTION

Economic growth in Thailand has been marked by the increasing power of the manufacturing sector. Expansion of manufacturing in the 1960s was dominated by protected industries, which were geared towards the domestic market for consumer goods. Since the beginning of the 1970s, when the domestic market was saturated, the country has moved towards an export-oriented strategy. The export of manufactured goods has gradually taken the place of the export of primary products.

Although industrialization is believed to be a major factor behind Thailand's economic growth record, its success and developmental role have been brought into question by the steady deterioration of the country's distribution of income. During the past three decades of industrialization and rapid growth, there has been a significant degree of protection for capital-intensive import-competing products, as well as a considerable rise in the export of labour-intensive products. At the same time, Thailand failed to distribute the benefits of economic growth equitably, and income distribution deteriorated. When the country started to lose its comparative advantage and economic growth began to slow in the middle of the 1990s, income inequality declined mildly.

The share of other sectors in gross domestic product (GDP) also expanded at the expense of agriculture. This trend was dominated by the increase in the share of the banking, financial institutions, insurance, and real estate (FIRE) sector that reached its peak in 1994. In 1995, the performance of the FIRE sector and the impressive record of the Thai economy started to manifest to show some problems. It is widely believed that the expansion of FIRE had a substantial impact on the allocation of, and the returns to, factors of production and on income distribution. While there is no study on the relationship between the FIRE sector and income inequality, some studies have attempted to establish a relationship between industrialization and income distribution

The author thanks Ratchanee Siboonthieng and Hatairat Juengjariyanon for their invaluable research assistance and Giovanni Andrea Cornia, Carolyn Jenkins, other participants at the UNU/WIDER project meeting held in Helsinki in December 1999, and Pasuk Phongpaichit, for the helpful comments and suggestions on this study.

in Thailand (Suganya and Somchai 1988; Pranee 1992; Teerana 1993; Orakoch 1999). However, these studies do not satisfactorily capture the relationship under examination. Basically, the explanations of Suganya and Somchai, Teerana, and Pranee are based on the fact that the share of manufacturing in GDP increased more rapidly than did the share of manufacturing labour in the total labour force. Consequently, output per worker increased more quickly in manufacturing than it did in agriculture, and the agricultural labour force was left with lower incomes. At the same time, income distribution deteriorated. Similarly, Orakoch states that economic growth and investment in manufacturing were among the factors that worsened income distribution.

This study attempts to re-examine the relationship among economic growth, structural change, and income inequality in Thailand. Section 16.2 provides a broad picture of the Thai economy. Section 16.3 reviews studies on the changes in income inequality from the 1960s through the beginning of the 1990s. Section 16.4 examines industrialization planning, industrial protection policies, regional income disparities, and the minimum wage bill over the past four decades. Section 16.5 analyses income inequality in 1988, 1992, and 1996 according to the subgroups and source decompositions of income. The final section summarizes.

16.2. ECONOMIC GROWTH AND STRUCTURAL CHANGE

The Thai economy has grown rapidly during the past four decades (Table 16.1). The annual average rate of growth of real GDP was approximately 8 per cent in the 1960s and 7 per cent in the 1970s. During the first half of the 1980s, the growth rate fell slightly to 5.7 per cent, but rose dramatically, to nearly 10 per cent, in the second half of the decade. With an annual population growth rate of about 2 per cent, the increase of per capita gross national product (GNP) reached 8 per cent during that period. The growth rate of GDP in the early 1990s was well above 8 per cent but dropped to 5.9 per cent in 1996 and contracted by 1.75 per cent for the first time in many decades in 1997. This change in the performance of the Thai economy is believed to have affected the distribution of income significantly.

The rapid growth of the Thai economy has been accompanied by profound shifts in its structure, from labour-intensive agriculture to capital-intensive manufacturing (see Sarntisart 2000: table 16.2). The share in GDP agriculture sharply declined, from nearly 40 per cent in 1960 to 25.9 per cent in 1970, 12.8 per cent in 1990, and 11 per cent

Table 16.1. *GDP growth at 1988 prices, 1980–97 (percentage)*

	1980	1985	1990	1991	1992	1993	1994	1995	1996	1997
GDP	6.91	5.45	10.41	8.07	8.08	8.38	8.95	8.90	5.93	−1.75
Agriculture	4.18	4.25	3.22	6.13	4.79	−1.34	5.38	2.93	3.57	−0.74
Manufacturing	10.03	4.91	15.12	11.47	11.30	11.20	9.35	11.37	6.90	0.17
Other	7.35	6.07	10.49	6.91	7.26	9.14	9.47	8.79	5.84	−2.97

Source: NESDB (various).

in the second half of the 1990s. The total share in agriculture of three major crops (paddy, cassava, and rubber) remained broadly constant at around 31 per cent. These changes were accompanied by a rapid expansion of manufacturing whose share in GDP rose from 12.5 per cent to more than 28 per cent over 1960–98. During the same period, the share of other sectors rose gradually, from nearly 48 per cent to more than 60 per cent.

A shift from simple processing in agriculture-based industries (food, beverages, tobacco, and snuff), which were discriminated against, to protected capital-intensive industries (petroleum refining and electrical machinery) also characterized the rapid expansion of the manufacturing sector. The share of other labour-intensive industries—such as clothing, leather, and textiles—that had increased from 13 per cent to about 21 per cent in the first half of the 1990s fell to around 19 per cent during second part of the decade, a period during which Thailand started to lose international competitiveness in these sectors.

Other sectors also expanded faster than agriculture during this period (Table 16.1). At the same time, following a sharp rise in foreign direct investment in the second half of the 1980s and financial liberalization in 1993, the share of the FIRE sector in the domestic output rose from around 2 per cent in the 1960s to almost 8 per cent in 1994. It should be noted that the rapid influx of FDI (mainly originating in Japan, Hong Kong, South Korea, Taiwan, and Singapore) was not solely the result of government policies but was also the effect of changes in economic conditions occurring in other regions of the world. Beginning in 1995, the share of the FIRE sector started declining gradually anticipating by 2–3 years the collapse of the speculative bubble that led to the 1997 financial crisis of the Thai economy. The performance of the FIRE sector affected the rate of profit and the return to labour in the sector, and it is widely believed that this affected the distribution of income.

During the past four decades of industrialization, manufacturing has become increasingly dominant. The expansion of manufacturing has been characterized by the reallocation of resources in favour of manufacturing and at the expense of agriculture, which employs most of the labour force. Between 1970 and 1997, for instance, the capital stock in agriculture expanded at relatively lower rates than that in the manufacturing and other sectors (Table 16.2).

The changes in the structure of output and capital accumulation were paralleled by changes in the structure of employment. Indeed, the labour force expanded at a much faster rate in manufacturing than it did in agriculture (Sarntisart 2000: table 16.4), though the majority of the labour force remained in agriculture. During the three decades prior to the 1990s, the average annual growth of the agricultural labour force, around 2–3 per cent, can be considered a result of natural growth rather than resource allocation. In the 1990s, the rate became negative. Coxhead and Jiraporn (1999) also point out that, after 1989, around 15 per cent of the 20-million strong agricultural labour force walked off the farm. However, the share of agricultural labour in the total labour force, which was about 82 per cent in 1960, was still above 45 per cent during 1995–8 and had dropped to only around 42 per cent by 1999. The share of labour employed in other sectors, which increased from 14 per cent of the total labour force in 1960 to 25 per cent in 1990, rose further to around 40 per cent over 1995–9.

Table 16.2. *Structure and growth of net capital stock at 1988 prices by sector, 1970–96*
(percentage)

	1970	1980	1985	1990	1991	1992	1993	1994	1995	1996
Total share										
Agriculture	19.62	14.42	11.09	8.30	7.79	7.38	7.18	7.00	6.83	6.73
Manufacturing	8.54	11.30	11.45	14.44	15.02	15.43	15.72	15.91	16.21	16.40
Other	71.85	74.28	77.46	77.25	77.18	77.19	77.10	77.08	76.96	76.87
Average	—	5.20	7.22	9.15	13.47	12.36	11.80	11.77	11.54	10.71
growth rate										
Agriculture	—	2.02	1.73	3.00	6.54	6.33	8.75	9.12	8.74	9.11
Manufacturing	—	8.20	7.50	14.35	18.00	15.43	13.91	13.12	13.64	11.97
Other	—	5.55	8.12	9.09	13.37	12.37	11.67	11.75	11.36	10.58

Source: NESDB (1998).

16.3. TRENDS IN INCOME INEQUALITY

The recent focus on income distribution arises from a mounting concern that structural change and rapid growth induced by international trade and industrialization have been followed in the Thai case by sharp increases in income inequality that have de facto excluded large segments of the population from the benefits of such growth.

Most of the earlier studies—based on household surveys carried out by the national statistical office—divide the Thai population into income quintiles and analyse changes in the income share of each quintile. The Gini index and other indices are used to summarize the extent to which the actual distribution of income deviates from a perfectly equal income distribution. Instead of using net income, previous studies generally relied on gross income. This reflects the fact that, in the view of Thai economists, the redistributive role of personal income tax and transfers has not been sizeable in Thailand (on this topic, see Chapter 10).

Medhi (1977) studied income inequality in 1963, 1969, and 1972. He used both money income and adjusted household income, which included income in kind and net retained corporate earnings. He finds that in each of the 3 years considered, 60 per cent of Thai households received less than 20 per cent of the country's income, while the income share of the top 20 per cent of households was nearly 66 per cent. Medhi concludes that income equality clearly deteriorated during these years (Table 16.3). The top 20 per cent in income had been the only group to gain a greater income share, and the top 1 per cent benefited the most. Given that poor households tended to be larger than rich ones, the worsening inequality was even more severe in per capita terms.

Suganya and Somchai (1988) studied income inequality in 1975/6, 1980/1, and 1985/6. Unlike Medhi *et al.*, they used income per capita. Since the size of poor households is generally larger than that of rich households and since the majority of the Thai population is poor, Gini indices of household income can be expected to be slightly lower than those reported by Suganya and Somchai. This is, however, not

Table 16.3. *Distribution of household income, 1963, 1969, and 1972*

	1963	1969	1972
Income share (%)			
20%-lowest	2.9	3.4	2.4
20%	6.2	6.1	5.1
20%-middle	10.5	10.4	9.7
20%	20.9	19.2	18.4
20%-highest	59.5	60.9	64.4
Top 1%	9.6	10.5	15.0
Gini index, money income	0.5627	0.5550	0.6051
Gini index, adjusted income	0.4559	0.4822	0.5348

Source: Medhi (1977: tables 9 and 10).

Table 16.4. *Distribution of per capita household income, 1975/6, 1980/1, and 1985/6*

	1975/6	1980/1	1985/6
Income share (%)			
20%-lowest	6.05	5.41	4.55
20%	9.73	9.10	7.87
20%-middle	14.00	13.38	12.09
20%	20.96	20.64	19.86
20%-highest	49.26	51.47	55.63
Top 10%	33.40	35.44	39.15
Gini index	0.426	0.453	0.500

Source: Suganya and Somchai (1988: table 2.2).

borne out by the data in Table 16.4, as, due to differences in income concepts and sample coverage, the results of the two studies are not comparable. Be as it may, inequality was shown to have increased also over 1975–85 (Table 16.4). The worsening of inequality was more severe between 1980/1 and 1985/6 than between 1975/6 and 1980/1, possibly because of the worsening of the agricultural terms of trade and the comparatively poor performance of agriculture during the latter period.

Income inequality in 1988, 1992, and 1996 has been calculated for this study using the same methodology as that of Suganya and Somchai (Table 16.5). In 1988, the shares of the three lower quintiles increased significantly, to 4.9 per cent, 8.5 per cent, and 12.4 per cent, at the expense of the upper two quintiles, for which the shares decreased to 19.7 per cent and 54.5 per cent. In terms of the Gini index, inequality fell from 0.500 in 1985/6 to 0.4929 in 1988.

It is notable that this was the first time in 30 years that Thailand recorded a decline in income inequality. Medhi *et al.* (1991) assert that this situation was similar to that

Table 16.5. *Distribution of per capita household income,*
1988, 1992, and 1996

	1988	1992	1996
Income share (%)			
20%–lowest	4.89	4.10	4.25
20%	8.45	7.22	7.62
20%–middle	12.43	11.23	11.85
20%	19.74	18.76	19.79
20%–highest	54.49	58.71	56.49
Top 10%	37.83	42.34	40.00
Gini index	0.4929	0.5310	0.5114
Shorrocks index	0.7929	1.7585	1.2791

Source: Calculated for 1988, 1992, and 1996 on the basis of household
surveys; see text for additional explanations.

in 1980/1. The major determinant of the reduction was crop prices, which were at
a peak in adjacent years. This improvement in equality coincided with an increase in
poverty between 1985/6 and 1988. The rise in poverty was an urban phenomenon.
During this period, municipal areas in almost every region experienced an increase in
poverty, except for Bangkok and municipal areas in the central region that were insu-
lated from these increases. Thus, the decline in inequality occurred at the expense of
urban residents who became poor.

Changes in inequality between 1988 and 1996 are very important for policy analysis.
Between 1988 and 1992, the changes in inequality followed the same trend as those in
previous years. Based on the Gini index and the Shorrocks index of order 2, inequality
increased, respectively, from 0.4929[1] and 0.7929 in 1988 to 0.5310 and 1.7585 in 1992.
This increase was mainly due to the gain in income share among the top 10 per cent,
from 37.8 to 42.4 per cent, while the shares of all other deciles fell. The trend was
reversed again in 1996, when the two indices showed a moderate decrease in inequality
from 0.5310 and 1.7585 to 0.5114 and 1.2791, respectively. This favourable change was
the result of the gain in the income shares of all lower deciles at the expense of the top
10 per cent. The reason behind the gain and the loss in the income share of the top
10 per cent between the two periods calls for further explanation.

The above discussion is based on gross income. The distribution of net income
would be less unequal than that of gross income if the structure of the personal income
tax were progressive. Chalongphob *et al.* (1999) analyse the incidence of the tax
between 1986 and 1996 and point out that the burden of the income tax fell more heavily on households in Bangkok and households in the upper income deciles. They also
add that the average income tax burden per household increased during the period. The
results of Suphanee (1995) differ slightly. Based on the 1990 tax burden on urban

---

[1] This is slightly different from the figure reported in Table 16.10; one reason may be different treatment
of outliers in the database.

households, Suphanee finds that the personal income tax had a progressive structure, and the tax burden fell mainly on wage and salary earners. By comparing the structure of the personal income tax in 1990 and 1992, Usarsee (1996) finds that taxation in 1992 was not more progressive than in 1990. Moreover, the 1992 regional and size distributions of post-tax income tended to be more unequal than the corresponding distributions of the pre-tax income. Thus, the results of previous studies indicate that, since not all households are subjected to income taxation, the redistributive impact of the progressive income tax may not be effective.[2]

16.4. FACTORS RELATED TO INCOME DISTRIBUTION

Many factors have influenced the distribution of the benefits of growth of the Thai economy. These include industrialization plans, protectionist policies, the minimum wage bill, direct foreign investments, trade liberalization, financial liberalization, land reform, and inequality in education. The extent to which the first three factors have influenced changes in income inequality are discussed in the following paragraphs. The impact of trade liberalization on inequality is borne out by the results of the studies on the relationship between industrial protection and income distribution mentioned earlier. Finally, although important, the role of financial liberalization, the failure of land reform, and the disequalizing impact of unbalanced educational expansion are not discussed in this study.

16.4.1. *Industrialization Plans*

Industrialization did not begin in Thailand until the late 1950s and the beginning of the 1960s. Since 1958, the policy of the Thai government has been to promote and guarantee private investment and to provide infrastructure. In its first development plan (1961–6), the government encouraged industrial expansion in the private sector, mainly by granting privileges and protection to industries producing in competition with imports. Then, after years of import substitution, Thailand moved slowly to abandon this policy through a gradual switch to export promotion. Although the second development plan (1967–71) did not actively promote exports, the aims of the plan laid more emphasis on agricultural and manufacturing exports and on the quality of exports.

Beginning with the third development plan (1972–6), the government attempted to promote the exportation of agricultural and manufacturing products making use of locally available raw materials. The two following plans (1977–81 and 1982–6) continued to focus on the export sector, but with more emphasis on marketing, industrial decentralization, and the promotion of heavy industry. Varying levels of special support were granted to selected firms in provincial areas. The purpose was to decentralize industries away from Bangkok and the surrounding provinces. The list of industries

---

[2] Chalongphob *et al.* (1999) and Sarntisart (1999) find that indirect taxes such as the business tax and VAT were slightly regressive.

benefiting from export promotion subsidies was enlarged, and the support offered to export industries increased. However, import-competing industries were still heavily protected. The next three development plans tended to be more concerned with distributional issues. The sixth plan (1987–91) placed more emphasis on the distribution of farmland, diversification of agricultural output, and the development of agro-based and small-scale industries; that is, measures that were expected to raise the incomes of the rural poor. The seventh plan (1992–6) focused more on structural adjustment in agriculture and industrial reallocation towards regional centres[3] that was expected to favour small-scale and cottage industries and reduce the regional income gap.

Finally, the eighth plan (1997–2001) assigns more importance to the development of human capital and the improvement of production technology and economic efficiency. However, attention has also been given to agriculture, agro-based industries, and selected manufacturing branches such as motor vehicles, electrical appliances, electronics, machinery, and telecommunications. Some of these industries have enjoyed monopoly rents. Though it will be a long time before the distributional consequences of these measures will be felt, the renewed attention placed on agriculture and agro-based industries is expected to generate favourable effects.

16.4.2. *Industrial Protection*

The theoretical arguments for industrial protection during industrialization are well known. Temporary protection may assist an infant industry to compete with foreign industry, while it develops its latent strengths. Protection raises the domestic prices of protected manufactures above world prices, bids up the return to mobile factors of production, and redirects the resources required for industrialization from agriculture to manufacturing.[4] In Thailand, it also involved the maintenance of low manufacturing wage rates through the provision of cheap agricultural produce for consumption by manufacturing workers. Consequently such policy, however, obstructed technological development and any move towards higher productivity and greater incomes. Moreover, protected industries are not encouraged to be more efficient, and thus tend to remain inefficient.

Generally, there are four objectives in industrial protection. First, in the case of Thailand, the initial objective was to raise revenue (Ingram 1971). Second, in an attempt to relieve the difficulties linked to the trade deficit, a high tariff was placed on consumer goods considered luxury items. Third, protection was regarded as an appropriate means to stimulate industrialization. The so-called infant industry argument asserts that temporary protection may be required to allow new firms to compete with established foreign firms. However, Nishimizu and Page (1986) found that infant industry arguments for protection in Thailand were supported empirically only for a minority of industries.

---

[3] These were Chiang Mai, Phitsanulok, and Nakhon Sawan in the north, Khon Kaen and Nakhon Ratchasima in the northeast, Saraburi and Ratchaburi in the central region, and Surat Thani and Songkhla in the south.

[4] Ikemoto (1991) and Sarntisart (1994) point out that the agricultural terms of trade deteriorated.

Fourth, the infant industry argument is frequently accompanied by the employment argument, which is often taken implicitly as a favourable distributional objective of protection. In the case of Thailand, a relationship between labour intensity and the level of protection runs counter to this argument. Estimates of the correlation among sectoral factor intensity, the ratio between the wage bill and the total non-wage bill, import duty rates, and import tax rates based on large number of sectors show that the degree of protection tends to be lower for labour-intensive industries (Sarntisart 2000: table 16.8). This relationship indicates that the employment argument is not valid, and the distributional impact of the 1995 protection system might be regressive. The estimates of Sarntisart (1994) on 1985 data point to a similar conclusion.

The distributional impact of protection has been discussed widely in the literature. In the neoclassical world of two countries, two sectors, and two factors of production, the Stolper–Samuelson theory states that an increase in the relative price of a product will raise the return to the factor used intensively in the production of that product and will reduce the return to the other factor. The Ricardo–Viner–Jones specific factors model, in which a factor is specific to some production sectors, states that the distributional impact of protection depends on the consumption basket of consumers. In the case of Thailand, where agriculture and the simple processing of its products are more labour intensive and constitute an important part of the consumption basket, the two theories point to the unfavourable impact of industrial protection.

A limited number of empirical studies have also attempted to establish a relationship in Thailand between income distribution and import tariffs. These studies fall into two categories. In Chalongphob *et al.* (1988) and Overbusch *et al.* (1988) the income-distribution impact of industrial protection was found to be ambiguous. Based on a computable general equilibrium (CGE) model, Chalongphob *et al.* assert that the impact of the replacement of import taxes through a proportional tax on household incomes in order to generate exactly the same tax revenue is unclear as their results depend on the economic closure of the model. Based on another CGE model, Overbusch *et al.* find that the distributive impact of government intervention in agriculture is inconclusive.

On the other hand, Fabers and Kennes (1982, cited in O'Mara and Le-Si 1985) and Sarntisart (1994) find that the distributional impact of industrial protection in Thailand is regressive. The results of Fabers and Kennes, based on a multisectoral macroeconomic model, indicate that a reduction in import tariff rates increases the share of agriculture significantly. By using a CGE model, Sarntisart shows that the structure of industrial protection in Thailand has favoured urban households, especially those in the upper expenditure deciles. This is supported by studies on the incidence of taxation, such as Suphanee (1995) and Chalongphob *et al.* (1999), which also point out that trade taxes are regressive.

16.4.3. *The Sectoral and Regional Bias of Protection*

The system of industrial protection in Thailand is based on many measures. These include tariffs, import and export licences, business taxes, and excise taxes. These are well discussed in the literature (e.g. Narongchai 1973; Pairote 1975; Paitoon *et al.* 1989; Sunee and Sombat 1996). In brief, while the protective effects of other measures are notable, tariffs are the most extensively used measures.

Many studies report estimates of the degree of protection since the 1960s. In most cases, the discussion focuses on aspects of the trade regime and the allocative impact of industrial protection. Despite differences in methodology and definition, these studies reach similar findings. According to Pairote (1975), Paitoon *et al.* (1989), and Sunee and Sombat (1996) import protection in Thailand in the 1970s, 1980s, and 1990s was characterized by the following features.

First, the tariffs increasingly protected the manufacturing sector, discriminated against agriculture, and were biased in favour of highly processed products. The protection for primary products in agriculture was less extensive than the protection for processed agricultural products. Thus, during the initial phase of industrial development, capital-intensive production was promoted. Second, although an export-oriented strategy has been attempted since the beginning of the 1970s, this has been far from successful, judged in terms of the nominal and effective rates of protection. The protection of import-competing industries is still relatively greater than that of export industries. During the 1980s, the protection of export industries increased slightly, while that for import-competing industries nearly doubled. Export promotion was merely added to existing policies to protect the import-competing industries. The focus on heavy protection for import-competing consumer goods led to a change in the structure of imports—which had consisted predominantly of consumer goods in the 1960s—to intermediate products and raw materials for the production of consumer goods and capital goods in the 1990s. Third, in terms of protection policies, Thailand is a patchwork of conflicting regional interests. On the one hand, industrial protection is raising the market prices for manufactured products, which are produced mostly in the central region and Bangkok, forcing buyers in other regions to pay higher prices for manufactures. On the other hand, discrimination or negative protection is lowering the market prices of agricultural goods, and thereby subsidizes non-farm consumers at the expense of farmers. Thus, one might expect sectoral and regional income disparities to follow upon industrialization in Thailand. This is discussed in Section 16.4.4.

16.4.4. *Regional Income Disparities*

During the past four decades, regional income disparities have been widening. Table 16.6 shows that the change in the gross regional products (GRP) of Bangkok and nearby regions contrasts sharply with the situation in other parts of the country. In 1960, the per capita GRP, at current prices, of the central region (including Bangkok) was about three times that of the poorest region, the north-east. By 1973, the gap had widened. The per capita GRPs of the central region and Bangkok were, respectively, more than three times and six times that of the north-east. More than 26 per cent of GDP went to Bangkok, where the population share was less than 10 per cent. By 1988, Bangkok's share in GDP had risen to 50 per cent. Its per capita GRP was much higher than the per capita GRP of other regions, namely, approximately 3 and 10 times that

Table 16.6. *Regional shares of GRP at current prices by industry, various years (percentage)*

	Total	Central	Bangkok	Northeast	Northern	Southern
1960						
Total economy	100.00	50.50	—	18.97	n.a.	n.a.
Agriculture	100.00	33.73	—	26.66	n.a.	n.a.
Manufacturing	100.00	67.79	—	11.59	n.a.	n.a.
Other	100.00	59.05	—	14.95	n.a.	n.a.
Per capita GRP	1.0000	1.6067	—	0.5569	n.a.	n.a.
1973						
Total economy	100.00	31.35	26.40	15.58	n.a.	n.a.
Agriculture	100.00	35.54	1.55	24.20	n.a.	n.a.
Manufacturing	100.00	41.91	40.14	6.71	n.a.	n.a.
Other	100.00	25.01	38.76	12.65	n.a.	n.a.
Per capita GRP	1.0000	1.4851	2.7155	0.4418	n.a.	n.a.
1988						
Total economy	100.00	16.91	50.08	11.91	n.a.	n.a.
Agriculture	100.00	22.89	9.43	22.88	n.a.	n.a.
Manufacturing	100.00	12.45	77.95	4.27	n.a.	n.a.
Other	100.00	17.10	49.82	12.03	n.a.	n.a.
Per capita GRP	1.0000	1.0077	3.1497	0.3436	n.a.	n.a.
1992						
Total economy	100.00	17.56	51.94	11.85	9.95	8.71
Agriculture	100.00	21.22	9.85	24.43	18.07	26.43
Manufacturing	100.00	20.42	69.29	4.31	3.94	2.05
Other	100.00	15.50	52.61	12.72	11.04	8.13
Per capita GRP	1.0000	1.0381	3.1289	0.3453	0.5220	0.6635
1996[P]						
Total economy	100.00	18.85	51.20	11.82	9.18	8.94
Agriculture	100.00	20.93	9.76	21.30	17.43	30.59
Manufacturing	100.00	25.42	63.65	5.10	3.82	2.01
Other	100.00	15.40	52.91	13.24	10.20	8.25
Per capita GRP	1.0000	1.1247	2.9457	0.3476	0.4943	0.6741

Notes: Since 1988, the GRPs of Samut Prakarm, Pathum Thani, Samut Sakhon, Nonthaburi, and Nakhon Pathom have been excluded from the central region and included in Bangkok. The total GRP of the southern region is the total GRP less the GRPs of the central region, Bangkok, the north, and the north-east. n.a. = not available.
[P] Predicted values.

Source: Calculated from unpublished data on gross regional products, Office of the National Economic and Social Development Board.

of the central and the north-east regions and the same trend continued in the 1990s. In 1992 and 1996, Bangkok accounted for more than 51 per cent of GDP. The per capita GRPs of the central region and the north during these 2 years were, respectively, 3.0 and 2.8 (1992) and 1.5 and 1.4 times (1996) that of the north-east.

I. Sarntisart

The causes of regional income disparities are difficult to document. They can be attributed to many factors, including the spatial immobility of labour, transportation costs, the endowment of natural resources, and productivity differences. Because of the variations in industrial mix among regions, intrasectoral productivity differences can also be regarded as a determinant of regional income inequality.

The differences in the industrial mix between Bangkok and other regions have been increasing over time. During the past three decades, the rapid expansion of the manufacturing sector in Bangkok and the central region has been a key factor in the fast growth recorded by these regions. Between 1960 and 1973, the share of Bangkok and the central region in the country's total manufacturing product rose from 67.8 per cent to 81.5 per cent. In 1988, the share of Bangkok and the central region in the gross manufacturing product was over 90 per cent. Of this 90 per cent, 87 per cent was accounted for by the Bangkok area.[5] In 1992 and 1996, Bangkok and the central region still represented around 90 per cent of the gross manufacturing product. However, because of the development of industrial estates along the eastern seaboard, the share of the central region in the gross manufacturing product had climbed by 1996 to more than 25 per cent, while the corresponding share of Bangkok had declined to 64 per cent.

The import protection policies favoured various manufacturing industries located in Bangkok and the central region. Before 1972, the systems of protection discriminated against food processing and construction materials. In the 1980s, protection of industries relying on agricultural raw material was mostly negative and that of food processing was low relative to the protection accorded to manufacturing. In 1960, more than 50 per cent of the output of the food processing industry originated from outside Bangkok and the central region. In contrast, except for rubber products, the highly protected industries—intermediate products, consumer goods, machinery, and transport equipment—were mostly located in Bangkok and the central region. In the 1970s and the 1980s, these highly protected manufacturing industries still tended to be located in Bangkok and the surrounding provinces. Since the beginning of the 1990s, because of the development of labour-intensive manufacturing in the Laem Chabang industrial estate and of heavy industry in the Map Ta Phut industrial estate, both of which are on the eastern seaboard, the bias of the protective system towards Bangkok and the surrounding provinces has been reduced and a growing share of the benefits of industrial protection has gone to the central region. That manufacturing in Bangkok and the surrounding provinces is more capital-intensive than manufacturing in other parts of Thailand is also well known (Somsak 1985). Thus, the productivity and wages income of the manufacturing labour force in Bangkok and the surrounding provinces are also higher. This fact, together with the concentration of manufacturing in Bangkok and the surrounding provinces, partly explains the widening regional income disparities and the deterioration in income inequality before the 1990s.

[5] The 1988 statistics provided by the national income account are for Bangkok and vicinity, rather than for Bangkok alone. The vicinity of Bangkok includes five provinces: Nonthaburi, Pathum Thani, Samut Prakarn, Samut Sakhon, and Nakhon Pathom.

16.4.5. *The Minimum Wage Bill*

After nearly two decades of rapid industrialization, a minimum wage bill was finally introduced on 14 February 1973. The minimum daily wage rate must be set by a tripartite committee consisting of representatives of employers, workers, and the government. The aim of the bill was to raise the minimum wage towards the average rate in each sector, to increase the competition between those employers who pay a fair wage rate and those who do not and to enhance economic development and income distribution. The bill covers employment in all non-agricultural sectors except the government sector.

Over the past three decades, the rate has been boosted significantly. It was first set at 12 baht[6] for unskilled workers in Bangkok and three surrounding provinces (Nonthaburi, Pathum Thani, and Samut Prakarn). Since then, the rate has been increased every 1 or 2 years in order to match the rising cost of living.[7] At the same time, more provinces have been added in the coverage of the bill. By the end of 1988, seventy-six provinces had been included in the bill. The minimum wage was set at 78 baht for Bangkok and five surrounding provinces, 75 baht for Phuket and two other provinces in the south, 70 baht for four growth poles in the central region, the north and the north-east, and 65 baht in the remaining sixty-three provinces. In 1997, the minimum wage rate was raised to 162 baht for Bangkok, the five surrounding provinces, and Phuket, 140 baht for the two southern provinces and the four growth poles, and 130 baht for the remaining provinces.

The bill was supposed to have a significant impact on the labour market and on income distribution. It was expected to encourage an improvement in labour productivity. As more provinces were covered by the bill, regional earnings gaps were expected to decline. Farm wages were supposed to rise, and thereby attract labour. It was anticipated that this would have a favourable long-term effect on income distribution. However, the introduction of the minimum wage (which is supposed to be higher than the market wage rate) has also created, according to some, an unemployment problem (on this, see also Chapter 8). Moreover, as the minimum wage in the Bangkok area is approximately 15–25 per cent higher than in other provinces, migration into Bangkok and the surrounding areas increased. In turn, this has aggravated many urban problems such as the expansion of slums and traffic congestion. Since some workers, such as the uneducated and ageing workers, are regionally and sectorally immobile and since farm and government workers are not covered by the bill, some regional and sectoral disparities were exacerbated by the minimum wage policy. Saowalak (2000) also points out that, according to the 1996 labour force survey of the national statistical office, only 26 per cent of all workers were protected by the bill and of these around 65 per cent were unskilled workers.

In sum, the overall income-distributional impact of the minimum wage bill is ambiguous. Moreover, during economic recession, when many workers are laid off, the disequalizing impact of the bill could be more severe and outweigh its equalizing impact.

---

[6] Approximately $0.50 at the time.

[7] Chutipongse (1996) has found that the various changes in the minimum wage rate have effectively outpaced the inflation rate.

16.5. ANALYSIS OF INCOME INEQUALITY IN 1988, 1992, AND 1996

This section reviews the decomposition analysis of income inequality contained in previous studies and examines changes in income inequality between 1988 and 1996. The decomposition is based on gross income, including incomes transferred from other households and the government. The aim of the review is to understand how previous studies have explained the trend in income inequality prior to 1988 and to use this to analyse the causes of changes in inequality that occurred subsequently up to 1996.

16.5.1. *Methodology*

Many indices of inequality are employed in the literature, with the most widely used one being the Gini coefficient. Its use, however, is limited by the fact that the aggregate value of the index is not decomposable among subcomponent groups.

Because of this, this study employs the Shorrocks index of order 2 (Shorrocks 1980). The index satisfies most of the important properties of inequality indices such as scale independence, variations to equal addition (subtraction), invariance to proportionate growth, transfer sensitivity, and aggregate decomposability. The latter property allows a detailed analysis of changes in inequality as follows. Let $Y = (Y_1, Y_2, Y_3, \ldots, Y_N)$ be the distribution of income among N individuals with mean income equal to M. The Shorrocks index of order 2 (I_2) is defined as

$$I_2 = (1/2\,N)\sum_i [(Yi/M) - 1]^2. \tag{16.1}$$

In order to analyse the importance of income from various sources in the distribution of overall income, Eq. (16.2) decomposes Eq. (16.1) by source of income:

$$I_2 = \sum_k (M_k/M)^2 I_{2k} + (1/M)^2 \sum_j \sum_k Cov(Y_j, Y_k), \tag{16.2}$$

where M_k = mean income from source k, I_{2k} = inequality in income from source k, and $Cov(Y_j, Y_k)$ = the covariance effect between incomes from different sources, $j \neq k$.

$$I_2 = \sum_g V_g \lambda_g^2 I_{2g} + (1/2)\sum_g V_g \lfloor \lambda_g - 1^2 \rfloor, \tag{16.3}$$

$$dI_2 = \sum_k \overline{\left(\frac{M_k}{M}\right)}^2 dI_{2k} + \sum_k \left[\overline{I_{2k}}\, d\left(\frac{M_k}{M}\right)^2\right] + \left[\sum_j \sum_k \overline{Cov\,(Y_j,\, Y_k)}\right] d\left(\frac{1}{M^2}\right)$$

$$+ \overline{\left(\frac{1}{M^2}\right)}\sum_j \sum_k dCov\,(Y_j,\, Y_k). \tag{16.4}$$

Equation (16.3) shows how previous studies have decomposed total income inequality at any point in time into two parts: Inequality among people in the same subgroup and inequality among people in different subgroups. Equation (16.4), in turn, can be used to analyse a change in income inequality occurring over a given period. It consists of four terms. The first term represents the impact of a change in inequality in income from source k. The second term is the impact of a change in income shares from various sources. The third term is solely the impact of a change in the overall mean income, that is, economic growth. The fourth term is the impact of a change in the covariation effect among income from different sources, that is, an error term.

16.5.2. *Subgroup Decomposition Analysis*

The decomposition of income inequality in this study relies on two prior studies by Suganya and Somchai (1988) and Orakoch (1999). The first study analyses the important features of changes in inequality and decomposed inequality in per capita household income in 1975/6, 1980/1, and 1988. The second study decomposes inequality in individual income in 1988, 1992, and 1996. Despite the difference in units of measurement, the results of the two studies are very important for policy analysis.

The analysis of Suganya and Somchai (1988) can be summarized as follows. First, by using multiple regression, Suganya and Somchai conclude that employment-related factors are the major causes of income inequality. Locational (community and region) and personal (human capital) variables are other important factors. Second, Suganya and Somchai (1988) disaggregate income inequality, as measured by the Shorrocks index, by various subgroups. Their results show that the benefits of development have become increasingly unbalanced. The relative inequality between people living in different locations, communities, and regions has increased compared to the inequality among people living in the same location, community, and region. The relative inequality among people in different socio-economic classes, different occupations, and different sectors of production and with different education levels has also risen pronouncedly.

The disaggregation of overall inequality by region, rural–urban residence, and sector of employment of the household head point to a widening of income disparities in all these dimensions (Table 16.7). For example, in 1975/6, 78.8 per cent of the national inequality was accounted for by within-sector inequality, while the remaining 21.2 per cent was due to between-sector inequality. Between 1980/1 and 1985/6, the contribution of within-sector inequality declined from 76.1 per cent to 71.5 per cent. During the same period, the contribution of between-sector inequality rose from 23.9 per cent to 28.5 per cent. This reflects the unfavourable distributional impact of the industrialization policies during the periods.

Based on individual income, Orakoch (1999) analyses inequality in 1988, 1992, and 1996 (Table 16.8).[8] According to the study, the Shorrocks index of order 2 shows that inequality rose from 1.4626 in 1988 to 2.8055 in 1992 to fall to 2.2837 in 1996. According to the subgroup decomposition, around 95 per cent of the overall inequality can be explained by inequality among individuals living within the same region or

---

[8] This is different from the inequality in Tables 16.6 and 16.7, which are based on per capita household income. However, the changes in inequality observed over the period are similar.

Table 16.7. *Subgroup decomposition of income inequality, 1975/6, 1980/1, and 1985/6 (percentage)*

Factor disaggregation	1975/6	1980/1	1985/6
Inequality (Shorrocks index)	0.304	0.347	0.427
Region			
Between group	16.18	19.87	24.90
Within group	83.82	80.13	75.10
Community			
Between group	20.20	21.77	28.15
Within group	79.80	78.23	71.85
Sector of production			
Between group	21.19	23.94	28.53
Within group	78.81	76.06	71.47

Source: Suganya and Somchai (1988: table 2.7).

Table 16.8. *Subgroup decomposition of income inequality, 1988, 1992, and 1996 (percentage)*

Factor disaggregation	1988	1992	1996
Inequality (Shorrocks index)	1.4626	2.8055	2.2837
Region			
Between group	4.31	4.05	3.50
Within group	95.69	95.96	96.50
Community			
Between group	5.61	5.09	4.57
Within group	94.39	94.91	95.43
Sector of production			
Between group	6.85	4.65	4.53
Within group	93.15	95.35	95.47

Source: Orakoch (1999: tables 5.2.5, 5.2.7, 5.2.11).

community, or working within the same sector of production. The contribution of within-group inequality rose slightly over the period considered. At the same time, the contribution of income disparities between regions, communities, and sectors of production, which explained only 5 per cent of overall inequality in 1988, declined moderately over time.

These results show that over 1988–96 the distribution of the benefits of development became more balanced from both a regional rural–urban and sectoral perspectives, possibly reflecting the success of the sixth and seventh development plans in achieving their distributional objectives.

16.5.3. *Decomposition Analysis by Income Source*

The intertemporal decomposition of individual income by source between 1988 and 1992 data can be used to evaluate the impact of the sixth development plan (1987–91), which aimed at raising incomes among the rural poor through a focus on agro-based industries and small-scale industrialization. In turn, a comparison between the 1992 and 1996 data can be used to evaluate the impact of the seventh development plan (1992–6), which aimed at decreasing the regional income gap through the reallocation of industrial activities from Bangkok and the surrounding provinces to a number of regional growth poles. Although available, the 1998 data on the distribution of house-hold income were excluded from the analysis to avoid the short-run impact of various government and international assistance measures that were introduced to relieve the hardship caused by the 1997 financial crisis.

The 1988, 1992, and 1996 data provide information by six sources of individual income: Wages and salaries, non-farm profit, farm profit, property income, transfer income, and other money receipts—these income categories are further described in the appendix to Sarntisart (2000). The importance of each source in the distribution of income is indicated by the relative share in the total (Table 16.9). Wages and salaries increasingly became the main source of income, representing approximately 41 per cent of the total in 1988 and 48 per cent in 1992 and 1996. During the same years, the share of farm profit in total income fell steadily while that of non-farm profits moved in the opposite direction. These changes reflect the structural shifts recorded by the Thai economy during this period, during which millions of rural settlers moved to the non-agricultural sector and became waged labourers. The shares of income from other sources, that is, transfer payments, property income, and other money receipts changed only slightly.

In turn Table 16.10 illustrates changes over time in overall income inequality, inequality by different income sources, and the contribution of each of them to overall inequality. Since the figures in this table are based on income earners, they are different from the ones presented in Table 16.8. As measured by the Shorrocks index,

Table 16.9. *Average individual income, by source, 1988, 1992, and 1996 (percentage)*

	1988	1992	1996
Wages and salaries	41.27	48.48	48.21
Non-farm profit	17.78	22.20	22.58
Farm profit	28.44	17.98	16.40
Transfer payments	9.05	7.01	8.69
Property income	1.71	2.50	2.31
Other money receipts	1.74	1.82	1.80

Note: Based on income earners.

Sources: Sarntisart (1997: table 7); Orakoch (1999: table 5.2.1).

Table 16.10. *Overall income inequality and its decomposition by source of income; 1988, 1992, and 1996*

Source of income	1988	1992	1996
Overall income	1.4754	2.9285	2.2837
	(100.00)	(100.00)	(100.00)
Wages and salaries	2.8769	2.8279	3.7108
	(33.22)	(22.70)	(37.77)
Non-farm profit	21.7740	38.3623	20.2804
	(46.65)	(64.58)	(45.30)
Farm profit	3.6251	8.8082	13.6768
	(19.87)	(8.93)	(16.11)
Transfer payments	13.9804	14.3257	8.8656
	(7.77)	(2.40)	(2.93)
Property income	107.0192	163.3968	102.5689
	(2.12)	(3.48)	(2.41)
Other money receipts	101.5663	217.9138	107.0148
	(2.09)	(2.48)	(1.52)
Covariance effect	(−11.72)	(−4.58)	(−6.02)

Notes: Based on individual income. Figures in parentheses are percentage contributions to overall individual income inequality.

Sources: Sarntisart (1997: table 8); Orakoch (1999: table 5.2.2).

overall inequality rose in 1988 to then decrease over 1992–6. Wage inequality fell marginally between 1988 and 1992 and then rose markedly between 1992 and 1996. Such increase was the result of the reallocation of resources following the rapid expansion of the FIRE sector. Although the growth this sector was brisk during the first half of the 1990s, it then slowed down—though the contractionary effect of such slowdown was not fully realized before 1996. The earnings of many professionals working in the FIRE sector were still relatively high and were far above the earnings of similar professional workers in other sectors. The trend in inequality in non-farm profit, which had jumped between 1988 and 1992 and then dropped in 1996, partly reflected the saturation of investment in the FIRE sector. The inequality in farm profit rose steadily over the period. This points to the widening gap among farmers in different agricultural subsectors and between traditional and modern farmers. The production of traditional agriculture was constrained by labour shortages due to outmigration towards the manufacturing sector.

As a result, the percentage of contribution of the different sources of income to overall inequality changed significantly during the period. The respective contributions of wages and farm profits first declined and then recovered. Thus, from 1988 to 1992, the importance of wages and farm profits in explaining overall inequality was reduced, but, from 1992 to 1996, it increased. On the other hand, the contribution of non-farm profits rose to 64.6 per cent by 1992 and then fell to 45.3 per cent by 1996. The changes in the contribution of other income sources to overall income inequality were minor.

16.5.4. *Decomposition of Changes in Income Inequality by Income Source*

This section traces the impact of changes in incomes from different sources on overall inequality. These changes are decomposed into four components: A change in the income shares by source; a change in the income inequality of each source of income; a change in overall mean income; and a change in the covariation effect among incomes from different sources. Mathematically, an increase (decrease) in the inequality of the distribution of income from a given source will increase (decrease) overall inequality. A change in the share of income from a source will also lead to a change in overall inequality in the same direction. While the interpretation of other components is straightforward, that of a change in overall mean income requires further explanation. If it has a positive sign, an increase (decrease) in overall mean income will lead to a decrease (increase) in income inequality. If it has a negative sign, an increase (decrease) in overall mean income will lead to an increase (decrease) in income inequality. Table 16.11 breaks down the changes in income inequality that occurred during 1988–92 and during 1992–6. The intertemporal decomposition reveals many important features of the changes in inequality during these two periods.

First, the shares of the FIRE sector and of the manufacturing sector played a significant role in the distribution of income. In the 1988–92 period, the total contribution of changes in the shares of the incomes from various sources to the increase in overall inequality was around 29 per cent. The major contributors were the increases in the shares of wages and salaries and of non-farm profit. This coincided with the rapid expansion of the FIRE sector and of the manufacturing sector that occurred during this period. The boom in these sectors raised the return to capital and wages, caused an upward shift in the costs borne by agriculture, and squeezed the rural sector. As the shares of the FIRE sector and manufacturing sector remained almost constant during the 1992–6 period, the contribution of changes in the shares of the incomes from various sources to the change in overall inequality was almost zero.

Second, the positive correlation between the changes in the inequality of non-farm profits and the changes in overall inequality is crucial. Between 1988 and 1992,

Table 16.11. *Decomposition of changes in overall income inequality by income source, 1988–92 and 1992–6*

	1988–92		1992–6	
	Share	Inequality	Share	Inequality
Overall income	29.05	70.95	−0.36	−99.64
Wages and salaries	12.84	−0.69	−1.29	31.07
Non-farm profit	37.01	46.69	7.53	−136.50
Farm profit	−21.00	20.41	−9.21	21.70
Transfers	−3.24	0.16	4.61	−5.12
Property income	3.12	1.80	−1.76	−5.31
Other money receipts	0.32	2.57	−0.23	−5.48

Source: See text.

the contribution of the increase in inequality in the income from non-farm profit to the increase in overall inequality was nearly 47 per cent. In the 1992–6 period, the decrease in inequality of non-farm profits reduced overall inequality by 137 per cent. Given a greater expansion in manufacturing in the central region during the first period than during the second, this indicates that after a few years industrial decentralization tended to enhance the distribution of non-farm profits and of total income.

Third, the increases in inequality in farm profit also raised overall inequality by more than 20 per cent in 1992 with respect to 1988 and in 1996 with respect to 1992. This points to the unfavourable impact of unbalanced agricultural development. The advances in agricultural commercialization and in agro–technology that led the growth in agriculture during these two periods were not well shared among farmers across regions and agricultural subsectors. Some groups of farmers were left behind along the path to agricultural development. In addition, exclusive of all other changes, the impact of changes in overall mean income and changes in the covariation among the incomes from different sources were insignificant in both periods. Thus, the analysis indicates that the role of higher overall mean income or rapid economic growth as an alternative to reduce income inequality in Thailand seems limited. This important issue requires further investigation.

16.6. CONCLUSION

The income distribution problem in Thailand has attracted considerable interest among economists and policy-makers. When the trend was towards an increase in national income, income inequality deteriorated. However, when economic growth began to slow down in the middle of the 1990s, there was a shift in the trend in income inequality. This phenomenon is very important for policy analysis and requires further explanation.

This study has examined the changing structure of the Thai economy and the relevant government development policies during the four decades from the 1960s to the 1990s. The industrial protection system tended to discourage agriculture and export industries, while import–competing industries were promoted. This policy led to the rapid expansion of the highly protected industries which came to dominate the industrial sector of the economy. Most of these protected industries were capital intensive and were not the most important sources of employment. The impact of such an approach to industrial protection on resource allocation was marked. While agriculture contracted, manufacturing and other sectors expanded. Because the manufacturing sector is concentrated in Bangkok and the surrounding provinces in the central region, the protection of industry favoured Bangkok and these provinces. Income disparities widened. However, beginning with the sixth development plan, industrial decentralization has been encouraged. Industrialization was shifted towards the central region as well as small-scale and agro-based industries. The favourable distributional impact of regional industrialization is indicated by a decline in the contribution of regional and sectoral inequality to total inequality.

Thus, without a mechanism to ensure that the distribution of non-farm profit is more egalitarian, industrialization can substantially raise income disparity. Such a mechanism could be industrial decentralization and the promotion of small-scale and agro-industries as proposed in the sixth and seventh development plans.

The expansion of other sectors, led by the rapid development of the FIRE sector, also had a significant unfavourable impact on overall inequality. During the boom period, resources were allocated to the FIRE sector at the expense of other sectors, which contracted. The expansion of the FIRE sector raised the return to capital and labour in this sector, but squeezed the output and the rate of return to agriculture. Thus, the expansion of a non-agricultural sector can be viewed as having disequaliz-ing influence on income distribution. Since it is widely believed that the rapid expansion of the FIRE sector was caused by the inflow of foreign capital (see Chapter 7), more research on the distributional effect of foreign investment is needed.

It should also be noted that, as the manufacturing and FIRE sectors expanded, more Thais became earners of wages and salaries. However, their earnings grew increasingly unequal. The cause could be the ineffectiveness of the personal income tax, the imperfectly competitive labour market for skilled workers, and the disequaliz-ing impact of education expansions, which undermined the favourable impact of industrial and financial development. Studies to clarify these points are needed and would be of paramount importance.

The rise in the skewness of the distribution of farm profits also points to the crucial influence of agricultural development on overall income inequality. There are many possible explanations for this (see Chapter 3). The advances in agricultural commer-cialization and agro-technology that led the growth in agriculture during these years were not well shared among the farmers in different regions and subsectors. Policies to diversify agricultural production did not show any substantial favourable impact on income distribution. The low productivity of the children and ageing farmers who were left behind to work the farmlands is also an explanation. Consequently, the income gap between traditional and modern farmers widened. Finally, the impact of changes in overall mean income on overall inequality was insignificant.

REFERENCES

Chalongphob, S., *et al.* (1999). *The Incidence of Government Spending and Taxation in Thailand, 1986–1996*, Thailand Development Research Institute Foundation, Bangkok, in Thai.

——, T. Pranee, and C. Tienchai (1988). The tax structure in Thailand and its distributional implications. Paper presented at the TDRI Year-End Conference on Income Distribution and Long-Term Development, Thailand Development Research Institute Foundation, Bangkok.

Chutipongse, B. (1996). The concurrence between minimum wage rates and economic conditions in Thailand. Master's thesis, Kasetsart University, Bangkok, in Thai.

Coxhead, I., and P. Jiraporn (1999). Economic boom, financial bust and the decline of Thai agriculture: Was growth in the 1990s too fast? *Chulalongkorn Journal of Economics* 11(1), 76–96.

Ikemoto, Y. (1991). *Income Distribution in Thailand: Its Changes, Causes and Structure*. Institute of Developing Economies: Tokyo.

Ingram, J. C. (1971). *Economic Changes in Thailand, 1850–1970*. Stanford University Press: Stanford.

Medhi, K. (1977). Income distribution among Thai households in 1972. *Thammasart Economic Journal* 10(1), 61–99, in Thai.

——,T. Pranee, and S. Suphat (1991). *Priority Issues and Policy Measures to Alleviate Rural Poverty: The Case of Thailand*. Asian Development Bank: Manila.

Narongchai, A. (1973). The manufacturing sector in Thailand: A study of growth, import substitution and effective protection, 1960–69. Ph.D. thesis, Johns Hopkins University: Baltimore.

NESDB (various). *National Income Account of Thailand*. Office of the National Economic and Social Development Board: Bangkok.

—— (1998). *Capital Stock of Thailand, 1970–96*. Office of the National Economic and Social Development Board, Bangkok.

Nishimizu, M., and J. M. Page Jr. (1986). Productivity change and dynamic comparative advantage. *Review of Economics and Statistics* LXVII(2), 241–7.

O'Mara, G., and V. Le-Si (1985). The supply and welfare effect of rice pricing policies in Thailand. World Bank Staff Working Papers 714. World Bank: Washington, DC.

Orakoch, K. (1999). Industrialization and income inequality. Master's thesis, Chulalongkorn University, Bangkok, in Thai.

Overbusch, *et al.* (1988). Income distribution and government interventions: Thailand agricultural Model-2. Paper presented at the workshop on modelling Thai agriculture, 29–30 October, Huahin, Thailand.

Pairote, W. (1975). The structure of differential incentives in the manufacturing sectors: A study of the Thailand experience during 1945–74. Master's thesis, Thammasart University: Bangkok.

Paitoon, W., C. Rachain, and T. Nattapong (1989). Trade in manufactured goods and mineral products. Paper presented at the TDRI Year-End Conference on Thailand in the International Economic Community, Thailand Development Research Institute Foundation, Bangkok.

Pranee, T. (1992). Industrialization and welfare: How poverty and income distribution are affected. Paper presented at the conference The Making of a Fifth Tiger? Canberra, 7–9 December.

Sarntisart, S. (1994). Trade liberalization in Thailand: Income distributional impact and financing problems. *Asian Economic Journal* 9(3), 261–91.

——(1997). Educational expansions and labour earnings inequality: The case of Thailand between 1988 and 1992. *Chulalongkorn Journal of Economics* 9(2), 127–74.

——(1999). The distributive welfare impact of value-added tax. Paper presented at the Conference in Celebration of the King's Seventy-Second Birthday, Chulalongkorn University, Bangkok, in Thai.

——(2000). Growth and structural changes in inequality: The experience of Thailand. WIDER Working Paper 207. UNU/WIDER: Helsinki.

Saowalak, W. (2000). The impact of minimum wages on unskilled labour in Thailand. Master's thesis, Chulalongkorn University, Bangkok, in Thai.

Shorrocks, A. F. (1980). The class of additive decomposable inequality measures. *Economica* 48(3), 613–25.

Somsak, T. (1985). Thai import demand Analysis. In D. Lim (ed.), *ASEAN-Australia Trend in Manufactures*. Longman Cheshire: Melbourne.

Suganya, H., and J. Somchai (1988). Thailand's income distribution and poverty profile and their current situations. Paper presented at the TDRI Year-End Conference on Income Distribution and Long-Term Development, Thailand Development Research Institute Foundation, Bangkok.

Sunee, B., and S.-H. Sombat (1996). *Tariff Reduction and Its Impact on Thailand's Competitiveness in the World Market*. Office of the National Economic and Social Development Board: Bangkok, in Thai.

Suphanee, C. (1995). The burden of taxation on urban households by income class, 1990. Master's thesis, Chieng Mai University, Bangkok, in Thai.

Teerana, B. (1993). Income distribution in the rapidly growing economy of Thailand. *Chulalongkorn Journal of Economics* 5(2), 109–35, in Thai.

Usarsee Khieorayab (1996). The impact of direct tax on income distribution in Thailand. Master's thesis, Kasetsart University, Bangkok, in Thai.

Index

438 *Index*